The Emotional Power of Music

Series in Affective Science

Series Editors
Richard J. Davidson
Paul Ekman
Klaus R. Scherer

The Emotional Power of Music

Multidisciplinary perspectives on musical arousal, expression, and social control

Edited by

Tom Cochrane, Bernardino Fantini,
Klaus R. Scherer

OXFORD
UNIVERSITY PRESS

OXFORD
UNIVERSITY PRESS

Great Clarendon Street, Oxford, OX2 6DP,
United Kingdom

Oxford University Press is a department of the University of Oxford.
It furthers the University's objective of excellence in research, scholarship,
and education by publishing worldwide. Oxford is a registered trade mark of
Oxford University Press in the UK and in certain other countries

© Oxford University Press 2013

The moral rights of the authors have been asserted

Impression: 1

Published in the United States of America by Oxford University Press
198 Madison Avenue, New York, NY 10016, United States of America

British Library Cataloguing in Publication Data
Data available

ISBN 978–0–19–965488–8

Printed and bound in Great Britain
by CPI Group (UK) Ltd, Croydon, CR0 4YY

Contents

Contributors

Brenno Boccadoro
Department of Musicology,
University of Geneva

Tom Cochrane
Department of Philosophy,
University of Sheffield

Lincoln John Colling
Radboud University Nijmegen, Donders
Institute for Brain, Cognition and Behaviour

Eduardo Coutinho
Swiss Center for Affective Sciences,
University of Geneva

Stephen Davies
Department of Philosophy,
University of Auckland

Bernardino Fantini
Institut d'Histoire de la Médecine et de la
Santé, University of Geneva

Penelope Gouk
School of Arts, Languages and Cultures
University of Manchester

Christine Jeanneret
Department of Musicology,
University of Geneva

Stefan Koelsch
Cluster Languages of Emotion,
Free University of Berlin

Joel Krueger
Department of Sociology, Philosophy and
Anthropology, University of Exeter

Daniel Leech-Wilkinson
Department of Music, Kings College London

Claude Victor Palisca (deceased)
Previously Professor Emeritus of music,
Yale University

Jackie Pigeaud
Honorary senior member,
Institut Universitaire de France

Jenefer Robinson
Department of Philosophy,
University of Cincinnati

Klaus R. Scherer
Swiss Center for Affective Sciences,
University of Geneva

Michael Spitzer
Department of Music, University of Liverpool

Jean Starobinski
Professor Emeritus of French literature,
University of Geneva

William Forde Thompson
Centre for Elite Performance, Expertise,
and Training, Department of Psychology,
Macquarie University

Wiebke Trost
Neuroscience of Emotion and Affective
Dynamics Laboratory, Department of
Psychology, University of Geneva;
Swiss Center for Affective Sciences, University
of Geneva

Ulrik Volgsten
School of Music, Theatre and Art,
Örebro University

Patrik Vuilleumier
Laboratory for Behavioral Neurology and
Imaging of Cognition, University of Geneva

Laurence Wuidar
Independent Researcher

Luca Zoppelli
Department of Musicology,
University of Fribourg

Interviewees:

Carter Burwell (composer)
Brian Ferneyhough (composer)
Gillian Keith (soprano)
Thomas Moser (tenor)
Christoph Prégardien (tenor)
Jean-Claude Risset (composer)
Lucy Schaufer (mezzo-soprano)
Bruno Taddia (baritone)

Translator:

Kristen Gray Jafflin
Department of Sociology, University of
California at Berkeley

Introduction

The field of music and emotion research is burgeoning. Since the 1990s, what could once be described as occasional bursts of activity has gradually become a sustained and steady flow as more and more researchers from different fields have converged on some of the most fascinating questions we can ask about the human mind and its culture: How can an abstract sequence of sounds so vividly capture the nature of emotional experience? What is it about music that can arouse such powerful reactions? Can the powers of music have therapeutic, or corrupting effects? It is the on-going pursuit of these questions that motivates the present volume.

With the amount of excellent research being produced on this subject it has not been too difficult to assemble a wide range of original papers representing the current state of the art. Our initial impetus was a 3-day conference organized by the Swiss Center for Affective Sciences in Geneva in June 2009 entitled "The Emotional Power of Music." Several workshops, organized jointly by academic centers and music institutions, were organized in the wake of this event. Additional contributors were also drawn into the project, some notably coming from another conference on the role of music in historical medical practice, organized by the Institut d'Histoire de la Médecine et de la Santé. The contacts between researchers on the one hand and composers and performers on the other also provided the opportunity to conduct some of the interview exchanges reported in this volume. Thus the scope of this volume has considerably evolved over the past 3 years, allowing us to present a broad and multifaceted perspective on the central themes of the volume.

All of the workshops and conferences contributing to this project were of course multidisciplinary, since this is a field that almost by definition combines the humanistic treatments of traditional music research with the experimentally oriented affective sciences. A researcher hoping to make a significant contribution to this area, even while firmly situated within their home discipline, must become at least conversant with the approaches of other disciplines relevant to the subject under study. There is simply too much of relevance being produced in these different fields for it to be safely ignored. As such, volumes such as this are becoming more and more essential for anyone seeking to get an overview of the field as it stands today.

We direct in particular the reader's attention to two other recent landmarks in music and emotion studies. First is Juslin and Sloboda's *Handbook of Music and Emotion: Theory, Research and Applications* (2010) which is an updated, and greatly expanded revision of its original 2001 edition. That volume presents an extraordinary breadth of views from the different scientific disciplines, focusing on both practical methodologies and theoretical approaches. The second landmark is the 2010 triple issue of *Music Analysis* focusing on music and emotion, edited by Michael Spitzer. That volume presents a number of in-depth analyses of the expressive techniques in specific musical works by Bach, Mozart, Schubert, and Skryabin, as well as analyses of particular emotions such as joy, jealousy, and fear in the work of different composers.

Our volume seeks to complement, rather than compete with, these other volumes. For even with a combined count of more than 1300 pages these volumes could not hope to cover everything in the field. For instance, a significant lacuna that the current volume helps to fill is in presenting perspectives from the performers and composers themselves. As the interview-centered chapters of Scherer and Cochrane reveal, these practitioners are often aware of the relevant theoretical debates, though they may regard them as rather blunt instruments when compared to subtleties of actual musical practice. Like the *Music Analysis* volume, the current volume also presents in-depth analyses of specific musical works (Spitzer; Zoppelli; Leech-Wilkinson) ensuring that the discussion does not remain at a purely abstract level. Our volume also brings together research on another aspect of the field which even multidisciplinary projects such as this sometimes neglect. This concerns the historical development of our conceptualizations of both music and emotion and the ways it has influenced medical practice (Fantini; Boccadoro) and social policy (Wuidar; Gouk; Volgsten).

Overall, our volume is organized into three sections; each addressing a central issue of the field from a range of different perspectives. The first section of the book addresses the issue of musical expressivity; the means by which listeners are able to recognize the music as representing, captur-ing, or possessing emotional qualities. In addition to theoretical treatments, this section is espe-cially concerned to address the practical role of performers and composers in providing expressive content to musical works and the ways in which techniques of musical expression have changed over time.

The second section then addresses the elicitation of emotions by music, which is widely regarded as central to the significance and power of music. The authors in this section present a number of views on the mechanisms potentially underlying the process of emotion elicitation or induction, often informed by particular theories of emotion. This includes research into the psychological and neurological mechanisms that underlie music listening, the features of the music that allow it to have its effects, and the relevance of the social context in which the listening experience is embedded. Some authors also address the ongoing debate concerning whether music can arouse extra-musical emotions or more unique "aesthetic emotions."

The third and final section explores the ways in which the societies of different historical periods have sought to manage or manipulate the powers of music. One strand is focused on the long theo-retical and practical tradition ranging back to ancient Greece that has sought to practically harness the special affective powers of music for alleviating the suffering of human beings, and the ways this has been informed by different models or metaphors regarding the qualities that music and emotions share. Another strand concerns the political constraints that have been imposed upon musical activities by those seeking to control its influence over ordinary people. Some cases involve overt attempts by political authorities to control the powers of music. Another more subtle case is explored in relation to present-day copyright law.

The authors in this volume represent the highest level of expertise for the issues they address. At the same time, we have emphasized maximal clarity and accessibility to readers outside of the particular disciplines represented. As such, we hope that both experts and the student seeking an introduction to the field will find much of value in the following pages. Prior to each section we also provide a more detailed summary of the chapters therein, allowing the reader to clearly dis-cern where the main lines of debate lie.

A volume such as this would not be possible without the assistance of a number of people. In addition to our contributors we would like to extend our thanks to Charlotte Green and Martin Baum at Oxford University Press, as well as the anonymous reviewers who provided many helpful suggestions. Thanks also to all those involved in the organization of the numerous conferences and workshops that contributed to this volume, in particular Miriam Spörri, Daniela Sauge, and Carole Varone. We acknowledge support of the Brocher Foundation, Geneva, the Swiss National Science Foundation, and the European Research Council for the organization of the original col-loquium and the preparation of the volume. Finally special thanks to Kristen Gray Jafflin who provided translations from the French for a number of our contributions.

Section 1

Musical expressiveness

Chapter 1

Section introduction

Tom Cochrane

Theoretical discussions concerning the expressive powers of music have been dominated by three major theories: the arousal, resemblance, and expression theories. Proponents of the arousal theory claim that we are able to recognize expressive qualities in music because we are aroused by certain emotions which we then projectively attribute to what we hear (see, e.g., Matravers 1998 for a review). So for example, in order to hear music as expressive of anger, listeners must at some level feel the emotion of anger, though they may not self-consciously realize that they feel this. As such, this theory is reliant on accounts of how music is able to arouse emotions. It must also specify a psychological process whereby the sense of an emotion is appropriately attributed to the music, since in contrast it is clear that although alcohol may causally arouse feelings of joy, we do not take alcohol to be *expressive* of joy.

Resemblance theorists, meanwhile, claim that we hear aspects of the music as resembling aspects of emotion, such as the movements associated with expressive behaviors (e.g. Davies 2005), the vocal expression of emotions (e.g. Kivy 1980, Juslin & Laukka 2003), or, in some formulations, the inner feelings of emotion (e.g. Budd 1995). This theory encourages analyses of the ways that the formal features of musical works may be taken to resemble features associated with emotions. A major issue is to explain how we manage to translate, presumably quite automatically, between patterns of sound and the movements or feelings correlated with emotions in humans. Resemblance theories must also explain what leads us to hear a resemblance to emotions in particular, rather than other natural phenomena that music might be taken to resemble (such as natural soundscapes).

Finally, expression theorists appeal to an empathic sense of a person to whom the emotion of the music could be attributed. Traditionally expression theories appealed to a recognition of the expressive intentions of the composer or performer. Modern formulations of this theory, known as "persona" theories, generally accept that there is no necessary connection between the feelings of the composer and the sound of the music, and rely instead on the listener *imagining* a person (be they real or entirely fictional) that is in some sense responsible for the emotion of the music (e.g. Levinson 2005). For example, the music may be heard as if it is spontaneously emanating from some imaginary person in the grip of an emotional state. Persona theorists must explain how music is able to engage the empathic faculties of the listener. They must also show that the essential experience of hearing emotions in music necessarily involves the imagining of a person (e.g. Cochrane 2011). Indeed it is important to note a distinction applicable to all theories of musical expressiveness between aspects of these theories aimed at explaining the causal processes involved in hearing emotions in music, and aspects aimed at explanations of the conscious experience of hearing emotions in music. Different accounts may be compatible at the causal level of explanation while incompatible as accounts of experience (see, e.g., Cochrane 2010).

Strands of all three of these major theories are to be found throughout this volume—as many of the contributors try to elucidate their different claims, and in some cases to synthesize them. In this section on musical expressiveness in particular, we are often concerned to examine how these theoretical considerations work out in the actual practice of musical production. As Michael Spitzer notes in Chapter 2, there are practically no existing studies that apply insights from psychologists and philosophers into how emotion unfolds as a process across an actual piece of music in any analytical detail. Spitzer begins to remedy this with an in-depth study of one of Schubert's greatest songs, "Trockne Blumen," from his song cycle "*Die schöne Müllerin.*" He begins by focusing on the role of highpoints in clarifying the distinction between vocal and instrumental affect. He then explores the song as an unfolding of sadness as a kind of human reflective behavior, defined by a more data-driven, bottom-up attention to musical detail. He follows writers such as Jack Katz in arguing that sadness is a scenario or indeed a "trajectory," encompassing episodes of memory and joy. The thrust of Spitzer's essay is that the persona theory of music can be extended to describe a work as imitating a person both in action and in thought.

Turning from a great historical composer to more modern practice, Tom Cochrane interviews three eminent composers working in three quite different spheres of musical production: Jean-Claude Risset (a pioneering electro-acoustic composer), Brian Ferneyhough, (one of the leading contemporary composers working within the classical tradition) and Carter Burwell (a highly distinguished film composer famous for his work on the Coen brothers' films, amongst many others). In these interviews each composer reflects on his motivations in producing music and the extent to which he conceptualizes the expressive qualities of music, its uses, and abuses. Providing examples from their own works, these composers provide a fascinating insight into the ways in which the different media they work within have an influence over the characteristics of their works.

We then turn to the performance of music. In Chapter 4, Daniel Leech-Wilkinson opposes a central supposition of Spitzer's analysis. Where Spitzer draws considerable expressive cues from a close study of Schubert's score, Leech-Wilkinson asserts that we must focus first and foremost on the performance event. Music, argues Leech-Wilkinson, is above all a negotiation between sound and the contents and mechanisms of the mind, and so it is within that space that the study of music's effects will be most illuminating. In particular, this negotiation is achieved most vividly in the performer's interpretation of the work. As such, it is not scores to which we should attribute musical meaning, but performances. Such an attribution may have its dangers in removing the constraints on the performer, but Leech-Wilkinson thinks it is a necessary clarification of the affective process involved in musical expression. Leech-Wilkinson provides some concrete examples of this process by exploring Alfred Cortot's 1934 recording of Chopin's *Étude*, Op. 25, No. 1 as well as examples from Schubert's songs. He is sensitive throughout to the issue of how the expressive nature of these performances is tied to the historical period in which they were produced.

We have reason to think that the performer plays a key role in the expressive meaning of musical works, but what do the performers themselves think about their expressive negotiations with the music? In Chapter 5 Klaus Scherer provides in-depth interviews with several internationally known opera singers—Thomas Moser (tenor), Gillian Keith (soprano), Lucy Schaufer (mezzosoprano), Bruno Taddia (baritone), and Christoph Prégardien (tenor). Scherer focuses the discussion around the issue of how much the performer must feel the emotion expressed by the music in order to communicate that emotion to the audience. In his analysis of the different singers' responses, however, Scherer argues that this dichotomy is too simple, and that in fact there are a number of different dimensions of performer engagement including the sense of spontaneity, credibility, control, and authenticity. Scherer's analysis is informed by his general theory of emotions, in particular the notion that a number of different components are synchronized in the arousal of an emotion. Performers can make use of these different components in quite practical ways to enhance their expressive success.

The physical immediacy with which singers relate to their chosen instrument may be a cause for envy in other performers. Yet all performers bear a complicated psychological relationship with the tools of their trade. Whether it is one's own voice box, or a complicated hunk of metal and wood, musical instruments are often stubbornly resistant to the intentions of the performer. In Chapter 6, Tom Cochrane examines the resistance of the instrument, arguing that it has a major influence over the pursuit and achievement of the different values embodied in the act of musical expression. Cochrane argues that from the perspective of both the performer and listener, the struggle to produce a sound can serve creativity, the stimulation of pleasure, and the sharing one's emotion with others. Cochrane discerns the influence of these values in the historical development of musical instruments with a particular focus on current technological applications. He then introduces an unusual case from his own research where the *transparency* between the performer's emotions and the music produced has apparently been maximized. Cochrane's system, called "the mood organ," uses physiological data indicative of the performer's emotional state to automatically generate music expressive of that emotion. As a consequence it can potentially bypass the skill and even intentions of the performer.

Chapter 7, by Christine Jeanneret, tackles a rather different aspect of performance, examining the influence that the gender of the performer has on the expressive quality of music. Jeanneret focuses on cantatas produced and admired in Rome during the Baroque period, typically performed by both female singers and castrati. The affect in which we are particularly interested here is love and erotic arousal, a perennial fixation, particularly in vocal music. Jeanneret shows the ways in which the sexual identity of the performer could dramatically alter the listener's appreciation of the work, and how the performances of these works were embedded within social settings aimed at maximizing the transmission of passions between performer and listener. She is also concerned to contextualize this practice with reference to the 17th-century medical theories concerning the difference between men and women's bodies, and associated personality features.

Taking a rather broader perspective on performance practice, Chapter 8 is a posthumous contribution from renowned music historian Claude Palisca, who died in 2001. In this previously unpublished work, Palisca explores the difficulties involved in reconstructing how musicians in the past have understood the expressive qualities of music, focusing in particular on writings from the Renaissance period. Musicians at this time were working within a tradition stretching back through medieval times to Ancient Greece, in which different modes were accorded specific emotional characteristics. The systems employed here extended not just to the scales employed, but also to other musical variables such as rhythm, melodic contour, and vocal range. Palisca shows that while musicians of this period mostly affirmed the basic theoretical commitment to the ethos of modes, it was clear that the ancient authorities could not provide unambiguous guidance for composers. At the same time, the rise of polyphonic music was providing another pressure on the requirements for musical expression, which ultimately undermined the authority of the ethos of modes.

Overall, the contributors to this section demonstrate that specific performance practices, the identity of the performer, the technical medium of the composer, and the historical traditions within which the performance is situated, all play a vital role in the expressive capacities of music. Further work is required to understand all of these factors, as well as their interactions within the different stages of musical production and reception. Greater understanding of these factors should also significantly enrich the major theories of musical expressivity, no doubt leading to further refinements and perhaps even entirely new approaches.

We also see that contemporary composers are driven by quite variable stylistic goals and concerns, and audience expectations regarding the music accordingly differ. The same degree of variation must apply to the musical works of the past, and as such, future research into musical expressivity will be aided by a richer appreciation of the historical variances of musical engagement in earlier eras. It is plausible that cultural sensibilities have changed to such a degree that we cannot immediately hear the music of the past in the same ways that listeners of those periods did. Changes in cultural sensibilities may even lead us to suspect that the quality of emotional experience in bygone eras may have differed from our own. It is a challenging task to discern universals of human emotion and musical experience while filling out the contextual factors that guide the subjective experience of a musical work in one way or the other.

Finally, accounts of musical expressivity are likely to develop in the future as the mechanisms by which music arouses emotion, and indeed the nature of emotional experience itself, are more clearly delineated. It will then become easier to trace the ways in which the composer and performer are influenced in intentionally or unintentionally expressing an emotional quality in the music, and what exactly is happening at a psychological level in the listener as he or she experiences the musical work. Fully understanding the impact of a musical work must combine detailed psychological and neurological data with a contextually situated analysis of the work and its performance. It is rare that a single researcher can develop expertise on both fronts. As such we should expect to see more collaborative studies between scientific and musicological researchers in the future. Due to numerous practical constraints, it is still uncommon to find empirical investigations of the experiences of listeners to complete musical works, let alone those situated in natural listening environments. A large number of interacting variables must be disentangled to properly tackle such real-life cases. But this is the target at which we must aim if we are to truly understand the expressive powers of musical works.

References

Budd, M. (1995). *Values of Art. Pictures, Poetry and Music*. London: Penguin.

Cochrane, T. (2010). A simulation theory of musical expressivity. *The Australasian Journal of Philosophy*, **88**, 191–207.

Cochrane, T. (2011). Using the persona to express complex emotions in music. *Music Analysis*, **29**, 264–75.

Davies, S. (2005). Artistic expression and the hard case of pure music. In Kieran, M. (ed.) *Contemporary Debates in Aesthetics and the Philosophy of Art*, pp. 179–91. Oxford: Blackwell.

Juslin, P. and Laukka, P. (2003). Communication of emotions in vocal expression and music performance: different channels, same code? *Psychological Bulletin*, **129**, 770–814.

Kivy, P. (1980). *The Corded Shell. Reflections on Musical Expression*. Guildford: Princeton University Press.

Levinson, J. (2005). Musical expressiveness as hearability-as-expression. In Kieran, M. (ed.) *Contemporary Debates in Aesthetics and the Philosophy of Art*, pp. 192–206. Oxford: Blackwell.

Matravers, D. (1998). *Art and Emotion*. Oxford: Clarendon Press.

Chapter 2

Sad flowers: analyzing affective trajectory in Schubert's "Trockne Blumen"

Michael Spitzer

"From the eyes may it go to the eyes"

Introduction

A fundamental strategic decision for any professional *Lied* composer—a gambit of which Schubert was the supreme master—was where in the piece to place the singer's highest note. In "Trockne Blumen," the 18th number in Schubert's song cycle *Die Schöne Müllerin*, the melodic apex is the G♯ of bar 37 (see Figure 2.1); the note also marks the emotional high-point of the song, and arguably of the entire cycle (for a comparative analytical study see Eitan 1999).

This coincidence of registral peak and emotional crux goes to the heart of the nature of musical structure in general, and of song composition in particular, and I shall use it as a peg on which to hang a number of observations on emotion, or affect, in music, in the course of an analysis of Schubert's song. Of course, it goes almost without saying that a *Lied* contains words, but I shall temporarily set to one side the emotional narrative explicated by Müller's poetry in order to explore what kinds of quintessentially *musical* devices Schubert exploits (for a more historical study of this song cycle orientated to the text see Youens 1992).

Why should a listener find a vocal high-point so affective? A high note requires more physical strain than simply striking a key on the piano. Writings on emotional contagion suggest that such physical effort may communicate directly to the listener (see Scherer and Zentner 2001).[i] Also, it is at high points that vocal utterances most resembles screams, where articulate language threatens to break down into direct expression. Opera studies have been captivated by psychoanalytic ideas on the nature of voice, especially the Lacanian "cry" (e.g. Tomlinson 1999, p. 85), but this literature would take us too far afield. I prefer to make the practical claim that a song or operatic composer's job is to defer this moment of cathartic release for as long as possible (Isolde's *Liebestod*, deferred by 5 hours, is the most accomplished performance of this technique). If so, then it turns upside down the widely held assumption that the natural trajectory of music is always downwards, submitting to the pull of musical gravity, acceding to "the gravitational slope of musical language," in Adorno's (1992) lovely phrase. Heinrich Schenker—the most important music theorist of the 20th century, whose ideas are still central in Anglo-American musicology—built his entire analytical system on the descent of a "fundamental line" (*Urlinie*) of structural "steps."[ii] Yet I would contend that perhaps this holds only for instrumental music, and that *rising contour* is more intrinsic to

Figure 2.1 Schubert, "Trockne Blumen", bars 28–47.

vocal music. That would certainly be in keeping with the Goethian notion of *Steigerung*, which massively influenced German music theory up to the early 20th century, before Schenkerism supplanted it. For Goethe, *Steigerung* is quintessentially the "intensification" of a flower's rising growth from root to blossom.[iii] I can't think of a more fitting metaphor for Schubert's "Trockne Blumen." The G♯s, beginning at bar 37, are the song's emotional "blossoms." If so, what are its roots?

Of course, a high vocal sound in itself isn't necessarily either pleasant or artistic; here, taken as a gross acoustic parameter, it is only a marker of a highly sophisticated formal strategy upon which it supervenes. Consider, first, that the G♯ at bar 37 is the occasion for the very first tonic authentic cadence in the piece, unfolded in fact by Schenker's requisite 3̂–2̂–1̂ linear descent, here G♯–F♯–E. Cadential descents are music's chief points of articulation and goal; following Schopenhauer, Schenker believed (and nearly all contemporary music theorists in the Anglo-American tradition still agree with him) that the musical notes "yearn"—through what he termed the "will of tones" [*Tonwille*]—towards these cadences. The fact that cadence and high-point coincide is crucial because highly unusual. It is far more common to set a vocal peak on a harmonically dissonant interval, such as the submediant, or sixth degree, whereby the tonal tension is an analog for vocal tension and registral extreme. Secondly, high-point and cadence co-recur not once but three times (again at bars 46 and 50). Schubert can't resist milking every last drop from this effect; I'm not aware of any other of his 600 songs which exploits this trick so theatrically (one normally associates this "one more time" technique with 19th-century Italian opera). Thirdly, this multiple climax is only the outward manifestation of a network of structural relations which feeds it. The bar 37 high-point is actually prepared by an obsessively repetitive seven-bar passage, each bar of which reiterates an inadequate form of the tonic–dominant cadence. What is wrong with these seven cadences, then? Firstly, the linear descents (a *sine qua non* for authentic cadences) happen in the bass rather than the melody, which hovers on the fifth degree and then *rises*. Secondly, the two would-be cadences to E at bars 35–36 are extremely odd, in approaching the tonic via a diminished seventh chord on A♯ rather than from the dominant (about which I shall have more to say). The G♯ high-point at bar 37 corrects these faulty progressions by triggering the first perfect authentic cadence in the piece, complete with the statutory 3̂–2̂–1̂ melodic descent. We can extrapolate backwards even further; to uncover the music's deepest motivations. Before we do so, however, I should say that my Schubert analysis is offered in support of the broad claim that music unfolds what I term an "affective trajectory."

Most approaches to musical emotion are static, insofar as they tend to either associate a (routinely very short) piece of music with a single emotional state, or track the music as a succession of affective "snap-shots." The exception to this tendency, ostensibly, is presented by theorists who analyze musical emotion as a change of intensity.[iv] Yet the latter approach shies away from identifying this affective process with any particular emotions, such as the basic emotional categories studied by Patrik Juslin: happiness, tenderness, fear, anger, and sadness.[v] My own approach, by contrast, analyzes a particular emotion—in the present case, sadness—as a goal-driven process: an "affective trajectory." I propose that affective trajectories in music are actually compound, being constituted by multiple parallel processes:

(1) First and foremost, especially in vocal music, is the trajectory towards cathartic release on a registral high-point, an outbreak of maximum immediacy within the work's stylistic constraints.

(2) An intensification [*Steigerung*] of musical features, such as acceleration, crescendo, expansion of melodic range, and thickening of texture.

(3) A rising linear pitch progression.

(4) An aesthetic transformation of opening materials.

There is something quintessential about vocal high-points as akin to the maximum expressive potency of screams. It would be unwise for a piece to begin with a "scream," since the music would have nowhere else to go without risking bathos or redundancy. A typical work, then, begins at a "low-point," and is pulled ineluctably towards its "high-point" through the logics both of music and affect. This, I argue, is the background affective trajectory of the work. But there can be screams of fear, of anger, of sadness, even of ecstatic joy: the affective trajectory is neutral with respect to the specific emotion expressed. This strengthens the case for the existence of a "core affect." Nevertheless, a core affective trajectory does not necessarily mean that its emotional specifics are purely a matter of extra-musical context, as Meyer proposed,[vi] or of performance practice, as Daniel Leech-Wilkinson contends.[vii] On the contrary, I argue that there are technical musical processes which elaborate core affective trajectories into trajectories of specific emotions. Consider the various musical features Juslin discovers to be associated with the expression of sadness: slow tempo, minor mode, dissonance, low sound level, moderate sound level variability, low pitch, narrow pitch range, etc. (Juslin and Lindström 2010, p. 335). Just as there are recognized, quasi-semiotic markers of affective states, there are markers of affective *processes*, once we recognize emotions as dynamic. Sadness isn't just an expressive mode; it signifies a state of mind or being. Sadness, as I shall show, is characterized by "separation anxiety," and is driven by a yearning to mend its breaches. In music, this trajectory is often marked by a turn from minor to major. It is a mistake, however, to interpret the progression from minor to major in "Trockne Blumen" as a change from one emotion to another: say, from sadness to happiness. In fact, I argue that the switch to major—and hence to happiness—plays out a single emotional scenario, that of sadness. Affective trajectories are richly dialectical processes. Words such as "sadness" are really just shorthand for complex packages of entailments. For instance, sadness connotes aspects such as "thoughtfulness," lyricism, and indeed lyrical reflection. The paradox is that lyricism is often considered to be a peculiarly static idiom; a symptom of this attitude is that we have no agreed scripts for slow movements to compare with the conventionality of sonata allegros. Otherwise put, a fast sonata form follows a conventional pattern; no such standard form exists for slow movements—or indeed for slow music in general. In this regard, a study of affective trajectory in a slow sad song cuts to the quick.

Emotion, sadness, and lyrical reflection

Like most German *Lieder*, "Trockne Blumen" starts with the trick of capturing a distinctive emotion with a characteristic figure (see Figure 2.2).

The monotonously plodding E minor triads in the piano introduction (bars 1–2) suggest the unresponsive fixity or turgid quality of extreme sadness or even depression. Even if we didn't know, via the text, that Schubert's miller is tragically unrequited in his love for the *Müllerin*, the music tells us that the song is sad. An extraordinary aspect of *Lieder*, seldom if ever appreciated by students of emotion, is that the affect established in the opening bars is normally sustained throughout the song, insofar as the characteristic figures are omnipresent. (This contrasts with the kaleidoscopically ever-changing emotional signs of a sonata or symphony (Agawu 1991).) The prolongation of emotion in songs runs counter to the theory, proposed by writers such as Ekman (2004), that emotional episodes are transient and fleeting (Sloboda 2005, p. 218 claims that "Emotions by their nature are immediate and evanescent: they do not survive long after the triggering event").[viii] The situation is in fact rather complex. One might expect emotion to fluctuate more in a song because it involves voice, and the intonations of speech change rapidly. Hence the prolongation of affect in songs is all the more striking. By contrast, the fast emotional change in a symphony—which would be considered crazy in a person—is sanctioned by the affective distance of abstract instrumental (or "absolute") music, which effects a kind of compression of emotional dynamics.

Perhaps, in this respect, the song's affect is not an emotion but a continuous *mood*, as Robinson (2007, p. 393) proposes, although she would probably allow that the words can give us a definite object and thus an emotion proper. However, given my argument that the music's sad affect is

Figure 2.2 "Trockne Blumen", bars 1–16.

discernible without comprehension of the words or knowledge of the song's title, the experience perhaps lies somewhere in between emotion and mood. In this case, we could say that, in submitting the opening figures (of sadness) to a process of incessant repetition, the song commutes them from transitive gesture to intransitive mood. With moods, we strike an attitude not towards anything or anyone in particular, but to "the world" at large. But I would go further, and situate musical moods in a spectrum between emotion (or perhaps even impulse) at one end, and personality at the other—or what Peter Goldie calls "dispositional character traits."[ix] The persona theory of music fits Romantic music particularly well (Robinson 2007, pp. 322–37), especially given the tradition of calling piano miniatures by Schubert, Chopin, Schumann *et al.* "character pieces." Schubert's stand-alone songs comprise a veritable *comedie humaine* of personality types; sung by a single character, the present song cycle presents different facets of a personality, or of successive staging-posts of their emotional journey. I am drawn towards Spinoza's theory of emotion as something which helps the person "endure," following Susan James's interpretation of his notion of passion as striving, or *conatus* (James 1997, p. 146):

> According to Spinoza, the reactions that are our passions are a manifestation of a striving to persevere in our being, which is our essence. [...] The whole of nature exhibits this striving or *conatus*, which constitutes the essence of the whole and each of its parts, so that everything possesses some power to maintain itself and resist destruction.

Spinoza's idea that emotions enable survival has become very widespread in post-Darwinian accounts. His take is distinctive, however, in suggesting that survival depends not on the accomplishment of a particular goal but in the perpetuation of our very essence. In musical terms, the desire of conation is not a yearning for a goal (as epitomized, after Meyer and Huron, in psychologies of expectation), but in a striving for *the same*, i.e. repetition. This valorizing of repetition is salutary for a modern aesthetic which has few—if any—rationales for appreciating the virtues of sameness. I thus hear Schubert's sustained characteristic figures as reiterated acts of character formation and endurance.[x] In purely sonic terms, of course, sheer repetition is required to keep the sound *alive*. Sloboda is not wrong, then; rather, we could say that song figuration sustains emotion by repeating "triggering events" indefinitely. Of course, whether these repeated motifs comprise dispositional character traits themselves or the *triggers* of such traits depends on our point of view. From the perspective of emotional induction in the listener, they are triggers which perpetuate a listener's feelings. From the perspective of emotional expression within the work, they are analogous to traits of the musical persona's imagined "character."

The sustained quality of the song's affect, concordant with notions of both mood and personality, is matched by analogous aspects of musical idiom and form. First and foremost is the music's idiom as *lyric*—by definition, a static style much less amenable to formal analysis than teleological forms such as sonata since, presumably, "nothing changes." Lyric forms (including dance, variation, fugue, as well as song) reflect on the opening material from different vantage-points, rather than truly moving or developing. This has consequences for the kind of material conducive to lyricism; it tends to comprise self-contained melodic units, which the listener aurally "gazes" upon. Far from all the songs in *Die Schöne Müllerin* are sad, but it could be argued that sad songs like "Trockne Blumen" are prototypical of lyricism, since they avoid the running or skipping gestures characteristic of more dynamic emotions. Moreover, as I shall argue later, sadness is an emotion of reflection.

The static nature of musical lyric is well served by the formal, melodic, and harmonic finger-prints of Schubert's personal style. Schubert perfected a technique called "strophic variation," whereby he sets each verse (strophe or stanza) of the poem with the same music, with slight changes. This is the case in "Trockne Blumen": the music of verse 1 (bars 1–16) is repeated almost exactly for verse 2 (bars 17–29). While the material of verse 3 seems new, it only makes sense as a transformation of the opening ideas. Within the first two strophes, repetition is remarkably recursive: the first part of the verse subdivides into a repeated four-bar phrase (bars 3–6 repeated in bars 7–10), while the second part of the verse constitutes a repeated two-bar phrase (bars 11–12 repeated in bars 13–14). This systematic repetition promotes the reflective function of lyricism—the repeated "reflection" on discrete musical materials.

Reflection is also promoted by Schubert's highly idiosyncratic melodic style. Melodies generally rise and fall in free curvilinear shapes, keeping a balance of disjunct leaps and linear formations, a phenomenon for which Huron (2006) has supplied much statistical evidence.[xi] Schubert's, by contrast, are often "axial," in that they circle a focal pitch, typically in widening orbits. Good examples are the opening horn melody of his ninth symphony, and the first subject of his great last piano sonata in B♭. In both cases, the melody creeps around the tonic center, venturing alternately a tone or two below and above. In the course of the movement, the circles gradually widen, encompassing greater intervals (thirds, fourths, etc.), creating the effect of wings being unfurled, a soul expanding. The melody in "Trockne Blumen" is partly of this type: fixing on B, rising a fourth above to E, falling a third below to G, then returning to B. It's slightly unusual, however, since one would expect the oscillations to be narrower at the beginning of the piece.

For the moment, I should explain why Schubert's axial idiom is effective on so many levels. It "centers" the voice, in the sense both of pitches and registers having much more of a "character" in vocal music than in instrumental, and also in the capacity of anchoring the subjectivity of the song. Moreover, the home pitch for a voice will tend to sit at the center of its range, whereas the tonic of a scale will by definition be the lowest note of a scale. Often, the singer's axial note *is* the harmonic tonic too. But in "Trockne Blumen," B is the *dominant*, which gives the emotion a certain restless character. By contrast, the two previous songs ("Die liebe Farbe" and "Die böse Farbe") are both in the key of B (respectively minor and major), and both utilize highly axial melodies. In both these songs, the B axis coincides with the tonic note. Interestingly, B is the pivot note connecting all three successive songs, drawing further attention to it as a central presence in the cycle. Finally, B is the source of note repetitions. One of this song cycle's most characteristic aspects is ostinato reiterations of the same pitch, a device which seems to be infinitely adaptable to different emotional scenarios. In "Die liebe Farbe," it expresses throbbing lamentation; in the final song, "Des Baches Wiegenlied," repeated Bs famously comfort the deceased miller with a morbid lullaby. Repeated Bs come to the fore in the second half of "Trockne Blumen," where the song takes a turn to the major. They are there in the right hand piano part, in the obsessively repetitive seven-bar phrase I have discussed as a prelude to the G♯ high-point (bars 30–36). Are they present also in the song's first part? The dotted B motives which frame the beginning and end of the first phrase (bars 2 and 4) are easy enough to spot. Much more subtle is the conceit that each of the verse's eight subdivisions (respectively, bars 2, 5, 7, 9, 11, and 13) begins on a B. The song projects a throbbing pulse of Bs slowed down so that each note is two bars apart. In the jargon of music theory, the B pulse is repeated as a "hypermeter" (meter writ large, with each bar analogous to a beat). If "Trockne Blumen" starts off with a slow hypermetrical pulse, then its natural trajectory is to accelerate it. There are inklings of a faster B pulse towards the end of the first two verses, at bars 11–13 and 25–27. But the pulse really starts to move, emerging to the surface as it were, at bar 30, with the modulation to E major.

The turn to E major brings us to perhaps Schubert's best-known trademark, his minor–major key shifts. In fact, this happens in the first half of the song too, since the respective lines of each couplet are in two different keys. The first line is in E minor, the second in G major. Altogether, "Trockne Blumen" slips into a major key along the two main pathways sanctioned by the musical grammar: first to the *relative* major, G (a third above E), in the second and fourth lines of verses 1 and 2; second, to the *parallel* major, E (the home key but with a G♯ rather than G♮), for verse 3. Unlike the tonic–dominant axis, relationships based on thirds are not intrinsically dynamic or form-defining. They are experienced, rather, as reinterpretations of the material in a different light or color, or from a new perspective. This makes them perfect for an idiom which specializes in reflection and memory. Major-key episodes in Schubert songs are typically associated with bittersweet recollections of past happiness in the midst of present woe. (Though interestingly, both the G and E major shifts in "Trockne Blumen" are future-orientated.) Schubert finds it very easy to slip between minor and major keys, often via the inflection of a single note. In sad songs like the present one, it bears out the dialectical model of crying proposed by the sociologist of emotion, Jack Katz, according to which sad and joyful crying are always defined against each other, and are thus co-present in the same emotional space. If sad crying typically "struggles to sustain a positive view of the person lost," then "Many joyful crying experiences have a bittersweet character because they celebrate a sense of relief at overcoming something terrible." That is why Katz's dialectical model has a symmetrical, chiastic character: "The overall relationship of sad to joyful crying can be described in a configuration in which an entity with a −/+ structure is related to one with a +/− makeup." (see Katz 1999, pp. 185–8).

In Schubert's hands, third relationships have a systematic dimension, kindred with the axial patterns of his melodies. The tonal architecture of "Trockne Blumen" is staked out by third cycles around the tonic, E. Thus a rising cycle of E–G–B is balanced by a descending cycle E–C♯–A♯. The first half of the song, verses 1–2, is dominated by the rising cycle, traversing first G major and then a half-close on the chord of B at the end of each verse (bars 14–15 and 28–29). The most dramatic aspect of the E major second half of the song—aside from the G♯ high-points—is the strong presence of C♯ minor (bars 33–34, bar 37 etc.). The falling scale in the piano left hand in bar 34 outlines the full descending third cycle: G♯–E–C♯–A♯, the last note—the lowest pitch in the song so far—supporting a darkly chromatic diminished seventh chord. Of course, the song's rising and falling tonal contour flows inevitably from the complementary positions of the E major and minor "shadows," a third *above E minor* (G major) in the first half, and a third *below E major* (C♯ minor) in the second.

A tonal architecture based on symmetrical third cycles around a central axis is static and synchronic. It doesn't partake of the long-range dramatic oppositions of keys—quintessentially tonic and dominant—which is fundamental to the Classical style. Third (or "mediant") relationships gradually eclipsed tonic–dominant dramas in all 19th-century music, including sonatas, quartets, symphonies, and operas. One of its main drivers, however, was the harmonic language of Schubert's songs. Schubert was the first composer to fully grasp the affinity between the static quality of axial tonality and the reflective character of lyrical emotion.

Spatial maps of tonality are pervasive in current music theory, configuring key relationships as two- (or even three-)dimensional lattices.[xii] Before we move on to track the affective trajectory of "Trockne Blumen," it is worth considering the suggestive—yet arguably misleading— analogy with maps of *emotional* space. The song's two tonal centers, E minor and E major, have opposite valence (roughly, "sad" and "happy"), as in the well-known circumplex model of Russell (1980). Nevertheless, the rising and falling cycles, emanating from E minor (E–G–B) and E major (E–C♯–A♯), respectively, can't be graphed according to an axis of high versus low arousal (see Figure 2.3). Such a mapping might be plausible for the circle of fifths, where a rising fifth (dominant) raises tension, whilst a falling fifth (subdominant) has a relaxing effect. But this principle doesn't apply for third progressions.

According to the circumplex model, the descent to C♯ and A♯ ought to induce progressive relaxation; in reality, Schubert's music at these points unfolds mounting excitement. A better model would flip the E major cycle 180 degrees so that the minor and major progressions face each other (see Figure 2.4). This would reflect the "rhyme" between the G♯ high-points, expressive of ecstatic excitement and affirmation, and the musical "question-marks" at the end of the two E minor verses. That is, the two E minor cycles both climax with an F♯ (on a B chord), the highest pitches in the song before G♯ is achieved (bars 14 and 27). By marking the two F♯s for consciousness in this way, Schubert helps the listener connect them with the subsequent G♯s: the listener "joins the dots," as it were (such over-arching registral connections are a staple of what Schenker called "Fernhören," or long-distance hearing). Thus, if the emotions at both these F♯ moments might be designated "distressed anxiety," they receive their answer in the G♯s' affirmative joy.

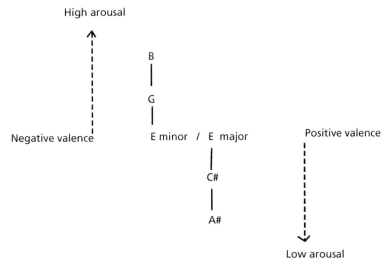

Figure 2.3 Putative map of Schubert's arousal space.

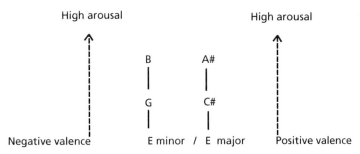

Figure 2.4 Improved map of arousal space.

Yet this interpretation rests on overriding the axis of tonal space (the vertical chain of thirds) with the dynamics of vocal contour, i.e. rising melodies raise tension no matter whether the *harmony* "rises" or "falls." The problem is that musical material is far too multidimensional to fit into standard models of emotional space. Even the notion of valence is problematic, in that Schubert's ostensible major-mode passages are famously ambivalent. If we slot Müller's words back in, then the notion of the miller joyfully embracing death becomes not just tragically ironic, but even rather disturbing. In fact, Kramer (1998, p.146), in his Lacanian interpretation of this moment, hears it as pathologically masochistic. Even without knowledge of this text, the complexity of Schubert's E major emotion is compounded by its C♯ minor "shadow." The emotional complexity is *in the music*. The origins of this "shadow" take us back to what I called the song's "affective trajectory."

Affective trajectories

The notion that the song's emotion, or affect, changes gradually in time would appear to go against both the common habit of labeling musical emotions with fixed adjectives, and the ostensibly static nature of lyrical reflection. Both of these assumptions can be challenged. According to Frijda (1986,

p. 70) all emotions, including sadness (encompassing the spectrum from mild melancholy to deep depression), include "action tendencies," entailing a kind of behavior or mode of cognition.

Exploring the influence of sadness on cognition and judgment, Keltner *et al.* (1993) find that when we are sad, we tend to be more analytical and attentive to detail. Oatley *et al.* (2006, p. 267) call the influence of emotion on cognition "processing style." Thus, whereas "positive mood facilitates use of already existing knowledge structures, such as heuristics and stereotypes, […] negative moods, in particular sadness, facilitates analytical thought and careful attention to situational details." How does this translate into sad lyric music? Such songs, as I have already argued, are more focused around the particularity of their musical material than is the case in fast, dynamic pieces. Conversely, fast music is naturally more schematic. It is common sense, of course, that the faster the music, the less time we have to attend to the musical detail. I need to define my terms with care here. I am not arguing that the song induces a sadness in the listener, which then inflects his or her cognition of the music in a feedback loop. Rather, I claim that the kinds of musical materials (tempo, minor key, melodic idiom) which produce the expressive *signs* of sadness are associated with a "data driven," "bottom up" cognition of this music (by contrast, happy sonata forms tend be more schematic in their material, inducing "concept driven," "top down" processing). I am careful here, then, to put the sadness in the music and its cognition in the listener, while leaving the fraught question of emotional induction completely out of the picture for now (the question will return). Thus I am not interested—yet—in whether or not the listener feels sad.

Actually, reflection doesn't happen only in the listener. The song also reflects on itself, insofar as each of Schubert's "strophic variations" comments upon and reinterprets earlier material. Music's hermeneutic circle has an "inner" and "outer" dimension, mediating its own self-reflection via the listener's thoughts and memories. But does reflection properly "move"? Yes, in that the variations unfold not so much a circle of repetition as a spiral of consciousness, gradually zooming in analytically on "problematic," or formally dissonant, aspects of the material. I'll end this chapter by conjecturing on the rationale and analyzing the musical detail of this "sadness spiral."

Investigating the sources of sorrow and grief in the brain, the neuroscientist Jaak Panksepp links these emotions to the severing of social bonding, creating a "separation anxiety." Thus, "To be alone and lonely, to be without nurturance or a consistent source of erotic gratification, are among the worst and most commonplace emotional pains humans must endure." (Panksepp 2005, p. 263). Certainly, the source of the Miller's distress is separation from his would-be lover. Sad music takes separation anxiety as an axiom; I argue that the trajectory of this music is to seek to recreate (recuperate, memorialize, return to) the severed social bonds. I draw this idea from Kramer's Lacanian interpretation of Schubert Lieder, in order to suggest that the chasm between neuroscience and psychoanalysis is bridgeable in places. Kramer (1998, pp. 14–26) argues that the course of a song such as the early (1815) "Erster Verlust" is motivated by the search to heal "the wound" of separation, i.e. the loss of love. Since true restoration or return is impossible within the genre of sad songs, the music reconstructs a semblance of the lost object out of its own materials, so that the sensuous beauty of the piece becomes an inner substitution. I would add two observations to Kramer's idea. First, cumulative beauty unfolding across the song can actually be fairly dissonant in character, appearing to luxuriate in the signs of musical pain. A sad song aestheticizes negative emotions, rendering them beautiful; this is not a premise, but an outcome of its formal process. Second, such "aestheticization" of negative emotions often happens even when the song stays in the minor key, instead of modulating to the major.

Nevertheless, a common strategy, as in "Trockne Blumen," is to associate the climax of this process with a turn to the bright major key. Looked at more carefully, the glorious, and seemingly joyful, music from bar 30, involving the enigmatic dissonance of C♯ minor, represents the "blossoming" of a darkness first mooted at the very opening of the song. The positively valenced E major half of the song doesn't represent the onset of a new emotion, as might first be thought. On the contrary, it follows very much within the scenario of sadness. This is further evidence for my claim that emotions in a song are not fragmentary or evanescent, but part of coherent affective scenarios. The happy, animated E major music is heard under the aegis of the sad E minor beginning, just as a major key inflects a minor. The new music completes and resolves the earlier material in all sorts of other ways. If the static monotones of the opening are now set in motion in skipping gestures, the hollow triads are filled in with rich textural figurations. Most strikingly of all, the E major melody finally escapes from its axial circle: rather than oscillating around B, the voice from bar 30 now *rises* to dramatic effect: a powerfully muscular ascent—first by step, then by leap—B–B♯–C♯–E–G♯. This is another reason why the G♯ high-point, the goal of this ascent, sounds so affirmatory.

And yet the leaps within this rising scale are disturbing in a way which confirms the persistent influence of the C♯ "shadow." Instead of resolving normatively via the dominant of E major (B) in a V–I progression, the melody leaps a third from C♯ to E, while the harmony substitutes the expected dominant chord with a diminished seventh (bar 35) or a submediant (bar 37). The sensuousness of the texture and the ecstatic high-point distracts us from this anomaly. The music's problem—rendered beautiful here—is the subversive role of the submediant. C♯ appears to have usurped the function of the dominant.

As before, we find that the dissonant "blossoms" of "Trockne Blumen" grow from seeds planted at the song's opening.[xiii] The turn from E minor to G major in the second lines of each of the verse's couplets involves the bass in an odd progression. The bass's opening E shifts, highly unusually, down a step to D natural at bar 5 (D natural is not part of the key of E minor), supporting a 6/4 cadence in the relative major. This E–D shift is also traced by the melody's broad outline (E at bar 3 rhyming with D at bar 5), suggesting a contrapuntally illicit parallel octave progression between the outer voices. What the E–D shift does is to commute the tonic, E, into a submediant of the new key, i.e. E is the sixth degree of G major. By undermining the tonic in this way, Schubert is suggesting that G major is the "real" key, which is of course a delusion. This is the fracture which the song's second half resolves. There can be no question that, from bar 33, C♯ minor is subservient to E major as submediant to tonic. Yet Schubert gives with one hand and takes with the other. At the same time as putting the submediant in its place, he explodes it. The "submediant problem" is now much more manifest, where it had been only latent in the song's first half. Thus the submediant "noise" comes to a head not just in the music's luxuriating in C♯ minor at bars 33–34, but in the kink in the rising scale initiated by the B of bar 30. Following the scale through (B–B♯–C♯), one expects the C♯ to climb to a D♯ in order to resolve by step to the E at bar 35. Instead, as we have seen, Schubert breaks the chain with a leap of a third directly from C♯ to E, supported by that anomalous diminished seventh cadence. If these two initial resolutions are broken-backed (eliding both melodic step and harmonic dominant), they are mended when the much-desired cadence is finally achieved after the G♯ high-point, discharging through a satisfying $\hat{3}$–$\hat{2}$–$\hat{1}$ linear descent to the tonic, and a rock-solid V–I progression. The affective trajectory of "Trockne Blumen" is thus the blossoming of a melodic–harmonic problem, or "seed." Thus we see that the simplest marks of musical change in the song—the linear ascent to G♯ and the broad transformation of musical features—are elaborated at the deepest level by a complex structural argument.

Conclusion: from trajectory to metamorphosis

Words of caution are salutary here to both emotion theorists and formalist music analysts. It behoves the emotion theorist to remember that a high-point like the G♯ is effective and *affective* only because it is supported by a sophisticated undercarriage of compositional strategy—comparable,

Figure 2.5 The song's linear spine.

as it were, to the invisible yet busily kicking legs keeping the graceful swan afloat on the surface (from a different angle, who cares about the high-points in songs of Schubert's forgotten contemporaries?). And music analysts should be reminded that elegant formal progressions are only symbols of broader principles. The linear "spine" of the song is the rising third, E–F♯–G♯; that is, a Schenkerian would hear the F♯ "question" (bars 14 and 28), which we found to "rhyme" with the G♯ "answer," as flowing from the E which is the song's previous melodic apex (in bars 3–13). These structural notes—the three respective apexes of E, F♯ and G♯—encapsulate the song's overall rise, its "Steigerung" (see Figure 2.5).

But this rise is interesting not only in itself but also as a notational trace of what I have called an "affective trajectory," interweaving several strands: a rise in activation or intensity; healing a "separation trauma" by constructing a semblance of a lost object of beauty, thereby aestheticizing a negative emotion; finally, cracking open the shell of articulate musical language so as to discharge a more immediate expressive idiom. I initially identified this expressive breakthrough with a "scream"; a better analogy might be with a sob, especially given the song's textual symbolism of "tear-soaked flowers," and the more general connection many critics have made between Schubert's music and weeping, as in Adorno's celebrated essay. "In the presence of Schubert's music," writes Adorno, "tears spring from our eyes without first consulting the soul" ["*ohne erst die Seele befragen*"]: they flow not metaphorically but tangibly within us. We cry without knowing why." (Adorno 1998). What Adorno seizes upon, in a critical–philosophical language very distant from current emotion theory, is that Schubert's tears are the occasion for affective contagion or empathy between music and listener. The tears don't first "consult the soul," or perhaps—in less elevated language—the *mind*. If the listener cries at all in response to this music, he or she is most likely to do so, perhaps, at these highly localized moments when the music itself "cries." In common-sense terms, listeners are most strongly aroused at what Sloboda (2005, p. 230) called "boundary cues [of musical structure], signifying the end (or the impending end) of one section and the start of the next"—as happens precisely at Schubert's high-point, which signals the onset of the final cadence. Such emotional contagion is famously recorded in the epigram Beethoven attached to his *Missa Solemnis*: "From the heart may it enter the heart". With Schubert, one could say that the emotion flows directly from the eyes of the song to the eyes of the listener.[xiv] "From the eyes may it go to the eyes."

This watery metaphor reminds us, initially, of the overall trajectory of the miller towards his grave within the stream in the last song; and also of an interesting asymmetry within Katz's +/− model of crying. "Sad crying expresses a dialectical narrative in that it *re*-presents loss," asserts Katz. Yet "Joyful crying is the upshot of a *consciousness about the dialectics of metamorphosis itself.*" Rites of passage (such as weddings, births, sunsets, sexual orgasms, etc.) "entail transformations in which an individual, a group or some element of nature is understood to become transformed in the most fundamental bases of identity. Events *of* metamorphosis are recognized *in* the corporeal metamorphosis of joyful crying." (Katz 1999, pp. 190–1). Schubert's "sad flowers" are of course "*dry* flowers," and the transformational course of the song entails a process irrigation: "All you flowers, whence so wet?"

In short, and in conclusion, understanding the affect of "Trockne Blumen" as emotional "character" or "personality" radicalizes the persona theory of music. Even Aaron Ridley's striking notion of musical expression imitating the expressive contour (or "dynamic melisma") of behavior (Ridley 1995, pp. 94–119) doesn't quite go far enough. Emotional behavior isn't *only* designative; angry people kill (and sad people like Schubert's miller sometimes kill themselves) not necessarily in order to communicate or express anything, but purely because that is what they do. Emotion is part of the broad ethology of behavior *tout court*, of which semiotic designation is only a subset. Other aspects of behavior include reflection and intentionality, and music, as we have seen, can mime the contour of that as well, in the course of unfolding its complex formal structure. Schubert's song is like a person in a richly self-reflective, cognitive way. It imitates the expressive behavior of sad *thought*, as well as sad gestures and intonations.

For the record, here are the words I have so far left out of the discussion. Müller's lyrics are beautiful; but Schubert's music is more so. We don't really need to know the words to fathom the emotion of Schubert's song, as is the case, I suggest, with many listeners who don't understand German, or who can't make out the words in *any* language in which a Romantic song is sung. To invoke a common trope of music aesthetics—itself a desiccated flower of rhetoric—the dry words are dissolved in the stream of tones.

> Dried Flowers
> All you flowers
> That she gave me
> They must put you
> With me in my grave.
> Why do you all look
> Upon me so sadly,
> As if you knew
> What has happened to me?
> All you flowers,
> Why withered, why pale?
> All you flowers,
> Why so wet?
> Alas, tears make
> No May green,
> Nor make dead love
> Bloom again.
> And spring will come,
> And winter will go,
> And flowers will
> Grow in the field.
> And flowers lie
> In my grave,
> All those flowers
> That she gave me.
> And when she walks
> Past the hill,
> And thinks in her heart:

He was true!
Then all you flowers
Come out, come out!
May has come,
And winter is over.[xv]

Notes

i   Scherer and Zentner discuss emotional contagion under the rubric of "empathy."

ii   Schenker's masterwork is his treatise, *Free Composition (Der freie Satz)*, translated and edited by Ernst Oster (Longman, 1979).

iii   Goethe's concept of *Steigerung*, with its entailments of intensification, ascent, variegation, polarisation, and spiralling return, was an all-encompassing analogy which he applied in botany (the evolution of his "*Urpflanz*"), optics (his color theory), and literature (as in novels waxing towards lyrical apotheosis). For an overview, see Spitzer (2004), especially pp. 294–95 and 330–41.

iv   See in particular two contributors to the *Music Analysis* special issue on "Music and emotion," Zbikowski (2010) and Hatten (2010). In particular, Hatten does not theorize his notion of "expressive trajectory" in relation to a specific emotional category.

v   For a recent refinement of Juslin's theory see Juslin and Lindström (2010).

vi   For a critical discussion of Meyer's theory of core affect versus current theories of discrete emotions see Spitzer (2009).

vii   See Leech-Wilkinson's essay in Chapter 4. The position of performance theory, that emotion arises through shaping the music in the act of performing it, seems to entail the corollary that the musical work is an emotionally neutral plasma. This position is curiously in line with Meyer's theory of "core affect." For an analysis of a specific emotion in another Schubert song see Spitzer (2010), in particular pp. 186–202, which looks at Schubert's *Der Erlkönig*.

viii   See also Scherer and Zentner (2001), for whom emotions are "relatively brief episodes" (p. 363).

ix   See the spectrum in Scherer and Zentner (2001, p. 363), which runs from preferences ("evaluative judgments of stimuli") to personality traits ("emotionally laden, stable personality dispositions"). See also Goldie (2000), especially pp. 151–60.

x   Lest the appeal to Spinoza seem anachronistic, two facts should be taken on board. First, Baroque arias (as in Bach cantatas) display the same consistency of figure and affect we find in Romantic *Lieder*. Second, this stylistic consanguinity between Baroque and Romantic music, noted by many music historians, parallels the resurgence of Spinoza in the late 18th century, leading to his strong influence on Hegel and Schelling.

xi   In particular, see Huron's theory of "regression to the mean," on p. 82.

xii   A particularly influential study is by Cohn (1999). A debating point is whether spatial lattices have "centers," like diatonic scale systems. By stipulating an axis round a center, my interpretation of Schubert's tonality is out of line with most so-called "Neo-Riemannian" theorists of chromatic harmony.

xiii   For a very different reading of the song see Zbikowski (1999).

xiv   Adorno devotees will be familiar with an enormous literature on the role eyes and gazing play in his and Walter Benjamin's work. Previous musicological treatments of this motif, I may venture, have tended to get lost in the maze of ocular symbolism, rather than make convincing connections either with music or the ethology of weeping.

xv   Author's translation.

References

Adorno, T. W. (1992). *Mahler: a Musical Physiognomy*, transl. E. Jephcott, p. 48. Chicago: University of Chicago Press.

Adorno, T. W. (1998). Schubert. In R. Tiedemann (ed.) *Gesammelte Schriften*, vol. 17, p. 33. Darmstadt: Wissenschaftliche Buchgesellschaft. (Translation by Max Paddison, private communication.)

Agawu, K. (1991). *Playing with Signs: a Semiotic Interpretation of Classic Music* Princeton: Princeton University Press.

Cohn, R. (1999). As wonderful as star clusters: instruments for gazing at tonality in Schubert. *19th-Century Music*, **22**, 213–32.

Eitan, Z. (1999) *Highpoints: a Study of Melodic Peaks*. Philadelphia: University of Pennsylvania Press.

Ekman, P. (2004). *Emotions Revealed: Understanding Faces and Feelings*. London: Phoenix.

Frijda, N. (1986). *The Emotions*. Cambridge: Cambridge University Press.

Goldie, P. (2000). *The Emotions: a Philosophical Exploration*. Oxford: Oxford University Press.

Hatten, R. (2010). Aesthetically warranted emotion and composed expressive trajectories in music. *Music Analysis*, **29**, 83–101.

Huron, D. (2008). *Sweet Anticipation: Music and the Psychology of Expectation*. Cambridge, MA: MIT Press.

James, S. (1997). *Passion and Action: the Emotions in Seventeenth-Century Philosophy*. Oxford: Clarendon Press.

Juslin, P. and Lindström, E. (2010). Musical expression of emotions: modelling listeners' judgements of composed and performed features. *Music Analysis*, **29**, 334–64.

Katz, J. (1999). *How Emotions Work*. Chicago: University of Chicago Press.

Keltner, D., Ellsworth, P., and Edwards, K. (1993). Beyond simple pessimism: effects of sadness and anger on social perception. *Journal of Personality and Social Psychology*, **64/5**, 740–52.

Kramer, L. (1998). *Franz Schubert: Sexuality, Subjectivity, Song*. Cambridge: Cambridge University Press.

Oatley, K., Keltner, D., and Jenkins, J. M. (2006). *Understanding Emotions*, 2nd edn, p. 267. Oxford: Blackwell.

Panksepp, J. (2005) *Affective Neuroscience: the Foundations of Human and Animal Emotions*. Oxford: Oxford University Press.

Ridley, A. (1995). *Music, Value, and the Passions*. Ithaca, NY: Cornell University Press.

Robinson, J. (2007). *Deeper than Reason: Emotion and its Role in Literature, Music, and Art*. Oxford: Clarendon Press.

Russell, P. A. (1980). A circumplex model of affect. *Journal of Personality and Social Psychology*, **39**, 1161–78.

Scherer, K. R. and Zentner, M. R. (2001). Emotional effects of music production rules. In P. Juslin and J. Sloboda (eds), *Music and Emotion: Theory and Research*, pp. 369–71. Oxford: Oxford University Press.

Sloboda, J. (2005). *Exploring the Musical Mind*. Oxford: Oxford University Press.

Spitzer, M. (2004). *Metaphor and Musical Thought*. Chicago: University of Chicago Press.

Spitzer, M. (2009). Emotions and meaning in music. *Musica Humana*, **1**, 155–96.

Spitzer, M. (2010). Mapping the human heart: a holistic analysis of fear in Schubert. *Music Analysis*, **29**, 149–213.

Tomlinson, G. (1999). *Metaphysical Song: an Essay on Opera*. Princeton: Princeton University Press.

Youens, S. (1992). *Schubert: die Schöne Müllerin*. Cambridge: Cambridge University Press.

Zbikowski, L. (1999). The blossoms of "Trockne Blumen": music and text in the early nineteenth century. *Music Analysis*, **18**, 307–45.

Zbikowski, L. (2010). Music, emotion, analysis. *Music Analysis*, **29**, 37–60.

Chapter 3

Composing the expressive qualities of music

Interviews with Jean-Claude Risset, Brian Ferneyhough, and Carter Burwell, by Tom Cochrane

Interview with Jean-Claude Risset

TC: *Do you believe that music arouses emotions in listeners? Are the emotions aroused by music like everyday emotions, or more uniquely musical in character?*

JCR: I think there is no doubt that music arouses emotions. I myself decided to engage into music because of the strong emotional power it had on me. I do not concentrate on expressing my own emotions in music, however. When I am overwhelmed with emotions, I am incapable of creating music. Yet it seems inevitable that the music can suggest certain emotions or mental states. It can be dynamogenic or depressing, active or meditative.

I would also add that while music can arouse more ordinary emotions, most emotions that music arouses in me are quite different from everyday emotions, even though they may have similar bodily effects when they are very strong: weeping of joy, shivering... I am an agnostic, but I feel the expressive qualities of music have the capacity to hint at transcendence and to elicit feelings that take us beyond ourselves. To me, the utmost musical emotion brings us a feeling of evidence that may have to do with creative mathematicians' intuitive and synoptic feeling for a demonstration that they have only to unfold.

There is an intriguing statement by Borges that I find relevant here: "Music, states of happiness, mythology, faces belaboured by time, certain twilights and certain places, try to tell us something, or have said something we should not have missed, or are about to say something; the imminence of a revelation which does not occur is, perhaps, the aesthetic phenomenon."

TC: *This reminds me somewhat of Stendhal's motto "Beauty is the promise of happiness." I suppose in both cases there is a recognition of the compelling powers of aesthetic objects. But when you also say there is a hint of transcendence, you suggest that music may (if only rarely) convey deeper meaning. How do you make sense of this meaning, given that non-vocal music contains no propositional content?*

JCR: Keats wrote: "A thing of beauty is a joy for ever." Indeed, I cannot speak clearly about the meaning of music, since music at its best seems to make sense in its own way. Beyond words, it conveys an unspeakable meaning, "*indicible*," as we say in French. Perhaps music has the virtue to speak to us about what is beyond us, beyond the grasp of our conscious intelligence and understanding.

Music cannot be translated: it does not need translation. It has its own coherence, its truth and evidence. To make sense out of simultaneous conversations, we have to extract one and ignore the others, but in music we can listen to different voices simultaneously. Harmony and counterpoint achieve synergy between components that keep their own identity: this is a metaphor for our dreams of a harmonious society. Music has a "religious" effect—from "re-ligare": it helps link people together, and it plays a role in the rituals of different religions.

Music can also attain a cosmic dimension, making us feeling strongly that we are part of an immense world and related to it.

TC: *How do you understand the way in which music arouses emotions?*

JCR: My own view of emotions in music is complex and quite a bit unclear, and I have hardly tried to unravel it. There has been a lot of debate between those who insist that musical meaning lies in the perception of musical form—from Hanslick to Stravinsky—and those who contend that music conveys extra-musical feelings, symbols, and meaning. Yet it seems artificial to separate these two aspects. Leonard Meyer considers that the listener plays the strongest role in bringing the formalist aspect or the emotional aspect into the foreground. According to Meyer, perception of music involves anticipation. What the listener expects depends of course on the style of the music and the extent to which he or she knows about it.

It seems to me that this view emphasizes the perception of relations between musical sounds, but that it does not consider enough the musicality of the sound itself. Varèse was turned off by music made with simplistic electronic sounds—"sounds for morticians"—not complex and lively enough to satisfy his demanding ears. Indeed hearing is performing complicated and effective cerebral operations even when concentrating on a single sound. For instance we can guess whether a tone arriving at the ear with a level of 30 dB has been produced by a powerful source far away or a soft source nearby. We can also localize precisely the direction of the source. This is quite remarkable.

Such discriminations help the predator find the prey or the prey escape the predator. One can reasonably believe that evolution has optimized our senses to provide information about the outside world that can help survival. Thus we are equipped to perform inquiries on acoustic sound, to guess where they come from (from what direction, how far) and what caused them. Music makes gratuitous use of our cognitive capacities: the ear may be frustrated if the sounds are too simple to enable such inquiries. Clearly these quests can produce emotional effects. For instance the "chorus" effect of many tones together may hint at a threatening crowd. So music is anchored in our perception, but the way perception has evolved is itself anchored in the physical reality of sounds in the outside world.

TC: *This exploration of the musicality of the sound itself seems to be an important aspect of your own work, and indeed quite characteristic of contemporary electro-acoustic music in general. Can you tell us more about how a composer such as yourself approaches or engages with these inner qualities of sound? Is it done in an intuitive or systematic way for instance? Are there emotional qualities at this level?*

JCR: Musicians have not waited for electrical sound to be preoccupied with the musicality of the sound itself. Much music outside the Western world demonstrates this, as well as the compositions of Berlioz or Debussy. Edgard Varèse complained that composers only concentrated on the grammar of music: he wanted to extend the vocabulary and produce a music of sounds rather than a music of notes, which he did even in his instrumental music—a path still followed today by George Crumb or Helmut Lachenmann. But Varèse was longing for electrical means to produce sound, which he finally used in his works *Déserts* and *Poème électronique*. Indeed electro-acoustic music has permitted composers to exert more elaborate control on the sounds, to the extent of composing the sound themselves.

In the early 1960s, I was encouraged by André Jolivet to compose instrumental music. I found that the traditional orchestra was a wonderful resource, but a limited one, more adapted to post-Romantic symphonies than to the quest for new musical paths. Also many instrumental sounds are highly referential: guitar tones irresistibly allude to Spain for instance.

So I was very intent on exploring the resources of electro-acoustic music. At that time, there were two dominant schools. In France, *musique concrète* had been started in the late 1940s by Pierre Schaeffer in the studios of the French national radio. Schaeffer and his followers, such as Pierre Henry, gathered recorded sounds of acoustic origin and assembled them into compositions using studio techniques (tape recorders, splicing, transposing, filtering, reverberating…). This method yielded dramatic works with a very rich variety of sounds. However, acoustic sounds had strong identity, and the means of transformation were relatively rudimentary compared with their richness, so one could hardly exert a truly compositional control upon them: it seemed to me difficult to escape an aesthetics of *collage*.

In Germany, the pioneers of *electronic music* were driven by the goal of producing very precise rendering of musical scores composed with complex serial procedures and very difficult to perform, special rhythms. So they used only sounds produced by electrical generators, for which they could precisely control parameters such as frequency or duration. Thus the elaborate compositional processes were rendered accurately, but the sounds were very peculiar. I found they lacked identity and richness, to the extent of turning off the ears of demanding listeners.

So, in the early 1960s, I was not satisfied with either *musique concrète* or *electronic music*, when I heard with puzzlement about computer synthesis of sound, a process implemented by Max Mathews at Bell Telephone Laboratories near New York City. Although I did not clearly understand the details, it seemed to me that the control available with the computer was very promising, and I hoped that the synthetic sounds could be made complex enough to be interesting, yet be accurately formatted to adapt to a compositional intent.

Indeed, the resources of computer synthesis were gradually developed so as to become musically useful and potent. Musicians contributed to this development, in particular John Chowning and myself: we had to do systematic exploration because auditory perception is very peculiar. Initially the specifics of hearing seemed surprising and arbitrary. Later we could understand them by considering that hearing extracts from the sound information about the environment that could be useful for survival. As a consequence, the ear is extremely sensitive to certain specific aspects of sounds. Its remarkable sensitivity to frequency can be understood in this perspective, since frequency is well preserved in sound propagation. Pitch has largely been exploited in music, but other significant aspects could hardly be thought of a priori. For instance, the ear seems to be more discriminant to the precise details of the sound when it can trace a plausible mechanical causality for this sound (blowing, scraping, hitting). One could almost speak of touching upon "erogenous" zones of hearing, which offer promises for musical expressivity provided they are dealt with in the right way. For his piece *Stria*, Chowning has chosen inner structure of the tones in relation to the steps of the frequency transposition scale he uses: the result is very novel, euphonious, and strong. In *Phone*, he transforms anonymous synthetic sounds into simulacra of human voices, a metamorphosis which means a lot to the listener.

Computer music thus elaborates its sound material, pushing the compositional control into the sonic domain: it attempts to compose sounds themselves, rather than merely composing with sounds. Beyond arranging sounds in time, the composer can play with time within the sounds. To use the words of the composer Denis Smalley, composing becomes an art of *spectromorphology*.

TC: *Do you think that music should generate emotions in listeners? Is this a priority for you?*

JCR: I think that music should be strong enough to generate emotions in listeners. However, this should happen as a consequence of the complex cognitive operations performed by the active and attentive listener, rather than as a result of systematic processes intended to make the music emotional by using tricks of the trade producing direct physiological effects. I believe that great music is demanding on the listener, so that its novelty is not exhausted at the first listening: immediate returns only produce shallow pleasure.

Composers for movies or computer games are often bluntly requested to arouse this or that emotion: more and more research is now channeled toward this goal. I disagree with Pierre Schaeffer, the pioneer of *musique concrète* and music research, when he describes himself as an engineer in emotions: working on the arousal of emotions seems akin to manipulation. I think the emotion should stem from some cognitive understanding rather than from raw effects.

I also consider that much popular music abuses of a few effects that are akin to manipulation: a sustained invariable beat, akin to military music; a strong tonal anchoring with dominance of degrees I (tonic, like C), IV (subdominant, F in C), V (dominant, G in C); and above all a high level of amplification, including energetic low and high frequencies that can affect the body beyond the sense of hearing. High sound intensities have intoxicating effects on the listeners, and they are detrimental to hearing (certainly for the performers themselves). Loud music can induce dependency (in French "*assuétude*") just as a drug.

TC: *So there is an ethical dimension to the composition of music then? Particularly with regard to its expressive powers?*

JCR: I think so. The emotional power of music can indeed be used to manipulate people toward certain goals. Strong music can alter the faculty of judgment or criticism. It can even be intoxicating. Musak Inc. made a fortune selling music designed to make people buy more goods. Military music is aimed at favoring subordination and weakening the fear of killing or being killed. Even art music can be deemed dangerously powerful. The playwright Bertold Brecht insisted that the infinite melodies of Wagner can induce an exhilaration, a kind of trance which tampers with the lucidity of the listener. Brecht advocated a form of opera that would allow the spectator to keep some distance and irony, so as to prevent him or her from being completed subdued: he claimed it was ethically important to resist whatever might facilitate social organizations exploiting people.

TC: *I think we can usefully distinguish between the manipulative use of clichés for expressive effect, and having some creative insight into how an expressive quality might be generated with basic acoustic properties. Are there any such cases from your own work of the latter that you can describe for us?*

In the 1960s, I was asked to compose music for the play *Little Boy* by Pierre Halet, a phantasmatic revival of the raid to Hiroshima to drop the first atomic bomb—code name "Little

Boy." The hero, or anti-hero, of the play is an historic character, Claude Eatherly, the pilot of the reconnaissance plane, who suffered severe guilt feelings after the raid and stayed a long time in a psychiatric hospital. The play stages Eatherly, under the effect of drugs, reviving a TV commemoration of the raid distorted by his own phantasms. The pilot identifies with the bomb "Little Boy"—an infantile regression according to the psychiatrists: when the bomb is dropped, he thinks he falls, but this is only an illusory psychic fall, a mental collapse. To illustrate this episode, I worked at making a continuous version of an endless descent. Roger Shepard had generated in 1964 twelve tones forming a chromatic scale that seem to endlessly go up when they are repeated. Ira Braus later traced this pitch circularity—A B C D E F G A…—in Western instrumental music. Shepard said in his 1964 article that he needed a gap between the tones. I could generate a continuous endless glissando by carefully controlling the synthesis. I extended this illusion to produce sounds that glided down yet were lower in the end than where they started. This produced strong and intriguing effects, which fit the theatrical demands.

Similar effects can be produced with rhythm. Around 1970, Kenneth Knowlton produced pulses that seemed to speed up endlessly. I could generalize this to envelopes modulating any tone to endow it with a constantly speeding-up rhythm, or with a beat that slows down but finally gets faster than it started. A "circular" speeding up does not get any faster in the long run, a slowing down does not get any slower: however, speeding up is much more dynamogenic than slowing down.

I could produce tones with stretched octaves that seem to go down in pitch when one doubles the frequencies of their components, and similarly beats that seem to slow down when one doubles the speed of the tape that reproduces them. Clearly pitch variations are not always isomorphous to frequency, and rhythm cannot be reduced to chronometric countings. Musicians should be aware of this, since "music is meant to be heard," as Schaeffer liked to say. Taking advantage of the idiosyncrasies of hearing yield paradoxical effects which can be surprising, expressive, or emotional.

Once I did avoid this technique for creating emotion, not because of any a priori *parti pris*, but because it induced negative emotions in myself. I encountered a poem by Henri Michaux, *La ralentie*, at a time when I had been working on the illusion of endless slowing. I decided to combine an endless rallentendo with an endless descent in pitch. After a couple of days experimenting to try to synthesize the strongest effect of rallentendo, I felt so depressed that I decided I did not want to go on: in addition, I did not feel I should impose such depressing effects on listeners.

I have to admit to the possibility of manipulation there: clearly powerful dramatic effects call for more than unemotional cognition. Illusions or paradoxes can introduce a certain poetic quality akin to magic. In fact Pierre Halet intended the play and the staging of *Little Boy* to give hints of the manipulating sensory effects used in the Second World War, and the music was supposed to play its part in this goal. Part of the music was written for acoustic instruments, and part was computer-synthesized: beyond producing pitch paradoxical behaviors, I also used synthesis to mimic instruments and produce an illusory phantasmatic mirror of the real world: sounds of immaterial instruments.

I have resorted to such confrontations, which induce emotional reactions. For instance, in my work *L'autre face* (1983), on a poem by Roger Kowalski, a soprano dialogues with computer-synthesized sounds. At some point the synthesized part tends to sound like a human voice, and it even becomes a convincing replica, a synthetic clone of the voice of the singer. This is intended to echo the poem: "*écoute: quelque chose ici n'est point de ce monde*" ("listen: something here is not from this world"). Here I am staging close encounters between the real world, with the voice of the singer, visible on the stage, and an illusory world, with sounds that are close enough to have the very special emotional quality of a voice—but it is not the voice of any person that could be seen or touched. The way the synthetic voice evolves makes the distinction clear to the listener, and the effect is intriguing.

In his work *Phone* (1981) John Chowning turned vocal metamorphosis into a powerful expressive resource: he developed ways to fine-tune the parameters of an anonymous synthetic tones (especially the vibrato) to mimic the gait of a human voice. The first time I tried to replicate his process on a computer in Marseilles, I knew exactly I was reproducing accurately a well-defined algorithm, yet I felt deeply moved when the computer began to sound just like a real person, giving a strong feeling of a presence.

Music relies on intersubjectivity. People are all different, but intersubjectivity allows the possibility of consensus. Yet personal experiences bear upon each one's emotional relation to music. In 1970, I played my piece *Mutations* to an audience of scientific researchers. This work, entirely synthesized by computer, ends with an endlessly ascending glissando lasting several minutes. Many listeners were intrigued (I was asked to play this paradoxical sound on a colloquium on infinity). Someone said he felt very anxious because the gliding sound reminded him of alarm sirens warning for a bombardment during the Second World War, thus causing gloomy feelings, negative emotions. Another one reacted, who on the contrary felt exhilarated: the endless ascent, liberated from gravity, evoked to him "*les corps glorieux*" (the glorious bodies after resurrection, evoked in the Catholic theology).

TC: *I am interested also in the way in which you combine natural sounds with synthesized sounds in your music—of which your composition* Sud *is a particularly striking example. Is the goal for a work like this to transport the listener to a different imagined environment? One also feels invited to meditate upon the musical qualities of such natural sounds as waves, birds, insects, and so on, is this your intent as well?*

JCR: My piece *Sud* is especially meaningful to me, because it attempts to marry electronic music and *musique concrète* to try to benefit from the strengths of both. I was not content with mixing synthetic sounds with sounds of acoustic origin: I tried to hybridize them. The piece was realized in 1984 at GRM [Groupe de Recherches Musicale], the birthplace of *musique concrète*.

I have often enjoyed the sonic beauty of the natural sounds along the sea shore near Marseilles: sea waves, winds blowing into the trees, songs of birds or chirps of insects. I wished *Sud* to evoke this by including soundscapes—plain recordings of a natural sonic scenes—hoping to induce listeners to reflect upon their musical quality and to appreciate natural sounds as music.

Thus *Sud* includes *phonographies*—sound photographies, mere recordings of natural sounds. The piece begins with phonographies. Then synthetic sounds are presented in sharp contrast: they are very different, they do not evoke nature but they follow a precise pitch scale. The scenario of *Sud* is the following: throughout the piece, the natural and synthetic sonic worlds will gradually intermingle though transformations bringing them closer to one another.

The initial phonography is a 15-second recording of sound waves breaking over a sandy beach on a quiet morning: a found sound object, which I decided to select as a germinal motif recalled in varied forms at different points in the piece. From this motif, I extracted profiles: curves of the time variations of the intensity or the spectral center of gravity. These profiles were used morphologically to shape different sounds or to determine melodic contours, and also metaphorically in terms of musical form.

The fact that many sounds refer to familiar scenes helps the listener to relate to these sounds, to follow their transformations throughout the piece, and to be insidiously taken from a "normal" sonic environment—an audible trace of a visible world—to a musically imagined one, suggesting an immaterial, illusory world, a separate internal reality. The gradual passage is suggested by transformations such as hybridizations of various sounds. For instance the energy flux of the sea will animate synthetic tones; the musical harmony chosen for the synthetic tones will be imprinted onto bird songs or sea surfs.

I started with a corpus of natural sounds—including phonographies which I had recorded myself—and a few synthetic sounds, the latter following a defective major–minor *scale* or *raga*. I initially imagined an overall form that would very gradually merge tones of natural and synthetic origins. I went through a long pre-compositional process of transforming the sounds of the corpus in various ways—including a form of hybridization called *cross-synthesis*. What I mean by this term is a transformation which starts with two sounds and generates a third sound that has certain properties of each of the two sounds, similarly to sexual procreation. Through this process, I could produce chimeras: birds–insects, waves of harpsichords. In fact I was trailing Cézanne, who wished to "marry curves of women and shoulders of hills." I brought *musique concrète* and *musique électronique* together by injecting the energy flux of natural sounds—the sea, the wind—into harmonically composed synthetic sounds, or by imprinting the scales and harmonies chosen for synthetic sounds onto natural sounds with indefinite pitch (e.g. sea sounds) or with pitches not selected by the composer (e.g. bird or insect sounds).

However, in the midst of the pre-compositional process, I stumbled on an unexpected and striking effect. I mixed a rough splashing sea sound with copies of this sound which I had slighted transposed by a small fraction of a semi-tone. Much to my surprise, this added to the sound a powerful glissando downwards, descending from the treble to extremely low frequencies. This was so effective a shock that I decided to take advantage of that "found" effect in a median section that would evoke a metaphoric tempest ending with a wreckage. This decision was made as a consequence of the emotion I felt then. *Sud* is probably my most emotional work.

TC: *How happy are you for listeners to derive their own interpretations of your music? For instance, if a listener projects a detailed narrative to fit your music or some symbolic meaning, would you regard this is as not properly taking the music on its own terms?*

JCR: I did get feedback from a number of young people who were asked in music classes to describe their experience listening to works such as *Little Boy* and *Sud*. I was rather unhappy when the music was simply described in a simplistic way such as "music of the outer space," which means that it was classified in a wide category of bizarre or unfamiliar. But when the detailed narrative was more elaborate, I found that the listener did relate in some way to the music, even if it was not the way I intended. Interpretations also encouraged me to look for ways to avoid simplistic evocations. I must admit that I can only suggest an interpretation of my music, but I cannot impose it. In fact I was excited by the variety of reactions it elicited. And I was happy to discover occasional symbolic or even mythical evocations which I found valid and suggestive.

TC: *It seems that electro-acoustic music has a quite definite sonic language and range of structural forms that require a good deal of effort to understand and appreciate. Are you concerned that an average listener more familiar with tonal music may be unable to appreciate your works? Do you envisage that this kind of music will eventually become more dominant in the wider musical world?*

JCR: As a composer, I am concerned by the fact that listeners may be unable to appreciate my works. However, I consider that it is not the primary concern of ambitious composers. Marketing is essential for commercial music, but art music should be innovative rather than derivative. The significance of art works is not linked with their immediate impact, but rather to their lasting value. It looks unlikely that electro-acoustic music—or any kind of art music—will become dominant: commercial music offers immediate gratification for people who are rushed and assaulted by all kinds of stimuli. The access to music through the world-wide web probably has a strong effect on the consumption of music: "songs" and "clips" have become the unit. The songs selected to be the hits of the year are trendy, simple, and easy to appreciate: they are bombarded to a large public through considerable and expensive exposure and publicity, and saturation wears them out quickly.

Some features of tonal music—especially the tonal cadenza and the satiation of chords on the tonic, the subdominant, and the dominant—constitute very clear articulations, rules forming a rudimentary musical grammar which is implicitly familiar to inexpert listeners: this grammar makes it easier to follow the music, and it is at work in most commercial music. But even strictly tonal works are not necessarily popular when their elaboration is complex. Beethoven's string quartets are highly regarded but not heard very often. Even though many music lovers admire and enjoy the atonal music of Schoenberg, a common opinion regards this music as cerebral, unpleasant, or inexpressive. Yet similar atonal music is perfectly admitted in movies—it is even recognized as very emotional.

There is indeed something special about electro-acoustic music. I do not agree that it has a quite definite sonic language: one can distinguish several dominant trends which are quite different. The fact that the origin of sounds is often difficult or impossible to identify has a strong bearing on the emotions it elicits. The composer Gerald Bennett has noticed that listeners to electro-acoustic music cannot see the sources of sound: they are in an "acousmatic" situation (an adjective qualifying Pythagoras' lessons heard behind a curtain and favored by the composer François Bayle), similarly to cave dwellers trying to detect the sounds of danger in the dark night. So anxiety or fear can be a powerful part of the expressive gamut of this music. The first works of *musique concrète* by Pierre Schaeffer and Pierre Henry keep a strong theatrical quality. But negative emotions can scare away many listeners who rather seek to be reassured by familiar sounds. In fact most listeners seem to want a sonic ambience hiding a threatening silence.

So curiosity is a requisite for being interested in the first place in new forms of music, especially electro-acoustic music. Then the familiarity gained by listening makes a listener more discriminating and interested in the properly musical issues. As the composer Jon Appleton demonstrated with his students, this will be even more so if the listener has an opportunity to directly manipulate sound, which is getting easy with present personal computers: in that case, the listener–actor gets more expert at appreciation and more demanding in quality.

I consider there are already powerful masterpieces in electro-acoustic music, and it is possible to speculate that this genre will gain in sophistication and acceptance. I cannot make predictions about which music will be dominant in the wider musical world. It much depends how society (societies?) will evolve from the present avidly consumerist state. Symphonic orchestras are economically threatened. Existing works of electro-acoustic music will only survive if they are carefully preserved and played. If art music is not supported, it may die— which would be a great loss, since commercial music has by no means the same enduring value.

Further reading

Braus, I. (1995). Retracing one's steps: an overview of pitch circularity and Shepard tones in European music, 1550–1990. *Music Perception*, **12**, 323–51.

Delalande, F., Formosa, M., Frémiot, M., Gobin, P., Malbosc, P., Mandelbrojt, J., and Pedler, E. (1996). *Les Unités Sémiotiques Temporelles—Éléments Nouveaux d'Analyse Musicale*. Marseilles: Edition MIM–Musurgia (with audio CD).

Meyer, L. B. (1956). *Emotion and Meaning in Music*. Chicago: University of Chicago Press.

Norman, K. (ed.) (1996). *A Poetry of Reality—Composing with Recorded Sound* (with an audio CD). (Special issue of the *Contemporary Music Review*, **15**.)

Risset, J. C. (1978). Musical acoustics. In E. C. Carterette and M. P. Friedmann (eds), *Handbook of Perception: Hearing*, Vol. IV, pp. 520–64. New York: Academic Press.

Risset, J. C. (1986). Pitch and rhythm paradoxes: comments on "Auditory paradox based on a fractal waveform." *Journal of the Acoustic Society of America*, **80**, 961–2.

Risset, J. C. (2008). *Du Songe au Son: Entretiens avec Matthieu Guillot*. Paris: L'Harmattan.

Biography of Jean-Claude Risset at <http://www.moderecords.com/profiles/jeanclauderisset.html>

Interview with Brian Ferneyhough

TC: *Do you believe that music arouses emotion in listeners?*

BF: Clearly music elicits various types of emotional response through a complex web of appellative injunctions. This indirect (subjunctive–speculative) mode is what distinguishes our emotive contact with art from that pertaining to everyday objects making demands on our emotional household. That is why the confusing overlap between these categories is especially (if perhaps puritanically) tasty. More interesting than confirming the mere fact, then, is examining the aspect of intentionality of the composer with respect to various degrees of explicitness of correlation between sonic icons and what one might term communally (implicitly) agreed-on emotive context. As with all art media, one is encouraged to introspective acts comparing what one 'should' feel with what, on any given occasion, one's specific subjective response might be. The result is a third thing, which one might, I suppose, term an informal aesthetic rejoinder. One is supplied with cultural hints as to which appropriately tinged locus quiddity is permitted to intercede in the apportionment of our raw emotive *volunté* to more public or private zones of emotive parsing.

TC: *So if I understand you correctly, the composer must navigate a kind of cultural–emotional milieu, that mediates and possibly constrains how one responds to the music. Do you think there is room here for a sincere form of communication, or shared experience between composer, performer, and listener?*

BF: I certainly espouse the former, with the proviso that 'sincerity' be not interchangeable with the abandonment of ambiguity. Shared experience is probably something that becomes increasingly persuasive over time; the intricate weave of experience needs to be continually retested against new subjective input. Even if, in the final analysis, there is no real way to confirm or disconfirm the degree of correspondence between productive, reproductive, and receptive models, I in no way feel that this invalidates the engagement that the mutual compact implies.

TC: *Do you think that music should generate emotions in listeners (or feelings of a particular kind)? Is this a priority for you?*

BF: I am doubtful of inserting 'should' into musical experience. Some types of music seem to elicit 'musical' emotions rather than evoking sensations of an extra-musical nature. Non-musicians might be forgiven for not perceiving the former, or at least not directly. As a composer, when I listen to, say, late Stravinsky, I am seized by a sense of optimism which takes the form of a desire to go away and work on my own music. Is this available to the educated listener?

TC: *So your own emotional reactions to music have been a significant source of inspiration?*

BF: Certainly. In my early twenties I was very moved by certain composers whose works manifested the sort of "sublimity" which I was beginning to seek in my own approach to compositional individuality. I was hit hard by the obvious virtuosity of technique of, say, the 'Sonata sopra "Sancte Maria" ' of Monteverdi's 1610 *Vespers*. Perhaps that is one reason why I find it difficult to separate emotional responses from the techniques which are their vehicle.

Of course, a composer seeks stimulation where and however he/she can find it; we are all magpies. But personally, I have come to appreciate other musics largely from this standpoint. Doubtless, one might argue that I am "missing something" in not being in a position to appreciate a musical work, as it were, by the application of cultivatedly disinterested faculties of apperception. There is room for all sorts.

TC: *Do you try to express your own emotions in music? Or other mental states?*

BF: I don't think I set out to put particular emotional experiences in direct contact with musical situations, although perhaps this happens without my direct knowledge. It's rather that experiencing emotions leads me to compose and, more importantly, to maintain the long-term pressure and focus which composing demands. I tend to assume that, as artists, we automatically maintain, recalibrate, and externalize subjective states in ways conducive to their insertion into, and subsequent modification of, cultural discourse. That is what artists do. At the same time, I have often been impelled to confront music with external intellectual disciplines in order to suggest mappings of a different order of cognition. The often jarring intersection of these discourses leads to a fluctuating field of intensities which, ideally, would empower subjective emotive reaction on a more complex level of evaluation.

TC: *Can you give an example of the external disciplines you have imposed on a work—and how this has led to a more complex set of reactions, particularly on your own part?*

Some of these constraint systems emerge directly from the nature of the sonic stuff with which one engages, and reflect, I suppose, aspects of my privileged position with respect to how and why things coalesced the way they did. In part, they reflect my understanding of the useful limits of variation, and how local variative techniques come to imply larger-scale categories of organization. This is probably true for all composers. Particularly in the earlier phases of my career I was very concerned with finding ways of confronting the "law of exceptions" which rules in individual works with historically grounded modes of organized perception—philosophical systems, alchemy, and so on. Perhaps some of these attempts might, in retrospect, be accused of well-meaning naivety; it was still worth, I think, the candle, given the degree to which certain tendencies of composition teeter between the mutually incompatible poles of *l'art pour l'art* and crudely prescriptive political manifestos.

TC: *Are there any techniques you employ for emotional expression in your music—for instance, imagining a persona in the music, narrative programs, resembling physical feelings or movement, or more specific rules?*

BF: No, not really, although it is indeed important that the forms of sonic rhetoric one employs correlate to some extent with imagined bodily actions. Imprecise parallels between the arts and the physical disciplines required to exercise their demands are very important to me: many of my works deliberately set out to encourage the performer to approach the text in a many-layered analytical mode emanating, in the final analysis, from highly specific physical configurations which can vary enormously from interpreter to interpreter.

TC: *In many of your works it seems that you are challenging the performer to physically accommodate him- or herself to the work. Is a sense of the actual physical means of producing the music an important part of its aesthetic content or value? That is, would it be a different work of art were the demands of production to change?*

BF: Yes to both these points. Performers are used to using their bodies as projective membranes. Composers should, ideally, bear this fact in mind when specifying performative acts. The hero-worship accorded to virtuosi throughout recent musical history can be seen as a crude acknowledgement of the sense of unease with which even educated listeners traverse the minefield of performative dexterity in quest of interpretative subtlety. The 1970s seemed to me a very fitting time to pose again the age-old question of how performers come to intimately know a work, and how this almost private intimacy comes to be transformed into a ritual of communication. This I attempted to anchor in the intertwining of form and practical realization.

TC: *Also I take it that you allow that performers may arrive at significantly different interpretations of your written scores. Are you concerned that certain aspects of the "meaning" or "intent" of the music may be lost in this process?*

BF: Yes, certainly. If one writes for performers, one must necessarily find a way of coming to terms with what they produce. In general, I feel myself privileged to have worked with several generations of interpreters whose approach to new works has been informed in equal measure by technical insight and dexterity, and aesthetic acumen. Obviously, this is not always the case, and one either learns to pass over such offerings in well-willing silence, or, perhaps, seeks to examine the discrepancies between score and realization in an extended sense (as, for instance, in the case of the Portsmouth Sinfonietta).

TC: *Are there any techniques you deliberately avoid with regards to emotions in music, e.g. methods you consider too clichéd or sentimental?*

BF: Your query implies that there is a broad spectrum of musical vocables which are held in common between composers and, by implication, listeners. Perhaps the music of the last 50 years has made this a questionable assumption. Music arises from active critical encounter with its current state of development (in a particular composer's work, say); thus, any and every method incorporated will necessarily be the result of an internal evolution of resources rather than a taxonomy of communally available correlates. If music is to be imagined, in part and highly conditionally, as something approaching a language, then individual expressive elements must be conceded their own diachronic evolution incompatible with an unchanging series of externally imposed affects. Any composer's individual idiolect will be assembled from elements which are at different stages of their evolution—sometimes immediately perceivable as new, not yet absorbed markers, choices emphasizing alienation as part of the receptive experience, at other times partially submerged, subliminally sensed forces which serve to order more recently inserted surface gestures. One cannot emphasize too much the need for musics capable of flexibly registering and redistributing the stratified temporal implications of diverse "vertical times" embodied by the material.

TC: *Can you say more about what you mean by "stratified temporal implications"?*

BF: Our perception of time is not monolithic, much as some branches of philosophy would like to persuade us of this. It is multilayered; events move at different rates both within themselves and with respect to other temporal motions. We naturally compare, I think, bodily motions with reasonably cognate external processes. My compositions tend to assume this embarrassingly disorderly quasi-chaos as an aesthetic given—not to celebrate it as such, but to prod it into locally unique intimations of all those things which your questions address.

Biography of Brian Ferneyhough at <http://www.edition-peters.com/composer/Ferneyhough-Brian>

Interview with Carter Burwell

TC: *I assume that you agree that emotional expression plays a big role in music?*

CB: Yes, I agree with that. Though it's probably not so much an issue of emotional expression as it is an issue of emotional manipulation. Because in what I do, the music serves the function of communicating to the audience emotional information.

TC: *So do you feel that you don't get a chance to personally express yourself when you produce a film score?*

CB: No I do feel that I get a chance to express myself, but it's really in the form of an actor. On a moment by moment basis, I'm not expressing my own emotions but I'm using my imagination to put myself in the world of the film and express that.

TC: *So do you try to empathize with the characters in the film, is that one of the methods?*

CB: Yes I do, very much so. That's not the only thing that film music does. It does many other things as well. But I do definitely try to empathize with the characters.

TC: *You've previously said that the music should add something to the film, not just parody what's already there, but add some more definite qualities. Can you tell me what kinds of things the film composer can add to the production?*

CB: It very much varies from film to film. There isn't a standard list of qualities that I go down when I'm doing this. But among the things that music can contribute to a film is suggest subtext. In other words, when music is expressing something that you're not seeing on screen, even if it's not specific semantically, which music isn't, still the very fact that you're hearing something different from what you're seeing, suggests that there's something else going on than what you see, and I think that that has an effect on the mind of the viewer.

Film music can also of course communicate story ideas. This is typically done through the use of motifs, where you associate a motif with a character or a story element and then you can call upon that musical motif at times when maybe that character or story element is not on screen but you imply that that element is important to what you're seeing right now, that it's related in some way. And of course one thing that I think myself and many film composers do is that we take that Wagnerian tradition of applying motifs to characters or plot elements and then try to interweave them throughout the film so that by the end there's some sort of satisfying whole, wherein the motifs come together and somehow resolve.

TC: *So it's definitely contributing to the narrative in that sense of how the characters are interacting and developing?*

CB: Very much so. And as I say it really depends upon what the film needs. But it's not unusual for the film to need some clarification of story or some clarification of character. And especially in so far as the music is one of the last things that goes into a film, the music is often called upon to do that.

TC: *There's this issue of how the music blends with the background of the film. You'll often hear it at prize-giving ceremonies, this idea that the greatest virtue of film music is to not be noticed, to seamlessly blend with what's going on. I guess someone like Ennio Morricone would vehemently deny that that's what film music should be doing. But what do you think about that kind of ideal?*

CB: Well again it really does vary from film to film. I think that there are times when you want the music to call attention to itself, but I would say those times are few and far between, that's not common.

TC: *Are there any principles to tell when that's what's called for?*

CB: It's an interesting question. Certainly it's going to be partly a question of cinematic style. There are times when you really want the viewer to be unaware of the art of cinema. You want them to not notice the editing, not notice the music… I don't have a cohesive explanation of why that's sometimes true and why sometimes it is not. I'll tell you that for myself, I encountered a very strong example of it in the Coen brother's film, *No Country for Old Men*, where we noticed that whenever we put anything that sounded like music against the picture it diminished the tension of the film. You suddenly knew you were watching a film instead of something that is more real. And I realize that what I just said is ridiculous, everyone knows that they're watching a film, but whenever we put music in, it reminded you of the artificiality of the experience. So we ended up only sneaking music in, in such a way that you never knew it was there. You never hear anything that sounds like a musical instrument, and you're never aware of its appearance, it's always slowly faded in. But that was an interesting example for me. We didn't know beforehand that that was going to be the solution to the film but it was.

However, I've done many films where they are also looking for tension and also looking for suspense and where the music is right up front, like *Psycho* where the music is telling you to be tense, even when you're just watching someone in a hotel room doing nothing. The art of the music is an important contribution to that experience. So I don't have a good cohesive explanation for when needs to be up front or when it needs to be in the back.

I think you have to remember that when discussing the aesthetics of film music, that it is just an element of the overall work of art. So coming up with a cohesive aesthetics of film music would be like coming up with a cohesive aesthetics of brushstrokes in a painting. It's hard to do. You may be able to come up with an aesthetics for art as a whole, but you're talking really about an element here, and it's just that there are going to be times when to want to see the brush strokes and times when you don't and they can all have strong, valuable aesthetic results for the viewer. But I think it's hard to over-generalize about one part of the work.

TC: *So I get the impression that you don't think there are real strong principles about film composition or indeed about film in general. You described taking an experimental approach and seeing what works in this particular example, and so you don't want to commit to definite principles of film composition or how it works.*

CB: Well that is true. I'd love to have a set of principles. It would be a fun thing to write about and talk about. But I have to say that I think it's more profitable to be empirical and take every film as its own world. And I have to say in my experience—and I've been doing this for a long time—I'm still constantly coming across new situations, new problems that need new solutions. And I don't find it easy to generalize except to say generally that there is no generalization. I think that the best thing for me has been to take each film as a world unto itself.

TC: *I suppose it's a collaborative process to a large extent as well. You'll get feedback from the director or producers and then you'll constantly refine the piece until you all agree it fits. Is that something you appreciate, do you think that kind of collaborative process makes the music better, that it really adds something to the music?*

CB: Well, I'll say I don't think it generally makes the *music* better because the feedback I'm getting usually has nothing to do with the quality of the music. The feedback I'll get from the director will be about how the music is affecting the film, but I do enjoy that. because the most interesting projects are those when it's not obvious what the music should be, and we go on a journey to figure that out. And in particular when I'm working with directors who have also written the film—so it's really their concept—I find that a very gratifying collaboration because we're getting at something deep there. I find sometimes with directors who are not writers, that they sometimes don't see as deeply into the subtext of the film, and sometimes I can't tell if we're ever really focusing in on the real meaning of the film. But I love working with directors who write and I'm fortunate to do that a lot of the time.

TC: *I guess this is connecting back to issues about personal expression. These directors who write are more engaged with expressing something, some meaning as you said, and there could be a sense in which you're helping that process of expression to happen.*

CB: It's true, and as an example, Joel and Ethan Coen, almost as a matter of principle, will not discuss the meaning of their films, almost as though they deny that they have meaning. And maybe they do feel that way, but it's very clear that there is still something at the heart of their films, something that made them want to write them. And I think now they have enough of a body of work that we can say that there is a cohesive whole there. And so I enjoy forcing them, dragging them, to find the heart of the thing. On the movie *True Grit* we had actually written all the score, the movie was virtually finished, and we got to the end of the movie and we realized that we couldn't figure out the meaning of one of the very last scenes. It's the one where the girl has been bitten by a snake, and the marshal carries her through the wilderness and collapses at the end. We had to write some music for it. We tried this, we tried that, and we realized we didn't really know what it was supposed to mean. Was it about his pride or his mortality? It seemed it must be about his feelings for the girl, but we realized that we had never really addressed their relationship satisfactorily. The film was full of scenes between the two of them, but nothing had ever established why he would do this almost impossible thing for her. So the Coens went back and shot a couple of shots of him looking at her when she's been bitten to show some empathy—very tiny things—but it was interesting how it was only when we got to the end of writing music for the film that we realized that there was a deep problem and we had to go backward and change things.

TC: *So although the Coen brothers might avoid specifying what the meaning of a certain scene is, you do feel that when you have it all put together and you see the music against the film, that you can tell when it's right, you can tell that 'OK we've captured the heart of something here'?*

CB: Yes, we always get to that point where either we feel that it's right or it's not and we have to keep working on it. Yes, we always get to that point.

TC: *But it's not necessarily something conscious where you could articulate what the meaning is?*

CB: I will go in and talk to them about it, even just having read the script and before they shoot. We'll talk a little bit about what we think is the important thing for the music to express or contribute, but we never really decide that until we've got the film in front of us, and I'm writing music and we're putting it in front of the film. And as I said we either feel it's right or feel it's wrong, and if it's not right then we start talking about what's missing, what it should do differently.

TC: *I'm curious about the kind of language you would use to describe what's missing or what's there. Do you appeal to metaphors, or is it more definite like; 'OK we want these two characters to really be in love with each other'?*

CB: Well I have to say in Joel and Ethan's movies it never comes down to two characters loving each other; that's a theme that never enters into their films. And one of the reasons it came up in *True Grit* was because it's not their original material, so there were unknowns in the story because they only existed in the mind of the writer of the novel. And adapting a novel to the screen involves removing a lot of stuff, you can't put it all up there, and of course you're telling a lot in terms of images instead of words. One of the things the music does in that movie, very consciously—this was a conscious decision of Ethan and myself—was to express the religiosity of the girl because it's on the page when you read the book, she's referencing it all the time, but it wasn't really there in the movie because she doesn't narrate the film. So that was a clear decision we made even before they shot the film, that the music would do that. But we got to that end, and it was an emotional space that was left. There might be some movies that Joel and Ethan make where you can end with emotional space, but they felt that this film, partly because of the nature of the book, and partly because of the people making the movie (Steven Spielberg was one of the producers), that emotional space was not going to be the right thing, there had to be some sense of connection between these two characters. I think there's maybe one more scene after that where she finds out the marshal is dead, that has to really mean something. And if they're not connected emotionally it's not going to.

TC: *You said before about getting an overview of all these films with the Coen brothers and that there is something cohesive you can extract from that. It seems to me that there is an aesthetic quality that a lot of these films share. When I think for instance about the use of the folk songs, or the kinds of stories which are told—focusing more on everyday lives than on epic events—that you could describe this quality as something like "American rustic". Do you think that's a fair description?*

CB: I think that's fair and they definitely have always been drawn to those kinds of stories, and those kinds of locales, and those kinds of characters, They are drawn to other things as well, but I think they're certainly exploring something about the tradition of America, and America's concept of itself and its frontier. That has always been interesting to them, it's true.

TC: *I'm particularly interested in your use of folk melodies in the scores. What is the attraction of using a folk melody?*

CB: While it's not what brought me to using them in the first place, I think in retrospect that one of the reasons why it has worked, especially in Joel and Ethan's movies like *Fargo* or *Miller's Crossing*, is that they have timeless qualities. Timelessness is not the right attitude exactly, but it transcends the moment. In other words we might be watching a movie that takes place in the 1930s like *Miller's Crossing*, but the melody clearly comes from hundreds of years before that. And the same thing with *Fargo*. The movie is taking place I guess in the 1970s, I'm not sure, but that melody clearly comes from a long time before and a long way away and it suggests that even though you're seeing a very specific character and a very specific location, there's still something bigger about what's going on, that somehow it isn't just about them. And because of the nature of Joel and Ethan's movies and themselves, they're not going to tell you what's bigger about it, they're not going to suggest that "oh, this is an archetype", they're not going to suggest anything like that. But the music implies it because of the folk element. And because what we've done in both cases is take the folk tune and then express it through an orchestral tradition that's sort of at odds with the folksiness of the melody, it opens up the canvas upon which these characters are acting.

TC: *I was also thinking about there are certain kinds of emotions associated with use of folk melody, emotions like nostalgia or melancholy, or the contentment of everyday life. Or being straightforward and having certain straightforward uncomplicated feelings. And then you're really putting it on a much larger canvas when you're orchestrating these things and there's different ways that could go emotionally. It could be somehow ironic or just more exaggerated in various ways.*

CB: In *Fargo*, the orchestral interpretation is typically pretty exaggerated. I wanted it to be exaggerated to help people to laugh at some of the violence. We wanted the audience to take the violence seriously, but also be able to laugh at it. And I think by using a certain amount of bombast in the score, I think that helps to solve the problem.

I will say that while there is something maybe comforting sometimes about folk melodies, I think that one of the things that Joel and Ethan like about folk melodies—and it's pretty obvious from the ones that they chose for *O Brother Where Art Thou*—is there's also a folk tradition of addressing the most abject pain and suffering of life through these tunes. If you listen to the words of these songs, they're often about death and loss. There's a simplicity often in the harmonies and chord progressions but there's also an edge—a bitter, tough edge to the melodies and the words. And that's certainly something that they're drawn to.

TC: *It reminds me of this funny contrast in the* Big Lebowski *where the rich Lebowski is listening to Mozart's* Requiem *and we're invited to scorn him and his overwrought emotionality. That's a very refined piece of music he's listening to which directly contrasts with the more down-to-earth, sincere emotional style that a folk melody will have.*

CB: It's true and yes, I think in that case it's very intentional.

TC: *So you mentioned before about writing serious music to go with a comedy film. I wanted to press you a little bit on that idea. I mean, how does that work? Are you just trying to forget that it's a comedy and take this situation, where often, as you said, a crime or a murder is happening, and do you pretend that you're taking this as seriously as possible when you write the music, or are you exaggerating for the comic effect as well?*

CB: Well it varies. In *Fargo* it was definitely an exaggeration. We knew right from the start that this was going to be a problem. When violence occurs in the film, which only happens occasionally in short little outbursts but does result in people dying, the Coens wanted the audience to take that seriously, to really believe that someone had died. But the people who are performing the violence, Steve Buscemi and Peter Stormare's characters, are also the buffoons of the film. So there's a question; how is the audience going to believe that they're actually killing people and at the same time be able to laugh at them? And the solution I proposed was to have the music really believe that this really was a true crime story, take it very seriously, and be so bombastic in its self-seriousness, that the music can't see any of the comedy. And then the fact that the music can't see the comedy is itself funny. It's like the music is the straight man who has no idea that anything funny is going on.

TC: *So it's not like the music is expressing the inner feelings of those characters who are fools in various ways. It's more the perspective of a third person who's seriously seeing, "yes this is a terrible situation here."*

CB: That's right. At the beginning of *Fargo* there's a card that comes up, that tells you this is a true crime story. So basically, that card is the point of view of the music. And you never see that card again, there isn't anyone who narrates the movie to tell you it's all true. But it's as though the music is playing what's on that card for the whole rest of the film, telling you it's a true crime story, and very serious.

TC: *So are you imagining how the audience is going to react to the music when you're producing it? I mean, are you trying to put yourself in the mind of the audience and thinking "OK this is funnier when it's like this"?*

CB: To be honest I'm imagining myself in the audience, I'm thinking for myself what would I want to see. What would I want to hear? What would make this the most entertaining, the most cinematic experience for me if I were in the audience? Especially in the Coen brothers' films I can easily imagine myself as an audience member for the films. But I do sometimes work on films where I'm not the audience. For the movie *Twilight*, for example, I'm clearly not the audience for that. So for that one, I did have to think that I was basically a teenager to do that.

TC: *Are you ever worried that you'll resort to clichés in order to do something like that?*

CB: Well I mean when I imagined myself to be a teenager I did not want this music to condescend to the teenaged audience. I wanted it to take their feelings and the adolescent amplification of feelings that happens at that age very seriously. So I tried very hard not to ever condescend or resort to clichés there. And with the director, Catherine Hardwicke, it was easy to do, we were able to do it. And the studio that was making the film disagreed with my approach, and we had vast arguments about it, they thought there were dissonances in the music that the audience would not accept etc. It was ridiculous. But I tried very hard to make sure that I was never condescending and not to use clichés. It's not for me to say. I probably resort to clichés all the time, but I'm at least trying to avoid them.

TC: *So you mentioned the studio pressures, I imagine there's a lot of pressures on you, not least having only a very limited time to write the music, I mean, to what extent are those quite dramatic constraints helpful or take you in a certain direction?*

CB: Honestly I don't that often hear creative notes from the studio. It almost never happens. *Twilight* was an exception in that sense. There have been other cases, but it doesn't happen that often. Usually it's just me and the director working with one another. But the time constraint is very serious and very severe and it really does have an effect on my work. I think the only time I've ever gotten a score to the point where I thought "this is really complete, I've done everything I can do with it" was *Miller's Crossing* and that's one film out of however many I've done. In every other case I've simply done the best that I can in the time allowed, and that's hard.

Biography of Carter Burwell at <http://www.thebodyinc.com/>

Chapter 4

The emotional power of musical performance

Daniel Leech-Wilkinson

Musical works

There has been much anxiety among musicologists and philosophers over the past few decades about the ontology of musical works (Talbot 2000; Ridley 2004; Cameron 2008), and with good reason. The easy assumption that music exists in works stored in scores that represent composers' wishes that performers make sound seems increasingly dubious, to put it mildly (Cook 2003, p. 204; Leech-Wilkinson 2009, ch. 2, para. 9). And yet the notion of musical works *existing* has become so deeply engrained in Western discourse over the past two centuries that, even in progressive musicological circles, it still underlies most discussion of music. Thus while some scholars have been arguing for years that the route from composer to listener is far less direct than it appears (Cook 1999, 2001a, 2007), it still seems self-evident to most that when we speak of, say, "Chopin's Berceuse," we are speaking of a work with a fixed identity determined by Chopin and on a par with that of, say, Turner's "Norham Castle, Sunrise," and that the job of a performer is to strive to *realize* Chopin's work as faithfully and perfectly as Turner realized his.

This notion has a history. The separation of composer from performer is a largely 20th-century phenomenon (until the middle of the last century most composers were still concert performers), but the separation of composition from performance was a gradual process that began much earlier. It was notation, developed with increasing specificity since the 9th century, that allowed composition to seem to generate objects of work. The writing, by existing, implied a thing that had a degree of fixity, even though performers were expected, even until the early 20th century, to provide some of the notes themselves. Then, as musicology gradually took shape between the late 18th and early 20th centuries, the process of talking and writing about compositions caused them to appear to exist in an increasingly concrete form: talking about them made them seem real.

But the most important change was commercial and (therefore) legal, namely the process by which publishers and composers began to gain rights to the music they produced. As one increasingly bought and sold pieces of music one increasingly accepted that they existed in a definitive form. Otherwise what was there to buy or sell? (See Volgsten in Chapter 25 for an extended discussion of this issue.) And this led to a slow but inexorable change in the relative status of composition and performance. As works became accepted as, in effect, the patented product of a composer, so it became increasingly agreed as self-evident that performances needed to be faithful representations in sound of the composer's conception. Put this together with the separation of composer from performer—meaning that, by the mid-20th century, fewer composers had a performer's acute awareness of the range of interpretative options—and inevitably, over time, the possibility that performance might play a major role in generating, not simply representing, music has come to seem dangerous and undesirable. In a thoughtful presentation of a view widely held among modern performers Alfred Brendel argues that "One should simply feel responsible towards the work—even more towards the work than the composer, for the work to a certain extent leads its own life after it has left the composer; it is an organism with its own rules which one should, where possible, adhere to" (Brendel 2002, p. 200). This gets neatly around the problem of the composer's intentions, much debunked by scholars in recent times (Dipert 1980; Taruskin 1995), but it does so at the cost of attributing to the work the power to limit the possibilities for its performance, and it is far from clear how it might do that. At any rate, it remains to be shown, presumably by a prolonged absence of new approaches to persuasive realization, that it has succeeded.

Similarly academic writers on music still routinely and unquestioningly speak of the power of compositions, that power being a function solely of the composer's handling of the musical material in relation to laws inherent in its grammatical and stylistic context, independent of any performance of the score, as if it were possible to gauge the composer's achievement without any conception of how the score might sound. But of course this is not actually how music is assessed. On the contrary, the power or greatness of a work is, in practice, agreed over time according to the extent to which it has moved many expert witnesses. What do those experts witness? Sometimes they hear real performances in which they find themselves moved: on other occasions, at their desk for example, they imagine the music, either recalling it from memory or reading a score. In the latter case what they are imagining is a performance made according to their expectations or ideals, that is to say, in the manner of the most persuasive performances they have heard, or perhaps, if they have really powerful aural imaginations, just a little bit better. The kind of music we are discussing here, then, comes not direct from the composer but is mediated by performers or fantasizing score readers. Yet this illusion of direct access is widely held, and achievement of it seen as the highest goal. "To me the greatest objective is when the composer disappears, the performer disappears, and there remains only the work" (Nadia Boulanger in Kendall 1976, p. 115).

It is obvious now that this attitude is highly questionable, obvious thanks to the easy availability of 100 years of recordings. Hearing the extraordinary diversity of approaches to the same repertoire of scores, so diverse indeed that it is sometimes not clear to modern listeners that the most celebrated performers from a century ago were musically competent (Leech-Wilkinson 2010), one cannot fail to appreciate that "the work," a core structure with meaning, changes hugely. It changes to such an extent that the way a composer expected to hear their music being performed may now be unacceptable, even laughable, to performers and audiences unless they are very familiar with, and sympathetic to, earlier performance styles. Portamento in Elgar, or indeed in Webern, is a symptomatic example, unacceptable in modern performance despite its being integral to those composers' expectations and tastes (Philip 2004, pp. 142–9; Leech-Wilkinson 2006b; Quick 2011). But almost every aspect of performance style has changed over the past century, and as a consequence we can see now that performance is far from transparent; it is subject to the grammar of performance habits which change over time. As with one's own accent, the existence of performance style is inaudible to the contemporary performer and listener; we all imagine we are playing and singing and reading scores in the only natural and plausible manner. Recordings prove to us that we are not: "Performance style, in short, is the elephant in the musicological room" (Cook 2011, p. 307).

This has profound consequences for our understanding of the identity and nature of music, consequences that it is extremely hard for either performers or writers to take fully on board, indoctrinated as we are by such a history of misconception, evolved through cultural selection in support of the buying and selling—the commodification and objectification—of music. The work has evolved as a grandiose, overblown extrapolation from a particular view of the nature and purpose of musical notation. Looking at the process afresh, it is clear that notation is nothing more than a set of suggestions, in the form of some notes (aptly named) and (in later scores) some hints on how to play them.

In being taught to see their role as representational rather than creative, performers have been hoodwinked into not recognizing the importance of what they do, although ironically their role is, compared with composers, not unfairly rewarded in their fees. In other words the market sees the truth of this revisionary view of performance, even if individuals cannot. Performers still create intensely, even if they do not recognize that that is what they are doing, and they get rewarded for it, and so to that extent it is arguable that their illusion matters much less than that maintained by writers on music. The writers (albeit unintentionally) are engaged in and rewarded for mis-representation. For in believing they have direct access to composers' minds, commentators have deluded themselves and their readerships into failing to see that what they are actually talking about when they speak of the character, relationships, and meanings of notes are the impressions experienced when those notes are sounded. Scores realized in one way on one occasion by histori-cally situated individuals, which could be realized very differently by others, still more differently at other times, cannot sensibly be thought of as containing expressive content that substantially defines their nature. Scores may well contain invariable expressive content—that is to say, expres-sive content that no performance whatsoever could change—but the research that would separate that out from expression provided by a performance or the imagination of a score reader has yet to be done. We do not know how far it extends (Leech-Wilkinson 2012). Whatever that content may eventually prove to embrace—and it is likely to be much less than we currently suppose—everything else emerges from individual performances (Cook 2001b).

It follows that when one speaks of the emotional power of music, one is speaking of its effect in performance, and indeed in a specific performance. Imagined in one's head, it will draw on performances one has heard and liked (been moved by). Or it may be a particular recorded per-formance, very likely a performance one "owns" which can be rerun on demand. But in any case, one's emotional experience is being shaped by the kinds of performances with which one is famil-iar. Responding to substantially different performances would involve a different experience. For we must assume, in the absence of strong evidence to the contrary, that performances in the past produced different kinds of emotional experiences. Certainly old performances do that for us: when we listen to an early 20th-century singer we are not having experiences quite like those we get from one of our contemporaries (Timmers 2007a,b). I think we should assume, as a working hypothesis, that their experiences were not like our experiences of their performances, and not like ours of our performances (Leech-Wilkinson 2012 discusses this further in relation to changes in writing about music). In other words we should assume that these very different sounds had effects we cannot experience today in the absence of the emotionally communicative environment that hosted them, and probably experiences unlike those we get from modern performances (unless we dare to assume that what I am calling the communicative environment has changed exactly in parallel with performance style, which seems a bold though interesting assumption).

Because these are difficult issues, thanks to the lack of any means for transmitting emotional experiences in all their complexity, and thanks to this being such a new set of issues with which to grapple, it is too early to say how musical performance relates to or reflects other kinds of period style. It seems reasonable to assume that there is a strong relationship with other forms of emotional communication, and so some insight may be available from film and from writings (Leech-Wilkinson 2009, ch. 7, para. 7). But in those cases, just as much as with recorded music, perception is period-bound and we are unlikely to be taking from words and acting the same emo-tional experiences they were designed to generate. There are many flavors of skepticism, embar-rassment, respectful dialogue, and loving conversation, for example, and their details depend on social customs that change (Reddy 2001). And so when we speak of the emotional power of music, even when we draw on the findings of controlled experiment, we can speak reliably only of its power for ourselves and our participants, not of transhistorical principles (Leech-Wilkinson 2007, pp. 214–15).

To return to our earlier example, what is "Chopin's Berceuse"? On one level it is a tradition of imagination, a collection of, or (in everyday usage) a selection from, beliefs about and performances of a collection of scores (manuscripts, prints), most (but not all) of whose written signs are the same, similar enough for them to seem obviously to constitute this piece and no other. And just as the notes may differ in different copies and editions, so in performance the writing on the page may be disobeyed to some extent, notes changed, omitted, or added, often with beneficial results for the musical experience. The added bass octaves in Cortot's performance of Chopin's *Étude* Op. 25, No. 1, which is discussed below, offer a case in point: we can assume that they would have been out of place in Chopin's performance, but they make powerful sense in Cortot's (see also Leech-Wilkinson 2009, ch. 2, para. 31); and making powerful sense is surely what we require of a musical performance.

You might say, then, that the identity of classical compositions is hard to pin down. And that is exactly the point. Music (all music) is highly adaptable. It meets a wide range of needs and circumstances precisely by being unfixed in its content and identity. This is just what theorists of musical evolution have suggested about music's social potential. It is thought to have had survival value through its varied uses in assisting social cohesion, moving and singing together enhancing physical and emotional cooperation (Cross 2009, p. 9). There is no need here to rehearse the multitude of uses to which music is put in our own world (DeNora 2000; Clarke *et al.* 2010).

One might go a step further. What has been said so far suggests that music has been seriously misrepresented, forced into existing molds in order to give us some way of handling it, especially some way of talking about it and making money from it. To see the other side of the argument we might, instead of seeing music in terms of other things, see other things in terms of music. Thus we might say "this room happens in time" rather than "this room exists in space." That is a more human-centered view, since it allows for the fact that the function and meaning, as well as the fabric, of the room changes as the people who use it change. This is not just to say that the room, or indeed the text, is the history of its receptions. It goes further, and says that the text, like the room, is an ongoing event, the dynamic of whose changing defines its being: more a phenomenological than a reception-historical approach, in other words. So instead of saying "music consists of a body of works" we might see what happens if we say, "a body of works is itself a musical process." Being moved by music, in this view, is not a trivial event of passing significance, of no relevance to the history and identity of the work, but rather the defining characteristic of music as it is, as a process: music does not exist, it happens through being—and to the extent that it is—experienced.

Musical events

So in considering the emotional power of music we must consider experiences of performances, not the content of scores, for music is the experience of listening to a performance (optionally a performance of a score). In a previous study I showed how radically this experience can alter, quite apart from the individuality of listeners, depending simply on the extreme differences that are possible between performances. My example there was a Schubert song, "Die junge Nonne," which I examined in recordings from different periods. Because of the text it is possible in a song to be quite specific about what the sounds made by a performer seem to imply. So in that case it is possible to say, expecting some measure of agreement among (modern) listeners, that one singer seems to represent the young nun as overjoyed, another as terrified, and a third as depressed or perhaps dying: radical differences from a single composition yet not outside the range of performance variability, as a century of recordings shows (Leech-Wilkinson 2007; to which I would add Schwarzkopf as an example of the protagonist as fearful).

Here is another example. Sound File 1 contains an extract (starting at "O frischer Duft") from the first stanza of Schubert's setting of Ludwig Uhland's "Frühlingsglaube." The complete text follows. The singer is Jo Vincent, accompanied anonymously, in a Columbia recording from the 1920s.

Frühlingsglaube	**Faith in Spring**
Ludwig Uhland	**Prose translation by Hyde Flippo**
Die linden Lüfte sind erwacht,	The gentle winds are awakened,
Sie säuseln und wehen Tag und Nacht,	They murmur and waft day and night,
Sie schaffen an allen Enden.	They create in every corner.
O frischer Duft, o neuer Klang!	Oh fresh scent, oh new sound!
Nun, armes Herze, sei nicht bang!	Now, poor heart, fear not!
Nun muss sich alles, alles wenden.	Now everything, everything must change.
Die Welt wird schöner mit jedem Tag,	The world becomes more beautiful with each day,
Man weiß nicht, was noch werden mag,	One does not know what may yet happen,
Das Blühen will nicht enden.	The blooming doesn't want to end.
Es blüht das fernste, tiefste Tal:	The farthest, deepest valley blooms:
Nun, armes Herz, vergiss der Qual!	Now, poor dear, forget the pain!
Nun muss sich alles, alles wenden.	Now everything, everything must change.

I suggest that what we experience, through Jo Vincent, is a fundamentally positive song, looking forward with optimism; everything is going to change for the better. Vincent is typical of earlier 20th-century *Lieder* singers in her quite literal reading of the song's surface meaning, focusing on its apparent message of hope in the coming of spring. (On this tendency see Leech-Wilkinson 2009, ch. 4, paras 19–22.)

In Sound File 2 we can hear Kirsten Flagstad accompanied by Gerald Moore in 1952. And to stack the evidence against me I have provided in this extract just the opening lines of the text, which on the face of it have no negative implication. Flagstad, however, seems to be looking back, focusing on the pain, or perhaps (or also) pessimistically looking forward, beyond spring to the inevitable dying of flowers that will follow: change will continue, and not for the better. She (again like most singers of her generation and the generations that followed, those who lived through the Second World War and sang after it) finds a message lying below the surface of the text. No longer do Schubert songs mean what they say; their greatness, we seem to believe, lies in those levels that Schubert finds beneath the surface. The song—the composition, the text, their combination—means something different, it feels different, and therefore the music (not the score, the music) is different.

It is that darker reading that has become the norm in modern times. To take a recent example, the young British singer Elizabeth Watts accompanied by Roger Vignoles in 2008 adopts a moderately slow speed and uses heavy accents made by crescendoing the first note on each beat and getting rapidly quieter through the second, modeling sighs, to suggest a sense of nostalgia, of something lost rather than eagerly anticipated (Sony/BMG 88697329322, track 12).

We need to understand this strategy in its wider context. Listening to 100 years of recordings of all sorts of compositions it is clear that performance styles change in consistent ways in particular directions. When recordings begin around 1900 we find we are hearing relatively plain performances, albeit with local rubato and a lot of portamento, but over the next 20 to 30 years musicians become much more emotionally expressive. Immediately after the Second World War there is a radical change to a different kind of expressivity, much less evident, in stricter time, with no portamento but with much deeper vibrato which becomes a kind of icon for expressivity—an index really, in the sense that the quavering voice is in real life a symptom of loss of control under overwhelming emotional pressure, but so formalized and mechanical as to become iconic. In the 1970s historically informed performance reacted violently against that, and since then there has been a gradual reintroduction of expressivity, which is now since the millennium quite unmistakable. It seems as if there is always a tendency over decades towards emotional inflation in musical performance, a tendency from which it is hard to step back without being accused of being lightweight. Suppose one were a young singer offering "Frühlingsglaube" to an audience today, especially an audience containing critics. Would one dare to sing that text at its sunnier face value? Probably not. Perhaps it is only when a whole culture changes that musicians lighten their performance styles. It took the Second World War and then later on the ideologically driven original-instrument movement to simplify performance styles in the 20th century. How far are we going to go with the current emotional inflation in musicianship before there is a switch, and what kind of event could drive it? We have too few models, because we have not had recorded performance for long enough, to know how this has worked in the past, but based on recent experience it seems that radical style change happens only in response to major shifts in belief in the wider culture.

We can take several lessons from this case study. First, during the past century we have changed Schubert's identity. Our Schubert is not the Schubert of 100 years ago. How he compares with Schubert's Schubert we cannot know, which is one reason why he remains so significant for each new generation. We can make him like us unhindered by the disapproving stare of historical fact. We may know things about Schubert's life, perhaps even about his personality and sexuality (Gibbs 2000), but we cannot know how his music sounded and to that extent (as I have argued above) we cannot know *his* music; making Schubert's scores into music is largely in our hands. Secondly, performances happen within a performance culture whose audible sign is its characteristic performance style. The performance culture consists of much more, however: attitudes to proper expressivity, to what is musical, to techniques that allow this particular kind of expressivity ("a tradition of imagining sound as music"; Cook 1990, p. 223); and in the wider context, as I have suggested, it must link to other kinds of expressive communication, to manners, conversation, love-making, acting, public speaking, and so to styles of interpersonal relationships. All of these are potentially analyzable in terms of the expressive gestures, and particularly the sound signals they use.

As I have already hinted in the discussion of the Elizabeth Watts recording, the vocal signals of these emotional states relate directly to signals we know—through inheritance, embodiment, and culture—from our experience of everyday life (for examples and discussion see Leech-Wilkinson 2006a and 2009, ch. 8). This will come as no surprise to anyone familiar with work in affective science on the vocal expression of emotions. Scherer *et al.* (2003), and Gabrielsson and Juslin (2003), for example, have outlined the principal vocal signs of a range of emotional states, and these apply in singing no less immediately than in speech, and in the performance of and response to art no less strongly than in everyday interaction. We know these signs from our lifetime's repeated use and observation. In the "Frühlingsglaube" examples, Flagstadt takes us an emotional degree beyond Watts in scooping up to accented notes, getting louder through them, and quietening much more slowly. The performance as a whole is slower, too, so the sounds she is applying to Schubert's score and Uhland's words are perhaps closer to moans than sighs. But to require an exact modeling is to miss the point. All that is required for us to experience a deeper sense of pain is for there to be some reference to, not a complete model of, an expressive vocal gesture we recognize from life, to which we respond automatically through empathy, contagion, or simply experience. (Suggestive studies include Neumann and Strack 2000 and Molnar-Szakacs and Overy 2006.) The promiscuity with which the brain makes connections between incoming sounds and sounds known already ensures that meanings are there to be found in profusion. So where I suggest a general likeness to a moan, others may prefer another. What we will agree on is very general, that this is not a joyful performance and that spring is not the prospect at the front of this protagonist's mind. That is enough. The details are a negotiation between the sounds and our individual minds, but mechanisms are not hard to suggest, given the wealth of research in recent years on emotional communication. (For outstanding recent collections see Davidson *et al.* 2003 and Juslin and Sloboda 2010.) In Vincent's performance (bear in mind that this is a different passage from the score) the accents are much more even, the speed faster, the dotted rhythm exaggerated, the note-attacks more immediate, the tone clearer. Reading across Juslin and Persson's table of expressive cues (Juslin and Persson 2002, p. 223) it is easy enough to see how many of the cues of happiness this performance sounds.

It may be objected that these processes and cue utilizations are obvious. But that is precisely what makes them powerful. They are obvious because they are so much a part of our deep-rooted and constantly reinforced modes of communication. Musical performance speaks the same language as all our other communicative acts, but speaks it without having to go through the medium of precise semantic meaning. It is therefore very good at undermining, contradicting, making more complex, more ambiguous, more nuanced, or simply less straightforward, the explicit meaning of a sung text. Yet it achieves this through the simplest and most direct—and therefore the most powerful—of means.

How does this same process work in instrumental performances? Sound File 3 offers Chopin's *Étude* Op. 25, No. 1 in A major, in a performance by Alfred Cortot recorded in 1934, chosen for its expressive intensity. And yet the score is relatively undifferentiated, a melody of (apparently) even crotchets, with many repeated pitches and melodic change mostly stepwise, supported by unvaryingly arpeggiated harmonies of no special complexity. If Cortot, by quite simple means, can make this score deeply engaging for the listener then there is probably something to be learned from his performance about pianistic expressivity.

Pianists can make extensive change in sound in only two dimensions, loudness and timing. Frequency is fixed and timbre is variable only to a small extent and only by the most expert players. So most of our attention can be focused on timing and loudness, their interrelation with each other and with the score. The range of loudnesses is 20 dB (attacks measured in Sonic Visualiser 1.8 using values returned by the "Power Curve: Smoothed Power" transform), and most of the performance lies within a narrower range of around 14 dB. As often with Cortot, loudness correlates with tempo, getting quieter as he slows and louder as be speeds up. This process works together with rubato. Like many of Cortot's performances this one often alternates longer and shorter bars and when that pattern varies it does so in relation to varying patterns in the score ("the compositional structure"). What makes these bars different lengths, though, is the placing of

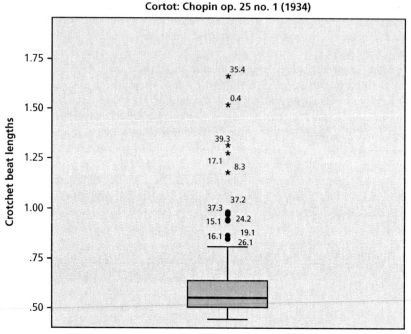

Figure 4.1 Beat lengths in seconds in Cortot's 1934 recording of Chopin's *Étude*, Op. 25, No. 1. The median value is shown as a horizontal bar within the shaded box. The box encloses the 50% of values around the median. The vertical lines ("whiskers") show the extent of the lowest 25% and the main spread of values within the highest 25%. The beats indicated above the upper whisker are outliers, exceptionally long beats which mark Cortot's points of greatest emphasis. The data are strongly skewed towards beats longer than the median.

longer crotchet beats in a purposeful way to make rhetorical points (there are further examples and detailed discussion of other Cortot performances in Leech-Wilkinson 2011). Cortot's crotchets sounding the melody vary in length from 0.44–1.67 seconds, but the median length is 0.55 seconds, so the majority of non-standard beats are longer than the norm; they are skewed towards a small number of much longer values (Figure 4.1). Where Cortot uses these much longer beats tells us most about his expressivity.

Figure 4.2 summarizes the functions of the longest beats, grouped into three bands according to the grouping evident in Figure 4.1. Clearly, function and length are very closely related. What is particularly interesting is that so many, and the longest, are not harmonic or melodic cruxes or key points of compositional structure but are rather signposts or pointers towards significant structural moments that are about to be reached. On the whole Cortot does not mark the starts of new structural units in the score by playing them more expressively; on the contrary he often speeds up through them. Rather, by unexpectedly lengthening a less important note he grasps the listener's attention just before the main points of structural interest so that they are attended to as he moves on through them. This is a rhetorical technique, a catching of the ear that both points out important moments in the score and yet avoids crassly stressing them.

Thomas Manshardt, who studied with Cortot and whose sense of Cortot's beliefs about technique and interpretation are transmitted in a book assembled by Manshardt's pupil Lawrence

Range of beat lengths	Function	Locations (longer to shorter: bar.beat)
1.66″ – 1.52″	Pointers to structural markers	35.4, 0.4
1.31″ – 1.18″	Pointers	39.3, 8.3
1.28″	Structural marker	17.1
0.98″ – 0.94″	Pointers	24.2, 37.2, 37.3, 39.2
0.94″	Structural marker	36.1
0.81″ – 0.94″	Harmonic accents	15.1, 16.1, 26.1, 4.3
0.81″ – 0.69″	Build-up to other markers	25.4, 35.3
0.76″ – 0.7″	Melodic accents	11.2, 2.1, 6.4, 22.3

Figure 4.2 Functions of the longest beats from Figure 4.1.

Amundrud—a somewhat tenuous link with Cortot therefore—seems to be describing exactly this kind of emphasis:

> Where a note of a phrase needs to be prolonged in order to give emotional significance to the moment it will usually be found that the anacrusis is the most desirable note to prolong. By holding the commencement of a phase a sense of emotional stress, of trying to move through a resistance, can be added. (Manshardt 1994, p. 120)

But listeners who bring different expectations (probably most listeners today, and perhaps, since few played like him, many among his contemporaries) have the option of hearing, perhaps can hardly avoid hearing, Cortot's emphases as pointing up unexpected moments in the score, not as pointing forwards, in other words, but as emphasizing the notes that are lengthened. A Cortot performance, therefore, can be a surprising experience, one whose meaning is hard to pin down and which leaves much for the listener to ponder, either because his intentions are now hard to read or perhaps because they were always intended to be. Daniel Barenboim has said of Cortot that "he looked for anything that was extraordinary. He always looked for something… totally removed from reality and from anything that distinctly could even be construed to be smelling of normality" (Barenboim 1999, at 55′ 45″). And here we can see how and why he does it. An element of the unexpected which somehow makes musical sense (amplifying the surprise) is key to Cortot's performance style and to his power as a communicator, a power that of course works differently now from the way it did in 1934.

One of the things this example shows is that expressive intensity in music (music as experienced through performance) can be achieved in more ways than seem obvious (i.e. than are current) at any one place and time, and in more ways, therefore, than can readily be conceived or codified at once. Some of this richness comes from the changes in performance style themselves, but much comes from our changing understandings of those styles as we reinterpret them in search of a logic compatible with our own expressive worlds. It is possible that over time recorded performance styles will have varied so much that most possibilities for expressivity will have been documented, but that is not going to happen soon. For the time being we shall have to be content with speaking in the most general terms about the underlying principles.

Juslin's lists of emotional cues provides a useful point of comparison (most recently in Juslin and Timmers 2010, especially p. 460 onwards, where much important work on the expression of emotion through music performance is cited). Most of these cues are vocal in origin, for the obvious reason that emotion is an experience that humans habitually express vocally (needing no musical training to do so); and how many of those can be taken over into instrumental musical performance depends on the similarity of the instrument to the voice. String players have many more options than pianists, and pianists more than harpsichordists, for example. But while it is easy to see that many kinds of performance expressivity draw on these cues, translating them into the vocabulary of particular instruments (irregular bursts of dissonant upper harmonics signaling anger, for example, in voice and string bowing, or quiet, even piano playing signaling calm), much of the most interesting music-making takes its power from less obvious likenesses to lived experience. A key concept here is embodiment, which helps us to understand how music engages us at deep levels without requiring deep knowledge of it. So in seeking to understand the principles that underlie this mapping from sound to emotional engagement we need to focus less on musicological facts and much more on bodily response. Mark Johnson's recent work (Johnson 2007) offers a useful route to follow.

Johnson is essentially concerned with the ways in which our experience of our bodies moving around and responding to our environment, day by day throughout our lives, provides us with models for experiencing other kinds of motion and apparent motion. Much of the metaphorical language of musical description draws on just these experiences. Music can sound halting and uncertain because we know what kinds of rhythmic and gestural movements arise from and signify uncertainty in life and we recognize the similarity when we hear these same movements in musical sound. The examples can be multiplied almost endlessly, covering everything we know through our bodies about sound and motion. In understanding expressivity in music, an obvious strategy is to look in performances for the ways in which musicians call on this deep-rooted form of knowledge which almost all of us share and apply automatically without having to know anything about the musical processes involved.

Cortot again can provide a clear example. His 1920 recording of Chopin's "Berceuse" (to pick up the example with which we began) shows embodiment being played with in several dimensions. Sound File 4 plays bars 1–14. First, Cortot alternates shorter and longer half-bars, so that the piece seems to expand during the second half of the bar, as the music slows, and to contract during the first half of the following bar as it speeds up again. In this way the music seems to breathe, and (thanks to the extent of the rubato) to breathe deeply, at the level of the bar, in a strikingly human way. I find that the depth of the breaths allied to their slow pace evokes a powerful mixture of calm and deep feeling: but I can only report how my body responds to it; a much wider study with many participants would be required before we could generalize towards meaning.

Secondly, in a rather uncommon move, Cortot matches the rising and falling of the principal melody with the slowing and speeding up of the beats. Whenever the melody rises Cortot slows, whenever it falls he speeds up. What this does is not just to amplify the effects of rubato and of melodic shape by reflecting one in the other; it also gives to the melody a sense of physical motion in a lifelike gravitational field, where going uphill is more effortful than going down; the climbing line generates tension, descending brings release. The quotation from Manshardt above continues thus:

> Forward impulsion of a phrase should move through an emotional resistance, otherwise it will sound facile, even glib. (Cortot said "Like running down a hill". Moving through a resistance he characterized as trying to get away while someone is holding on to you.) (Manshardt 1994, p. 120)

In other words, Cortot aimed to trigger exactly this sense of physical motion through a landscape, which is one of Johnson's basic musical schemas. It is hard not be engaged through one's body with a performance that behaves in this way.

Thirdly, and closely related, Cortot takes longer over the upward leaps; that is to say, the note before a leap up is lengthened. The sense that the leap takes longer because there is further to travel adds another dimension to the lifelike quality of this performance. The sense that the music involves space as well as time, gravitational forces, a set of bodily processes, contributes vitally (quite literally vitally) to the power of this performance.

Cortot's 1920 recording now seems an extreme example, but that is why it is a good one to study. In more typical performances these same processes are likely to be operating effectively but on a much subtler scale. His 1923 and 1926 recordings of the same piece, in which the rubato is less pronounced, are easier to understand once one has seen what is happening in 1920 (Cortot 1923, 1926). In his late 1949 recording the note lengths are still nearer to equality, the performance of a much more typical pianist (Cortot 1949). Most performances we know are less radical than Cortot's, but nonetheless we can better understand how they work on and in us in the light of his more extreme cases.

The breadth of performance traditions of scores varies greatly. I have focused on examples with relatively rich traditions. That of "Die junge Nonne" is so wide as to encompass readings from joyous to suicidal. "Frühlingsglaube" extends from optimistic to pessimistic. As an instrumental piece the *Étude* is less amenable to this kind of labeling, but it is not hard to see how different patterns of loudness and rubato might lead to different effects. Just how different we can hear from a 1933 recording by Solomon (Sound File 5), who finds a drama quite unknown to Cortot. Indeed, aside from the superficial facts of the score these two performances seem to generate substantially different music (compare Sound File 3). The more examples we hear the clearer seems the implication that expression of emotion in performances of composed scores is constrained more by tradition among performers than by anything inherent in the notes.

Some scores, however, vary very little in their realizations over time, and these have an interest of their own, for once one has become aware of the variety of musics that emerge from a single score it seems almost odd that a score could continue to be read in one manner over several generations. Cortot may change his approach to the "Berceuse" substantially during his later life, but listening to dozens of recordings from across the last century suggests that either this is not a score with many options (but one might have thought that of the *Étude*) or that in some way the score contains only limited potential for persuasive readings. Of course there are many other limiting pressures. A performer needs to please in order to earn a living, and a piece that for so many listeners encapsulates a dreamy calm is not an invitation to cause interpretative havoc (or perhaps it is, but if so we are still waiting). There is an element of self-policing: once a composer's intentions become enshrined in mythology, performers who believe that to realize those is their highest task will find it perverse to break away. And then there are titles and texts, which do a great deal to predispose performers to treat the score in a particular way, according to their (or performance tradition's) understanding of what a text or title means (which may not be at all what it meant to its author, needless to say).

Perhaps a more interesting example, taking the argument one step further, is Schubert's setting of Goethe's "Erlkönig," recorded hundreds of times, by men, women, and children, with piano and orchestral accompaniment, and yet always essentially a gothic horror tale, its character little changed by so many performers. In a case like this it is very tempting to collapse score into work and to see "the music" as something that remains sufficiently stable to be thought of as existing with a full identity separate from any performance (for a fine analysis of the score from this perspective see Spitzer 2010). But of course that is not what has transpired. It is simply that there is a strong performance tradition which the public expects will be followed, and so the various performances of "Erlkönig" have tended to be rather similar. But that is not to say that they have to be. It would be entirely possible to perform the notes of that score at the tempo habitually given to the first movement of Beethoven's "Moonlight" sonata, say crotchet = 64, and what would emerge would be not a terrifying piece but rather an intensely sad one. The story described in its text, assuming it could be sung at all (my point is not what Schubert intended but what is expressively possible, and a piano reduction would make the point perfectly well), would be presented as a dream, which might in fact seem more plausible than the literal reading we are usually given.

Similarly, the "Moonlight" sonata works, rather successfully in a sympathetic performance, at radically different speeds, and with correspondingly different dynamics and articulation, from those we are used to. I invite pianists to try the first movement at minim = 75, the whirlwind of conventional "Erlkönig"; the second movement slow and rather beautiful at crotchet = 112 (with the Trio faster, say 130); and the final movement, much slower and more thoughtful than Beethoven probably expected, at crotchet = 68. A sensitive musician can make these notes work at these speeds. So the expressive content of these scores, that is to say the expressivity inherent in the notes alone, independent of any performance, is not nearly as specific as we assume. The notes are conventionally read with many assumptions about expression, but that expression is provided by the performer, not definitively encoded within the notes by the composer. Composer and performer may once have shared assumptions, but that does not give the notes themselves much specific emotional power. Moreover, given the huge differences we hear in earlier recordings, increasing as we go further back from the present, and given the long distances in time that separate these composers from even the earliest recordings, we cannot sensibly assume that those assumptions are shared today, still less that we know in detail what was really expected.

Conclusion

The extent to which the emotional power of music depends on performers has been disastrously underestimated—disastrously because so much writing on music over the past two centuries has been focused on the wrong phenomenon, attributing meanings and effects to scores which in fact emerge from imagined, remembered, or revisited performances. It follows that when we attribute powers of persuasion to specific composers and compositions—power to change our state of mind, often to move us as deeply as almost anything we experience—we are in fact misattributing much. This conclusion brings with it all sorts of dangers, particularly for performers from whom it removes much comforting constraint, but at the same time it clarifies our task for those who study music's affective process. Music is above all a negotiation between sound and the contents and mechanisms of the mind, and so it is within that space that the study of music's effects will be most illuminating.

In this sense music is uniquely revealing of individual minds. It depends to such a high degree, compared with other emotionally charged experiences, on our own internal constructions of meaning which have neither the opportunity nor the need to be challenged or modulated by those of other listeners, that it can be regarded as a potential key to opening up many other parts of a personality to study and understanding. The same evidently goes for the brain in general, as the ubiquity of music studies in psychology and neuroscience has already shown. But the use of musical response as a way into individual minds, though enabling remarkable work in music therapy, is still in its infancy. The potential for varied approaches to performance to play a controlled part in this process needs much more consideration. First, though, we shall need to find out a lot more about performance, its components, and their effects on us.

Music, as we have seen, does not exist, it happens, and in a multitude of different ways. Even with composed scores, endless re-formations and re-presentations create new kinds of powerful experiences on each occasion and for each listener. We need to be able to keep that diversity at the forefront of our understandings of what music is and how it works.

References

Barenboim, D. (1999). Contribution to: *The Art of Piano: Great Pianists of the 20th Century*. DVD 3984-29199-2. NVC Arts.

Brendel, A. (2002). *The Veil of Order: Alfred Brendel in Conversation with Martin Meyer*, transl. R. Stokes. London: Faber.

Cameron, R. P. (2008). There are no things that are musical works. *The British Journal of Aesthetics*, **48**, 295–314.

Clarke, E., Dibben, N., and Pitts, S. (2010). *Music and Mind in Everyday Life*. Oxford: Oxford University Press.

Cook, N. (1990). *Music, Imagination, and Culture*. Oxford: Oxford University Press.

Cook, N. (1999). Words about music, or analysis versus performance. In N. Cook, P. Johnson, and H. Zender (eds), *Theory into Practice: Composition, Performance, and the Listening Experience*, pp. 9–52. Leuven: Leuven University Press.

Cook, N. (2001a). Between process and product: music and/as performance. *Music Theory Online*, 7/2.

Cook, N. (2001b). Theorizing musical meaning. *Music Theory Spectrum*, **23**, 170–95.

Cook, N. (2003). Music as performance. In M. Clayton, T. Herbert, and R. Middleton (eds), *The Cultural Study of Music: a Critical Introduction*, pp. 204–14. London: Routledge).

Cook, N. (2007). Imagining things: mind into music (and back again). In I. Roth (ed.), *Imaginative Minds*, pp. 123–46. Proceedings of the British Academy, 147. Oxford: Oxford University Press (for the British Academy).

Cook, N. (2011). Off the record: performance, history, and musical logic. In I. Deliège and J. W. Davidson (eds), *Music and the Mind: Essays in Honour of John Sloboda*, pp. 291–309. Oxford: Oxford University Press.

Cortot, A. (1923). *The Complete Acoustic Victor Recordings*, CD 2, track 11. Biddulph LHW 014-15, issued 1993.

Cortot, A. (1926). *Chopin, Œuvres Pour Piano, Cortot*, CD 1, track 10. EMI Classics CZS 7 67359 2, issued 1991.

Cortot, A. (1949). *Great Pianists: Cortot*, track 27. Naxos Historical 8.111023, issued 2005.

Cross, I. (2009). The nature of music and its evolution. In I. Cross, S. Hallam, and M. Thaut (eds), *The Oxford Handbook of Music Psychology*, pp. 3–13. Oxford: Oxford University Press.

Davidson, R. J., Scherer, K. R., and Goldsmith, H. H. (eds) (2003). *Handbook of Affective Sciences*. Oxford: Oxford University Press.

DeNora, T. (2000). *Music in Everyday Life*. Cambridge: Cambridge University Press.

Dipert, R. (1980). The composer's intentions: an examination of their relevance for performance. *The Musical Quarterly*, **66**, 205–18.

Gabrielsson, A. and Juslin, P. N. (2003). Emotional expression in music. In R. J. Davidson, K. R. Scherer, and H. H. Goldsmith (eds), *Handbook of Affective Sciences*, pp. 503–34. Oxford: Oxford University Press.

Gibbs, C. H. (2000). *The Life of Schubert*. Cambridge: Cambridge University Press.

Johnson, M. (2007). *The Meaning of the Body: Aesthetics of Human Understanding*. Chicago: University of Chicago Press.

Juslin, P. N. and Persson, R. S. (2002). Emotional communication. In R. Parncutt and G. E. McPherson (eds), *The Science and Psychology of Music Performance: Creative Strategies for Teaching and Learning*, pp. 219–36. Oxford: Oxford University Press.

Juslin, P. N. and Timmers, R. (2010). Expression and communication of emotion in music performance. In P. N. Juslin and J. A. Sloboda (eds), *Handbook of Music and Emotion: Theory, Research, Applications*, pp. 453–89. Oxford: Oxford University Press.

Juslin, P. N. and Sloboda, J. A. (eds) (2010). *Handbook of Music and Emotion: Theory, Research, Applications*. Oxford: Oxford University Press.

Kendall, A. (1976). *The Tender Tyrant: Nadia Boulanger, a Life Devoted to Music*. London: Macdonald and Jane's.

Leech-Wilkinson, D. (2006a). Expressive gestures in Schubert singing on record. *Nordisk Estetisk Tidskrift*, **33–34**, 50–70.

Leech-Wilkinson, D. (2006b). Portamento and musical meaning. *Journal of Musicological Research*, **25**, 233–61.

Leech-Wilkinson, D. (2007). Sound and meaning in recordings of Schubert's "Die junge Nonne." *Musicae Scientiae*, **11**, 209–36.

Leech-Wilkinson, D. (2009). *The Changing Sound of Music: Approaches to Studying Recorded Musical Performance* [online] London: CHARM. <http//www.charm.kcl.ac.uk/studies/chapters/intro.html>

Leech-Wilkinson, D. (2010). Listening and responding to the evidence of early twentieth-century performance. *Journal of the Royal Musical Association*, **134** (Special Issue no. 1), 45–62.

Leech-Wilkinson, D. (2011). Making music with Alfred Cortot: ontology, data, analysis. In H. von Loesch and S. Weinzierl (eds), *Gemessene Interpretation—Computergestützte Aufführungsanalyse im Kreuzverhör der Disziplinen*, pp. 129–44. Mainz: Schott.

Leech-Wilkinson, D. (2012). Compositions, scores, performances, meanings. *Music Theory Online*, 18/1 <http://mtosmt.org/issues/mto.12.18.1/mto.12.18.1.leech-wilkinson.pdf>

Manshardt, T. with contributions by Amundrud, L. (1994). *Aspects of Cortot*. Hexham: Appian.

Molnar-Szakacs, I. and Overy, K. (2006). Music and mirror neurons: from motion to "e"motion. *Social Cognitive and Affective Neuroscience*, **1**, 235–41.

Neumann, R. and Strack, F. (2000). "Mood contagion": the automatic transfer of mood between persons. *Journal of Personality and Social Psychology*, **79**, 211–23.

Philip, R. (2004). *Performing Music in the Age of Recording*. New Haven: Yale University Press.

Quick, M. (2011). *Performing Modernism: Webern on Record*. PhD thesis, King's College London.

Reddy, W. M. (2001). *The Navigation of Feeling: a Framework for the History of Emotions*. Cambridge: Cambridge University Press.

Ridley, A. (2004). *The Philosophy of Music: Theme and Variations*. Edinburgh: Edinburgh University Press.

Scherer, K. R., Johnstone, T., and Klasmeyer, G. (2003). Vocal expression of emotion. In R. J. Davidson, K. R. Scherer, and H. H. Goldsmith (eds), *Handbook of Affective Sciences*, pp. 433–56. Oxford: Oxford University Press.

Spitzer, M. (2010). Mapping the human heart: a holistic analysis of fear in Schubert. *Music Analysis*, **29**, 143–213.

Talbot, M. (ed.) (2000). *Musical Work: Reality or Invention?* Liverpool: Liverpool University Press.

Taruskin, R. (1995). Last thoughts first: wherein the author gently replies to a few of his critics and takes tender leave of the topic. In Taruskin R. (ed.) *Text and Act: Essays on Music and Performance*, pp. 3–47. Oxford: Oxford University Press.

Timmers, R. (2007a). Vocal expression in recorded performances of Schubert songs. *Musicae Scientiae*, **11**, 237–68.

Timmers, R. (2007b). Perception of music performance on historical and modern commercial recordings. *Journal of the Acoustical Society of America*, **122**, 2872–80.

Sound examples

All sound examples may be found at <www.oup.co.uk/companion/cochrane>.

Sound File 1: Columbia D 10036, matrix F660-2, 32″–1′ 08″. Transfer by Andrew Hallifax, © King's College London 2009. The complete track may be downloaded via the CHARM sound file search at <http://www.charm.kcl.ac.uk/sound/sound_search.html>.

Sound File 2: HMV DB 21554, matrix 2EA16677-2A, 19″–51″. Transfer by Andrew Hallifax, © King's College London 2009. The complete track may be downloaded via the CHARM sound file search at <http://www.charm.kcl.ac.uk/sound/sound_search.html>.

Sound File 3: HMV DB 2308, matrix 2B7255-2, band 1. Transfer by Daniel Leech-Wilkinson, © King's College London 2011 .

Sound File 4: Victor 74623, matrix C22502-5. Transfer by Ward Marston, © Ward Marston 2011. I am extremely grateful to Mr Marston for making this transfer for me and allowing me to use it here.

Sound File 5: Columbia LX 314, matrix ©AX6225–1, band 2. Transfer by Daniel Leech-Wilkinson, © King's College London, 2011.

Chapter 5

The singer's paradox: on authenticity in emotional expression on the opera stage

Klaus R. Scherer

with contributions by Thomas Moser, Gillian Keith, Lucy Schaufer, Bruno Taddia, and Christoph Prégardien

Introduction

The question of how emotions should be displayed on the stage has been an object of debate ever since antiquity. An extremely naturalistic view would suggest that the actor should actually feel the emotions required by the plot in order to convincingly express them. One of the first documented cases for this strategy goes back to the 4th century BC and is owed to the Greek actor Polus who, in the role of Electra mourning Orestes, took the ashes from the tomb of his son who had recently died and thus expressed real grief in his performance (Strasberg and Chaillet 2008). In contrast, in the Natyashastra, an ancient Indian treatise on the performing arts, an extremely artistic manner of emotional expression precisely prescribes conventionalized movements for the expressions of certain emotions, down to configurations of finger movements (Hejmadi *et al.* 2000). An intermediate condition is to produce seemingly spontaneous expressions that are artfully engineered to look natural.

It is this option that Diderot opposes to the extremely naturalistic one in his famous Socratic dialogue on the actor's paradox (Diderot, 1880/1883):

> But they say that an actor is all the better for being excited, for being angry. I deny it. He is best when he imitates anger. Actors impress the public not when they are furious, but when they play fury well. In tribunals, in assemblies, everywhere where a man wishes to make himself master of others' minds, he feigns now anger, now fear, now pity, now love, to bring others into these diverse states of feeling. What passion itself fails to do, passion well imitated accomplishes.

Diderot's treatise has stimulated a lively debate (see Roach 1993) which is likely to continue for some time to come. An interesting approach was taken by William Archer who reported in his book *Masks or Faces?* (Archer 1888/1957) the results of responses to a questionnaire on actors' preferences in the matter which he had sent to leading English and French actors of his time. The first question read as follows:

> In moving situations, do tears come to your eyes? Do they come unbidden? Can you call them up and repress them at will? In delivering pathetic speeches does your voice break of its own accord? Or do you deliberately simulate a broken voice? Supposing that, in the same situation, you on one night shed

real tears and speak with a genuine lump in your throat and on the next night simulate these affections without physically experiencing them: on which occasion should you expect to produce the greater effect upon your audience?

Based on his own intuitions and the responses to his questionnaire, Archer concluded that actors both "lived" the characters they represented and "acted" them, suggesting that a superior performance could be achieved by direct affective involvement. Roach (1993) has given a detailed account of the debate on "to feel or not to feel" in acting in theatre.

Here I would like to extend the discussion to singing on the opera stage where the same question can be asked: will a singer achieve a stronger effect on the audience when he or she actually experiences at least part of the emotion that is expressed in an aria or recitative? The situation is complicated by the fact that whereas the actor has only the playwright's text and can freely choose, within the constraints set by the director, the non-verbal expression in voice, face, and body, the opera singer is additionally constrained by the structure and dynamics of the composer's music. As asserted by many of the contributors to this volume, the music itself will convey strong emotional meaning. In addition, the opera singer has to sing rather than speak the text, exactly as prescribed by the composer's notes and interpretation notations which adds further constraints and difficulties. However, the basic question remains the same—should the singer artfully feign the expression of the respective emotion of the character in the plot, as specified by the libretto, the music, and the director's and conductor's interpretations of the same, or actually experience, at least in part, the appropriate emotion and express the innermost feeling through voice, face, and gestures? In honor of Diderot, I will refer to this as the paradox of the opera singer, or, for short, the *singer's paradox*.

In order to appropriately frame what follows, it should be noted that the emphasis is here on theater and opera that are conceived in the dramatic rather than the epic style (Goethe 1827), in other words, the emphasis is on the immediate experience of the individual character, on realistically presented actions and emotions rather than on a more distant, more neutral narrative of a broader range of past events. Most classic theater pieces and most operas are conceived in this style, although there are many cases of mixed forms (especially in Baroque opera), where narrative, epic passages alternate with more immediate, dramatic scenes and the representation of an individual's thoughts and emotions. In contrast, some more recent work has focused on a less emotional, more rational and didactic form of theater and opera, in particular Brecht's "epic or dialectic theater" (Bernardino Fantini, personal communication).

Before approaching this issue in an analytical fashion from the vantage point of emotion psychology, I will first reproduce selected passages from interviews I conducted with internationally known singers, in part during the conference upon which this volume is based, following Archer's pioneering effort, to obtain some first-hand insights into how the issue is perceived by the opera singers themselves.

Thomas Moser (tenor)

[The singer's need to control emotion]

First of all I would have to make a differentiation between singers and actors, because I am convinced that actors can allow themselves to do things on the stage that a singer can't, because a singer must remain in complete control of his body at all times otherwise he can't sing. So I can't let myself go with the emotion when I'm singing. I have to understand what it is I wish to express but I can't just let myself go or very quickly I'll be out of voice altogether. I also think there has been a change between the time of Diderot and today because acting has changed even if we are just talking about straight theater. In Diderot's time one declaimed a text which today, no matter how wonderful the interpretation, would be considered to be terribly stiff. I would imagine that perhaps Racine ought to be delivered in this way but we're in a period of time in which fashion and the presence of the microphone have changed the way in which actors deliver text. Singers don't have the microphone so they have to sing the way they were trained to do which is to fill the room with their voices without help. If I were an actor in a normal theater in Europe today, I could probably allow myself to go with the emotion and be practically voiceless at the end of a soliloquy and have the audience in tears because I was actually living out in front of them what I was supposed to portray. Whether that is the way it ought to be in the theatre or not, it can't be that way on the musical stage.

Total control in singing may be difficult in some operas. For instance, when I was young I hated Wagner. I didn't like Wagner at all. I liked Mozart, anything that was clear and that had a certain transparency, also Schubert. I was already having trouble with Brahms. I liked modern composers because there was certain clarity in the things they composed. I overcame my dislike of Wagner when it simply came to the fact that I was going to have to sing his works. That seemed to be the next stage and everyone around me advising me thought that this was the thing to do. Then I got into it and became fascinated by it. This is a composer who touches one, at least touched me in the work that I was doing so profoundly that there was the danger that I could allow myself to be carried by the emotions and stop thinking about what I was doing.

Of course, the emotion in the music has an influence but it's not ruling me. It's not taking me over. I try to feel it, it's there, but I know that I have to know what it is I'm trying to express. I had a student once who came to me and said "I just assumed that if the emotion is right the singing will be OK." But you can't sing with emotion. You have to express emotion but you can't sing with emotion. For instance, I used to sing the *Lied* "Guten Abend, gut Nacht" [Brahms] at the end of recitals. It took me years before I could sing that without crying. I'm getting tears in my eyes now because the emotions are there because of singing it to my daughter when she was a baby. I have to say, my emotions are very close to the surface, but I have to keep the control over myself, because of the singing, or my voice will fail. But of course they are there, alongside with "What's my colleague doing now. Oh God I just stepped on my costume; how do I get out of this," while I am singing and trying to look graceful. Or the conductor just indicated that I am a little bit behind, that I have to catch up. There are about 50 things going on simultaneously and one is certainly the emotion I am trying to express.

[Different tracks of consciousness while singing]

Some people tell me that this is the wrong way to think but my impression of myself on the stage is that, at least in the most difficult moments, there are two of me there: the one who is doing it and the one who is telling the one who is doing it how to do it and reminding him not to let himself run away with the feeling and keep the control. A singer has to do everything with a certain peace. You have to pull your breath through your body. Regardless of how mad what you are doing is, you have to be in a situation of peace even if you don't look like you are to the audience, because you are trying to play it as well as sing it. But you've got to be there, you have got to find in this part of your body that thing that will allow you to support what you are doing vocally. I always feel that there is another me invisible to everyone else saying "Watch out, that moment is coming, be careful. Remember the voice lesson. Remember how you are supposed to do it. Enjoy it." Or I see someone in the audience who, in the heat of the moment, looks like my teacher. In reality, when the lights come on he doesn't look like him at all. But I need him and he is there.

…

It's like having my brain split and one half is working on the technical aspect. I have heard singers who say: "You know, by the time I get on the stage I know the role so perfectly technically that I don't need to think about anything except what I want to express." My personal answer to that has to be "Bullshit." I don't believe that you can go through an entire evening of singing and never have to think about having to correct yourself. Never being in danger of going somewhere you don't want to go, unless you just stand there and all you are doing is singing, which is expressing nothing. I get the gooseflesh occasionally while I'm singing but that is something that doesn't affect the singing. But if my heart is racing….

[Interpreting the emotion of a character]

The emotional interpretation of a character is clear in the text. Normally, I always have a text to work with. If you had to tell a singer who didn't know how to learn the material what he had to do, the first thing to tell him to do would be to study the text. Learn the text and speak the text in rhythm. Then learn the melody and add it to the text because the composer wouldn't have written that melody if he hadn't had that particular text to do it with. I'm sure that he wanted the words to be understood. There are some singers who will tell you that, for instance if you are singing an art song, it is sufficient to sing the melody properly and to speak the words as perfectly as you can, of course with all of the dynamic changes and so on. I don't believe that. For instance, someone once commented on my singing in Parsifal "B…b…l…löder, taumelnder Tor" [Stupid, tumbling fool: emphasis on stop consonants]. Some people would not have given as much weight to that "bl." If you care about language and you love language and text and it is important to express the content, then you are given utensils. Whereas if you only have a vowel and you say "sing that vowel and mean love or hate or despair," I don't really know how great the difference will be. However, I am capable of hearing something in a language that I don't understand and still being touched by it and that the mental picture that I get from the song or the aria may be different from what the words are describing. I've listened to Nicolai Gedda sing Russian songs, but I have no idea about Russian. I learnt a Russian text once phonetically, but it gave me no pleasure at all to sing that way, it was just like it will be singing syllables. I knew what I was singing about but I kept thinking "I can't create any sort of nuance in my voice because the words do not mean anything to me." And then I decided that from that point on I would only sing in languages that I can understand.

[Effects of emotion on singing]

At a particular performance, I was having a very difficult personal moment in which there was an awful lot of negative energy going on and I managed to turn that energy around and use it in a positive way in the performance. I can't really tell you how that happened, I don't know. I know that I simply invested all of what I had that was coming in a negative way in trying to funnel all this energy into the person that I was playing. If I have an argument with another character on the stage, she is no longer Mrs So and So, she is the character. And besides, one of the lovely things about emotions is that when you get to the extremes (love–hate) the intensity is very similar. You can sing as long as you are not clenching your teeth. You can sing with all of your negative intensity the beautiful words of love and someone will probably believe you. I think one of the reasons that I chose music or that music chose me was because from early on there were things that for me were difficult to express. I found a craft in which I could express those things and I found within the craft a language and that was singing. I started out with piano but it didn't satisfy me. I discovered theater and singing for myself more or less simultaneously. And I knew that was what I wanted. I didn't believe that I could have it but it was what I wanted.

Gillian Keith (soprano)

[Effects of emotion on singing]

The effects of emotion on singing are varied, depending on the emotion being expressed. I'll use an example of a role I've sung that involves emotional extremes, and how these emotions affected my singing. The opera is Harrison Birtwistle's *Punch and Judy* and my role was Pretty Polly. In the two opening scenes the emotion is extreme excitement and agitation, and this is written very clearly into the vocal line. It's almost like screeching or screaming. The character is very tense and anxious, like a child who cannot calm down. The choreography that was set was extremely jerky and fast. I would move my head side to side and shake with my whole body. The prop that I was holding needed to shake and tremble as well. In the rehearsal process I discovered that because everything was so fast and tense, (both music and movement) my throat would get very tight if I let myself be carried away by these extreme emotions. But I couldn't let that happen and sing at the same time. This is a good example of when I had to step back; I needed to find other physical movements that would allow me to express the same level of excitement, but also allow me to keep my throat relaxed enough to sing. I had to keep my voice free, yet it had to convey tension and anxiety. These emotions (excitement, agitation, tension, anxiety) come quite close to fear, I guess. So it could be the same kind of situation if you were expressing fear through your singing. You might get sweaty hands, dry in the mouth, and short of breath. If you're trying to express that on stage obviously you don't want a dry mouth, sweaty hands, and shortness of breath. Those things would be very impractical for singing. The same could apply if you were expressing sadness or despair and found yourself crying whilst singing. Crying creates mucus in the nose and mouth and makes singing difficult. There have to be other ways to show these emotions rather than experiencing them for real. In these instances we have to simulate the feelings, and add certain colors to the voice to convey the emotion.

[Feeling genuine emotion]

There are situations in which feeling genuine emotion will be beneficial to the performance. If the performer is able to relate to the emotion in a very real way, the performance will surely be enhanced. If I am singing a religious or spiritual work in a particular setting, for example a beautiful cathedral, I might feel a certain sense of awe and admiration coming into my voice as I am being moved by the music in these particular surroundings. I believe that one would be able to hear these things in the voice as my singing was lifted by the other-worldliness and the spirituality of the occasion. I always try to pick an experience in my own life that comes as close as possible to what I'm trying to portray through the music. I think you can use personal experience and take it to the extreme; put it into another example or situation, and allow yourself to be right there inside it. It's about allowing yourself to imagine something that might seem a little ridiculous to say out loud, but you don't have to tell anyone, you just try to embody it. With some emotions this will be more obvious to a listener and with others it may be more subtle. This depends on how your body reacts to the different emotions.

[The importance of the text]

Text is obviously important to convey meaning and for telling the story. The way we choose to sing text is linked to the emotion we are trying to express. But when there is no text (for example in the singing of a vocalise) can we still express the emotion? I believe that emotion will affect the color and timbre of the voice with or without text. When singing passages without text a challenge for me is to keep the intention and the emotion going through the whole line. Visualization techniques as well as physical intention help this journey outside of the text. Body language, when linked to the emotion we are trying to express, will color the voice even when we are not singing words. Feelings of anger might tighten the jaw and feelings of joy will activate our facial muscles as we smile. We don't need to be singing text for a listener to be able to hear these emotions in our voices.

[The role of the audience]

An audience inevitably changes the way we sing and perform. An audience may make us nervous, which has varying effects on our bodies. Nerves can cause the voice to tremble or the breath to be shallow. An audience can also give an adrenaline rush in the way they respond to a performance. This could give a feeling of excitement or confidence that we couldn't simulate on our own. I've had an experience before; when I just couldn't find the right energy in the rehearsal room. I don't know if it was the room, the casual situation, or the lack of air in the space. We were in a big building without windows or natural light, and we didn't have costumes. There was one section I kept singing under pitch. And I would always get the nod from the conductor, "You're sounding flat." I knew I was, but I was really having to manufacture something artificial and probably a bit tense just to get through the section. As soon as we got to a situation where we had audience, all of a sudden, the energy was there. And it changed my body. Everything just flowed the way it needed to flow. It could just be a simple fact of adrenaline. But I think it's something more than that. There were emotions of pride and excitement that I was feeling which I believe came directly as a result of being in front of an audience. And this is what brought my performance to a much higher level.

Lucy Schaufer (mezzo-soprano)

[How to generate the emotion appropriate to the character]

The process of choosing an emotion which is appropriate to your character is similar to the proverbial question of "how long is a piece of string?" The options are endless. Yet we singing actors have many clues to how a character might feel at any one time during the span of a performance: how the composer orchestrates a scene, how the text is phrased or turned, how the drama unfolds, how a specific director conceptualizes the work, and, most importantly, how the individual performer responds to these stimuli. The personal responses to these clues, these stimuli, are the core to how I build my emotional through-line in a performance. My imagination and previous personal experiences provide a wealth of choices and help to guide me to choose the appropriate emotion. Though the nomenclature sounds definitive, an appropriate emotion can be any emotion the actor chooses—when substantiated dramatically and musically.

Memory and imagination go hand in hand when creating a character. My goal is to create a character that is as truthful to the human condition as possible; even when in a production which might be surreal and highly conceptualized because the audience must identify with the experience being portrayed on the stage. We are the mirror to the world. So I try to choose honestly by reacting to the above mentioned stimuli. If playing Cio-Cio San in *Madama Butterfly* and I've never had a baby, then I must think of something similar or imagine what it would be like to lose your child by perhaps identifying a situation in my own life in which a relationship went wrong and painful loss was experienced.

A few years ago I played Margaret Johnson in *The Light in the Piazza*, a musical in which a mother copes with the aftermath of an accident which leaves her daughter Clara mentally diminished after being kicked by a pony at a birthday party—when Margaret had turned away to answer the telephone instead of staying and watching the children. Much of the story tells of how Margaret tries to protect Clara and how Margaret eventually learns to let her go. What did I have in my life that I could draw upon and inform my choices to make Margaret believable? My sister had a daughter who was killed in an accident on the family farm. My sister, like Margaret, had turned to answer the telephone when the incident occurred. From watching my sister grieve all these years for her daughter and replay scenarios of actions taken or not taken, I have observed what it's like to experience such a level of guilt and responsibility. It was finding that base level of understanding in my own bones from my memory which allowed me to take that next leap into making it Margaret's story using my imagination. I was never truly thinking of about being my sister, picking up the phone—it is only the leaping off point.

My toolbox for making these choices might be labeled Stanislavski or method acting. The leaping off point where you the singing actor makes the choice of the appropriate emotion must be informed, and I prefer to plumb the real or authentic to find my choices. Being in the moment of appropriate emotional choice is being in Margaret's moment not your own personal memory because if you remain in your personal memory, I think you remain too inward in your thinking, close down your energy and stop communicating to the audience. It's indulgent, which is where the misunderstanding and criticism about method and Stanislavski occurs. It is the emotional memory of your own, of your personal life or imagined life which informs your choices and what eventually you identify as your character. If you only keep it to yourself and do not leap from that personal point then you will never fully inhabit your character and your choices will not be "appropriate."

Memory and imagination inform, then your voice and body will follow suit creating specific colors and shapes which result in a personal and individual performance. This is the route by which you create your Anna Bolena, Blanche Dubois, Wozzeck, or Cherubino—claim it as your own because there is only one you, why copy what has gone before? Develop your toolbox to include memories, observations, and a playfulness in rehearsal and performance which allows your brain to imagine all the possibilities. Embrace the leaping off point: it is exactly where the personal and the imagined merge, where the voice and the body combine to make a fully integrated performance, one in which it is not just sound for sound-sake, but a beautifully fully human story telling soundscape.

Bruno Taddia (baritone and philosopher)

The foundations of a singer's/actor's work could be defined and described by all those linguistic formulations that evoke the concept of transformation, or the idea of "becoming other." When a performer finds himself in front of a text, his body is nothing but a blank page on which to write the part to play; and the gestures, the exclamations, and emotions will be the ink; thus the starting point appears to be a dichotomy to be integrated into a unity. Expressed as a formula:

Performer's body + text to interpret = character played.

If the equals sign represents the purpose of the actor/singer and indicates its fulfillment, the plus sign represents his intention to become on stage the character he wants to be in the most believable way possible, except for fortuitous situations. Therefore the will of the actor is the key to that process, which comes in the form of a will to change and an intention to become different. As a result, from a purely theoretical point of view, we can say that the process involving the performer implies giving up on what he is, hence he can create what he wants (or has to) become. The nature of this transformation is the most fascinating subject of the whole history of the theater and it also seems to be one of the most formidable enigmas: should it remain completely rational, calculated, or once engaged by the will, can it be experienced in its deep emotivity?

In the theatrical process, the body of the actor, who is the protagonist of the transformation above-mentioned, tries to replace some of its distinctive features, with new features necessary for the creative process and functional to the achievement of a result. To summarize, the body of the actor loses some of its specific features to adopt new features, sometimes unknown, in a way in which the subject-actor can transform himself and become the subject-character. For example: Maria Callas becomes Norma at the Rome Opera House, so A becomes B. However, it should be noted that the actor, who becomes a character because of the process we mentioned above, is always the place of this change, so Maria Callas is Norma at the Rome Opera House, then A is B. Therefore, we have the paradoxical situation of something that becomes something else, being both at the same time. In other words, the actor (Maria Callas, A) in becoming a character (Norma at the Rome Opera House, B), really is this character (Maria Callas is Norma at the Rome Opera House, A is B). This example shows the enigma of the actor's situation where something that is itself is something else at the same time. This extraordinary situation is not only possible, but necessary; a place in which the unthinkable, shows itself as thinkable. Therefore this strange transformation belongs to the sphere of "madness," as Western culture defines it.

The working material in this creative process of the singer/actor is the body. The promise of a character's communication, and more generally of human communication, is in the body. He can use it for verbal and non-verbal language, to express emotions, as a sign and/or a silent movement, or via the logical ordering of language. The body communicates and brings in its own flesh the ability to communicate intentions, feelings, and evaluations of an event, even beyond the intentionality of the subject. For example, sometimes we accept for compelling reasons an offer which we would rather reject, and yet we reveal our struggling: the language follows our will to communicate, whereas the body betrays our struggle and reveals it. In such a situation the body denounces the conscious and/or unconscious refusal of the behavior our rationality suggests as convenient. However, this betrayal reveals the profound link between corporality and emotionality, as well as the eidetic communicative strength of this bond, sometimes difficult to inhibit, beyond the will of the subject himself.

We often use the term "technique" when we talk about the theatrical process, a complex word that is difficult to define here. To simplify we will employ it using its common definition of a set of rules and practices concerning a certain activity. Critics, singers, conductors, and people who work in the music industry talk often about technique. This kind of discussion is raised because the subject of "play well" is really important. It is related to attempts to find mentally stored "knowledge" that can be intentionally activated to serve in the practice of acting. This process is also called a method. However, often lost in this operation, the subjects are distracted by some details and lose sight of the finishing line. If we consider the etymology of the word "technique," we find that it means "know-how." However, the meaning of this word is often misrepresented as a calculating thought only able to assert itself, whereas it should be considered as a way to "know how to express" the language of the body in the presence of an impelling emotion. Nevertheless this manifestation is the very expression of an emotion. Therefore the technique exists when it evaporates and transubstantiates in the expression it chooses to turn its attention to. For example: if I have a key, this will help me to open a specific door, nevertheless only when I open the door will I have the expressiveness of the key. The expression of the key is in the act of opening the door and not in the fact that the key is a metal object. There are many keys, but not many door openings…

The act of singing involves the larynx, the vocal cords, the diaphragm, and the muscles, so it is only normal that one of the first subjects to be studied is about the physical problems a singer can have when interpreting the sounds written on a score. Therefore the first step is to identify the body's feelings required to perform a song. When studying, these feelings are transformed into a fixed body memory corresponding to a particular way of singing. On the other hand a singer does not have to produce just some phonemes; otherwise the expression of his work would stop at the pure sound and the process will end there. The real goal is semantic, which aims to capture, in a kind of hermeneutic circle, the deep meaning of a dramatic situation. Implicitly, this is what Fischer-Dieskau evoked when he was asked about the most important skills that a singer should have, and answered—shocking his audience—that it was the imagination and not the voice as everyone would have expected. That is the real goal, as per one great baritone: to shed light, to illuminate as far as possible the deeper and unknowable essence that is what we call a "man" by using the imagination. The theatrical performance tries to achieve this kind of illumination and focuses more on the aesthetic aspect, which should progressively prevail, once the technique has employed its prerogatives on the body of the singer, solving the problems we commonly call "technical." During this creative moment the singer must transform himself into a character. Therefore he is forced to do some long and thorough work, which sometimes reaches some almost hypnotic excesses, trying to transform the physical sensations (we might say "technical sensations") which previously have dissolved the roughness of the song by using imaginative and psychagogic processes, into internal sensations of the character. These sensations constitute the expression of the emotions that will act on the expressive power of the character's body, intended as communication while singing, as well as an expression of the body acting on stage. Only in this perspective can the body become expressive and lose that ability of representation that inevitably will appear (because of the expressive power of the body we analyzed earlier) in case this is intended to maintain a purely technical vision based on the theatrical act. It should be noted that the inner transformation of the performer matches the contradictory experience of the actor we analyzed at the beginning. This applies to both to the actor's behavior and to the behavior of a raving man who falsifies his own experience, altering the reality considering it as acting and the acting as the real life. When acting on stage the performer feels like a blind man who ventures into a known location which becomes astonishing and unexpected because of his blindness. This blindness implies an uncertainty that no technique will be able to reproduce. Therefore the theatrical experience is the interpreter of the vertigo in which there lives together a man's sense, which he has built for his own safety, and the madness that haunts him and keeps questioning him; both of them are difficult to separate. For that reason Diderot's question of whether the performer has to be rational or sensible has only one answer to me—I do not know—and this not knowing expresses itself as an unspeakable and inextricable aesthetic "knowledge."

Christoph Prégardien, tenor

[How to use emotional imagery in a performance]

For myself, there is not only one way to do this. Sometimes I have to evoke memories of personal situations, but I try not to use special memories for special pieces, because I think it is important that you, when you are on stage and create a tale, that you live it at that moment, and that you trust yourself and your own experience and fantasy, that in the right moment, the right pictures come up. And those pictures are not always the same. There are some pieces you have to sing quite often, and there is the danger, if you sing the same role very often, that you always get into the same mood, evoking the same pictures. And of course, I have a broad repertoire and that makes it easy for me. But some pieces do come up quite often. But what I experience for myself, and what makes it so interesting, if it is good music, well composed music with a good text, I don't have any problems with my fantasy to create new pictures in myself.

[Difference in expressing emotions in singing opera or Lieder]

There is not such a great difference. Because of the nature of music, be it opera or instrumental music, or song, it is always human beings finding themselves in a certain human situation, in an emotional situation, and you have to show what that situation is like, you have to show how the composer put the text into music, and so you act like a kind of medium between the composer and the author on the one hand, and the audience on the other. Because music is always written for an audience. It is not written for a museum or for the composer himself. Composers want to express themselves through their music. And we have to bring that music to life. And this is not dependent upon what repertoire it is, whether it's *Lied* or opera. The way of expressing emotions, I think, is always the same.

[The role of text in determining emotions]

I think that is a question of the where the text comes from. If you have text from the 20th century, the emotional impact and the emotional content is different from that of a 19th century, text because the authors of the 19th century, especially of the Romantic period, wrote texts that are different from both modern authors and authors from the 17th or 16th centuries; they have different approaches to emotions. And of course you also have to take into account what the situation of the normal people was at that time. Thus, to provide a good interpretation of Schubert's music, you should know how life was in Vienna at that time. One big theme in Schubert's music is death. And why was so much music written about death at that time, and why were composers drawn to poetry dealing with this theme? Because death was omnipresent at that time. All over Europe, there were many diseases, because conditions of hygiene were different from today. In consequence, death was much more frequent, and people lived in different circumstances. They had big families, children were born, old people died, and this was a very normal thing. People had a different relationship to these themes than we do today. They also had a different relationship with nature. And they had a different notion of expressing emotions, like love, loss, or desire. I think it was just more normal to talk and to write about this. In addition, I think it's easier for a composer to write about sad things than about beautiful or easygoing things. I think much of the music comes from the dark side of the human soul.

The singers I consulted on their personal views about the role of emotion in singing largely confirmed the responses that the theatre actors gave on William Archer's questionnaire in the 1880s—the emotions of the character in the play have to be acted according to the plot but it is helpful if the singer can get into an emotional feeling that is similar or complementary to the character's emotion, as long as the bodily concomitants do not interfere with the physical action of singing. It would be interesting to examine the effect of the typical repertoire of a singer (e.g. more oriented toward the epic or dramatic style) on the approach to emotional interpretation (Bernardino Fantini, personal communication), but this would lead us too far astray in the current context. I will now turn toward a more detailed analysis of the underlying processes from the point of view of emotion psychology, in particular the work on emotional expression.

Real versus fake—genuine versus acted

In analyzing the singer's paradox from a psychological point of view, I will first question the widespread assumption that there is a clear dichotomy between real, genuine feelings, actual experience, authentic expression, etc. on the one hand, and artificial portrayals, feigned or faked feelings, acted emotions, and the like. This distinction is increasingly made in research on the expression of emotion in psychology and affective computing in engineering and the computer sciences, the study of former becoming the sought after ideal and the latter increasingly criticized and shunned (see Scherer, 2013). A similar tendency is emerging in the world of theater. There as well, the role of reality, immediacy, genuineness, authenticity, and credibility in contrast to fiction, staging, performance, and artificiality, is a burning issue. Matzke (2006) shows how much of contemporary theater is looking for authenticity and wants to put "real" human beings with high "strong claims for truth" on the stage, pointing out the inherent contradictions of this ideal of convincingly staged authenticity. It is likely that this analysis especially applies to the expression of emotions on the stage. A similar tendency is observable in modern stagings of classic operas by directors intent on innovation (especially in the recent German fashion of "Regietheater," in which authenticity is often equated with rather crude examples of human folly and suffering).

I want to show here that the supposed dichotomy between "real people" and "professional actors" and between "natural, genuine, authentic, uncontrolled, spontaneous, credible" and the exact opposite of all this, is not tenable and actually impedes advances in our understanding of emotional expression in real life and on the stage. Here are the two main arguments: (1) in accordance with one of the great pioneers of social science research on emotions, the anthropologist Erving Goffman (1959), one can affirm: "We all play *emotion theater* most of the time"; (2) a detailed analysis of the emotional process and the role of the expression shows that we have to consider the attributes of naturalness, control, authenticity, and credibility as separate, if not even orthogonal dimensions.

Emotion theater in everyday life

With precise observations in the field, Goffman (1959) was able to demonstrate convincingly that we always stage our daily lives and not only protect ourselves with a variety of ingenious strategies but also present our ideal self depending on the context. In doing so, acted emotions as well as masked emotions play a central role, since on the one hand inappropriate emotional expressions can damage our self-presentation, and on the other hand strategically produced emotional expressions play an important role in shaping our self-presentation in order to reach our goals in social interaction. The latter has been known since the beginning of thinking about human emotions.

Aristotle, a pioneer of the concept of "emotional intelligence," indicates that it was important to express one's anger at the right time, at the appropriate intensity, and directed at the proper person, in order not to be regarded as a social fool. Already in ancient times, teachers of rhetoric highlighted the central strategic function of facial and vocal expression in their textbooks. The control and masking of spontaneous emotional expression, depending on situational context, social norms, and their own action plans, has been addressed again and again in expression research. Thus Ekman and Friesen (1969) proposed the notion of culturally defined "display rules" which survey and modify the expression programs generated by genetically grounded affect programs. In modern psychology, emotion regulation (often based on proprioceptive feedback from motor expression on the subjective feeling state) plays a central role in the study of emotional expression (Gross 2007).

Thus, one can reasonably assume that completely spontaneous, involuntary emotional expressions are likely to be the exception rather than the rule and are limited to emotional outbursts or "affect bursts" (Scherer 1994). In the vast majority of cases, emotional expression constitutes a central instrument of individual regulation of emotion and strategic communication in social interaction. I have therefore proposed to distinguish between two separate determinants of emotional expression: (1) internal *push factors*, which "push" the expression characteristics in a certain direction due to the effect of physiological changes underlying emotional arousal, and (2) external *pull factors*, which "pull" the emotional expression towards a specific target pattern as a result of socio-cultural conventions.

Push factors are defined as changes in organismal subsystems that have a direct impact on the nature and intensity of motor expression. They work largely in an involuntary fashion, but their effects can be influenced to some extent (e.g. by suppression). The effect of these factors on facial and gestural expression and on vocalizations is almost exclusively determined by the type and strength of physiological changes. The resulting expression pattern is therefore independent of socio-normative guidelines or target patterns. In contrast, the pull factors are represented by exactly these external specifications or standards. They trigger the production of expression patterns (such as specific patterns of facial or vocal expression), which are shaped by standardized social situation demands, by signal transmission conditions, or self-presentation purposes as mentioned earlier. In other words, trigger mechanisms of push factors are the causes (such as physiological changes), while the resulting expression phenomenon is the consequence. In contrast, in the case of pull factors, the expression patterns to be generated are the independent variables, and the required production mechanisms are the dependent variables.

It can be assumed that both push and pull factors occur only very rarely in pure form since most spontaneously occurring behaviors are monitored and checked immediately. On the other hand, the strategic manipulation of expression is often due to the strengthening of a rudimentary involuntary expression. Both expression determinants interact with each other, and their respective degree of influence is dependent on the person's strategic intent and the specific situational context. In other words, we all constantly play *emotion theater*. Thus the distance from real life to professional acting is not nearly as clear-cut as it is usually made out to be.

The push–pull distinction can be directly applied to the singer's paradox, as nicely illustrated in the examples provided by the singers themselves. In singing a specific role in an opera, their expressions are determined by a large number of pull factors, including the specification of the character's emotions and expressions by the libretto, the emotional meaning that the composer has given to the score, the interpretation imposed by the director, socio-cultural rules about what is "proper" for display in an opera house, the specific expectations of the audience, and, most importantly, the control required by the technical feat of producing complex sequences of elaborate sounds with their voices. But there are also many different push factors. Some of these may be quite incompatible with the desired or expected emotional expression, as in the case of emotions generated by the personal situation off stage, emotional reactions to the behavior of other singers, the director, the conductor, or the audience, concern about one's vocal capacity, or just general stage fright. Others may actually serve the desired expression and thus be sought out or even encouraged, such as appropriating emotion memories from one's own experience, imagination, induction by the emotional meaning in the music, or emotional contagion from others on the stage. Just like in everyday life, many of these push and pull factors are active simultaneously and the resulting expression is often a compromise between the respective influences.

Yet, while we all play emotion theater in juggling push and pull effects, actors and particularly singers are the professionals at this game and it may be enlightening to examine their objectives and the mechanisms they employ to reach their goals. Given the theories and treatises on acting from antiquity to today, one could venture the hypothesis that one of the main aims is to express the character's emotions in a way that the audience will consider as natural, genuine, authentic, uncontrolled, spontaneous, and credible. This, by the way, is very similar to what we all attempt to produce in our daily emotion theater.

Dimensions of expression production and expression effects

The terms used to qualify expression such as natural, genuine, authentic, uncontrolled, spontaneous, credible are often, at least implicitly, considered as synonyms or at least highly correlated. On the other hand it is often assumed that these properties can easily be distinguished from their opposites. I will try to show that both assumptions stand on very shaky ground.

First we need to separate the expression production mechanism from the impression processing mechanism. "Spontaneous versus arbitrary" and "controlled versus uncontrolled" are production mechanisms, which can be detected with neuroscience and physiological methods (although, of course, observers draw conclusions in this regard). In contrast, credible versus not credible (and probably also natural versus artificial) are just subjective impressions of quality, which heavily depend on personal experiences, values, and preferences. Furthermore, there is the question of the possibility of clearly distinguishing these poles.

Spontaneous, reflexive versus intended, arbitrarily, controlled. Let us first distinguish between spontaneous, reflexive action versus intentional or willful control, using the example of affective vocalizations. Similar to other patterns of behavior, it seems impossible to clearly distinguish between spontaneous and intended control behavior. Let us take the reflexive pain cry "aaaaah" as an example: even though this is an emotional outburst ("affect burst"), the phonological sound-form (/a/, the "schwa" in phonetics) can be produced softer or louder, shorter or longer, with lower or higher pitch, or even completely suppressed (to hide one's own suffering, often without conscious intention), or alternatively to make it more noticeable (in order to arouse compassion, as often encountered in small children tripping over). At the same time there are language-specific conventionalized emotional emblems (such as "ouch" in English or "aua" in German), which are likely to be produced spontaneously without explicit informational purposes. On the other hand, an accidental outbreak of emotion is not entirely reflexive even if there are no observers, since the control of vocalization can also be caused involuntarily by typical self-presentation or role definition mechanisms.

Most likely, the majority of all patterns of human expression (except possibly unbearable pain) are controlled and surveyed by the central nervous system with monitoring structures which suppress, enhance, or change the behavior. For this reason, it makes little sense to distinguish sharply between reflex-like outbreaks and intended controlled expressions. Similar to the above-mentioned determinants of expression, there is a continuum, with extreme cases occurring occasionally but the large majority consisting of mixed cases in which both determinants are present and interact, with one or the other being more dominant.

Genuine, authentic versus inauthentic, artificial. I propose a similar continuum for the dimension "genuine, authentic versus inauthentic, artificial." In contrast to the preceding dimension, the fundamental determinant of the particular position on the continuum is not the type of production, i.e. the degree of conscious, voluntary control, but the *object* of the expression production. To rephrase the question, is the specific form of expression only the visible sign, which is an automatically occurring *symptom* of the underlying emotional reaction pattern, or is it the intended *goal* of expressive behavior? For example, does a high frequency of the voice reflect an increased tone of the vocalis muscle caused by sympathetic excitement or has it been achieved by a targeted effort to produce a specific voice frequency level for strategic purposes? One can argue that the former is a reflexive push effect, while the latter is a conscious–volitional pull effect and therefore question the independence of the proposed dimensions. In fact, the dimensions are probably not independent, but correlated. Nevertheless, the distinction makes sense if one considers that the regulation of emotion, consciously or unconsciously, is part and parcel of the emotion process. Highly controlled and modulated pain sounds would still be genuine when they truthfully reflect both the push by physiological changes and the pull exerted by social conventions, especially if the dynamic changes from the onset of the outbreak to the regulated affect emblem are faithfully reflected. This outbreak is genuine and authentic, in the sense of an "original," if it reflects a complex emotional process that can also contain some conscious regulation components. Generally an expression can be considered as inauthentic or contrived, i.e. a "copy," when it only mimics certain elements of a true expression and produces a stereotyped, often static expression.

But how can we specify this subtle difference? I propose to use one of the major characteristics of emotion episodes for this purpose. Emotional episodes are mainly characterized by the synchronization of their various components, reflecting the subsystems of the organism. This synchronization reflects the organism's effort to mobilize as much energy as possible in order to master a critical situation (in the negative and positive sense). It is costly because it affects the normal functioning of the subsystems and therefore should only occur if it is really necessary (see Scherer 2001, 2009 and Chapter 10).

A direct consequence of this assumption is that the deliberate production of a specific emotional expression—which is basically an affective emblem—does not lead to a complete synchronization of all major systems (as this would be too costly for the organism). It appears likely that only some of the most visible indicators of the emotion—especially facial expression, which is easily and effortlessly controlled—will be produced. We would therefore expect very little synchronization between changes in expression and changes in physiological signals for symbolically represented emotions—affective emblems included. A further consequence of this hypothesis would be that in the case of a *conscious attempt* to synchronize and integrate the various components, the results would be artificial and less perfect than synchronization which is generated by real, ongoing appraisal processes. It is to be expected that the attempt to deliberately synchronize vocal and facial expression leads to differences from the natural, on-line synchronization with a regard to synchronizing the beginning and end, the duration and intensity as well as in other dynamic properties (e.g. symmetry of facial expression) of the two expressive channels. This also concerns the sequential and cumulative nature of the synchronization process (as predicted by the component process model of emotion; Scherer 2001, 2009). If the model is correct, the characteristics of the expressive sequence will occur in a fixed sequence during the synchronization process, with cumulative effects. In the case of a false, pretended expression, one would expect a simultaneous rather than sequential occurrence of all subfeatures of the expression process due to a single voluntary motor command producing a single integrated movement.

Credible versus not credible. As mentioned earlier, the dimension of credibility is based on subjective evaluation, as determined by the sensory organs, experiences, and value system of the viewer ("in the eye of the beholder"). An objective determination of the credibility of expressions of emotion is therefore difficult, unless one trusts the convergence of observers' judgments. The more a particular emotional expression is considered to be credible, the more readily one will accept the particular expression as "original" (real, authentic). An interesting example of this was observed during the presidential election contest between Nicolas Sarkozy and Ségolène Royal in France in the spring of 2007. This is relevant because, after all, politicians are also actors on a stage, playing to the audience. In the crucial TV debate, Royal took her rival's declaration of his intention to facilitate the school enrollment of disabled children in mainstream schools as an opportunity to show a strong anger reaction extending over several utterances. Already in journalists' comments immediately after the broadcast and consequent press reports persistent doubts about the authenticity of this outbreak of anger were expressed. What is the basis of this convergent doubt?

Mortillaro, Mehu, and Scherer (2013) studied Ségolène Royal's facial and vocal expressions as well as her gestures in the widely distributed video clip. The results show that Royal, despite repeated verbal voicing of her pretended anger and aggressive deictic gestures on accented syllables in her voice, showed only very few of the typical signs of physiologically determined anger arousal (pull effects). Thus, the fundamental frequency of her voice (pitch) was less high than in earlier television shows in which she let her anger run freely. Furthermore, the energy distribution in the spectrum is not indicative of an extreme form of this emotion. Most importantly, based on the discussion above, a decisive indicator for the impression of a lack of authenticity is the absence of synchronization between the different modes of expression. Thus, the verbal marked manifestation of anger is rarely accompanied by the typical facial muscle movements (such as frowning) or by the typical angry voice modulations. The gestures are repetitive and are only coordinated with the speech rate or word accents.

Thus, perceived credibility seems to be strongly related to perceived authenticity, based on coordinated expressions in different modalities, probably because the latter can be considered as external signs of a genuinely unfolding dynamic emotion process—as theory would predict. Of course, such examples have only an illustrative function—the postulated relationships still await empirical testing. In this context, it would be interesting to examine to what extent credibility assessment is related to the role of the expression in Lipps' (1903) theory of empathy. One might expect that a rudimentary imitation of the observed expression processes can only lead to a clear result when the individual elements of the expression are consistently coordinated with each other and therefore able to activate particular interpretation schemes.

Credible emotion expression on the stage

What conclusions can we draw from the preceding considerations for the performance of the emotions on stage in general and for the singer's paradox in particular? First of all, one should abandon the idea that, for the sake of complete authenticity, actors should live through "real emotions" on the stage. As we have seen, emotions are almost always regulated due to many different sorts of constraints. In consequence, the notion of "natural" or uncontrolled emotion expression is practically unattainable. In addition, at least for singers, there is the constraint that the technical control of the voice required for their vocal performance would suffer. Furthermore, it seems unlikely that the real emotions singers could experience on the stage, which by definition must be based on events that are highly relevant to themselves, fit the emotional script contained in the libretto and the music.

A quote from Stanislavski's *An Actor Prepares* (Stanislavski 1936, pp. 40–41) is instructive here:

> On the stage there cannot be, under any circumstances, action which is directed immediately at the arousing of a feeling for its own sake. To ignore this rule results only in the most disgusting artificiality. When you are choosing some bit of action leave feeling and spiritual content alone. Never seek to be jealous, or to make love, or to suffer, for its own sake. All such feelings are the result of something that has gone on before. Of the thing that goes before you should think as hard as you can. As for the result, it will produce itself.

In terms of modern emotion psychology one can interpret Stanislavski's claim "All such feelings are the result of something that has gone on before" as referring to the lawful unfolding of emotion episodes, including specific emotional expressions, as a result of specific configurations of appraising events in terms of their relevance for oneself (see Chapter 10). Thus, specific emotional expressions are credible, i.e. appear authentic, when they can be seen as generated by appraisals that fit the respective circumstances. Here is another quote from Stanislavski (1936, pp. 51–2), who asks of an actor "Sincerity of emotions, feelings that seem true in given circumstances":

> By true seeming we refer not to actual feelings themselves but to something nearly akin to them, to emotions reproduced indirectly, under the prompting of true inner feelings.... In practice, this is approximately what you will have to do: first, you will have to imagine in your own way the "given circumstances" offered by the play, the regisseur's production, and your own artistic conception. All of this material will provide a general outline for the life of the character you are to enact, and the circumstances surrounding him. It is necessary that you really believe in the general possibilities of such a life, and then become so accustomed to it that you feel yourself close to it. If you are successful in this, you will find that "sincere emotions," or "feelings that seem true" will spontaneously grow in you.... However, when you use this third principle of acting, forget about your feelings, because they are largely of subconscious origin, and not subject to direct command. Direct all of your attention to the "given circumstances." They are always within reach.

I suggest that the frequently claimed requirement of authenticity on the stage should be defined in terms of the credibility of the emotional expression given the character, the emotional development of the plot, and the music (which is often intimately linked to the text). Based on the analysis proposed above, the singer would be required to be emotionally credible given these constraints, projecting sincere emotions—or at least producing a deceptively genuine copy. This means that in order to succeed he or she must: (1) select the correct expression elements for the respective emotions in the various modalities (voice, face, body) and combine them dynamically, in a psycho-biologically correct fashion, i.e. reflecting the physiological and psychological factors in the situation; (2) a precise coordination to achieve synchronization of the respective processes, letting the expression unfold in an appropriate fashion, and (3) to handle the situational development appropriately in terms of its dynamic flow or contextually necessary regulation efforts. This is a list of requirements, which obviously demand the highest amount of professionalism when the voluntary representation of a certain dynamic forms of expression is the object of effort.

Perhaps the task is easier if singers can rely on emotional experiences that have stuck in their memory. Results from affective neuroscience show that these also contain an important somatovisceral component. This includes motor expression patterns, as experienced in real situations as a reflection of the ongoing cognitive and physiological processes. It can be assumed that the reproduction of such patterns from their own experience, or their use as a realistic blueprint, is much more automatic and coherent than a deliberate production of hypothetical patterns. This idea may have been at the basis of Stanislavski's fundamental idea which has influenced the method acting approach referred to by Lucy Schaufer. Here is a central passage from Stanislavski's "textbook" for actors (Stanislavski 1936, p. 177):

> Never lose yourself on the stage. Always act in your own person, as an artist. You can never get away from yourself. The moment you lose yourself on the stage marks the departure from truly living your part and the beginning of exaggerated false acting. Therefore, no matter how much you act, how many parts you take, you should never allow yourself any exception to the rule of using your own feelings. To break that rule is the equivalent of killing the person you are portraying, because you deprive him of a palpitating, living, human soul, which is the real source of life for a part.... Always and for ever, when you are on the stage, you must play yourself. But it will be in an infinite variety of combinations of objectives, and given circumstances which you have prepared for your part, and which have been smelted in the furnace of your emotion memory. This is the best and only true material for inner creativeness.

Given the nature of emotion expression and the cues used by observers to infer emotionality and authenticity, this method would create at least a certain degree of authenticity, which may be hard to achieve by consciously and deliberately constructed forms of expression. In fact, Stanislavski stressed the fact that his method used conscious means to achieve unconscious results. Most likely, the type of synchronization of all organismal systems that I have postulated as the central criterion for authenticity is achieved more organically and convincingly if it is the result of imagining, and partly reliving, emotions rather than the conscious effort of manipulating different expressive means.

To conclude, I will return to Diderot. The words "feigning" or "imitating" in the opening quote to this chapter may suggest that he had skilful but superficial acting in mind. However, by "passion well imitated" he had a much more complex procedure in mind, one that in many ways already foreshadowed Stanislavski's method, including the notion of emotional memory. Here is a succinct summary by Roach (1993):

> A great actor will first create within himself the "*modèle idéal*" of the character he is portraying. Only after he has "considered, combined, learnt, and arranged the whole thing in his head," even down to the last "twentieth part of a quarter of a tone," is he ready to present his grand illusion of being not himself—a Regulus, Ninias, or Macbeth—free from threat of random intrusions by merely personal emotions. The "inner model" acts as a kind of linear matrix and template: it structures sequences of passions, not still expressions, and directs all subsequent embodiments of the illusion, so that the great actor who plays from "reflection" and "memory" will "be one and the same at all performances." [p. 133]
>
> Memory has two implications in Diderot's theatrical scheme: first, in terms of performance, it means the training of muscles into patterns of facial and bodily movement as in mime or ballet; second, in terms of the creation of the inner model, it means wealth of stored sense impressions and associations known generally to the eighteenth century as decaying sensations or "vibratiuncles," but which later theorists, retracing ground first covered by Diderot, categorized as "affective memories." Emotional events, sharply experienced by the body, become intelligible—and hence useful to the actor—only in retrospect; they are anything but intelligible as they occur, palpitating the diaphragm and shocking the mind. The passage of time permits reflection to order violent experiences into coherence, while imagination serves to revive at least some of their original piquancy. [p. 145].

To sum up. In this chapter I have tried to argue that we need a theoretically grounded notion of emotional authenticity on the stage that avoids the pitfalls of both the naïve notion of "real emotions" conjured up by the actor/singer and the cynical notion of a skilled professional who can effortlessly manipulate his/her expressive machinery to achieve a convincing semblance of "real emotions." As so often, the middle ground may be more promising than the extremes. After analyzing the many underlying dimensions of the notion of authenticity, including spontaneity, credibility, absence of control, genuineness, I have suggested defining authenticity in the sense of the credibility of the expressed emotion in terms of a plausible result of the appraisal processes that can be assumed to underlie the state of a character at a particular point in the plot, given the constraints, for the opera singer, of the libretto, the music, and the director's interpretation. I have argued that the perception of a high degree of synchronization of the different expressive channels, as would be produced by the result of an emotion-antecedent appraisal process, is a necessary condition for the actor/singer to be seen by the public as "inhabiting" the emotion of the character rather than just going through the motions. This synchronization may be easier to achieve in an unconscious fashion through the evocation of emotional memories which contain traces of the different emotion components, such as physiological change and expressive movements that are synchronized during an emotion episode than through effortful intentional motor commands. Maybe not surprisingly, these preliminary suggestions, which will need much further elaboration, seem to be highly compatible with reflections on the art of acting over the centuries—from Diderot, to Stanislavski, to Strasberg, to mention only some of the most well-known names. Thus it may be possible in the future to provide both theoretical and empirical underpinnings to the theoretical proposals and teachings of some of the major figures in this domain. Last but not least, as demonstrated by the testimonials of five professional opera singers, this approach does not seem too far from what is currently practiced by these experienced artists. Maybe there is a solution to the singer/actor's paradox after all.

References

Archer, W. M. (1888). *Masks or Faces? A Study in the Psychology of Acting*. London: Longmans, Green & Co. [Reprinted in *The Paradox of Acting and Masks or Faces?* Introduction by Lee Strasberg. New York: Hill & Wang, 1957.]

Diderot, D. (1880). *Paradoxe sur le comédien*. Paris: Sautelet et Cie. [Translated as *The Paradox of Acting* by W. H. Pollock, 1883. Reproduced in *The Paradox of Acting and Masks or Faces?* Introduction by Lee Strasberg. New York: Hill & Wang, 1957.]

Ekman, P. & Friesen, W. V. (1969) The repertoire of nonverbal behavior: categories, origins, usage, and coding. *Semiotica*, **1**, S49–S98.

Goethe, J. W. (1827). Ueber epische und dramatische Dichtung [letters Goethe/Schiller]. In *Goethe–Ueber Kunst und Alterthum*, Band 6, Heft 1, pp. 1–26. Stuttgart: Cotta.

Goffman, E. (1959). *The Presentation of Self in Everyday Life*. Garden City, NY: Doubleday.

Gross, J. J. (ed.) (2007). *Handbook of Emotion Regulation*. New York: Guilford.

Hejmadi, A., Davidson, R. J., and Rozin, P. (2000). Exploring Hindu Indian emotion expressions: evidence for accurate recognition by Americans and Indians. *Psychological Science*, **11**, 183–7.

Lipps, T. (1903). *Ästhetik: Psychologie des Schönen und der Kunst: Grundlegung der Ästhetik*, Erster Teil. Hamburg: L Voss.

Matzke, A. M. (2006) Von echten Menschen und wahren Performern. In E. Fischer-Lichte (ed.), *Wege der Wahrnehmung: Authentizität, Reflexivität und Aufmerksamkeit im zeitgenössischen Theater*, pp. 39–47. Berlin: Theater der Zeit.

Mortillaro, M., Mehu, M., and Scherer, K. R. (2013). The evolutionary origin of multimodal synchronisation and emotional expression. In: E. Altenmüller, S. Schmidt, & E. Zimmermann (eds.). *Evolution of Emotional Communication: From Sounds in Nonhuman Mammals to Speech and Music in Man*, pp. 3–25. Oxford: Oxford University Press – Series in Affective Sciences.

Roach, J. R. (1993). *The Player's Passion: Studies in the Science of Acting*. Ann Arbor: University of Michigan Press.

Scherer, K. R. (1994). Affect bursts. In S. van Goozen, N. E. van de Poll, and J. A. Sergeant (eds), *Emotions: Essays on Emotion Theory*, pp. 161–96. Hillsdale, NJ: Erlbaum.

Scherer, K. R. (2001). Appraisal considered as a process of multi-level sequential checking. In K. R. Scherer, A. Schorr, and T. Johnstone (eds), *Appraisal Processes in Emotion: Theory, Methods, Research*, pp. 92–120. New York: Oxford University Press.

Scherer, K. R. (2009). The dynamic architecture of emotion: evidence for the component process model. *Cognition and Emotion*, **23**, 1307–51.

Scherer, K. R. (2013). Vocal markers of emotion: comparing induction and acting elicitation. *Computer Speech and Language*, **27**, 40–58.

Stanislavski, K. (1936). *An Actor Prepares*. London: Methuen [paperback edition 1988].

Strasberg, L. & Chaillet, N. (2008). Acting. In *Encyclopedia Britannica*. (Retrieved 25 May 2012, from <http:// www. britannica.com>)

Web links to performer biographies

Gillian Keith <http://www.musichall.uk.com/>

Thomas Moser <http://www.fischerartists.com/thomas-moser.html>

Christoph Prégardien <http://www.pregardien.com/>

Lucy Schaufer <http://www.lucyschaufer.com/>

Bruno Taddia <http://www.brunotaddia.com/>

Chapter 6

On the resistance of the instrument

Tom Cochrane

Emotional expression is often regarded as central to the purpose and meaning of art. In large part this is because it encompasses a number of different values, each more or less present as a product of the awareness, deliberation, inventiveness, and social coordination to be found in the expressive act (cf. Scherer in Chapter 5). My goal here will be to outline these values in an act of musical performance, highlighting the role played by the *resistance* of the instrument to the immediate realization of the musician's intentions. Resistance is also something that comes in degrees, and by examining some recent trends in musical instrument technologies, I will argue that relative *transparency* is also a viable choice, depending on the values to which one aspires.

Let us begin by discerning the values to be found at a general level in the expression theory of art. A classic statement of the theory is R. G. Collingwood's (1938) book *The Principles of Art*. Here Collingwood articulates the view that the business of art "proper" is to express the emotional state of the artist. Collingwood means something very specific by the term "expression," however. It is not simply a matter of revealing one's emotion. In a famous passage, he describes the process involved:

> At first, he is conscious of having an emotion, but not conscious of what this emotion is. All he is conscious of is a perturbation or excitement, which he feels going on within him, but of whose nature he is ignorant. While in this state, all he can say about his emotion is: "I feel... I don't know what I feel." From this helpless and oppressed condition he extricates himself by doing something which we call expressing himself.

The artist begins with a vague, inchoate impulse which he or she then clarifies by means of expression. This is a matter of bringing the state to full articulate consciousness, so is quite unlike the casual betrayal of one's emotional state (which could occur without the awareness of the subject). Collingwood is also keen to emphasize that the artist does not simply reproduce some pre-conceptualized idea, for that would be mere craft. He rather gives form for the first time to a *new* mental state, individualized in its own unique way in the act of expression. Thus while the value of expression might sometimes be conceptualized in terms of its cognitive benefit, of enabling an individual to gain some self-understanding, it is also rooted in the value of creativity. The struggle to express oneself is a means towards self-manifestation or self-becoming. And if it is engaged in sincerely, it cannot help but result in something original, because it will be a product of the artist's individual experience.

A similar theme is to be found Hegel's (1835) *Lectures on Fine Art*:[i]

> The universal and absolute need from which art (on its formal side) springs has its origin in the fact that man is a *thinking* consciousness, i.e. that man draws out of himself and puts *before himself* what he is and whatever else is. Things in nature are only *immediate* and *single*, while man as spirit *duplicates* himself.... This aim he achieves by altering external things whereon he impresses the seal of

his inner being and in which he now finds again his own characteristics. Man does this in order, as a free subject, to strip the external world of its inflexible foreignness and to enjoy in the shape of things only an external realization of himself. Even a child's first impulse involves this practical alteration of external things; a boy throws stones into the river and now marvels at the circles drawn in the water as an effect in which he gains an intuition of something that is his own doing…. [Introduction, Section 6i]

Both Hegel and Collingwood, then, align artistic creativity with a supposedly universal drive; to make manifest our inner natures. Artistic expression simply brings this drive to its highest pitch of sophistication. And why should we want to make manifest our inner natures? Its motivation seems to be drawn from the fundamental will to live and to flourish. As such, no further justification seems necessary. That's just the kind of creature we are.

At the same time, however, Collingwood recognizes that the artist is interested in sharing his impressions with the wider community. Art to some extent is a public service since the artist expresses emotions on behalf of the audience. The artist "is singular in his ability to take the initiative in expressing what all feel, and all can express" (Collingwood 1958, p. 119). This is no mere side-benefit to expression, but an important part of bringing the artist's expressive intent to fruition. For if other people cannot re-create the artist's emotional state by engagement with the work, then the artist cannot be sure that he or she has had a genuine aesthetic experience (Collingwood 1958, pp. 311–15).

For Tolstoy, the value of sharing one's emotions is paramount. Adopting a fairly simplistic theory of expression as a kind of emotional contagion he claims that, "every art causes those to whom the artist's feeling is transmitted to unite in soul with the artist, and also with all who receive the same impression" (Tolstoy 1899, p. 163). Indeed, so important is the value of sharing for Tolstoy that he demands that art only express emotions that everyone can share; emotions such as merriment, pity, cheerfulness, and tranquility or "feelings flowing from the perception of our sonship to God and of the brotherhood of man" (Tolstoy 1899, p. 164). All other arts either unite some people at the expense of alienating others (such as patriotic arts) or are inaccessible to the masses. An unfortunate consequence of this view acknowledged and accepted by Tolstoy is that Beethoven's Ninth Symphony turns out to be an inferior piece of work because it is rather complicated. Collingwood, in contrast, takes the rather more sympathetic line that the artist need only share his emotions with a limited subset of likeminded fellows—and indeed that it would be insincere for the artist to play to the lowest common denominator.

We have seen that for Collingwood, the main point of expressing oneself is that it brings one's creative insight to fruition. The value of sharing is somewhat subservient to the value of creativity or self-realization (including perhaps, the self-realization of certain members of the audience). However, Tolstoy clearly regards the value of sharing emotions in different terms. There are strong moral overtones to Tolstoy's discussion; that art should contribute to the interpersonal harmony of the community. And it is plausible that sharing emotions through art can stimulate feelings of belonging; of overcoming loneliness or the more profound worry that others cannot understand what it's like to be you. While we need not insist with Tolstoy that art is best when it promotes a quantitatively maximal level of sharing, we can still recognize that the sharing of emotions is a valid goal for art. And again, like the drive for creativity, we can derive the value of sharing from the basically social nature of humans. We are just the kind of creatures that thrive in mutually supportive environments.

There is also another, less frequently noted value to be found in expression, that of pleasure. It is a value compatible with both Tolstoy's ideal of emotion sharing and Collingwood's ideal of creative articulation. But we also find it explicitly discussed in Dewey's (1934/1980) *Art as Experience*, particularly in connection with the resistance that the environment offers to one's emotional impulses:

> Nor without resistance from surroundings would the self become aware of itself; it would have neither feeling nor interest, neither fear nor hope, neither disappointment nor elation. Mere opposition that completely thwarts, creates irritation and rage. But resistance that calls out though generates curiosity and solicitous care, and, when it is overcome and utilized, eventuates in elation. [pp. 59–60]

Dewey has a rather broad notion of resistance that encompasses the whole struggle of the artist to bring objective form to his or her expressive intent. As the above passage indicates, Dewey regards resistance as a necessary condition for self-consciousness since a creature that never met resistance to its impulses could not become conscious of the independence of the world to its will, and thus its distinction from the world. But in addition to all this metaphysical talk, we also see the elation that accompanies a successful expressive act. To *express*, in the traditional sense of expelling something, of overcoming some resistant material, feels good.

We can now see the ways in which the various values of expression are drawn out in the act of musical performance. Beginning with the value of pleasure, we observe that the challenges involved in getting a good sound out of a musical instrument are, for the musician at least, an important part of their *experience* of the music. There is an immediate connection between the energy required to do something and one's sense of power, or between the ability to transcend the limitations of the instrument and one's sense of grace or freedom. Eric Clarke (2006) for instance describes the pleasures involved in interacting in a controlled and fluent manner with an instrument that is often "unbearably uncomfortable or uncooperative." He cites a case in which a pianist reports enjoying the use of his thumb in a certain passage even though it is not the most efficient fingering available. He also describes his own heightened enjoyment of violin music when performing in a comfortable key.

Since these various feelings of enjoyment, power, or gracefulness are generated as a result of interacting with the musical instrument, the physical act of performance must contribute to the emotional state felt by the performer. Were the instrument *not* to a degree resistant to the intentions of the musician, their emotional state would be different. As such, these pleasures are not incidental to the act of expression. If the performer is engaging in a Collingwoodian act of creative *self-expression*—the kind of immediate creative articulation found not just in improvisation but any creative interpretation of a score—the physical interaction with the instrument will also shape that mental state expressed by the performer in the musical event. In these circumstances, then, we should recognize that the instrument is not merely a means to the end of realizing some pre-existing expressive sentiment, but a vital part of shaping expressive content from the beginning.

In a previous paper (Cochrane 2008) I described at length how the performer may use the instrument to think through his or her emotion, and that the music and its means of production may even be construed as a literal component of the musician's mental state. My concern in that paper was to establish the point that musicians may use music to physically extend the cognition of emotions. What I would like to elaborate on here, however, are the ways in which the interaction with a musical instrument also serves the *values* that motivate the act of musical expression in the first place. We may note, for instance, that while the pleasure of performance is perhaps most intensely felt by the performer, the audience is also capable of vicariously enjoying that pleasure by empathically re-creating the performer's movements. When we watch a concert pianist, even if we have no experience of playing a piano ourselves, we have a rough idea of what it takes to press on a piano key and produce a sound. As a result, the way that the pianist moves about the instrument has the potential to convey a great deal of information about the attitude of the performer (cf., again, Clarke 2006). We can detect, for example, flamboyance in movements which we know to be quite unnecessary to the production of the sound. The point generalizes to the full range of emotional attitudes that may be conveyed in the interaction with an instrument; the sense of rage conveyed by an aggressive strike, or desolation conveyed in trying but failing to produce a sound. As such, the physical resistance afforded by the instrument is a significant means by which such emotional information may be shared.

We should admit here that at least some of the performer's movements may simply be the product of tics or ingrained habits. Moreover, some of the performer's gestures are likely to be intentional and communicative, where others unconsciously betray emotional attitudes, and still others are determined by purely physiological factors. In many cases it may be impossible to separate these various influences. Still, this is no different from the complexities and ambiguities that attend the interpretation of everyday body language. We are nevertheless prone to draw inferences about personality and attitude on observing such behavior. Collingwood would no doubt wish to exclude non-intentional movements from the artistic event properly so-called, but I find myself unwilling to draw such sharp distinctions in this regard. Any musician performing in front of an audience must accept that the audience will sensitively engage with the entire perceivable event. And if we were to learn that the groans and expressive behaviors of a pianist like Glenn Gould were entirely unconscious, I do not believe this would be sufficient grounds to exclude these factors from our appreciation of his performances, or indeed of him as a person.

In addition to the value of emotion sharing, the resistance of the instrument also serves the value of creativity. It is in exploring the capacities of the instrument that the musician's creative imagination is stimulated because it allows him or her to see what is possible (see again Cochrane 2008 for discussion). But the performer must often also seek inventive ways to adjust to the physical constraints of the instrument in the pursuit of his or her expressive intent. Stravinsky (1956) makes this point in his *Poetics of Music* when he observes that constraints are necessary to stimulate the creative imagination. And Tōru Takemitsu makes a similar point in with regards to the traditional Japanese string instrument, the biwa:

> The biwa could be called the mother of Japanese music. The major characteristic that sets it apart from Western instruments is the active inclusion of noise in its sound whereas Western instruments, in the process of their development, sought to eliminate noise. It may sound contradictory to refer to "beautiful noise," but the biwa is constructed to create such a sound. That sound is called sawari, a term that also has come to be used in a general sense… The term sawari, which also means "touch," may additionally mean "obstacle." Thus, sawari is the "apparatus of an obstacle" itself. In a sense it is an intentional inconvenience that creates a part of the expressiveness of the sound. Compared to the Western attitude toward musical instruments, this deliberate obstruction represents a very different approach to sound…. The monthly biological function in women is also referred to in Japanese as the 'monthly sawari'—a natural inconvenience for women but essential in producing children. For me there is something symbolic about this: the inconvenience is potentially creative. In music the artificial inconvenience in creating sound produces the sound. The resulting biwa sound is strong, ambiguous, deeply significant. [Takemitsu 1995, pp. 65–6]

What Takemitsu is describing here is a traditional way to resolve aesthetic problems; to ironically embrace the imperfection, to intensify it, marking it out as an intended aesthetic feature, thereby allowing us to appreciate its beauty. It once again underlines the way in which the artist's expression is guided by his or her physical medium; accepting and celebrating the natural qualities of the object. But while Takemitsu is correct to claim that the development of Western instruments has often sought to eliminate noise, he is wrong if he also wishes to imply that Western music is not also guided by the embrace of imperfections or the more general creative interplay with the resistant instrument. These seem to be musical universals. Note for instance the rise of "extended technique" in a number of instrumental performance practices. For example, oboists now quite commonly employ multiphonic effects—where all those cracks and whistles that were once the bane of the oboe performer's life are now deliberately employed.

The same guiding values can be seen in the rise of computer music. Synthesized sounds have permitted the average individual, lacking access to a backyard orchestra, to employ a far more diverse range of sounds in their creative endeavors. Naturally the sounds produced by keyboard synthesizers are often flat and homogeneous in comparison to what can be achieved with the original instruments—though the capacity of computers to reproduce the characteristics of different instruments has greatly improved. A greater worry for computer-based musicians is that when programming musical performances, the regularities of timbre, attack, and rhythm result in a sound that is inexpressive and dull. As a result, computer musicians often spend a great deal of time reintroducing irregularities; the mistunings or distortions of an more intense attack, or slight inconsistencies of timing that the music sound "more human." What we see here then is that the opening up of creative capacities is supplemented by a desire to simulate the feeling of a live performance, of a real performer with whom the listener can enjoy a sense of sharing; perhaps not sharing emotions specifically, but certainly a sense of life.

A similar issue is faced in recent developments in interfaces for musical expression; a general movement in present-day musical practice towards designing new instruments for employment in live performance, typically mediated by electronics. The same drive that pushes us to diversify the sonic palette also pushes us to find new ways to interact physically with sound, implicitly recognizing that the attitude taken towards the device shapes expressive content. At the same time, a common complaint about such instruments is that it is opaque to the listener what the performer is actually doing to get the sounds out of them. This problem is compounded by the frequent use of algorithmic routines, and even probabilistic outputs, such that a significant aspect of the music is not controlled directly by the performer at all. Where there is a disconnection between the electronic generation of the sounds and the physical means to activate these processes, we have no idea to what extent the performer's movements express emotional content, or even attitudes as basic as success or failure of intent (see Fels 2004; Gurevich and Fyans 2011 for discussion). This may be somewhat alienating for the audience. As such, the new-interface community is faced with finding effective ways in which the intention of the performers, their skill, and expressive goals, can be communicated to the audience, again, to satisfy the listeners' and performers' values of sharing.

We have seen how the resistance of the instrument contributes to the creative act of the performer. For the listener also, an appreciation of the physical resistance of the instrument contributes to a significant degree to their sense of what is going on with the performer, and as a consequence their empathic sense of the performer's feelings. There is, however, a counter-trend in the development of instrument technologies seemingly aimed at *reducing* the resistance of the instrument—that is, increasing the transparency between the performer's state of mind and the musical results. One important recent development in the new interfaces movement is the use of physiological sensors to measure such variables as heart rate, skin conductance (sweat), facial expressions, muscle tension, and skin temperature. It is now possible to directly sonify these signals to produce sounds (e.g. Knapp and Lyon 2011).

In particular, it has been the goal of my own research of late to use these signals to generate music that appropriately matches the actual emotional state of the performer—with the operational target that listeners can identify the self-reported emotion of the performer with a success rate comparable to our capacity to detect emotions in facial and vocal expressions, if not better. I call this system "the mood organ."[ii] An important theoretical component of the mood organ is that the various signals collected by the physiological sensors contribute proportionally to dimensional measures of emotional experience. For instance, muscle tension and heart rate contribute to the emotion dimension of power (similar, though more narrowly specified, than the common dimension "arousal"—see Cochrane 2009 for discussion). Changes in mouth corner position and heart rate variability contribute to the dimension of valence (rises in these measures tend to signal more positive emotions). The correlations here are not always entirely unambiguous—heart rate variability also increases in the emotion of disgust—clearly a negative emotion (see Kreibig 2010 for an extensive review). Yet when the various physiological signals are combined, dimensional correlates can be more reliably discerned. These dimensions are then fairly straightforwardly used to manipulate musical variables. For instance, a rise in positive valence can be made to increase the harmonic consonance of the music. Because the physiological signals continuously update the dimensional variables, I use looping samples than can be triggered and gradually adjusted in various ways, comparable to minimalist music. But the music also tends to fluctuate expressively in ways that we never find in minimalist music, leading to a musical result that is surprisingly unpredictable—displaying a striking *lack* of long-term emotional narrative.

Now to the extent that anyone off the street can put on the various sensors, and allow music to be produced regardless of his or her intentions, this system could not, according to Collingwood and Dewey, count as expressive. The sounds produced would *not* be art properly so called, but craft, or the mere betrayal of emotion. Moreover, since I have been extolling the virtues of instrumental resistance for promoting the values of emotion sharing, creativity, and pleasure, one might be forgiven for asking, what is the point of this system?

While it is true that the naïve use of such a system is not artistic, we could understand my role in developing the device as comparable to that of an architect who shapes the experiences of others. I have of course had to make musical choices as to what particular sounds should accompany what physiological changes. And although the mood organ is mechanically translating bodily states, it also *feels like something* to hear one's bodily states so translated, and it cannot help but affect the on-going development of one's emotional state. Subject and sound are locked into a tightly reciprocal relationship, just as we find in the attempt to express one's emotions with a traditional musical instrument. Moreover it is anticipated that, after prolonged use, some people will develop expertise in controlling their physiological responses by means of this musical feedback (though sweat and heart rate variability are rather more difficult to control than facial expression and muscle tension). As a consequence, some people should be able intentionally plan the music produced and give it a long-term narrative structure of their choosing.

The difference between this system and ordinary musical expression is also somewhat analogous to that between photography and painting. That is, there is a causal mechanism involved in this system that reliably produces an "image" of the performer's current bodily state. But as in the case of photography, it should still be possible to adapt the system to one's own ends in controlling the content that is imaged. In photography, we also appreciate that we are witnessing scenes that have concrete reality, or at least did so, and there are interesting effects concerning whether the subjects of a photograph are aware of being photographed. Similarly, the listener to a mood organ production may appreciate the glimpse into the actual inner workings of another person's body, and may contemplate shades of sincerity and emotional commitment that should be quite distinct from that of traditional musical performance, since it is often the case that traditional performers must remain calm if they are to successfully carry off the physical demands of the music (though see Scherer in Chapter 5 for a discussion of the variations involved here).

Besides the various creative uses to which this system might be put, however, the value that this system is primarily designed to promote is that of sharing emotions. This is not meant in the sense that a listener may read off the emotional state of the performer by listening to the music produced (though certain scientific goals may be achieved in that way) but that it provides a way for multiple performers to mutually engage in the formation of their emotional states. In particular, having established ways to transform an individual's bodily responses into music, the idea is to perform the same procedure for several people at once. This can be achieved in a number of different ways. We can simply allow that several performers individually produce music in a common setting (perhaps restricting ways in which the music produced can clash). Alternatively, we can divide up responsibility over the musical product such that one individual's physiological responses are responsible for one aspect of the music (for instance the harmony) while another's responses are responsible for its rhythm. Or finally, we may simply take an average of the group's signal and use that to generate our musical variables. In all these cases, we can observe the way the performers' mutual awareness of the music produced results in natural adjustments and synchronizations of their emotional states, and quite possibly feelings of intense rapport, as a consequence of their mutual awareness of this synchronization.

Naturally it is possible for performers of traditional instruments to engage in the collaborative expression of emotional states in comparable ways. But the mediation of instrumental skill presents considerable barriers to the sincere committal towards one's own and other's musical productions, because one is typically occupied with a critical stance towards the quality of the music produced, and is often unsure of the emotional committal of the other participants. A certain standardization and automaticity of the expressive means helps to alleviate these worries, just as it does in ordinary verbal communication—where we are (relatively) more confident in sharing common meaning for our terms.[iii]

Compare this with the historical development of instrumental technologies and we see that the rise in complexities and variances of expression are often tempered by moves towards standardization. Take for example the way that the shape of the violin bow has evolved since the Baroque period. The straight long bows that we find today were not established as a standard until the early 19th century. Prior to this time, a number of different shapes were employed. Bows of the Baroque period are often shorter, with an arch-shaped frame and pointed tips. These qualities make it harder to produce an even tone. Yet violinist Girolamo Bottiglieri has emphasized that they afford the player a greater range of possible sonorities. Similarly the oboe of the Baroque period is a considerably less complex instrument than today's oboe with its mass of silver keys and piping, and as a result it is much less stable and more difficult to play. Yet the oboist Béatrice Zawodnik describes the older oboe as more flexible, and thereby possessing a greater expressive potential (Bottiglieri and Zawodnik 2009).

In both cases, the demand for an instrument that can more reliably produce a certain sort of sound has resulted in developments that have sacrificed a certain degree of personal flexibility. When one must perform ensemble music, or follow the instructions of a musical score, there is a pressure to conform to certain standards. And given enough time, these pressures will, in a manner analogous to natural selection, result in instruments that can more effectively satisfy these pressures. The value ultimately behind these developments is, I submit, the value of the shared engagement in musical performance, because they are essentially solving a coordination problem. They allow many people to coordinate the expression of their emotions, guided towards an ideal of shared emotion. The mood organ is geared towards the same ideal.

Conclusion

Expression theory synthesizes a number of different values: the value of creativity, sharing, pleasure, and associated values of (self-) understanding and moral harmony. Different authors prioritize these values in different ways, while still pointing to basically the same, quite fundamental behavior—the act of expression—an act common to our everyday communicative behaviors, brought to its highest pitch or fluency in the creation of art.

Developments in musical instrument technologies have continued to be driven by the values inherent in artistic expression, particularly with respect to enriching our capacities for creativity, and sharing our emotions with others. Neither of these fundamental human values is in any danger of being undermined in our musical culture. For while they may sometimes seem to be in tension, as soon as we develop new ways to satisfy one value we tend to seek ways to satisfy the other as well. At the same time, we should recognize that musical expression is achieved not just at the individual level but also at the group level, and that as a consequence what may appear to be conflicting developments (i.e. towards complexity or simplification, towards resistance or transparency) may simply reflect the same ideals pursued at different levels of human organization.

Finally, while new technological developments certainly offer exciting new musical opportunities, there is no suggestion here that our means of expression are superior to those of the past. Because musical expression is essentially geared towards the self-realization of the individual, and how we understand each other, it is something that must be renewed in each generation, making use of the materials at hand.

Acknowledgments

The preparation of this chapter was made possible by support from the Swiss National Science Foundation, grant PBSKP1-130854 "The Mood Organ: Putting Theories of Musical Expression into Practice."

Notes

i   This is not surprising, since Hegel was a major influence on Benedetto Croce (1902/1992), who was himself major influence on Collingwood. Thanks to Jenefer Robinson for pointing this out.

ii This is after a fictional device described in Philip K. Dick's book *Do Androids Dream of Electric Sheep?* which is used to regulate emotions.

iii The automaticity of the system will also free-up the "performers" to emotionally interact with each other in more everyday ways.

References

Bottiglieri, G. and Zawodnik, B. (2009). Les affects et les emotions dans la musique instrumentale. Conference presentation at the University of Geneva, 8–9 May 2009.

Clarke, E. F. (2006). Making and hearing meaning in performance. *Nordic Journal of Aesthetics*, **18**(33–34), 24–48.

Cochrane, T. (2009). Eight dimensions for the emotions. *Social Science Information*, **48**, 379–420.

Cochrane, T. (2008). Expression and extended cognition. *Journal of Aesthetics and Art Criticism*, **66**, 329–40.

Collingwood, R. G. (1938/1958). *The Principles of Art*. London: Oxford University Press.

Croce, B. (1902/1992). *The Aesthetic as the Science of Expression and of the Linguistic in General* (transl. C. Lyas). Cambridge; Cambridge University Press.

Dewey, J. (1934/1980). *Art as Experience*. New York: Perigree Books.

Fels, S. (2004). Designing for intimacy: creating new interfaces for musical expression. *Proceedings of the Institute of Electrical and Electronics Engineers*, **92**, 672–85.

Gurevich, M. and Fyans, A. C. (2011). Digital musical interactions: performer–system relationships and their perception by spectators. *Organised Sound,* **16**, 166–75.

Hegel, G. W. F. (1835/1975). *Aesthetics. Lectures on Fine Art,* 2 vols (transl. T. M. Knox). Oxford: Clarendon Press.

Knapp, R. B. and Lyon, E. (2011). The measurement of performer and audience emotional state as a new means of computer music interaction: a performance case study. *Proceedings of the International Computer Music Conference, University of Huddersfield, UK, 31 July–5 August 2011.* Accessed 15 February 2013 at <http://quod.lib.umich.edu/i/icmc/bbp2372.2011?rgn=full+text>

Kreibig, S. (2010). Autonomic nervous system activity in emotion: a review. *Biological Psychology,* **84**, 394–421.

Stravinsky, I. (1956). *The Poetics of Music in the Form of Six Lessons.* Cambridge, MA: Harvard University Press.

Takemitsu, T (1995). *Confronting Silence; Selected Writings* (transl. Y. Kakudo and G. Glasow). Berkeley, CA: Fallen Leaf Press.

Tolstoy, L. (1899). *What is Art?* (transl. A. Maude). London: Walter Scott Ltd.

Chapter 7

Gender ambivalence and the expression of passions in the performances of early Roman cantatas by castrati and female singers

Christine Jeanneret

More than in subtle artifices, [the masters of our time] emphasize the affects, the graces and the vivid expression of the senses of what is sung. And this is what really ravishes and makes one goes into ecstasies. (Della Valle 1640, pp. 152–3)[i]

More than any other genre, solo singing in the 17th century is associated with the expression of the passions. During the first half of the century, Rome saw an unparalleled production of cantatas, performed for an exclusive audience. Women as well as castrati singing in performance were considered highly erotic and sometimes even threatening. The expressive power of music was enhanced by this ambivalent and alluring gender issue. The study of the context and the content of these sensual performances sheds some light on their link with the expression of emotions. The poetical texts that were sung clearly refer to the medical theory of the time, in particular with the idea of the perfect male body, the less perfect and womanish body of the castrato and the even worse female body. Gender ambivalence is also reflected in the ambiguous position of the narrator. Poems were written mostly by men, but sung by women or castrati alike, whereas the audience could be made up of listeners of both sexes. The narrator of the poetic text could be either male or female, and could even shift from one gender to another during the same piece. In a purely Baroque fashion, the repertory and the performance of cantatas toys with an ambivalent game of erotic expression of the affects, in which the audience does not want to expose women publicly but nevertheless wants to see them sing; and in which a female singer might embody a male lover singing of his lovesickness, and/or a castrato might embody a wretched female lamenting her fate. The transcription and analysis of two unpublished pieces composed by castrati on texts written by male poets, and sung by a professional female singer will illustrate this transgressive play on gender roles in social settings of music (see Appendix, p. 359).

Performances of lavish operas given by the Roman aristocracy were much advertised but fairly rare, because they were reserved for the period of Carnival or for special occasions, such as prestigious visits. The most common and most practiced genre at the time was the vocal chamber cantata for soprano voice.[ii] It was sung for very selected circles in private gatherings or at academies, in particular at the *Accademia degli Umoristi*, the most famous Roman circle of *literati* (Antolini 1989). The favorite subject for conversations at the academies was obviously love. Or as one academician, the poet Gianfrancesco Maia Materdona (1629), puts it in the preface of his *Rime*:

> If the subject of my verses are of love's love and of the vulgar Venus, it is the fault of corrupted human nature, which senses more the latter than the former. And if in this very subject, you might find some joke of juvenile affect, remember that poets rely more on the plausible ("*verosimile*") than on the true; that their quills do not always follow love's design; and that sometimes, they also have to express others' affects, besides their own.

Baldassare Castiglione's (1987) Renaissance ideal of the noble poet and singer disappeared during this period. For the most part, the aristocracy shifted from being performers to becoming the audience, from active participants to passive voyeurs. Dedicating themselves to patronage and art collecting, they yielded the stage to the new social category of professional singers and their prodigious virtuosity.[iii] However, many Roman prelates or noblemen (such as Giulio Rospigliosi—the future pope Clement IX—and Pietro Della Valle, nobleman, composer, librettist, writer, and ethnographer) wrote *poesie per musica*, both for operas and cantatas. Some of the most celebrated poets in the cantatas' manuscripts include Domenico Benigni, Francesco Melosio, and Francesco Balducci, and the librettist Giovanni Filippo Apolloni (Holzer 1990; Leopold 1990). The music was composed by prominent and mostly Roman composers such as Carlo Caproli, Giacomo Carissimi, Pietro Antonio Cesti, Marco Marazzoli, Luigi Rossi, Mario Savioni, and Antonio Francesco Tenaglia, among others. The most famous singers who performed this repertory in Rome were Ippolita Recupito, the castrati Marcantonio Pasqualini, Atto Melani, and Loreto Vittori, Adriana Basile and her two daughters Leonora and Caterina Baroni, Margherita Costa, and Francesca Caccini—daughter of the author of the *Nuove Musiche*—during her stay in Rome (Murata 1979a, 1981; Hammond 1994; Hill 1997; Brosius 2009; Cusick 2009; Freitas 2009). While most cantatas were composed for solo soprano with basso continuo, there are some rarer examples for lower voices, and for two or three voices and continuo. Almost never committed to print, this repertory survives almost exclusively in manuscripts, ranging from gorgeous collector's pieces to functional composers' scribbles (Murata 1993, pp. 254–5). The manuscripts were commissioned by avid music lovers, who jealously preserved them and shared them parsimoniously within an elite circle, both in Italy and abroad (Morelli 2006). The volumes are strikingly similar, attesting to their Roman provenance (Ruffatti 2007). The collector's volumes present lavish bindings realized in the *bottega* of the Andreoli, bookbinders to the Vatican; they are often written by professional copyists in an extremely elegant calligraphy and many pieces are decorated by elaborate ornate letters. Several pieces are anonymous or present conflicting attributions with other manuscripts. Previous studies of cantatas have tended to focus either upon individual composers and issues of attribution,[iv] or upon the purely social aspects of performance (LaMay 2005; Feldman and Gordon 2006; Brosius 2009). The former tend to ignore the social dimension of cantata performance; the latter have focused almost exclusively upon written testimony and gender issues, and do not engage the music in any great depth. Opera scores, which are more accessible, have been the main focus of studies (Heller 2003; Gordon 2004).[v] The purpose of this chapter is to fill this gap by examining the cantatas in a broader perspective, including social setting, medical theory, performance, and a direct confrontation between the written testimonies on singers and the texts set to music. The relationship between the body and the expression of passions brings a new insight on the poetical texts. By contextualizing the cantatas' repertory in performance, including audience and patronage, it is possible to unveil a conscious play of gender equivocation.

When dealing with early modern women musicians, a scholar has to face a critical problem: the almost complete disappearance of female musicians from sources, as well as women poets and the scarce testimony for women listeners. In the 17th century, the visibility of women in public was strictly regulated by conventions and edicts. Decent women were expected not to exhibit themselves in any kind of public action, unless they wanted to be considered as sirens (Bianconi and Walker 1975, pp. 441–2, Durante 1987, Rosselli 1993, Glixon 1995, Heller 2003, pp. 1–25). Saint Paul's ban, *mulieres in ecclesiis taceant*, had enduring consequences on silencing the voices of female musicians, and not only in church. In certain circumstances, it was acceptable for a woman to perform at court for a small, select audience, but it was an entirely different matter to appear publicly on the opera stage. Exhibition was equated with lack of decency and was directly linked to the suspicion of being a courtesan. Therefore, decent women tended to remain aloof from such public activities and—if they were musicians—tended to choose some sort of private practice, carefully canceling all traces of their activity, except for the most famous or the most scandalous ones. The domestic practice of music leaves almost no traces; these women were not paid; their names do not appear in the archives. Their musical activities can be reconstructed only by indirect evidence: for instance, payments made by a noble family to buy instruments, or music paper, or to have a harpsichord tuned for an unidentified lady-in-waiting. For the sake of decency, the visibility of female patrons is submitted to an identical dissimulation, albeit to a lesser degree. Roman noblewomen tended to sponsor private music gatherings rather than grandiloquent public events (De Lucca 2011).

The female singer represented, more than any other, an object of desire embodying male expectations, as a fascinating, ambiguous, and transgressive icon. She was equated with a courtesan at best or, at worst, a prostitute, as this contemporary qualification of the scandalous Neapolitan *prima donna* and impresario Giulia di Caro detta La Ciulla (1646–97) testifies: "Comediante Cantarinola, Armonica Puttana" (Rosselli 1993, p. 84; Croce 1992, p. 168; Maione 1997, p. 13).[vi] The taste for castrati in Italy was linked to the ban on women's voices in the church at first and then to the rise of opera (Durante 1987; Rosselli 1988; Barbier 1996; Bergeron 1996; Freitas 2003, 2009). It was a convenient and highly ambivalent strategy to obtain a high voice in an adolescent or adult male body. Boys represented a supreme ideal of love for men, being superior to women physically and spiritually. With their high voices, round baby faces without beard, and soft skin, the castrati were a representation of this ideal boy. They also had a phenomenal virtuosity, for physiological and sociological reasons. Castration caused them to grow bigger than normal, to develop huge lungs and, as a result, an extremely large breath capacity. Trained since childhood, they had no viable career path other than being extremely good singers. Freitas (2003, pp. 218, 223) rightly defines the castrato as a temporally extended boy, representing a suspension between masculinity and femininity. The ambivalence of the sexual boundaries between castrati and female singers justifies the interchangeability of women and castrati on the stage but also in chamber performances, as we will see.

To better understand why a female singer was both threatening and appealing, it is necessary to consider how body, sex, and gender were apprehended in the 17th century. Medicine still largely relied on Hippocratic and Galenist medical traditions, with the theory of the four humors and animal spirits (Siraisi 1990, vol. 1 pp. 281–91; Nutton 1993; Wear 1995, pp. 215–73; Gouk 2000, pp. 184–5). Health, both physical and psychological, was determined by a good balance of blood, phlegm, and yellow and black bile. Man was dry and hot, whereas woman was wet and cold, or as Galen (1968, p. 650) explains it:

> Now just as mankind is the most perfect of all animals, so within mankind the man is more perfect than the woman, and the reason for his perfection is his excess of heat, for heat is Nature's primary instrument. Hence in those animals that have less of it, her workmanship is necessarily more imperfect, and so it is no wonder that the female is less perfect than the male by as much as she is colder than he.

This difference in temperature determined very different psychological qualities: honor, bravery, strength of body and spirit for the man; instability, deceptiveness, depravity, and uncontrollable sensuality for the woman (Laqueur 1990, p. 108).[vii] Yet the division into male and female, considered as different entities in the way that they are today, did not exist as such at this time (Laqueur 1990, pp. 25ff.). There was instead what Laqueur calls a "one-sex model." The male was considered the most perfect manifestation of the body, whereas the woman was just a lesser version of man. She was considered to have the same genitalia as the man, but turned inside instead of outside. The difference was due to vital heat, which shaped the body and the humors, and it was gradual, hierarchical, and quantitative, not qualitative. Men were therefore in a real danger of losing their virility and becoming womanish. According to these theories, being a man or a woman implied a social role and not yet an ontological difference. Or in other words, the real difference was one of gender and not one of sex.

With regard to the function of the organ of singing, vocal chords had not yet been discovered in the early Baroque.[viii] From Aristotle[ix] to Athanasius Kircher, the voice was still considered to be a wind instrument (Kircher 1650, vol. 1, p. 20; Pangrazi 2009, pp. 23–42). Women and children consequently had high voices because they were weak and could move only slight quantities of air. Men had deep voices because they were strong. Castrati were situated exactly in the middle of this continuum and exhibited female qualities (Aristotle 1943, pp. 550–1):

> All animals when castrated change over to the female state, and as their sinewy strength is slackened at its source they emit a voice similar to that of females. This slackening may be illustrated in the following way. It is as though you were to stretch a cord and make it taut by hanging some weight on to it [...] when the weight is removed from the cord or from the warp; and as this slackens, the source (or principle) which sets the voice in movement is correspondingly loosened. This then is the cause on account of which castrated animals change over to the female condition both as regards the voice and the rest of their form: it is because the principle from which the tautness of the body is derived is slackened.

This view remained unchanged from antiquity to the early modern period (Paré 1634, p. 27 as quoted in Freitas 2003, p. 204):

> Eunuchs [...] seeme to have degenerated into a womanish nature, by deficiency of heate; their smooth body and soft and shirle [i.e. shrill] voyce doe very much assimulate weomen.

Even more crucial to our subject is the fact that singing produced heat, which was carried by the vital spirits created in the heart. Made out of blood and air, the vital spirits were distributed through the arteries which maintained inherent natural heat. Medically, music was recommended in several cases (Gouk 2000, p. 185). Singing was a simple exercise able to stimulate the pulse and balance the humors. Listening to music was beneficial for digestion, could relax the listener before sleep, and was even believed to ease the process of childbearing. And due to its affinities with the passions, music was especially powerful in bringing alterations in the body's humors, either in a positive or negative way. A woman or a creature of womanish complexion such as the castrato augmented their temperature while singing, which made them more similar to men, transgressing a border and threatening male identity. This transgression was viewed as both appealing and disgusting, sensual and dangerous, according to the tastes of the listener.

All the testimonies on the performance of solo singing emphasize the erotic aspect of such performances, either focusing on the beauty or the danger of it according to the taste or disgust it aroused (Lorenzetti 1994). It is interesting to notice that the descriptions—always related from a male point of view, and generally inclined to celebrate the singer—all use the same rhetoric to describe the effects of this marvelous singing. Seeing a beautiful singer performing, be it a castrato or a female, creates a rapture in the listener. Pietro Della Valle (1640, p. 164) wrote about the famous Roman singer Leonora Baroni: "Who isn't taken out of himself when listening to Leonora with her archlute so freely and ingeniously ("francamente e bizzaramente") played?" The French violist André Maugars (1639/1993, pp. 22, or p. 123 in the translation by MacClintock) describes an evening at the Baronis' house, hearing Adriana Basile singing with her two daughters, Leonora and Caterina Baroni:

> This concert, composed of three beautiful voices and three different instruments, so affected my senses and so ravished my spirit that I forgot my mortal condition and thought I was among the angels enjoying the delights of the blessed.

Female voices exert a fascination on the audience, which is described in terms of a sensual experience qualified as ecstasy and could very well applied to an erotic experience, only discreetly disguised as a spiritual ecstasy in Maugars' terms.[x]

Indeed, the interesting point is that the description does not change whether the singer is a female or a castrato.[xi] Both create the same erotic rapture in the listener. The following is a description the famous castrato Atto Melani in the role of Achille in *La Finta Pazza* (Francesco Sacrati/ Giulio Strozzi) (Rosand 1991, p. 415, transl. by Freitas 1998, p. 42):

> The youth, who was a most valorous little singer from Pistoia, began to sing so delicately that the souls of the listeners, as if exiting through the portals of the ears, raised themselves to heaven to assist in the enjoyment of such sweetness.

Or again Della Valle (1640, pp. 163–4) on the castrati:

> The sopranos of today [are] persons of judgment, maturity, sentiment, and mastery in this exquisite art, they sing with grace, with taste and real elegance. Cloaking themselves in the affects, they enrapture the listener.

Thus, female singers and castrati are described in the same language. However, the descriptions use a different rhetoric when they applied to a male singer who is not a castrato. If they also emphasize the ability of the singer to arouse the affects of the text in the listener, they never use an erotic vocabulary. Lower male voices do not ravish the listeners in ecstasy as the soprano voices do.[xii]

But how did these sopranos enrapture the listeners? All the commentators use a strikingly similar language to describe the performances. These singers were incredible virtuosos, they had obviously a perfect mastery of their voice and could exert extraordinary control every subtle nuance. But there was more to it, as Vincenzo Giustiniani (1628, pp. 108, 121) explains in his *Discorso sopra la musica*:

> Furthermore, they [the singers] moderated or increased their voices, loud or soft, heavy or light, according to the demands of the piece they were singing; now slow, breaking off with sometimes a gentle sigh, now singing long passages legato or detached, now groups, now leaps, now with long trills, now with short, and again with sweet running passages sung softly, to which sometimes one heard an echo answer unexpectedly. They accompanied the music and the conceit with appropriate facial expressions, glances and gestures, with no awkward movements of the mouth or hands or body which might not express the conceit of the song. They made the words clear in such a way that one could hear even the last syllable of every word, which was never interrupted or suppressed by passages and other embellishments [p. 69 of MacClintock's translation]. […] Above all, they make the words clear, using one note for each syllable; now piano, now forte, now slow, now fast—by the expression of their faces and by their gestures giving meaning to what they are singing, but with moderation and not in excess [p. 77 of MacClintock's translation].

The singer performed a "staging" of the affects expressed by the text, by acting them out physically with gestures, movements of the face and the eyes. Singing was therefore received by the audience not only as a purely aural experience, but also as a visual one (see Chapter 15). Eyes and ears were enticed simultaneously, thereby reinforcing the erotic power of singing. Sight was the sense by which love penetrated the soul in the neo-Platonic theory of love (Couliano 1987, pp. 21, 29–30). The image of the beloved literally penetrates the lover, entering through his eyes as a pneumatic spirit and taking possession of his soul. The singer is an impersonation of the loved one. This is why descriptions of singers always present them as extremely beautiful and chaste, except for ranting misogynists such as Ottonelli and Leti. It was of no relevance if the singers were ugly, because they became beautiful by singing and embodying the beloved. Both Adriana Basile and her daughter Leonora were praised in printed sonnets written by the Roman prelates, noblemen, and poets. They exaggeratedly emphasize their beauty along with their virtuosity: *virtuose*, both in terms of technical mastery and chastity (*Teatro* 1623; *Applausi* 1639; *L'Idea* 1640).[xiii] Etymologically, virtuosity comes from the Roman idea of the full manliness ("vir") and the Renaissance ideal of a man's "virtù." There was undoubtedly a transgression if a woman or a castrato became "virtuosi," a clear allusion to the fact that by singing they augmented their body temperature and became more masculine. Of course, the object of love was expected to firmly repel the advances of her lovers and never succumb to the temptation of earthly love. Sexual desire was supposed to be sublimated into the perfect spiritual love of God. At least in theory: in practice notorious affairs abounded between male and female singers and aristocrats, even including cardinals.[xiv] If some singers were openly courtesans, most of them, along with their admirers, struggled hard to preserve a reputation for virtue by avoiding public exposure. In her old age, Leonora did not appreciate being remembered as a singer: "Leonora prides herself on having her place as a lady […] she doesn't want to be known as a singing girl" (Trinchieri Camiz 1996, p. 288). Her suitors constantly and excessively insisted on presenting her as modest, chaste, and virtuous, a woman who only reluctantly agreed to exhibit herself after much pleading. The poet Domenico Benigni states that she allegedly didn't even want to publish her own poetry (*L'Idea* 1640, p. 212):

> The first [compositions] are by Signora LEONORA. There are not many, because it was necessary to steal them; but a single one would have been enough to immortalize her name.

The combination of music and love was indeed powerful and threatening. This is exactly why the Jesuit Athanasius Kircher (1650, vol. 1, pp. 560–61, translated by Blackburn and Holford-Stevens, pp. 65–67; Bianchi 2011) prudently suggests hiding the singers from sight:

> So prevalent even in [music] is the vice of vanity—commonly called singers' temperament—which in certain people is the greater the less their education. […] Some people were right to hold that musicians should be shut away and not seen by anyone, least by the unseemly movement of their bodies they should break the power of harmony. It is therefore of great importance for arousing the emotions that performers should take care to combine a seemly deportment of the body and controlled movements with seemly delivery and seemly suppleness of voice.

It is no coincidence that sight and hearing were also the two senses celebrated in the poetic texts set to music. Rich in metaphors and deliberately frivolous, cantata poems celebrate love in all its forms (Bianconi 1986, p. 355). Unlike the texts used for the madrigal which were pre-existing, and drew on a remarkable tradition of poetry from Petrarch to Tasso, cantata texts were written to be set to music. When published separately, they almost always present the mention *per musica*, emphasizing the fact that they did not exist as a purely literary genre *per se*. The texts usually combine freely rhymed verses of *settenari* and *endecasillabi* with regular verses, sometimes strophic or sometimes of different length.[xv] Composers did not always conform to the expected text-setting (aria for a strophic form and recitative for *versi sciolti*), but sometimes turned a recitative into an arioso, building free sequences of narrative, *secco* recitative, expressive recitative, florid recitative, syllabic arias in duple or triple meter, etc. (Murata 2005, pp. 412–15). It is an innovative and simpler literary genre, made of recurring lines and parallel syntax to better fit the musical setting. The texts focus on love, expressed in mythology, religion, Ancient Roman, or contemporary history, and the much appreciated pastoral. Sacred and profane love rub shoulders in the same manuscripts without any distinction. The lexical field of love reduces the beloved to its component parts in trivial synecdoches, focusing strongly on the eyes (the organ by which love throws its arrows on one side, and penetrates the lover on the other) and the mouth (the organ by which the song is projected toward the listener/lover to penetrate his soul). This emphasis is made clear by some cantata caption titles. Among the many examples, we might cite just a few: "Occhi, lingue di bellezza, voi parlate sì, sì, sì" (Eyes, tongues [i.e. voices] of beauty, you are speaking, yes, yes, yes) by Antonio Francesco Tenaglia (manuscript I-Rc 2466, ff. 197$_r$–199$_r$); "Due labbra di rose fan guerra al mio core" (Two lips of roses make war on my heart) and "Lo splendor di due begl'occhi, di due labbra l'armonia" (The splendor of two beautiful eyes, the harmony of two lips) both set by Luigi Rossi.[xvi] Love is of course always unrequited, causing all sorts of pains and despair that often lead to death. Oscillating between cold and hot, the lover is consumed by the fire of passion and frozen by the unwavering and icy cruelty of his beloved. The constant references to such dangerous changes in temperature are a clear reference to the medical view of lovesickness. Again a few incipits will illustrate the point: "Han tal forza due nere pupille / ch'ogni core per vinto si rende, / son carboni ch'esalan faville / sembran spenti ma han foco ch'incenda" (Two black eyes have such strength that any heart surrenders, they are coals exhaling sparks, they seem extinguished but have a burning fire) by Pier Simone Agostini (I-Rc 2471, ff. 111$_r$–16$_v$); "Io mi struggo in lento foco" (I am consumed by a slow-burning fire) by Carlo Caproli (I-Rsc G.885, ff. 123$_r$–126$_v$); "Eh potesti lasciarmi / e stabilir con sì mortal decreto, / di non vedermi più, / io resto, io gelo, / attonita, insensata" (Ah, should you leave me and decide with such a deadly decree to see me no more, I'll stay, I'll freeze, dazed, insane) by the castrato Marcantonio Pasqualini;[xvii] and "Misero cor che non ti struggi in pianti / un picciol marmo invola / il tuo nobil thesoro / ond'infelice e sola / io manco io gelo io moro" (Wretched heart that is not consumed in tears, a little marble robs your noble treasure where I, miserable and alone, pass away, I freeze, I die) set by Virgilio Mazzocchi on a text by Giulio Rospigliosi.[xviii]

A closer look at the beginning of "Scrivete occhi dolenti" (Freitas 2009, pp. 248–50, 266–9) allows us to shed some light not only on the metaphors and lexical fields used in the texts, but also on the ambiguous position of the narrator. The text by Francesco Melosio (1609–1670) was set to music by the castrato Atto Melani:

Scrivete occhi dolenti	Write, pained eyes
con inchiostro di pianto	in ink of tears
sùl foglio del mio volto i vostri affanni	on the paper of my face your troubles
narrate i miei tormenti	narrate my torments,
rigistrate i miei danni	record my losses
e dite à chi nol crede	and tell her who does not believe it
ch'amar tacendo ogni martire eccede	that to love in silence exceeds every martyrdom
per un labro vezzoso	for charming lips
che uccide, mà diletta	that kill but delight
per un ciglio amoroso	for amorous eyelashes
che piace mà saetta	that please but pierce

per un seno di neve	for a snow-white breast
che mirar non si può senz'adorarlo.	that one cannot look at without adoring
Ardo, piango, sospiro e pur non parlo	I burn, I cry, I sigh and still I do not talk.
sì, sì taccia la lingua	Yes, yes, let my tongue be silent
ma favellino i lumi	but let my eyes tell
Dolor, tu detta i carmi, Amor correggi	Pain, you dictate the poems, Love, you correct
Occhi scrivete, e tu mi vita leggi.	eyes you write, and you my life, read.[xix]

The beloved is again reduced to his/her most seductive and dangerous body parts: a charming but lethal mouth ("labro vezzoso che uccide"), eyes that shoot arrows ("ciglio amoroso che […] saetta"), as well as a less threatening, but no-less-enticing breast, qualified as snow-white, therefore evoking a cold temperature ("seno di neve").

An interesting point in our perspective is the position of the narrator in these texts, which is ambiguous in several respects. First, in the text itself the narrator is often shifting, changing or multiplying himself. The most common form, known as "monody" in Greek lyrical poetry and amply used in the madrigals, is what classicists term the "I–You" stance (Murata 2005, pp. 412–14). Ideal for expressing the passions, and highly subjective, the poet or singer addresses directly a "you" generally identified with the beloved. The monolog is a different form of direct discourse, where the narrative voice expresses his passions by speaking to himself, or addressing non-humans such as nature, or animals (Murata 1979b). Many texts, however, cloud the issue by switching from indirect to direct discourse. They are introduced by an external and undefined narrator, naming the character(s) and the situation, usually in recitative. For instance in Antonio Cesti's (1623–1669) "Del famoso oriente," a Jewish mother is thus introduced (Cesti 1986, pp. 15–20; source GB-ChCh Musis MS 83, pp. 27–32):

Del famoso orïente	From the famous Orient
[…]	[…]
di già languia Gerusalemme oppressa	Jerusalem oppressed already languished
quando una madre ardita	when a daring mother
che in digiun disperato i dì traea,	who spent her days in a wretched fast,
avida sol di vita,	avid only for life,
il figlio uccise, indi così dicea:	killed her son and then spoke thus:

Often, after a dramatic expression of passions—especially in this case, where the mother eats her own son—the piece ends by returning to the cold third-person narration, functioning as a closure. The same structure is found in many cantatas, for instance in "Tirsi ch'omai disciolto" by Lorenzo Corsini.[xx] Tirsi's monolog is also introduced by an external narrator, but in this case it is even more interesting, because, after a few verses, Tirsi himself speaks for his former lover and replaces the narrator:

Tirsi, ch'omai disciolto	Tirsi, now freed
Per novella beltà dal laccio antico	from his old bond for a new beauty
[…]	[…]
Agitato tal'hor così dicea:	Then agitated, he spoke thus:
Pur al fin quella tiranna,	Finally that merciless tyrant
che' l mio core	who forever condemned
a sì barbaro dolore,	my heart
dispietata ogn'hor condanna,	to such barbarous pain
pur al fin vint'è schernita,	finally conquered, scorned
E pentita	and repentant
del suo error sospirerà,	will she sigh for her error

E dirà:	and say:
Chi troppo il laccio al prigionier ristinge,	Who ties the cord around the prisoner too tightly
a fuggir disperato al fin lo spinge.	will push him to flee at last in desperation.

These successive impersonations by the singer were exactly the kind of sophisticated game appreciated by the elite and highly literate audience at the Roman gatherings where cantatas were performed. The audience was often made up of the very poets who wrote the texts, of various members of the academies, and of the Roman nobility and clergy. Shifting rapidly between dispassionate, neutral narration and highly expressive and emotional lyrics, the singer was expected not only to embody the passions evoked in the poem, but to stage them theatrically by impersonating the various characters, their changing affects, and, more than anything else, transmitting them to the listeners. Inscribed in the larger frame of the academies or private meetings, the songs were one among other games of eloquence. In the introduction to *L'Idea della veglia*—one of the eulogistic volumes containing poems celebrating Leonora Baroni—the poet Domenico Benigni describes in detail a fascinating game called the "Oracle," played during an evening at the Baronis' house, which does not seem to have attracted scholarly attention yet (*L'Idea* 1640, pp. 10–36). One of the guests played the narrator and related a real or imaginary event. The guest designated as the Oracle—in this case Adriana Basile—then utters a single word. On the basis of the oracle's "prophecy" the other guests are expected to extemporize narrations for and against the different perspectives of the initial story. In the end, the Oracle settles the matter and assigns a penalty to the most inadequate narration, which can be paid by composing some poetry. In this case, as always, the topic is love.[xxi] Benigni, who was chosen as the narrator, relates the story of two knights enamored of the same lady, who ordered them to leave her. One of them stays, the other leaves. The Oracle's hint was "*cielo*" (sky). Then four guests, including Leonora and Caterina Baroni, argue for and against both knights' decisions, drawing on philosophy, astrology, puns, and the entire Baroque rhetorical arsenal. The shifts from one point of view to the other, as well as the games of impersonation, extemporization, and theatricality, are exactly the ones a singer was expected to perform.

To return to the issue of gender, it is highly revealing that at any stage the narrator could be either male or female, in complete accordance with Laqueur's theory of the one-sex body. The poet was usually a male, but not always. Several literate women (sometimes female singers themselves) wrote texts to be set to music (Morandini 2001): Francesca Caccini, Brigida Bianchi, Margherita Costa, Leonora, and Caterina Baroni.[xxii]

The gender ambivalence found in poetic texts was also to be found in the performance of their musical settings. The pieces were sung by women or by castrati, who were considered as almost female. The narrator in the texts could be either male or female, sometimes switching gender in the middle, as we have just seen in Corsini's piece, when Tirsi impersonates his Clori. Traditionally, laments were narrated by a female voice, but could just as easily be sung by a castrato. In "Toglietemi la vita" (Marazzoli), the female narrator laments her fate and directly addresses her cruel lover in an "I–You" form (Marazzoli 1986, pp. 2–13, 174; source I-Rvat Chigi Q.VI.81, ff. 209$_v$–15$_r$). "Ferma lascia ch'io parli" (Carissimi on a text by Giovanni Filippo Apolloni 1635–1688) portrays the Catholic queen Mary Stuart before her executioner (Carissimi 1986, pp. 129–37, 174; source GB-Lbl Harley MS 1265, ff. 1$_r$–12$_v$). And in a text written by Margherita Costa,[xxiii] the narrator is also female. Set to music by Marazzoli for two sopranos, this is a very interesting case, where the narrator is female, but she starts by immediately introducing her impersonation of the male lover (Marazzoli 1986, pp. 138–43, 280; source I-Rvat Chigi Q.VIII.177, ff. 15$_v$–18$_r$):

Oh Dio, voi che mi dite:	Oh God, what are you saying to me:
"Bella ch'il cor mi leghi,	"Beauty who ties my heart,
cruda che mi tormenti,	cruel one who torments me,

sorda che non mi senti,	deaf one who does not hear me,
empia che non ti pieghi."	ruthless one who does not yield to me."

She then abruptly switches to the "I–You" form, addressing her lover:

voi mi burlate, se pensate ancora	you are making fun of me, if you still believe
ch'io creda che il mio volto	that I think that my face
possa darvi tormento in su quest'ora!	can torment you any more at this time!

And then, even more suddenly, she shifts to an introspective and sad monolog on her age, at the end of which she again addresses her lover and clearly identifies herself as female (*pazza*):

Non son più soavissimi i miei lumi e mi	My eyes are no longer sweet and the mirror
dice la spera	tells me
ch'il mio volto non è di primavera.	that my face is no longer springlike.
Io non m'inganno e mi conosco bene	I do not delude myself and I know myself well
[…]	[…]
credete a me ch'io non son pazza affatto.	believe me because I am not mad at all.
O voi non ci vedete, o sete matto.	Either you don't see, or you are mad.

The second soprano enters in the second part of the piece, in a three-strophe lyric duet *Amanti fuggite / cadente beltà* (Lovers, escape a decaying beauty). The second voice does not impersonate the male lover, but reinforces the first voice in a subjective and expressive reflection on old age, taking the audience as interlocutors and addressing them as lovers. The gender confusion in this case is quite illuminating: the poet is a woman, the composer is male, the narrator female accompanied by another high voice of undetermined sex. The singers might have been two females, or two males, or one of each. Castrati who were composers also frequently used female narrators in the pieces they set to music.[xxiv]

The audience plays an important role as the recipient of these performances and does not escape the gender ambivalence. The audience was mostly male, but again not exclusively. Several female patrons of music are well known in 17th-century Rome: Maria Mancini Colonna, Christine of Sweden, and Olimpia Aldobrandini Borghese the younger (1623–1681) (De Lucca 2009). They are harder to find in the early *Seicento*, but as mentioned earlier, women tend to disappear from the sources, or carefully tried to wipe their traces in order to avoid a dubious reputation. A heated controversy surrounding the production of the opera *La Catena d'Amore* (Rome, 1626, music by Domenico Mazzocchi on a libretto by Ottavio Tronsarelli) shows that women participated in many aspects of music patronage. The elder Olimpia Aldobrandini Borghese (1567–1637), the grandmother of Olimpia the younger, played an important role in the casting of the opera. A strong rivalry developed between two famous Roman singers considered to be courtesans, Margherita Costa and Cecca del Padule, for the roles of Venus and the maga Falsirena, and passionately divided the Roman nobility. Eventually Olimpia Aldobrandini defused the crisis by dismissing the two *prime donne* and substituting them with two castrati.[xxv] In such a society, it is hard to understand what female desires were. Does the incident indicate that Olimpia enjoyed castrati singing rather than women, as her male counterparts enjoyed the chaste Leonora and her sensual singing? Or is it simply the dubious (real or constructed) morality of Margherita and Cecca that pushed her to this decision? Whatever the answer is, the issue in this controversy is clear: Olimpia's will overpowered that of her son's, Giovanni Giorgio Aldobrandini, who commissioned the opera.

That women were actively involved in commissioning music is also made clear by the fact that indications of female patronage can be found on the bindings of some cantata manuscripts. Some of these have impaled coats-of-arms, doubtlessly testifying that the books were intended for, and most probably committed by a noblewoman (Morelli 2008). A female aristocrat retained her blazon when she got married and coupled it with her husband's, whereas the latter did not change his own. These kinds of blazons can be found on several manuscripts and indicate the possessor, for instance Maria Cristina Altemps, wife of Ippolito Lante della Rovere, and two yet unidentified noblewomen.[xxvi] Other testimonies are the mentions of some rare explicit female presences in the audience. This is a very rare testimony of an all-female musical evening:

> Wednesday evening the lady Ambassador held a late evening gathering in her chambers, where la Cecchina [Francesca Caccini] was singing, and a lady was excellently playing the double harp. The attendees were the Lady Duchess Sforza, the wifes of Signor Orazio Magalotti, of Falconieri, of Signor Neri Capponi and another woman.[xxvii]

Finally, an important part of female patronage can be unveiled in the dedications of printed music poetry, or libretti. For instance the above-mentioned *L'Idea della veglia* is dedicated to Olimpia Aldobrandini Borghese the younger. The presence of the noblewoman at the *conversazioni* is made clear in the dedication (*L'Idea* 1640, pp. 7–8):

> Compositions in which the name of famous sirens live, must be dear to Your Excellence, since you, taking delight in making concerts of singers, renew the ancient nobility of kings and emperors. […] With happy ambition, this book takes courage to present to Your Excellence, among the works of others, those of these ladies [the Baroni sisters], that you sometimes were pleased to enjoy, and it has been judged that, where the virtues of those ladies have Rome as theatre, they can also have princesses as spectators.[xxviii]

It is interesting to note that it was considered a "daring" undertaking to publish poetry written by women. The same princess Aldobrandini is also the dedicatee of one of the extremely rare published volumes of cantatas by the castrato Loreto Vittori, *Arie a voce sola* (1649).

Finally, another very rare trace of a female musician is to be found in the manuscript I-Rn 71.9.A.33 (olim MS Mus. 141). Beautifully bound in gilt mosaic leathers, this large volume contains 42 cantatas and twice gives the indication of its possessor in garlands framing ornate letters: *Cecilia Musica* (f. 47$_r$) and *Libro della Signora Cecilia* (f. 59$_r$). Arnaldo Morelli has identified this singer as a professional Roman musician mentioned by Marazzoli in the 1640s. Her name might be Cecilia Flavi or Cecilia Scuttari (Morelli 2005). This manuscript is a very precious testimony. Since we know it belonged to a female singer, we can take a closer look at what her repertory was with respect to the ambivalent narrator position. Interestingly enough, one text was written by a female comedian named Brigida Bianchi. The other identified authors are all male and all from Rome: Sebastiano Baldini, Giovanni Lotti, Salvator Rosa, and Theodoli for the poets and Carlo Caproli, Giacomo Carissimi, Antimo Liberati, Marco Marazzoli, Marcantonio Pasqualini, Luigi Rossi, Mario Savioni, Antonio Francesco Tenaglia, and Loreto Vittori for the composers. Three of them were castrati: Pasqualini and Vittori sopranos and Savioni alto castrato. Their pieces, "Lasciatemi o pensieri" (ff. 177$_r$–188$_r$) and "Così cruda e così fiera" (ff. 189$_r$–192$_v$) both have male narrators and were undoubtedly sung by Cecilia in this case. The manuscript bears many indications of performance and was in no way only a collector's object made for the eye. Figured bass, corrections, tempi, and ornaments indications attest that it was used in performance, most certainly in one of those elite gatherings of Roman nobility.

To give a clearer idea of the repertory, two contrasting pieces from the *Libro della Signora Cecilia*, never published before, are given here (see Appendix p.359). Composed by two castrati on texts written by male poets and sung by Cecilia, they concretely illustrate the ambiguity and erotic games in this repertoire on one hand. On the other, they exemplify how the music expresses the affects of the suffering lover and the dangerous changes of temperature to which he is exposed. The above-mentioned "Così cruda e così fiera" in G minor has no concordances whatsoever, while the other piece by Mario Savioni, "Bizzarre pupille che fare vi credete" (ff. 88$_r$–91$_v$) in B♭ major, appears in a Neapolitan manuscript with an attribution to Carlo Caproli.[xxix] Vittori's piece is a simple stophic canzonetta set in eight-syllable lines (*ottonario*) alternating rhymes. Typical for this lighter genre are the numerous repetitions in the text—both of words and parallel syntax—that are mirrored in the musical setting. To create more variety and freedom in the setting, composers played with irregular verse length, which is exactly what Vittori is doing here by displacing some verses metrically, either by postponing or anticipating their entries on weaker beats. The canzonetta was also considered the best form to express the passions of love and a diversity of affects. In fact Vittori does not strictly respect the strophic setting: the second strophe is varied to follow the affects expressed by the text. The lover's sufferings are uttered in a light tone, both in text and music, playing on simple ascending and descending motives, alternating with leaps in the second stanza, and some simple chromaticisms. Savioni's setting presents a wider range of expression: two very distinctive parts with change of character and of meters. The first stanza is set in a lyrical slow triple meter. The second stanza moves to a much faster duple meter to illustrate the burning flames evoked by the text, whereas the last stanza starts with recitative. The typical rhetoric of body parts (the eyes in both cases) and the narrator's ambiguous position are recurring: from monolog to direct discourse and back to monolog in Vittori's piece; and in Savioni's piece the narrator oscillates from direct address to the eyes of the beloved to monolog, and direct discourse either to the loved one or to Love himself. *Bizzarre pupille* is an especially interesting case for the very precise performance indications specified in the score (tempi, nuances, and ornaments).

The contextualization of cantata performances in their social and cultural settings brings new insights on this typical Baroque form of entertainment. Sung for a selected audience, it was one element of sophisticated forms of entertainments where readings or improvisation of poetry, discourses on love, games of eloquence, and music all shared the same purpose, rather of *delectare* than *docere*. Castrati and female singers played an ambivalent erotic part in these games, embodying the beloved, singing the poets' words, and embodying all sorts of male or female narrators to express the passion of love and to move the souls (and not only) of the listeners. While the strong impact played by the body of the singer in performance is undeniable, my research emphasizes the idea of sexual ambiguity on various levels. The ambivalent positions of the narrators and the performers, even including the audience. This play on male and female identities reinforces the erotic aspect of performance. As a form of entertainment, acting both on the eye and the ear, music was especially powerful in expressing the affects of love.

Appendix (see p. 359)

Appendix (see p. 359)

Loreto Vittori, "Così cruda e così fiera" and Mario Savioni [or Carlo Caproli], "Bizzarre pupille che far vi credete", in Libro della Signora Cecilia, I-Rn 71.9.A.33 (olim MS Mus. 141), ff. 189r–192v and 88r–91v. Edited by Christine Jeanneret.

Acknowledgement

My gratitude goes to Eric Bianchi, Margaret Murata, Valeria De Lucca, and Lorenzo Bianconi for their precious help and suggestions.

Notes

i   Translations are mine unless otherwise stated.

ii The terms *cantata, aria, arietta, recitativo,* or *canzonetta* were equally used to define them. For a discussion of terminology, see Holzer (1990, pp. 226–54).

iii   On the shift from performance to collection with regard to cantatas see Murata (in press) and Jeanneret (in press).

iv   Catalogues of cantatas by Antonio Cesti, Luigi Rossi, Mario Savioni, Alessandro Stradella, Giacomo Carissimi, Alessandro and Atto Melani were published in: Jander (ed.) (1964–72). Facsimiles of the manuscripts by Rossi, Carissimi, Marazzoli, Pasqualini, Cesti, Atto and Alessandro Melani, Mario Savioni, among others, were then published in the series edited by Gianturco (1985–1986).

v   Gordon's book unfortunately is full of unforgivable imprecisions as well as very questionable positions.

vi   The quotation is from Fuidoro, I. (1934–9). Giornali di Napoli dal MDCLX al MDCLXXX. Naples: Società Napoletana di Storia Patria, notizia del 11/VIII/1671.

vii   This view on woman can be found in Aristotle (*History of the Animals*, book 9, ch. 1): "The fact is, the nature of man is the most rounded off and complete, and consequently in man the qualities or capacities above referred to are found in their perfection. Hence woman is more compassionate than man, more easily moved to tears, at the same time is more jealous, more querulous, more apt to scold and to strike. She is, furthermore, more prone to despondency and less hopeful than the man, more void of shame or self-respect, more false of speech, more deceptive, and of more retentive memory. She is also more wakeful, more shrinking, more difficult to rouse to action, and requires a smaller quantity of nutriment." (transl. W. D'Arcy). Available at: <http://classics.mit.edu/Aristotle/history_anim.9.ix.html> (accessed 5 September 2011).

viii   Discovered by Antoine Ferrein in 1741 (Gordon 2004, pp. 10–46).

ix   In Aristotle, On the Soul (transl. J. A. Smith). Available at <http://classics.mit.edu/Aristotle/soul.2.ii.html> (accessed 5 September 2011).

x   More threatening and misogynist accounts of female singing can be found in Ottonelli (1645) and Leti (1667).

xi   Here we completely disagree with Brosius (2009, pp. 260–61) who think that castrati and women were apprehended in a totally different way by the audience.

xii   One example among many is the description of the tenor Jacopo Peri singing the part of Orfeo in *Dafne* (Gagliano, 1608, p. 81): "I would even say that someone who hasn't heard these arias sung by [Peri] himself, cannot completely understand their grace and their strength because [he] gives them such grace and style that he imprints in the other the affect of these words, be it strength, tears, or joy, as he wishes." Other examples can be found in Giustiniani (1628, p. 110; translated by C. MacClintock, p. 71): "And they all sang, whether bass or tenor, with a range consisting of many notes, and with exquisite style and passage-work, and with extraordinary feeling and a particular talent to make the words clearly heard."

xiii   The 19th-century scholar Ademollo (1895, p. 7) did not understand this point when he wrote, referring to Leonora's portrait by Fabio Della Corgna: "With all respect to Monsignor Rospigliosi and to his fifty-six fellows competing in singing on every tone and in every meter the beauties of Leonora Baroni, we can attest that the sweet siren of their hearts was ugly."

xiv   Myth or reality: Cardinal Antonio Barberini both with Leonora Baroni and the castrato Marcantonio Pasqualini, Duke Carlo II of Mantua with Atto Melani, Countess Elena Forni with Giovanni Francesco Grossi (detto Siface), Grand Prince Ferdinando de Medici with the castrato Francesco de Castris (detto Cecchino), Cardinal Camillo Pamphili with Leonora Baroni. (Freitas 2003, p. 216; Brosius 2009, p. 335).

xv   For detailed studies of the poetic texts see Holzer (1990) and Leopold (1990).

xvi   Both pieces are in the manuscript I-Rc 2464, ff. 31$_r$–38$_v$ and ff. 77$_r$–94$_v$. They present several concordances with other sources.

xvii   I-Rc 2478, ff. 91$_r$–95$_v$, anonymous in I-Rc 2475, ff. 71$_r$–76$_v$, anonymous but in Pasqualini's hand in I-Rvat Barb. lat. 4220, ff. 93$_r$–95$_v$, where the text is attributed to Giovanni Lotti.

xviii I-Rc 2505, ff. 112$_r$–113$_v$, aria for Erisilda, from act 4, scene 9 of *La Genoinda*. (Rome, 1641), libretto by G. Rospigliosi, no surviving score of the opera.

xix See Holzer (1990, pp. 946–54) for complete text, translation, and Melani (2005, pp. xxxv, 60–72), for a slightly different translation and music.

xx Published in Corsini (1640, pp. 5–11). The complete text, translation, and transcription is given in Holzer (1990, pp. 696–7).

xxi "Limiting themselves always to subjects that are either moral or amorous, even if the latter seems to be favoured by everybody as one that can grant the most delightful successes" (*L'Idea* 1640, p. 10).

xxii *L'Idea* (1640) contains poems by both sisters, pp. 215–21 for Leonora, including one "Canzonetta per Musica" and one sonnet dedicated to the *Umoristi* with the interesting mention of Leonora participating: "For the Gentlemen Academicians *Humoristi* on the occasion that [Leonora] was received in their Academy," and pp. 223–36 for Caterina, with another sonnet dedicated to the *Umoristi*: "For the Academy of the Gentlemen *Humoristi*, alluding to their undertaking."

xxiii The author might have been Margherita's sister, Anna Francesca, also a singer, as suggested by Antolini (1984). The attribution is given by Marazzoli in this autograph manuscript *Della Signora Costa*.

xxiv Pasqualini (1986, pp. 75–85, 220–1; source I-Rvat Barb.lat.4223, ff. 87$_r$–92$_r$): "Oh Dio, come farò"; Melani (2005, respectively pp. xxvi–xxvii, xxix–xxxii, xxxvi for the texts and 3–13, 29–37, 77–80 for the music): "A più sventure ancora," "Fileno idolo mio," "La più dolente, e misera che viva" (text by Sebastiano Baldini), with the interesting mention *The unfortunate lady*, a beautiful Lady being much afflicted by various misfortunes, gave the subject of the following melancholic recitative, "M'abbandona la sorte," "Sola tra le sue pene"; Vittori (1649, pp. 4–11): Lament of the Princess of Tunis "Per l'affricana riva" (text by himself). Other laments by Luigi Rossi (not a castrato) with female narrators include: the Turk Zelemì in "Con occhi belli e fieri" (text by Fabio Della Corgna), Zaida in "Spars'il crine e lagrimosa" (text by Fabio Della Corgna), and a beautiful female sinner (*la bella peccatrice*) in "Pender non prima vide" (Rossi 1986, respectively pp. 77–89 and 264, 123–6 and 266, 155–69 and 268–9).

xxv The anecdote is narrated by G. V. Rossi (1648, vol. 3, pp. 150–1) with his usual malicious misogyny.

xxvi The coat-of-arms of the families Lante/Della Rovere/Altemps figure on the manuscripts I-Rc 2467 and 2483; of the family Scaglia and probably Antonacci on I-Rc 2475 and 2479; and of the family Biscia and an unidentified blazon on I-Rc 2466 and 2477.

xxvii Letter of the literate Antimo Galli to Dimurgo Lambardi, 25 November 1623, quoted in Crinò (1960, p. 181).

xxviii The dedication is signed by Cosimo Ruggieri, Rome, 3 January 1640.

xxix I-Nc, 33.4.12, ff. 149$_r$–54$_v$, "Carlo del Violino."

References

Ademollo, A. (1895). *La Leonora di Milton e Clemente IX*. Milano: Ricordi.

Antonlini, B. M. (1984). Margherita Costa. In: *Dizionario Biografico Treccani* [online]. Available at <http://www.treccani.it/enciclopedia/margherita-costa_(Dizionario-Biografico)/> (accessed 5 September 2011).

Antolini, B. M. (1989). Cantanti e letterati a Roma nella prima metà del Seicento: alcune osservazioni. In F. Della Seta and F. Piperno (eds), *In cantu et in sermone: for Nino Pirrotta on his 80th Birthday*, pp. 347–62. Firenze: Olschki.

Applausi poetici alle glorie della signora Leonora Baroni (1639). Bracciano: Francesco Ronconi.

Aristotle (1943). *Generation of Animals* (transl. A. L. Peck), pp. 550–1. London, Cambridge, MA: Heinemann/Harvard University Press.

Barbier, P. (1996). *The World of the Castrati: the History of an Extraordinary Operatic Phenomenon*. London: Souvenir.

Bergeron, K. (1996). The castrato as history. *Cambridge Opera Journal*, **8**, 167–84.

Bianchi, E. (2011). *Prodigious Sounds: Music and Learning in the World of Athanasius Kircher*. PhD dissertation, Yale University.

Bianconi, L. (1986). Il Cinquecento e il Seicento. In A. Asor Rosa (ed.). *Letteratura Italiana*, vol. 6. *Teatro, Musica e Tradizione dei Classici*, pp. 319–63. Torino: Einaudi.

Bianconi, L. and Walker, T. (1975). Dalla *Finta pazza* alla *Veremonda*: storie di Febiarmonici. *Rivista Italiana di Musicologia*, **10**, 379–454.

Brosius, A. (2009). *"Il suon, lo sguardo, il canto": Virtuose of the Roman Conversazioni in the mid-Seventeenth Century*. PhD dissertation, University of New York.

Carissimi, G. (1986). *Cantatas*, ed. G. Massenkeil. New York: Garland.

Castiglione, B. (1987). *Il libro del cortigiano* (introduction by A. Quondam). Milano: Garzanti. (Transl. Opdycke, L. E. (2000). *The Book of the Courtier*. Ware: Wordsworth Classics.)

Cesti, A. (1986). *Cantatas*, ed. D. Burrows. New York: Garland.

Corsini, L. (1640). *Musiche di Lorenzo Corsini romano. Libro quinto*. Rome: Andrea Fei.

Couliano, I. P. (1987). *Eros and Magic in the Renaissance*. Chicago: University of Chicago Press.

Crinò, A. M. (1960). Virtuose di canto e poeti a Roma e a Firenze nella prima metà del Seicento. *Studi Secenteschi*, **1**, 175–93.

Croce, B. (1992). *I Teatri di Napoli: dal Rinascimento alla fine del Secolo Decimottavo*. Milan: Adelphi.

Cusick, S. G. (2009). *Francesca Caccini at the Medici Court: Music and the Circulation of Power*. Chicago: University of Chicago Press.

Della Valle, P. (1640). Della musica dell'età nostra. In A. Solerti (ed.) (1903). *Le origini del melodramma*, pp. 143–79. Turin: Bocca. (Partially translated by Murata, M. (1998). From "Of the music of our time." In O. Strunk (ed.). *Source Readings in Music History*. New York, London: Norton, pp. 544–51.)

De Lucca, V. (2009). *"Dalle sponde del Tebro alle rive dell'Adria": Maria Mancini and Lorenzo Onofrio Colonna's Patronage of Music and Theater between Rome and Venice (1659–1675)*. PhD dissertation, Princeton University.

De Lucca, V. (2011). Strategies of women patrons of music and theatre in Rome: Maria Mancini Colonna, Queen Christina of Sweden, and women of their circles. *Renaissance Studies*, **25**, 371–92.

Durante, S. (1987). Il cantante. In L. Bianconi and G. Pestelli (eds), *Storia dell'Opera Italiana*. Vol. IV: *Il Sistema Produttivo e le sue Competenze*, pp. 347–415. Turin: EDT.

Feldman, M. and Gordon, B. (eds.) (2006). *The Courtesan's Arts: Cross-Cultural Perspective*. New York: Oxford University Press.

Freitas, R. (1998). *"Un Atto d'ingegno": a Castrato in the Seventeenth Century*. PhD dissertation, Yale University.

Freitas, R. (2003). The eroticism of emasculation: confronting the Baroque body of the castrato. *Journal of Musicology*, **20**, 196–249.

Freitas, R. (2009). *Portrait of a Castrato: Politics, Patronage, and Music in the Life of Atto Melani*. Cambridge: Cambridge University Press.

Gagliano, M. (1608). Preface to *Dafne*. In A. Solerti (ed.) (1903). *Le origini del melodramma*, p. 81. Turin: Bocca.

Galen (1968), *On The Usefulness of the Parts of the Body* (transl. M. T. May), p. 650. Ithaca: Cornell University Press.

Gianturco, C. (ed.) (1985–1986). *The Italian Cantata in the Seventeenth Century*. New York: Garland.

Giustiniani, V. (1628). *Discorso sopra la musica de' suoi tempi*. In A. Solerti (ed.) (1903). *Le Origini del Melodramma*, pp. 103–28. Torino: Bocca. (Transl. by C. MacClintock in Bottrigari, E. (1962). *Il Desiderio / Giustiniani, V. Discorso sopra la musica*. Rome: American Institute of Musicology.)

Glixon, B. L. (1995). Private lives of public women: prima donnas in mid-seventeenth-century Venice. *Music & Letters*, **76**, 509–31.

Gordon, B. (2004). *Monteverdi's Unruly Women: the Power of Song in Early Modern Italy*. Cambridge: Cambridge University Press.

Gouk, P. (2000). Music, melancholy, and medical spirits. In P. Horden (ed.), *Music as Medicine: the History of Music Therapy since Antiquity*, pp. 173–94. Aldershot: Ashgate.

Hammond, F. (1994). *Music and Spectacle in Baroque Rome: Barberini Patronage under Urban VIII*. New Haven: Yale University Press.

Heller, W. (2003). *Emblems of Eloquence: Opera and Women's Voices in Seventeenth-Century Venice*. Berkeley: University of California Press.

Hill, J. W. (1997). *Roman Monody, Cantata, and Opera from the Circles around Cardinal Montalto*, 2 vols. Oxford: Clarendon Press.

Holzer, R. R. (1990). *Music and Poetry in 17th century Rome: Settings of Canzonetta and Cantata texts of Francesco Balducci, Domenico Benigni, Francesco Melosio, and Antonio Abbati*. PhD dissertation, University of Pennsylvania.

Jander, O. (ed.) (1964–72). *Wellesley Edition Cantata Index Series*. Wellesley, MA: Wellesley College.

Jeanneret, C. (in press). Roman cantata manuscripts (1640–1680): a musical cabinet of curiosities. In H. Schulze (ed.), *Musical Text as Ritual Object*. Turnhout: Brepols.

Kircher, A. (1650) in Scharlau, U. (ed.) (1970). *Musurgia universalis*. Hildesheim: Olms. (Partially transl. by B. Blackburn and L. Holford-Stevens (1995). *The Perfect Musician*. Krakow: Musica Iagellonica.)

L'Idea della veglia (1640). Roma: Heredi di Corbelletti.

LaMay, T. (ed.) (2005). *Musical Voices of Early Modern Women: Many-Headed Melodies*. Cambridge: Cambridge University Press.

Laqueur, T. W. (1990). *Making Sex: Body and Gender from the Greeks to Freud*. Cambridge, MA: Harvard University Press.

Leopold, S. (1990). *Al modo d'Orfeo: Dichtung und Musik im italienischen Sologesang des frühen 17. Jahrhunderts*, 2 vols (*Analecta Musicologica*, **29**). Rome: Deutsches Historisches Institut.

Leti, G. (1667). *Il puttanismo romano* (ed. E. Bufachi, 2004). Rome: Salerno.

Lorenzetti, S. (1994). "Quel celeste cantar che mi disface": immagine della donna ed educazione alla musica nell'ideale pedagogico del Rinascimento Italiano. *Studi Musicali*, **23**, 241–61.

Maia Materdona, G. (1629). *Rime*. Venice: Vangelista Deuchino.

Maione, P. (1997). *Giulia De Caro "Famosissima armonica" e il bordello sostenuto del signor don Antonio Muscettola*. Naples: Luciano.

Marazzoli, M. (1986). *Cantatas*, ed. W. Witzenmann. New York: Garland.

Maugars, A. (1639/1993). *Response faite à un curieux sur le sentiment de la musique d'Italie*, ed. H. Wiley Hitchcock. Genève: Minkoff. (Transl. in MacClintock, C. (1982). *Readings in the History of Music in Performance*. Bloomington, IN: Indiana University Press.)

Melani, A. (2005). *Complete Cantatas*, ed. R. Freitas. Middleton, WI: A-R Editions.

Morandini, G. (2001). *Sospiri e palpiti: Scrittrici italiane del Seicento*. Genova: Marietti.

Morelli, A. (2005). Una cantante del Seicento e le sue carte di musica: *Il Libro della Signora Cecilia*. *Analecta Musicologica*, **36**, 307–27.

Morelli, A. (2006), Perché non vanno… La cantata romana del pieno Seicento: questioni di trasmissione e di funzione. In P. Russo (ed.), *Musica e Drammaturgia a Roma al Tempo di Giacomo Carissimi*, pp. 21–39. Venezia: Marsilio.

Morelli, A. (2008). For a material history of cantata: some reflections on the Roman manuscript sources. Unpublished lecture presented at the 13th Biennial International Conference on Baroque Music, Leeds, 2–6 July 2008.

Murata, M. (1979a). Further remarks on Pasqualini and the Music of MAP. *Analecta Musicologica,* **19**, 125–45.

Murata, M. (1979b). The recitative soliloquy. *Journal of the American Musicological Society,* **32**, 45–73.

Murata, M. (1981). *Operas for the Papal Court, 1631–1668.* Ann Arbor, MI: UMI Research Press.

Murata, M. (1993). La cantata romana tra mecenatismo e collezionismo. In C. Annibaldi (ed.), *La Musica e il Mondo: Mecenatismo e Committenza Musicale in Italia tra Quattro e Settecento,* pp. 253–66. Bologna: Il Mulino.

Murata, M. (2005). Image and eloquence: secular song. In T. Carter and J. Butt (eds), *The Cambridge History of Seventeenth-Century Music,* pp. 378–425. Cambridge: Cambridge University Press.

Murata, M. (in press). The score on the shelf: valuing the anonymous and unheard. In H. Schulze (ed.), *Musical Text as Ritual Object.* Turnhout: Brepols.

Nutton, V. (1993). Humoralism. In W. F. Bynum and R. Porter (eds), *Companion Encyclopedia of the History of Medicine,* pp. 281–91. New York: Routledge.

Ottonelli, G. B. (1645). *Della pericolosa conversatione con le donne, o poco modeste, o Ritirate, o Cantatrici, o Accademiche.* Florence: Franceschini & Logi.

Pangrazi, T. (2009). *La Musurgia Universalis di Athanasius Kircher: Contenuti, Fonti, Terminologia.* Firenze: Olschki.

Paré, A. (1634). *The Workes of Ambrose Parey,* transl. T. Johnson. London: Cotes and Young.

Pasqualini, M. A. (1986). *Cantatas,* ed. M. Murata. New York: Garland.

Rosand, E. (1991). *Opera in Seventeenth-Century Venice: the Creation of a Genre.* Berkeley: University of California Press.

Rospigliosi, G. (1641). *Argomento dell'opera musicale intitolata L'innocenza difesa [La Genoinda].* Rome: Nella stamparia della Rev. Cam. Apost.

Rosselli, J. (1988). The castrati as a professional group and a social phenomenon, 1550–1850. *Acta Musicologica,* **60**, 143–79.

Rosselli, J. (1993). *Il Cantate d'Opera: Storia di una Professione (1600–1990),* pp. 79–99. Bologna: Il Mulino.

Rossi, G. V. [alias Iani Nicii Erithraei] (1648). *Pinacotheca Imaginum Illustrium,* 3 vols. Köln: Kalcovium.

Rossi, L. (1986). *Cantatas,* ed. F. Luisi. New York: Garland.

Ruffatti, A. (2007). Curiosi e bramosi l'oltramontani cercano con grande diligenza in tutti i luoghi. *Journal of the Seventeenth-Century Society,* **13** [online] Available at <http://www.sscm-jscm.org/v13/no1/ruffatti. html> (accessed 5 September 2011).

Siraisi, N. G. (1990). *Medieval and Early Renaissance Medicine: an Introduction to Knowledge and Practice,* vol. 1, pp. 281–91. Chicago: University of Chicago Press.

Teatro delle glorie della signora Adriana Basile (1623). Venice: Deuchino.

Trinchieri Camiz, F. (1996). "La bella cantatrice": i ritratti di Leonora Barone e Barbara Strozzi a confronto. In F. Passadore and P. Rossi (eds), *Musica, Scienza e idee nella Serenissima durante il Seicento,* pp. 285–94. Venezia: Levi.

Vittori, L. (1649). *Arie a Voce Sola del Cavalier Loreto Vittori.* Venice: Vincenti.

Wear, A. (1995). Medicine in early modern Europe 1500–1700. In L. Conrad, M. Neve, V. Nutton, and R. Porter (eds), *The Western Medical Tradition 800 BC to AD 1800,* vol. 1, pp. 215–73. Cambridge: Cambridge University Press.

Chapter 8

The ethos of modes during the Renaissance[i]

Claude Victor Palisca

In the final years of the 15th century, we begin to find the assertion that a polyphonic composition's characteristics must conform to the subject treated in the text and that the best means of achieving this goal is by choosing an appropriate mode (Gaffurio 1496). Around 1540, at least two authors—Matteo Nardo[ii] and Giovanni del Lago (1540)—considered the choice of mode decisive; they asserted that the first thing a composer must do was to study the text or the subject treated by the piece in order to choose, on this basis, the composition's mode.[iii] In the second half of the 16th century, a rather consistent theoretical literature asked the composer to form his work in a mode adapted to its subject.

Given the importance granted to the choice of mode, it is surprising to note how little consequence is given to the characterization of the eight modes' emotional associations or ethos in polyphonic music. While, on the technical level, most discussions of modality derive from analyses of either plainsong or polyphonic practice, remarks on ethos derive from a hybrid genealogy. Some of the characterizations derive from a modal system foreign to both plainsong and polyphonic practice, notably the classical Greek system. Others have independent medieval origins, intrinsic to the plainsong tradition and descended from, on the one hand, Guido d'Arezzo[iv] and Johannes dictus Cotto vel Affligemensis (n.d.) and, on the other hand, the church father's literature, in particular from Clement of Alexandria, Saint Ambrose, and Saint Augustine. Finally, a certain number of moral, ethical, and emotional associations appear to be based on the experience of polyphonic music.

Before examining how norms regarding the ethos of modes were articulated during the Renaissance, we ought to review the diverse modal system and the factors that were supposed to affect their moral, ethical, and emotional character. In general, we accept that in Greek music, ethos was not only attributed to the octave's aspects [*species*] but also to the vocal range, that is to say to the pitch, to certain melodic qualities, to its *genera*—diatonic, chromatic, and enharmonic—and to rhythm and meter. Until the humanists' discoveries in the last third of the 16th century, Western musicians viewed the Greek modes as those described by Boethius around 500 in his *De Institutione Musica*[v]: the Hypodorian, the Hypophrygian, the Hypolydian, the Dorian, the Phrygian, the Lydian, the Mixolydian, and the Hypermixolydian. These names were given to eight transpositions, identical in terms of intervals, from the double octave system to four tetrachords. Boethius had also enumerated the octaves' aspects. As seen in his diagrams, these appeared in the median octave when the modes, or *tonoi*, were planned on a three-octave system, which we generally represent between La–la‴[vi]; however, Boethius did not give them an ethnic nomenclature. Nor did he speak of the ethos of modes, which concerned the transposition of the double-octave system or of the octave's aspect.

During the 19th century, the terms Hypodorian, Hypophrygian, etc. were applied to the ensemble of octave's aspects, starting from La (Chailley 1965). In ascending order, this aspect's initial notes were separated by a tone, a half-tone, a tone, a tone, a half-tone, a tone, a tone, as in la's natural range. Later, the last mode, Hypermixolydian, was lowered one fifth on the Mixolydian plagal mode or the Hypochlorhydria.[vii] As a consequence, aside from a few rare exceptions, musicians and theorists believed that plainsong modes were identical to their Greek homonym modes and that the characteristics ancient authors attributed to the Greek modes could be transposed to those found in plainsong.

However, we must remember how different Greek modes are at their base from modern musical modes. How was it possible that Greek modes awoke diverse passions, virtues, or moral attitudes among listeners? If we solely consider pitch, the Greek literature is ambiguous. Nevertheless, we can highlight some general correspondences. To this end, we will distinguish pitch keys or *tonoi* from octaves' aspects, sometimes known by the name of *harmoniai*. The *tonoi* or tonalities can be divided into hypatoide or deep, mesoide or middle, and netoides or high. Aristides Quintilian associates deep voices with tragic compositions, middle voices with dithyrambs, and high-pitched voices with nomic compositions (see Table 8.1). With regards to ethos, Aristides also differentiates melodic compositions, which he divides into three classes: the diastolic, which awakens the mind, the middle [*hesichastic*], which calms the soul, and the systolic, which awakens painful passions (Mathiesen, 1983). Thanks to Cleonide,[viii] we can associate these three ethical categories to vocal ranges and to types of composition. Covering the deepest region of the voice, the diastolic ethos expresses majestic and virile moods; it is well-suited to expressing heroic events and tragic poetry. The *hesychastic* (middle) ethos, occupying middle ranges, inspires a calm and peaceful disposition; it is suitable for hymns, paeans, eulogies and didactic poetry. The systolic ethos, which draws from the highest-pitched part of the vocal register, carries the spirit into a humble and effeminate state; it is appropriate for expressing erotic emotions as well as dirges and lamentations.

One of Bellermann's anonymous pieces couples, among others, the parts of the vocal range with particular *tonoi*. The hypatoide region includes the tonalities found between the Hypodorian's *hypate meson* and the Dorian's *mese*; the middle, or mesoide, region includes those between the Phrygian *hypate meson* and the Lydian *mese*; and the third those from the Lydian *mese* up to its *nete synemmenon*. (The anonymous author adds still a fourth region below these; Najock 1972). All of these associations are united in Table 8.1, which, for the record, is a synthesis derived from disparate sources.

Table 8.1 Classical categories of ethos associated with pitches

Vocal region	Modes	Ethos	Genres	Emotions
Deep (hypatoide) [si–la]	Hypophrygian, Hypolydian, Hypodorian	Diastolic	Poetry	Majestic, peaceful, tranquil, virile
Middle (mesoide) [fa'–do']	Dorian, Phrygian, Lydian	Hesychastic	Hymns, paeans, eulogies; didactic, dithyrambic and heroic poetry	Calm, peaceful
Sharp (netoide) [do'–sol']	Mixolydian, Hypermixolydian	Systaltic	Dirges, lamentations, nomic	Humble, erotic, sorrowful, feminine

Some individual mode's expressive powers are based on pitch. For example, Pratinas of Phlius, a contemporary of Aeschylus, urged musicians to play neither intense music nor loose Iastian music, but to work the middle path, and especially the Eolian mode (Abert 1899, pp. 64–8; translated in Anderson 1966, pp. 47–8). Presumably the Iastian later became the Hypophrygian and the Eolian the Hypodorian. By intense music, Pratinas may have meant the Mixolydian. Plato and Aristotle also opposed intense and loose music, that is to say, modes found in the sharp and deep regions. Plato even rejected two classes of modes: the threnodies—"the Mixolydian, the Syntono-lydian and others of that sort," and softened or user-friendly modes—the loose Lydian and the Iastian (*Republic* 398e). He only supported the Dorian and Phrygian (*Republic* 399a). Evidently, there was a "syntonic" Lydian, intense or sharp, and a softened or deep Lydian, the Dorian and Phrygian being found between the two, in a more central range.

Thus, at least a part of the ethical energy of Greek modes depended on pitch, while plainsong modes are distinguished more by their intervals' aspect than by their pitch. Clearly, there was only a slim possibility for the ethical effects of ancient modes truly to transfer to modern ones.

In contrast, another aspect of the ancient ethos was more compatible with modern modes. This aspect was associated with the system of *harmoniai*, which, according to one school of modern commentators, was an octave scale similar to plainsong modes. These scales could be represented by their octave aspects, but they were undoubtedly more complex ensembles of melodic formulae. Numerous associations that are tied to entities called Dorian, Phrygian, etc. probably refer to the *harmoniai*'s qualities. Thus, while Heraclides Ponticus praised the Dorian as male and majestic, and pseudo-Plutarch praised it as steady and having a principally masculine ethos, they were making allusion to its melodic content.

Heraclides considered the Hypodorian proud, pompous, and a bit vain.[ix] Aristotle described the Phrygian as enthusiastic, violently exciting, emotional, and capable of awakening religious ecstasy (*Politics* 1340b, 1342b). It is said that Timothy used this mode to encourage Alexander to rise from the banquet table, to put on his armor, and to go into battle.[x] This story may account for the attempt to establish this as the traditionally martial mode. A certain understanding about the Mixolydian, which Plato called melancholic (*Republic* 398d), Aristotle plaintive and reserved (*Politics* 1340b), and pseudo-Plutarch passionate (*De Musica* 1136d), also existed.

How the *harmoniai* produced such different effects remains a mystery. The interval aspect alone seems insufficient. The *harmoniai* offered neither finales nor dominants nor internal relations which could have established a hierarchy of tensions and points of rest. On the other hand, it is possible that the *mese* could have exerted a gravitational role, if we are to believe Aristotle's *Problems*, where we read that the melody frequently returns to the *mese* (*Problems* 19.20.919a). But it isn't clear whether it was the dynamic *mese* at the center of the key or the central note of the double octave's original scale. When projecting tones in the median octave from the *hypate meson* to the *nete diezeugmenon*, the [dynamic] *mese* of each key falls on a different note in the octave: for example, that of the Mixolydian is near the peak, that of the Dorian in the middle, on the thetic *mese*, and that of the Hypodorian is on the central octave's deep note. If a melody tends to complete an octave and to return to the *mese* within it, the attraction toward the high note exercised by the Mixolydian *mese*, the stability of Dorian, and the attraction descending from that of the Hypodorian certainly influenced the melody's emotional character.

Another factor affecting this ethical character was without a doubt the arrangement of tones, half-tones, and micro-intervals in the *harmoniai*'s scale. The *harmoniai* shared this characteristic with ecclesiastic and polyphonic modes. Both the Greek systems and their Christian correlates were limited to the seven available aspects of the diatonic octave. However, Christians rejected one of them and applied an ethnic nomenclature to the aspects of individual octaves different from

Table 8.2 Classical and Christian nomenclature for octaves' aspects

Greek nomenclature	Part of the octave	Christian nomenclature
Mixolydian	S T T S T T T [b–b']	None, later Locrian
Lydian	T T S T T T S [c–c']	None, Glarean: Ionian
Phrygian	T S T T T S T [d–d']	Dorian
Dorian	S T T T S T T [e–e']	Phrygian
Hypolydian	T T T S T T S [f–f']	Lydian
Hypophrygian	T T S T T S T [g–g']	Mixolydian
Hypodorian	T S T T S T T [a–a']	Hypodorian, Glarean: Aeolien

that used by the Greeks. If we classify the aspects and their nomenclature according to Cleonides and the ecclesiastic tradition (Table 8.2, left and right columns, respectively), we find that only one aspect has the same name in each system, the Hypodorian—and that wasn't even always the case.

If the disparities between the Greek and Christian systems seem evident to us today, they weren't for the users and theorists of Christian modes. So much so that the ethical characteristics of the Greek modes became unconsciously associated with the Christian modes of the same name. This misunderstanding particularly affected the four authentic modes: the Dorian, the Phrygian, the Lydian, and the Mixolydian. Thus Gaffurius (1518, bk 4, ch. 2, p. 180) spoke of the modesty and the constancy of the Dorian (see Table 8.3), while Glarean (1547, bk 2, ch. 21, p. 118) qualified it as majestic and deep, adding that it was particularly well-suited to heroic poetry.

Gaffurius thought the Hypodorian full of inertia and weakness. Aron (1525, ch. 25) found it well-suited to tears and lamentations, while Glarean (1547, bk 2, ch.16, p. 102) judged it serious, sinister and submissive. These characteristics of the Hypodorian persist up to Bermudo (1555, bk 5, ch.33, fol. Q1v), Vicentino (1555, bk 3, ch. 6), Hermann Finck (1556, ff. R$_r$3$_v$)[xi] and Zarlino (1558, bk 4, ch.6, p. 58).

A tenacious tendency considered the Phrygian as inciting anger and war (Gauffurius, Aron, Nardo, Glarean, Finck).[xii] The Hypophrygian's characteristics are less constant, maybe because classical literature offered few indications: deep and tranquil (Gaffurius 1518, bk 4, ch.8); restful and tranquil (Aron 1525, ch. 25); melancholy and plaintive (Glarean 1547, bk 2, ch.18, p.110); and well-suited to texts that were serious, spiritual and to lamentations (Finck 1556, f. R$_r$4$_r$).

The Lydian, described as gentle, convivial, and relaxed by Plato, was considered jovial and pleasant by Gaffurius, although he also mentioned its use in dirges and lamentations in earlier times (Gaffurius 1518, bk 4, ch. 5, p. 183). Aron (1525, ch. 25) thought the Lydian capable of assuaging melancholy, anxiety, and pains. Glarean, citing ancient authorities, affirmed that it was convivial and bacchic (Glarean 1547, bk 2 ch. 25, p. 127), while it is lascivious and sensual for Bermudo (1555, bk 3, ch. 9). The Hypolydian, in contrast, was tearful and sad.

The Mixolydian, which had the reputation of being funereal, plaintive, and simultaneously passionate and restrained in the classical literature, retained its general character among certain authors (Ramos de Pareja 1482, tract. 3, ch. 3, p. 57; Gaffurius 1518, bk 4, ch. 5, p.184), while others found it lascivious (Aron 1525, ch. 25; Zarlino 1558, bk 4, ch. 24, p. 72)[xiii] and still others proud and haughty (Bermudo 1555, bk 5, ch. 3 f. Q2$_v$; Vicentino 1555, bk 3, ch. 11). I purposely ignore the Hypomixolydian, as no classical tradition existed for this modal form. Some of the above characteristics are summarized in Table 8.3.

Table 8.3 The ethos of modes: antiquity–Renaissance comparison

Mode	Antiquity	Gaffurius (1518)	Aron (1525)	Glarean (1547)
I Dorian	Majestic, masculine, constant	Constant, severe, moves phlegm	Content, joyous; excites all of the passions	Grave, prudent, dignified, modest
II Hypodorian	Haughty, pompous, pretentious	Slow, backward, lazy	Plaintive, grave	Serious, daunting, submissive
III Phrygian	Exciting, martial	Incites anger and war	Combative, irritable, funereal	Incites rage and battle
IV Hypophrygian	Austere, calms anger	Tranquil, grave, calms excitement	Calm, tranquil	Melancholic, plaintive
V Lydian	Funereal, sad, convivial	Gloomy, suitable for lamentations	Assuages melancholy and burdens	Hard, convivial, bacchic
VI Hypolydian	Bacchic, intoxicating	Tearful, suitable for lamentations	Incites tears and compassion	Pleasant, not elegant
VII Mixolydian	Threnodic, piteous	Exciting, restrained	A mix of modesty and joviality	Well-suited to praise
VIII Hypomixolydian		Sublime, without corruption	Joyous, content	Naturally charming, sweet

In addition to the tradition regarding ethos based on the coincidence in their names, there was another, which seems to be based on the plainsong experience (cf. Table 8.4). Authors like de Zamora (n.d.) and Ramos de Pareja (1482, tract. 3, ch. 3) represent it. Some of their theories are taken up by Aron and German theorists, like Hermann Finck(1556, bk 4). It should be noted that this medieval tradition wasn't free from ancient contaminations and that it also was influenced by later changes inspired by the polyphonic experience.

Yet another approach to modal ethos existed during the Renaissance: the practical approach. It issues from recognition of the technical resources of combinations of a mode's intervals, which are both successive and simultaneous, as well as the tempers that they awaken. This practical reaction to music corrected some of the most inappropriate medieval and Renaissance characterizations. Two authors who followed this pragmatic approach were Zarlino and Vicentino. Zarlino (1558), who cited most of the ancient associations in his historical chapter 5 of the fourth book of *Le Istitutioni Harmoniche*, ended this same chapter with a cynical commentary in which he attributed the variety of contradictions in modal characteristics to changing habits and customs, to writers' lack of understanding, and to errors of transcription. In book 4's practical chapters—on plainsong modes and polyphony—as well as in the preceding chapter on counterpoint, Zarlino sought musical properties that had an expressive potential. What he writes about this first mode is typical:

> The first mode has a certain effect, between sadness and joy, because of the minor third, which is heard in the contrapuntal relations above the fourth and fifth's extreme notes, and because of the absence of the major third in the deep part [of the fifth]. This mode's nature is religious and devote as well as a little sad; that is why it is best used with words full of gravity that treat high and edifying subjects [*Le Istitutioni Harmoniche*, bk 4, ch. 8, p. 58].

Table 8.4 The ethos of modes: the medieval ecclesiastical tradition

Mode	de Zamora (n.d., c. 1240)	Ramos de Pareja (1482)	Finck (1556)
I Dorian	Flexible, suitable for all emotions	Supple, suitable for all emotions; moves phlegm, awakens and assuages laziness and sadness	Brings on drowsiness, assuages pain and affliction; purges phlegm
II Hypodorian	Severe, funereal	Severe, funereal	Funereal, heavy, serious, humble
III Phrygian	Severe, exciting, healthful	Severe, exciting, well-suited to proud, irritable and wild men	Moves anger and bile, well-suited to battles, elevated gestures
IV Hypophrygian	Caressing, talkative, flattering	Caressing, talkative, flattering, lascivious, without charm	Represents the servant who serves his master's pleasures
V Lydian	Modest, charming; gentle and assuages despair	Delicious, modest, joyous; gladdens sad and desperate people	Nicer emotions; calms those who are perturbed; modest, delicious, joyous; consoles the afflicted and desperate
VI Hypolydian	Incites tears and piety	Incites tears and piety	Opposite of the Lydian
VII Mixolydian	Erotic and joyous, represents adolescence	Erotic and joyous, represents adolescence	Used for invectives, terrifying, not serious for aged people
VIII Hypomixolydian	Sweet and somber, like solitary people	Sweet and somber, like solitary people	Soothing, calms anger through gentleness

With regards to the third mode, and rejecting all that had historically been said about this martial mode, Zarlino affirmed:

> If the third mode isn't mixed with the ninth mode [Aeolian on la], and if it is listened to alone, its harmony has something hard, however, being tempered by the ninth mode's fifth and by the cadence on la, which is used very often, some people think that it incites tears. As a consequence, they use it to accompany tearful words that are full of lamenting [*Le Istitutioni Harmoniche*, bk 4, ch. 20, p. 64].

Zarlino's manner of speaking of the emotional quality of the twelve modes in his book on counterpoint is equally significant. It notes that, among imperfect consonances, the major third and sixth, as well as their combinations, are lively and joyful, while the minor third and sixth, although sweet and round, are sad and languid. As a consequence, when the major third and sixth are found in the finale or in the note that divides the octave into fourths and fifths, as in the fifth, sixth, seventh, eighth, eleventh, and twelfth modes, these modes are "gay and lively." This is in part, because the major third is placed below the minor third, that is to say that the fifth is harmonically divided, according to natural sounds. The other modes are sad or languid because the minor third is found in the finale or in the median note, as in the first, second, third, fourth, ninth, and tenth modes. In these cases, the fifth is divided arithmetically, which is less natural for the ear (Zarlino 1558, bk 3, ch. 10, pp. 21–2).

Vicentino, who wrote in the same period as Zarlino, was more credulous. He adapted ancient features to practical experience in a pragmatic and eclectic fashion. After all, the intention of

L'Antica Musica ridotta alla Moderna Prattica was adapting ancient music to modern practices. Thus, he considered the first mode agreeable and devout, more virtuous than licentious; but he couldn't stop himself from adding that the Dorians sang their praises and their heroic acts in this mode (Vicento 1555, bk 3 ch. 5). He declared that the second mode was, by nature, similar to the first, but more joyous and modest, because the fourth's aspect was present above the fifth. He considered that the third mode carried little consolation if not accompanied by a chromatic and enharmonic mix, even if it could be joyous with four voices. All reference to choleric nature and its Greek homonym was absent. He saw the fourth mode as funereal, and the fifth as proud and haughty, even while joyous, characteristics which he also granted to the Mixolydian.

What was the relationship between this theory about ethos and the manner in which music was composed and heard? We know that a certain number of composers conscientiously observed the limits and musical identity of the modes they chose for their compositions. Thanks to the works of Bernhard Meier (1974),[xiv] Harry Powers (1981), Jessie Ann Owens (1986), James Haar (1987), and Robert Luoma (1977), some composers have been identified. They include Adrian Willaert, Cipriano de Rore, Orlando di Lasso, and Giovanni da Palestrina. I will only discuss one of them, Rore. He published two collections of madrigals divided according to modal criteria and which, as a consequence, show the composer's deliberate choice of mode.[xv] In the first book of madrigals in five voices, published in 1542, the order of texts is arbitrary—in contrast to Lasso's "Penitential Psalms," for example, which are also classified by mode, but in an order predetermined by the texts. As a consequence, we can hypothesize that, in Rore's 1542 collection, it was the nature of the text that determined the choice of mode.

How well do Rore's choices (see Table 8.5) agree with associations established in the theoretical literature? Of the three madrigals written in the first mode, the third, "Poggian'al ciel," meshes best with the Dorian's recognized character. It includes praises of a woman who remains virtuous, despite a seduction and Cupid's repeated attempts against her: the poet can't find noble enough words to properly honor the woman for her virtue. However, the first madrigal, Giovanni Brevio's "Cantai, mentre chi arsi," does not contradict the Dorian's conventional spirit, as the poet tranquilly remembers the romantic ardor that inspired the verses written for his lady. The music is restrained and preserves the ideal qualities of seriousness, nobility, and moderation, association with the classical Dorian. The famous sonnet of Petrarch, "Hor che'l ciel e la terra e'l vento tace," doesn't correspond as well with stereotypes. Rore sought, first of all, to depict dormant nature in a mode that, according to Finck, awakens people from sleep. Then, at the words "veggio, penso, ardo, piango," the text radically changes, and Rore introduces so many alterations that the mode's flavor is erased for a moment. The sonnet's *sestina*, which alternates between hope and despair, may correspond better to Zarlino's description of the first mode as between sadness and joy.

The two following madrigals, both based on Petrarch's texts, are in the Hypodorian or second mode. "Quand'io son tutto volto" begins by affirming that Laura is the poet's light, and that the poet fears she will go out. Then, he loses this light and wanders blindly—in silence, because his words can only express few things—fleeing the thought of death, crying and solitary. The subject accords with the ancient description of the mode, which characterizes it as threnodic, with Gaffurius' conception of it as funereal and with Zarlino's description of it as apt for representing tears, sadness, solitude, captivity, and calamity. Aside from frequent flat notes in the sixth degree before the finale, Rore maintains the mode throughout the interior of the piece.

"Solea lontana in sonno," written during Laura's terminal illness, is no less pessimistic; it tells how dreaming of Laura consoles the poet, who now remembers how, the night when she left him in tears, she didn't have the courage to tell him that he would never see her again on earth. Rore maintains the mode, rarely altering the characteristic minor thirds.

Table 8.5 Correlations between modes and subjects in books 1 to 5 of Cipriano de Rore (1542)

Text	Works	Mode	Subject
1. "Cantai, mentre ch'i arsi" Giovanni Brevio	2: 1–4	1 (tr)	I sing and I burn—my ears hear my ardor. No peace for lovers
2. "Hor che'l ciel e la terra" Petrarch no. 164	2: 4–9	1 (tr)	Nature sleeps; I think, burn, cry. I am at war. Her hand could care for me, I die a thousand deaths
3. "Poggian'al ciel" (Anon)	2: 9–14	1(tr)	My lady, Cupid loses his erotic wings in your presence. I lack both the genius and the ink necessary to honor you
4. "Quand'io son tutto volto" Petrarch 4. no. 18	2: 14–19	2 (tr)	Laura is his light; without her image, he flees blindly, dying for lack of her; tears, solitude
5. "Solea lontana in sonno" Petrarch no. 250	2: 20–24	2 (tr)	Dreaming that she consoles him, recalling that she told him that he would never see her again on this earth
6. "Altiero sasso" Francesco Maria Molza	2: 25–29	3	Stones, streams, waves of signs; the day of sorrow has arrived
7. "Strane ruppi, aspri monti" Nicolo Amanio	2: 29–34	3	Strange rocks, craggy mountains, trembling ruins, etc. I wander, crying, among those who listen to me
8. "La vita fugge" Petrarch no. 272	2: 34–40	3	I am at war with everything, past, present, and future, life flees, return to port [death] with a broken ship; the lights are out
9. "Tu piangi" (Anon.)	2: 40–44	4	You cry while she laughs; dead, she looks down and laments the [living] death that was her life on earth
10. "Il mal mi preme" Petrarch no. 244	2: 44–50	5	Consolation for Giovanni de'Dondi, cheated by love; tells him to scorn his heart and place his faith in God
11. "Per mezz'i boschi" Petrarch no. 176	2: 51–56	5	The forest pleases him because he sees Laura's image everywhere; but an image too far from the true Laura
12. "Quanto più m'avvicino" Petrarch no. 32	2: 56–62	6	Closer to death, closer to peace; this isn't the time to speak of love; difficult times approach
13. "Perseguendomi amor" Petrarch no. 110	2: 62–69	6	He was ready for the worst, but he saw Laura's ghost; she greeted him quietly without his hearing
14. "Chi vol veder quantunque" Petrarch no. 248	2: 69–75	7	He who wishes to see the biggest miracle of nature [Laura] must hurry, before she dies; her praises are inadequate
15. "Qual sempre acerbo" Petrarch no. 157	2: 76–81	7	He remembers the day when he saw Laura cry; he describes her face, her voice, her crystal tears
16. "Far potess'io vendetta" Petrarch no. 255	2: 81–87	8	He imagines that her words torture him, softened by the sight of her. Do imaginary kisses interrupt his sleep?
17. "Amor, che vedi" Petrarch no. 163	2: 87–93	8	He tells Cupid how much he has suffered, how hard it was to ascend towards Laura; Cupid must not be unhappy about his sighs

tr, transposed.

The martial character that the ancient tradition associated with the Phrygian could have suggested the use of the third mode for the next two texts. Francesco Maria Molle's poem, "Altier cassot, 2 mentions the "grandiose honors that the ancients made to the god, Mars" and Petrarch's "La vita fugue" speaks of a poet in a perpetual state of war against everyone. The last madrigal in this mode, Nicola Amanite's "Strand rupin, esprit Monti" better corresponds to Zarlino's characterization, which considered this mode rude and inciting listeners to tears. Here, Rore intensifies these sentiments by using a motif of four notes descending by tones, le sol fa mi, at the beginning. The inconclusive progression from the major sixth to the fifth, and the successive delays contribute to the painful humor. "La vita fugue" is one of the sonnets "in morte di Madonna Laura," written after Laura's death. Rore strictly sticks to this mode, except in " E la morte vien dietro a gran giorno", where he seeks a discordant effect in alternating minor and major chords.

There is only one piece in the fourth mode, "Tu piangi," based on an anonymous text. Vincentino's description of this mode as funereal and Zarlino's as suitable for words of lamentation lead me to think that this was a conscious choice for this poem, about a dead lover who laments the living death of the poet's life on earth. A significant gap in modal purity is produced at the words "Dolc'harmonia per ogni parte ascolta": an allusion to celestial harmony surrounding the beloved is depicted by major triads, spaced in order of "number sounds," that is to say, in combining intervals (from deepest to highest) of the major fifth, fourth, and third or of the octave and the major fifth, fourth, and third. Rore choose the fifth mode for two texts, which correspond to conventional expectations about the Lydian. It should be noted, however, that the composer flattens the si, as was normal, identifying the fifth's aspects with those of the seventh and eighth modes. The main theme connecting the descriptions of this mode is its aptitude for relieving melancholy and anxiety. Thus, it was a judicious choice for Petrarch's sonnet "Il mal mi preme," consoling Giovanni de' Dondi's lover's despair. Petrarch's "Per mezz'i boschi" is a scene outside, in which forests, rivers, and birds all evoke Laura's image; this consoles the poet's grief for a moment, until he realizes, in the last line, that too large a part of his "sun" had faded in the picture.

The two compositions in the sixth mode, characterized by most writers as funereal and piteous, are constructed on rather neutral and abstract texts, even though they indicate optimism. Petrarch's "Quanto più m'avvicino al giorno estremo" speaks about approaching death and the futility of thinking and sighing over love. In "Perseguendomi amor," Petrarch touches a joyous note; arming himself against somber thoughts, the poet spies a familiar ghost, which suddenly reveals itself to be Laura herself, greeting him quietly.

The seventh mode, the Mixolydian, is a paradoxical mode because ancient tradition used it for lamentations, while modern authors saw erotic, joyous, and invective-laden potentials in its homolog. Petrarch's "Chi vol veder quantunque" is ambiguous, containing a panegyric to Laura's beauty, which invites the world to admire her in flesh and blood, because the poet's verse cannot do her justice. He who waits will cry from regret forever; in effect, she dies 19 sonnets later. The sonnet, "Quel sempre acerbo et honorato giorno," is bitter-sweet, describing the sight of Laura in tears with an interior ardor and vivid imagery. Whether intentionally or not, in these two madrigals, Rore seems to have brought about a compromise between ancient and modern traditions concerning the Mixolydian.

Zarlino's description of the eighth mode as sweet and filling the spirit with joy isn't contradicted by Rore's two madrigals in this mode, based on two of Petrarch's dream-poems, "Far potess'io vendetta" and "Amor, che vedi ogni pensiero aperto."

If I have identified the dominant emotions in these poems as Rore would have interpreted them, his choice of mode seems to be based partially on the conventional doctrines of the ancients, medievals, and moderns concerning modes' ethos and partially on polyphonic resources inherent to modern modes. These polyphonic resources includes the distinct aspects of the fourth and fifth, impacts, regular and irregular cadence, the song's range, and triads constructed on the mode's and finale's degrees.

I'm not sure that I have convincingly proven that Rore chose the modes based on their recognized associations in his madrigals. What I have presented does not constitute solid proof, but, in fact, rests on a moving and slippery base. That said, I nonetheless think that there are significant correlations between what was thought about the ethos of modes and Rore's choices. This collection's composer was free to chose the text that best suited him and to arrange it in any order; for example, he didn't arrange Petrarch's sonnets in the same order as the *Canzoniere*. He must have planned to limit the number of madrigals in each mode to two or three from the outset. Rather than choosing the mode for a given subject, he could search for subjects which were best fitted to the required modes. Then, the modes gave the opportunity, while the texts were the means of taking advantage of it. Another possibility is that he had a great number of madrigals already composed and that he chose only those that fitted the modal grid, an alternative wherein the subject comes first and the choice of mode follows. Finally, he could have begun by choosing the 17 poems and composed arbitrarily in the modes required to fill the quotas. This last possibility seems improbable because Rore was very concerned about musical expression and would not have neglected any recognized means of achieving it. In addition, with all the discussion about the ethos of modes carried out by Aron, Nardo, and Egnazio in Venice, where Rore worked in Willaert's shadow, he was not well placed to ignore this doctrine.[xvi]

Conclusions

Musical theorists during the Renaissance formed and mingled extra-musical associations for modes arising from different origins: from ancient Greek writings, from medieval writings about the plainsong repertoire and from their experience of listening to and composing polyphonic music. There was not enough material in these analogies to provide consistent guidance to composers. Furthermore, there wasn't a clear affective profile for modes as they were practiced in polyphonic composition. Differences between them, which could have been harnessed, were too subtle for even intelligent listeners and musicians to detect. Moreover, as theorists sometimes recognized, a good composer could contort any mode to serve his purpose.

The ethos of modes was a humanist fashion that came and went relatively quickly in the second half of the 16th century. The polyphonic style based on an extreme sensitivity to the text it served disappeared with it. The same humanist movement which made the ethos of modes *à la mode* also gave it its *coup de grâce* by invalidating the associations inspired by ancient tradition, thus depriving this doctrine of authority and leaving the way clear for a variety of ethico-musical coordinations in a disjointed network of associations.

Notes

i   French translation by Christine Jeanneret and English translation by Kristen Gray Jafflin.

ii   Matteo Nardo, undated letter, fragmentary copy. Città del Vaticano, Biblioteca Apostolica Vaticana, MS Vat. lat. 5385, f. 57$_v$.

iii For an English translation of del Lago's passage see HarràNewn (1973).

iv   *Micrologus* (ed. 1955 Jos. Smits van Waesberghe, American Institute of Musicology, ch. 15). Translation in Babb (1978, p. 69).

v   Boethius, Anicius Manlius Torquatus [Severinus], *De Institutione Musica*, bk 2 (ed. 1867 G. Friedlein, Leipzig, pp. 4.15–4.17). Translated and edited by Bower and Palisca (1989).

vi   Editors' note: between A above middle C and A2.

vii Hermannus Contractus in Elliwood (1952).

viii In Strunk (1950).

ix   Athenaeus, *Deipnosophistae*, 19.642d (cf. Michaelides 1978).

x   Reported in the Greek Lexicon by Suidas.

xi   For an English translation of the section on modes in book 4 see Beebe (1976, pp. 445–54).

xii For example, Gaffurius (1518, bk 4, ch. 5), Aron (1525, ch. 25), Nardo (f. 57$_v$, see note ii), Glarean (1547, bk II, ch. 23) and Finck (1556, f. R$_r$4$_r$x).

xiii The third part of Zarlino was translated in Marco and Palisca (1968) and the fourth in Cohen and Palisca (1983).

xiv See also Meier (1963).

xv   These two collections, *Primo libro a 5 voci*, 1542 and *Primo libro a 4 voci*, 1550, are analyzed with regards to key, the finale, and the mode by Owens (1986).

xvi For more on the value of the methods of Egnazio see Palisca (1985, pp. 343–5).

References

Abert, H. (1899). *Die Lehre vom Ethos in der griechischen Musik*. Leipzig: Breitkopf & Härtel.

Anderson, W. (1966). *Ethos and Education in Greek Music*. Cambridge, MA: Harvard University Press.

Affligemensis, J. (n.d.) *De Musica cum Tonario*, ch. 16. (Reprinted in: Smits van Waesberghe, Jos. (ed.) (1950). *Corpus Scriptorum de Musica 1*. Middleton, WI: American Institute of Musicology.)

Aron, P. (1525), *Trattato della Natura et Cognitione di tutti gli tuoni di Cantofigurato*. Venice. (Reprinted 1970, Bolgna: Forni.)

Babb, W. (transl.) (1978). *Hucbald, Guido, and John on Music: Three Medieaval Treatises*, with introductions by C. V. Palisca (New Haven: Yale University Press).

Beebe, E. S. (1976). *Mode, Structure, and Text Expression in the Motets of Jacobus Clemens non Papa: a Study of Style in Sacred Music*. PhD dissertation, Yale University.

Bermudo, J. (1555). *Declaración de Instrumentos Musicales*. Ossuna. (Reprinted 1957, Kassel: Bärenreiter.)

Chailley, J. (1965). *Alia Musica*, pp. 137–8, 198–9 [critical edition with commentary and an introduction on the original of pseudo-Greek modal nomenclature in the Middle Ages] (Paris: University of Paris Institute of Musicology).

Cohen, V. (ed.) (1983). *On the Modes*, with an introduction by C. V. Palisca. New Haven: Yale University Press.

Elliwood, L. (ed.) (1952) *Musica Hermanni Contracti*, ch. 8, p. 32 and ch. 20, p. 65. Eastman School of Music, University of Rochester, NY.

Finck, H. (1556). *Practica Musica*. Wittenberg. (Reprinted 1971, Hildesheim: Georg Olms Verlag.)

Gaffurio, F. [Gaffurius] (1496). *Practica Musicae*, bk 3, ch. 15. Milan. (Reprinted 1972, Bologna: Forni.)

Gaffurius (1518). *De Harmonia Musicorum Instrumentorum Opus*. Milan. (Translated by C. Miller, 1977. Middleton, WI: American Institute of Musicology.)

Glarean, H. (1547). *Dodekachordon*. Basel: H. Petri.

Haar, J. (1987). A case study in the use of mode: the *Capriccio* of Giachet Berchem (1561). Unpublished paper. Presented at conference on "Tonal Coherence in Pre-Tonal Polyphony, *c.* 1450–1650," Princeton University.

Harràn, D. (1973). The theorist Giovanni del Lago. *Musica Disciplina*, **27**, 107–51.

del Lago, G. (1540). *Breve Introduttione di Musica Misurata*, section 39. Venice. (Reprinted 1969, Bologna: Forni.)

Luoma, R. G. (1977). Relationships between music and poetry (Cipriano de Rore's "Quando signor lasci-aste"). *Musica Disciplina*, **31**, 135–54.

Marco, G. A. and Palisca, C. V. (1968). *The Art of Counterpoint*. New Haven: Yale University Press.

Mathiesen, T. J. (1983). *Aristides Quintilianus: on Music in Three Books* (translation, with introduction, commentary, and annotations), pp. 92–3. New Haven: Yale University Press.

Meier, B. (1963). Foreword on Cipriano de Rore. In B. Meier (ed.), *Opera Omnia*, vol. II *Madrigalia*, pp. III–IV. Middleton, WI: American Institute of Musicology.

Meier, B. (1974). *Die Tonarten der klassischen Vokalpolyphonie*. Utrecht: Oosthoek. (Translated 1988 by E. S. Beebe as *The Modes of Classical Vocal Polyphony*, with revisions by the author. New York: Boude Brothers)

Michaelides, S. (1978). Ethos. *The Music of Ancient Greece*, pp. 110–13. London: Faber and Faber.

Najock, D. (1972). Anonyme III 63–64. *Drei anonyme griechische Traktate über die Musik: eine kommentierte Neuausgabe des Bellermannschen Anonymus*, pp. 112–14. Kassel: Bärenreiter.

Owens, J. A. (1986). Modes in the madrigals of Cipriano de Rore. Paper presented a the 14th Annual Conference on Medieval and Renaissance Music, King's College. London, August 1986. (Published in Charteris, R. (ed.) (1990). *Altro Polo: Essays on Italian Music in the Cinquecento*. Sydney: Frederick May Foundation for Italian Studies.)

Palisca, C. V. (1985). *Humanism in Italian Renaissance Musical Thought*. New Haven: Yale University Press.

Powers, H. (1981). Tonal types and modal categories in Renaissance polyphony. *Journal of the American Musicological Society*, **34**, 428–70.

Ramos de Pareja, B. (1482). *Musica Practica*. Bologna. (Modern edition Wolf, J. (ed.) (1901) Leipzig: Publikationen der Internationalen Musikgesellschaft.)

Strunk, O. (1950). *Source Readings in Music History*, p. 45. New York: Norton.

Vicentino, N. (1555). *L'Antica Musica ridotta alla Moderna Prattica*. Rome. (Reprinted 1959, Kassel: Bärenreiter.)

de Zamora, J. A. (n.d.). *Ars Musica*. (Reprinted in: Robert-Tissot, M. (ed.) (1974) *Corpus Scriptorum de Musica 20*, ch. 15, pp. 100–105. Middleton, WI: American Institute of Musicology.)

Zarlino, G. (1558). *Le Istitutioni Harmoniche*. Venice. (Reprinted 1969, Bologna: Forni.)

Section 2

Emotion elicitation

Chapter 9

Section introduction

Klaus R. Scherer

The multiple ways in which music can express and represent emotions and other affective states, discussed in Section I, has been metaphorically referred to over the centuries as the "language of the emotions." The parallel notion that music can have strong effects on listeners and evoke or arouse different emotions has also been commented upon by scholars since time immemorial, often invoking a link between the representation of emotion in musical structure and the emotional effects of music. However, despite the ubiquity of the claim, and the number of strong opinions voiced in the literature (e.g. Hanslick 1854), attempts to render the issue amenable to scientific investigation have been few and far between. In the pioneering volume on music and emotion (Juslin and Sloboda 2001), Scherer and Zentner (2001) reviewed the field and proposed a systematic listing of the factors involved in the elicitation of emotion through music and the various "routes" by which this might occur. More recently, Juslin and Västfjäll (2008) have attempted to define some of these routes as concrete *mechanisms*, partly tied to underlying neural structures. The ensuing debate has been lively and has served to render the underlying issues salient for researchers in different disciplines. Three questions loom particularly large in this debate: What kinds of emotion are generally elicited or aroused by different kinds of music? What are the routes, principles, or mechanisms involved in this process? Does music evoke the emotions that it expresses or represents? This section of our volume on the emotional power of music provides an overview of current thinking and research in this area, testifying to the lively research activities that are currently ongoing.

In Chapter 10, Klaus Scherer and Eduardo Coutinho update the earlier overview by Scherer and Zentner (2001), providing a more detailed description of (and reviews of the literature on) the possible routes of musical emotion elicitation: (1) specific types of appraisal (such as novelty, unexpectedness, pleasantness), (2) music-related memory associations, (3) contagion and empathy, (4) entrainment and proprioceptive feedback, and (5) facilitation of preexisting emotions (disinhibition). They advocate a functional approach to understanding the determinants of, and processes underlying, the elicitation or induction of emotion through music by postulating production rules which imply complex interaction between many different factors such as musical structure, the interpreter's performance, the state of the listener, and a variety of contextual factors. The authors also address the issue of the kind of emotions generated by different kinds of music, contrasting music-elicited aesthetic and epistemic emotions with the utilitarian emotions of everyday life.

The subtlety and complexity of the processes involved jointly in the musical representation and elicitation of emotion is nicely illustrated by Luca Zoppelli's case study in Chapter 11 of fear-arousing features in Verdi's *Messa da Requiem*. The author advocates a multilayered perspective, postulating the simultaneous interaction of different systems of coding and perceived meaning at different biological and cultural levels (emotional coding, intrinsic meaning, and extrinsic symbolization) and proceeds to illustrate these processes by a minute analysis of the multiple ways in which Verdi skillfully uses the different coding principles in his piece. Importantly, Zoppelli also highlights the important role of musical traditions and historical listening attitudes in contextualizing the emotional effects.

Starting from the assumption that theories of emotion may have something to offer with respect to the issue under scrutiny, Jenefer Robinson in Chapter 12 provides a detailed review of three major theoretical traditions in psychology—appraisal theories, Frijda's action tendency theory, and embodied feeling theories based on William James. Her chapter applies the respective frameworks to the elicitation of emotion through music, particularly the nature of the emotional responses with respect to motivation and bodily reactions. In this process, she provides an important comparison with the views proposed by music theorists, such as Kivy and Nussbaum. Robinson concludes that each stage of the emotion process—appraisal, action readiness, feeling—has its own distinct mechanism for emotional arousal. Like many other authors in this section, she also highlights the effect of the proprioception of musically induced bodily changes.

Stephen Davies, the author of Chapter 13, has been a long-standing advocate of the notion that music elicits emotion through a process of emotional contagion. Concretely, he defines contagion as a sort of "mirroring" response—the listener is moved to feel the emotion that the music expresses. In his chapter Davies further develops this notion and contrasts it with various psychological theories of imitation or mimicry. Davies analyzes the important aspect of the object of a musically induced emotion. He forcefully argues that the music is not the emotional object of the response because the listener does not believe anything of the music that would make it the intentional object of a sad response, namely, that the music is unfortunate, suffering, or regrettable.

A much appreciated developmental perspective is contributed by Joel Krueger in Chapter 14 in his discussion of shared musical experiences, affording affectively powerful, and developmentally primitive, forms of empathic connectedness. Focusing on neonate music therapy, he suggests that shared musical experiences are often dynamic processes of joint sense-making (e.g. between infant and care-giver) through skilful engagement with music within a supportive environment. Krueger stresses the important role of the body which is actively utilized as an expressive vehicle from birth, suggesting that even the earliest encounters with music are simultaneously encounters with the lived body. The consequence is that music can train the listener to attend to the subtle rhythms and dynamic valences of affect and movement that constitute primitive forms of bodily self-experience, interwoven with the experience of being in relation to others.

The body, and in particular bodily action, also occupies center stage in Chapter 15 by Lincoln Colling and William Thompson. These authors argue that the emotional responses to music can be explained by viewing music listening as an embodied experience that engages sensory–motor processes. Their claim is based on the multimodal nature of music, reviewing extensive experimental evidence that mere observation of the actions that accompany music performance greatly influences our perception and interpretation of the acoustic dimension of music; the properties of the music that we hear. They propose a theoretical framework that views perception and action as inextricably linked, and suggest that music engages predictive sensory–motor processes in listeners and thus elicits emotional responses (providing a direct link to expectancy-based models of musical emotions).

The two final chapters in this section, while addressing the same general issues, stand apart in that they directly address the level of the neurophysiological underpinnings of the routes, principles, or mechanisms discussed in the earlier chapters. Adding this perspective brings in not only new methodologies for measuring the nature of emotional responses but also provides valuable contributions to the study of the processes involved in emotion elicitation through music. In Chapter 16 Wiebke Trost and Patrik Vuilleumier focus on rhythmic entrainment as an underlying mechanism for emotion induction and contagion by music. They hypothesize that, as most music is based on a metrical structure, music is likely to synchronize internal rhythms of brain and body to the periodicities that are present in the temporal structure of the music. Rhythmic entrainment processes are expected to occur at different levels, including the perceptual, the physiological, the motor, and the social level. The authors review evidence from neuroscience that the mere processing of timing features in the music (such as rhythms) can trigger specific neural processes, which contribute to the induction of certain emotional states as measured through self-reported feeling and physiological markers.

In Chapter 17 Stefan Koelsch focuses on different positive emotions induced by music listening, such as reward-related episodes of "having fun," feelings of gentle positive emotions, or strong pleasurable experiences such as "chills," and provides a comprehensive overview of the neurophysiological correlates of such affective experiences. He describes the two major brain systems that are involved in evoking these different types of emotion. The first of these (diencephalon-centered), commonly glossed as a "reward system," is implicated in the generation of pleasure/pain, experiences of reward/punishment, and the subjective feeling of attraction/aversion, a system that is of vital importance for the survival of the individual by preparing adaptive behaviors. The second system (hippocampus-centered) is hypothesized to be involved in the generation of attachment-related emotions, such as joy, happiness, tenderness, and love. The author reviews functional neuroimaging studies showing that the reward circuitry is activated by music that is perceived as pleasant and exciting by the listener, whereas the attachment-related regions tend to be activated upon listening to happy and sad music (possibly linked to the engagement of social functions that support communication and cooperation between humans).

The contributions by the authors represented in this section provide exciting new insights and hypotheses on the processes involved in the elicitation of many different kinds of emotion by many different kinds of music. There seems to be convergence towards the view that there are a fairly large number of routes, principles, or mechanisms (there is some hesitation as to how exactly to label this process of mediation) involved in the induction process and that these may often be operative simultaneously in an interactive fashion. Several authors also explicitly reject narrow determinism and acknowledge that individual differences and contextual factors play a major role. While many of the contributors to this section provide more detailed descriptions and justifications of the mechanisms they favor, in some cases with suggestions for experimental investigation, much remains to be done with respect to theoretical refinement of the specification of the underlying factors and processes and their empirical assessment. This is particularly the case for many of the body-centered mechanisms proposed as major protagonists in several chapters—entrainment, contagion, mimicry, or proprioceptive feedback. This is all the more the case as several authors insist that the descriptions or definitions that researchers in psychology have provided for the respective phenomena cannot be directly applied to elicitation of emotion by music. The same is true for the notion of empathic responding, for which, despite its great popularity in recent years, little agreement is to be found in the literature.

One of the central issues for further development is the question to what extent the type of emotions expressed or represented in the music (see Section I) determine the nature of the emotions aroused or elicited in the listener. Clearly, future advances on this important issue depends on a much higher degree of collaboration and exchange between scholars working on expression or representation on the one hand and those working on elicitation or emotional response on the other.

It will be important for the future discussion of these issues to overcome the tendency to separate processes in the mind (the "cognitive approach") and in the body (the "embodiment approach"). It is increasingly obvious, last but not least because of the advances in neuroscience research, that little is to be gained by such a distinction, as central and peripheral processes are essentially intertwined. It is worth noting that the pioneer of embodiment, William James, 10 years after his "revolutionary" redefinition of emotion stated that "The same bear may truly enough excite us to either fight or flight, according as he suggests an overpowering 'idea' of his killing us, or one of our killing him" (James 1894, p. 518), thus highlighting that the nature of the organic excitement, which he considered the central cause of emotional feeling, depends on the cognitive appraisal of the situation. Since then, as several of the chapters in Section II show, there has been a major advancement in our knowledge concerning the interactions between mental and bodily (or central and peripheral) factors in emotion.

Judging from the views expressed in different chapters, there is clear disagreement about the nature of the emotions evoked by music. Are they the same or very similar to everyday emotions or are they in some way special, given the way they are produced? Future discussion of this issue would benefit from clear distinctions with respect to several important variables such as: Do emotions elicited by listening to music differ from those aroused by playing music? What difference does it make if the listening or playing occur individually or in a group? What is the role of the genre of the music? Is it the musical content (e.g. structural features) or the occasion that evokes the emotion? Is music listening a goal (e.g. to relax) comparable to other goal-oriented activities (e.g. taking a drink to relax)? Finally, it may be helpful for further advancement of research on elicitation of emotion by music to agree on a convergent definition of "emotion" itself, given the massive variation one finds in the literature (see Mulligan & Scherer, 2012).

References

Hanslick, E. (1854). *Vom Musikalisch-Schönen* [The beautiful in music]. Leipzig: R. Weigel.

James, W. (1894). The physical basis of emotion. *Psychological Review*, **1**, 516–29.

Juslin, P. N. & Sloboda, J. A. (2001). *Handbook of Music and Emotion: Theory, Research, Applications*. New York : Oxford University Press.

Juslin, P. N., & Västfjäll, D. (2008). All emotions are not created equal: reaching beyond the traditional disputes. *Behavioral and Brain Sciences*, **31**, 600–12.

Mulligan, K. & Scherer, K. R. (2012). Toward a working definition of emotion. *Emotion Review*, **4**, 345–57.

Scherer, K. R. and Zentner, K. R. (2001) Emotional effects of music: production rules. In P. N. Juslin and J. A. Sloboda (eds), *Music and Emotion: Theory and Research*, pp. 361–92. Oxford: Oxford University Press.

Chapter 10

How music creates emotion: a multifactorial process approach

Klaus R. Scherer and Eduardo Coutinho

Introduction

As demonstrated by many of the chapters in this book, the intimate connections between emotions and music have multiple facets that have fascinated musicians, scientists, and listeners to music since the dawn of time. There are two major ways in which music and emotion are related. First, music *represents* (iconically, indexically, or symbolically; Peirce, 1868) emotion. This is why music is often called the "language of emotion," referring to the causal effect of emotion on music in the sense that composers integrate emotional elements into their scores, interpreters imbue their performances with emotional qualities, and listeners attribute emotional meaning to different parts of a piece of music. Second, music *creates* real, felt emotions. Here music plays a causal role in producing a specific mental and bodily process in the listener that is commonly called emotion.

A large corpus of literature has consistently reported that listeners often agree rather strongly about what type of emotion is expressed in a particular piece or even in particular moments or sections, thus forcefully suggesting the ability of music to convey emotional meaning (see reviews in Gabrielsson and Juslin 1996; Juslin and Laukka 2003; Juslin and Sloboda 2010). However, the perception of emotion in music is fundamentally a sensory and cognitive process that does not necessarily mirror what a listener is actually feeling. For instance, one does not necessarily become sad while listening to a sad-sounding piece of music. Indeed, emotions perceived (or expressed by the music) and felt by listeners may differ, and there is evidence that the relationships between perceived and felt emotions are manifold (Gabrielsson 2002). Whereas the emotions expressed in a piece of music seem to rely mostly on the arrangement of acoustic and musical features (Gabrielsson and Lindström 2010), the emotions experienced by listeners can be triggered by, and are a collective function of, many parameters, including the mood and psychological state of the listener, memories and other previous listening experiences, environmental and other situational aspects, individual preferences and attitudes, and cultural conventions, among others (Scherer and Zentner 2001).

In this chapter we primarily address the issue of *emotion induction*, explore how music produces emotions in listeners, and identify the major factors or determinants involved. In addressing these issues we first have to clarify what exactly an emotion is, as this is by no means universally agreed. Hence, we will first provide our view of the current convergence on this definitional issue. We will then explore the possibility that emotions may come in many forms rather than constituting a homogeneous type of human reaction. Here, we will propose that there may indeed be different types of affective reactions, of which true emotions are only one manifestation, and that even among those emotions there may be different types that are more or less conducive to musical elicitation. Then, we will propose an integrated framework that links the perception and cognition of music (and other associated objects and events) to the production of emotion by means of psychobiological pathways (*routes*) recruiting various subsystems of the central and autonomic nervous systems. We will show that this theoretical framework describes the nature and substrate of a wide range of emotional experiences with music, considering a variety of possible modulatory effects. We will also suggest that certain emotional experiences with music are emergent routes in our framework.

What is an emotion?

William James posed that question in 1884 and started a debate that is still ongoing. There are many definitions that have been proposed over the years and it almost seems as though every researcher is intent upon producing his or her own (see Scherer 2005). Here we adopt a position that represents a convergence on some of the major constitutive elements that seem to be required in order to diagnose the presence of an emotion.

Frijda and Scherer (2009) have summarized the constitutive features of a definition of emotion that seem to be shared by a majority of emotion theorists and researchers in different disciplines.

(1) Emotions are elicited when something relevant happens to the organism, having a direct bearing on its needs, goals, values, and general well-being. Relevance is determined by the appraisal of events with regard to a number of criteria, in particular the novelty or unexpectedness of a stimulus or event, its intrinsic pleasantness or unpleasantness, and its motivational consistency, i.e. its conduciveness to satisfy a need, reach a goal, or uphold a value, or its "obstructiveness" to achieving any of those (Scherer 2001; Ellsworth and Scherer 2003).

(2) Emotions prepare the organism to deal with important events in its life and thus have a strong motivational force, producing states of action readiness (Frijda 2007).

(3) Emotions engage the entire person urging action and/or imposing action suspension, and are consequently accompanied by preparatory tuning of the somato-visceral and motor systems. This means that emotions involve several components, subsystems of the organism that tend to cohere to a certain degree in emotion episodes, sometimes to the point of becoming highly synchronized (Scherer 2005).

(4) Emotions bestow control precedence (Frijda 2007) on those states of action readiness, in the sense of claiming (not always successfully) priority in the control of behavior and experience.

These elements of a definition of emotion are also constitutive for emotion episodes as described by the component process model (CPM) of emotion (Scherer 1984, 2001, 2009). The CPM focuses on the dynamic unfolding of an emotion in which emotion is defined as a "bounded episode in the life of an individual that is characterized as an emergent pattern of synchronization between changing states of different subsystems of the organism (the components of the emotion), preparing adaptive action tendencies to relevant events as defined by their behavioral meaning (as determined by recurrent appraisal processes) and thus having a powerful impact on behavior and experience" (see Scherer 2005, 2009). Figure 10.1 shows a graphic representation of the model in terms of the most important recursive causal relationships between the components.

The CPM suggests that an event and its consequences are appraised through a set of criteria (the appraisal components). This does not necessarily require a complex cognitive assessment, and can also occur in an automatic, unconscious, and effortless fashion. Leventhal and Scherer (1987) have suggested that the type of processing with respect to content (types of appraisal) and the level of processing (sensory–motor, schematic, and conceptual) is determined by the need for the evaluation to arrive at a conclusive result. The result of the appraisal will generally have

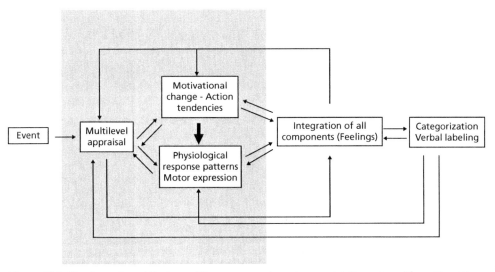

Figure 10.1 The dynamic architecture of the component process model. Reproduced from *Cognition and Emotion*, **23**(7), The dynamic architecture of emotion: evidence for the component process model, Klaus R. Scherer, pp. 1307–1351 © 2009, Taylor and Francis, reprinted by permission of the publisher, Taylor & Francis Ltd (<http://www.tandf.co.uk/journals>).

a motivational effect, often changing or modifying the motivational state that existed before the event occurred. Based on the appraisal results and the simultaneous changes in motivation, there will be effects in the autonomic nervous system (e.g. in the form of cardiovascular and respiratory changes) and in the somatic nervous system (in the form of motor expression in face, voice, and body). All of these components—appraisal results, action tendencies, somato-visceral changes, and motor expressions—are centrally represented and constantly fused in a multimodal integration area (with continuous updating as events and appraisals change).

Parts of this centrally integrated representation may then become conscious and subject to assignment to fuzzy emotion categories which may then lead to labeling with emotion words, expressions, or metaphors. The feeling component could also be instrumental in language and music since it allows the organism to regulate and adjust its communication depending on its own emotional experience, which in turn can reflect that of others. For this to occur, subjective experience needs to integrate and centrally represent all information about the continuous patterns of change of the components and their coherence with other components, especially if it is to serve a monitoring function.

Figure 10.2 shows a Venn diagram in which a set of overlapping circles represents the different aspects of feeling. The first circle (A) represents the sheer reflection or representation of changes in all synchronized components in some form of monitoring structure in the central nervous system. The second circle (B), which only partially overlaps with the first, represents that part of the integrated central representation that becomes conscious. This circle corresponds most directly to what is more generally called "feelings" or *qualia*. Scherer has suggested that the degree of synchronization of the components (which might in turn be determined by the pertinence of the event as appraised by the organism) generates awareness (Scherer 2005; see also Grandjean *et al.* 2008). Circle C represents the categorization and verbalization (labeling) of feelings (for example in social sharing of emotional experiences).

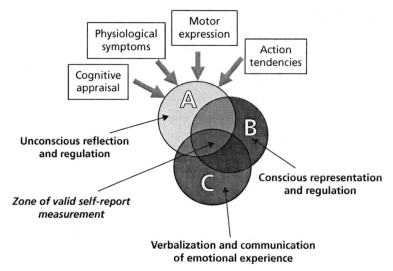

Figure 10.2 The reflection of component emotion processes in a monitor system.

Past definitions of emotion, as well as the CPM model of the emotion process described above, tend to emphasize the adaptive reactions to relevant events, often stressing physical survival and well-being, as in the case of "basic emotions." To be able to describe certain musical experiences as emotional, we need to broaden this definition and consider emotions as adaptations at various levels with different types of relevance, as determined by goals such as experiencing pleasure, regulating arousal, or engaging in social bonding. Such a broader definition of the functions and response patterns of emotion is entirely compatible with the CPM and most other componential emotion theories. For the sake of ecological validity, we must first identify the types of emotional experiences that pertain to music, because it is fundamental to understand these in order to interpret musical emotions, relate them to psychophysiological processes, and integrate them within a general framework of emotion.

The types of emotion elicited by music

In much of the literature it is been tacitly assumed that music elicits the general set of so-called "garden variety" basic emotions. Recently, Juslin and Västfjäll (2008) have attempted to lend credence to this belief by arguing that music-evoked emotions are indistinguishable from other emotions in both their nature and underlying mechanisms, and that music just induces some emotions more frequently than others. Several of those who have discussed their article (Madison 2008; Malmgren 2008; Moors and Kuppens 2008; Robinson 2008; Scherer and Zentner 2008; Vuust and Frith 2008) have taken issue with this claim. The central problem is that the mechanisms involved in elicitation of emotion are ubiquitous, and that many phenomena are produced by an interaction of multiple determinants, and by different mechanisms at different times. In consequence, the fact that some mechanisms are shared by different emotion manifestations cannot be interpreted to mean that all of these belong to the same class. To use a concrete example from another domain, the fact that printing presses are used to produce books, magazines, and newspapers does not mean that all these products are indistinguishable because the production process is comparable.

In trying to disentangle the types of emotional experiences conveyed by music, it is fundamental to start by considering the potential differences between different kinds of affect. To this end, Scherer (2005) has suggested using design feature analysis (Hockett 1960) to distinguish different types of affective phenomena: preferences, emotions, moods, interpersonal stances, attitudes, and personality traits. The design features used to distinguish these different classes of affective states are based on the constitutive elements of the CPM (described in the previous section). Table 10.1 (adapted from Table 2 in Scherer 2005) shows the proposed classification of the different states based on the extent to which the relative importance of certain design features are constitutive to label an affective state by the respective term.

It should be noted in passing that music can be expected to elicit simple preference responses (e.g. to like or not like the music), moods (e.g. music inducing a pensive mood), or interpersonal stances (e.g. music inducing tender feelings toward others). These effects will not be discussed here; rather, we focus on emotional responses, and particularly on the three subclasses shown in Table 10.1—utilitarian, aesthetic, and epistemic emotions.

Utilitarian emotions are most often studied in emotion research—for example the "basic emotions" of anger, fear, disgust, and sadness. These are utilitarian in the sense of having major functions in the adaptation and adjustment of individuals to events that have important consequences for their physical survival and well-being by preparing action tendencies (fight, flight) and recovery and reorientation (grief, work). But emotions can also serve many other important functions such as social bonding (joy, compassion), enhancement of motivation (pleasure, pride), social obligations and reparation (shame or guilt), among others. Such utilitarian emotions tend to engender relatively high-intensity reactions, often involving a synchronization of many subsystems, including changes in the endocrine, hormonal, and autonomic nervous systems as well as in the somatic nervous system, which are driven by the appraisals in the central nervous system. Some of these utilitarian emotions can also be elicited or modulated through music, such as communal singing and dancing, preparation for fighting, or ritual purposes (see Lewis, 2013).

We suggest that a major difference between utilitarian emotions on the one hand and aesthetic and epistemic emotions on the other is the fact that appraisals concerning goal relevance and coping potential involve different criteria (such as different goals and coping mechanisms) in aesthetic or epistemic emotions compared with utilitarian ones. In other words, an aesthetic or epistemic emotional experience is not triggered by concerns with the immediate relevance of an event for one's survival or well-being, nor with how well one can cope with the situation. Rather, the appreciation of the intrinsic qualities of a piece of visual art or a piece of music, or the degree of discovery or insight one achieves through novel and complex stimulation in different modalities, is of paramount importance. This corresponds in many ways to Kant's well-known definition of aesthetic experience as "*interesseloses Wohlgefallen*" (disinterested pleasure; Kant 1790/2001), a definition which insists on the need for a complete absence of utilitarian considerations.

The apparent absence of direct personal relevance in aesthetic or epistemic emotions does not mean that they are completely disembodied. Indeed, we know that music (but also other forms of art) produces physiological and behavioral changes (see Hodges 2010 and Västfjäll 2010 for reviews). It should be emphasized though that these changes typically seem to serve behavioral readiness (Frijda 1986), particularly with respect to attention, sharpening of sensory perception, and arousal regulation (stimulation versus relaxation) rather than fight/flight reactions. Thus they are not proactive but rather diffusely reactive. For example, the most commonly reported bodily symptoms for intense aesthetic experiences are goose pimples, shivers, tingling in the spine, or moist eyes—all rather diffuse responses which do not serve any obvious adaptive purposes—which

Table 10.1 Design feature differentiation of different types of affective phenomena. Adapted from *Social Science Information*, 44(4), Scherer, K. R., What are emotions? And how can they be measured? pp. 693–727, table 2 © 2005, Sage Publications, with permission.

Type of affective state: brief definition (examples)	Design features								
	Intensity	Duration	Synchronization	Event focus	Intrinsic appraisal	Transactional appraisal	Rapidity of change	Behavioral impact	Prob. of music elicitation
Preferences: evaluative judgments of stimuli in the sense of liking or disliking, or preferring or not over another stimulus (*like, dislike, positive, negative*)	L	M	VL	VH	VH	M	VL	M	H
Utilitarian emotions: relatively brief episodes of synchronized response of all or most organismal subsystems in response to the evaluation of an external or internal event as being of major significance for personal goals/needs (*angry, sad, joyful, fearful, ashamed, proud, elated, desperate*)	H	L	VH	VH	M	VH	VH	VH	H
Aesthetic emotions: evaluations of auditory or visual stimuli in terms of intrinsic qualities of form or relationship of elements (*moved, awed, full of wonder, admiration, feelings of harmony, rapture, solemnity*)	L-M	L	M	H	VH	L	H	L	VH
Epistemic emotions: evaluations of auditory or visual stimuli in terms of their information content and contribution to knowledge or insight (*surprised, feelings of interest, insight, discovery; enthusiastic, fascinated, bored*)	L-M	L	L-M	H	L	L	H	M	VH
Moods: diffuse affect states, most pronounced as change in subjective feeling, of low intensity but relatively long duration, often without apparent cause (*cheerful, gloomy, irritable, listless, depressed, buoyant*)	M	H	L	L	M	L	H	H	M
Interpersonal stances: affective stance taken toward another person in a specific interaction, coloring the interpersonal exchange in that situation (*distant, cold, warm, supportive, contemptuous*)	M	M	L	H	L	L	VH	H	L
Attitudes: relatively enduring, affectively colored beliefs and predispositions towards objects or persons (*loving, hating, valuing, desiring*)	M	H	VL	VL	L	L	L	L	M
Personality traits: emotionally laden, stable personality dispositions and behavior tendencies, typical for a person (*nervous, anxious, reckless, morose, hostile, envious, jealous*)	L	VH	VL	VL	L	VL	VL	L	L

VL, very low; L, low; M, medium; H, high; VH, very high.

Table 10.2 Mean ratings of importance for different determinants of emotional reaction. Reproduced from Scherer, K. R., Zentner, M. R., & Schacht, A., Emotional states generated by music: A exploratory study of music experts. Musicae Scientiae. The Journal of the European Society for the Cognitive Sciences of Music (Special issue), pp. 149–171 (c) 2002, Sage Publications, with permission.

	Total	**Classical**	**Non-classical**
Other	4.54	4.38	4.67
Musical structure	3.88	**4.53**	**3.36**
Acoustic features	3.82	3.58	4.00
Interpretation	3.45	3.47	3.44
Technical quality	3.08	3.34	2.88
Listener's mood	2.88	2.70	3.02
Affective involvement	2.88	2.92	2.85
Context factors	2.67	2.35	2.92
Personality	2.46	2.14	2.71

Significant difference ($t = 10.73$, $P = 0.002$) indicated in bold.

contrast strongly with the arousal and action-oriented responses for many basic emotions that prepare for emergency reactions.

Following this rationale, our group has empirically studied with what frequency different emotion words indexing the different categories are reported by music listeners. Based on extensive empirical work (identifying which labels listeners to different kinds of music prefer to use to refer to their emotional experiences) we have demonstrated the need for a domain-specific approach to assessing emotional experiences and have developed and validated the Geneva Emotional Music Scale (GEMS), consisting of nine scales: wonder, transcendence, tenderness, nostalgia, peacefulness, power, joyful activation, tension, and sadness (Zentner *et al.* 2008). In a study in which listeners evaluated their emotional reactions to a set of standard musical stimuli in the laboratory and in a free listening task in their homes, using basic emotion scales, dimensional ratings, and the GEMS, we could show that listeners preferred the GEMS, that they agreed more on their judgments on the GEMS, and that the GEMS ratings more successfully discriminated the musical excerpts There is now copious empirical evidence that the listening to music is likely to generate more frequently and more consistently the types of emotions that can often be glossed as aesthetic in comparison to basic (see Sloboda 2010; Zentner and Eerola 2010), and current studies using the GEMS consistently support the underlying rationale (e.g. Miu and Baltes 2012; Trost *et al.* 2012).

We continue to develop appropriate measurement tools based on the notion of domain-specific emotion labels, particularly short forms of the GEMS (see Zentner and Eerola 2010, p. 206) that can be used economically in different field settings. It is important to note that even though Zentner *et al.* (2008) could show satisfactory validity of the GEMS for several music genres (specifically classical, jazz, rock, and pop music in different contexts), we cannot assume that the nine scales of the GEMS exhaust all relevant dimensions. For example, using a short form of the GEMS at a festival for contemporary music (which originally contained nine categories corresponding to the GEMS with three adjectives each), we found that it was essential to add scales covering the domain of the epistemic emotions as listener often added labels, such as "feelings of interest and discovery" or "insight," in the space provided for additional comments following the regular scale.

We concluded that one needs to include more epistemic knowledge and insight-related emotions to study the emotional effect of music and we are currently developing a new, expanded rating instrument to be used in naturalistic settings (Coutinho and Scherer 2012).

The effort of distinguishing between different classes of affective states, and further identifying different types of emotion, does not imply that we postulate sharp and reliable boundaries between these classes. On the contrary, we expect that there are very fuzzy boundaries and we have to consider this domain as consisting of a multidimensional space rather than one of sharply defined categories. In addition, the meaning of the respective emotion words for the respective classes (see Table 10.1) are difficult to define and are multiply interrelated (see Fontaine *et al.*, 2013, on the semantics of emotion terms). We also acknowledge that music can produce various types of emotions. Nevertheless, as past work in this area has almost exclusively focused on a small set of basic emotions (applied indiscriminately in music studies), here we highlight the preponderance of those emotions that are aesthetic (and also epistemic) in character (i.e. in cases where appreciation of intrinsic qualities is a determining factor). Aesthetic and epistemic emotional responses to music are in urgent need of further examination, because it is fundamental to understand the nature of the wide variety of emotional responses to music in order to establish the relevance of music for the individual and to assert its power to elicit emotions. We do not exclude, however, that music may in certain circumstances produce utilitarian emotions. Music might produce sadness, fear, and anger in certain cases. However, one cannot be sure that these have the same quality as the sadness, fear, and anger produced by the loss a loved one, a bear coming towards us, or being insulted. Also, we do not consider that aesthetic emotions are limited to music (they are equally found in the visual and dramatic arts). In fact, there is empirical evidence that emotions relating to nostalgia, love, wonder, and transcendence are experienced equally often in non-musical everyday life contexts as in musical contexts (Zentner *et al.* 2008, p. 515).

From musical experiences to emotion: a functional account

We now turn to the process of elicitation of emotion in the listener. Our starting point is the effort of Scherer and Zentner (2001) to identify the *production rules* that underlie the induction of emotion through music; they argue that generally there is an interaction between a multitude of factors in the production of emotional effect distinguishing structural (e.g. tones, intervals, chords, melodies, fugues), performance (e.g. physical appearance, expression, technical and interpretative skills, current affective and motivational state), listener (e.g. musical expertise, stable dispositions, current motivational and mood state), and context (e.g. location and event) features. It is suggested that these features can, individually or in combination, produce the different affective states described above, assuming a multiplicative interaction function between features, such as:

experienced emotion = effect of structural features × performance features × listener

features × contextual features (see Scherer and Zentner 2001 for further details).

Our group conducted a study with music experts (Scherer, Zentner and Schacht 2002) examining the relative importance of some of these determinants and the potentially underlying production rules for both classical and non-classical music. Musical structure was given the highest rating of the list of determinants based on the production rules, but technical, acoustic, and interpretational features also received high ratings (see Table 10.2). It is interesting to note that the experts mentioned many other factors, like listener personality or motivation, that could not be subsumed to one of the above classes and show up as "Other" in the table, demonstrating the need to extend the model.

In the rest of this chapter we will develop this model further. We divide our presentation into three main parts. First we will discuss the role of music structure in the elicitation of emotion. Then we will identify relevant aspects related to the listening context and briefly exemplify how they modulate and sometimes determine the emotional experience. Finally, we will identify and describe the main routes (and mechanisms involved) whereby emotions may actually be produced by music. It should be stressed that due to space restrictions we will mainly focus on contemporary music activities, such as concerts and individual listening, with a strong emphasis on music as a means to achieve some sort of emotional experience. Nevertheless, we will also touch upon various other everyday musical activities (which are of many types) and contextualize them within our framework.

Music structural features

Earlier, we discussed the types of emotions that music is often likely to induce. Here, we will briefly discuss how music structure contributes to (and may drive) those experiences.

Music structural features encompass a range of aspects that describe the music signal. At the most basic level, the music (as an acoustic signal) is encoded as an auditory signal. At this level music is mapped onto a new domain which preserves relevant features of its structure for further analysis, but various invariant properties related to microstructural organization are immediately conveyed. The basic auditory perceptual attributes involved in music perception are loudness, pitch, contour, rhythm, tempo, timbre, spatial location, and reverberation. While listening to music, our brains continuously organize these dimensions according to different *Gestalten* and psychological schemas. Most of the time, the percept reflects the properties of the music's acoustic objects and events very accurately, but the transduction process involves various transformations involving innate as well as culturally determined processes. Some of these schemas involve further neural computations on extracted features which give rise to higher-order musical dimensions (e.g. meter, key, melody, harmony), reflecting (contextual) hierarchies, intervals, and regularities between the different structural elements. Others involve continuous predictions about what will come next in the music as a means of tracking structure and conveying meaning, both through *Gestalt* and learned expectations (Meyer 1956; Huron 2006). Furthermore, the development of mental schemata reflecting musical and socio-cultural (implicit and explicit) knowledge of some sort (e.g. through music training or exposure to a particular music culture or subculture) also plays a critical role in music perception, cognition, and emotion.

In sum, music structural features range from microstructural properties of the acoustic signal that very closely describe the features of the emanating source and surrounding environment to a much higher level of structural organization and abstraction, which can convey, for instance, form and style. By attending to the structural aspects of the acoustic signal at these various levels, listeners construe emotional meaning and, although the way that different levels interact is still largely unknown, there is evidence of specific structural cues and patterns communicating similar emotions to all listeners (see Gabrielsson and Lindström 2010 for an in-depth review). There is also convincing evidence that music can express emotions that are recognized universally, a phenomenon that is also associated with acoustic profiles which transcend all cultural boundaries (Balkwill and Thompson 1999; Balkwill *et al.* 2004; Fritz *et al.* 2009).

Interestingly, the most consistent relationships between musical structure and emotional qualities pertain to the effects of basic variables in human audition, such as loudness and timbre, and motion (e.g. tempo). Concerning higher levels of music perception and cognitive structure retrieval, their expressive power seems to be more complex and dependent on the musical context (i.e. other structural factors). Furthermore, it is important to mention that there is now converging evidence that points to the existence of acoustic profiles common to the expression of emotion in both speech and music, with particular acoustic codes consistently associated with particular categories (Juslin and Laukka 2003; Ilie and Thompson 2006, 2011) and dimensions (Coutinho and Dibben 2010, 2012) of emotion. These and other studies provide a strong basis on which to purport the existence of a general mechanism for the expression and recognition of emotions in the acoustic domain (Scherer, 2013).

In addition to acoustic-related features it is also fundamental to mention, if only briefly, that music can also convey meaning in other sensory modalities. Indeed, music structure can also convey meaning outside the auditory domain, for example visuo-spatial and motor (Eitan and Granot 2006; Chapter 15 this volume), as well as tactile (Eitan and Rothschild 2010) metaphors. Such cross-modal interactions in the perception of music can have a strong influence on emotional responses to music, by conveying emotional meaning across multiple modalities which can lead to more intense and multifaceted emotional experiences. For that, some sort of invariant perceptual quality must be obtained from the acoustic signal or some aspects of music itself convey some sort of indexical meaning (e.g. sound movement can index a spatio-temporal representation of a gesture; rhythm and tension can also generate indexical sound gestures priming specific targets in the music).

Lastly, it should be mentioned that music-related cues are not the only sensory and perceptual inputs with an impact on the emotional state of the listener in a given circumstance. Other inputs, and particularly visual ones, which have an impact on the emotional response are mentioned throughout this chapter at various moments since they become relevant for the description and operation of some of the routes (and when concomitant with music). Nonetheless, because our focus is music as the object of emotion, we restricted ourselves here to the identification of pertinent levels of interaction between music structure and the emotions of the listener.

The listening context

We identify three main groups of features related to the listening context that may affect listeners' emotional responses to the music at various levels: performance features, listener (or individual) features, and contextual features. In the context of our framework, all these features may have, directly or indirectly, an influence on the emotions produced by music in a particular listener or group of listeners. As will be shown, these features have a modulatory effect not only on the emotional experience itself but most importantly on the actual routes of emotion production. Thus, in certain circumstances, cues related to the listening context may determine the nature of an emotional experiences or even block it, and, as we will also see, many of these features may have similar effects across listeners, thus also leading to stereotyped responses.

Performance features

Performance features include two distinct, although intertwined, dimensions, both with a major impact on the perception and induction of emotion. One is intrinsic to the aural experience and corresponds to the way in which a piece of music is executed by a singer and/or one or more instrumentalists. Cues of tempo, dynamics, timing, timbre, and articulation are amongst the most important acoustic building blocks used by performers as a means of achieving emotional expression (e.g. Juslin and Timmers 2010). The second dimension refers to the effects of iconic, indexical, and symbolic information communicated during the performance. It includes the stable identity (physical appearance, expression, reputation) and ability (technical and interpretative skills) of the performer as well as transient performance-related variables, which we will call the performance state (interpretation, concentration, motivation, mood) and performance manners (body movements, gestures, stage presence, audience contact, etc.) (e.g. Huang and Krumhansl 2011). All these aspects, isolated or in combination, directly or indirectly, and in the context or a particular listening situation, affect the emotional experiences of a musical performance.

Listener features

The individual and socio-cultural identity of the listener and the symbolic coding convention prevalent in a particular culture or subculture are also fundamental modulatory cues in emotional experiences with music. These features can be summarized into musical expertise, including cultural expectations about musical meaning, and stable dispositions (related or unrelated to music). Musical expertise includes those musical capacities acquired through exposure to music with or without the help of explicit training. It should be noticed that the capacities derived from "implicit" exposure achieve very high levels of sophistication, such that they enable untrained listeners to respond to music as explicitly trained listeners do (Bigand and Poulin-Charronnat 2006). Nevertheless, explicit training can alter listeners' emotional experiences by priming the understanding of the musical structure in various ways and through an awareness of details in the music that impact their emotions (even at the level of brain function, e.g. Dellacherie *et al.* 2011).

Stable dispositions refer to individual differences in age (e.g. motivational and selective neuropsychological decline) and gender, in memory (including learned associations and conditioning; see Jäncke 2008), in inference dispositions based on personality (e.g. Rusting and Larsen 1997), socio-cultural factors (e.g. Basabe *et al.* 2000), prior experiences (e.g. Bigand and Poulin-Charronnat 2006), physiological reactivity (Penman and Becker 2009), coherence between emotional experience and physiology (e.g. Sze *et al.* 2010), among others. In addition, transient listener states such as motivational state, concentration, or mood may also affect emotional inference from the music (cf. Cantor and Zillmann 1973). Stable dispositions are also intertwined with exposure to particular music systems (and thus sensitivity to performance features and emotional communication). Although listeners across cultures seem to be capable of decoding emotional meaning from unknown musical systems (e.g. Fritz *et al.* 2009), exposure to a particular system and familiarity with the style or a particular piece seem to be determining factors in shaping the level of sensitivity (e.g. Daynes 2010).

Contextual features

By contextual features, we refer to certain aspects of the performance and/or listening situation. The location of a performance and/or a listening situation may be a concert hall, church, party, street, car, or home. The dominant material surrounding the listener/performer may be wood, glass, stone, metal, or none. In addition to the location, the particular event may be a wedding, a funeral, a ball, or the celebration of an outstanding achievement. The music may be transmitted through loudspeakers, headphones, or without any technical support. The music may be heard without interruption or the sirens of an ambulance or the coughing of a concert visitor may disturb it. We submit that all these features can have an influence on the acoustics, the ambience of the location, or the behavior of the audience, which in turn may lead to different emotional effects due to objective features of the situation or subjective perceptions of the listeners.

Routes

With this initial formalization of the output (emotions), the input variables (structural features), and mediating factors (performance-, listener-, and context-related) involved in emotional responses to music, we can now inquire into particular ways by which emotion may be generated by music. Given the diverse nature of these, Scherer and Zentner (2001) called these *routes* and provided a number of examples: I1) specific types of appraisal (such as novelty, unexpectedness, pleasantness), (2) music-related memory associations, (3) contagion, and empathy, (4) entrainment and proprioceptive feedback, and (5) facilitation of pre-existing emotions (disinhibition). The term *routes* was chosen to emphasize the assumption that only major pathways through the cognitive and emotional systems involved can be traced, with each of these recruiting a large number of neural and somatic structures and many different mechanisms in terms of the underlying machinery.

More recently, Juslin and Västfjäll (2008) have suggested a list of "mechanisms" which is quite reminiscent of the list of routes proposed by Scherer and Zentner (2001), except for the notable lack of the appraisal route. These authors consider a revised version of this proposal as a unified theoretical framework called BRECVEM (see also Juslin *et al.* 2010) which is an acronym for brainstem reflex, rhythmic entrainment, evaluative conditioning, contagion, visual imagery, episodic memory, and musical expectancy. Three of these mechanisms can be subsumed under the appraisal route described by Scherer and Zentner: brainstem reflex as a low-level novelty and intrinsic pleasantness check; evaluative conditioning is the precondition for creating valenced associations for many types of appraisal; and musical expectancy corresponds to what is described as part of the discrepancy of expectation check. Episodic memory is covered under the memory mechanism, as is visual imagery in the form of memory-dependent constructive imagination. Empathy and emotional contagion cover Juslin and colleagues' contagion mechanism, but go much beyond this single mechanism. Rhythmic entrainment was covered under proprioceptive feedback, which also contains mechanisms lacking in BRECVEM (which does not cover the facilitation emotion route).

While the review of the literature provided in Juslin and Västfjäll (2008) is useful, the status of the proposal as a "unified theoretical framework" is dubious. It is doubtful whether the seven mechanisms listed are an exhaustive set of possible or even likely mechanisms (e.g. brainstem reflexes). The "mechanism status" of several entries in the list is unclear if one applies Marr's (1982) distinction between three levels of function—the computational, the algorithmic, and the implementational levels. For example, contagion seems to operate on the computational level, evaluative conditioning on the algorithmic level, and brainstem reflexes on the implementational level. Thus, the proposed mechanisms seem to be situated on different levels of function. Furthermore, as multiple mechanisms are likely to operate in many cases, a unified framework would require a discussion of potential interaction. The complete absence of multilevel appraisal as a central mechanism underlying several of the phenomena discussed, in particular musical expectancies, is also difficult to understand. And it seems unfortunate that the appraisal of goal conduciveness in the framework of music listening motivation (covered by several chapters in Juslin and Sloboda 2010) is completely neglected. In spite of these problems, the renewed emphasis on the mechanisms underlying the emotional power of music is to be greatly encouraged as it is essential to conduct more theory-guided research, using appropriate experimental paradigms, to elucidate at least some of the many open questions.

Here, we extend and reformulate the suggestions made by Scherer and Zentner (2001) in an attempt to systematize the proposal and illustrate the suggestions with concrete examples. The following subsections describe the major routes or pathways underlying the production of emotions in listeners. In order to tie these routes to the emotion architecture proposed by the CPM, we will use Figure 10.3, an extension of Figure 10.1, to illustrate the major routes, as identified by the bold arrows in the figure labeled from A to E. In addition we will illustrate the concrete mechanisms that might be recruited for specific routes. Concretely, we postulate five major routes: A, appraisal; B, memory; C, entrainment; D, emotional contagion; and E, empathy.

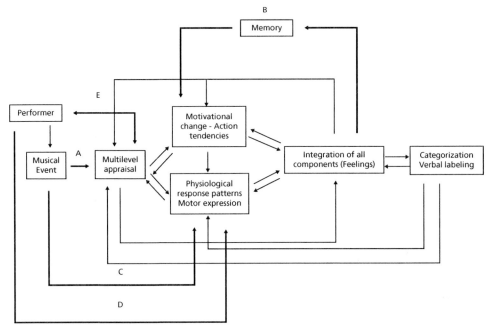

Figure 10.3 Adaptation of Figure 10.1 to musical events. Adapted from Cognition and Emotion, 23 (7), The dynamic architecture of emotion: Evidence for the component process model, Klaus R. Scherer, pp. 1307–1351 (c) 2009, Taylor and Francis, reprinted by permission of the publisher (Taylor & Francis Ltd, http://www.tandf.co.uk/journals).

Appraisal (route A)

Given that the term "appraisal" is now used, in some form or function, by almost all emotion theorists (Moors and Scherer, in press), there seems to be convergence about the central role of appraisal in the emotion process. It is thus to be expected that the mechanisms described by emotion psychologists may also be applicable to the study of induction of emotion via music. Indeed, appraisal seems to have a pervasive role in emotional induction through music—on the one hand because music structure percepts and representations must be evaluated at some point for their emotional meaning and/or relevance to the individual and on the other because appraisal is central to the process of emotional induction by continuously driving and coordinating activity on the various subcomponents of emotion.

As outlined in the description of the CPM, the appraisal process may occur in a rudimentary, automatic fashion at lower levels of the central nervous system (mostly the limbic system, including the brainstem), especially for evolutionarily "prepared" stimuli, or in a series of more elaborate and effortful processes involving the higher regions of the central nervous system. Indeed, music structural features can trigger low-level emotional appraisals by means of innate detection mechanisms of relevant affective information. For instance, considering the link between vocal and musical expression of emotion mentioned earlier (see p. 130), it is plausible to assume that musical stimuli that share the acoustic characteristics of, for instance, fear vocalizations (sudden onset, high pitch, wide range, strong energy in the high-frequency range) may be appraised by the evolutionarily low-level but extremely powerful detection systems and may provoke physiological defense responses in a similar way to pictures of spiders or facial expressions of fear (see Vuilleumier 2005). It should be also noted that similar automatic evaluation processes can occur for auditory stimuli that are not themselves evolutionarily prepared but that have been conditioned to such stimuli by occurring repeatedly at the same time (LeDoux 1996).

Similar low-level detection mechanisms can be demonstrated for the appraisal criteria of suddenness/novelty and intrinsic pleasantness (see Scherer 2009). There is some evidence that musical sounds can generate strong suddenness/novelty (particularly for evolutionarily prepared stimuli as discussed later) and, in particular, intrinsic evaluations of pleasantness. A good example is perceived roughness, and particularly sensory dissonance. For instance, studies of infants' perception of music show a preferential bias favoring consonance over dissonance as early as 4 months, suggesting that the human infant might possess a biological preparedness that makes consonance more attractive than dissonance (Zentner and Kagan 1996, 1998).

Appraisals of music structure can occur at the various structural levels outlined in the section "Music structural features," (p. 129) although the object and context of such evaluations is not always clear. An interesting possibility that has not been much explored in the psychology of emotion so far is that, either as a part of intrinsic detection of importance or as a separate mechanism, there may be an automatic evaluation of aesthetic qualities. Thus, it could be that there are some universal criteria of beauty that are evaluated automatically on the basis of visual and auditory stimulation and give rise to an affective response. Such a prepared aesthetic response has been postulated for landscape preferences, a claim which has found some empirical support (Kaplan and Kaplan 1989).

Turning now to the operationalization of appraisal, including higher-level appraisals, we will provide some examples of how the different appraisal checks briefly outlined in our description of the CPM model can apply to the generation of emotion in listening to music, grouped by the major aims of appraisal. It should be noticed, nevertheless, that due to the generality of appraisal checks, they apply to musical and non-musical objects. Hence, the various checks have different levels of predominance in musical and non-musical contexts which is also related to the fact that different types of goals may be involved (sometimes even dependent on the music activity itself). Future work should explore the extent to which the various appraisals checks may be weighted differently for music during the integration of top-down processes providing contextual information that alter the contribution of a particular check of an appraisal. In addition, new checks, eventually not preponderant for non-musical stimuli, such as domain-specific musical expectations, may play an important role in music appraisal.

The first group of checks evaluates the *relevance* of the sensory input. A stimulus event is considered as requiring attention deployment, further information processing, and potential action. Three subchecks are involved:

- *Novelty*: Here we can distinguish three further subchecks: suddenness, familiarity, and predictability. All three of these are highly pertinent to music. As mentioned above, very abrupt onset of sound, sharp attack of the amplitude and pitch envelopes, and sudden tone shifts (processed at the automatic level) can produce strong emotional effects through low-level appraisal. As we have already emphasized, familiarity has a strong impact on the listener's emotional experiences. To appraise familiarity we need to proceed to pattern matching with stored schemata and/or association-based processing, a process strongly modulated by the listener's musical background. This is turn is linked to predictability. For instance, there is evidence for increasing anticipation of emotional events with familiarity (Daynes 2010), and musical sounds conforming to the Western system of harmony are more predictable to Western listeners than Asian music systems (Balkwill *et al.* 2004).

- *Intrinsic pleasantness*: This is a central aspect of musical emotions and it is often processed at the automatic level (e.g. consonance and dissonance). But there can also be other levels of processing involved—for example, the conscious determination of whether a particular musical structure corresponds to a classic ideal of beauty or the result of repetitive exposure to particular music pieces, genres, and cultures.

- *Goal relevance*: Does the event have consequences for my needs or goals? For aesthetic emotions, where the main goal of the activity is, at least in part, the experience of certain positive emotions or at least bittersweet emotions, an important consequence might be whether I will really enjoy the music and experience one of the coveted emotions. Or else it could be a quest for new experience, to gain insight or acquire knowledge (the epistemic emotions). Nevertheless, the pervasiveness of music in everyday life and its concomitance with various physical and cognitive tasks points out other levels of relevance in engaging in musical activities. Furthermore, music is known to support and powerfully modulate cognition as well as to regulate arousal and emotion, and thus pleasure and emotional regulation can also be goal states (e.g. to pass the time, keep awake, achieve the desired level of arousal).

The second group of checks concerns *implications*. Following attention deployment, the pertinent characteristics of the stimulus event and its implications or consequences for the organism are determined. There are four subchecks that evaluate this criterion:

- *Outcome probability*: How likely is it that the desired consequences will occur? For a familiar piece of music this may depend on the performer, for an unknown piece this might be an important criterion for some emotions to occur (e.g. boredom). For the purpose of emotional regulation, a pervasive use of music, it may depend on the achievement of a target emotional state.

- *Discrepancy from expectation*: How different is the situation from what I expected it to be? This check is extremely important for music processing as it ties in directly into the central issue of musical expectancies, which has been one of the earliest music-related appraisals highlighted by the pioneering work of Leonard Meyer (1956) on emotional meaning. Importantly, the appraisal of the discrepancy of temporal or melodic expectancies can occur at a microlevel, within phrases, or in much larger time frames. The operation of the expectancy check has been copiously studied and there is now a large amount of literature on the topic (e.g. Huron 2006; Lerdahl and Krumhansl 2007; Patel 2008). The inputs to this check are not only low-level proximal cues but also the results of various hierarchical neural computations applied to those. These provide crucial information about the stimulus at different levels of music perception and cognition, making use of innate and acquired mappings and models. These processes are strongly mediated by individual factors such as, familiarity, exposure, and expertise (e.g. Daynes 2010).

- *Conduciveness*: Is the event conducive or obstructive to reaching my goals? This is of course determined by the goals underlying the choice of listening to music or by the present goals of an individual when hearing music was not a choice. In both cases this subcheck is central for the outcome—in music as for all other types of stimulations or events.

- *Urgency*: How urgently do I need to react? This appraisal is important for utilitarian emotions but unlikely to play a major role in listening to music, especially as the time frame for the listening experience is generally well circumscribed.

The third group of checks concerns coping potential. Once the nature of the event and the consequences are known sufficiently well, the organism checks its ability to cope with the consequences to be expected:

- *Agent and intention*: Who was responsible for a particular expected consequence and what was the reason? The most important factor in the case of listening to music is probably the decision about whether it is the composer, the performer, or oneself as a listener who is responsible, for example for expectancy violations or goal obstruction consequences. An important qualification is the estimation of whether this is due to competence, effort, or intentionality.

- *Control*: Can the event or its consequences be controlled by human agents? *Power*—do I have sufficient power to exert control if possible? *Adjustment*—if control is impossible, how well can I adjust to the consequences? All of these checks are unlikely to play a major role in passive listening as the control and power relationships are pretty much mapped out for ritual occasions of music listening. However, one interesting factor for the resulting emotion might be if one can stop the music or easily move out of earshot. In the case of active practice of music in a social context this may well be a rather important factor. It should be stressed that music can lead to undesirable effects that are much stronger than mere displeasure. Some physical effects (e.g. raised blood pressure and stress hormones) may be hard to deal with for some listeners, and, although rare, unwanted loud music can even trigger seizures among some people with epilepsy. Control is certainly a fundamental subcheck in these situations.

The fourth and final group of checks concerns *normative significance*, the overall assessment of the event with respect to its compatibility with one's self-concept, and values on the one hand and the dominant social-norms, and moral rules on the other. The evaluation of the compatibility of a stimulus event with external standards (norms, cultural values) and internal standards (personal values) as part of the appraisal process is highly relevant for the elicitation of emotion via music. There seem to be prescriptions specific to culture and/or historical periods as to what is aesthetically pleasing, beautiful, and even what is to be rejected as a violation of 'good taste' (Farnsworth 1969; Kenyon 1991; see also Lynxwiler and Gay 2000 for an interesting recent example). Throughout musical history, the criterion of social norms or standards has been involved in powerful emotional reactions towards 'modern' music, which was seen as violating established standards of morality and decency. The well-known scandal provoked by the première of Igor Stravinsky's dissonant and polyrhythmic *Sacre du printemps* or that of Edgar Varèse's surreal *Deserts*, both in Paris, are just two particularly drastic examples of strong emotional reactions to the perceived disregard of established standards. In relation to one's values and musical identity, it is important to mention the use of music as a means and source for developing individual identities, to conform to a particular group, or to society in general. Obviously, the role of other society members plays a fundamental part in this process, but also the way that we define ourselves in relation to music (e.g. Hargreaves *et al.* 2002).

Memory associations (route B)

Memory is fundamental for music. Auditory signals unfold over time, thus it is necessary to keep track of ongoing information to coherently construct multidimensional perceptual objects from sequentially ordered sounds. This is a process in which the working memory plays a major role, as in speech processing. In terms of their involvement in routes of elicitation of emotion, there are two particularly important memory mechanisms to be mentioned: episodic and associative. Episodic memory permits specific (strong) emotional reactions that an individual has experienced in the past to resurge in memory, spontaneously or triggered by a specific cue or evoked due to an instruction to vividly imagine the event (Blaney 1986; Christianson 1992). Expressive and physiological reaction patterns to emotion-inducing events are likely to be stored in the memory together with the experiential content (Lang 1979; LeDoux 1996). Music, like smell, seems to be a very powerful cue for bringing emotional experiences from episodic memory back into awareness. This is not surprising, for two reasons. Firstly, music is quite a pervasive element of social life and accompanies many highly significant events in an individual's life, such as religious ceremonies, marriage, burial rites, dancing, and other festivities, etc. Thus, there are many associations between musical elements and emotionally charged memories. Second, music, again like smell, may be treated at lower levels of the brain that are particularly resistant to modifications by later input (e.g. LeDoux 1996). There may be other aspects of the memory system involved in this route, for example perceptual and semantic memory, which we cannot cover here for lack of space.

By means of associative memory, in addition to straight recall of events or objects from the past, it is possible to associate and combine elements of memory to construct scenarios or visual images and auditory impressions via the imagination. It is often claimed that recall of past emotional experiences from memory and imagination can evoke similar emotional reactions to the original experience. The empirical evidence for such memory-induced resurgence of expressive and physiological reactions is still scarce (see review by Jäncke 2008).

Entrainment (route C)

Music is likely to produce emotion states through a route that is independent of appraisal or memory—via a direct influence on the peripheral nervous system and spread to other emotion components. One potential candidate for such influence is *entrainment via rhythm*. We all know the contagious effects of strong musical rhythms, at least on susceptible individuals who find it difficult not to move their heads or their legs in unison with the rhythm (e.g. in the case of dance rhythms, marches, or techno beat; see also Zentner and Eerola 2010). Recent evidence suggests that such coupling of internal rhythms to external movements, as originally described by Byers (1976), might be present already at a very early age (Rochat and Striano 1999). If there is indeed a fundamental tendency for synchronization of internal biophysiological oscillators to external auditory rhythms (entrainment), such coupling may provide a promising explanation for the emotion-inducing effects of music (see Bispham 2006; Fitch 2012).

As discussed earlier, an internal or external object or event can lead to the activation of various response systems including the autonomic and somatic nervous systems. But the opposite can also happen, that is, the state of the response systems can also become the event that triggers an emotional episode. Currently, neurobiological models of emotion recognize not only the importance of higher neural systems on visceral activity (top-down influences) but also influences in the opposite direction (bottom-up) (see Berntson *et al.* 2003 for an overview). While the top-down influences allow cognitive and emotional states to match the appropriate somato-visceral substrate, the bottom-up ones serve to bias emotion and cognition towards a desired state (e.g. guiding behavioral choice; Bechara *et al.* 2003).

An important aspect of physiological activation is its interaction with other components of emotion. Indeed, physiological activation can also affect the subjective feeling of an emotion, a process known as peripheral feedback. Its role as a mechanism for generating emotion from music is based on the idea that the emotion system consists of integrated components and that the system as a whole can be activated by manipulating the patterning of one of its components, that is, it can have multiple initiation points (see Ekman *et al.* 1983). The general idea is also consistent with proprioceptive feedback theories (e.g. facial feedback; McIntosh 1996) which claim, in their strong form, that subjective feeling can be produced or, in their weak form, enhanced or intensified, by increased or uninhibited motor expression (see also Laird 2007). In the context of music, Dibben (2004) investigated the role of physiological arousal in determining the intensity and hedonic value of the emotion experienced while listening to music. Results show that the group of participants with induced physiological arousal reported "feeling" more intense emotions than those without, providing strong evidence that physiological arousal influences the intensity of emotion experienced with music. Furthermore, Coutinho and Cangelosi (2011) have suggested that consideration of peripheral physiological activity in addition to proximal cues can improve the accuracy of prediction of subjective feelings of emotion in response to music.

Emotional contagion (route D)

In the case of the routes involving the mechanisms and processes described above (appraisal- and memory-mediated routes), we focused mainly on elicitation of emotion based on the processing of intrinsic proximal cues, i.e. those inherently psycho-acoustic. However, as mentioned, emotional reactions can be elicited by direct effects of extrinsic cues which can be derived from the aural stimulus itself (e.g. audio-tactile metaphors, images of motion) as well as from externally observed cues of emotional expression in others (e.g. body movements, facial expressions). One somewhat speculative but interesting possibility is that mirror nervous system mechanisms might be involved (Overy and Molar-Szakacs 2009).

As an example, we can be infected by the joy of others at a successful party, the essential feature here being the observation of the motor expressions of the persons concerned. The assumption is that the mere observation of strong motor expressions can produce similar muscular reactions in ourselves, a process generally called "motor mimicry;" this has been at the center of a theory of emotional inference suggested by the German philosopher and psychologist Lipps (1909). He argued that our understanding of the emotions of others occurs through *Einfühlung* (a term for which "empathy" is not quite the correct translation), based on our mimicking, at least in a rudimentary fashion, the expressive patterns we see in the other (i.e. a contagion, at least of the expressive movement). This process may occur in quite an unconscious fashion, simply by observing and possibly internally mimicking the expressive movements. In this case, one would experience similar emotions to the observed models (or at least change our experiences towards those models). In the case of a musician performing a musical piece, there is evidence that the expressive movements and practice methods of the performer(s) lead to emotional contagion, and may even influence the perception of music structure (e.g. Vines *et al.* 2011).

In Chapter 13 Davies proposes that:

> [...] music is expressive because we experience it as presenting the kind of carriage, gait, or demeanor that can be symptomatic of states such as happiness, sadness, anger, sassy sexuality, and so on. If contagion operates through mimicry, we might expect the listener to adopt bodily postures and attitudes (or posturally relevant muscular proprioceptions) like those apparent in the music's progress. Vocal mimicry, in the form of subtle tensing or flexing of vocal muscles, would also be a predictable response to vocal music or to acts of subvocal singing along with instrumental music. And where the flux of music is felt as an articulated pattern of tensing and relaxing, this is likely to be imaged and mimed within the body, perhaps in ways that are neither subpostural nor subvocal.

Juslin and Laukka (2003), having established a large degree of overlap in the acoustic cues indexing emotions in speech and music, suggest that musical instruments may serve as "superexpressive voices" and that this may produce empathy or contagion with an imaginary speaker. However, it remains to be established whether a detour via vocal imagery is necessary for contagion or whether the iconic character of the specific acoustic patterns for certain types of emotions is sufficient. In general, even for facial mimicry, which has been very frequently studied in recent years, the precise mechanisms have not yet been established with precision, and much more work on the vocal/acoustic domain remains to be done in this respect.

Empathy (route E)

Emotions can also be elicited by observing another person being affected by an event that is very important to him/her but not necessarily to oneself. Through *empathy* we have feelings of concern for other people, we experience the emotions that others feel, and we "know" what others are thinking and what one would expect to feel in a particular situation. Such a socio-emotional competence is crucial in human interactions (e.g. mother–child bonding) because it smudges the line between self and other (Decety and Svetlova 2012). Thus, the process of empathy is different from simple contagion (which can work through expression only) in that the observer has to put him/herself into the shoes of the observed and simulate the latter's motivation and appraisal processes; this helps us to understand the other person's emotion and feel compassion.

In the case of music, empathy is particularly important in live performances and in social listening settings (e.g. parties) and, as in the case of emotional contagion, non-musical cues play an essential role. For instance, emotional responses may be mediated by empathy through an understanding of the performers' (or other listeners') emotional states, as well as their possible relation to imaginary events or underlying "ideas." Naturally this process is concomitant with the perception of emotional expressions and music structure, and thus the emotional contagion and appraisal routes, with which may interact in multiple ways. Interestingly, music-induced emotions (including physiological arousal) are also generally affected by manipulations of empathy towards the performers (Miu and Baltes 2012) and by individual differences on empathy scores (Wöllner 2012). It is also worth noticing that empathy may facilitate the induction of negative emotions (Vuoskoski and Thompson 2012).

Conclusion and outlook

In this chapter we have attempted to review possible answers to the question of how music creates emotions in listeners. We have emphasized that a precondition for answering this question is to agree on the nature of the reaction of a listener to piece of music that one wants to qualify as *emotional*. We have acknowledged that music can evoke many different affective states, including preferences and moods. However, we focused on a more constrained definition of properly emotional reactions to music as based on convergent definitions in the current literature and using Scherer's CPM of emotion as a guide. Importantly, we have suggested differentiating between three fuzzy sets (as there may be multiple blending) of emotions—utilitarian, aesthetic, and epistemic. These classes differ in the nature and importance of the eliciting objects and events, the central appraisal criteria involved, and the nature of the response patterns in the different components. We submit that this distinction is useful for promoting empirical research on the induction of emotion by music as it not only provides a theoretical framework, generating concrete hypotheses to be tested, but also informs the development of research tools such as scales for the assessment of self-reported emotional reactions (as we have shown using the example of the development of the GEMS and its offshoots).

The bulk of the chapter presented an extension and further development of a theoretical framework proposed by Scherer and Zentner in 2001. Starting from the notion that research on induction of emotion by music should focus on music characteristics, more precisely the musical structure and performance variables, we also accounted for the modulation of these central effects through factors related to characteristics and states of the listener as well as a host of contextual features.

We mostly illustrated the types of factors by providing examples, as restricted space did not allow us to review the pertinent work in this area in a comprehensive fashion. We feel that such a review would be timely, especially if it were to adopt a systematic theoretical organization that could help to encourage research designs that do not focus on single factors but attempt to examine multifactorial interactions.

In particular we aimed to extend and enrich the discussion on the precise mechanisms that are involved in the process of the elicitation of emotion through music. We tried to demonstrate that the mechanisms underlying the production of emotion through music are various and ubiquitous. Furthermore, we have tried to show that these mechanisms can be recruited (in various combinations) at several levels of the emotion induction process. Hence, the process of induction of emotion through music is better operationalized as routes, that is, psychobiological pathways recruiting various subsystems of the central and autonomic nervous systems. In this way, it is possible to describe the nature and substrate of eclectic emotional responses to music, and the variety of possible modulatory effects that pertain to particular or all mechanisms.

Routes also relate to the nature and function (implicit or explicit) of the various musical activities. For instance, music can be used as a source of emotional experience or a means for emotional regulation, and in this case most routes described are likely to be implied in one way or another. But emotional experiences with music also exist (and are at the base of some of its uses) in the context of cognitive enhancement or physical recovery, and not only when listening to music is at the very center of the listener's goals. In these cases, it is more likely that other ongoing processes, appraisals, and the background emotion state have an impact on the listener.

We also emphasize that, in this chapter, we have only discussed the production of emotions where there were none before, although the enhancement of existing emotions has been touched upon. However, emotions induced by music are not absolute phenomena, and they largely depend on the listener's ongoing processes and appraisals. Thus, emotional responses to music can be blocked or potentiated by factors extraneous to the music or situation but nevertheless of relevance to the listener. This seems to be a natural consequence of emotion mechanisms being shared by musical and non-musical stimuli. Another potential effect of listening to emotionally arousing music can be the weakening or the elimination of control or regulation over emotional expression. Due to socio-cultural display and feeling rules, or because of strategic considerations, emotional reactions are often highly controlled or regulated, both with respect to motor expression and subjective feeling.

It is to be hoped that the recent theoretical activity, including critical debate, concerning the issue of induction of emotion by music and the underlying mechanisms will help to generate empirical research to test and validate some of the major assumptions proposed here and in other work on the topic. Given the theoretical framework that we have proposed here, one of the major preconditions for successful research ventures in this area would seem to consist in the development of methods that allow us to determine, using objective criteria, whether or not an emotional process, as defined by the synchronization of response patterns in different components, is indeed occurring. While verbal self-report of emotional experiences, the most frequently used dependent variable in this research, remains a major means of access to processes internal to the listener, it should be complemented, whenever possible, by other indicators of appropriate response patterns such as motor expressions (facial, postural) or neurophysiological responses. In addition to allowing a more comprehensive assessment of a listener's reactions, the latter behavioral indicators have the advantage of allowing continuous measurement—and thus the possibility of closely aligning them with the dynamic changes in musical structure.

As mentioned at the outset, the emotional effects of music have fascinated scholars for the last two millennia. As we have seen, there are no simple answers given the huge number of factors involved and their intricate interactions. But the explosive development of research activities in this area, the progress being made in both theory and methodology, and in particular, the nascent tendency of composers, performers, and an informed part of the public to interact with researchers, promise to further our understanding of the emotional power of music in the near future.

References

Balkwill, L.-L. and Thompson, W. F. (1999). A cross-cultural investigation of the perception of emotion in music: psychophysical and cultural cues. *Music Perception*, **17**, 43–64.

Balkwill, L.-L., Thompson, W. F., and Matsunaga, R. (2004). Recognition of emotion in Japanese, Western, and Hindustani music by Japanese listeners. *Japanese Psychological Research*, **46**, 337–49 [special issue "Cognition and emotion in music"].

Basabe, N., Paez, D., Valencia, J., Rime, B., Pennebaker, J., Diener, E., and Gonzalez, J. L. (2000). Sociocultural factors predicting subjective experience of emotion : a collective level analysis 1. *Psicothema*, **12**, 55–69.

Bechara, A., Damasio, H., and Damasio, A. (2003). The role of the amygdala in decision-making. *Annals of the New York Academy of Sciences*, **985**, 356–69.

Berntson, G. G., Sarter, M., and Cacioppo, J. T. (2003). Ascending visceral regulation of cortical affective information processing. *European Journal of Neuroscience*, **18**, 2103–9.

Bigand, E. and Poulin-Charronnat, B. (2006). Are we "experienced listeners"? A review of the musical capacities that do not depend on formal musical training. *Cognition*, **100**, 100–30.

Bispham, J. C. (2006). Rhythm in music: What is it? Who has it? And Why? *Music Perception*, **24**, 125–34.

Blaney, P. H. (1986). Affect and memory: a review. *Psychological Bulletin*, **99**, 229–46.

Byers, P. (1976). Biological rhythms as information channels in interpersonal communication behavior. In P. P. G. Bateson and P. H. Klopfer (eds), *Perspectives in Ethology*, vol. 2, pp. 135–64. New York: Plenum.

Cantor, J. R. and Zillmann, D. (1973). The effects of affective state and emotional arousal on music appreciation. *Journal of General Psychology*, **89**, 79–108.

Christianson, S. A. (ed.) (1992). *The Handbook of Emotion and Memory: Research and Theory*. Mahwah, NJ: Lawrence Erlbaum Associates.

Coutinho, E. and Cangelosi, A. (2011). Musical emotions: predicting second-by-second subjective feelings of emotion from low-level psychoacoustic features and physiological measurements. *Emotion*, **11**, 921–37.

Coutinho, E. and Dibben, N. (2010). Music, speech and emotion: psycho-physiological and computational investigations. In R. Timmers and N. Dibben (eds), *Proceedings of the International Conference on Interdisciplinary Musicology: Nature versus Culture (CIM '10)*, pp. 47–8). Sheffield: University of Sheffield.

Coutinho, E. and Dibben, N. (2012). Psychoacoustic cues to emotion in speech prosody and music. *Cognition and Emotion*, doi: 10.1080/02699931.2012.732559

Coutinho, E. and Scherer, K. R. (2012). Towards a brief domain-specific self-report scale for the rapid assessment of musically induced emotions. *Proceedings of the 12th International Conference of Music Perception and Cognition (ICMPC12)*, Thessaloniki, Greece. Available at: <http://icmpc-escom2012.web.auth.gr/sites/default/files/papers/229_Proc.pdf>

Daynes, H. (2010). Listeners' perceptual and emotional responses to tonal and atonal music. *Psychology of Music*, **39**, 468–502.

Decety, J. and Svetlova, M. (2012). Putting together phylogenetic and ontogenetic perspectives on empathy. *Developmental Cognitive Neuroscience*, **2**, 1–24.

Dellacherie, D., Roy, M., Hugueville, L., Peretz, I., and Samson, S. (2011). The effect of musical experience on emotional self-reports and psychophysiological responses to dissonance. *Psychophysiology*, **48**, 337–49.

Dibben, N. (2004). The role of peripheral feedback in emotional experience with music. *Music Perception*, **22**, 79–115.

Eitan, Z. and Granot, R. (2006). How music moves: musical parameters and listeners' images of motion. *Music Perception*, **23**, 221–47.

Eitan, Z. and Rothschild, I. (2010). How music touches: musical parameters and listeners' audio-tactile metaphorical mappings. *Psychology of Music*, **39**, 449–67.

Ekman, P., Levenson, R. W., and Friesen, W. V. (1983). Autonomic nervous system activity distinguishes among emotions. *Science*, **221**, 1208–10.

Ellsworth, P. C. and Scherer K. R. (2003). Appraisal processes in emotion. In R. J. Davidson, H. Goldsmith, and K. R. Scherer (eds). *Handbook of the Affective Sciences*, pp. 572–95. New York: Oxford University Press.

Farnsworth, P. R. (1969). *The Social Psychology of Music*, 2nd edn. Ames, IA: Iowa State University Press.

Fitch, W. T. (2012). The biology and evolution of rhythm: unraveling a paradox. In P. Rebuschat, M. Rohrmeier, J. Hawkins, and I. Cross (eds), *Language and Music as Cognitive Systems*, pp. 73–95. Oxford: Oxford University Press.

Fontaine, J. R. F., Scherer, K. R., and Soriano, C. (2013). *Components of Emotional Meaning: a Sourcebook*. Oxford: Oxford University Press.

Frijda, N. H. (1986). *The Emotions*. Cambridge: Cambridge University Press.

Frijda, N. H. (2007). *The Laws of Emotion*. Mahwah, NJ: Lawrence Erlbaum Associates.

Frijda, N. H. and Scherer, K. R. (2009). Emotion definition (psychological perspectives). In D. Sander and K. R. Scherer (eds), *Oxford Companion to Emotion and the Affective Sciences*, pp. 142–3. Oxford: Oxford University Press.

Fritz, T., Jentschke, S., Gosselin, N., Friederici, A. D., and Koelsch, S. (2009). Universal recognition of three basic emotions in music. *Current Biology*, **19**, 573–6.

Gabrielsson, A. (2002) Emotion perceived and emotion felt: same or different? *Musicae Scientiae*, Special Issue 2001–2002, 49–71.

Gabrielsson, A. and Juslin, P. N. (1996). Emotional expression in music performance: between the performer's intention and the listener's experience. *Psychology of Music*, **24**, 68–91.

Gabrielsson, A. and Lindstrom, E. (2010). The role of structure in the musical expression of emotions. In P. N. Juslin and J. Sloboda (eds), *Handbook of Music and Emotion: Theory, Research, Applications*, pp. 367–400. Oxford: Oxford University Press.

Grandjean, D., Sander, D., and Scherer, K. R. (2008). Conscious emotional experience emerges as a function of multilevel, appraisal-driven response synchronization. *Consciousness and Cognition*, **17**, 484–95.

Hargreaves, D. J., Miell, D., and MacDonald, R. A. R. (2002). What are musical identities, and why are they important? In R. A. R. MacDonald, D. J. Hargreaves, and D. E. Miell (eds), *Musical Identities*, pp. 1–21. Oxford: Oxford University Press.

Hockett, C. F. (1960). The origin of speech. *Scientific American*, **203**, 88–96.

Hodges, D. A. (2010). Psychophysiological measures. In P. N. Juslin and J. A. Sloboda (eds), *Handbook of Music and Emotion: Theory, Research, Applications*, pp. 279–312. New York: Oxford University Press.

Huang, J. and Krumhansl, C. L. (2011). What does seeing the performer add? It depends on musical style, amount of stage behavior, and audience expertise. *Musicae Scientiae*, **15**, 343–64.

Huron, D. (2006). *Sweet Anticipation: Music and the Psychology of Expectation*. Cambridge, MA: MIT Press.

Ilie, G. and Thompson, W. F. (2006). A comparison of acoustic cues in music and speech for three dimensions of affect. *Music Perception*, **23**, 319–29.

Ilie, G. and Thompson, W. F. (2011). Experiential and cognitive changes following seven minutes exposure to music and speech. *Music Perception*, **28**, 247–64.

James, W. (1884). What is an emotion? *Mind*, **9**, 188–205. [Reprinted in Arnold M. B. (ed.) (1968). *The Nature of Emotion: Selected Readings*, pp. 17–36. Harmondsworth: Penguin.]

Jäncke, L. (2008). Music, memory and emotion. *Journal of Biology*, **7**. doi: 10.1186/jbiol82

Juslin, P. N. and Laukka, P. (2003). Communication of emotions in vocal expression and music performance: different channels, same code? *Psychological Bulletin*, **129**, 770–814.

Juslin, P. N. and Sloboda, J. A. (eds) (2010). *Handbook of Music and Emotion: Theory, Research, Applications*. New York: Oxford University Press.

Juslin, P. N. and Timmers, R. (2010). Expression and communication of emotion in music performance. In P. N. Juslin and J. A. Sloboda (eds), *Handbook of Music and Emotion: Theory, Research, Applications*, pp. 453–89. New York: Oxford University Press.

Juslin, P. N. and Västfjäll, D. (2008). All emotions are not created equal: reaching beyond the traditional disputes. *Behavioral and Brain Sciences*, **31**, 600–12.

Juslin, P. N., Liljeström, S., Västfjäll, D., and Lundqvist, L.-O. (2010). How does music evoke emotions? Exploring the underlying mechanisms. In P. N. Juslin and J. A. Sloboda (eds), *Handbook of Music and Emotion: Theory, Research, Applications*, pp. 605–42. New York: Oxford University Press.

Kant, I. (1790/2001) *Kritik der Urteilskraft*. Hamburg: Meiner.

Kaplan, R. and Kaplan, S. (1989). *The Experience of Nature: a Psychological Perspective*. Cambridge: Cambridge University Press.

Kenyon, N. (ed.) (1991). *Authenticity and Early Music*. Oxford: Oxford University Press.

Laird, J. D. (2007) *Feelings: the Perception of Self*. New York: Oxford University Press.

Lang, P. J. (1979). A bio-informational theory of emotional imagery. *Psychophysiology*, **16**, 495–512.

Lang, P. J., Kozal, M. J., Miller, G.A., Levin, D. N., and MacLean, A. (1980). Emotional imagery: conceptual structure and pattern of somato-visceral response. *Psychophysiology*, **17**, 179–92.

LeDoux, J. E. (1996). *The Emotional Brain*. New York: Simon and Schuster.

Lerdahl, F. and Krumhansl, C. (2007). Modeling tonal tension. *Music Perception*, **24**, 329–66.

Leventhal, H. and Scherer, K. R. (1987). The relationship of emotion to cognition: A functional approach to a semantic controversy. *Cognition and Emotion*, **1**, 3–28.

Lewis, J. (2013). An anthropological perspective on music, dance, narrative. In M. A. Arbib (ed.), *Language, Music and the Brain: a Mysterious Relationship*. Cambridge, MA: MIT Press.

Lipps, Th. (1909). *Leitfaden der Psychologie*. [Primer of Psychology]. Leipzig: Engelmann.

Lynxwiler, J. and Gay, D. (2000). Moral boundaries and deviant music: public attitudes toward heavy metal and rap. *Deviant Behavior*, **21**, 63–85.

Madison, G. (2008). What about the music? Music-specific functions must be considered in order to explain reactions to music. *Behavioral and Brain Sciences*, **31**, 587.

Malmgren, H. (2008). Identifying and individuating the psychological mechanisms that underlie musical emotions. *Behavioral and Brain Sciences*, **31**, 587–8.

Marr, D. (1982): *Vision. A Computational Investigation into the Human Representation and Processing of Visual Information*. San Francisco: W. H. Freeman and Company.

McIntosh, D. N. (1996). Facial feedback hypotheses: evidence, implications, and directions. *Motivation and Emotion*, **20**, 121–47.

Meyer, L. B. (1956). *Emotion and Meaning in Music*. Chicago, IL: University of Chicago Press.

Miu, A. C. and Baltes, F. R. (2012). Empathy manipulation impacts music-induced emotions: a psychophysiological study on opera. *PLoS ONE*, **7**(1): e30618. doi: 10.1371/journal.pone.0030618

Moors, A. and Kuppens, P. (2008). Distinguishing between two types of musical emotions and reconsidering the role of appraisal. *Behavioral and Brain Sciences*, **31**, 588–9.

Moors, A. and Scherer, K. R. (2013). The role of appraisal in emotion. In M. Robinson, E. Watkins, and E. Harmon-Jones (eds), *Handbook of Cognition and Emotion, pp. 135–155*. New York: Guilford.

Overy K. and Molar-Szakacs I. (2009). Being together in time: musical experience and the mirror neuron system. *Music Perception,* **26,** 489–504.

Patel, A. (2008). *Music, Language, and the Brain.* Oxford: Oxford University Press.

Peirce, C. S. (1868). On a new list of categories. *Proceedings of the American Academy of Arts and Sciences,* **7,** 287–98 [presented 14 May 1867]. Reprinted in *Collected Papers,* vol. 1, paras 545–59; *Writings of Charles S. Peirce: a Chronological Edition,* vol. 2, pp. 49–59; *The Essential Peirce,* vol. 1, pp. 1–10. Arisbe Eprint.

Penman, J. and Becker, J. (2009). Religious ecstatics, "deep listeners," and musical emotion. *Empirical Musicology Review,* **4**(2), 49–70.

Robinson, J. (2008). Do all musical emotions have the music itself as their intentional object? *Behavioral and Brain Sciences,* **31,** 592–3.

Rochat, P. and Striano, T. (1999). Emerging self-exploration by 2-month-old infants. *Developmental Science,* **2,** 206–18.

Rusting, C. L. and Larsen, R. J. (1997). Extraversion, neuroticism, and susceptibility to positive and negative affect: a test of two theoretical models. *Personality and Individual Differences,* **22,** 607–12.

Scherer, K. R. (1984). On the nature and function of emotion: a component process approach. In K. R. Scherer and P. E. Ekman (eds), *Approaches to Emotion,* pp. 293–317. Hillsdale, NJ: Lawrence Erlbaum Associates.

Scherer, K. R. (2001). Appraisal considered as a process of multilevel sequential checking. In K. R. Scherer, A. Schorr, and T. Johnstone (eds), *Appraisal Processes in Emotion: Theory, Methods, Research,* pp. 92–120. New York: Oxford University Press.

Scherer, K. R. (2005). What are emotions? And how can they be measured? *Social Science Information,* **44,** 693–727.

Scherer, K. R. (2009). The dynamic architecture of emotion: evidence for the component process model. *Cognition and Emotion,* **23,** 1307–51.

Scherer, K. R. (2012). Neuroscience findings are consistent with appraisal theories of emotion. But does the brain "respect" constructionism? *Behavioral and Brain Sciences,* **35,** 163–4.

Scherer, K. R. (2013). Emotion in action, interaction, music, and speech. In M. A. Arbib (ed.), *Language, Music and the Brain: a Mysterious Relationship.* Cambridge, MA: MIT Press.

Scherer, K. R. and Zentner, M. (2001) Emotional effects of music: production rules. In P. N. Juslin and J. A. Sloboda (eds), *Music and Emotion: Theory and Research,* pp. 361–92. Oxford: Oxford University Press.

Scherer, K. R. and Zentner, M. (2008). Music evoked emotions are different–more often aesthetic than utilitarian. *Behavioral and Brain Sciences,* **31,** 595–6.

Scherer, K. R., Zentner, M. R., & Schacht, A. (2002). Emotional states generated by music: A exploratory study of music experts. *Musicae Scientiae. The Journal of the European Society for the Cognitive Sciences of Music, (Special issue),* 149–171.

Sloboda, J. A. (2010). Music in everyday life: the role of emotions. In P. Juslin and J. Sloboda (eds), *Handbook of Music and Emotion: Theory, Research, Applications,* pp. 493–514. New York: Oxford University Press.

Sze, J. A., Gyurak, A., Yuan, J. W., and Levenson, R. W. (2010). Coherence between emotional experience and physiology: does body awareness training have an impact? *Emotion,* **10,** 803–14.

Trost, W., Ethofer, T., Zentner, M., and Vuilleumier, P. (2012). Mapping aesthetic musical emotions in the brain. *Cerebral Cortex,* **22,** 2769–83.

Vastfjall, D. (2010). Indirect perceptual, cognitive, and behavioural measures. In P. Juslin and J. Sloboda (eds), *Handbook of Music and Emotion: Theory, Research, Applications,* pp. 255–78. New York: Oxford University Press.

Vines, B. W., Krumhansl, C. L., Wanderley, M. M., Dalca, I. M., and Levitin, D. J. (2011). Music to my eyes: cross-modal interactions in the perception of emotions in musical performance. *Cognition*, **118**, 157–70.

Vuilleumier, P. (2005). Staring fear in the face. *Nature*, **433**, 22–3.

Vuoskoski, J. K. and Thompson, W. F. (2012). Who enjoys listening to sad music and why? *Music Perception: an Interdisciplinary Journal*, **29**, 311–17.

Vuust, P. and Frith, C. D. (2008). Anticipation is the key to understanding music and the effects of music on emotion. *Behavioral and Brain Sciences*, **31**, 599–600.

Wöllner, C. (2012). Is empathy related to the perception of emotional expression in music? a multimodal time-series analysis. *Psychology of Aesthetics, Creativity, and the Arts*, **6**, 214–23.

Zentner, M. and Eerola, T. (2010). Self-report measures and models of musical emotions. In P. Juslin and J. Sloboda (eds), *Handbook of Music and Emotion: Theory, Research, Applications*, pp. 187–223. New York: Oxford University Press.

Zentner, M. R. and Kagan, J. (1996). Perception of music by infants. *Nature*, **383**, 29.

Zentner, M. R. and Kagan, J. (1998). Infants' perception of consonance and dissonance in music. *Infant Behavior and Development*, **21**, 483–92.

Zentner, M., Grandjean, D., and Scherer, K. R. (2008). Emotions evoked by the sound of music: characterization, classification, and measurement. *Emotion*, **8**, 494–521.

Chapter 11

"Mors stupebit": multiple levels of fear-arousing mechanisms in Verdi's *Messa da Requiem*

Luca Zoppelli

As a musicologist—and a musicologist particularly interested in the way that music functions as a means of communication—my attention is drawn to the subtle and complex mechanisms by which music evokes and transmits certain aspects of human experience. Emotion is central in this respect—after all, the idea of music as a means to express and arouse emotional states has a long history in Western culture, reaching back to antiquity. There are, however, many different mechanisms by which this transmission of emotional states can occur. Some are based on the primary functions of music with respect to the construction of experience and the induction of kinesthetic responses. Others manipulate and exploit the listener's logical/syntactical competence based the internalization of codes belonging to a particular musical language. Others still are linked to the important semantic qualities of music and their capacity to evoke different imaginary forms or mental representations, which in turn can engender emotional responses.

As my case study, I have chosen the particular emotional state of fear, and a piece of music supposed to evoke or transmit this emotion. It is well known that music can play a central role in inducing states of fear, dread, or panic. It is able to accomplish this, on the one hand, by directly "creating" such an emotional effect as fear and, on the other hand, by recalling the forms and objects of fear imagery. I hope to demonstrate that it is impossible, within musical language, to dissociate between "pure" or "direct" (neurological) emotional responses—not to be found, or at least less important, in verbal language—and responses induced by syntactical and semiotic mechanisms (which evoke a network of culturally dependent signifier codes).

Our knowledge of the textual frame (in my case, the liturgical text of the sequence *Dies irae, dies illa*, from the Mass of the Dead) allows us to "verify" the pertinence of such associations. Admittedly, there is a danger in wanting to find at all cost what amounts to a pre-formed mental expectation shaped by the verbal text within musical technique. I hope, however, that a rigorous approach towards the codes involved will allow me to avoid the trap of such wishful thinking. The poetic text acts as an anchor, but does so within a semantic field expressed by music.

I shall begin by giving a short summary of what I consider to be the main mechanisms of musical communication. These mechanisms function at different levels, occurring either separately or in parallel, and I would stress that their merging makes it difficult, in certain cases, to make clear distinctions between them.

(A) Emotional coding. This type of mechanism distinguishes itself by its (at least partially) biological or pre-cultural basis originating in our adaptive responses. I am thinking of recent research which has underlined the importance of intrauterine and infant sound perception (Peretz 2001; Imberty 2004): maternal cardio-rhythm and its emotional decoding; affective tuning through vocal interaction; "affective prosody" implied in melodic profiles; decrypting real situations by classifying sound stimuli according to their danger level (through association with the mother's perceived emotional states or through biological heritage). This type of mechanism demands the least cultural mediation, involving, according to Scherer and Zentner (2001), a "primitive but extremely powerful" evolutionary detection system. It may explain both the existence of a more or less universal activity as "useless" as music, and the fact that it should be considered in many cultures (such as our own) as a sort of "original" emotional language, an idea which already found a particularly vivid description in the work of Jean-Jacques Rousseau. According to him, if the first human language still existed, people would sing rather than speak, "l'on chanteroit au lieu de parler" (Rousseau c. 1755/1995, p. 383).

(B) Intrinsic meaning. Within this category I group the types of mechanisms studied in the seminal work of Leonard Meyer (1956; for a recent reappraisal of Meyer's work see Spitzer 2009). Following Roman Jakobson, these mechanisms are called "intramusical referring" or "introversive semiosis" in Jean-Jacques Nattiez (1990) and other studies. A given musical language is based on internal codes such as tonal systems (with their gravitational laws), rhythmic models, syntax (organization of phrases, according to the style of the time), rhetorical functions (introductory or finishing formula) and formal structures. For the listener educated within a given tradition, any manipulation of these internalized structures generates responses which can be defined in terms derived from his or her real experience: feelings of accomplishment, surprise, acceleration or deceleration, change of direction, frustration, etc. This means that even this type of "logical" or "structural" signification can be experienced as having a referential, and at least partially emotional, value. Further, as musical experience is associated with kinetic neurological reflexes (beginning in the prenatal state), these dynamics can be experienced either on a purely psychic level (emotional dynamics, in the sense listed above under category A), or projected towards a visual imagination, in order to suggest a series of movements or exterior events linked along a temporal axis in the real, phenomenal world ("pantomimic" function, "mickeymousing" soundtracks, etc.). This in turn brings us to something resembling the extrinsic category (C2) of iconic meaning, which will be described next.

(C) Extrinsic symbolization. This designation (Nattiez 1990, where we also find "extroversive semiosis") indicates the relation to elements from the external world: music referring beyond itself by means of a sort of symbolic coding. However, such a category requires some further, more precise, distinctions: there are imitations in the direct sense of phenomena which already have an acoustic nature (C1) and thus do not require a process of the type called "intersemiotic translation." Further we find visual "madrigalisms" or "iconisms," which can suggest an image or movement by graphic or kinetic analogy, through a particular melodic profile or other temporal organization of sounds (C2). Next one can distinguish topoi systems (pastoral, warrior, religious…) based on the association of sound patterns with idiomatic types of musical writing traditionally or historically linked to certain human environments or activities (C3, though it may also qualify as a complex case of C1: the reference in the "real world"—music performed in a given context—is already a phenomenon having an acoustic nature). This type of codified musical semantic unity is also called "exogenous" (Noske 1977, 1978), which underlines its belonging to a communal linguistic competence. By contrast we could describe as "endogenous" a sound element which is given an arbitrary meaning through visual or paratextual indexations, within a given piece (C4). This final type is represented by recurring ideas, identification motifs, and other *Leitmotivs* often found in genres such as the symphonic poem, romantic opera, or *Musikdrama*. In order to function, such elements must be presented in connection with the designated concept, either through visual coincidence (on stage) or through the reading of a program.

The aim of this list, admittedly too synthetic to cover the complex system of production of musical meaning, is to draw attention to the multiple levels at work in all musical expressivity. On the one hand, the categories themselves are far from being "pure": where is the exact border between a biological emotional response and cultural coding? Is the *pianissimo* string tremolo, suggesting a shiver of fear, only a topos, which we have finally come to consider "natural"? Or is it based on a simple homology easily associated with universal physiological phenomena? Does culture simply "refine" natural associations, or does it "invent" something that seems natural? Does melody simply "imitate" the affective prosody of vocal expression (mechanism C1), thus creating a form of cognitive recognition informing us on the nature of the affective state being referred to, or does it reactivate primary affective experiences (mechanism A) based on sound interaction?

Such a multilayered perspective, moreover, could help to de-dramatize the traditional opposition between "emotivism" ("music elicits real emotional responses in listeners") and cognitivism ("music expresses/represents emotions"). It is clear that category A demands a more direct, uncontrolled, "emotionalist" response, while categories B and C can have a no less powerful emotional impact, but only on listeners sharing the cultural codes implied (and indeed sharing the presupposition that music *should* be listened to in an emotionally charged way). The different balance between mechanisms A, B, and C in one piece can thus affect its tendency to rely mostly on "induction" or "representation." Moreover, the response seems not to be an absolute one, but historically and socially determined. Individuals, social groups (as described in Adorno 1962, ch. 1) and adepts of different aesthetic tendencies adhere to the one or the other "style" of listening; one and the same person can listen the same piece in a "emotional" or in a "cognitive" detached way in different moments; social norms and situations can compel the listener to inhibit a given type of response.

On the other hand, each piece of music relies on multiple parameters which, in turn, make use of several different mechanisms: Wagner's *Leitmotivs*, for instance, are admittedly "arbitrary" (C4), but at the same time, they are charged with both intrinsic and exogenous semantic (B, C) as well as affective (A) levels (see Zoppelli 2009, on fear mechanisms in *Siegfried*). So it is precisely this multiplicity that allows composers to adapt their strategies to evoke real/imagined experience (and our supposed emotional responses thereto) according to their aesthetic aims. This is what I would like to show with the help of the following example.

Composed between 1869 and 1874, Verdi's *Messa da Requiem* is not only one of the most remarkable settings of the liturgical text of the *missa pro defunctis*, it is also one of its most controversial specimens, since the composer—an avowed agnostic—treated the sacred text according to a tragic perspective: the act of prayer seen as an expression of human suffering and dread (Zoppelli 2003). At the heart of this work we find the *Dies irae, dies illa* sequence, in which Verdi pushes to an extreme both the evocation of apocalyptic imaginary (within the aesthetic categories of the sublime) and the focalized representation of an imaginary witness's terror. In a certain sense, the *Dies irae* text is conceived as an eschatological role game, projecting us into the situation which will be ours on Judgment Day. Verdi engages in a game with the narrative status of this imaginary witness.

In the two first sections ("Dies irae" and "Tuba mirum"), the apocalypse and the trumpets of Judgment Day are evoked by, on the one hand, an incredible phonic violence and, on the other hand, a radical destabilization of music linguistic structural landmarks. Despite the use of material usually belonging to the scales of G and D minor, no tonal center is clearly detectable during the four first sections of the piece, before the cadence at measure 177 (in the mezzo's solo "Liber scriptus"). Rough thematic elements follow one another in a seemingly chaotic order. Only in the seventh verse of the poetic text does the imaginary participant's subjective point of view become explicit, when the discourse moves to the first person ("Quid sum, miser, tunc dicturus?"). Verdi, however, prepares this focalization in the preceding verses. For example, he first brings in the Judgment Day trumpets in stereophonic disposition; he then proceeds to show them as a gradual perception becoming clearer and clearer through the double chromatic ascension and the dynamic use of repetitions, as if heard from within the scene. In this section, the rapid sequence of musical gestures leads to an almost unbearable summit of intensity, abruptly cut short: the last sounds of the "Tuba mirum," which bear no clear functional relation with what came before (A major following a section in A♭), stops abruptly, as if cut off by an axe. This in itself suffices to ignite certain mechanisms of signification: the interrupted sound perception—silence—homologically suggests the interruption of visual perception—darkness. Further, our syntactic "competence" tells us that this music did not stop as a result of the musical discourse's natural conclusion, but rather was subjected to a violent interruption. This puts us in a situation similar to that of humanity "creating"— according to the anthropologist Pascal Boyer's analysis—the presence of the supernatural: due to our evolutionary heritage, our inference system pushes us to "sur-detect the presence of agents" rather than to "sub-detect" it (Boyer 2004). Thus we will explain the brutality of such an interruption—with the help of the anchoring furnished by our knowledge of the liturgical text—as the violence of a superior force which "turns out the light," leaving us in fear and uncertainty. In this case, the manipulation of the "logical" mechanism of a given musical language becomes a factor of affective response: a linguistic decoding rule (functioning only with listeners sharing the same cultural background) pushes us to react appropriately in term of imagery.

The following section, "Mors stupebit," describes the resurrection of the dead. Awoken by these terrifying trumpets, the deceased emerge from their tombs to be judged:

Mors stupebit, et natura	Death will be stunned, and so will nature
Cum resurget creatura	When the creature awakes
Iudicanti responsura.	To answer the Judge.

This is precisely the section I would like to focus on. First the sudden and prolonged silence, an ancestral mechanism linked to survival strategies: although a primitive one, it is very effective in creating an attitude of spasmodic waiting. Next a musical gesture in the strings, *pppp*. The low dynamic level forces us to heighten our perceptive activity, linked to our typical reaction in situations of possible danger. That is probably why low dynamics produces an emotional state of fear, as is well confirmed by music psychological research (Juslin 2001, in particular the table on p. 315).

The "thing" which emerges next (ω in the musical example, Figure 11.1) is equally worrying, for other reasons. Its topical character is clear: it is a typical fragment from a funeral march in binary measure. Why a funeral march? Because such a topos evokes the idea of a procession linked to the semantic field of death. Let us remember that the situation here is of a procession of corpses emerging from their tombs to present themselves for judgment by the Almighty. However, the worrying nature of the scene is mainly occasioned through other parameters:

(1) A march module is, by definition, continuous: here, however, after the motif has been announced, everything falls back into silence. This happens twice, so that the rhythm only

very gradually begins to fall into a continuous pattern. We have here a conflict between the topos and the kinetic model.

(2) The two ornamental notes at the beginning, in the context of short, staccato, "brilliant" articulation, are taken from the vocabulary of comic and dance music: applied here, they lend a grotesque and shocking atmosphere to the scene. As an upsetting construction of opposing elements, a combination of sublime and caricature, and a subversion of classifications grids for experience, the grotesque plays an important role in the tradition of the "demonic" supernatural. The disorientation it engenders can lead to discomfort, loss of reference, and, ultimately, fear, easily entering into the realm of the sinister and the *unheimlich*. One need only think of the role this category assumes in the topos (pictorial and musical alike) of the *danse macabre*. In music as in other media, grotesqueness is achieved through the juxtaposition of elements belonging to opposite categories, irreconcilable topical frames. So we realize that topoi, as well as grammatical/syntactic patterns, set a system of expectations, which can be matched or denied through the others parameters, for the purpose of fixing and describing emotional reactions.

(3) If one accepts that this section refers to the tonality of D minor (which is what the key signature suggests; the A major chord at the end of the former section would then serve as a dominant, while the "Mors stupebit" ends on another A major chord), then the motif itself never touches the tonic, but stays suspended, undetermined. Yet the last note of extract ω (circled in the musical example, Figure 11.1) is an A: its position suggests that it probably has a dominant function, and would thus enforce the tonal gravitation of D minor. However, Verdi treats it in a way which confuses the recognition of its pitch: the double bass pizzicato alone and *pppp* (so in the critical edition of the orchestral score, Verdi 1874/1990) in a very low register, sounds almost like an indefinite pitch, especially in combination with the muffled sound of the bass drum (which has no definite pitch). Then, as passage ω is transposed, the double basses (still accompanied by the bass drum) stay fixed to that A. The sound is thus treated as a pedal, but without its usual stabilizing function. Its metrical position also evokes the typical rhythmic features of a funeral march, but with a destabilizing effect due to the irregular intervals at which the beats are set. Tonal and metrical incertitude, due to failing grammatical structure, generates a response of alienation and fear.

At the same time, however, the muffled and very low frequency beat of the bass drum creates a physical vibration felt directly as a trembling within the body. This in turn triggers an absolutely ancestral response linked to a reaction in the presence of agents whose footsteps make the ground tremble (see the nocturnal sequence preceding the tyrannosaurs' appearance in *Jurassic Park*). This sound alone activates at least three different tools to generate affective responses: cultural references (to the tradition of *danse macabre*), grammatical competence (failing dominant pedal, collapse of rhythmic regularity), and ancestral adaptive responses.

One must also consider the treatment of the vocal part. Although the poetic text is extradiegetic, and projected into the future, Verdi chooses to use it as phonetic material for a second-degree statement. It is treated as a "live" commentary of someone in the clutch of fear, who is watching the appalling spectacle—first faintly, punctually, then more and more continuously—unfold beneath his eyes. The emotional response is here a matter of "narrative" strategies: as simple as this may seem, the effect of fear comes from listening to a voice "which is afraid" (intradiegetic strategies are an essential component in literary traditions of the fantastic and horror; see Viegnes 2006). The voice begins with an uninterrupted syllabic scansion of the words, a sort of non-singing, on the edge of silence, anticipating the beginning of the text. It then enounces the entire text in groups of repeated syllables reduced to the note sequence E–A–C–E♭: this ascent corresponds, in terms of "affective prosody," to the unfolding of a terror scream which culminates on a note foreign to the given tonality, and what is more harmonized with a diminished 7th (marked with a dotted line in Figure 11.1). This chord denotes terrifying supernatural phenomena and characters throughout the tradition of Western music; see the commander's statue in *Don Giovanni*, Samiel in *Freischütz*, and others. If reaction to affective prosody is a matter of direct emotional dynamics, recognition of tonal functions is a matter of grammatical competence, and recognition of the topos is a matter of cultural competence: again, many levels are at work simultaneously. This chord is also accompanied by the only intervention, *fortissimo*, of the brass: this is based on a topos which associates fanfare sound with scenes of judgment (as, for example, in the fourth act of *Aida*) and puts into musical language the idea of a "call to appear" before the supreme court. After another terrifying silence, the voice drops down to D to begin—with isolated syllables, repeating the word "mors" and sung "*cupo*" (darkly)—a descent towards the dominant A. After each syllable, the orchestra echoes an answer (marked with χ in the Figure 11.1) with the "grotesque" head of passage ω and the beat of the double basses/bass drum. This complex marks the most extreme disaggregation of a musical language reduced to the simple kinetic depictions of grotesque fragments in motion. As for the voice, its affective response is extreme: after having sung D, C♯, and C♮, it is unable to continue, sinks into aphasia, and leaves the orchestra with the task of pursuing the progression. Finally, it re-enters on B♭ to announce the verb ("stupebit") and descend to A, which the strings harmonize as an A major chord. This can be perceived as a hinge dominant between the two sections conceived in a doubtful D minor, but it also works as a surprising, offset sonority conveying "stupor" and astonishment.

Figure 11.1 Giuseppe Verdi: *Messa da Requiem* (1874), vocal score. "Mors stupebit" section.

We have evoked categories belonging to aesthetics and poetics such as the grotesque, the uncertain, the invisible (accomplished here through perceptive distortions which prevent a clear recognition and classification of the "funeral march"), and last but not least, silence. Silence characterizes the most extreme moment of fear experiences, the situation of unutterable horror: authors well know the strategy of writing "which leads to a meaningful aphasia" (Mellier 1999). Musical language is equally well equipped for obtaining this kind of effect: it makes use both of "relative" silence (the singing voice, carrier of an intradiegetic perspective, falls silent: other sounds take over in order to say the inexpressible) and of absolute silence (the total absence of sound). This absence gains meaning through its structural relation with the sonorities surrounding it.

With this example, I do not claim to have thoroughly explained how Verdi's "Mors stupebit" evokes fear, but I hope to have given a convincing plea for the recognition of the stratified, multilevel functioning of affective arousal in such complex cultural artefacts as works belonging to so-called "art music." No single type of mechanism could be responsible, at least as far as this type of music is involved, for what we call "the emotional power of music." In my opinion, any attempt to explain the emotional and conceptual effectiveness of such a musical work should be based on a comprehensive survey of this complex and multilayered process.

References

Adorno, Th. W. (1962). *Einleitung in die Musiksoziologie*. Frankfurt: Suhrkamp.

Boyer, P. (2004). *Et l'homme créa les dieux. Comment expliquer la religion*. Paris: Gallimard.

Imberty, M. (2004). Le bébé et le musical. In J.-J. Nattiez (ed.), *Musiques. Une encyclopédie pour le XXIe siècle*, vol. II, *Les savoirs musicaux*, pp. 506–26. Arles: Actes Sud.

Juslin, P. (2001). Communicating emotion in music performance: a review and a theoretical framework. In: P. Juslin and J. Sloboda (eds), *Music and Emotion: Theory and Research*, pp. 309–37. Oxford: Oxford University Press.

Meyer. L. B. (1956). *Emotion and Meaning in Music*. Chicago: University of Chicago Press.

Mellier, D. (1999). *L'écriture de l'excèse. Fiction fantastique et poétique de la terreur*. Paris: Champion.

Nattiez, J.-J. (1990). *Music and Discourse. Towards a Semiology of Music*. Princeton: Princeton University Press.

Noske, F. (1977). *The Signifier and the Signified. Studies on the Operas of Mozart and Verdi*. Den Haag: Nijhoff.

Noske, F. (1978). Das exogene Todesmotiv in den Musikdramen Richard Wagners. *Die Musikforschung*, **31**, 285–302.

Peretz, I. (2001). Listen to the brain: a biological perspective on musical emotions. In P. Juslin and J. Sloboda (eds), *Music and Emotion: Theory and Research*, 105–34. Oxford: Oxford University Press.

Rousseau, J.-J. (c. 1755/1995). Essai sur l'origine des langues. In *Oeuvres complètes V: Écrits sur la musique, la langue et le théâtre*, pp. 371–429. Paris: Gallimard (Bibliothèque de la Pléiade).

Scherer, K. and Zentner, R. (2001). Emotional effects of music: production rules. In P. Juslin and J. Sloboda (eds), pp. 361–92. *Music and Emotion: Theory and Research*. Oxford: Oxford University Press.

Spitzer, M. (2009). Emotions and meaning in music. *Musica Humana*, **1**, 155–96.

Verdi, G. (1874/1990). *Messa da Requiem*. Critical edition by D. Rosen. Milan/Chicago: Ricordi/University of Chicago Press.

Viegnes, M. (2006). *Le fantastique*. Paris: Garnier-Flammarion.

Zoppelli, L. (2003). Eine Erzählung im Kirchengewande? Liturgische Struktur und narratologische Perspektive in Verdi's "Messa da Requiem." *Musiktheorie*, **18**, 21–38.

Zoppelli, L. (2009). Petite sémiologie musicale de l'épouvante. In M. Viegnes (ed.), *La peur et ses miroirs*, pp. 151–68. Paris: Imago.

Chapter 12

Three theories of emotion—three routes for musical arousal

Jenefer Robinson

Introduction

In *Deeper than Reason* (Robinson 2005) I tried to show that there are multiple mechanisms whereby music arouses emotions in listeners, and I suggested that a major reason why the emotions music arouses are often said to be "ineffable" is that they are the products of different mechanisms all working simultaneously (Robinson 2005, ch. 13). In one passage or sequence of passages in a piece of music there might be conflicts among different emotions, blends of different emotions, and a morphing of one emotion into another. Moreover, the various emotions that blend or conflict or morph could themselves be produced by different mechanisms. In this chapter I want to pursue this line of argument from a slightly different angle by showing how different mechanisms of emotional arousal are emphasized by different theorists of emotion making different theoretical assumptions about emotion.

Cognitive appraisal theorists emphasize that emotions are caused by appraisals of the environment: anger is caused by an appraisal that one (or a member of one's group) has been offended and sadness is caused by an appraisal of serious loss, etc. According to appraisal theorists, without loss of some kind sadness is—logically—impossible. On the other hand, those who think that emotions are action tendencies in response to affordances in the environment focus on the role of emotions as states of action readiness:[i] sadness is viewed as a form of withdrawal from the world in response to a world perceived as full of loss. In this respect it is like shame, which may indeed be a kind of sadness, namely, sadness that one hasn't measured up to important societal norms in some way. Finally, those who identify emotions with feelings of bodily change emphasize the importance to emotions of bodily responses. As William James famously observed, without feelings of bodily change there would be no emotionality in emotion, but merely a "cold and neutral state of intellectual perception" (James 1981, p. 1067), i.e. what today's theorists would call a "cognitive appraisal."

In my view, emotions are best thought of as processes in which all three of these components play an important role. Emotions are processes designed both to focus attention on whatever in the environment is appraised as significant to our survival and/or well-being and that of our "group," as well as to get us to act appropriately to the environment so appraised. The response itself is a bodily and behavioral response, which is typically experienced as an "emotional feeling." Emotions look both inward and outward: outwardly at the world which demands to be appraised and acted upon, and inwardly at feelings of bodily response.[ii] But whether we think of these different approaches as competing theories of emotion or as theories that focus on one component in a more complex emotion process, it remains true that each of these theories underwrites a different mechanism of emotional arousal, including emotional arousal by music. In this chapter I propose to examine the different mechanisms of emotional arousal underwritten by these different theories. It's my view that each of these theories has something to teach us about the emotional effects of music.[iii]

Cognitive appraisal theories

I think it's fair to say that most theorists of emotion not only in psychology but also in philosophy, anthropology, and other disciplines defend a "cognitive appraisal" theory of emotions—the idea that some evaluation or interpretation of a situation is the most important element in the emotion process in that it is what sets the whole process in motion. The relevant appraisals have to do with events or objects or people that impinge on one's values, wants, or goals in an important way, whether positively or negatively.

Emotions have so-called intentional objects, something that the emotion is about or to which it is targeted. If you tread on my toe and I interpret or appraise this action of yours as a deliberate insult, this angry appraisal is what sets off my anger response. A similar response (red contorted face, increased heart rate etc.) caused by extreme physical effort would not count as an angry response because it has the wrong type of cause. The "object" of the relevant appraisal is the object of the emotion: I appraise you as insulting me and I am angry at you for your insult. Moreover, we distinguish different emotions largely by the kinds of appraisal they involve: in fear we appraise or evaluate the stimulus as a threat, in anger as an offense, in joy as a boon, and in sadness as some sort of loss. The psychologist Richard Lazarus (1991) calls these types of intentional object "core relational themes," because they define "adaptational encounters"—types of interaction with the environment with important significance for survival and/or well-being—that all human beings face.

For appraisal theorists, musical emotions are a puzzle.[iv] When music makes us sad or happy (if it does) there doesn't seem to be any "adaptational encounter" with the music: nothing has happened to make us happy or sad. I haven't won a prize or suffered the death of a friend. The music does not seem to be the intentional object of my sadness or happiness; it's not the target of my sadness or what my happiness is about.[v] It's for this reason that the philosopher of music Peter Kivy argues that music simply cannot make us happy or sad, or induce any other of the so-called "garden variety" emotions such as fear, anger, sadness, and so on (Kivy 1990). Nevertheless, Kivy acknowledges that music does arouse people emotionally. He explains this by imputing it to emotions such as "enthusiasm, or excitement, or ecstasy" which are "directed at the music as its intentional object" (Kivy 2006, p. 280). In other words, there is an adaptational encounter with the music after all. In listening to a piece of music with understanding, I may appreciate its beauty and the skillful way the composer has crafted the structure of the piece, and I am emotionally excited by this. Maybe it's a double fugue such as occurs towards the end of Verdi's *Falstaff*, or a magisterial passacaglia as in the last movement of Brahms' Fourth Symphony.

Why should such things induce excited admiration? Kivy does not speculate, but perhaps people are so constructed as to be pleased and thrilled when they encounter something beautiful and well made. At any rate, there is probably some evolutionary story to tell about this phenomenon.[vi] Kivy is surely right that appreciating music in this way does evoke emotions. The trouble with his account is not that it is wrong but that it is incomplete. For according to Kivy these emotions of excitement and ecstasy directed at the music itself are the only emotions that music can arouse, and this seems palpably false.

As a formalist about music, Kivy thinks that the emotions he's talking about are aroused primarily by formal or structural qualities in music. They are emotions that occur after we have recognized the double fugue or the passacaglia and are appreciating how beautifully and skillfully it has been composed. Elsewhere I have referred to these emotions as "emotions of appreciation."[vii] But there are other emotions that are aroused in the very process of grasping the musical structure. I have in mind the kinds of emotional states that Leonard Meyer (1956) discusses in *Emotion and Meaning in Music*. Meyer points out that those who have little or no training in music theory but have listened to a great deal of music can be said to understand a particular piece if they have the "right" emotions at the "right" places in the music. Meyer is thinking primarily of music in the Classical and Romantic style, roughly speaking from the mid 18th to early 20th century. A paradigm for him is sonata form and the way that sonata form leads the listener to have certain expectations about what will happen as the music unfolds. Once sonata form has been well established, the composer can write with audience expectations in mind. He can play with these expectations, leading the listener to expect one thing but doing something else, such as delaying the arrival of an expected resolution, and eventually bringing everything to a conclusion in an unexpected way. Reacting to these events is a bit like reacting to the twists and turns in the intricate plot of a detective story. We can be pretty confident that the murderer will be revealed but we don't know who the murderer is, and how, why, and when he'll be discovered. Similarly, we can be pretty confident that the tonic will return at the end of a mid-18th-century piece in sonata form, but we don't know how and when. Consequently, as we listen to the piece, especially if we are not trained music theorists, we experience a sequence of emotional states such as surprise, disappointment, bewilderment, and relief, which are directed towards structural features of the music.

Now, these emotions are triggered by "appraisals" but they are not likely to be deliberate or even conscious appraisals. I can react with emotion to the unusual appearance of an F minor harmony without formulating the proposition that "the introduction of F minor here is very unusual." Most experimental psychologists think of "cognitive appraisals" as within the capability of at least "lower" animals (especially primates) and hence believe that the appraisals necessary to emotion don't have to be deliberate or articulate and are not always propositional in form. Klaus Scherer has written that "many appraisal theorists, rather than limiting the term to a cortically based propositional calculus, adopt a broader view of cognition and assume that appraisal can occur, in more or less complex forms, at several levels of processing" (Scherer *et al.* 2001, p. 370). Whereas an experienced but theoretically untrained listener can sense only the presence of "strange occurrence," the trained music theorist can identify the unusual harmonic shift into F minor in a piece in sonata form that is dominated by F♯ major. Hence although a great deal of learning is necessary before either listener has the requisite expectations about sonata form, once those expectations are in place, the listener's reactions can be more or less automatic. Moreover, as Nico Frijda has noted, when something surprising or unexpected occurs it's probably a good idea for human beings (and other organisms) to react emotionally so as to be able to deal with a potentially threatening situation. Similarly, when things turn out as expected we respond by relaxing our guard. Most likely, listeners' reactions to what is appraised as unexpected in music and then to what is appraised as a comforting return of the expected are a by-product of a generally adaptive pattern of behavior.[viii]

There are no doubt other ways in which cognitive appraisals of music can arouse emotions in listeners. I have written elsewhere about emotional responses to musical topoi, for example, as when we begin to feel stirred by what we recognize as martial music or we feel solemn and reverent in listening to what is appraised or recognized as a hymn. And of course there are personal associations to music that make people emotional when they recognize a piece as associated with some memorable and important event in their own lives.[ix] Nevertheless, even after enumerating all these ways in which appraisals of the music can generate emotions, they don't seem sufficient to explain the overpowering emotional effects that listeners claim to experience on listening to at least some music.[x] Moreover, many listeners think that they do experience "garden variety" emotions as a result of listening to music—feeling anxious as a result of listening to anxious music or happy as a result of listening to happy music—emotions that the appraisal theory has difficulty explaining. Hence it seems unlikely that the appraisal theory as sketched so far can explain all the sources of music's emotional power.

Frijda's theory

The psychologist Nico Frijda (1986, 2007) endorses the idea that emotions appraise the world in terms of the personal significance of the "adaptational encounter." But for Frijda the key point for emotion theory is that emotions do not merely appraise the world, they also get us ready to deal with the world as so appraised. Emotions are action tendencies and emotional experience "is to a large extent awareness of action tendency" (Frijda 1986, p. 71). More precisely, emotions are "modes of relational action readiness," usually in the form of "tendencies to establish, maintain, or disrupt a relationship with the environment," as in emotions such as anger, fear, or love, and sometimes in the form of "mode of relational readiness as such," as in the case of generalized excitement or apathy (Frijda 1986, p. 71). Emotional experience is defined as

> awareness of some mode of action readiness of a passive and action-control-demanding nature, involving readiness to change or maintain relationships with the environment (or intentional objects generally); which action readiness is experienced as motivated or caused by situations appraised as relevant, urgent, and meaningful with respect to ways of dealing with it; which situations are felt to affect the subject, and affect him bodily (Frijda 1986, p. 257).

In emotional experience we perceive the world as calling for action or action tendencies: in this sense we perceive Gibsonian "affordances" (Frijda 1986, p. 325). Frijda emphasizes that emotional experience involves a perception, "a mode of appearance of the situation": emotional experience is "perception of horrible objects, insupportable people, oppressive events" (Frijda 1986, p. 188), all of which typically require to be dealt with in some way.

Now, this theory might seem every bit as difficult to apply to music as the appraisal theory. Music doesn't seem to be calling for action, except insofar as it is march music calling for marching, or a hymn calling for us to get on our knees, or dance music demanding to be danced to. Beethoven's *Fifth Symphony*, by contrast, just seems to demand that we listen to it, and if we are in the modern concert hall, that we listen to it without tapping our feet or humming along or engaging in any other overt activity.

In an interesting book, *The Musical Representation*, Charles Nussbaum has argued that, on the contrary, actions or action tendencies are elicited all the time as we listen to complex art music such as Beethoven's Fifth, although these action tendencies are typically suppressed in the contemporary concert hall.[xi] Indeed, in order to understand a complex piece of music as it unfolds it is imperative that we enact in imagination the "action plan" of the music. On the basis of the "action plan" of a particular piece of music, listeners construct a (constantly updated) musical mental model that represents "the features of the layouts and scenarios" (Nussbaum 2007, p. 82) through which listeners move in their imagination. Listening to music with understanding is imagining moving on a route through the virtual space and time of the music, and enacting the virtual movements (slow and labored, or quick and flowing etc.) specified by the action plan of the music.[xii]

For Nussbaum a musical performance is what the philosopher Ruth Millikan has called a "push-mi–pullyu" representation: it both indicates the musical plan, "the hierarchical representations[xiii] whose content is the organized musical surface" (Nussbaum 2007, p. 99), and at the same time it prescribes the listener to "implement" the plan by making it her own: "certain bodily sets must be adopted, and motor areas of the brain activated" (Nussbaum 2007, p. 99). In other words, "the listener must act the music out" by playing or—"more likely"—singing it as well as by moving through its virtual space in imagination and simulating "the virtual entities contained in this space" (Nussbaum 2007, p. 99). Listening to a piece of music with understanding should be thought of as "an attempt to grasp a complex plan by trying it out, adopting it, and acting on it by way of simulation or in imagination" (Nussbaum 2007, p. 214).

Nussbaum makes the striking claim that "all Western tonal art music since 1650, including so-called pure music, is program music" having "extra-musical significance" ((Nussbaum 2007, p. 126) because "the contents of the mental models it motivates are layouts and scenarios in which the listener acts off-line" (Nussbaum 2007, p. 126). The listener who is striving with some success to understand how a piece of music is unfolding is constructing a mental model that maps not just various structural relations such as repeats, inversions, modulations, and the like, but "scenarios, objects, and events in virtual musical space" (Nussbaum 2007, p. 123) that can in turn model so-called "extra-musical content" (Nussbaum 2007, p. 126). This mental model is continually updated as the music proceeds. And these "scenarios, objects, and events" are not merely thought about or observed from afar but are actually encountered in imagination. Thus when we say that music goes up and down, leaves home and returns, we are pointing to the way we enact the music's "action plan" in imagination as we listen. "If the musical plan generates appropriate mental models and puts the listener's body into appropriate motor states off-line" (Nussbaum 2007, p. 140), the musical mental models can then map extra-musical content. For example, a string quartet might exemplify a friendly conversation among four people. The musical conversation is a "scenario" that "incorporates bodily sets and sequenced behaviors" (Nussbaum 2007, p. 125) of the four "participants," such as accosting, replying, disputing, questioning, acceding, and so on. The performers attempt to enact this scenario and listeners attempt to simulate their actions or action tendencies as they listen.

Borrowing from Frijda's idea that emotions are changes in action readiness in response to perceptions of Gibsonian affordances, Nussbaum claims that an emotion is "a valent perception of an object, situation, or event relating to a core relational theme and accompanied by one or more modes of arousal as well as a change in action readiness"[xiv] (Nussbaum 2007, p. 199). He then argues that music arouses emotion "by motivating virtual (off-line) actions afforded in musical space" (Nussbaum 2007, p. 190):

> Musical affective feelings .... arise out of an ongoing attempt to negotiate a musical virtual terrain, to act in accordance with its musical affordances, dealing with surprises, impediments, failures, and successes on the way, and requiring the constant reevaluation of strategy to which emotional response is keyed. (Nussbaum 2007, p. 214).

In the string quartet "conversation" the questions and ripostes are not merely heard as angry or comic. The listener hearing an angry-sounding musical riposte will respond empathetically, in imagination responding with the action tendency or "body set" of anger; when the music switches to a light-hearted comic interchange, the listener will in imagination respond by smiling and relaxing his or her guard, with consequent bodily feelings of relaxation and contentment.

In some ways Nussbaum's view is reminiscent of Meyer's theory of musical understanding. According to Meyer (1956), as we engage with a piece or passage of music, we grasp its structure in the very act of responding emotionally to surprising, puzzling, and satisfying events. However, Nussbaum's view is different in at least one important respect. A long-standing objection to Meyer's account is that it assumes that we are always surprised and puzzled by the way a piece of music unfolds even if we have heard it countless times and know exactly what is going to happen. What

Nussbaum suggests is that we do not merely *listen* to the unfolding musical structure—we *move through* the virtual musical terrain, encountering obstacles, moving freely and smoothly through open stretches, struggling with conflicting tendencies, wondering which way to turn, and so on. And we experience the feelings of these action tendencies. In re-enacting a virtual journey through the music, we know in some sense that a "surprise" is due, but since we *encounter* it in imagination rather than merely "*cognizing*" it, the effect of the "surprise" does not wear off after repeated listenings.

Do we experience emotional feelings or genuine emotions when listening to music? Nussbaum seems to think that usually it is emotional feelings—feelings of action tendencies—that we experience. Sometimes, however, what we experience are emotions and emotional feelings that are analogous to the simulated "off-line" emotional reactions that we experience for characters and plot developments in a novel. Listening to a string quartet as a conversation may be like this, as we simulate the angry musical rebuffs or comical musical ripostes by the participants as well as perhaps simulating a concerned bystander.[xv] Either way, the listener in imagination implements the action plan of the music and hence gets put into actual bodily states. These bodily states are typically inhibited, since the corresponding actions are merely simulated, but if they weren't they would be the bodily states that signal a certain state of mind: concerned, angry, amused, etc. In short, music can arouse genuine emotions even if the corresponding action tendencies—and hence feelings—are inhibited, and at times, no doubt, in the privacy of our own homes the action tendencies induced will be overtly expressed, as when listening to the swelling triumphal music of Beethoven's *Egmont* overture, we find ourselves "conducting" the music with broad triumphal gestures.

Nussbaum's view has the merit of linking in a new and original way the emotionally expressive character of music to the emotions it arouses in listeners. The expressive character of a musical episode is founded on the responses induced by enacting the musical action plan in imagination. As Nussbaum puts the point, "… the expressive character of the work is founded on mirroring responses" (Nussbaum 2007, p. 230). *Till Eulenspiegel*, for example, is music expressive of a mischievous state of mind. This means that a successful performance of *Till Eulenspiegel*

> enjoins the listener to implement a plan (off-line), which puts him into certain active bodily states whose muscular effects are inhibited, effects that, if not inhibited, would eventuate in the sort of behaviors, including deliberate inhibition of action, that comport with a mischievous state of mind. (Nussbaum 2007, p. 230)

And of course we might not be so inhibited if we are listening to mischievous music in a situation where we can be more expressive in a bodily way.[xvi]

I have myself distinguished between expression and expressiveness in the arts and have suggested that expressiveness can be analyzed in terms of simulation theory.[xvii] In my view an artwork that expresses an emotion in an expressive way is one that reveals something of what it is like to be in such an emotional state. In art as in life this often means that the artwork succeeds in evoking a responsive emotion in audiences. Elsewhere (Robinson 2007) I have illustrated the point with respect to dance:

> The audience at a work of dance mimics in imagination the bodily movements of the dancers on the stage. Because of this, they can actually feel what the dancers are expressing. Of course the audience is not actually dancing about in the aisles; their own bodily activity is largely suppressed. But their muscles may tense, their blood may race, and they may feel as if they are extending their arms, flexing their legs, and so on even as they are sitting quietly in the theater. Moreover, because dance evokes bodily responses in the audience, it is peculiarly capable of communicating what it feels like to be proud and resentful or in the throes of young love or stricken with grief or rage.[xviii]

What I said about dance is very similar to what Nussbaum claims about music. In listening to music we virtually encounter affordances which call for particular action tendencies which in turn are perceived as emotional feelings of various sorts.

Anthony Newcomb (1984) has introduced the idea that some symphonies in the Romantic period, notably the symphonies of Beethoven, exemplify a "musical plot" with "extra-musical" significance. So, for example, we might think of the structure of Beethoven's Fifth as exemplifying the "plot archetype" of a "struggle to victory." According to Nussbaum's way of thinking, we not only hear a struggle to victory in the music, we also enact that very struggle, and in so doing we experience the emotions of the person struggling.[xix] There is an opportunity here for powerful participatory emotions to be aroused, because we ourselves are in imagination involved in the struggle represented by the music.

How plausible is Nussbaum's theory? Formalist critics are likely to deny both that music comprehension requires enacting an "action plan" of the piece and that on the basis of this action plan the music mandates the formation of mental models that represent virtual scenarios of various sorts. But for those who experience musical structure as having significance beyond its mere beauty or complexity, the idea that in "following" a piece of music we are performing virtual movements that the plan of the music mandates or suggests is very appealing.[xx] Among its advantages are: (1) that it makes listening to music with understanding a necessarily emotional process, and (2) that it explains how music can bear "extra-musical" meaning. Moreover, (3) it accurately reflects the experience of many listeners to music of moving through a virtual environment replete with obstacles to be surmounted and surprising turns of events to be dealt with. It seems to me that Nussbaum has explored an intriguing new way in which music can arouse emotion or emotional feelings in listeners, and one that is closely tied to a proper comprehension of the music.

The Jamesian theory

Both the appraisal theory and the action readiness theory focus on the input side of the emotion process, on what initiates that process. The main rival to the appraisal and action readiness theories about the emotions is William James's theory, which focuses more on the output side. As is well known, James argued that the common-sense view of emotions gets things back to front: "Common sense says, we lose our fortune, are sorry and weep; we meet a bear, are frightened and run; we are insulted by a rival, are angry and strike." But on James' view "*the bodily changes follow directly the PERCEPTION of the exciting fact*," and "*our feeling of the same changes as they occur IS the emotion*" (James 1981, p. 1065). Hence it is accurate to say that "we feel sorry because we cry, angry because we strike, afraid because we tremble" (James 1981, p. 1066). James gives a three-part argument in favor of his theory: first we do in fact respond automatically and instinctively to events in the environment that are important to our survival and/or well-being (i.e. "adaptational encounters"); secondly, these responses are bodily and especially visceral responses which are felt as soon as they occur; and thirdly—the "vital point" of his theory—if we imagine some strong emotion "and then try to abstract from our consciousness of it all feelings of its bodily symptoms, we find we have nothing left behind," except "a cold and neutral state of intellectual perception" (James 1981, p. 1067). James has been interpreted in different ways, but if we take him literally here, he is saying that the emotion IS the conscious awareness of bodily changes. Without an awareness of bodily changes there will be no emotionality, just "a cold and neutral state of intellectual perception." It is our feelings of the different bodily reactions characteristic of different emotional states that James identifies with different particular emotions.[xxi]

James takes it as good evidence for his theory that deliberately taking on the typical bodily expression of an emotion is a good recipe for changing the way you feel:

> Smooth the brow, brighten the eye, contract the dorsal rather than the ventral aspect of the frame, and speak in a major key, pass the genial compliment, and your heart must be frigid indeed if it do not gradually thaw! (James 1981, p. 1078)

James's theory is notoriously a piece of armchair theorizing, but in recent years there has been a great deal of empirical work designed to test his hypothesis. In his recent book, *Feelings: the Perception of Self*, the psychologist Jim Laird has catalogued a large number of experiments purporting to show that feelings follow and provide information about our bodily states and actions: our feelings are generated by a "process of self-observation and interpretation," which he calls "self-perception" (Laird 2007, p. 9). Laird examines different categories of bodily state, including emotional expressions (facial expressions, vocal expressions), posture, and autonomic arousal, and finds good evidence that emotional feelings follow the deliberate induction of such bodily changes. Examples of experiments cited include the well-known study by Dutton and Aron in which male subjects encountered "an attractive female confederate" after they had crossed one of two bridges over a river, one "low and wide," and the other "high, narrow, and shaky" (Laird 2007, pp. 82–3). The woman had given all the men her phone number on some pretext. After the experiment, more men who had crossed the scary bridge called her than those who had crossed the "safe" bridge. The idea is that the men on the scary bridge felt aroused by the scary bridge because they were afraid, but they falsely attributed their feelings to how they felt about the woman. Laird says: "When people have been aroused by fear, anger, or physical exercise, they then report being more strongly attracted sexually or romantically" (Laird 2007, p. 83). In another ingenious experiment Strack *et al.* (1988) asked subjects how funny a series of cartoons was. Half of the subjects were asked to hold a pen in their mouth by pursing their lips and the other half to hold it with their teeth. Those who were induced to look angry reported feeling less amused than those who had been induced to "smile."

Laird departs from James in pointing out that we don't always feel the bodily reactions that occur in emotional states. There are individual differences among people as to how sensitive they are to their own bodily states, and even those who are sensitive don't always realize how they are reacting in a particular situation. He notes, however, that this point supports James's basic view that feelings are not the cause of behavior, but "the consequences of behaviors":[xxii] feelings function as "information about the behaviors that are going on, in relation to the context in which the person is acting" (Laird 2007, p. 109). They provide information about states of action readiness, and hence cannot occur until the states of action readiness are already in place.

We might wonder whether what's induced in the experiments cited by Laird is a genuine emotion or merely an "emotional feeling." In the report of their experiment, Strack *et al.* explicitly say that it is emotional feelings that are altered by alterations in facial expression. In the Dutton and Aron experiment, by contrast, it looks more as if generalized autonomic arousal merely increases the likelihood of genuine emotions being aroused. As in the Schachter and Singer (1962) experiment, which is in a similar vein, the agent is aroused, feels himself to be aroused, and looks around for an explanation for his state of arousal.[xxiii] In this case, it seems, feelings are aroused which are interpreted as emotional, but it is unclear whether or not genuine emotions are aroused. And of course everything is complicated by the fact that when one feels aroused and then begins to believe that one is feeling attracted by an attractive member of the opposite sex, genuine attraction rapidly follows. And similarly with respect to the belief that one is feeling cheerful or angry: once I identify my feeling as one of cheerfulness or anger, I begin to appraise the world in the appropriate way.

A third possibility is that what's aroused is, strictly speaking, neither an emotion nor an emotional feeling but a mood. The reason why this might seem to be a plausible alternative is precisely because although the feelings in question are feelings of bodily change, they are not initiated by an "appraisal" as emotions typically are. Certainly those who hold the cognitive appraisal theory are likely to think, contra both James and Laird, that these "emotional feelings" cannot be feelings of genuine emotion because the feelings are aroused by awareness of bodily changes and not by an appraisal of some "intentional object."

Laird does not make a sharp distinction between emotion and mood in his book. However, many of his examples are not plausibly analyzable as moods. The subjects in the Dutton and Aron experiment came to have a *romantic attachment* to somebody; some of those in the Strack *et al.* experiment experienced feelings of *amusement*. In both cases the agent interpreted the feeling state as emotional and a specific intentional object appeared to which the feeling state was then attached. All the elements of an emotion were then present; it's just that the process did not originate in an appraisal of an intentional object. Emotions are malleable: they hook on to whatever in the environment seems appropriate. If I'm autonomically aroused and there's a handsome guy before me, I assume the feeling is caused by that guy and proceed to act as if it indeed it were. So it looks as if the Jamesian mechanism is indeed a mechanism for (indirectly) inducing emotions, not just moods or emotional feelings. Of course, this does not rule out the possibility that moods can also be generated by interpreting one's feelings of bodily change as indicative of one's mood.

There is some neuroscientific support for the self-perception hypothesis. Antonio Damasio has identified specific areas of the brain that monitor the current and ongoing state of the body and found that these areas are active when people "recalled and re-experienced personal life episodes marked by sadness, happiness, anger, or fear" (Damasio *et al.* 2000). He identifies the "feeling" of an emotion with a "mapping" by the brain of a pattern of bodily changes that occurs in that emotion. In experiments in which subjects were asked to think about an emotional episode in their past life while being given a positron emission tomography (PET) scan, all the "body-sensing areas" they studied—the cingulate cortex, the somatosensory cortices of insula and SII, the nuclei in the brainstem tegmentum—"showed a statistically significant pattern of activation or deactivation," indicating that "the mapping of body states" had been modified during these episodes of feeling. (Damasio 2003, pp. 99–100). As Laird notes, for Damasio, bodily feedback plays an important role in generating feelings, which in turn function as useful data on which to base decisions.

What has all this to do with music? There is a great deal of evidence that music affects its listeners in a bodily way, and if music can directly affect the motor system, posture and gesture, facial expression, and/or action tendencies, then, if James and Laird are right, it should be able to induce emotional feelings of these bodily changes that are interpreted by the agent as emotions. (This is what I have labeled in Robinson (2005) the "Jazzercise effect.") In their article "Emotional effects of music: production rules," Scherer and Zentner (2001) summarize a number of ways in which music can arouse emotions, among them bodily feedback mechanisms.[xxiv] They report on studies that seem to show that music listening has an effect on autonomic measures such as heart rate, blood pressure, respiration, finger temperature, and galvanic skin response. For example, one study showed statistically significant differences in cardiorespiratory activity in people listening to music independently identified as sad, happy, calm, or excited (Nyklicek *et al.* 1997). Another study purported to show that happy music induced subliminal smiles and sad music subliminal frowns (Scherer and Zentner 2001). Sandra Trehub has shown that when infants listened to their mother's singing, the cortisol in their saliva modulated arousal, i.e. the babies calmed down (Trehub 2003). These kinds of results are supported by self-reports: people claim that music does indeed calm them down, stir them up, and make them happy or sad. As for inducing emotional feelings through inducing behavior, including action tendencies or motor activity, much music is composed with specific behavior patterns in mind, such as marches, lullabies, and dance music. Rhythm is presumably particularly important in these activities. The neuropsychologist Daniel Levitin (2006) has noted the massive connectivity between the cerebellum, which is a center of motor control linked to our sense of timing, and emotional brain centers such as the amygdala.

Interestingly, psychologists often simply assume that music can induce moods, since they use music as a "mood-induction procedure." They have found that music with a happy or sad character has systematically differentiated effects on perception, memory, and various cognitive abilities. These results are consistent with Laird's self-perception theory: they suggest that music affects behavior, action tendencies, and motor responses, and the feelings of these responses are interpreted as feelings of some particular mood or emotion. Thus, a funeral march such as Purcell's music for the death of Queen Mary would seem to induce a certain kind of solemn, heavy-footed movement, which in turn can be experienced as a feeling of sadness. Moreover, if I think I feel sad I may indeed become sad, and the usual cognitive effects of sadness will ensue: I see more sadness in ambiguous faces;[xxv] I more readily remember past events in which I was sad;[xvi] I more readily recognize words like "sad";[xxvii] and so on. This phenomenon probably extends to feeling states that are not always identified as emotional. Laird points to a number of studies that indicate that "acting as if confident and proud makes people feel confident and proud" (Laird 2007, p. 124), although he thinks confidence is not a genuine emotional state (Laird 2007, p. 124). Some music does indeed sound "confident and proud," and such music may well induce a corresponding posture and stance towards the world, which in turn induces confident feelings.

Although the Jamesian theory seems to have some real consequences for music listening, I think we have to admit that it plays a lesser role in musical understanding and appreciation than the cognitive appraisal and action readiness theories. Listening to complex music of the sort discussed—in their different ways—by Kivy and Nussbaum evokes emotions that can help us to understand and/or appreciate how the music is structured and what it expresses. By contrast, moods, emotional feelings, and even genuine emotions that are elicited by the Jamesian mechanism are usually induced without awareness and play only a background role in music listening. A sad piece of music can temporarily sadden me; a languorous piece may unawares put me into a slightly calmer mood. But taken by themselves these effects are often weak and transient.

It may now seem that there is no difference between the Jamesian mechanism for emotion induction and the Nussbaumian mechanism discussed earlier. But notice that in Nussbaum's view listeners (in imagination) actually *encounter* affordances in the music, such as obstacles and surprises, which result in corresponding states of action readiness. Feelings of these states are feelings of the appropriate emotion. And sometimes we experience genuine emotions that are analogous to the simulated "off-line" emotional reactions that we experience when we engage with a literary fiction. By contrast, the Jamesian mechanism requires no such imaginative activity. It consists simply in the arousal of bodily changes which are interpreted as emotional feelings and then "labelled" accordingly. On the other hand, as I noted at the very beginning of this chapter, several different mechanisms for emotional arousal may be operating simultaneously as we listen to music. Certainly the automatic Jamesian mechanism, whereby music-induced movement and posture and autonomic changes, etc. are experienced as emotional feelings, can reinforce the enactive imaginative engagement with virtual layouts and scenarios emphasized by Nussbaum.

In conclusion, I would like to reiterate that although this essay has focused on three important mechanisms of emotional arousal by music, there are doubtless many more. Indeed, Juslin and Vjästfäll (2008) have suggested a number of mechanisms that I have ignored here.[xxviii] My goal has been primarily to show how different theories of emotion privilege different mechanisms of emotional arousal. But if, as I believe, emotion is a *process* in which appraisals result in states of action readiness which are then (often) experienced as emotional feelings, then what this chapter demonstrates is that each stage of the emotion process—appraisal, action readiness, feeling—has its own distinct mechanism for emotional arousal. This is not very surprising at the input stage. It is more surprising at the output stage. Nevertheless, however weak and transient their effects, it does seem as if emotional feelings can indirectly induce actual emotion by the Jamesian mechanism.

Acknowledgment

Thanks to Tom Cochrane for his helpful critical comments.

Notes

i   Nico Frijda is the best-known exponent of this idea and he also clearly acknowledges the importance of appraisals to emotion.

ii In some theories all three aspects are even more tightly connected. In Robinson (1995) I defended the view that bodily responses themselves register emotionally significant events. Jesse Prinz has elaborated with great subtlety the idea of emotions as "embodied appraisals" or "gut reactions" (Prinz 2004).

iii I am not claiming that my list of mechanisms of emotional arousal by music is complete. For example, I say nothing about how we may respond emotionally to music that sounds like a human vocal expression, something that Patrik Juslin (2001) in particular has stressed. See also Juslin and Vjästfäll (2008).

iv They are also a puzzle for the "embodied appraisal" theory. Prinz (2004) explains emotions aroused by music as perceptual illusions like the Müller–Lyer illusion.

v   Of course I might be sad about the horrible horn-playing or glad that my daughter is conducting the orchestra, but such emotions are not induced by or directed at the musical piece per se.

vi See Dutton (2009) for one recent account of how a delight in the beautiful and well-crafted may have evolved.

vii See Robinson (2009, pp. 651–80). Many of the issues I touch on here are given a more detailed treatment in that article.

viii Kivy (2002, p. 97) has a different explanation. He argues that what Meyer is talking about are points of tension and release *perceived in* the music, not emotions *aroused by* it. This is also how he deals with expressiveness in music: to say a piece of music expresses melancholy is simply to say that it has a certain aesthetic property that is perceived but not felt.

ix But these emotional responses are not typically relevant to musical understanding or appreciation, which is what matters for Kivy and Meyer.

x   See Robinson (2005, ch. 13).

xi Nussbaum confines his attention to "western tonal art music since 1650" (Nussbaum 2007, p. 20). He is not talking about folk music or rock concerts or atonal music or the music of Indonesia or Ghana (to name but a few).

xii Nussbaum explains how music can be experienced as spatial by pointing out that there is a homology "between the acousticolateral nuclei of fishes" which enable the fish to "detect and locate moving objects in the water" and "the human cochlear nucleus" (Nussbaum 2007, p. 52) especially the organ of Corti. Just as fish detect predators by means of "sequential stimulations on the skin surface" (Nussbaum 2007, p. 53), i.e. by a kind of touch, so "sequential mechanical stimulations along the frequency-tuned length of the organ of Corti" enable humans to experience musical sounds in a tactile way as having location and direction.

xiii   For Nussbaum these hierarchical representations are given by Lerdahl and Jackendoff tree structures.

xiv   Strictly speaking, as we saw earlier, a perception of affordances is an "emotional experience" for Frijda rather than an emotion. Thanks to Tom Cochrane for pointing this out.

xv   Nussbaum seems to think that we typically simulate our own actions as we move (in imagination) through the music, but I assume we may also simulate a distinct persona in the music as when we imagine the "hero" of Beethoven's Fifth as he struggles with his fate and finally triumphs over it.

xvi   I owe this point to Kathleen Higgins (2009).

xvii   See Robinson (2007). See also Cochrane (2010).

xviii   See for example Rizzolatti et al. (1996). The discovery of so-called mirror neurons has spawned a wealth of philosophical speculation about emotional contagion and empathy.

xix   And also perhaps of those witnessing this struggle and feeling uplifted by it.

xx   I find it interesting that Kivy's account of what we appreciate in music focuses on the "puzzle" element in music listening, for example, how we try out different possibilities ("hypotheses") in our minds for what is likely to happen and how we play "hide and seek" with the main themes. Both these activities may turn out to be implemented (perhaps unconsciously) by the motor system (see Kivy 2002, ch. 5).

xxi   James points out that the same bodily responses can occur not only to simple stimuli that we might be pre-programmed to respond to, but also to more cognitively complex stimuli of the same general type: threats of whatever type elicit a fear response, offenses of whatever type elicit an angry response, losses of whatever type elicit a sad response and so on.

xxii   The philosopher Laura Sizer (2006) has independently made a similar point: emotions and feelings have different functions, in that emotions cause behavior and feelings inform us about how we are behaving.

xxiii   Schachter referred to this as a "labeling" process.

xxiv   See also Robinson (2005, ch. 13).

xxv   Scherer and Zentner (2001, p. 374). See also Niedenthal (2001).

xxvi   Bower (1981, p. 141).

xxvii   Niedenthal et al. (1997) and Sloboda and Juslin (2001, p. 84).

xxviii   Some of the mechanisms they identify are mechanisms I have discussed here, e.g. "musical expectancies," which produce the emotions I discussed in relation to Meyer. Some are mechanisms that are not directly related to the understanding and/or appreciation of the music in question, such as "episodic memory," i.e. "the process whereby an emotion is induced in a listener because the music evokes a memory of a particular event in the listener's life." In this case it is the memory that causes the emotional response rather than the music per se: the music may have a different character from the memory, as when I associate a melancholy event with a cheerful tune.

References

Bower, G. (1981). Mood and memory. *American Psychologist*, **31**, 129–48.

Cochrane, T. (2010). A simulation theory of musical expressivity. *The Australasian Journal of Philosophy*, **88**, 191–207.

Damasio, A. (2003). *Looking for Spinoza: Joy, Sorrow, and the Feeling Brain.* Orlando, FL: Harcourt.

Damasio, A., Grabowski, T. J., Bechara, A., Damasio, H., Ponto, L. L. B., Parvizi, J., and Hichwa, R. D. (2000). Subcortical and cortical brain activity during the feeling of self-generated emotions. *Nature Neuroscience*, **3**, 1049–56.

Dutton, D. (2009). *The Art Instinct: Beauty, Pleasure, and Human Evolution*. Oxford: Oxford University Press.

Frijda, N. (1986). *The Emotions*. Cambridge: Cambridge University Press.

Frijda, N. (2007). *The Laws of Emotion*. Mahwah, NJ: Lawrence Erlbaum Associates.

Higgins, K. (2009). Comments on Nussbaum's *The Musical Representation*. American Society for Aesthetics Pacific Division.

James, W. (1981). *The Works of William James*, ed. F. H. Burkhardt, 3 vols. Cambridge, MA: Harvard University Press.

Juslin, P. (2001). Communicating emotion in music performance: a review and a theoretical framework. In P. Juslin and J. Sloboda (eds), *Music and Emotion: Theory and Research*, pp. 309–37. New York: Oxford University Press.

Juslin, P. and Vjästfäll, D. (2008). Emotional responses to music: the need to consider underlying mechanisms. *Behavioral and Brain Sciences*, **31**, 559–75.

Kivy, P. (1990). *Music Alone: Philosophical Reflections on the Purely Musical Experience*. Ithaca, NY: Cornell University Press.

Kivy, P. (2002). *Introduction to a Philosophy of Music*. Oxford: Clarendon.

Kivy, P. (2006). Mood and music: some reflections for Noël Carroll. *Journal of Aesthetics and Art Criticism*, **64**, 271–81.

Laird, J. D. (2007). *Feelings: the Perception of Self*. New York, Oxford University Press.

Lazarus, R. (1991). *Emotion and Adaptation*. New York: Oxford University Press.

Levitin, D. (2006). *This is Your Brain on Music: the Science of a Human Obsession*. New York: Dutton.

Meyer, L. B. (1956). *Emotion and Meaning in Music*. Chicago: University of Chicago Press.

Newcomb, A. (1984). Once more "between absolute and program music": Schumann's Second Symphony. *19th Century Music*, **7**, 233–50.

Niedenthal, P., Halberstadt, J., and Setterlund, M. B. (1997). Being happy and seeing "happy": emotional state facilitates visual word recognition. *Cognition and Emotion*, **11**, 594–624.

Niedenthal, P., Brauer, M., Halberstadt, J. B., and Innes-Ker, A. H. (2001). When did her smile drop? Facial mimicry and the influences of emotional state on the detection of change in emotional expression. *Cognition and Emotion*, **15**, 853–64.

Nussbaum, C. (2007). *The Musical Representation: Meaning, Ontology, and Emotion*. Cambridge, MA: MIT Press.

Nyklicek, I., Thayer, J. F., and van Doornen, L. J. P. (1997). Cardiorespiratory differentiation of musically-induced emotions. *Journal of Psychophysiology*, **11**, 304–21.

Prinz, J. (2004). *Gut Reactions: a Perceptual Theory of Emotion*. New York: Oxford University Press.

Rizzolatti, G., Fadiga, L., Gallese, V., and Fogassi, L. (1996). Premotor cortex and the recognition of motor actions. *Cognitive Brain Research*, **3**, 131–41.

Robinson, J. (1995). Startle. *Journal of Philosophy*, **92**, 53–74.

Robinson, J. (2005). *Deeper than Reason: Emotion and its Role in Literature, Music, and Art*. Oxford: Clarendon.

Robinson, J. (2007). Expression and expressiveness in art. *Postgraduate Journal of Aesthetics*, **4**(2), 19–41.

Robinson, J. (2009). Emotional responses to music: what are they? how do they work? and are they relevant to aesthetic appreciation? In P. Goldie (ed.), *Oxford Handbook of Philosophy of Emotion*, pp. 651–680. Oxford: Oxford University Press.

Schachter, S. and Singer, J. (1962). Cognitive, social, and physiological determinants of emotional state. *Psychological Review*, **69**, 379–99.

Scherer, K. and Zentner, M. (2001). Emotional effects of music: production rules. In P. Juslin and J. Sloboda (eds), *Music and Emotion: Theory and Research*, pp. 361–92. Oxford: Oxford University Press.

Scherer, K. R., Schorr, A., and Johnstone, T. (2001). The nature and study of appraisal: a review of the issues. In *Appraisal Processes in Emotion: Theory, Methods, Research*, pp. 369–91. Oxford: Oxford University Press.

Sizer, L. (2006). What feelings can't do. *Mind and Language*, **20**, 108–35.

Sloboda, J. A. and Juslin, P. N. (2001). Psychological perspectives on music and emotion. In P. N. Juslin and J. A. Sloboda (eds), *Music and Emotion: Theory and Research*, pp. 71–104. Oxford: Oxford University Press.

Strack, F., Martin, L. L., and Stepper, S. (1988). Inhibiting and facilitating conditions of facial expression: a nonobtrusive test of the facial feedback hypothesis. *Journal of Personality and Social Psychology*, **54**, 768–77.

Trehub, S. (2003). Musical predispositions in infancy: an update. In R. J. Zatorre and I. Peretz (eds), *The Cognitive Neuroscience of Music*, pp. 3–20. Oxford: Oxford University Press.

Zentner, M., Grandjean, D., and Scherer, K. (2008). Emotions evoked by the sound of music: characterization, classification, and measurement. *Emotion*, **8**, 494–521.

Chapter 13

Music-to-listener emotional contagion

Stephen Davies

Introduction

It was in 1980 and 1983 that I first published on the relation between music's expressiveness and the listener's response. I do not subscribe to the so-called arousal theory, according to which "the music is sad" is true if and only if the music disposes a suitably qualified and interested listener to feel sad. I regard music's expressive properties as possessed independently of their effects (for details see Davies 1994, pp. 184–99, 2006). Nevertheless, I do think that music's expressiveness can induce an emotional reaction and that, in the interesting case, the listener is moved to feel the emotion that the music expresses.[i] I call this a "mirroring" response and describe the communication of emotion from music to listener as emotional "contagion" or "infection." I am not wedded to the medical metaphor, however; I also describe the connection as involving transmission, communication, or osmosis.

Apart from the musical case, it is commonly held that we can be affected in our affective states by the expressive character that we are inclined to attribute to other inanimate aspects of our environments, such as the color of the room or the tone of the weather. Again, the effect, if it exists, presumably relies on some mode of contagion.

Here is a more formal characterization of emotional contagion (from Davies 2011):

> one emotional state, appearance, or condition is transmitted to a person (or creature) who comes to undergo the same emotion; the display of the first emotional state plays a causal role in the process of transmission and the first emotional state must be perceived, either attentionally or non-attentionally, by the emotion's recipient; the first emotional state is not the emotional object of the response, however, because the responder does not hold about the first emotional state beliefs that make it an appropriate intentional object for the response in question.

Some psychologists, including Juslin and Västfjäll (2008a), identify emotions as involving appraisals and objects that are appraised, even where contagion is involved.[ii] Let me make it clearer what I mean by saying that music is not the *emotional object* of the listener's mirroring response. Though it is true that background music of which the hearer is not consciously aware might affect her feelings by way of contagion, that is not the relevant case. And though the intentional object of one's response can drift apart from its perceptual object under conditions of error, as when one fears the presence of a lion when one mistakes the shadow of a mop for the shadow of a lion, that again is not the relevant case. Rather, the important point is that even where the mirroring response of sadness targets and tracks the music, one is not sad *for* or *about* the music. The *intentional object* of the emotion, or in Anthony Kenny's (1963) terminology the *emotional object* of the emotion, is the object that is perceived with belief as falling under the emotion-relevant description; for instance, where the emotion is envy of another, its emotional object is the person who I believe to possess something that I do not have and desire. While the listener's contagious response of sadness is reflected back to the sad music and in that sense takes the music as its object, and while this response clearly involves appraisals of the music's expressive character, the music is not the *emotional object* of the response because the listener does not believe of the music what would make it the intentional object of a sad response, namely, that the music is unfortunate, suffering, or regrettable. The music is not brought under the characterization that picks out the *emotional object* of sadness. And provided that nothing else is brought under that characterization, the response lacks an emotional object though the music remains its perceptual object.

Person-to-person emotional contagion involves "catching" the other's emotional state, but should be distinguished from cases that are outwardly similar in that two people come to experience the same emotion (Davies 2011). The following are not instances of emotional contagion as I have characterized that notion. We both feel the same emotion because our emotions have a common intentional object about which we both hold the same emotion-relevant beliefs. (We both laugh at the same joke.) I react to your emotion by feeling the same, because I believe the basis of your reaction will also provide me with a reason to react similarly. (Seeing you flee in terror, I do the same without waiting to discover what you are terrified of.) Your emotion is the emotional object of my response and our emotions are the same. (You are angry that we are delayed, and I am angry that you are angry because you promised you would keep your cool.) I try to work out what you are feeling by imaginatively simulating your situation, or I use knowledge of your character and circumstances, and thereby empathically share your state.

Also to be distinguished from emotional contagion are certain social or situational influences on our reactions, for example, that people laugh more with others who laugh out loud, that they may feel a sense of community through shared emotion, or that they may become self-conscious and embarrassed to react as others do.

I

At the time I first published my views, psychologists apparently had not clearly isolated and studied the phenomenon of emotional contagion, though there had been much work on empathy and sympathy. The pioneering work *Emotional Contagion* by Elaine Hatfield, John Cacioppo, and Richard Rapson came in 1994. Of course, those earlier researchers were not interested in the musical case; they studied the human-to-human transmission of affect. And their primary interest, unlike mine, was in the mechanism causally responsible for inducing in one person what is felt by the other. In brief, they described this mechanism as follows:

(1) in attending to person A, her interlocutor, person B tends unconsciously to ape A's facial expressions, vocal tone, etc.;

(2) as part of working out what she feels, B monitors her facial expression, vocal tone, etc.;

(3) so, if A feels some emotion and betrays it in her appearance, tone, and action, B is inclined to come to feel the same emotion.

In a different work, Teresa Brennan (2004) surmises that the mechanism involves the subconscious detection of pheromones. However, if there is emotional contagion between music and humans, or between colors or the weather and humans, it cannot be facial mimicry or pheromones that underpin it because music, colors, and the weather do not present a human physiognomy or give off pheromones. The error of these psychologists is to equate the phenomenon with causal mechanisms that apply only in the cases of contagion that interest them. We need a more careful characterization of the phenomenon, such as I offered earlier.

When psychologists searched for an analogous role for music in the induction of emotion, it was in the context of testing how background music affects the mood and behavior of diners and shoppers and in the use of music as therapy.[iii] Neither kind of study specifically targets music-to-listener emotional contagion, as opposed to more general interactive effects between music and mood, and in many cases the concern is with effects that do not involve the hearer's attention to the music as such. As a result, these studies do not provide useful paradigms for the study of emotional contagion where this results from the listener's close attention to the music's expressive character in a context of trying to follow the music with understanding.

Psychologists concerned with music-to-listener emotional contagion of the attentional variety tend to return to the human-to-human model. For instance, Juslin and Västfjäll (2008a, p. 565) describe music-emotional contagion as:

> a process whereby an emotion is induced by a piece of music because the listener perceives the emotional expression of the music, and then "mimics" this expression internally, which by means of either peripheral feedback from muscles, or a more direct activation of the relevant emotional representations in the brain, leads to an induction of the same emotion.… Recent research has suggested that the process of emotional contagion may occur through the mediation of so-called mirror neurons discovered in studies of the monkey premotor cortex in the 1990s.

The problem with this is that it appears to turn what is supposed to be literal for human-to-human contagion into something metaphorical. It is not as if the music has muscles, the movements of which can be mimicked, or a premotor cortex with neuronal activity that can be mirrored in the brains of listeners. Because of their apparently metaphorical character, the explanatory power of such characterizations of the relevant mechanisms is questionable.

Yet talk of emotional contagion seems perfectly apt in such cases. In part this is because talk of musical movement, pattern, tension, and expressive appearances is literal, or so I would maintain. Such attributions are secondary, in that the meanings of the relevant terms are not first taught by reference to such examples, but once the secondary extensions of these meanings are acquired, the terms have the kind of shared interpersonal use that live metaphors lack. For instance, dictionary definitions of words like "sad" frequently mention the case of music or art, whereas live metaphors do not appear in such reference works. Moreover, whereas metaphors can easily be replaced with non-synonymous terms, talk of spatial movement and the use of emotion-terms in describing the music's character seem to be ineliminable.[iv] If this is so, talk of listeners mimicking the music is not merely poetic; even if there are no musical muscles or neuronal patterns to be imitated or mirrored, there can be musical movement and process, patterns of tension and release, and the like.

How then does emotional contagion operate in the musical case? That is for scientists to discover, but it is possible to offer some speculative suggestions. I favor the view that music is expressive because we experience it as presenting the kind of carriage, gait, or demeanor that can be symptomatic of states such as happiness, sadness, anger, sassy sexuality, and so on.[v] If contagion operates through mimicry, we might expect the listener to adopt bodily postures and attitudes (or posturally relevant muscular proprioceptions) like those apparent in the music's progress.[vi] Vocal mimicry, in the form of subtle tensing or flexing of vocal muscles, would also be a predictable response to vocal music or to acts of subvocal singing along with instrumental music.[vii] And where the flux of music is felt as an articulated pattern of tensing and relaxing, this is likely to be imaged and mimed within the body, perhaps in ways that are neither subpostural nor subvocal. Finally, there is the possibility that music works on the brain, not only by eliciting physical-cum-physiological changes that nudge the subject as she becomes aware of them toward affective appraisals and responses, but also more immediately, by directly stimulating cortical regions linked with emotional recognitions and responses.[viii] Many and diverse routes of emotional transmission might be involved, perhaps simultaneously.

II

There are many mechanisms by which an emotional response to music might be induced. Juslin and Västfjäll (2008a) identify six, of which emotional contagion is only one, the others being brain-stem reflexes, evaluative conditioning, visual imagery, episodic memory, and musical expectancy. Some of these—for example, increased tension when a prediction about the course of the music is defeated or the reflex induction of a startle response by an unexpected loud chord—perhaps should not count as emotions. And others—for example, happiness when music triggers memories of a happy occasion—reveal more about the experiences of the listener than the nature of the music. One reason for focusing on the mirroring response, then, is that it is usually identified as a fully fledged emotion that is directly connected to and is revealing of the music's expressive character. More important for the philosopher, perhaps, is that the mirroring response is intriguingly problematic in two respects.

First, this type of response violates the cognitive theory of the emotions, which is a theory put forward by Kenny (1963) and Robert C. Solomon (1976) among others. Not everyone went so far as Solomon, who declared that emotions are no more than judgments, but the cognitive theory maintains that emotions are to be characterized in terms of the kinds of beliefs or epistemic commitments one holds about their objects. It cannot be fear for myself I feel unless I believe of something that it poses a threat to me; I cannot envy you unless I think you possess something that I do not have and desire. The cognitive theory stresses the cognitive dimension of emotions, their intentionality or object-directedness, and the public aspect of the expressive behaviors that are in part constitutive of them, and contrasts with a purely physiological, often pneumatic, view that sees emotions as inner stirrings that precede cognition and are distinguished one from the other by their distinctive phenomenological profiles.[ix]

Now, the mirroring response to music does not align with the cognitive theory because, as I observed earlier, the listener does not believe of sad music what would make it an appropriate emotional object of the sad response she experiences, namely, that there is something about the music that is unfortunate or regrettable. She does not believe the music is sentient, and hence does not believe that it suffers the sadness it expresses, so there is nothing here for her to get sad about, yet she does become sad. Not all her sad attentional responses to the music are of this kind; she might be saddened by the music's banality and execrable execution. Such responses match the cognitive theory and are otherwise unproblematic.[x] But the attentional mirroring response of sadness does not rely on her believing of the music that it is unfortunate or regrettable (which she does not), and where she thinks the music is good—is indeed better for its expressiveness—such beliefs as she has are at odds with the sad response she feels.

The second respect in which the mirroring response is problematic is this: it appears to be non-rational, yet notwithstanding this we often would acknowledge such a response as evidence that the listener follows the music with understanding. Typically, we justify our emotions by showing that their emotional objects have the emotion-relevant qualities that we believe them to have. I justify my fear for myself by pointing to the dangerous qualities of the apparently hungry lion that shares the room with me, for instance. But in the case of the mirroring response, the listener does not hold beliefs about the music appropriate for her response to its expressiveness. She cannot justify her response of sadness in the usual way, by indicating what is unfortunate and regrettable about the music or its expressiveness.[xi]

III

There are several ways one might try to address the first worry. One possibility is that the emotion takes something other than the music as its emotional object. Perhaps the listener believes the composer must have experienced loss and suffering to compose such sad music, and her sadness is directed to him. It seems implausible to suggest that all mirroring responses could be explained away in this fashion, however; after all, composers often were happy to be commissioned to write sad requiems. A second, more promising approach is to argue that make-believe can substitute for belief in securing an emotion to its object. And it is quite plausible to suggest that our responses to fictional novels, dramas, paintings, and movies involve making believe that one is seeing (or hearing about) actual events, and that this grounds the response, whether we call it a genuine emotion or not.[xii] Moreover, such a move answers the second concern as well as the first; we can justify the rationality of the response by reference to what is true in the fiction, that is, to the truths that the audience make-believedly entertains under the artist's direction (Davies 1983). But what is one supposed to make-believe on hearing an "abstract" musical work without a sung text, program story, or literary title? Several philosophers have suggested that the listener make-believes that the music provides a narrative about the experiences of a hypothetical persona.[xiii] The listener feels sad because she hears the music as a direct expression of that fictional persona's suffering, just as she feels sad on reading *Anna Karenina* or weeps at the end of *La Bohème* though she knows that Anna and Mimi are no more real than is the persona imagined as being in the music.

I agree that the cognitive theory should be modified to include make-believe as well as belief (and perhaps other modes of mental representation as well) and that this allows us to make sense of our responses to fictional narratives and depictions. Moreover, I allow that the hypothetical persona account does capture an important aspect of our experience of music's expressiveness, namely, that it is more like a direct encounter with someone who feels an emotion and shows it, than it is like being told about or reading a description of such matters. Nevertheless, I am not convinced that the hypothetical persona theory correctly characterizes music's expressiveness and our mode of reacting to this (see Davies 1983, 1997, 2006). In brief, many listeners who both recognize music's expressiveness and experience a mirroring response to that expressiveness are not aware of the acts of make-believe posited by the theory. Besides, unlike a fictional novel or movie, instrumental music does not possess a definite propositional or depictive content, so our imaginative engagement with such music is not controlled and directed to the extent that it is when we read a novel or see a movie. Where one listener imagines a single, changing persona, another might hear a series of different personas; where the first imagines youthful depression, the other hears aged tiredness; where the first hears flight away, the other senses running toward; and so on. Those who propose and defend the persona account aim not only to explain why we hear music as expressive but also to acknowledge the strength of interpersonal agreement over what it expresses. But given how free instrumental music leaves our imagination, I believe the theory fails in the second task as well as the first.

IV

My response to the first issue did not take the form of a defense of, or friendly amendment to, the cognitive theory of the emotions. A number of problem cases for that theory are widely recognized: phobias (which do not involve beliefs appropriate to the emotion experienced) and moods (which are apparently not targeted on any specific intentional objects and therefore do not involve emotion-relevant object-directed beliefs). The musical case does not fit in either of these camps, but is a new kind of counterexample that was not widely recognized as such. This does not mean that the musical case is one peculiar to the aesthetic context, however, which is a good thing because the application of emotion terms under circumstances that bear no resemblance to the wider context of their use, as in talk of sui generis artistic emotions or responses, is rightly regarded with suspicion by modern philosophers of art. In fact, appealing to what I took to be commonplaces of folk psychology, I claimed that emotional contagion is familiar as a response to our fellow humans. We often catch or are affected by the mood of others. Moreover, the outcome is not necessarily diminished when we move to modes of expression that do not involve sentience. I speculate that a person would be more likely to be depressed working on the production of masks of tragedy than on the production of masks of comedy. And moving yet further from the human case, as I noted previously it is widely held that the weather and colors can affect our emotions, and we predicate expressive properties to both the weather and to colors. So my response to the first concern, that the musical mirroring response is not consistent with the cognitive theory of the emotions (even if amended to include make-believe alongside belief) can be summarized this way: yes, the musical reaction is an exception to the cognitive theory of the emotions, but there are other exceptions to the theory, including ones that parallel the musical case.

As for the second problem—that the listener does not have the beliefs that could justify her response—one should admit that it has some force. It is not obvious that we should criticize someone who is not moved to sadness by sad music, because it is not as if he thereby betrays callousness or lack of sympathy. But we can also argue that, if the mirroring response does occur, it can be justified, not by reference to emotion-relevant beliefs but rather in the sense that no other non-cognitively directed response is equally apt. By comparison with the person who is typically cheered by sad music and depressed by happy music, but without believing or make-believing about either anything that makes it a fit object for happiness or depression, the person who is cheered by happy music or saddened by gloomy music seems normal and has the appropriate response. Or to make the point differently, there seems to be a place prepared in our natural history for the mirroring response in a way that is not true for alternatives that are similar in also not being cognitively directed. It is for this reason that the listener's response can be taken as indexing her sensitive comprehension of the music's character.

We might draw a parallel here with emotional responses to what are known to be fictions. Some philosophers regard these as paradoxical and irrational. After all, why should I fear the movie monster that I know not to exist and, hence, not to be able to harm me? Whatever one says in answer to this paradox, it seems reasonable to suggest that it is more rational to fear the monster than the cowering, little old lady that it is threatening in the film.[xiv] In the same way, it is more rational to be saddened by sad music and gladdened by happy music, even if I think the music expresses no one's feelings in either case and even if I hold no other emotion-relevant beliefs about the music, than it is to feel the reverse.

Notes

i   Psychologists have recorded the effect; see Evans and Schubert (2008).

ii   By the way, I agree with Robinson (2008) that Juslin and Västfjäll (2008a) frequently depart from their definition in their paper in which they give it.

iii   On shopping, see Bruner 1990; Milliman 1982, 1986; North and Hargreaves 1997; on therapy, see Bunt and Pavlicevic 2001.

iv   For further discussion see Davies (1994, pp. 148–65) and Budd (2008, chs 6–9).

v   For details see Davies (1980, 1994, pp. 221–58, 2006).

vi   For relevant empirical data see Janata and Grafton (2003).

vii For relevant empirical data see Koelsch *et al.* (2006). Juslin and Laukka (2003) and Juslin and Västfjäll (2008a), who postulate that the response to music can be explained as involving emotional contagion, make the comparison not with facial mimicry but with the communication of affect through vocal cues. See Patel (2008) on how this hypothesis might be tested via brain imaging. Simpson *et al.* (2008) suggest their brain-imaging results—that instrumental music is not processed by parts of the brain concerned with the voice—show that contagion is not a mechanism for the arousal of emotion by music. Their conclusion is unwarranted because they do not consider alternatives to the suggestion by Juslin and his fellow researchers that music is experienced as a super-expressive voice. (Juslin and Västfjäll 2008b reject their criticism for other reasons, of course.)

viii For further discussion of related possibilities, see Cochrane 2010.

ix   For a subtle account of the issues written with the advantage of hindsight, see Solomon (2003). And note that there is much weaker form of cognitivism to which many psychologists subscribe according to which emotions involve appraisals of one's self or situation, where these appraisals may be very fast, automatic, and not present to consciousness. In other words, there is cognitive (or at least bodily) processing but there need not be the adoption of propositional attitudes such as belief.

x   Peter Kivy (1987) is one philosopher who argues that all emotional responses to music are of this kind and that the mirroring response never occurs.

xi   There is a third issue, specifically about the sad (rather than the happy) mirroring response, that I will not consider here, namely, why we enjoy and return to music that makes us feel sad. For discussion see Davies (1994, pp. 307–20).

xii Carroll (1990, 1997) and Lamarque (1981) count these as genuine emotions, Walton (1990) does not.

xiii For example see Levinson (1996, 2006) and Robinson (2005).

xiv For discussion of the alleged paradox of responding emotionally to what are recognized to be fictional characters and situations and of the rationality of such responses see Davies (2009).

References

Brennan, T. (2004). *The Transmission of Affect*. Ithaca: Cornell University Press.

Bruner, G. C. (1990). Music, mood, and marketing. *Journal of Marketing*, **54**, 94–104.

Budd, M. (2008). *Aesthetic Essays*. Oxford: Oxford University Press.

Bunt, L. and Pavlicevic, M. (2001). Music and emotion: perspectives from music therapy. In P. N. Juslin and J. A. Sloboda (eds), *Music and Emotion: Theory and Research*, pp. 181–201. Oxford: Oxford University Press.

Carroll, N. (1990). *The Philosophy of Horror or Paradoxes of the Heart*. New York: Routledge.

Carroll, N. (1997). Art, narrative, and emotion. In M. Hjort and S. Laver (eds), *Emotion and the Arts*, pp. 190–211. Oxford: Oxford University Press.

Cochrane, T. (2010). A simulation theory of musical expressivity. *Australasian Journal of Philosophy*, **88**, 191–207.

Davies, S. (1980). The expression of emotion in music. *Mind*, **89**, 67–86.

Davies, S. (1983). The rationality of aesthetic responses. *British Journal of Aesthetics*, **23**, 38–47.

Davies, S. (1994). *Musical Meaning and Expression*. Ithaca: Cornell University Press.

Davies, S. (1997). Contra the hypothetical persona in music. In M. Hjort and S. Laver (eds), *Emotion and the Arts*, pp. 95–109. Oxford: Oxford University Press.

Davies, S. (2006). Artistic expression and the hard case of pure music. In M. Kieran (ed.), *Contemporary Debates in Aesthetics and the Philosophy of Art*, pp. 179–91. Oxford: Blackwell.

Davies, S. (2009). Responding emotionally to fictions. *Journal of Aesthetics and Art Criticism*, **67**, 269–84.

Davies, S. (2011). Infectious music: music-listener emotional contagion. In P. Goldie and A. Coplan (eds), *Empathy: Philosophical and Psychological Perspectives*, pp. 134–48. Oxford: Oxford University Press.

Evans, P. and Schubert, E. (2008). Relationships between express and felt emotions in music. *Musicae Scientiae*, **12**, 75–99.

Hatfield, E., Cacioppo, J. T., and Rapson, R. L. (1994). *Emotional Contagion*. New York: Cambridge University Press.

Janata, P. and Grafton, S. T. (2003). Swinging in the brain: shared neural substrates for behaviors related to sequencing and music. *Nature Neuroscience*, **6**, 682–87.

Juslin, P. N. and Laukka, P. (2003). Communication of emotion in vocal expression and music performance: different channels, same code? *Psychological Bulletin*, **129**, 770–814.

Juslin, P. N. and Västfjäll, D. (2008a). Emotional responses to music: the need to consider underlying mechanisms. *Behavioural and Brain Sciences*, **31**, 559–75.

Juslin, P. N. and Västfjäll, D. (2008b). All emotions are not created equal: reaching beyond the traditional disputes. *Behavioral and Brain Sciences*, **31**, 600–12.

Kenny, A. (1963). *Action, Emotion, and Will*. London: Routledge & Kegan Paul.

Kivy, P. (1987). How music moves. In P. Alperson (ed.), *What Is Music?: an Introduction to the Philosophy of Music*, pp. 149–63. New York: Haven.

Koelsch, S., Fritz, T., von Crammon, D. Y., Müller, K., and Frederici, A. D. (2006). Investigating emotion with music: an fMRI study. *Human Brain Mapping*, **27**, 239–50.

Lamarque, P. (1981). How can we fear and pity fictions? *British Journal of Aesthetics*, **21**, 291–304.

Levinson, J. (1996). Musical expressiveness. In *The Pleasures of Aesthetics*, pp. 90–125. Ithaca: Cornell University Press.

Levinson, J. (2006). Musical expressiveness as hearability-as-expression. In M. Kieran (ed.), *Contemporary Debates in Aesthetics and the Philosophy of Art*, pp. 192–204. Oxford: Blackwell.

Milliman, R. E. (1982). Using background music to affect the behavior of supermarket shoppers. *Journal of Marketing*, **46**(3), 86–91.

Milliman, R. E. (1986). The influence of background music on the behavior of restaurant patrons. *Journal of Consumer Research*, **13**, 286–9.

North, A. C. and Hargreaves, D. J. (1997). Music and consumer behaviour. In D. J. Hargreaves and A. C. North (eds), *The Social Psychology of Music*, pp. 268–89. Oxford: Oxford University Press.

Patel, A. D. (2008). A neurobiological strategy for exploring links between emotion recognition in music and speech. *Behavioral and Brain Sciences*, **31**, 589–90.

Robinson, J. (2005). *Deeper than Reason: Emotion and its Role in Literature, Music, and Art*. Oxford: Clarendon Press.

Robinson, J. (2008). Do all musical emotions have the music itself as their intentional object? *Behavioral and Brain Sciences*, **31**, 592–3.

Simpson, E. A., Oliver, W. T., and Fragaszy, D. (2008). Super-expressive voices: music to my ears? *Behavioral and Brain Sciences*, **31**, 596–7.

Solomon, R. C. (1976). *The Passions*. Garden City: Anchor.

Solomon, R. C. (2003). Thoughts and feelings: what is a "cognitive theory" of the emotions and does it neglect affectivity. In *Not Passion's Slave: Emotions and Choice*, pp. 178–94. Oxford: Oxford University Press.

Walton, K. L. (1990). *Mimesis as Make-Believe: on the Foundations of the Representational Arts*. Cambridge, MA: Harvard University Press.

Chapter 14

Empathy, enaction, and shared musical experience: evidence from infant cognition

Joel Krueger

Introduction

Empathy is a kind of intimacy, an immediate sharing of experience and understanding.[i] In what follows, I consider how shared musical experiences can bring individuals into intense forms of communion and understanding—even during the earliest stages of life. The basic idea is that music can be thought of as an "aesthetic technology" (DeNora 2000) for co-constructing, with others, new relationships and shared experiences; it is a tool jointly used to create opportunities for empathic connection and basic forms of communication. The more radical idea defended below is that music dynamically motivates even the earliest infant–caregiver interactions. Various studies indicate that infants seem poised from birth to respond to music in relatively sophisticated ways, perceptually speaking. They are active perceivers. Moreover, within these early interactions, music plays—or at least *can* play—a crucial role in drawing out and guiding early communicative exchanges. And these early instances of active and shared musical experiences, I suggest, provide insights into how we interact with music both alone and with others later in life. This chapter is therefore a consideration of shared experiences of music—specifically, a consideration of how music functions as a tool for driving rudimentary forms of empathic connectedness. Most of the discussion that follows focuses on how infants hear and respond to music. I use "empathy" fairly broadly to refer to our basic capacity to experience and engage with the thoughts, feelings, and intentions of others in an immediate (i.e. non-inferential) way.[ii] Music is thus a tool for driving primitive but experientially rich forms of empathy.

In developing this idea, I stress the enactive character of shared musical experience.[iii] Shared musical experiences depend crucially on sensorimotor features of the animate body. To highlight this feature of shared musical experience, I characterize such experiences as dynamic processes of (1) joint *sense-making*, enacted via temporally extended patterns of (2) *skillful engagement* with music that are (3) synchronically and diachronically *scaffolded* by the surrounding environment. The discussion below treats these three aspects in turn, arguing that they collectively afford the unique sort of intimacy—empathy—possible within shared listening experiences.

So what?

What is the theoretical significance of this way of thinking about the social and enactive dimensions of musical experience? There are at least two reasons why this thesis is philosophically compelling. First, it challenges what the psychologist John Sloboda calls the "pharmaceutical model" behind many philosophical and psychological treatments of music listening. According to Sloboda, this model rests on the idea that music listeners "are the passive recipient of musical stimuli which have the psychological effect they do because of the way that the human brain is constructed, on the one hand, and the way that music is constructed, on the other" (Sloboda 2005, p. 319). Music listening is thus largely a passive experience. Listeners passively contemplate a musical work and respond to it in a purely structural way, that is, in terms of whatever musical meanings a composer has seen fit to embed within a piece's compositional structure. However, this is a quite restricted way of thinking about musical experience in that it overlooks the active way that musical meanings are dynamically constructed, even by infants. Listeners, I suggest, have a great deal of perceptual autonomy in what they do with music: how they listen, what sort of meanings they choose to enact, and how they actively engage with music to forge relationships and shared experiences.

Second, there is a tendency in some circles to see music and musical experience as somehow inessential to the business of everyday life. Steven Pinker (1997) famously calls music "auditory cheesecake." Since it has no clear adaptive function, according to Pinker, music is ultimately a pleasurable but evolutionarily irrelevant artifact lacking developmental sustenance:

> Compared with language, vision, social reasoning, and physical know-how, music could vanish from our species and the rest of our lifestyle would be virtually unchanged. Music appears to be pure pleasure technology, a cocktail of recreational drugs that we ingest through the ear to simulate a mass of pleasure circuits at once. (Pinker 1997, p. 528)

I argue that this pharmaceutical view of musical experience is simply mistaken. Not only does it ignore the active dimension of musical experience, it also overlooks the ways that music and musicality are deeply embedded in everyday life, informing and shaping our relationships and communicative practices. Indeed, without music as a regulating force, our social and emotional lives would change dramatically.[iv] Moreover, as the discussion below will show, "musicality" is an essentially quality of fundamental forms of embodied interpersonal communication. Basic rhythms and expressive contours of these pre-linguistic bodily engagements have an inherently musical character. Music itself is, once again, a crucial aesthetic technology that we regularly employ to deepen social intimacy and to train the young in communicative practices essential to their social being. In short, music enhances and refines our affective capacities and empathic relatedness. It plays a critical role in shaping our sociality.

Intersubjectivity and "communicative musicality"

The notion of a developmentally primitive "communicative musicality" (Malloch 1999) has recently received much attention.[v] It captures the musical patterns that are part of the infant's earliest social engagements with others—that is, the affectively governed dynamics of "coordinated companionship" characterizing healthy infant–caregiver interactions (Trevarthen and Malloch 2002, p. 11). Importantly, this early musical interaction is pre-linguistic. It is contoured through the fine-grained inflection of expressive vocal and bodily gestures that bring infant and caregiver into a state of felt attunement (Malloch 1999) or a kind of musical empathy. For instance, caregivers around the world intuitively adopt certain forms of expression calibrated to stimulate the infant (Trainor and Heinmiller 1998, p. 78). This includes things like exaggerated movements, facial expressions, and gestures, as well as "infant-directed" speech consisting of raised pitch, slowed tempo, elongated vowels, and slow pitch contours with large frequency ranges modified to capture the infant's attention and draw out their innate communicative capacities (Stern *et al.* 1985; Papousek and Papousek 1987; Malloch 1999). These exaggerated sound features are often found in music, giving these structured patterns of engagement a quasi-musical character.[vi] Additionally, these mutually coordinated patterns appear to facilitate interpersonal understanding. They afford an immediate and direct kind of experiential access to the thoughts, feelings, and intentions of others insofar as these are articulated in and through the dynamics of bodily expressiveness (Gallagher 2008; see also Zahavi 2001; Thompson 2001; Krueger and Legrand 2009; Krueger 2011b). The notion of "communicative musicality" thus emphasizes the immediate way that feelings and experiences are coordinated and shared within interpersonal contexts via the musicality of the expressive body.

According to Colwyn Trevarthen and Stephen Malloch (Trevarthen and Malloch 2002; Malloch and Trevarthen 2009), communicative musicality harbors three dimensions: *pulse*, *quality*, and *narrative*. "Pulse" refers to "the regular succession of discrete behavioral events through time, vocal or gestural, the production and perception of these behaviors being the process through which two or more people may coordinate their communications" and anticipate future communicative interactions (Malloch and Trevarthen 2009, p. 4). Communicative pulses provide the forward momentum driving our interpersonal exchanges. "Quality" refers to "the modulated contours of expression moving through time" (Malloch and Trevarthen 2009, p. 4). This includes both psycho-acoustic attributes of various vocalizations as well as attributes of direction and intensity of bodily gestures. Pulse and quality come together to form temporally extended "narratives" of expression and intention which emerge within sequences of joint gesture and vocal exchange. These affect-driven "'musical' narratives allow adult and infant, and adult and adult, to share a sense of sympathy and situated meaning in a shared sense of passing time" (Malloch and Trevarthen 2009, p. 4). Just as these qualities are essential to music, so, too, the argument goes, are they integral dimensions of our interpersonal engagements. It is the common "musicality" of our skillful bodily-affective encounters that, even before the development of language, allows us to "share time meaningfully together, in its emotional richness and its structural holding" and to forge communicative connections that link us in immediate, and immediately *felt*, ways (Malloch and Trevarthen 2009, p. 5). If infants can sensitively engage with these quasi-musical qualities, it appears that they emerge from the womb ready to enact the expressive rhythms and melodies that establish basic forms of social understanding.

I now want to further explore this notion of "communicative musicality" by looking at ways that music, particularly in shared listening contexts, facilitates a deep form of empathy and interpersonal intimacy. For while communication may in fact have a musical character, as Trevarthen and Malloch suggest, music itself, I suggest, is immediately recognized (even by the very young) as an environmental structure that affords the cultivation of social relationships and shared experience. With their suggestive notion of "communicative musicality," Trevarthen and Malloch seem to use "musicality" in a metaphorical way when describing the character of early forms of social interaction. But music, I suggest, can be a tool for refining our inherent socio-communicative musicality—bodily skills at the root of our capacity for empathy. An extended consideration of neonate music therapy will demonstrate how this is so.

Shared musical experience: joint sense-making

Christopher Small (1998) has coined the verb "musicking" to emphasize the active and situated nature of musical experience in all its variegated forms. According to Small, musicking is "to take part, in any capacity, in a musical performance, whether by performing, by listening, by rehearsing or practicing, by providing material for performance (what is called composing), or by dancing" (Small 1998, p. 9). This broad definition is Small's attempt to situate music and musicality within the common practices of everyday life. Additionally, it is compatible with Malloch and

Trevarthen's notion of "communicative musicality." According to Small, the primary function of music is to establish interpersonal relationships. Small thus argues that "music's primary meanings are not individual at all but social," and that they are, moreover, "fundamental to an understanding of the activity that is called music" (Small 1998, p. 8).

To return to the main thesis, the first proposal that I want to defend is that, as a form of active and socially situated musicking, shared listening episodes are episodes of "joint sense-making": cooperative processes of meaning construction and appreciation. Sense-making within the literature on enactive cognition is seen as a relational and affect-laden process by which an organism actively generates a meaningful world (Varela *et al.* 1991; De Jaegher and Di Paolo 2007). By "joint sense-making," I also have in mind something akin to what the phenomenologist Alfred Schutz, in writing about musical experience and communication, has called a "mutual tuning-in relationship": a primitive, bodily-affective resonance and empathic understanding that grounds all antecedent forms of linguistic communication (Schutz 1951, p. 161; see also Gendlin 1997). Schutz defines this connection as a relationship in which "the 'I' and the 'Thou' are experienced by both participants as a 'We' in vivid presence," one which "originates in the possibility of living together simultaneously in specific dimensions in time" (Schutz 1951, pp. 161, 162). Making music together—which, like Small, Schutz insists includes both performing as well as listening since the interpretive activity essential to the latter is itself a kind of experiential composition (Schutz 1951, p. 170)—is thus a cooperative activity. It discloses the primitive way that subjects share experiences, feelings, motives, and, most crucially, *felt understandings* independently of linguistic expression. This is because the "meaning structure" of such communicative episodes, according to Schutz, "is not capable of being expressed in conceptual terms; they are founded upon communication, but not *primarily* upon a semantic system used by the communicator as a scheme of expression and by his partners as a scheme of interpretation" (Schutz 1951, p. 159). Rather, the resonance and understanding within these instances is established by a pre-linguistic, affectively charged relation— again, what Malloch and Trevarthen term "communicative musicality."

Joint sense-making, at least in the form I am concerned with here, is therefore a process that unfolds prior to linguistic competence. As the notion of communicative musicality is meant to highlight, infants are motivated from the start by a primitive drive for affective connection, a basic need to affiliate that quickly blossoms into more articulate desires to share experiences and enter into sympathetic communion with others (Rochat 2009, p. 23). A great deal of empirical research supports the idea that newborns emerge from the womb with an innate or "primary intersubjectivity" (Trevarthen 1979): a range of embodied practices, such as imitative capacities (Kugiumutzakis 1999) and an attunement to the timing and emotional quality of bodily expressions (Gopnik and Meltzoff 1997; Nadel *et al.* 1999) that allow the infant to interact with caregivers in meaningful (and musical) ways. Part of this "primary intersubjectivity" also consists of a perceptual sensitivity to the emotive values carried by harmonic and melodic parameters of the human voice (Trevarthen 2002, p.25). As Trevarthen observes there:

> [The] expressive signals of the whole body, but especially of face, voice and hands, are coherent in a single subjective or "embodied" time and space from birth. While the infant's knowledge and skills are at their most rudimentary, a vitality of action awareness is already there.

This action awareness and perceptual sensitivity to the musicality of communicative interactions is the root of joint sense-making.

To see how shared musical experiences are episodes of joint sense-making, consider the interactive character of neonate music therapy. Music therapy refers to a cluster of music-based practices, techniques, and clinical interventions designed meet an individual's social, psychological, physical, and spiritual needs within an ongoing therapeutic relationship (Magee and Davidson 2000). These interventions are designed to give patients of all ages the opportunity to explore and share emotions (Bunt and Pavlicevic 2001). While traditionally geared toward adults and children with various disabilities or mental health problems, there has in recent years been an increased focus on music therapy for neonates. This focus has arisen in response to what Tia DeNora terms the "paradox of cure in the neonatal unit"—namely, the idea that the very environment created to help the infant thrive (i.e. the neonatal intensive care unit or NICU) may instead exhibit features that inhibits their healing and psychological and physiological well-being (DeNora 2000).

A major problem is that the NICU furnishes an exceedingly unfriendly sonic world for the infant. In addition to the consistent flow of doctor and nurse activity, this sonic world is peppered with myriad sonic disturbances (e.g. the sound of respirators, bottles clanking on top of the incubator, amplifications of the infant's disorganized state via the heart monitor, etc.) generated by the very technology used to care for the infant (DeNora 2000, p. 80; see also Haslbeck 2004). This uninviting soundworld has the adverse effect of upsetting basic life processes and neonatal biorhythms which, in turn, negatively affect sleep regulation and state lability (Kaminski and Hall 1996, p. 46). So, after many months of becoming accustomed to soothing intrauterine sounds and rhythms, the transition from the womb to the NICU is a particularly harsh journey—one which may impede the neonate's healthy development (Collins and Kuck 1991, p. 24). Neonate music therapy has thus been developed to counteract this possibility.

Though research in this area is relatively young, there appear to be many positive benefits of neonate music therapy: reducing stress; providing stimulation in stimulation-deprived environments; promoting bonding with parents; facilitating neurologic, communication, and social development; exhibiting calming effects on pre-term and full-term infants; increasing oxygen saturation levels and shortening hospitals stays (Standley 2001, p. 213); facilitating various kinds of physiological and microbehavioral stability including stable heart rate, blood pressure, color, feeding, changes in posture, muscle tone, less frantic movements, rhythmic crying, cessation of grimacing, and regularization of sleep/wake cycles (DeNora 2000, p. 81). Beyond these psycho-biological benefits, neonate music therapy (as we will see below) also helps cultivate bodily skills essential to communication—including, for example, the temporal coordination of bodily movement and affective expression as well as sensitivity to the timing and rhythm of interactive turn-taking.

Given these psycho-biological benefits, playing music for babies within therapeutic contexts might be thought of as a form of "entrainment": the alignment or coordination of bodily features with recurrent features of the environment (Haslbeck 2004; Clayton *et al.* 2005).[vii] And the positive outcomes of music therapy—again, the fact that neonates are entrained to regulate their internal bodily states and expressive movements with positive recurrent features of this musical environment—affirms that music is an aesthetic technology being successfully "employed to meditate tensions between endogenous (bodily) and exogenous (environmental) processes within neonatal intensive care units" (DeNora 2000, p. 79). Music, it would seem, is balm for the neonate's embodied soul.

But why characterize neonate music therapy as an instance of joint sense-making? I suggest that there are three dimensions to this process that mark it as an instance of joint sense-making. First, the music is mutually (if implicitly) recognized as *experientially salient*, as a meaningful environmental structure to be attended to and engaged with. Second, the music is also mutually recognized as *affording communicative possibilities* between joint listeners. Third, the musical context is mutually used to generate *a shared attentional framework* which establishes a new domain of felt intimacy.

Like adults, infants, too, seem to appreciate and respond to music as an experientially salient feature of their perceptual environment. They implicitly recognize music as presenting an auditory structure qualitatively distinct from the unstructured ambient noise of their surroundings—and in music therapeutic contexts, as something they can use with others in meaningful ways. For example, both full-term and pre-term infants attend more fixedly to music than they do to other ambient noises; this suggests a preference for the sonic coherence and organizational structure of music in contrast to contingent environmental noise (Butterfield and Siperstein 1972; Standley 2001). Though infant activity tends to decrease in response to auditory stimuli generally, the most significant decreases are caused by music, further suggesting that music is a preferred auditory stimulus (Kagan and Lewis 1965). Other studies have found that infants are surprisingly discriminating listeners. Beyond merely tuning in to overarching musical patterns, they are also able to pick out and attend to fine-grained auditory properties of music such as pitch, melody, tempo, and musical phrase structure (Trehub and Trainor 1993; Trehub and Schellenberg 1995; Schellenberg and Trehub 1996; Trehub et al. 1999). Three- to six-month-olds can vocalize a matched pitch to sung tones (Wendrich 1981) and learn to turn toward a loudspeaker whenever they perceive a change in background melody (Trehub et al. 1987). Another study found that 2-month-olds are capable of remembering short melodies and later discriminating a remembered melody from other melodies (Plantinga and Trainor 2009). Infants are thus capable of hearing and responding to the particular sound features that carry a piece's expressive content. Even the very young possess the perceptual skills needed to find music perceptually captivating because of its emotional expressivity (Nawrot 2003).

Beyond merely exhibiting the perceptual skills needed to discriminate between music and noise, however, infants also seem to experience music as affording communicative possibilities. For example, Haslbeck (2004) found that, over the course of several music therapy sessions, the pre-term neonates in her study gradually became active participants within the sessions, intentionally seeking interpersonal contact via the music (which consisted of slowly sung melodies supplemented with a hand resting gently on the infant's chest or back). This interpersonal contact emerged via bodily entrainment. The infants enacted whole-body "rhythmic dialogues" with the music (Haslbeck 2004, p. 9). These dialogues (i.e. instances of communicative musicality) were established via a coordinated rhythmic alteration between the sung lullaby and the infants' bodily responses. Both sucking/swallowing and regularized patterns of respiration were observed to mimic the rhythmic alterations of the sung melody (e.g. sucking at the end of melodic phrases) (Haslbeck 2004, p. 9). More tellingly, the infants gradually initiated eye contact, summoned an increasingly attentive and engaged posture, and exhibited increased mouth movements (playing with the tongue, mouthing the vowels being sung, such as "o" and "u") and vocalizations during the sessions. Other movements included opening and closing of hands, wrinkled brows, and eyes opening and closing in sync with the rising or falling of the sung melody (Haslbeck 2004, p. 11). This opportunity for social contact within music therapeutic contexts is crucial—something that the infants in Haslbeck's sessions actively sought out—given the isolation of the pre-term infant's life inside the incubator.

Finally, the infants, working in concert with the caregiver, used the musical context to enact a shared attentional framework which, in turn, generated a new domain of felt intimacy. This was accomplished by a mutual temporal orientation to features of the rhythmic dialogue being shared. Haslbeck found that some of the infants responded to variations of melodic phrasings (e.g. pauses in the singing or changes in timing) by coordinating their own movements (e.g. respiration, sucking, hand movements, etc.) with these perceived variations. Describing an instance of this mutual temporal orientation, Haslbeck writes that one infant, Nelly, "does not only recognize a temporal structure, she creates this temporal experience. She begins to orient herself, perceives my offer of contact and actively performs a first continuous interaction" (Haslbeck 2004, p. 10). To return to Schutz, it thus appears that, within the music therapeutic context, the infant appreciates and responds to the opportunity to enact a musically informed "mutual tuning-in relationship" with the caregiver, one that "originates in the possibility of living together simultaneously in specific dimensions in time" (Schutz 1951, p. 162).

An objection to this line of argument is that these descriptions simply attribute too rich a musical phenomenology to infants by suggesting that they are capable of hearing (much less appreciating) music *as* music.[viii] First, it may be objected that prolonged attention is in itself insufficient to establish aesthetic preference and/or appreciation. For example, passers-by tend to stare intently at road accidents, and it's unlikely that they are responding appreciatively to the aesthetic properties of the scene. Why assume that something like this is going on when babies attend fixedly to music? Second, being affected by music (as it appears babies are) does not establish that they can pick out music as qualitatively distinct from noise; rather, it merely affirms the relatively trivial point that they can perceptually distinguish between different kinds of noise. Moreover, non-human animals are also affected by music but we're unlikely to attribute aesthetic appreciation of music to them. For example, in an unpublished study, the psychologists Adrian North and Liam MacKenzie found that a thousand Holstein cows at two dairies produced 3% more milk over a 9-week trial period when played slow, relaxing music than when played fast music (i.e. over 120 beats per minute) or no music at all.[ix] Similarly, a 1998 study found that "playing the radio to chickens is an easy practicable way of enriching their environment and, perhaps, of helping to reduce their fear of new noises" (Jones and Rayner 1999). Sixteen per cent of 100 farmers surveyed in the study claimed that playing music increased egg production. But again, it's unlikely that the cows or chicken hear the music *as* music.

In response, it surely must be granted that speculating about the phenomenology of infant consciousness—much less animal consciousness—is a difficult affair. However, given the totality of behavioral evidence, it's not clear that these objections stick. First, the claim here is not that prolonged attention is both necessary and sufficient to establish musical appreciation. Rather, prolonged attention—when embedded within a repertoire of other behavioral responses comprising what I discuss above and below under the rubric of bodily entrainment—indicates that infants are, or can become, selectively aware of and orient themselves toward distinctively musical environments. In other words, the analogy with car crashes fails. Unlike with musical cases, no processes of bodily entrainment issue from prolonged attentiveness to car wrecks. Yet infants seem to implicitly recognize music as affording entrainment, and they often respond accordingly.

As I discuss below, part of these responses consists of active, self-initiated engagements with music. Moreover, it's not necessary that infants possess propositional knowledge of music to hear it as such (I shall say more about this later). Rather, it's sufficient for the purposes of this discussion that they simply pick it out of their sonic environment as qualitatively distinct from other noises—that is, as experientially *different* in terms of presenting an exploratory profile inviting bodily entrainment. For instance, studies have found that pre-verbal infants spontaneously display tempo-sensitive rhythmic motions of their body with music—this rhythmic bodily motion is, moreover, a source of positive affect—but that they don't exhibit this behavior in response to speech or other arrhythmic ambient noise (Zentner and Eerola 2010). Other studies have found that some parrots are capable of similar rhythmic coordination (Patel *et al.* 2009; Schachner *et al.* 2009). So, evidence suggests that infants and possibly some non-human animals hear and respond to music as music—that is, as phenomenally distinct from ambient noise, and as affording distinctive exploratory profiles and entrainment possibilities—even if they lack the necessary propositional or conceptual capacities to classify it as such.

A similar line of objection concerns whether or not music therapeutic interactions involving neonates are cases of genuine sense-making, that is, shared processes in which partners actively construct mutually appreciated *meanings*.[x] Again, it might be argued that neonates simply lack the necessary cognitive capacities to appreciate the significance of these experiences to character-ize them thus. However, the sort of sense-making (and simultaneously, meaning-*appreciating*) activity I am attributing to infants is not equivalent to a reflective or higher-order cognitive appre-ciation of the encounter. Rather, it is something more basic. It is inherent within the temporally flexible rhythms and mutual coordination of expressiveness that motivates these interactions.

To elaborate further: it is well-known that babies become distressed when their mother, after actively engaging with the infant for some time, suddenly assumes a still and unexpressive face—despite the infant's efforts to continue the interaction (Tronick *et al.* 1979). However, babies also become agitated and distressed when, while interacting with their mother in real-time via a double TV monitor, the live footage of the mother is suddenly replaced with recorded footage from earlier within the same interaction (Murray and Trevarthen 1985). In the latter case, the temporal coordi-nation of that interaction has been disrupted; the infant's sensorimotor expectancies are no longer being fulfilled in a reliable and satisfying way. In other words, the interactive normalcy of the encounter—as well as the interpersonal meaning associated with this normalcy (i.e. the fact that the infant actively solicits a unique response based upon its own expressive contributions to the engagement)—is compromised, and the infant's distress response reflects an appreciation of this fact. Likewise, the infant's sensorimotor responses to the touch and singing of the music therapist indicate a similar appreciation of the interactive normalcy governing music therapeutic encoun-ters. The infant seems to be responsively attuned to the interpersonal salience of the singing and the touch—and they intentionally enact a range of temporally sensitive entrainment responses to further motivate the back-and-forth dynamic of the encounter. Their active and intentional par-ticipation is in this way a primitive grasp of the meaning of the interactive episode. They skillfully perceive and respond to the particular expressive contingencies that give that interaction a unique social character. They play an active role in regulating this instance of social coupling.[xi]

Shared musical experience: skillful listening

In addition to comprising an instance of joint sense-making, shared musical experiences are also instances of skillful perceptual engagement. These cooperative "musickings" are jointly enacted musical *doings*. To continue with the discussion of neonate music therapy: infants, I suggest, pos-sess an implicit sensorimotor knowledge that allows them to use music in an active, skillful, and self-aware way, to regulate their affective states and to establish and refine interpersonal relation-ships. This implicit sensorimotor knowledge is what gives all of us (including neonates and infants) experiential access to the expressive qualities of music.[xii] Additionally, it allows us to access music as something that we can use to actively do things with.

The sensorimotor knowledge I am here concerned with is the skills-based knowledge of how modulations of bodily movement and attentional focusing affect sensory change. For instance, when we perceive a visual scene, movements of the head or body change the way that occluded objects (e.g. part of a bush obscured by a tree standing in front of it) gradually reveal themselves as we move closer to or around them. We possess similar knowledge of how bodily movements and attentional modulations shape the character and content of musical experience. Rudimentary sensorimotor knowledge is thus the implicit practical understanding that, as an embodied agent,

I possess the sensorimotor skills needed to secure experiential access to different features of my world by using my body in different ways.[xiii] Being sensitive to the sensorimotor contingencies (i.e. the reliable ways that movement modulates experiential content) governing my relation to perceptual objects is what it means to be a "skilled" embodied perceiver (see O'Regan and Noë 2001).

In developing his sensorimotor account of perceptual consciousness, Alva Noë offers two conditions under which an object can be said to be perceptually available in experience (Noë 2009). A perceiver must implicitly understand

> in a practical, bodily way, that there obtains a physical, motor-sensory relation between the perceiver and the object or quality, satisfying two conditions:
> (i) Movement-dependence: movements of the body manifestly control the character of the relation to the object or quality
> (ii) Object-dependence: movements or other changes in the object manifestly control the character of the relation to the object or quality. (Noë 2009, p. 476)

When I say that babies know how to do things with music, what I mean is that babies implicitly recognize that the sensorimotor relation between themselves and the expressive qualities of music satisfy these two conditions. That is, they immediately recognize music (including the particular sound features that convey its expressive content) as something they can do things with, and they also immediately recognize how to use their bodies to do the things they want to with music. So, they know, for example, that moving their head slightly in one direction will allow for more focused attention to an especially pleasing part of a musical piece, bringing about a desired affective response; and they know that allowing their head to linger in that position will continue to afford this focused listening and affective response, at least until the sound source moves and they must adjust their body accordingly. Similarly, they know that turning their head the other way will suppress or push away (if ever-so-slightly) unpleasant aspects they find sonically uninviting. Babies thus have an implicit mastery of basic sensorimotor contingencies that govern the way that they are responsively attuned to different affordances in their environment—including expressive sound features within music. Musical qualities afford this interactional engagement.

As we saw in the previous section, neonate music therapy is a kind of coordinated interpersonal engagement—an active sharing of expression and feeling. This coordinated engagement emerges from a primitive sensitivity to the rhythm and direction of movement in others, which is "the natural regulator of social life for even very simple animals" (Trevarthen 2002, p. 26). This sensitivity is also manifest in the infant's responsive sensitivity to the dynamic qualities (e.g. rhythm and direction) of musical expression. The ability to appreciate the expressive aspects of music and coordinate shared interpersonal responses around these aspects is itself a sensorimotor skill. It is an example of active and skillful perceiving, I suggest, because within musical contexts neonates exhibit (1) a *selective orientation* to musical sounds, along with (2) a more fine-grained *critical discrimination of particular musical sound features*, both of which are enacted via (3) a *sensorimotor (i.e. vocal and gestural) engagement* with the music. Again, this is what it means to say that babies know how to use their bodies to do things with music.

As was noted earlier, neonates exhibit a selective orientation to musical sounds. They attend more fixedly to music than to other ambient noises (Butterfield and Siperstein 1972; Standley and Madsen 1990; Standley 2001). And via turning and focusing on the music (or conversely, fidgeting and turning away), they can actively foreground it within their perceptual field (or actively make it recede). Infants thus pick out music as something they can do things with, as something that affords unique experiences by virtue of the fact that "[a]coustically, music is unlike any other sound; it is more pleasant, soothing, and interesting than noise and uses highly preferred frequencies and harmonics selected through centuries of refinement and development of a specific music type" (Standley 2001, p. 212). Moreover, as was also noted above, infants are surprisingly discriminating listeners. They are able to perceive fine-grained musical properties such as pitch, melody, tempo, and musical phrase structure (Trehub and Trainor 1993; Trehub and Schellenberg 1995; Schellenberg and Trehub 1996; Trehub et al. 1999). In this sense, they emerge from the womb as skilled listeners.

However, not only can neonates and infants perceptually discriminate between music and noise. Beyond this, neonates and infants present the perceptual skills needed to actively *appropriate* music for emotion regulation and interpersonal coordination. This is an important distinction. For it is one thing to hear music as music, but it is something else to *use* music, to act on music as an experientially salient environmental structure. However, there are empirical indications that infants both pick up on and exploit music in this way. Multiple studies have indicated that infants prefer listening to, and show heightened emotional responses toward, infant-directed "musical" speech, as opposed to adult-directed speech, where the former refers to "sing-song" speech intentionally modified to be pleasing to the infant: raised pitch, slowed tempo, elongated vowels, and slow pitch contours with large frequency ranges (Trainor and Heinmiller 1998, p. 78). Infants focus on (i.e. "use") musical speech since it affords emotionally pleasant and stimulating exchanges with caregivers.

They seem to do something similar with music, too. Despite the fact that they have no conceptual knowledge of musical scale structure or prior exposure to music, infants display an evaluative preference for consonant over dissonant musical intervals.[xiv] Not only can they perceptually discriminate consonant from dissonant interval notes, their prolonged looking indicates an affective preference for the former—even when they are embedded within a more sonically complex "naturalistic context" (Trainor and Heinmiller 1998, p. 83).[xv] Zenter and Kagan (1998) found similar results. However, not only did infants look significantly longer at consonant melodies, the infants in Zenter and Kagan's study also *used* the consonant melodies to regulate their affective states, that is, to bring about a more inquisitive and emotionally balanced state in relation to their sonic environment. The infants fretted less, exhibited less motor activity (i.e. they were less fidgety and more absorbed in the music), and vocalized more (i.e. expressed interest in the music) during the consonant melodies (see also Leonard 1993). Similarly, recall Haslbeck's (2004) findings that, over the course of multiple sessions, the pre-term infants in her study would synchronize bodily movements such as sucking (both rhythm and intensity), tongue and mouth protrusions, and eye opening and closing, with the rising and falling of sung lullaby melodies. So, it appears that the infants in these and other studies engaged with and actively appropriated the sonic structures in their immediate environment by engaging bodily with the music.

With age and experience these sensorimotor skills continue to develop and become more refined. Other research indicates how infants develop a richer understanding of how the ways that we move shape what we hear. For example, Jessica Philips-Silver and Laurel Trainor found that movement influences auditory encoding of rhythm patterns in both infants (Philips-Silver and Trainor 2005) and adults (Philips-Silver and Trainor 2007). In the earlier series of experiments, 7-month-old infants were trained by listening to an ambiguous 2-minute rhythmic pattern (i.e. a pattern lacking accented beats). During this training, half of the infants were bounced on every second beat and half were bounced on every third beat. As a result, the infants expressed a more prolonged interest in the auditory test stimulus with the metrical form [every second beat accented (the duple form) in one stimulus, and every third beat (the triple form) in the other] that matched the metrical form of their training bouncing (Philips-Silver and Trainor 2007, p. 1430). This was also the case when they were blindfolded. A further experiment showed that personal bodily movement was necessary to establish this metrical preference. Watching the experimenter bounce during the ambiguous rhythm training failed to establish a preference for either of the auditory stimulus versions (Philips-Silver and Trainor 2007, p. 1430).[xvi] A similar set of experiments was later done with adults (Philips-Silver and Trainor 2007). Unlike the infants, of course, the adults could engage in their own "bounce training." But like the infants, the adults' synchronized movements of their bodies determined how they heard an ambiguous musical rhythm (Philips-Silver and Trainor 2007, p. 543). Once again, they had to personally bounce their own bodies, and not watch a video of another doing it, in order for their experience of the ambiguous rhythm to covary relative to their particular bounce training (e.g. bouncing on every second or on every third beat). But their sensorimotor training determined how they enacted the content of their experience of the ambiguous rhythm.

Bodily movements in this way modulate the listener's enactive relation to different features of the musical piece, such as meter and melody. Bodily gestures are a form of attentional focusing and the vehicle of perceptual construction. The animate body becomes a vehicle for voluntarily drawing out features of a musical piece (e.g. expressive aspects, rhythmic beats, or melodic progression) and foregrounding them in our attentional field. This drawing out is an enactive gesture in response to felt affordances within the music. The listener perceives the inner space of the piece as a space that can be entered into, experientially, and by doing just this shapes how the experiential content of the piece-as-given becomes phenomenally manifest. In short, "we hear what the body feels" (Philips-Silver and Trainor 2007 p. 544). What the body feels are sensorimotor contingencies—possibilities for interaction, movement, and coordination that determine the character and content of musical experience. Sensitive music listening is thus a kind of skilled coping with a sonic world, a kind of listening with our muscles. As Dewey (1934/1980, p. 237) notes, "sounds *come* from outside the body, but sound itself is near, intimate; it is an excitation of the organism; we feel the clash of vibrations throughout our whole body".[xvii] Musical pieces are therefore not simply constellations of acoustic properties or "pre-ordained gestures" (Iyer 2004, p. 168) collectively transferred from composer to listener (i.e. as within the pharmaceutical model of musical experience). Rather, even for neonates, a piece is actively engaged with in a bodily way. It contains sonic information that summons forth the perceptual and motor skills of the attentive listener absorbed within its spatial, temporal, and rhythmic duration.[xviii]

Shared musical experience as social scaffolding

The bodies we use to engage with music in active ways are always *situated* bodies, embedded in encompassing biological, social, and cultural worlds. Ideally, the infant's world is a socially rich world, full of stimulation and opportunities for interpersonal engagement. But beyond merely providing a rich phenomenological buffet of information from which the infant can selectively pick and choose, the environment plays a crucial enabling role in the development of the infant's social skills and interpersonal sensitivity. With respect to our burgeoning sociality, the dyadic unit of infant–caregiver interaction becomes an intimate relational circuit that drives and nurtures the child's psychological and physiological development. This dyadic unit itself—and again, the relational spaces and gestural and vocal transactions that compose it—is "scaffolding" guiding the child's communicative endeavors and supporting its burgeoning social intelligence.[xix] This persistent environmental scaffolding makes an active contribution to the development of social skills and cognitive processes. Environmental scaffolding, in the sense I am using the term here, thus plays two essential roles in driving cognitive processes and guiding behavior. First, it provides persistent *structures* supporting both the synchronic and diachronic development of emotional and communicative performances. Second, it places *organizational constraints* on the development of these processes. The context determines both the form these processes take as well as the developmental trajectory they assume. Music, I suggest, often serves as environmental scaffolding that makes an active contribution to both the development and form of our social intelligence.

To begin to see how this is so, consider first Kenneth Kaye's work on the origins of social intelligence. Kaye has shown that breastfeeding—which consists of affective cycles of touch and movement—may play a crucial role in the infant's cognitive development (Kaye 1982). Kaye observes that breastfeeding constitutes the most immediate and complex form of social interaction that neonates and mothers engage in soon after the child is born (Kaye 1982, p. 37). He further notes that human infants are the only mammalian infants who breastfeed in short bursts. When human infants pause in their feeding, all mothers—including new mothers who report never having held a baby before their own—instinctively jiggle the infant as a bodily prompt to resume feeding. This jiggling seems to work; infants are more likely to resume feeding in the pause just after jiggling than they are during the jiggling or if they had not been jiggled at all (Kaye 1982, p. 38). This behavioral interaction is significant in that it is arguably one of the earliest instances of social understanding. The mother communicates a non-verbal intention; the infant perceives and responds to this intention. The give-and-take dynamic of this exchange provides the temporal template for the infant's future communicative encounters: "the mother's actions serve to organize this most basic and repetitive interaction between infant and mother, providing the prototype… for turn-taking interactions in general" (Wexler 2008, p. 111). The infant's behavior is guided and supported by the persistent presence of the mother's touch, as well as the bodily prompting provided by the jiggling. This interactive turn-taking is thus a primitive social skill; it is first learned within the physically intimate, gestural proto-conversation of breastfeeding. This and other research (some of which was cited earlier) indicates that infants are born with

> highly organized action systems that allow them to maintain close physical contact with caretakers they depend upon for their survival… It all starts with an innate endowment of prefunctional action systems to which caretakers are in turn instinctively attuned in order to dispense with the intensive care neonates need for their survival. (Rochat 2009, p. 25)

But again, the point is that the interactive dyadic unit *as a whole* is the social scaffolding upon which these social skills develop and emerge.[xx]

Music is a kind of social scaffolding. Music affords the cultivation of primitive social skills like interactive turn-taking and the temporal coordination of bodily movement and affective expression. As we've already seen, neonate music therapy (much like the majority of our day-to-day musical experiences) doesn't consist of mere passive listening. Rather, it is an enactive and embodied *doing*, a form of skillful perceiving. Moreover, it involves ongoing affective cycles of touch and movement—in addition to the active perceiving of the music itself. As Trevarthen and Malloch observe, "[w]hile the primary mode of awareness for the music therapist is aural, touch and observed bodily gesture also play a part in the reception of interpersonal 'presentations' that hold therapist and client in relationship" (Trevarthen and Malloch 2000, p. 5).

Infant-directed sing-song speech is a persistent auditory feature of the infant's early environment. This gives the infant's world an inherently musical character from the start. As was discussed earlier, caregivers around the world instinctively fall into musical patterns of communication and expression with infants. And they use similar intonation contours in similar contexts—for instance, employing rising contours to attract an infant's attention; smooth or falling contours to calm the infant; and sharp, flat contours to discourage naughty behavior (Fernald

1991; Papousek 1992). Moreover, caregivers sing to infants with the intuitive understanding that lullabies promote both emotion regulation (i.e. alter an infant's affective state) as well as sleep (Trehub and Trainor 1993, 1998). Attentive caregivers "are exquisitely sensitive to the perceptual abilities of their infants, singing to them more slowly, at a higher pitch, with exaggerated rhythm, and in a more loving or emotionally engaging manner than when singing alone" (Trainor and Heinmiller 1998, p. 78). As was briefly noted earlier, infants exhibit a clear preference for and heightened emotional response toward this sort of melodically expressive speech (Trainor and Heinmiller 1998), preferring happy-sounding melodically expressive speech to neutral-sounding speech (Singh *et al.* 2002).

Musical speech thus scaffolds the infant's behavior and emotional responses in two senses. First, it *synchronically* supports particular episodes in particular contexts. Within a specific encounter, the infant negotiates emotional feedback received from the caregiver (in addition to musical speech, accompanying cues like facial expressions, movements, gestures, and touch) by reciprocating with her own vocal and gestural responses—responses which in turn govern the tone, intensity, and affective coloring of the caregiver's subsequent responses. The ongoing dynamics of this temporally extended reciprocal feedback, unique to the context of that particular encounter, shape the character of the infant's emotions and communicative intentions within that context. Second, infant-directed, musical speech *diachronically* scaffolds the development of the infant's broader repertoire of emotional, social, and communicative skills. By repeatedly encountering infant-directed musical speech as a persistent feature of its social world, the infant progressively exploits this speech (and again, the accompanying non-verbal emotional cues) to cultivate the skills central to social life: skills like perceptual sensitivity to the open-ended, turn-taking processes and shared temporality of interpersonal exchanges; the ability to coordinate affect and expression; tuning in to the face as a rich source of emotional and social information, etc. As environmental scaffolding, infant-directed speech is thus a tool that infants use to develop and refine their emotional life.

As should now be clear, music can fulfill a similar scaffolding function. This is, in part, because babies are almost constantly surrounded by music. In addition to using musical patterns of speech, there is much evidence that we naturally sing to babies—and we do it almost constantly. Mothers in every culture sing to their infants (Trehub and Trainor 1998). This particular sort of maternal singing, in contrast to other forms of singing, is contoured with greater emotional expressiveness, higher pitch level, and slower tempo (Trainor *et al.* 1997; Trehub *et al.* 1997). Though fathers sing less to infants than mothers do, when they do sing it is characterized by a heightened emotional and expressive character (Trehub *et al.* 1997; O'Neill *et al.* 2001). Other research has found that even pre-schoolers sing more effusively in the presence of infant siblings (Trehub *et al.* 1994). It is clear that "the presence of a baby seems to influence the emotions of caregivers or bystanders, one consequence of which is highly expressive singing" (Trehub 2002).

Music and musical speech surround infants as a persistent informational structure within their environment. Given their sophisticated listening skills, as well as their preference for music and musical speech, it is thus an ever-present feature of their world, ready-to-hand for exploiting and exploring emotional expression. Within a music therapeutic context, the scaffolding function of music is manifest in both a diachronic as well as a synchronic sense. Within these contexts, music becomes a focused and intensified manifestation of the musicality that shapes the infant's social world. As argued above, music therapy sessions are instances of shared listening. Moreover, they are processes of joint sense-making, processes of mutual musical engagement in which a shared attentional framework is erected and a new domain of felt intimacy emerges. Synchronically, music facilitates fine-grained affective attunement between infant and caregiver. The coordination or bodily entrainment that occurs is a result of the infant perceiving and responding to regularities within the music (e.g. textural qualities and melodic and rhythmic patterns[xxi]), regularities that beckon for deeper perceptual exploration.

In addition, within the synchronic or short-term temporal context of individual encounters, music, such as the sung lullaby of a caregiver, scaffolds the infant's affective negotiation of that context. Rising melodic contours, for instance, beckon the infant to engage further, to remain alert and poised for further interaction; downward contours indicate the conclusion of an interactive period. As the evidence surveyed above indicates, the infants perceive and respond to these melodic vitality affects (Stern 1985). They pick up on the expressive character of the music; the whole-body rhythmic dialogues they enact (e.g. coordination of respiration, sucking, eye movement, vocalizations, etc. with melodic contours of the music) reflect an ongoing appropriation of the music as a persistent informational structure within the infant's environment. More simply, they appreciate the music as something they can do things with (i.e. as affording communicative possibilities, as well as possibilities for emotional self-regulation)—and crucially, *they do things with it*.

In a long-diachronic sense, repeated encounters with music assist the infant in developing and fine-tuning emotional and social skills (Shenfield *et al*. 2003). Music entrains the infant to enter into and creatively participate within the shared time of interpersonal exchanges and to negotiate the melodic contours of these exchanges. To reaffirm an earlier point, perhaps the most important social skill that music (and musical speech) entrains is sensitivity to the flexible temporal parameters of interpersonal engagement, a sensitivity that is a precondition for negotiating meaningful shared experience. Music scaffolds the developmental acquisition of key features of the infant's emotional and social repertoire. It is, once again, a tool that infants actively exploit in the cultivation of their social being and the bodily skills essential for their empathic access to others.

Final thoughts

In this chapter I have investigated shared musical experiences, particularly insofar as they afford affectively powerful, and developmentally primitive, forms of empathic connectedness. Focusing especially on neonate music therapy, I have argued that shared musical experiences are very often dynamic processes of (1) joint sense-making, enacted via temporally extended patterns of (2) skillful engagement with music that are (3) synchronically and diachronically scaffolded by the surrounding environment. The animate body has been an important part of this story. For, as is now clear, the body is actively utilized as an expressive vehicle from birth. But an intriguing suggestion, which has emerged throughout the course of this investigation, is that even the earliest encounters with music are simultaneously encounters with the lived body. Thus music can train the young (and surely, the not-so-young!) in using the musicality inherent within the expressive capacities of the lived body. Research on neonate music therapy seems to confirm this, drawing our attention to the subtle rhythms and dynamic valences of affect and movement that fund primitive forms of bodily self-experience—as well as, importantly, the way that these subtle experiences are crucially interwoven with the experience of being in relation to others. The face, voice, hands, and feet—as well as an embodied appropriation of time and space (i.e. the temporal and visuo-spatial dynamics of our communicative exchanges)—from the very beginning are used to construct and convey shared motives and feelings. Music affords an active exploration of these embodied social skills, one that then continues as we mature both physiologically and aesthetically.

Notes

i   I am grateful for exceedingly helpful critical comments from Stephen Davies, Jenefer Robinson, and Tom Cochrane on an earlier draft of this essay. I am also grateful for comments from audiences in Durham and Copenhagen.

ii   This "direct perception" way of characterizing empathy is in line with the model of empathy found within the phenomenological tradition. See, for example, Zahavi (2001), Gallagher (2008), and Krueger (2012).

iii By "enactive," I mean to emphasize the way that skillful bodily action and perceptual experience are fundamentally intermingled. On this active view of perception, perceptual experience is enacted, or brought forth, by an agent's actively doing things in and to the world (see Varela *et al.* 1991; Noë 2004). For a longer discussion of enaction within the context of musical experience see Krueger (2009).

iv   This is not to suggest that all cultures use and relate to music in precisely the same way. Music plays different roles in different cultures. But the fact that nearly every known culture practices some form of music (singing, dancing, religious rituals, etc.), or has a form of communication that can be called "musical," suggests that music is universally recognized as a potent tool for social bonding and organization (see DeNora 2000).

v   See Malloch and Trevarthen (2009) for an extensive collection of papers devoted to this topic.

vi   According to the *super-expressive voice* theory (e.g. Juslin 2001), music's expressiveness stems from its ability to sound like and, in many ways, *exceed* (in terms of speed, intensity, timbre, etc.) the expressive aspects of the human voice.

vii Similarly, Trevarthen and Malloch (2000, p. 11) note that "music is therapeutic because it attunes to the essential efforts that the mind makes to regulate the body, both in its inner neurochemical, hormonal and metabolic processes, and in its purposeful engagements with the objects of the world, and with other people."

viii Many thanks to Stephen Davies for raising this objection.

ix   See <http://news.bbc.co.uk/2/hi/science/nature/1408434.stm>

x   I'm very grateful to Jenefer Robinson for pressing this point.

xi   For more on the notion of "sense-making" and interactive meaning from an enactive perspective see De Jaegher and Di Paolo (2007)and Fuchs and De Jaegher (2009).

xii For more on this idea, see Krueger (2009, 2011a).

xiii This pre-reflective experience of being an embodied and situated agent, i.e. an ecological sense of embodied selfhood, seems to already be in place at birth, and to provide the infant with a minimal form of basic self-consciousness long before it acquires a conceptual or reflective awareness of self (see Gallagher 2005, pp. 65–85).

xiv Roughly speaking, consonant intervals are stable (i.e. pleasant-sounding) and require no resolution. Dissonant intervals exhibit a "tense" quality that requires resolution to a consonant interval (see Huron 2006).

xv   Instead of simply playing bare notes for the infant, a second experiment modified a Mozart minuet to produce different versions with predominantly consonant or dissonant intervals, which was then played to the infant.

xvi See http://www.sciencemag.org/cgi/content/full/308/5727/1430 for samples of the experimental sound stimuli.

xvii For more on this idea, see Nussbaum (2007) and Walton (1997).

xviii Trevarthen (1999) and Trevarthen and Malloch 2000) report a vivid example of this sort of sensorimotor engagement. They describe a 5-month-old baby, born blind, who "without prompting or training, and, indeed without her mother being aware of her graceful rhythmic gestures, conducts portions of the melodies of famous Swedish baby songs . . . with her left arm and hand" (Trevarthen and Malloch 2000, p. 13). Trevarthen describes how the infant's arms rise and hands widen when the swelling of the song intensifies, and how her hands suddenly close and drop when the stanza concludes. Presumably, the infant experientially feels that the dynamic qualities of the music afford this sort of active engagement.

xix   I readily admit that "scaffolding" is an inelegant term. Moreover, it is potentially misleading given the rather static picture the term summons (in contrast to the inherently dynamic character of music). However, the idea of environmental scaffolding plays an important role in work on situated cognition, according to which the very context in which cognition takes place provides essential enabling conditions for the cognitive processes needed to experience that environment. In this sense, then, I want to take a situated approach to musical experience—and the ugly term "scaffolding" helps emphasize this situated character.

xx   Some may object to characterizing this interaction as a case of genuine social understanding since it is not immediately clear that the infant recognizes the mother's intention in resuming feeding; experimental data show that children take several years to become genuine mind-readers (i.e. capable of recognizing and responding to others' intentions). But this presupposes that mind-reading or "mentalizing" (Whiten and Perner 1991) is necessary for even rudimentary forms of social understanding and thereby begs the question. However, this mentalizing presupposition has recently been challenged from multiple perspectives in both philosophy and psychology. This debate is too large to discuss here (see, e.g., Hobson 2002; Gallagher 2008; Gallagher and Zahavi 2008; Reddy 2008; Fuchs and De Jaegher 2009; Rochat 2009 Krueger 2011b, 2012).

xxi   By musical "textures" I am referring to the overall quality of a piece of music, its sonic complexity. Gentle music with "thin" textures and no abrupt modulations of volume or tempo reduces alerting responses in infants (Standley 2001, 2002) and thus affords a stable and inviting sonic world for the infant. For more on how infants perceive and appropriate specific sonic invariants such as musical textures and patterns see Krueger (2011a).

References

Bunt, L. and Pavlicevic, M. (2001). Music and emotion: perspectives from music therapy. In P. N. Juslin and J. A. Sloboda (eds), *Music and Emotion: Theory and Research*, pp. 181–201. Oxford: Oxford University Press.

Butterfield, E. and Siperstein, G. (1972). Influence of contingent auditory stimuli upon nonnutritional suckle. In J. Bosma (ed.), *Oral Sensation and Perception: the Mouth of the Infant*, pp. 313–33. Springfield, IL: Charles C. Thomas.

Clayton, M., Sager, R., and Will, U. (2005). In time with the music: the concept of entrainment and its significance for ethnomusicology. *ESEM Counterpoint*, **11**, 3–75.

Collins, S. and Kuck, K. (1991). Music therapy in the neonatal intensive care unit. *Neonatal Network*, **9**(6), 23–6.

De Jaegher, H. and Di Paolo, E. (2007). Participatory sense-making. *Phenomenology and the Cognitive Sciences*, **6**, 485–507.

Denora, T. (2000). *Music in Everyday Life*. Cambridge: Cambridge University Press.

Dewey, J. (1934/1980). *Art as Experience*. New York: Perigree Books.

Fernald, A. (1991). Prosody in speech to children: prelinguistic and linguistic functions. *Annals of Child Development*, **8**, 43–80.

Fuchs, T. and De Jaegher, H. (2009). Enactive intersubjectivity: participatory sense-making and mutual incorporation. *Phenomenology and the Cognitive Sciences*, **8**, 465–86.

Gallagher, S. (2005). *How the Body Shapes the Mind*. Oxford: Oxford University Press.

Gallagher, S. (2008). Understanding others: embodied social cognition. In *Handbook of Cognitive Science*, pp. 437–52. San Diego: Elsevier.

Gallagher, S. and Zahavi, D. (2008). *The Phenomenological Mind: an Introduction to Philosophy of Mind and Cognitive Science*. New York: Routledge.

Gendlin, E. (1997). *Experience and the Creation of Meaning*. Evanston, IL: Northwestern University Press.

Gopnik, A. and Meltzoff, A. (1997). *Words, Thoughts, and Theories*. Cambridge: MIT Press.

Haslbeck, F. (2004). Music therapy with preterm infants: theoretical approach and first practical experience. *Music Therapy Today* [online], **5**(1), 1–15.

Hobson, P. (2002). *The Cradle of Thought: Exploring the Origins of Thinking*. London: Macmillan.

Huron, D. (2006). *Sweet Anticipation: Music and the Psychology of Expectation*. Cambridge: MIT Press.

Iyer, V. (2004). Improvisation: temporality and embodied experience. *Journal of Consciousness Studies*, **11**(3–4), 159–73.

Jones, R. B. and Rayner, S. (1999). Music in the hen house: a survey of its incidence and perceived benefits. *Poultry Science*, **78**(**S1**), 110.

Juslin, P. N. (2001). Communicating emotion in music performance: a review and theoretical framework. In P. N. Juslin and J. A. Sloboda (eds), *Music and Emotion: Theory and Research*, pp. 309–37. Oxford: Oxford University Press.

Kagan, J. and Lewis, M. (1965). Studies of attention in the human infant. *Journal of Developmental Psychology*, **11**, 95–127.

Kaminski, J. and Hall, W. (1996). The effect of soothing music on neonatal behavioral states in the hospital newborn nursery. *Neonatal Network*, **15**(1), 45–54.

Kaye, K. (1982). *The mental and social life of babies: How parents create persons*. Chicago: Chicago University Press.

Krueger, J. (2009). Enacting musical experience. *Journal of Consciousness Studies*, **16**(2–3), 98–123.

Krueger, J. (2011a). Doing things with music. *Phenomenology and the Cognitive Sciences*, **10**, 1–22.

Krueger, J. (2011b). Extended cognition and the space of social interaction. *Consciousness and Cognition*, **20**, 643–57.

Krueger, J. (2012). Seeing mind in action. *Phenomenology and the Cognitive Sciences*, **11**, 149–73.

Krueger, J. and Legrand, D. (2009). The open body. In A. Carassa, F. Morganti, and G. Riva (eds), *Enacting Intersubjectivity: Paving the Way for a Dialogue between Cognitive Science, Social Cognition, and Neuroscience*, pp. 109–28. Lugano: Universita della Svizzera Italiana.

Kugiumutzakis, G. (1999). Genesis and development of early infant mimesis to facial and vocal models. In G. Butterworth and J. Nadel (eds.), *Imitation in Infancy*, pp. 127–85. Cambridge: Cambridge University Press.

Leonard, J. E. (1993). Music therapy: fertile ground for application of research in practice. *Neonatal Network*, **12**(2), 47–8.

Magee, W. and Davidson, J. (2000). Identity in chronic neurological disability: finding an able "self" in music therapy. In C. Woods, G. Luck, R. Brochard, S. O'Neill, and J. Sloboda (eds), *Proceedings of the 6th International Conference on Music Perception and Cognition*. Department of Psychology, Keele University, Staffordshire, UK [CD-ROM only].

Malloch, S. (1999). Mothers and infants and communicative musicality. *Musicae Scientiae* (Special issue on Rhythms, Musical Narrative, and the Origins of Human Communication), 29–57.

Malloch, S. and Trevarthen, C. (2009). Musicality: communicating the vitality and interests of life. In S. Malloch and C. Trevarthen (eds), *Communicative Musicality: Exploring the Basis of Human Companionship*, pp. 1–11. Oxford: Oxford University Press.

Murray, L. and Trevarthen, C. (1985). *Emotional regulation of interactions between two month-olds and their mothers.* In T. Field and N. Fox (eds), *Social Perception in Infants*, pp. 101–25. Norwood, NJ: Ablex.

Nadel, J., Carchon, I., Kervella, C., Marcelli, D., and Réserbat-Plantey, D. (1999). Expectancies for social contingency in 2-month-olds. *Developmental Science*, **2**, 164–73.

Nawrot, E. S. (2003). The perception of emotional expression in music: evidence from infants, children and adults. *Psychology of Music*, **31**, 75–92.

Noë, A. (2004). *Action in Perception.* Cambridge, MA: MIT Press.

Noë, A. (2009). Conscious reference. *The Philosophical Quarterly*, **59**, 470–82.

Nussbaum, C. O. (2007). *The Musical Representation: Meaning, Ontology, and Emotion.* Cambridge, MA: MIT Press.

O'Neill, C. T., Trainor, L. J., and Trehub, S. E. (2001). Infants' responsiveness to fathers' singing. *Music Perception*, **18**, 409–25.

O'Regan, J. K. and Noë, A. (2001). A sensorimotor account of vision and visual consciousness. *Behavioral and Brain Sciences*, **24**, 939–1031.

Papousek, M. (1992). Early ontogeny of vocal communication in parent-infant interactions. In H. Papousek, H. Jurgens, and M. Papousek (eds), *Nonverbal Vocal Communication: Comparative and Developmental Approaches*, pp. 230–61. Cambridge: Cambridge University Press.

Papousek, H. and Papousek, M. (1987). Intuitive parenting: a dialectic counterpart to the infant's integrative performance. In J. Osofsky (ed.), *Handbook of Infant Development*, 2nd edn., pp. 669–720. New York: Wiley.

Patel, A. D., Iversen, J. R., Bregman, M. R., and Schulz, I. (2009). Experimental evidence for synchronization to a musical beat in a nonhuman animal. *Current Biology*, **19**, 827–30.

Philips-Silver, J. and Trainor, L. (2005), Feeling the beat: movement influences rhythm perception. *Science*, **308**, 1430.

Philips-Silver, J. and Trainor, L. (2007), Hearing what the body feels: auditory encoding of rhythmic movement. *Cognition*, **105**, 533–46.

Pinker, S. (1997). *How the Mind Works.* New York: Norton.

Plantinga, J. and Trainor, L. J. (2009). Melody recognition by two-month-old infants. *Journal of the Acoustical Society of America*, **125**, 58–62.

Reddy, V. (2008). *How Infants Know Minds.* Cambridge, MA: Harvard University Press.

Rochat, P. (2009). *Others in Mind: Social Origins of Self-consciousness.* Cambridge: Cambridge University Press.

Schachner, A., Brady, T. F., Pepperberg, I. M., and Hauser, M. D. (2009). Spontaneous motor entrainment to music in multiple vocal mimicking species. *Current Biology*, **19**, 831–6.

Schellenberg, E. G. and Trehub, S. E. (1996). Natural musical intervals. *Psychological Science*, **7**, 272–7.

Schutz, A. (1951). Making music together: a study in social relationship. *Social Research*, **18**, 76–97. (Reprinted 1971 in Schutz, A. *Collected Papers II: Studies in Social Theory*, ed. A. Brodersen, pp. 159–78. The Hague: Martinus Nijhoff.)

Shenfield, T., Trehub, S. E., and Nakata, T. (2003). Maternal singing modulates infant arousal. *Psychology of Music*, **31**, 365–75.

Singh, L., Morgan, J., and Best, C. (2002). Infants' listening preferences: baby talk or happy talk? *Infancy*, **3**, 365–94.

Sloboda, J. A. (2005). *Exploring the Musical Mind: Cognition, Emotion, Ability, Function.* Oxford: Oxford University Press.

Small, C. (1998). *Musicking: the Meanings of Performing and Listening.* Middletown, CT: Wesleyan University Press.

Standley, J. (2001). Music therapy for the neonate. *Newborn Infant Nursing Reviews*, **1**, 211–16.

Standley, J. M. (2002). A meta-analysis of the efficacy of music therapy for premature infants. *Journal of Pediatric Nursing*, **17**, 107–13.

Standley, J. M., and Madsen, C. K. (1990). Comparison of infant preferences and responses to auditory stimuli: Music, mother, and other female voice. *Journal of Music Therapy*, **27**, 54–97.

Stern, D. (1985). *The Interpersonal World of the Infant: a View from Psychoanalysis and Developmental Psychology*. New York: Basic Books.

Stern, D., Hofer, L., Haft, W., and Dore, J. (1985). Affect attunement: the sharing of feeling states between mother and infant by means of intermodal fluency. In T. Field and N. Fox (eds), *Social Perception in Infants*, pp. 249–68. Norwood, NJ: Ablex.

Thompson, E. (2001). Empathy and consciousness. *Journal of Consciousness Studies*, **8**(5–7), 1–32.

Trainor, L. J. and Heinmiller, B. M. (1998). The development of evaluative responses to music: infants prefer to listen to consonance over dissonance. *Infant Behavior and Development*, **21**, 77–88.

Trainor, L. J., Clark, E., Huntley, A., and Adams, B. (1997). The acoustic basis of preferences for infant-directed singing. *Infant Behavior and Development*, **20**, 383–96.

Trehub, S. E. (2002). Mothers are musical mentors. *Zero to Three*, **23**, 19–22.

Trehub, S. E., and Schellenberg, E. G. (1995). Music: its relevance to infants. *Annals of Child Development*, **11**, 1–24.

Trehub, S. E. and Trainor, L. (1993). Listening strategies in infancy: the roots of music and language development. In S. McAdams and E. Bigand (eds), *Thinking in Sound: the Cognitive Psychology of Human Audition*, pp. 278–327. Oxford: Oxford University Press.

Trehub, S. E. and Trainor, L. J. (1998). Singing to infants: lullabies and play songs. *Advances in Infancy Research*, **12**, 43–77.

Trehub, S. E., Thorpe, L. A., and Morrongiello, B. A. (1987). Organizational processes in infants' perception of auditory patterns. *Child Development*, **58**, 741–9.

Trehub, S. E., Unyk, A. M., and Henderson, J. L. (1994). Children's songs to infant siblings: parallels with speech. *Journal of Child Language*, **21**, 735–44.

Trehub, S. E., Unyk, A. M., Kamenetsky, S. B., Hill, D. S., Trainor, L. J., Henderson, J. L., and Saraza, M. (1997). Mothers' and fathers' singing to infants. *Developmental Psychology*, **33**, 500–7.

Trehub, S. E., Schellenberg, E. G., and Kamenetsky, S. (1999). Infants' and adults' perception of scale structure. *Journal of Experimental Psychology*, **25**, 965.

Trevarthen, C. (1979). Communication and cooperation in early infancy: a description of primary intersubjectivity. In M. Bullowa (ed.), *Before Speech: the Beginning of Interpersonal Communication*, pp. 321–47. Cambridge: Cambridge University Press.

Trevarthen, C. (1999). Musicality and the intrinsic motive pulse: evidence from human psychobiology and infant communication. *Musicae Scientiae*. (Special issue on Rhythms, Musical Narrative, and the Origins of Human Communication), 157–213.

Trevarthen, C. (2002). Origins of musical identity: evidence from infancy for musical social awareness. In R. Macdonald, D. Hargreaves, and D. Miell (eds), *Musical Identities*, pp. 21–38. Oxford: Oxford University Press.

Trevarthen, C. and Malloch, S. (2000). The dance of wellbeing: defining the musical therapeutic effect. *Nordic Journal of Music Therapy*, **9**(2), 3–17.

Trevarthen, C. and Malloch, S. (2002). Musicality and music before three: human vitality and invention shared with pride. *Zero to Three*, **23**, 10–18.

Tronick, E. Z., Als, H., and Adamson, L. (1979). Structure of early face-to-face communicative interactions. In M. Bullowa (ed.), *Before Speech: the Beginning of Interpersonal Communication*, pp. 349–70. Cambridge: Cambridge University Press.

Varela, F. J., Thompson, E., and Rosch, E. (1991). *The Embodied Mind: Cognitive Science and Human Experience*. Cambridge, MA: MIT Press.

Walton, K. (1997). Listening with imagination: is music representational? In J. Robinson (ed.), *Music and Meaning*, pp. 57–82. Ithaca: Cornell University Press.

Wendrich, K. (1981). Pitch imitation in infancy and early childhood: observations and implications. Unpublished doctoral dissertation, University of Connecticut, Storrs.

Wexler, B. (2008). *Brain and Culture: Neurobiology, Ideology, and Social Change*. Cambridge, MA: MIT Press.

Whiten, A. and Perner, J. (1991). *Fundamental Issues in the Multidisciplinary Study of Mindreading*. Oxford: Blackwell.

Zahavi, D. (2001). Beyond empathy: phenomenological approaches to intersubjectivity. *Journal of Consciousness Studies*, **8**(5–7), 151–67.

Zentner, M. R. and Eerola, T. (2010). Rhythmic engagement with music in infancy. *Proceedings of the National Academy of Sciences of the United States of America*, **107**, 5768–73.

Zentner, M. R. and Kagan, J. (1998). Infants' perception of consonance and dissonance in music. *Infant Behavior and Development*, **21**, 483–92.

Chapter 15

Music, action, and affect

Lincoln John Colling and William Forde Thompson

Music is a powerful tool for generating and shaping emotional experiences. The emotional power of music operates through a number of distinct mechanisms. Listening to music can lead to emotional experiences through its ability to evoke memories or images, or by repeated association with emotional states. A piece of music may be reminiscent of a sad time in one's life, and this episodic memory, in turn, may trigger feelings of sadness. The various sonic attributes may remind a listener of the sound of a waterfall, wind blowing through trees, or a vast and isolated landscape. These images and ideas may also trigger emotional associations. Music can also evoke emotions because of social, cultural, or political associations. A national anthem can, for some, evoke powerful emotions of pride and joy no matter how tortured the rendition. Conversely, music that is beautifully composed and sensitively performed may, if used as propaganda in a racist campaign, evoke sinister associations and negative emotions. In all these examples, the music itself is not the primary object of the emotional experience. Emotional experiences are partly triggered by the music, but the memories, imagery, or associations are what actually drive the emotional experience.

In this chapter, we outline a model that aims to explain how music, as the paradigm example of an embodied signal, can be the *direct object* of powerful emotional experiences. We will argue that the direct, unmediated emotional responses to music can be explained by viewing music listening as an embodied experience that engages sensory–motor processes. First, we illustrate the multimodal nature of music by reviewing evidence that merely observing the *actions* that accompany music performance greatly influences our perception and interpretation of the *acoustic* dimension of music: the properties of the music that we hear. Second, we introduce a theoretical framework that views perception and action as inextricably linked, and that construes music as a unique type of multimodal behavior specialized for engaging predictive sensory–motor processes in listeners. By this means, our perception of the qualities of music can directly guide the arousal of emotions. Moreover, we demonstrate that this framework allows for a unification of action-based models of emotion with expectancy-based models of musical emotions.

Music and gesture

Before the invention of the gramophone and the rise of the recording industry, music was almost always experienced as a multimodal phenomenon containing auditory, visual, and kinesthetic dimensions. Moreover, before the rise of concert halls, music was rarely observed passively, but was actively experienced; music making was often social, collaborative, accompanied by dance, and had weak or absent boundaries between performer and audience.[i] Indeed, people are highly attuned to the human movements that are used to produce musical sounds. Movements such as banging on a drum or plucking a guitar string function not only to produce musical sounds; they provide a visual signal to others engaged in the musical activity. Visual signals, such as facial expressions and bodily movements (which we broadly call gesture), are integral to musical communication and they shape the way music is perceived, understood, and experienced. Research conducted over the past decade has rediscovered and confirmed the multimodal, embodied nature of music experience: how visual and bodily dimensions of music (both on the part of the performer and the audience) inform and interact with the acoustic dimension of music, giving rise to complex psychological and social effects.

The influence of gesture on music perception

Groundbreaking research over 30 years ago illustrated that the facial movements that accompany speech have striking effects on how speech sounds are perceived. McGurk and Macdonald (1976) asked participants to listen to spoken syllables (such as [ga] or [ba]) and to report the syllable that they heard. Participants performed the task with correct identification of syllables in over 90% of trials. However, performance was dramatically altered when the acoustic signal for one spoken syllable was synchronized with the mouth movements used to produce a different spoken syllable. When the acoustic signal of [ba] was synchronized with a video of the mouth movements required to produce the syllable [ga], participants often reported hearing the syllable [da]. This illusory percept, known as the McGurk effect, was dependent on the presence of the visual signal: by closing their eyes, participants could once again accurately identify the vocalized syllable.

In a similar fashion, movements that accompany music performance influence the perception of musical structure. Thompson *et al.* (2005, experiment 1) found that facial expressions and gestures that occur during music performance influence the perception of "musical dissonance." Musical dissonance occurs when a pitch or pitch combination is perceived to clash with (learnt) harmonic or tonal expectations, resulting in music that sounds discordant or in need of resolution.[ii] It is differentiated from sensory dissonance—the sensation of beating and roughness associated with interactions among sound waves (amplitude fluctuations) and the inner ear's ability to resolve spectral components.

In order to examine the role of facial expressions and gestures on perceived musical dissonance, twenty excerpts from an audio-visual recording of B. B. King playing the blues were selected. Ten of these excerpts contained facial expressions that conveyed a sense of dissonance (dissonant set) while the other ten excerpts contained more neutral facial expressions (neutral set). The actual level of musical dissonance in the two sets of excerpts was similar, so the only systematic difference between sets was the type of facial expressions used. Facial expressions and gestures in the dissonant set included wincing of the eyes, shaking of the upper body, a grimace, and a rolling of the head in a back-swung position. Such expressions may have resulted from an increased (or feigned) difficulty of performing dissonant notes, but they may also be introduced to signify a performer's interpretation of musical structure. Participants viewed both sets of excerpts under audio-visual and auditory-only conditions and judged the level of dissonance for each excerpt. Dissonance was explained to participants as "occurring when the music sounds discordant (i.e. conflicted or negative) and in need of some sort of resolution." (Thompson *et al.* 2005, p. 189). In the audio-visual condition, excerpts that contained dissonant facial expressions and gestures were rated as more dissonant musically than excerpts that contained neutral facial expressions. However, when those same passages were presented in the absence of facial expressions (audio-only condition), ratings of dissonance were no different in the two sets. That is, the inclusion of facial expressions and gesture was wholly responsible for the perceived dissonance of the excerpts. These results are consistent with the notion that visual information associated with musical performance can significantly influence how audiences perceive and encode consonance and dissonance.

If facial expressions during music performance can influence the way acoustic information is perceived, then it stands to reason that such facial expressions might influence the perception of musical structure. Thompson *et al.* (2005, experiment 2) examined whether facial expressions used by singers could communicate to audience members the size of a melodic interval they were singing. Participants were asked to view (video-only) or listen to (audio-only) a trained musician sing four intervals that ranged in size between two and nine semi-tones. For both audio-only and video-only presentations, ratings of interval size by musically untrained participants were highly correlated with the actual size of the intervals, illustrating that musical structure is conveyed not only by the acoustic dimension of music, but also by visual signals arising from the facial expressions and gestures of musicians. Even more striking, the effect of facial expressions was evident even when acoustic information was present (Thompson *et al.* 2005, experiment 3). For example, ratings of interval size were significantly higher if an auditory signal arising from a small melodic interval (two semi-tones) was paired with facial expressions associated with the production of a large melodic interval (nine semi-tones) than when it was paired with facial expressions associated with the production of a small melodic interval (two semi-tones).

Subsequent research was conducted to identify specific facial features associated with melodic interval size. Thompson and Russo (2007) asked participants to judge the size of a sung interval from silent video recordings. As with Thompson *et al.* (2005, experiments 2 and 3), participants' ratings were strongly correlated with actual interval size. The authors also measured several types of facial movements in their stimuli. These included head and eyebrow displacement (measured as the maximum distance relative to start positions) and the size of mouth opening (measured as the maximum distance between the upper and lower lip). All movements measured were correlated with interval size suggesting that participants have access to multiple and partially redundant visual cues for extracting melodic interval size.

Musicians may produce these movements for a number of reasons. First, they may reflect production constraints: producing a large interval requires a large change in vocal cord tension, but the muscles used to implement this change in vocal tension might inadvertently recruit muscles that control facial features. Second, such movements may be an explicit attempt by musicians to communicate the size of a pitch interval. Third, facial movements may be an implicit form of communication built into conventional expressive actions and gestures among performers because of their success at enhancing musical communication and, hence, enjoyment. Fourth, they may reflect arousal states associated with pitch movements (e.g. see Scherer 2003). Large intervals typically reflect dramatic moments in music: if a performing musician experiences this dramatic effect as heightened arousal, then facial expressions associated with that affective state might naturally arise. Such facial expressions may not always be evident, however; elite singers, for example, may actively suppress facial expressions that negatively impact on the quality of their vocal output.

Thompson *et al.* (2010) probed the nature of these visual cues in more detail. Participants were asked to judge the size of a sung interval from a video recording of a musician singing various ascending melodic intervals. By overlaying a mask onto the video, parts of the face were occluded in some conditions. They determined that participants were able to accurately judge interval size even when only head movements were visible (all facial features occluded). The ability to evaluate interval size was increased further when facial features were visible, suggesting that subtle movements of individual facial features provide detailed information about melodic structure. Three-dimensional motion capture was next used to track the movements of the singers. Movement analyses confirmed that the magnitude of head displacement and mouth opening correlated well with actual interval size (the size as sung by the performer), corroborating the results of Thompson and Russo (2007).

What processes underlie such effects? Do viewers consciously consider head and facial movements when judging interval size or is there an unconscious process by which auditory and visual input are automatically integrated? To answer this question, participants were asked to perform a distracting secondary task (counting digits that appeared on the screen) while judging sung interval size from audio-visual recordings of singers (Thompson *et al.* 2010, experiments 2 and 3). The secondary task was designed to occupy attentional resources thereby reducing the capacity of participants to use these resources to judge interval size. The presence of the secondary task did not alter the effect of visual information. That is, judgments of interval size were modulated according to the type of visual information present (congruent or incongruent), and this effect was observed regardless of the difficulty of the secondary task, or whether participants were explicitly told to ignore visual signals. These results suggest that visual information is automatically and pre-attentively combined with auditory information, and that our experiences and interpretations of music represent a balance between these cues.

The influence of gesture on affective judgments

The movements produced by musicians also carry emotional information. Thompson *et al.* (2005) examined whether the perceived emotional valence of a sung melodic interval is influenced by the facial expressions adopted by the singer. Audio-visual recordings of a sung minor third (usually associated with a negative emotional valence) and a sung major third (usually associated with a positive emotional valence) were edited to yield congruent audio-visual conditions (e.g. sung minor interval combined with facial expressions used to produce that same minor interval) and incongruent conditions (e.g. sung minor interval combined with facial expressions used to produce a major interval). By comparing judgments for congruent and incongruent conditions, it was possible to determine that facial expressions significantly influenced the perception of emotional valence in sung intervals. That is, a performing musician can significantly alter the emotional valence of music merely with the accompanying facial expressions.

This effect was present even when participants were engaged in a distracting secondary task and when they were explicitly asked to ignore facial expressions and make their judgments exclusively on the auditory information (Thompson *et al.* 2008). As with the influence of facial expressions on the perceived size of a melodic interval, the influence of facial expressions on the perceived valence of music occurs pre-attentively, without the need to consciously attend to facial cues. This influence is not restricted to isolated sung intervals but is also evident for longer and more naturalistic performances. Thompson *et al.* (2005, experiment 5) examined the influence of facial expressions and gestures on emotional judgments of excerpts from sung performances by Judy Garland. Groups of participants were shown either an audio-visual excerpt or an audio-only excerpt from each performance. Participants then judged the emotional valence of the performance using a Likert scale (sad to happy). The group exposed to the audio-visual recording was instructed to base their judgments exclusively on the audio signal alone. Emotional judgments differed significantly depending on whether listeners had been exposed to the complete audio-visual excerpt or only the audio component. That is, the emotional quality of the performance was again influenced by the presence of visual information (even though the group exposed to audio-visual materials was instructed to ignore the visual information). The direction of this effect was dependent on the excerpt presented, suggesting that Judy Garland used facial expressions differently depending on her emotional goals for the song. For some songs, the inclusion of facial expressions and gestures led to an increase in the perceived emotional valence (judged more happy); in other excerpts it led to a decrease in perceived emotional valence (judged more sad).

The preceding studies indicate that the facial expressions and gestures of performers can profoundly affect the way music is perceived, interpreted, and experienced. Movements and facial expressions can shape the perception of musical structure (interval size) as well as the emotional messages communicated by the music. What are the mechanisms by which such movements exert their influence? One hint comes from the observation that music listening is rarely, if ever, a passive activity. Indeed, recent evidence suggests that movements produced by the *perceiver*—a kind of "mirroring" behavior—might play a part in how the music is perceived, and may in turn influence the emotional character.

Livingstone *et al.* (2009) employed an emotional-production synchronization paradigm whereby participants were asked to observe and then imitate sung phrases. The phrases were sung with varying emotional intentions (along with a neutral control condition), and participants were asked to pay close attention to the emotional content of the sung phrases as they observed them so that they could then imitate the expressed emotion. The facial expressions of the observers were monitored during the observation phase, immediately after the observation phase as they planned their own imitation (pre-production phase), during their imitation of the sung phrase (production phase), and after their imitation (post-production phase). Facial expressions were monitored with three-dimensional motion capture (experiment 1) and electromyography (EMG; experiment 2).

For the motion capture analysis, markers were placed on the eyebrows, lip corners, and lower lip. Movements of the eyebrows and lip corners reflect eyebrow furrowing and smiling, respectively. Movements of the lower lip should occur during any vocalization, but these movements do not tend to vary with emotional intentions. Analyses revealed that there was an effect of emotion on the movement of the eyebrow marker during the planning, production, and post-production phases. This suggests that movements related to the production of "sad" facial expressions begin before participants start to imitate sung phrases with "sad" emotional connotations. With the lip corner marker, the effect of emotion was present in all four phases, including the perception phase. This suggests that movements related to the production of "happy" facial expressions begin not only prior to production but even while participants are merely *observing* sung phrases.

Motion capture analysis was supplemented by the use of EMG to measure activity of zygomatic muscles (near the cheeks) and corrugator muscles (near the eyebrows), which are associated with positive and negative affect, respectively (Schwartz *et al.* 1976; Dimberg *et al.* 2000). As part of the analysis, a composite score was calculated by summing together zygomatic muscle activity while observing or imitating a happy sung phrase with corrugator muscle activity while observing or imitating a sad sung phrase. This analysis indicated that emotional facial expressions occurred during perception, pre-production, production, and post-production phases. As with the motion capture data, the EMG data suggest that observing emotional singing can immediately trigger a process of emotional mimicry. However, as participants in this investigation were explicitly instructed to imitate sung phrases, additional research is needed to determine whether emotional mimicry for sung phrases occurs automatically.

Music and action

The experimental findings outlined above can be explained within a theoretical framework that grounds perception within action. Psychologists have long been interested in the link between perception and action. For example, William James (1905) argued strongly that perception and action were tightly intertwined. According to the ideomotor principle outlined by James (1905), actions are represented in terms of their perceptual consequences. Such action–perception associations operate in two directions: an action plan can trigger a representation of the perceptual outcome of that action; and perceiving an action can trigger action plans that lead to such a perceptual outcome. Gibson (1986) also viewed perception and action as mutually dependent. According to this "ecological" approach, the environment is perceived in terms of the action possibilities available to the organism, called *affordances*. For example, a cup might be perceived in terms of the grip that would be required to manipulate it, and a chair might be perceived in terms of the act of sitting down. Furthermore, Gibson (1986) observed that actions themselves are often used to extract valuable information from the environment. Along similar lines, the common-coding hypothesis argues that there is a common representational code for perception and action (e.g. see Hommel *et al.* 2001). Perception leads to the formation of action plans, and action plans lead to perceptual predictions. Several lines of evidence have been used to support this hypothesis.

Experiments on stimulus response compatibility provide some of the most well-known examples of perception influencing action planning (e.g. Simon, 1969). Stimulus response compatibility refers to the way in which the perception of certain stimuli can activate action plans. Drost *et al.* (2005) measured reaction times for pianists who played a musical chord in response to a visual stimulus. The visual stimulus depicted the chord that was to be played, but it was also accompanied by one of the following auditory stimuli: (1) the same chord (congruent); (2) a different chord (incongruent); or (3) non-tonal sounds (control). The results showed that pianists responded faster to the visual stimulus when it was accompanied by a congruent auditory signal. That is, perceiving the predicted sensory consequence of an action (the sound of the chord) was sufficient to activate action plans for the production of the corresponding action, thereby priming and expediting the execution of the action.

The connection between perception and action has also been examined directly by measuring the effects of perception on motor regions of the brain. This approach has revealed action plans in the brain in the absence of any physical movement. Grahn and Brett (2007) found that listening to musical rhythms resulted in activation of motor regions in the brain, including the supplementary motor area, dorsal pre-motor regions, and the basal ganglia. Importantly, there was no activation of *primary* motor regions, suggesting that motor activation was not related to actual movement but action plans. They were also able to exclude motor *preparation* as a possible cause of motor activation by focusing their analysis on experimental trials in which no motor planning or preparation was required. Not only do rhythmic stimuli activate motor regions in the brain, neurological diseases that destroy motor regions in the brain can lead to deficits in rhythm discrimination. Grahn and Brett (2009) found that patients with Parkinson's disease perform poorly on a rhythmic discrimination task when compared with healthy controls. Thus, not only does a regular beat induce movement and activate the motor system, a functional motor system might be required for veridical perception of a regular beat.

Overlapping patterns of activity in motor regions have also been observed for perception and performance tasks. Bangert *et al.* (2006) have shown that motor regions are activated when musicians either listen to music or perform actions related to music making. In this study, musicians and non-musicians either listened to novel music or arbitrarily pressed keys on a silent piano keyboard. Musicians showed significantly more motor activity than non-musicians during the listening tasks. Similarly, Haueisen and Knösche (2001) found that when pianists listened to piano sequences, there was activation in motor regions normally associated with the production of piano sequences. These results suggest that a common motor network underlies the perception and the performance of music.

Recent neurophysiological evidence has illustrated the ubiquity of common coding for perception and action. For example, specialized neurons, called *canonical neurons*, have been shown to be active both when a monkey performs a particular action, such as a precision grip, and when they observe an object that can be manipulated by means of a precision grip (Fadiga *et al.* 2000). That is, the mere observation of an object directly generates an action plan for interacting with that object.

Another class of perceptual-motor neurons, called *mirror neurons*, are selective not for objects but for actions. Mirror neurons are active both during the observation of actions performed by conspecifics and during the production of action (for a review, see Rizzolatti and Craighero 2004). That is, merely perceiving an action is sufficient for generating action plans in the observer. The activity of mirror neurons has also been observed following the perception of action *effects*, including the sounds that are produced by actions (Kohler *et al.* 2002). These *auditory mirror neurons* (or echoic neurons) may play an important role in music perception. Indeed, regions thought to contain mirror neurons were shown to be active during the music perception tasks studied by Grahn and Brett (2007) and Bangert *et al.* (2006), outlined above. Mirror neurons do more than simply copy the actions that are perceived: they also help to predict the consequences of observed actions (Wilson and Knoblich 2005).

Common-coding theory states that perception of action influences action planning, and action (and action planning), in turn, influence perception. Repp and Knoblich (2007) found that trained pianists were more likely to report two ambiguous tones as ascending in pitch if they produced those tones with a left-to-right key press sequence on a piano keyboard. That is, participants were more likely to hear an ascending pitch sequence when they pressed the piano keys in an order that was compatible with an ascending pitch sequence. Similarly, Phillips-Silver and Trainor (2007) found that movements made concurrently with musical stimuli influenced how those stimuli were perceived, encoded, and subsequently remembered. They trained participants to make rhythmic (bouncing) body movements in time with rhythmically ambiguous sounds. The body movements could be produced in either duple or triple form. After the training session, they asked participants to identify the sounds that they heard during the training session. Even though all participants were presented with rhythmically ambiguous sounds during the training sessions, participants were more likely to select sounds that explicitly conformed to the rhythmic pattern of the movements they made during the training session. That is, the rhythmic patterns of participants' movements shaped their perceptions of the acoustic signal.

If the perception of action can generate action plans, and action plans can modulate perception, then it stands to reason that the perception of action can modulate perception. That is, our action systems may modulate the way in which we perceive actions, or auditory stimuli accompanied by actions. The most commonly cited example is the McGurk effect (McGurk and Macdonald 1976) outlined above (p. 198). However, the empirical studies performed by Thompson and colleagues, detailed earlier (p. 200), also provide evidence for this claim. In these examples, the observation of facial expression and gestures activate action representations that modulate the incoming acoustic signal such that sung melodic intervals accompanied by sad facial expressions (facial expression produced when singing a minor third) are sadder *sounding* than the same sung intervals accompanied by "happy" facial expressions (facial expression produced when singing a major third). Considered within the common-coding framework, the findings of Thompson and colleagues can be explained by grounding emotional experience in the body. Observing the body movements and facial expressions of a musical performer should lead to the activation of action plans in the observer. These action plans should, in turn, modulate the perception of the expressive content contained in the audio-visual signal. Furthermore, the findings of Livingstone *et al.* (2009), which suggest that observers initiate action plans while merely observing emotional singing, also supports the notion that bodily actions help listeners "get the feel" of the music.

Action and emotion

Action-based accounts of emotion have a long history. The theory of emotion developed by James (1884) directly linked emotions with sensory–motor processes in the brain. James (1884) noted that emotions are tightly correlated with particular patterns of bodily change. For James (1884), it is not our emotional states that lead to bodily changes such as a racing heart. Rather, "bodily changes follow directly the perception of the exciting fact, and... our feeling of the same changes as they occur is the emotion" (James 1884, p. 449). This assumption led James to further argue that, "[w]e feel sorry because we cry, angry because we strike, afraid because we tremble" (James 1884, p. 450). James also asked his readers to imagine a strong emotion, and then try and remove from this imagining all bodily changes. Without those bodily changes, he believed that there would be nothing left of the emotion.

Other authors have also emphasized the link between action and emotion. For example, Frijda (1987) equated each emotion with a particular profile of action tendencies, called an action readiness profile. The emotion of happiness might be associated with an increased "tendency to stay in proximity of" and "exuberance [or] free activation, [and] increased generalized action readiness" (Frijda 1987, p. 133). The perceptual theory of emotion developed by Jesse Prinz (2005) combined the views expressed by James (1884) and Frijda (1987). On this account, the link between emotion and the body (and action) is bi-directional. That is, emotions are perceptual states registering bodily change but they also motivate bodily changes and control action. Behavioral and neuroimaging studies have supported the notion that emotional experience is grounded in action and the body. Zuckerman et al. (1981) found that participants reported an increased intensity of emotional experience when asked to produce exaggerated facial expressions while observing emotionally laden video clips. Similarly, Strack et al. (1988) found that participants' ratings for the "funniness" of cartoons was attenuated by restricting facial movements by asking participants to either hold a pen between their lips or the teeth. Holding a pen in the lips prevented the participants using their zygomatic muscles (used for smiling) because this would have resulted in the pen falling from the mouth. Thus, it is possible to infer the emotional state one is in by registering the bodily changes that one experiences. And these bodily changes can modulate, or interfere, with the emotional content of perceived emotions in, for example, the music.

Support for grounding the phenomenology of emotion in the body also comes from patients with spinal cord lesions. In a study of 25 patients with various types of spinal injuries, Hohmann (1966) found that sustaining an injury that decreased sensation from the body led to changes in the phenomenal character of emotions. Nearly all patients reported a decrease in the emotional feelings of fear and anger after their injury, and it was found that, where these emotions remained, they were primarily abstract and detached in nature and lacking the somatic phenomenal descriptions that had usually been associated with them.

Neuroimaging has also implicated somato-sensory regions in emotional experience. In a study by Damasio et al. (2000), participants were asked to recall an emotional episode from their life while undergoing brain scanning using positron emission tomography. Although different patterns of neural activity were observed for the different emotions that were recalled, all emotions activated regions associated with body perception, such as the somato-sensory cortex, and regions receiving sensory signals from the viscera.

Links between music and action are increasingly incorporated into theories of the emotional power of music. The Shared Affective Motion Experience (SAME) model of musical emotion proposed by Molnar-Szakacs and Overy (Molnar-Szakacs and Overy 2006; Overy and Molnar-Szakacs 2009) draws heavily on the common coding of action-perception and action-production performed by mirror neurons. They argue that the mirror neuron system is a key mechanism that allows emotion to be transmitted by music. The mirror neuron system is thought to provide access to a musician's emotional state by representing music in terms of motor commands. Auditory signals that arise from music are imbued with emotional intentions because they imply actions that are themselves emotional. When auditory signals are transformed into a motor representation in a listener's brain, the listener can "work backwards" from this motor representation to the emotional intentions that gave rise to the music.

In this view, music is perceived as an "intentional, hierarchically organized sequence of expressive motor acts" (Overy and Molnar-Szakacs 2009, p. 492). How is this done? Most listeners lack the specialized knowledge needed to infer the specific motor acts required to produce musical sounds. For example, only a highly trained pianist can appreciate the fine-grained movements required to perform a Bach fugue on the piano. Overy and Molnar-Szakacs (2009) proposed that depending on the listener's level of musical ability, they can extract movement information at different levels of the motor system. Whereas a skilled musician may have access to fine-grained actions used to perform music, a musically unskilled listener may interpret emotional intentions with respect to gross actions such as clapping or tapping, which mirror the overall beat. In support of this model, Overy and Molnar-Szakacs (2009) cited the tight links between music and movement, along with evidence demonstrating that music can directly activate motor regions in the brain.

An important assumption of the SAME model is that emotional intentions are inferred directly from this motor activity. This assumption is derived from the early "mind-reading" model of mirror neuron function proposed by Gallese and Goldman (1998). Although the idea that we have neurons specialized for mind-reading is intriguing, it has been heavily criticized. In particular, Jacob and Jeannerod (2005; see also Jacob 2008) have argued that the perception–action transformations performed by mirror neurons cannot underlie the process of mind-reading (or inferring intentions from actions) because the replication of motor commands performed by mirror neurons is not sufficient for replication of a mental state. Intentions and actions have a many-to-one relation, so it is rarely possible to "work backwards" from an action to an intention. A wide range of intentions can lead to the same motor response. For example, the act of picking up a pen may occur because an agent is sad and is writing a note of sympathy about a deceased friend, or because an agent is angry and has decided to tender a resignation. Similarly, identical scalpel movements can be used by a doctor trying to save a patient's life or by a madman torturing a victim (Jacob and Jeannerod 2005).

Moreover, mirror neuron activity is not necessary to understand the intentions behind actions. In particular, experiments have shown that observers readily provide mentalistic explanations for the behavior of agents in displays consisting of simple geometric shapes (e.g. see Castelli *et al.* 2000). Simple geometric shapes lack human bodies and, therefore, do not lend themselves to mirror neuron activity. Furthermore, electrophysiological evidence (e.g. Umiltà *et al.* 2001) suggests that, rather than decoding the goal of an action, mirror neuron activity is dependent on the observer already understanding the goal of an observed action.

While this evidence suggests that mirror neurons are neither necessary nor sufficient for mind-reading, it is still possible that mirror neurons may form part of a larger system for inferring intentions from actions. However, this hypothesis awaits further evidence. We believe there is a more parsimonious way to account for the interconnections between music, the mirror neuron system, and emotion. Specifically, we argue that the action plans generated by mirror neurons function for perceptual *prediction*.

Consistent with this argument, Wilson and Knoblich (2005) propose that mirror neurons form part of an emulator system used for predicting the actions of other agents. They suggest that during action observation, mirror neurons are used to simulate the actions of others by mapping the actions of observed agents onto an internal model of the observer's own motor system. This internal model can then be used to stand in for actual sensory input and this allows an observer to track the movements of an observed agent in real-time—even when they are obscured from view—or to generate predictions of the unfolding motor act. Thus, mirror neuron activity may be used to predict the sensory consequences of observed motor action (Knoblich *et al.* 2002; Flach *et al.* 2003) or it may be used to plan anticipatory actions in response to unfolding observed motor acts. This system may underlie the ability to engage in synchronous action (e.g., Colling *et al.* 2010) including ensemble music performance (Keller *et al.* 2007).

Action production need not be overt. It can also take the form of simulated perception–action couplings. The ability of music (as human action) to engage processes of *synchronization* may represent one of the defining characteristics of music experience and may be critical for generating emotional responses to music.

Expectancy, action, and emotion

Having examined the role of action in how we perceive the emotional quality of music, we now turn our attention to how the same system can lead to the arousal of emotions. The power of common coding of perception and action, and synchronization driven by motor simulation, is that it provides a framework for linking action-based accounts of music perception with action-based and prediction-based (expectation) accounts of musical emotion. If perception is linked to action plans and action plans are also linked to perceptual prediction, then action-based and expectation-based accounts of musical emotion are two sides of the same coin.

The landmark work of Meyer (1956) draws heavily on melodic expectancies as the psychological basis for emotional responses to music. For Meyer (1956), musical meaning was conveyed by the manner in which one musical event built expectancies for musical events to follow. Similarly, Huron's (2006) ITPRA theory outlines multiple ways that expectancy (prediction) can account for emotional responses to music. Huron (2006) proposed five subsystems of musical expectancies that are relevant to the emotional power of music: imagination, tension, prediction, reaction, and appraisal. The first two subsystems mediate responses that occur before the expected/unexpected event (pre-outcome responses) and are related to guiding behavior by means of predicted future emotional experiences and physiological and psychological preparation for predicted future events. The final three subsystems mediate responses that occur after the event (post-outcome responses), and their activity is related to whether the event was accurately predicted, as well as pre-attentive and conscious assessment of the event once it has occurred.

The pre-outcome response of *imagination* is an important motivator for action. It can be used to preview future events and to predict/simulate what these future events might feel like and what emotional responses they may evoke. In this way, imagination is used to generate and test out action plans and simulate the emotional consequences of these action plans. These simulated emotional states act as a reward or punishment that can guide action selection. The pre-outcome response of *tension* refers to preparation for an expected event. Preparation may involve preparing cognitive resources through heightened attention or it may take the form of increasing action readiness, through physiological arousal, in preparation for predicted future events.

After the occurrence of the event the *prediction* response provides a reward for accurate prediction or a punishment if there was a failure to predict the event. As suggested by the common-coding hypothesis, the action plans generated by the musical stimulus, and pre-outcome responses may drive these predictions. A positively valenced emotional response serves as a reward and a negatively valenced emotional response serves as a punishment. The emotional experience evoked by the prediction response serves to fine-tune the predictive mechanisms so that future predictions are more accurate. The prediction response is not dependent on the nature of the event; it merely depends on whether the event was accurately predicted.

The nature of the event (whether it was a positive or negative event) drives two post-outcome responses—reaction and appraisal. *Reaction* responses are rapid assessments of the events that occurs pre-attentively and outside of conscious awareness. Reaction responses may also take the form of mild surprise evoked by violations of expectancies, and can result in action consequences such as rapid "knee-jerk" bodily actions or visceral responses. *Appraisal* responses are deliberate, conscious assessments of an event that operate over longer time frames and are heavily dependent on context. They operate independently of reaction responses, and reaction responses that may initially evoke a negatively valenced emotional response may, upon reflection or *appraisal*, turn into a positively valenced emotional experience. For example, initial negative feelings evoked by violations of harmonic expectancies may, upon reflection, be appreciated on intellectual grounds. Because of the independent action of these different response subsystems, Huron (2006) argued that expectancies and prediction are able to generate complex, dynamic, and highly nuanced emotional experiences.

Perceptual predictions are directly and bi-directionally linked with action plans. Therefore, expectancies such as those described in Huron's (2006) model may be functionally equivalent to action plans. Indeed, Huron (2006) explicitly links action with pre-outcome responses, such as tension, and post-outcome responses, such as reaction. As such, expectancy-based accounts of musical emotion may be seen as a special case of more general action-based accounts of emotion.

A feedback-controlled synchronization model

Recently, work by Carver and Scheier (2009) has sought to develop a general account of the link between action and emotion. Key to Carver and Scheier's (2009) framework is the notion that behavior is goal-directed and controlled by feedback processes. Emotional experiences are the natural outcomes of the attainment of or the failure to attain goals. The feedback generated by the attainment of or failure to attain goals is fed into a *behavior control system* in order to modify future behavior. Goals may include static end-states (e.g. catching a ball or passing an exam) or dynamic goals that evolve over time. Goal-directed behavior may also take the form of generating expectancies, where the goal of an expectation is the accurate prediction of the environment. Synchronizing covert or overt bodily actions with music may be a particularly important form of goal-directed behavior that occurs during music listening. Synchronization relies on expectancies that are derived from predictive action plans generated by the musical signal. These expectancies need to be constantly updated so as to match the ongoing dynamic music signal. By unifying expectancies and goal-directed action, Carver and Scheier's (2009) model can account for many of the same phenomena discussed in Huron's (2006) model of expectancy in music.

In any system, whether artificially engineered or biological, the maintenance of goal-directed behavior occurs through *feedback control*. Feedback control systems can be broken down into four parts: an input value, a reference value, a comparison mechanism, and an output. Inputs provide a measure of the current state of the system or a prediction or expectancy that the system has generated. The reference value serves as a target value with which the input is compared. This reference value, or goal state, can take the form of an action goal or it can be a measure of the value that the system is attempting to predict. A comparison process then computes the discrepancy between the input value and the reference value and generates an error signal. The error signal is then sent as output to be fed back into the controller of the system. The output signal can then be used to modify the behavior of the system or to update the predictions that the system is generating.

The behavior of the system can be modified in one of two ways. In positive-feedback systems, the output signal modifies the system's behavior so as to increase the discrepancy between the input value and reference value. This type of feedback system is used to guide the behavior of a system away from a possibly negative stimulus. In negative-feedback systems, the output modifies the behavior of the system so that the input values approach the reference value. In the case of predictive systems, which generate expectancies, negative feedback is used because expectancies have the goal of accurate prediction or minimal discrepancy between the predicted values/events and actual values/events.

In Carver and Scheier's (2009) model, positive and negative feedback do not directly generate emotional experience. Instead, the valence of an emotional experience is determined by the action of a secondary loop that runs simultaneously and in parallel with the primary, or behavior-guiding, loop. This secondary, or affect, loop monitors the progress of the behavior-guiding loop, with the error signal generated by the primary loop serving as the input for the affect loop. In the case of negative-feedback systems, the affect loop monitors the rate at which the primary loop's error signal is decreasing over time, corresponding to the progress that the system is making towards achieving its goal. Carver and Scheier (2009) suggest that the error signal that is generated by this second loop manifests phenomenologically as an experience of emotion. Valence is determined by comparing the pace or rate of change in the error signal from the primary loop with a criterion or expected rate of change. If the discrepancy is being reduced at a rate that is better than expected, then the error signal generated by the affect loop leads to a positive emotional experience. If the discrepancy is decreasing at a rate that is worse than expected, then the error signal generated by the affect loop leads to a negative emotional experience. Thus, positive and negative emotional experiences indicate to the system how well the behavior-guiding loop is doing at achieving its goal.

Carver and Scheier's (2009) model provides a plausible mechanism underlying emotional effects arising from music expectancies (see also Thompson and Quinto, 2011). Perceptual experiences that occur during music listening activate action plans and, hence, expectancies. More generally, music engages processes of synchronization that are underpinned by dynamic action-prediction–action-production loops. This is evident in cases where people feel compelled to move "in time" with music.

Within the common-coding framework, listening to music is functionally equivalent to engaging in goal-directed behavior. By manipulating how goals are achieved and violated, composers control valence and arousal dimensions of emotional experience. The activity of the primary (behavior-guiding) loop, which is directly activated by action plans initiated by music listening, may allow composers to control the arousal dimension of emotional experience. The activity of the secondary (affect) loop means that the emotional valence of music shifts as listeners or performers are able to increase or decrease their level of synchronization over time. Together, the actions of the behavior-guiding and affect loops create a rich and complex emotional experience.

Figure 15.1 provides a sketch of the synchronization feedback model. The model places the performing musician front and center in the emotional experience. By observing or imagining the actions of performers, audiences generate action plans and expectancies through the common coding of perception and action. Action plans and expectancies work together to drive the process of synchronization. The level at which listeners can synchronize is dependent on their level of motor experience. Skilled musicians may be capable of detailed and fine-grained synchronization and can generate detailed expectancies. Unskilled, musically naïve listeners may instead

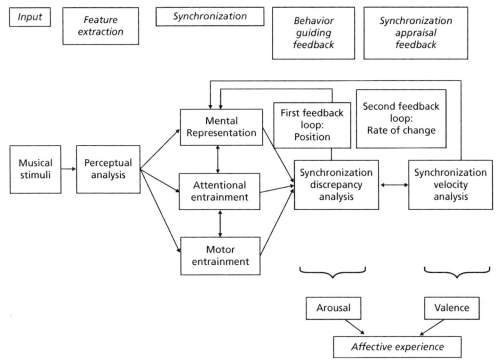

Figure 15.1 An illustration of the synchronization feedback model (reprinted by permission from Thompson and Quinto 2011).

synchronize using gross actions such as clapping, tapping, and dancing or by synchronizing with expressive movements by performing actual or simulated movements, such as "air guitar" (see also Schubotz, 2007). Musical expectancies also arise from observing or inferring the actions of performers. Surprising or predictable actions in the stream of patterned motor activity that make up a musical signal are just as effective at evoking emotions as surprising or predictable acoustic events. By controlling the interplay between the fulfillment and violation of these expectancies along with the fulfillment and violation of expectancies generated by the acoustic signal (as in the case of B. B. King or Judy Garland detailed on p.200), performers can evoke a dynamic and highly nuanced emotional experience.

Musical expectancies need not only occur for immediate effects. Some expectancies can occur over larger time scales and can possess more abstract content. For example, immediate expectancies may occur as a direct result of action plans generated by the beat, or tactus, of a musical piece. Simultaneously, expectancies related to higher-order melodic, harmonic, or phrasing structure may also be generated. The results of more immediate expectancies may interact with these higher-order expectancies in order to create a multilayered emotional experience. Furthermore, bodily changes induced by the effect of music on the motor system may operate on a longer time scale in order to modulate the phenomenology of emotional experiences evoked by processes of synchronization. Thus, the emotions aroused by the music are not necessarily the same as those that we perceive the music to be expressing. The model of expression we endorse states that we infer emotions from the motor activations that result from the actions we take to be responsible for producing the music. Meanwhile, our model of emotion states that one's emotional valence is due to one's success or failure at predicting the musical action. It is possible then for one to have a positive emotional experience in response to predicting musical action that is perceived as emotionally negative. It is the confluence of these effects that may account for the powerful emotional responses to music.

Acknowledgments

Some of the research described in this chapter was supported by a discovery grant from the Australian Research Council to the second author. We thank John Sutton and Thomas Cochrane for helpful comments.

Notes

i   See Freeman (2000) for a discussion of music as a technology for social bonding.

ii   For a discussion of dissonance see Huron (2006, pp. 310–12) and Thompson (2009, pp. 48–50).

References

Bangert, M., Peschel, T., Schlaug, G., Rotte, M., Drescher, D., Hinrichs, H., Heinze, H., and Altenmüller, E. (2006). Shared networks for auditory and motor processing in professional pianists: evidence from fMRI conjunction. *NeuroImage*, **30**, 917–26.

Carver, C. S. and Scheier, M. F. (2009). Action, affect, and two-mode models of functioning. In E. Morsella, J. A. Bargh, and P. M. Gollwitzer (eds), *Oxford Handbook of Human Action*, pp. 298–327. Oxford: Oxford University Press.

Castelli, F., Happè, F., Frith, U., and Frith, C. (2000). Movement and mind: a functional imaging study of perception and interpretation of complex intentional movement patterns. *NeuroImage*, **12**, 314–25.

Colling, L. J., Sutton, J., and Thompson, W. F. (2010). Action synchronisation with biological motion. In W. Christensen, E. Schier, and J. Sutton (eds), *ASCS2009: Proceedings of the 9th Conference of the Australasian Society for Cognitive Science*, pp. 49–56. Sydney: Macquarie Centre for Cogntive Science.

Damasio, A. R., Grabowski, T. J., Bechara, A., Damasio, H., Ponto, L. L. B., Parvizi, J., and Hichwa, R. D. (2000). Subcortical and cortical brain activity during the feeling of self-generated emotions. *Nature Neuroscience*, **3**, 1049–56.

Dimberg, U., Thunberg, M., and Elmehed, K. (2000). Unconscious facial reactions to emotional facial expressions. *Psychological Science*, **11**, 86–9.

Drost, U. C., Rieger, M., Brass, M., Gunter, T. C., and Prinz, W. (2005). Action-effect coupling in pianists. *Psychological Research*, **69**, 233–41.

Fadiga, L., Fogassi, L., Gallese, V., and Rizzolatti, G. (2000). Visuomotor neurons: ambiguity of the discharge or "motor" perception? *International Journal of Psychophysiology*, **35**, 165–77.

Flach, R., Knoblich, G., and Prinz, W. (2003). Off-line authorship effects in action perception. *Brain and Cognition*, **53**, 503–13.

Freeman, W. (2000). A neurobiological role of music in social bonding. In N. L. Wallin, B. Merker, and S. Brown (eds), *The Origins of Music*, pp. 411–24. Cambridge, MA: MIT Press.

Frijda, N. H. (1987). Emotion, cognitive structure, and action tendency. *Cognition and Emotion*, **1**, 115–43.

Gallese, V. and Goldman, A. (1998). Mirror neurons and the simulation theory of mind-reading. *Trends in Cognitive Sciences*, **2**, 493–501.

Gibson, J. J. (1986). *The Ecological Approach to Visual Perception*. New York: Psychology Press.

Grahn, J. A. and Brett, M. (2007). Rhythm and beat perception in motor areas of the brain. *Journal of Cognitive Neuroscience*, **19**, 893–906.

Grahn, J. A. and Brett, M. (2009). Impairment of beat-based rhythm discrimination in Parkinson's disease. *Cortex*, **45**, 54–61.

Haueisen, J. and Knösche, T. R. (2001). Involuntary motor activity in pianists evoked by music perception. *Journal of Cognitive Neuroscience*, **13**, 786–92.

Hohmann, G. W. (1966). Some effects of spinal cord lesions on experienced emotional feelings. *Psychophysiology*, **3**, 143–56.

Hommel, B., Müsseler, J., Aschersleben, G., and Prinz, W. (2001). The theory of event coding: a framework for perception and action planning. *Behavioral and Brain Sciences*, **24**, 849–78.

Huron, D. (2006). *Sweet Anticipation: Music and the Psychology of Expectation*. Cambridge, MA: MIT Press.

Jacob, P. (2008). What do mirror neurons contribute to human social cognition? *Mind and Language*, **23**, 190–223.

Jacob, P. and Jeannerod, M. (2005). The motor theory of social cognition: a critique. *Trends in Cognitive Sciences*, **9**, 21–5.

James, W. (1884). What is an emotion? *Mind*, **9**, 188–205.

James, W. (1905). *The Principles of Psychology*, vol. 2. New York: Henry Holt and Company.

Keller, P. E., Knoblich, G., and Repp, B. H. (2007). Pianists duet better when they play with themselves: on the possible role of action simulation in synchronization. *Consciousness and Cognition*, **16**, 102–11.

Knoblich, G., Seigerschmidt, E., Flach, R., and Christensen, W. (2002). Authorship effects in the prediction of handwriting strokes: evidence for action simulation during action perception. *Quarterly Journal of Experimental Psychology: Section A*, **55**, 1027–46.

Kohler, E., Keysers, C., Umiltà, M. A., Fogassi, L., Gallese, V., and Rizzolatti, G. (2002). Hearing sounds, understanding actions: action representation in mirror neurons. *Science*, **297**, 846–8.

Livingstone, S. R., Thompson, W. F., and Russo, F. (2009). Facial expressions and emotional singing: a study of perception and production with motion capture and electromyography. *Music Perception*, **26**, 475–88.

McGurk, H. and Macdonald, J. (1976). Hearing lips and seeing voices. *Nature*, **264**, 746–8.

Meyer, L. B. (1956). *Emotion and Meaning in Music*. Chicago: University of Chicago Press.

Molnar-Szakacs, I. and Overy, K. (2006). Music and mirror neurons: from motion to "e"motion. *Social, Cognitive, and Affect Neuroscience*, **1**, 235–41.

Overy, K. and Molnar-Szakacs, I. (2009). Being together in time: musical experience and the mirror neuron system. *Music Perception*, **26**, 489–504.

Phillips-Silver, J. and Trainor, L. J. (2007). Hearing what the body feels: auditory encoding of rhythmic movement. *Cognition*, **105**, 533–46.

Prinz, J. J. (2005). Passionate thoughts: the emotional embodiment of moral concepts. In D. Pecher and R. A. Zwaan (eds), *Grounding Cognition: the Role of Perception and Action in Memory, Language, and Thinking*, pp. 93–114. New York: Cambridge University Press.

Repp, B. H. and Knoblich, G. (2007). Action can affect auditory perception. *Psychological Science*, **18**, 6–7.

Rizzolatti, G. and Craighero, L. (2004). The mirror-neuron system. *Annual Review of Neuroscience*, **27**, 169–92.

Scherer, K. R. (2003). Vocal communication of emotion: a review of research paradigms. *Speech Communication*, **40**, 227–56.

Schubotz, R. I. (2007). Prediction of external events with our motor system: towards a new framework. *Trends in Cognitive Sciences*, **11**, 211–18.

Schwartz, G., Fair, P., Salt, P., Mandel, M., and Klerman, G. (1976). Facial muscle patterning to affective imagery in depressed and nondepressed subjects. *Science*, **192**, 489–91.

Simon, J. R. (1969). Reactions toward the source of stimulation. *Journal of Experimental Psychology*, **81**, 174–6.

Strack, F., Martin, L. L., and Stepper, S. (1988). Inhibiting and facilitating conditions of the human smile: a nonobtrusive test of the facial feedback hypothesis. *Journal of Personality and Social Psychology*, **54**, 768–77.

Thompson, W. F. (2009). *Music, Thought, and Feeling : Understanding the Psychology of Music*. Oxford: Oxford University Press.

Thompson, W. F. and Quinto, L. (2011). Music and emotion: psychological considerations. In E. Schellekens and P. Goldie (eds), *The Aesthetic Mind: Philosophy and Psychology*, pp. 357–75. Oxford: Oxford University Press.

Thompson, W. F. and Russo, F. A. (2007). Facing the music. *Psychological Science*, **18**, 756–7.

Thompson, W. F., Graham, P., and Russo, F. A. (2005). Seeing music performance: visual influences on perception and experience. *Semiotica*, **156**, 203–27.

Thompson, W. F., Russo, F., and Quinto, L. (2008). Audio-visual integration of emotional cues in song. *Cognition and Emotion*, **22**, 1457–70.

Thompson, W. F., Russo, F. A., and Livingstone, S. R. (2010). Facial expressions of singers influence perceived pitch relations. *Psychonomic Bulletin and Review*, **17**, 317–22.

Umiltà, M. A., Kohler, E., Gallese, V., Fogassi, L., Fadiga, L., Keysers, C., and Rizzolatti, G. (2001). I know what you are doing: a neurophysiological study. *Neuron*, **31**, 155–65.

Wilson, M. and Knoblich, G. (2005). The case for motor involvement in perceiving conspecifics. *Psychological Bulletin*, **131**, 460–73.

Zuckerman, M., Klorman, R., Larrance, D., and Spiegel, N. (1981). Facial, autonomic, and subjective components of emotion: the facial feedback hypothesis versus the externalizer–internalizer distinction. *Journal of Personality*, **41**, 929–44.

Chapter 16

Rhythmic entrainment as a mechanism for emotion induction by music: a neurophysiological perspective

Wiebke Trost and Patrik Vuilleumier

Abstract

Music is a form of art that lives in the time domain. Therefore, likewise, the appreciation of music fluctuates over time and affects the listener in a dynamic, time-varying fashion. As most music is based on a metrical structure, music is thought to let different rhythms in the brain and the body resonate and eventually tune these internal rhythms into alignment with the same periodicities presented in the temporal structure of the music. In this chapter we discuss this notion of "rhythmic entrainment" and its role as a possible mechanism of emotion induction via music listening. We will describe the processes that take place in the brain when rhythmic aspects in the music are perceived and show how these processes may interact with the production of emotions. Furthermore, a distinction between rhythmic entrainment processes at different levels is suggested, including the perceptual, the physiological, the motor, and the social levels. We review the existing neuroscience approaches in the music literature to answer the question of how the temporal structure of music influences perceptions and affective reactions. We conclude that the mere processing of timing features in the music (such as rhythms) can trigger specific neural processes, which contribute to the induction of certain emotional states. However, we also underscore that this does not represent an automatism and argue that subjective aspects like musical preferences, familiarity, and training can act as important modulators.

Introduction: musical emotions in time

Igor Stravinsky stated that, "The phenomenon of music is given to us with the sole purpose of establishing an order in things, and particularly, the coordination between man and time" (Strawinsky 1937). Music could in this sense be regarded as an art that draws the attention of the listener to time itself, and to changes that are engendered over time. In accord with this, several psychological studies have shown that listening to music influences the perception of time (Olivers and Nieuwenhuis 2005, Noulhiane *et al.* 2007). More relevantly here, however, it is also most likely by virtue of its temporal properties that music is intimately associated with experiences of emotions. By nature, emotions are regarded as transient processes emerging and transforming themselves in time. In this respect music and emotions share an important characteristic, as they both fluctuate in time.

Koelsch (2010 and Chapter 17 this volume) moreover claims that in order to make music together *coordination*, *cooperation*, *communication*, and *social cognition* have to be established in a group, which in turn strengthen *contact*, *co-pathy*, and *social cohesion* (see also Chapter 17). These activities implicate spending time together, but also being in time together, i.e. being in "sync" in a strong and complete sense of this term.

The connection between music and emotion therefore appears well suited to be studied with special regard to its temporal quality. In particular, as our affective reactions to music are expressed, like other "everyday life" emotions, in a variety of physiological changes, emotional states evoked by music can be studied by measuring the temporal fluctuations of different physiological systems like respiratory or cardiac effort. Thus in this chapter we will present a short review of the recent literature on emotional reactions measured by physiological techniques, and discuss a particular aspect of the mechanisms of emotion induction by music in the temporal domain.

Music perception and emotions

First, it is necessary to ask how music is perceived in order to understand how it can evoke strong emotions. Further, is there any direct interaction between the way music is perceived and how it generates feelings?

Being an auditory stimulus, music is perceived in the inner ear, activates the cochlea, and is then submitted to a first analysis of low-level acoustic features (roughness, intensity, pitch, timbre, etc.) in the brainstem. Further on the acoustic signal reaches the auditory cortex via the thalamus, where its musical features are analyzed and categorized more in detail, taking into account the harmonic and rhythmic structure and integrating them according to *Gestalt* principles to a common percept (Koelsch 2010). From the auditory cortex, information is projected via feedforward and feedback loops to several regions in the brain, which monitor the signal for meaning and emotional value. Neuroimaging studies in humans (Blood *et al.* 1999, Brown *et al.* 2004, Koelsch 2005) have shown that, apart from the auditory cortices, listening to music activates several distributed networks including the limbic system (e.g. hippocampus, amygdala, cingulate cortex, etc.), sub-cortical striatal (putamen, caudate nucleus), and cortical motor circuits (e.g. motor cortex, supplementary motor area, pre-motor cortex, cerebellum), as well as higher-order associative areas (e.g. pre-frontal areas). (See Chapter 17 for an overview of neuroimaging studies on music perception and emotions.)

"Musical emotions" specifically refer to the (consciously or unconsciously) felt emotional experience during music listening, and we use this term accordingly throughout this chapter. As musically induced emotions do not have a proper goal (in terms of behavioral adaptation), which is a defining requirement for an "emotion" to arise according to many emotion theories (Scherer and Zentner 2001), they are generally considered to be different from everyday life emotions. Yet, it is difficult to deny that music does induce powerful affects even without any obvious (immediate) goal. Moreover, music can affect brain activity in a way that is similar to changes produced when a person is experiencing an emotion (see Koelsch 2010). For example, different music types activate ventral striatum, amygdala, or insula, all key brain regions typically responding to rewards, fear and anxiety, or arousal, respectively. In this sense, music puts the brain in a state of activity "as-if" a real emotion would be processed in response to other biologically or motivationally significant events. In addition, this does not preclude that more "direct" or "basic" emotions can also be evoked by music or music-related information, such as surprise for unexpected chords or performance, and even more complex feelings associated with social settings of the performance. A complex combination of these different factors, including aspects that concern the music itself, but also non-musical issues like the personal state, context, and culture, may trigger these processes. The latter aspects of music listening may resemble Damasio's somatic markers theory (Damasio 1996), which claims that decision-making is facilitated by simulating one's own state given a certain decision and observing the internal affective response "as-if" an emotional evaluation were to take place. According to Damasio, such a simulation can take place via a purely "internal" as-if loop retrieving cortical representations of particular affective states, but also via a body loop that lead to measurable changes in peripheral physiological states (Damasio 1999; Cochrane 2010). Thus, it appears particularly valuable to study the neural mechanisms responsible for musical emotions in order to unveil the psychological and neural underpinnings of subjective emotional experiences.

Mechanisms of emotion induction

A second important aspect of musical emotions concerns the question of which kinds of affective states can actually be induced by music. In fact, in the literature on the psychology of music, no consensus has yet been reached. On the one hand, a large number of psychologists claim that emotions constitute several discrete categories, including basic emotions such as joy, power, or anger (Ekman 1992). On the other hand, some theorists suggest that emotions occupy continuous dimensions (such as valence and arousal) and can be related to each other by measuring the distance between them in the space spanned by these dimensions (Russell 2003). Still another, intermediate, approach was put forwards by Zentner and colleagues (Zentner *et al.* 2008) who argue that musical emotions are special kinds of "esthetic emotions" that are different from "utilitarian" goal-related emotions, although they can partly overlap with general affective dimensions (Trost *et al.* 2012).

Another debate concerning emotions relates to the mechanisms that induce them. For esthetic emotions, Scherer and Zentner (2001) proposed that several distinct "production rules" might explain emotional experiences during music listening. According to these authors, musical structure, performance, listener, and contextual features all contribute to shaping the actual experienced emotion. Structural features can be divided into segmental features and supra-segmental features of the musical composition. Performance features are defined by the skills and the state of the performer. Listener features are differentiated into musical expertise, stable dispositions, and the current mood or motivational state of the listener, as well as his or her cultural background. The location and the form of the event of music listening are contextual features. However, these production rules essentially represent a formal differentiation of factors influencing the emotional experience of the listener, but do not make any suggestion about the underlying mechanisms (at the cognitive or neural level) that create the actual emotional reaction.

Juslin and Vjästfjäll (2008) recently suggested a unified theoretical framework that attempts to better explain the mechanisms of music induction. The authors claim that several different mechanisms might potentially be responsible for evoking emotions in the listener via music, and that they can operate largely in a parallel, additive, or interactive manner. They suggested that these mechanisms include *brainstem responses*, *evaluative conditioning*, *emotional contagion*, *visual imagery*, *episodic memory*, *music expectancy*, and *cognitive appraisal* (Juslin and Västfjäll 2008). Critically, in the latest version of this model, another mechanism was added which the authors called *rhythmic entrainment* (Juslin *et al.* 2010). Juslin and colleagues explain this principle by stating that "an emotion is induced by a piece of music because the powerful, external rhythm of the music interacts with an internal body rhythm of the listener such as heart rate" (Juslin *et al.* 2010). By becoming aware of these physiological changes, the listener consequently feels emotionally engaged. Thus, Juslin and colleagues suggest that entrainment processes linking the temporal structure of music inputs with physiological activity, such as heart or respiration rate, play a causal role in emotion induction. However, there is still little empirical evidence in favor of this view, although music clearly seems to be associated with entrainment effects as we will present below.

Physiological reactions to music

Since ancient Greek times, the strong impact of music on the body has been well known. In fact, psychophysiological reactions are a very important component of the emotional reaction. These bodily reactions occur, to various degrees, whenever an emotional stimulus is perceived by the senses (audition, vision, touch, smell) and is processed by the brain, reflecting a propagation of neural signals to the peripheral nervous system. However, it remains a matter of debate whether distinct emotions are associated with clearly distinct patterns of physiological change.

The peripheral nervous system is divided into the somatic nervous system, which is responsible for the voluntary control of skeletal muscles and transmission of sensory signals, and the autonomic nervous system, with the latter consisting of two subcomponents,—the sympathetic part and the parasympathetic part. The sympathetic division has a stimulating function, which is responsible for the release of several neurotransmitters (e.g. adrenaline) and thus mobilizes the body for action. The parasympathetic system is responsible for the coordination of physiological processes in the body at rest (e.g. intestinal activity). Both components are antagonists but their interplay is important for the maintenance of homeostasis.

Abundant research has tried to distinguish exactly which physiological pattern is associated with which affective state (Feldman-Barrett 2006, Cacioppo *et al.* 2007). These patterns can imply very explicit behavioral changes like body movements and facial expressions, including tears, along with implicit and more "hidden" changes in heart or respiration rate, skin conductance, pupil size, or blood pressure. The sympathetic and parasympathetic autonomic pathways drive many of the latter changes.

Among others, one reason for ambiguous results in past emotion research on physiological reactions could stem from the fact that the type of emotion induction differs widely between studies. Even from a purely perceptual point of view, it seems possible that looking at emotional pictures would probably engender a slightly different physiological pattern than generating a comparable emotion by means of a smell. For music, this perceptual effect is further complicated by the fact that in most styles of music, a rhythmic structure is present containing certain periodicities, and some changes in the stimulus flow are closely related to induced feelings. As several physiological processes are also of a dynamic and periodic nature, they might be particularly prone to interact with stimulus variations over time, and important synchronization or entrainment effects between the physiology and the music might come into play. In this respect, respiratory and cardiac activity might provide a unique window into the temporal unfolding of emotion induction, and therefore be of special interest when studying emotional reactions to music.

Respiration

Respiratory effort is influenced by both the sympathetic and the parasympathetic branches of the autonomic nervous system (Lorig 2007), but can also be controlled voluntarily. Different measures of respiration can be recorded using a respiration monitor belt around a person's chest. Inhalation and exhalation time, breathing volume, and the number of respiratory cycles can be computed. However, the most frequently reported measure is the respiration rate during a task. In general, it has been shown that a higher respiration rate is associated with elevated arousal or discrete emotions like fear, anger, and happiness. On the other hand, a decrease in respiration rate has been reported for low arousal, or emotions like sadness or content (Kreibig 2010).

Similar results have been described in music research. Several studies showed an increase of respiratory effort when listening to highly arousing music as compared with less arousing music (Krumhansl 1997; Blood and Zatorre 2001; Baumgartner *et al.* 2006; Gomez and Danuser 2007).

Moreover, it has been suggested that temporal features of the music could directly influence respiratory activity, as shown by some studies where participants started to adapt their respiratory cycles to the tempo of the music (Baumgartner *et al.* 2006; Etzel *et al.* 2006). Furthermore, non-musical aspects of rhythmic auditory stimuli can also influence the respiratory effort, such as familiarity, musical preferences, and subjective evaluations (Salimpoor *et al.* 2009).

Cardiac activity

Cardiac effort itself is not under voluntary control but is regulated by both the sympathetic and the parasympathetic components of the autonomic nervous system (Berntson *et al.* 2007). As for respiratory effort, cardiac activity is mostly measured as heart rate and heart rate variability using plethysmography or an electrocardiogram. In general, heart rate also increases with emotional arousal or for distinct emotions like anxiety or surprise. Conversely, it is decreased in resting conditions or in response to emotions like contentment, sadness, and disgust (Kreibig 2010). Another measure of cardiac activity that is also studied is heart rate variability. Here the results have shown a clearer picture for emotional stimuli, suggesting that pleasant emotions are associated with low heart rate variability (Orini *et al.* 2010). However, as we are primarily interested in studying synchronization processes we will focus in this chapter only on the beat frequency of cardiac activity.

In the music research literature, several ambiguous results have been reported concerning heart rate. Some studies have suggested that, regardless of the level of arousal, listening to music may decrease heart rate in participants (Krumhansl 1997; Rickard 2004), whereas other studies have claimed that the musical tempo is an influential factor that can drive changes in heart rate (Etzel *et al.* 2006; Gomez and Danuser 2007). As a fast tempo is generally present in highly arousing music and a slow tempo in music with low arousal (Gabrielson and Juslin 2003), it could thus be suggested that only the level of arousal should directly be related to changes in cardiac activity. However, there is recent evidence that heart rate also seems to be sensitive to the pleasantness (i.e. valence) of the music (Sammler *et al.* 2007; Witvliet and Vrana 2007; Salimpoor *et al.* 2009; Orini *et al.* 2010). It is therefore possible that one of the reasons for discordant results on heart rate in previous studies on musical emotions might stem from the fact that the stimuli in different studies were not well controlled for the level of pleasantness, or with regard to their temporal structure.

Other physiological measures

Apart from respiration and cardiac effort, other physiological measures are often employed to study emotional reaction, like skin conductance, blood pressure, pupil diameter, body temperature, or muscle tension, (via an electromyogram). However, as these measures do not represent periodic signals allowing a test of entrainment processes, we will not discuss them further in this chapter (for a review see Hodges 2010).

Entrainment as emotion induction

In general, entrainment refers to a process in which two independent oscillators interact and phase lock to each other (for a review see Clayton *et al.* 2005). Entrainment is a very general and basic phenomenon that is present in many circumstances in nature. First a physical phenomenon, it was then realized to represent a general principle also occurring in biological and even social contexts. For example the synchronization of hand clapping in an audience is a very common experience, or the synchronization of movements in a group of people (Kirschner and Tomasello 2009). In the musical context, the potential importance of synchrony is somewhat obvious. In order to produce music jointly, a fine-tuned synchronization and adaptation of movements and actions has to be established. However, not only in music production, but also in music perception, entrainment processes may play an important role and arise relatively automatically. But what is the evidence for such entrainments by music in humans?

Perceptual entrainment

Most musical styles are based on a metrical structure (with some exceptions for example in traditional Arab music or contemporary Western music). This means that the notes of the music are placed in time according to a specific organization, and meter represents the invariant in these temporal patterns (London 2004). Within this temporal grid a specific hierarchy is defined between the notes. The metric allocates relative importance to every instance of the metrical unit with respect to the other time points of the unit. The impression of this hierarchy is created as specific structural elements in the music reoccur with a certain periodicity. The slower the periodicity, the higher the level in the structural hierarchy. The theory of dynamic attending (Jones 1987) claims that in order to perceive this hierarchy between the musical beats, the perceptual system has to take up these periodicities and synchronize to it. These adaptations are possibly enabled by neural synchronization processes in the auditory cortex and sensorimotor circuits which are also implicated in the processing of temporal expectancies (Coull 2009). Accordingly, studies using electroencephalography (EEG) showed that when listening to isochronous metronome beats, the periodicity of beats creates expectations (Brochard *et al.* 2003) and can be tracked in the brain waves (Will and Berg 2007; Nozaradan *et al.* 2011). However, the precise neural basis of meter perception is still an issue of research.

In fact, it is a feature of expressive music to also play with tempo variations, adding to expectations and violations thereof that can also be induced by melodic features. Meyer (1956) as well as Huron (2006), state that music is a powerful tool for generating melodic, harmonic, and, through the metrical structure, also temporal expectations. Both authors claim that either meeting this expectancy or disappointing it can produce an emotion. However, disappointment of expectation in this sense means only slight deviations from the metronomic tempo, for example small accelerations and decelerations, or anticipations of a note. Thus, these kinds of deviations, which are essential to the expressiveness of music, do not disturb the global metrical structure of the music but reconfirm the regularities of the composition and help to reinforce entrainment processes.

Motor entrainment

Entrainment by the beat of music may have other overt and stimulating effects. The common phenomenon of the urge to move with the music is one classic example of such an entrainment process. In fact it was shown that several motor circuits become activated when listening to metrical music (Grahn and Brett 2007). This might imply an internal preparation of actions and explain the spontaneous initiation of movements when music is heard. Several studies also showed that the basal ganglia, a crucial subcortical relay in motor pathways, are consistently implicated in rhythm processing (Grahn 2009; Kotz *et al.* 2009; Schwartze *et al.* 2011). In Parkinson patients, who have problems with initiating movements (including with gait) due to basal ganglia dysfunction, astonishing improvements have been documented in response to music (Pacchetti *et al.* 2000). Listening to marching music, with strong and pronounced beats, some patients could be helped to walk very smoothly and without hesitation. This effect is probably due to a stimulation of the basal ganglia via the rhythm of the music, which in consequence facilitates the execution of gait movements. The basal ganglia are also strongly implicated in the processing of pleasant emotion. For example, activations in the striatum are associated with different forms of reward, like food, sex, and monetary gain (Berridge and Robinson 1998; Small *et al.* 2003) but also with pleasant music (Blood and Zatorre 2001; Brown *et al.* 2004; Menon and Levitin 2005). The basal ganglia therefore seem to represent an ideal candidate for an anatomical and functional basis of interactions of rhythm and emotion processing, as they are involved in both the dopaminergic reward system and the motor circuits.

Finally, it has been reported that several traditionally motor-related brain regions like the supplementary motor area, cerebellum, and Rolandic operculum may all exhibit an increase in activity in response to music, particularly when comparing pleasant und unpleasant music (Blood and Zatorre 2001; Koelsch *et al.* 2006). Kornysheva *et al.*(2009) further showed that the pre-motor cortex and cerebellum were more strongly activated when the music stimuli contained a rhythm that was subjectively preferred as compared with a non-preferred stimulus. These results suggest that there might be a strong interaction between rhythm perception and the experience of emotion due to the implication of different structures within the motor system (basal ganglia, supplementary motor area) in both contexts. Yet, the precise mechanisms of interaction in emotion and rhythm processing still remain unresolved.

Moreover, other findings link the motor system and physical effort with increased physiological activity. Notably, not only performing but also watching or imagining actions performed by another person with a certain effort also induces an increase in physiological reactions like heart and respiration rate (Paccalin and Jeannerod 2000). It can be envisioned that a similar link also applies for music listening. For example, perceiving rhythmical structures might be associated with the physical effort made by performers, which could thus activate motor circuits and evoke changes in respiratory activity.

Physiological entrainment

Many studies have confirmed that listening to music can induce changes in respiration and heart rate (for a review see Hodges 2010). For example, already when listening to simple metronomic beats participants synchronize involuntarily the length of their respiration cycles (Haas *et al.* 1986). From music psychology, it is also known that tempo represents one of the most important determinant of mood induction via music (Gabrielson and Juslin 2003; Schubert 2004). Therefore, entrainment processes are supposed to be important for the generation of emotional reactions to music through an induction of synchronized changes in physiological processes like respiration.

Etzel *et al.* (2006) compared the cardiovascular and respiratory patterns for listeners to happy, sad, and fearful music. They found that the physiological responses could mainly be explained by the tempo-related differences between the different types of stimuli. Khalfa *et al.* (2008) further tested this hypothesis by presenting to their subjects not only the normal version of the music but also a modified version with rhythm or tempo alone. These authors found that entrainment was established in the tempo alone condition for respiration rate, but disappeared when rhythm and melody were added. Thus, rhythmic entrainment seems to be established as soon as there are clear beats in an auditory signal, but other musical ingredients like pitch and rhythm can abolish this effect. This might be due to the fact that these musical characteristics are responsible for the production of an emotional experience.

In a recent study, Salimpoor *et al.* (2009) asked participants to bring their favorite music to the lab and counterbalanced the stimuli in such a way that each participant was listening to his preferred music and to the favored music of another participant as a control condition. The physiological reactions between preferred music and control condition differed enormously. As the pieces were different for each participant, no conclusion can be drawn regarding the tempo entrainment. However, this study shows clearly that subjective pleasantness and musical preferences can drastically change the physiological reactions to music. This result might be explained by the fact that recognizing one's preferred music will trigger a state of high arousal and interest. This effect could also be described by an induction mechanism that Juslin *et al.* (2010) called "evaluative conditioning," simply representing a conditioned physiological response triggered by a familiar stimulus. Another study by Bernardi *et al.* (2006) investigated more directly the influence of musical expertise on physiological entrainment. The authors found that musicians adapted their respiration rate more precisely to the tempo of the music than did non-musicians.

In spite of the influence of pleasantness, familiarity, or expertise, these results do not rule out the existence of more automatic effects on physiological entrainment, since it is possible that these effects might be weaker and covered by averaging the results over different musical stimuli.

Social entrainment

When considering the listening contexts, entrainment also has an important social component. As stated in our Introduction, Koelsch (2010) argued that music plays an important social role, as it can coordinate actions, advance cooperation and communication, and strengthen social cohesion. These aspects can all be regarded as forms of entrainment in a broader sense. In fact the term "entrainment" is also widely in use in the ethnomusicology literature (Clayton *et al.* 2005; Cross and Morley 2008; Becker 2010). Entrainment is here one mechanism to describe musical rituals in different cultures. In this sense, a musical trance experience through collective drumming (Szabo 2006) or ecstatic dancing to music (Becker 2010) are described as very strong emotional experiences including an altered state of consciousness. These experiences can lead to a strong feeling of being connected to someone else (God, in the case of dancing Sufis) or to something "transcendental," but also to be close to other members of the group sharing the musical experience. In this way entrainment could be interpreted as socialization with other in-group members, and even as a form of empathy.

Empathy is a pro-social human process, which implies the ability to understand the feelings of other people and to sympathize with them, often associated with the mirror neuron system. Mirror neurons in humans are supposedly located in the posterior parietal and ventral pre-motor areas of the brain, and have primarily been related to motor functions and action understanding (Freedberg and Gallese 2007). These mirror neurons are characterized by the fact that they fire when an action is observed, as well as when the person is performing the action herself. Furthermore, Overy and Molnar-Szakacs (Molnar-Szakacs and Overy 2006; Overy and Molnar-Szakacs 2009) suggest that rhythmic entrainment could help confirm the existence of the mirror neuron system in humans. It is thought that, via mirror neurons, the actions required to produce the heard music are simulated in the brain, which thus also include rhythmic movements (Lahav *et al.* 2007). Overy and Molnar-Szakacs (2006) propose that motor pathways within the brain and other sites mimic these processes, which altogether lead to what they call a "shared affective motion experience." Interestingly, it has been shown that pleasant rhythms activate the ventral pre-motor cortex (Kornysheva *et al.* 2009) where mirror neurons might be present. This finding hints at how the different levels of entrainment can be interrelated, as brain regions that are implicated in rhythm processing play also a role in the generation of empathic feelings.

Summary and discussion

This chapter has highlighted how and why rhythmic entrainment might constitute a possible mechanism of emotion induction via music. We considered the different principles and varieties of entrainment in the context of music listening. In particular, we distinguished entrainment proc-esses at different levels and describe the putative neuropsychological aspects of "rhythmic entrain-ment" for each of these scales.

Our review suggests that regarding the mechanism of physiological "rhythmic entrainment," a major differentiation between familiar and non-familiar music should be made. Based on sub-jective familiarity, other induction mechanisms like "evaluative conditioning," "emotional conta-gion," or "episodic memory" will determine the exact type of emotional reaction. But when music is unfamiliar, which represents the most genuine music experience, auditory signals must be ana-lyzed along the multistep auditory pathways according to general acoustic features, including their temporal structure and evolution over time. To extract and encode this musical structure, neural entrainment processes might have to take place in sensory circuits (perceptual level). The rhythmic aspects of the signal might also activate motor circuits including the basal ganglia (motor level). As the basal ganglia are not only implicated in the learning and guidance of motor sequences, but also in emotion processing and reward prediction (especially striatum), some functional crosso-ver between motor and affect processes might take place in these circuits. This could initiate a release of dopamine and therefore trigger emotional reactions or motivational changes, which could manifest in changes in peripheral physiology, like an increase in respiration rate or heart rate (physiological level). Finally, as a function of the listening context, an evoked emotion might be revealed by distinct movements and actions with other individuals (social level).

Further research is needed in order to better understand the relations between the different lev-els at which entrainment can take place, and to determine whether and how these levels might be interrelated. For example it would be interesting to study whether stronger entrainment at the per-ceptive level (attentional entrainment) can influence the entrainment of physiological processes. It would also be important to elucidate how exactly aspects of musical preference and familiarity influence these processes along the chain of music-induced reactions. It could be possible that entrainment processes are also intensified by familiarity, as more attention and anticipation would be paid to musical features, including the rhythmic structure. Furthermore, these processes might represent a cyclic mechanism with feedback loops, such that felt pleasantness in the music could in turn also facilitate entrainment processes. In the above review, for simplicity, we mainly focused on one direction of causation according to which "entrainment induces emotion." However, what about the opposite direction? Although to date there is no clear evidence that an emotion itself would engender entrainment, it is entirely plausible that feedback mechanisms might strengthen the entrainment process when the music is experienced as pleasant or familiar, consistent with the fact that pleasant music or rhythms activate both sensory and motor circuits more strongly (Kornysheva et al. 2009). This sort of hypothetical feedback loop would corroborate the notion of entrainment, and to some extent the existence of such mechanisms would be crucial for mainte-nance of the synchronization.

It is important to highlight that rhythmic entrainment represents just one of the multiple music induction mechanisms which might be at play. As argued by Juslin et al. (2010), a complex inter-play of several induction principles is likely to be necessary to explain the full range of emotions that can be evoked by music. Juslin and colleagues suggested that other processes associated with autobiographical memory, brainstem reflexes, auditory perception, or cognitive appraisal all might contribute to varying degrees in eliciting musical emotions. The kind of emotion that is typically induced via rhythmic entrainment alone might be particularly related to aspects of pleasantness. Moreover, being in synchrony with either an external beat or a group of musicians is generally regarded as a very pleasant state, and these effects might be exploited by the many varieties of dance in different cultural and social contexts. However, this does not implicate that music with the most stable temporal structure will always evoke the strongest or most positive emotional reactions. In fact, musical expressivity and its emotional impact seem in particular to increase when structural regularities and created expectancies are violated and deviated, as suggested by Meyer (1956). The joint effects of entrainment by rhythmic structure and its variations or violations, which can impact on sensory and motor processing as well as attention and internal physiological rhythms, are undoubtedly a potent source for the deep effects of music on cognitive and affective processes.

Taken together, the research discussed here suggests that rhythmic entrainment is a concept that has only recently become scrutinized in psychology and neuroscience, but is now increasingly recognized to make an important contribution to the generation of musical emotions. We believe that this mechanism deserves to be further explored and understood, as it closely reflects the specificity of musical emotions in the time domain.

References

Baumgartner, T., Lutz, K., Schmidt, C. F., and Jancke, L. (2006). The emotional power of music: how music enhances the feeling of affective pictures. *Brain Research*, **1075**, 151–64.

Becker, J. (2010). Exploring the habitut of listening: antrhopological perspectives. In P. N. Juslin and J. A. Sloboda (eds), *Handbook of Music and Emotion: Theory, Research, Applications*, pp. 127–57. Oxford: Oxford University Press.

Bernardi, L., Porta, C., and Sleight, P. (2006). Cardiovascular, cerebrovascular, and respiratory changes induced by different types of music in musicians and non-musicians: the importance of silence. *Heart*, **92**, 445–52.

Berntson, G. G., Quigley, K. S., and Lozano, D. (2007). Cardiovascular psychophysiology. In J. T. Cacioppo, L. G. Tassinary, and G. G. Berntson (eds), *Handbook of Psychophysiology*, pp. 182–210. New York: Cambridge University Press.

Berridge, K. C. and Robinson, T. E. (1998). What is the role of dopamine in reward: hedonic impact, reward learning, or incentive salience? *Brain Research. Brain Research Reviews*, **28**, 309–69.

Blood, A. J. and Zatorre, R. J. (2001). Intensely pleasurable responses to music correlate with activity in brain regions implicated in reward and emotion. *Proceedings of the National Academy of Sciences of the United States of America*, **98**, 11818–23.

Blood, A. J., Zatorre, R. J., Bermudez, P., and Evans, A. C. (1999). Emotional responses to pleasant and unpleasant music correlate with activity in paralimbic brain regions. *Nature Neuroscience*, **2**, 382–7.

Brochard, R., Abecasis, D., Potter, D., Ragot, R., and Drake, C. (2003). The "ticktock" of our internal clock: direct brain evidence of subjective accents in isochronous sequences. *Psychological Science*, **14**, 362–6.

Brown, S., Martinez, M. J., and Parsons, L. M. (2004). Passive music listening spontaneously engages limbic and paralimbic systems. *NeuroReport*, **15**, 2033–7.

Cacioppo, J. T., Tassinary, L. G., and Berntson, G. G. (2007). Psychophysiological science: interdisciplinary approaches to classic questions about the mind. In J. T. Cacioppo, L. G. Tassinary, and G. G. Berntson (eds), *Handbook of Psychophysiology*, pp. 1–16. New York: Cambridge University Press.

Clayton, M., Sager, R., and Will, U. (2005). In time with the music: the concept of entrainment and its significance for ethnomusicology. *European Meetings in Ethnomusicology*, **11**, 3–142.

Cochrane, T. (2010). A simulation theory of musical expressivity. *Australasian Journal of Philosophy*, **88**, 191–207.

Coull, J. T. (2009). Neural substrates of mounting temporal expectation. *PLoS Biology*, **7**, e1000166.

Cross, I. and Morley, I. (2008). *The evolution of music: theories, definitions and the nature of the evidence*. In S. Malloch and C. Trevarthen (eds), *Communicative Musicality*, pp. 61–82. Oxford: Oxford University Press.

Damasio, A. R. (1996). The somatic marker hypothesis and the possible functions of the prefrontal cortex. *Philosophical Transactions of the Royal Society B: Biological Sciences,* **351**, 1413–20.

Damasio, A. R. (1999). *The Feeling of What Happens: Body and Emotion in the Making of Consciousness.* New York: Harcourt Brace.

Ekman, P. (1992). An argument for basic emotions. *Cognition and Emotion,* **6**, 169–200.

Etzel, J. A., Johnsen, E. L., Dickerson, J., Tranel, D., and Adolphs, R. (2006). Cardiovascular and respiratory responses during musical mood induction. *International Journal of Psychophysiology,* **61**, 57–69.

Feldman-Barrett, L. (2006). Are emotions natural kinds? *Perspectives on Psychological Science,* **1**, 28–58.

Freedberg, D. and Gallese, V. (2007) Motion, emotion and empathy in esthetic experience. *Trends in Cognitive Sciences,* **11**, 197–203.

Gabrielson, A. and Juslin, P. N. (2003). Emotional expression in music. In R. J. Davidson, K. R. Scherer, and H. Hill Golsdsmith (eds), *Handbook of Affective Sciences,* pp. 503–34. New York: Oxford University Press.

Gomez, P. and Danuser, B. (2007). Relationships between musical structure and psychophysiological measures of emotion. *Emotion,* **7**, 377–87.

Grahn, J. A. (2009). The role of the basal ganglia in beat perception: neuroimaging and neuropsychological investigations. *Annals of the New York Academy of Sciences,* **1169**, 35–45.

Grahn, J. A. and Brett, M. (2007). Rhythm and beat perception in motor areas of the brain. *Journal of Cognitive Neuroscience,* **19**, 893–906.

Haas, F., Distenfeld, S., and Axen, K. (1986). Effects of perceived musical rhythm on respiratory pattern. *Journal of Applied Physiology,* **61**, 1185–91.

Hodges, D. A. (2010). Psycho-physiological measures. In P. N. Juslin and J. A. Sloboda (eds), *Handbook of Music and Emotion: Theory, Research, Applications,* pp. 279–311. Oxford: Oxford University Press.

Huron, D. (2006). *Sweet Anticipation.* Cambridge, MA: MIT Press.

Jones, M. R. (1987). Dynamic pattern structure in music: recent theory and research. *Perception and Psychophysics,* **41**, 621–34.

Juslin, P. N. and Västfjäll, D. (2008). Emotional responses to music: the need to consider underlying mechanisms. *Behavioural and Brain Sciences,* **31**, 559–75 [discussion 575–621].

Juslin, P. N., Liljeström, S., Västfjäll, D., and Lundqvist, L. O. (2010). How does music evoke emotions? Exploring the underlying mechanisms. In P. N. Juslin and J. A. Sloboda (eds), *Handbook of Music and Emotion: Theory, Research, Applications,* pp. 605–42. Oxford: Oxford University Press.

Khalfa, S., Roy, M., Rainville, P., Dalla Bella, S., and Peretz, I. (2008). Role of tempo entrainment in psychophysiological differentiation of happy and sad music? *International Journal of Psychophysiology,* **68**, 17–26.

Kirschner, S. and Tomasello, M. (2009). Joint drumming: social context facilitates synchronization in preschool children. *Journal of Experimental Child Psychology,* **102**, 299–314.

Koelsch, S. (2005). Investigating emotion with music: neuroscientific approaches. *Annals of the New York Academy of Sciences,* **1060**, 412–18.

Koelsch, S. (2010). Towards a neural basis of music-evoked emotions. *Trends in Cognitive Science,* **14**, 131–7.

Koelsch, S., Fritz, T., Cramon, V., Muller, K., and Friederici, A. D. (2006). Investigating emotion with music: an fMRI study. *Human Brain Mapping,* **27**, 239–50.

Kornysheva, K., von Cramon, D. Y., Jacobsen, T., and Schubotz, R. I. (2009). Tuning-in to the beat: aesthetic appreciation of musical rhythms correlates with a premotor activity boost. *Human Brain Mapping,* **31**, 48–64.

Kotz, S. A., Schwartze, M., and Schmidt-Kassow, M. (2009). Non-motor basal ganglia functions: a review and proposal for a model of sensory predictability in auditory language perception. *Cortex,* **45**, 982–90.

Kreibig, S. D. (2010). Autonomic nervous system activity in emotion: a review. *Biological Psychology,* **84,** 394–421.

Krumhansl, C. L. (1997). An exploratory study of musical emotions and psychophysiology. *Canadian Journal of Experimental Psychology,* **51,** 336–53.

Lahav, A., Saltzman, E., and Schlaug, G. (2007). Action representation of sound: audiomotor recognition network while listening to newly acquired actions. *Journal of Neuroscience,* **27,** 308–14.

London, J. (2004). *Hearing in Time: Psychological Aspects of Musical Meter.* Oxford: Oxford University Press.

Lorig, T. S. (2007). The respiratory system. In J. T. Cacioppo, L. G. Tassinary, and G. G. Berntson (eds), *Handbook of Psychophysiology,* pp. 231–44. New York: Cambridge University Press.

Menon, V. and Levitin, D. J. (2005). The rewards of music listening: response and physiological connectivity of the mesolimbic system. Neuroimage, **28,** 175–84.

Meyer, L. B. (1956). *Emotion and Meaning in Music.* Chicago: University of Chicago Press.

Molnar-Szakacs, I. and Overy, K. (2006). Music and mirror neurons: from motion to "e" motion. *Social Cognitive and Affective Neuroscience,* **1,** 235–41.

Noulhiane, M., Mella, N., Samson, S., Ragot, R., and Pouthas, V. (2007). How emotional auditory stimuli modulate time perception. *Emotion,* **7,** 697–704.

Nozaradan, S., Peretz, I., Missal, M., and Mouraux, A. (2011). Tagging the neuronal entrainment to beat and meter. *Journal of Neuroscience,* **31,** 10234–40.

Olivers, C. N. and Nieuwenhuis, S. (2005). The beneficial effect of concurrent task-irrelevant mental activity on temporal attention. *Psychological Science,* **16,** 265–9.

Orini, M., Bailon, R., Enk, R., Koelsch, S., Mainardi, L., and Laguna, P. (2010). A method for continuously assessing the autonomic response to music-induced emotions through HRV analysis. *Medical and Biological Engineering and Computing,* **48,** 423–33.

Overy, K. and Molnar-Szakacs, I. (2009). Being together in time: musical experience and the mirror neuron system. *Music Perception,* **26,** 489–504.

Paccalin, C. and Jeannerod, M. (2000). Changes in breathing during observation of effortful actions. *Brain Research,* **862,** 194–200.

Pacchetti, C., Mancini, F., Aglieri, R., Fundaro, C., Martignoni, E., and Nappi, G. (2000). Active music therapy in Parkinson's disease: an integrative method for motor and emotional rehabilitation. *Psychosomatic Medicine,* **62,** 386–93.

Rickard, N. (2004). Intense emotional responses to music: a test of the physiological arousal hypothesis. *Psychology of Music,* **32,** 186–8.

Russell, J. A. (2003). Core affect and the psychological construction of emotion. *Psychological Review,* **110,** 145–72.

Salimpoor, V. N., Benovoy, M., Longo, G., Cooperstock, J. R., and Zatorre, R. J. (2009). The rewarding aspects of music listening are related to degree of emotional arousal. *PLoS One,* **4,** e7487.

Sammler, D., Grigutsch, M., Fritz, T., and Koelsch, S. (2007). Music and emotion: electrophysiological correlates of the processing of pleasant and unpleasant music. *Psychophysiology,* **44,** 293–304.

Scherer, K. and Zentner, M. (2001). Emotional effects of music: production rules. In P. N. Juslin and J. A. Sloboda (eds), Music and Emotion: Theory and Research, pp. 361–92. Oxford: Oxford University Press.

Schubert, E. (2004). Modeling perceived emotion with continuous musical features. *Music Perception,* **21,** 561–85.

Schwartze, M., Keller, P. E., Patel, A. D., and Kotz, S. A. (2011). The impact of basal ganglia lesions on sensorimotor synchronization, spontaneous motor tempo, and the detection of tempo changes. *Behavioural Brain Research,* **216,** 685–91.

Small, D. M., Gregory, M. D., Mak, Y. E., Gitelman, D., Mesulam, M. M., and Parrish, T. (2003). Dissociation of neural representation of intensity and affective valuation in human gustation. *Neuron,* **39,** 701–11.

Strawinsky, I. (1937). *Erinnerungen*. Zürich: Atlantis-Verlag.

Szabo, C. (2006). The effects of listening to monotonous drumming on subjective experiences. In D. Aldridge and J. Fachner (eds), *Music and Altered States*, pp. 51–9. London: Jessica Kingsley Publishers.

Trost, W., Ethofer, T., Zentner, M., and Vuilleumier, P. (2012). Mapping aesthetic musical emotions in the brain. *Cerebral Cortex*, **22**, 2769–83.

Will, U. and Berg, E. (2007). Brain wave synchronization and entrainment to periodic acoustic stimuli. *Neuroscience Letters*, **424**, 55–60.

Witvliet, C. V. O. and Vrana, S. R. (2007). Play it again Sam: repeated exposure to emotionally evocative music polarises liking and smiling responses, and influences other affective reports, facial EMG, and heart rate. *Cognition and Emotion*, **21**, 3–25.

Zentner, M., Grandjean, D., and Scherer, K. R. (2008). Emotions evoked by the sound of music: characterization, classification, and measurement. *Emotion*, **8**, 494–521.

Chapter 17

Striking a chord in the brain: neurophysiological correlates of music-evoked positive emotions

Stefan Koelsch

Summary

Music can evoke different positive emotions, such as reward-related experiences of "fun," the experience of "tender positive" emotions, or extremely pleasurable experiences such as "frissons." This makes music an interesting and important tool for studying emotion and its neural correlates. This chapter describes two different brain systems that are involved in generating different types of positive (and different types of negative) emotion: the first one is a diencephalon-centered system involved in the generation of pleasure/pain, experiences of reward/punishment, and the subjective feeling of attraction/aversion. This system is primarily responsible for basic behavioral patterns that are crucial for the survival of the individual (although this system is not the only system responsible for such patterns). Among its main structures are the thalamus and hypothalamus, as well as diencephalo-fugal pathways such as the so-called reward pathway which includes the ventral tegmental area with projections to the striatum (of which the ventral part hosts the nucleus accumbens). A typical characteristic of the activation of this "reward pathway" are feelings of pleasure and "fun" (e.g. when basic homeostatic needs are fulfilled). Several functional neuroimaging studies have shown that this reward pathway is activated by music that is perceived as pleasant by the individual (and this system also appears to be involved in experiences of music-evoked "frissons").

The second system is a hippocampus-centered system (including the hippocampus, the para-hippocampal gyrus, the temporal poles, and the amygdala). This affect system is hypothesized to be involved in the generation of attachment-related emotions (and corresponding behaviors). These emotions are subjectively experienced as tender positive emotions, such as joy, happiness, and love (on the other hand, pathological depression, involving sadness, is correlated with functional and structural impairment of this system). Several functional neuroimaging studies using happy and sad music reported activity changes within this hippocampus-centered affect system. Activation of this system during music listening (and perhaps even more so during music making) is perhaps due to the engagement of social functions that support the emergence of attachments between humans (such as communication and cooperation). Participating in these functions fulfills human needs, and can evoke strong positive emotions. The activation of the reward pathway as well as of the hippocampus-centered affect system by music has important implications for the use of music in the therapy of diseases related to dysfunctions within these systems.

Introduction: what are "music-evoked emotions"?

Some researchers advocate that music can evoke a wide spectrum of "real" emotions, whereas others argue that emotions evoked by music are artificial (and not real). For example, Zentner et al. (2008, p. 496) state that "musical antecedents do not usually have any obvious material effect on the individual's well-being and are infrequently followed by direct external responses of a goal-oriented nature," and thus reject the notion that music can evoke real joy, sadness, anger, or fear. Similarly, Scherer (2004, p. 244) writes that "music is unlikely to produce basic emotions," Noy (1993, p. 126) states that "the emotions evoked by music are not identical with the emotions aroused by everyday, interpersonal activity," and Konečni (2003, p. 333) claims that "instrumental music cannot directly evoke genuine emotions in listeners." The assumption that music would not have material effects on the individual's well-being is also taken as an argument for the notion that music cannot evoke basic emotions related to survival functions (Kivy 1991; Scherer 2004; Zentner et al. 2008). Based on these assumptions, Scherer (2004) proposed to distinguish between goal-oriented *utilitarian* emotions (which are elicited in order to "adapt to specific situations that are of central significance to the individual's interests and well-being," Scherer and Zentner 2008), and *aesthetic* emotions (which are elicited without "obvious material effect on the individual's well-being and only rarely leading to specific goal-oriented responses"; Scherer and Zentner 2008).

However, the assumption that music-evoked emotions are not goal-relevant conflicts with the assumption that making music in a group supports the emergence of several evolutionarily adaptive social functions: engagement in such functions is associated with goal-relevant motivations to fulfill social needs (such as the "need to belong"; Baumeister and Leary 1995), and the fulfillment of these needs evokes emotions such as feelings of reward and pleasure, and possibly attachment-related emotions such as love and happiness (see also the "seven Cs" in the section "From social contact to social cohesion—the seven Cs"). Moreover, the assumption that music cannot evoke "real" emotions conflicts, for example, with the experience that music can "hale souls out of men's bodies" (William Shakespeare, *Much Ado About Nothing*, Act II, Scene 3), and it conflicts with therapeutic effects of music-evoked emotions. In the following, several arguments will be offered that speak for the notion that music making and music listening (1) have material effects, and (2) can serve the fulfillment of basic needs and thus serve the achievement of goals related to the survival of the individual.

Juslin and Västfjäll (2008) argued that several psychological mechanisms underlying the evocation of emotion with music are shared with mechanisms underlying the evocation of "a wide range of both basic and complex emotions in listeners." In this regard, it is worth noting that listening to music can evoke changes in the three major reaction components of an emotion, namely in *physiological arousal* (as reflected, for example, in changes in autonomic and endocrine activity),[i] *subjective feeling* (such as feelings of pleasantness, happiness, sadness, etc.), and *motor expression* (e.g. Grewe et al. 2007a; Lundqvist et al. 2009). In addition, music listening often elicits *action tendencies* (dancing, foot tapping, clapping, etc.). Finally, music can modulate activity in all so-called limbic and paralimbic brain structures (that is, in those structures that generate emotions, this will be elaborated further below), suggesting that music-evoked emotions are not merely illusions of the mind, but that music can indeed evoke "real" emotions.

Several arguments support the notion that music can evoke "basic" emotions such as joy, fear, anger, sadness, and disgust:[ii] Many individuals experience joy and happiness while making music, or while listening to music (this is a frequent motivation for listening to music, e.g. Juslin *et al.* 2011). It has also been shown that music can elicit surprise (Koelsch *et al.* 2008a; see also Meyer 1956; Huron 2006), and some participants in an earlier study Koelsch *et al.* (2006) reported to us that continuously highly dissonant stimuli (used in that study) evoked a feeling of disgust and vertigo. Most people get quite angry when they have to listen to music that they utterly dislike, and music is sometimes used to stimulate anger and aggression (e.g. the "hate music" of neo-Nazis; Messner *et al.* 2007).

With regard to sadness, it has been argued that music cannot evoke "real" sadness, because it is assumed to have no "real implications for the individual's well-being" (Zentner *et al.* 2008), and because in "real" life, sadness tends to be experienced as a negative state, which most people try to avoid. By contrast, some individuals "do not usually turn off the radio when a sad song hits the air" (Zentner *et al.* 2008; other individuals, however, will turn off the radio when a sad song is played). Thoughts about why humans seek negative emotional experiences in the arts date back to Aristotle's *Poetics*, and have been summarized for the musical domain by Levinson (1990). Here, suffice it to say that the experience of sadness during art reception (or production) can have several rewarding effects (such as emotional catharsis, identifying expression, empathic emotional responses, understanding one's own feelings, emotional simulation, distraction from the extra-musical world, reward of expressive potency, emotional communication, realizing that no true loss occurred, etc.). Such rewarding effects are experienced as feelings of pleasure, or fun, and they correlate with activity of reward circuits in the brain (as will be described further below). A crucial point is that some of such rewarding effects (particularly emotional catharsis, empathic emotional responses, understanding one's own feelings, and emotional simulation) are only possible because "real" sadness occurred prior to the experience of reward—otherwise there would be no reason for the elicitation of such rewarding effects. Therefore, music-evoked sadness must be congruent, at least for brief episodes, with the sadness evoked by a "real" event.

The fact that music usually does not evoke all basic emotions equally often does not mean that music is not capable of evoking these emotions (e.g. music usually evokes happiness more often than disgust). Moreover, even if music does not evoke a basic emotion in an individual with the same intensity as a particular "real life" situation, the underlying brain circuits are nevertheless presumably the same (whether I feel strong or moderate fear—the emotion is still fear). The assumption that music has no goal relevance, and no relation to the survival of an individual, will be dealt with in the next section.

Music and goal relevance: survival functions

Music can have effects on the well-being of an individual, often including regenerative autonomic, endocrine, and immunological effects. Although such effects are not material in the sense that the individual can eat, drink, or even touch them, they nevertheless involve matter (hormone and immune molecules and cells which also modulate expenditure of glucose, fat, and minerals).[iii] Moreover, as will be described in more detail in the next section, music activates, and facilitates, social functions such as communication, cooperation, and group cohesion. Engaging in such social functions fulfills the basic needs of an individual, and is vital for the well-being of an individual. Notably, the engagement of humans in social functions was (and is) critical for the survival of the human species. Therefore, the pleasure of engaging in these social functions is related to survival functions, arguing against the notion that music cannot evoke basic emotions related to survival.

From social contact to social cohesion—the seven Cs

Music making is an activity involving several social functions. The ability, and the need, to engage in these social functions is part of what makes us human, and the emotional effects of engaging in these functions include experiences of reward, fun, joy, and happiness. Exclusion from engaging in these functions represents an emotional stressor, leads to depression, and has deleterious effects on health and life expectancy (Cacioppo and Hawkley 2003).[iv] Therefore, engaging in such social functions is important for the survival of the individual and the species. These functions can be categorized into seven areas:

(1) When individuals make music, they come into *contact* with each other. Being in contact with other individuals is a basic need of humans (Harlow 1958), and social isolation is a major risk factor for morbidity as well as mortality (House *et al.* 1988; Cacioppo and Hawkley 2003). As will be outlined further later, a plausible hypothesis is that social isolation results in damage of the hippocampal formation and that, on the other hand, contact with other individuals promotes hippocampal integrity.

(2) Music automatically engages *social cognition*. During music listening, individuals automatically engage processes of mental state attribution ("mentalizing," or "adopting an intentional stance"), in an attempt to figure out the intentions, desires, and beliefs of the individuals who actually created the music (also often referred to as establishing a "theory of mind"). A study by Steinbeis and Koelsch (2008c) showed that listening to music automatically engages brain structures dedicated to social cognition (i.e. a network dedicated to mental state attribution in the attempt to understand the composer's intentions). These processes are also required when making music together in a group, for example when varying tempo and/or loudness, during improvisation, etc. Interestingly, individuals with autistic spectrum disorder (ASD) seem to be surprisingly competent in social cognition in the musical domain (Allen *et al.* 2009). This supports the notion that music therapy can aid the transfer of socio-cognitive skills in the musical domain to non-musical social contexts in individuals with ASD.

(3) Music making can engage *co-pathy* in the sense that inter-individual emotional states become more homogeneous (e.g. reducing anger in one individual, and depression or anxiety in another), thus decreasing conflicts and promoting cohesion of a group (e.g. Huron 2001). With regard to positive emotions, for example, co-pathy can increase the well-being of individuals during music making or during listening to music.[v] The term "co-pathy" is used here (instead of "empathy") because co-pathy refers to the social function of empathy. Moreover, empathy has many different connotations, due to various definitions of empathy provided by different researchers. By using the term co-pathy I not only refer to the phenomenon of thinking what one *would* feel if one were in someone else's position. Instead, I refer to the phenomenon that one's own emotional state is actually affected in the sense that it occurs when one perceives (e.g. observes or hears), or imagines, someone else's affect, and that this perception or imagination evokes a feeling in the perceiver which bears strong congruency with what the other individual is feeling (for a review of the concept of empathy see Singer and Lamm 2009). Co-pathy should be differentiated from (a) *mimicry* (a low-level perception–action mechanism of imitating another individual's emotional expression, e.g. contraction of the musculus zygomaticus major when looking at a smiling face),[vi] and (b) *emotional contagion* (a short-term spread of a behavior which is presumably a precursor of co-pathy, for example children laughing because other children laugh).[vii] Both mimicry and emotional contagion contribute to co-pathy. They may occur outside of awareness, and do not require a self/other concept. By contrast, co-pathy requires self-awareness and self/other distinction, i.e. the capability to make oneself aware that the affect may have been evoked by music made by others, although the actual source of one's emotion lies within oneself. Moreover, co-pathy should be differentiated from (c) *sympathy, empathic concern*, and

compassion, which do not necessarily involve shared feelings (e.g. feeling pity for a jealous person, without feeling jealous oneself; for details see Singer and Lamm 2009).

(4) Music involves *communication* (notably, for infants and young children, musical communication during parent–child singing of lullabies and play-songs appears to be important for social and emotional regulation, as well as for social, emotional, and cognitive development; Trehub 2003, Fitch 2006). A number of neuroscientific and behavioral studies revealed considerable overlap of the neural substrates and cognitive mechanisms underlying the perception of music as well as of language, with regard to the processing of syntax (e.g. Koelsch *et al.* 2005; Steinbeis and Koelsch 2008b; Slevc *et al.* 2009), and with regard to the processing of meaning (Koelsch *et al.* 2004; Daltrozzo and Schön 2009; Steinbeis and Koelsch 2008a, 2011; Grieser-Painter and Koelsch 2011; Schön *et al.* 2010; Goerlich *et al.* 2011). With regard to speech and music production, a study by Callan *et al.* (2006) also showed a strong overlap of the neural substrates of speaking and singing. Because music is a means of communication, active music therapy (in which patients make music) can be used to train skills of (non-verbal) communication (Hillecke *et al.*, 2005).

(5) Music making also involves *coordination* of actions. This requires individuals to synchronize to a beat, and to keep a beat. The coordination of movements in a group of individuals appears to be associated with pleasure (e.g. when dancing together), even in the absence of a shared goal (apart from deriving pleasure from concerted movements; see also Huron 2001). Interestingly, a study by Kirschner and Tomasello (2009) reported that children as young as 2½ years synchronized more accurately to an external drum beat in a social situation (i.e. when the drum beat was presented by a human play partner) compared with non-social situations (i.e. when the drum beat was presented by a drumming machine, or when the drum sounds were presented via a loudspeaker). This effect might have originated from the pleasure that emerges when humans coordinate their movements with each other (see also Overy and Molnar-Szakacs 2009; Wiltermuth and Heath 2009). The capacity to synchronize movements to an external beat appears to be uniquely human among primates, although other mammals (such as seals) and some song birds (such as cockatoos) might also possess this capacity. A current hypothesis (e.g. Patel 2006, 2008) is that this capacity is related to the capacity of vocal learning, which might depend (in mammals) on a direct neuronal connection between the motor cortex and the nucleus ambiguus. The nucleus ambiguus is located in the brainstem and contains motor neurons innervating the larynx (the motor cortex also directly projects to brainstem nuclei innervating the tongue, jaw, palate, and lips; e.g. Jürgens 2002).

(6) A convincing musical performance by multiple players is only possible if it also involves *cooperation* between players. Cooperation involves a shared goal, and engaging in cooperative behavior is an important potential source of pleasure. For example, Rilling *et al.* (2002) reported an association between cooperative behavior and activation of a reward network including the nucleus accumbens (described in more detail later). Cooperation between individuals increases inter-individual trust, and increases the likelihood of future cooperation between these individuals. It is worth noting that only humans have the capability to communicate about coordinated activities in order to cooperatively achieve a joint goal (Tomasello *et al.* 2005).

(7) As an effect, music leads to increased *social cohesion* of a group (Cross and Morley 2008). A wealth of studies showed that humans have a "need to belong" (Baumeister and Leary 1995), and a strong motivation to form and maintain enduring interpersonal attachments

(Baumeister and Leary 1995). Meeting this need increases health and life expectancy (Cacioppo and Hawkley 2003). Social cohesion also strengthens the confidence in reciprocal care (see also the "caregiver hypothesis"; Trehub 2003, Fitch, 2005), and the confidence that opportunities to engage with others in the mentioned social functions will also emerge in the future.

Although it should be clearly noted that music can also be used to manipulate other individuals, and to support non-social behavior (e.g. Brown and Volgsten 2006), music is still special in that it can engage all of these social functions at the same time (similar, for example, to cooperative forms of play). This is presumably one explanation for the emotional power of music. Therefore, music does serve the goal of fulfilling social needs (the human need to be in contact with others, to belong, to communicate, etc.). In this regard, music-evoked emotions are related to survival functions and to functions that are of vital importance for the individual (for a discussion on the role of other factors, such as sexual selection, for the evolution of music see Huron 2001 and Fitch 2005).

As will be described later in this chapter, engaging in social functions during music making evokes activity of neural "reward pathways," and we (Koelsch *et al.* 2010b) have previously suggested that activity of these reward pathways is subjectively experienced as "fun." In addition to experiences of fun, music making can also evoke attachment-related emotions (due to the engagement in the mentioned social functions), such as love, joy, and happiness. These emotions presumably involve activity of the hippocampal formation (as will be elaborated further later). In this regard, music can not only be fun, it can also make people happy. Note that the engagement in social functions is not the only principle that can give rise to (positive) emotions while listening to music or making music. The next section (Emotional responses to music—underlying principles) will provide a systematic overview of further principles underlying the evocation of emotions with music. These principles are not confined to music, but can be extrapolated to emotion psychology in general.

Emotional responses to music—underlying principles

Everyone knows the experience of music-evoked emotion, but how does music evoke emotions? Several authors described "mechanisms" that "induce" emotions with music (Scherer 2004; Juslin and Västfjäll 2008). The use of such terms gives the impression that specific musical antecedents determine a specific emotional effect. This, however, does not seem to be the case (otherwise, depressive patients could easily be healed with happy music). Therefore, instead of using the term *mechanism*, the term *principle* will be used here. Likewise, the term *music-evoked emotion* will be used (instead of *music-induced emotion*), to emphasize that some emotional effects cannot be caused (or intended) in a deterministic way. In the following, several principles underlying the evocation of emotion with music (as well as relations to music perception, syntactic processes, musical meaning, and social functions) will be suggested. Some of these principles were suggested previously by Juslin and Västfjäll (2008).

(1) One principle is *evaluation*. Evaluative processes may occur on a number of other levels. For example, Scherer (2001, p. 103) noted that evaluative processes can occur on a sensory–motor, a schematic, and a conceptual level.[viii] For example, "brainstem reflexes" (Juslin and Västfjäll 2008) to music are the result of a sensory evaluation on the level of the brainstem (for details see, e.g., Garcia-Cairasco 2002; Brandão *et al.* 1988; Koelsch 2011). Note that evaluative processes can be (a) automatic and non-cognitive (e.g. evaluative processes occurring on the level of the brainstem or the thalamus), (b) automatic and cognitive, but without

awareness (probably involving processes on the level of the orbitofrontal cortex; Siebel *et al.* 1990), or (c) cognitive with involvement of conscious awareness (processes on the level of the neocortex). On each of these levels, several evaluative processes can be carried out: In his sequential check theory of emotion differentiation, Scherer (2001) proposed several *sequential checks* underlying the evaluation (appraisal) of stimuli.[ix]

Evaluative processes are major antecedents for emotions (Scherer 2001), and are therefore considered here as one principle underlying the evocation of emotion in response to music. Scherer and Zentner (2001) have outlined a number of appraisal processes with regard to music (referred to as "production rules" by the authors; see also Chapter 10 in this volume). These appraisal processes are determined by the musical structure, the quality of the performance, the expertise and current mood or motivational state of the listener, as well as by contextual features such as location and the form of the event.

(2) Another principle is emotional *contagion*, i.e. the evocation of an emotion due to an individual perceiving an emotional expression (facial, vocal, gestural, and/or postural), and then copying this expression internally in terms of motor expression and physiological arousal. For instance, music might express joy (due to faster tempo, large pitch variation, etc.), this expression is copied by the listener in terms of smiling, and the (peripheral) feedback of these motoric acts evokes an emotion (Hatfield *et al.* 1993). As mentioned above, contagion may contribute to fully fledged empathic phenomena (also involving self-awareness and self/other distinction).

(3) The *memory* principle refers to the evocation of an emotion due to the activation of a memory representation (this implies that emotions, and stimuli associated with emotions, can be memorized). With regard to music, a musical stimulus might be associated with a memory of an autobiographical event, and the perception of the music might evoke an emotional memory representation leading to an emotional response (see also the "episodic memory" mechanism in Juslin and Västfjäll 2008).[x] Moreover, a musical stimulus might repeatedly be paired with a certain emotion elicited by another stimulus, so that music can become a conditioned stimulus and trigger an emotional response (see also Juslin's "evaluative conditioning" in Juslin and Västfjäll 2008). Although episodic memory, semantic memory, and evaluative conditioning involve different learning processes, and rely on different neural correlates,[xi] they are all (long-term) memory functions, and thus categorized here under a *memory* principle.

(4) The principle of musical *expectancy* states that the build-up, fulfillment, and violation of expectancies has emotional effects (such as surprise, tension, suspense, or relaxation).[xii] A detailed account on this principle goes beyond the scope of this chapter (for details see Koelsch 2012 and Chapter 15 in this volume), but it is important to note that, in addition to emotional effects due to musical expectancy, emotional effects due to a "mere exposure" (Moors and Kuppens 2008) are also related to predictive (and thus expectancy-related) processes: although the mechanisms underlying the *mere exposure effect* are unclear, it appears that the ability to predict upcoming events (thus facilitating processing fluency) correlates with perceived pleasure (Armstrong and Detweiler-Bedell 2008). Complete predictability, on the other hand, can easily lead to boredom.[xiii]

(5) Another principle is *imagination*, which refers to the emotional effects of being resourceful, inventive, curious, or creative, and to the emotional effects of trying something out. The imagination principle is related to Juslin and Västfjäll's principle of "visual imagery" (Juslin and Västfjäll 2008; note, however, that visual imagery can also lead to processes of evaluation,

for example because imagined objects or scenes usually have an emotional valence). During music production, imaginative processes can have emotional effects due to improvisation, interpretation, or composing.

(6) Emotional effects also arise from *understanding*. With regard to music, an individual might understand an extra-musical meaning, the (intra-musical) meaning of a musical structure, the "logic of musical ideas and their progress" Davies (1994), the musical discourse, etc. Perlovsky (2007) argued that humans (and perhaps other species as well) have an inborn need to understand (or "make sense of") how elements of contexts, or structures, are synthesized into coherent entities. This need is referred to as the *knowledge instinct* by Perlovsky (2007).[xiv] The fulfillment of this need to understand is experienced as rewarding (the "aha moment," or "eureka moment"), and presumably involves activity of the dopaminergic reward pathway, although this remains to be specified empirically.

(7) Finally, as described in "From social contact to social cohesion—the seven Cs," *engaging in social functions* during music making (or during listening to music) may evoke emotional responses. It was also mentioned that engaging in social functions has positive effects on human health, which relates this emotion principle to the potentially regenerative effects of music perception (and music making) on the immune system (for a review see Koelsch and Stegemann 2012). Note that such regenerative effects only emerge in the absence of (physical and psychological) violence. Thus, social functions are inherently linked to experiences of *beauty*, and thus to *aesthetic experience* (see also Siebel *et al.* 1990).[xv] Beyond the aesthetic experience of social functions during music making (and in part also during music listening), it is assumed that the beauty of musical sounds, contents, and structures can also evoke emotions (for example, Kivy 1999 argued that "music moves us emotionally is by its sheer musical beauty"). Aesthetic experience refers here to emotions that are due to the experience of beauty, not simply to the evaluation of "how beautiful something is," or "how good or bad something is." Therefore, aesthetic experience is not conceived here as a case of the evaluation principle.[xvi]

Note that it is often difficult to investigate one particular principle underlying the evocation of emotion with music, because several principles are usually at work at the same time (making it difficult to tease apart emotional effects evoked by different principles).

Neural correlates of positive emotions

A particular advantage of music is that it can evoke a range of positive emotions; this makes music a useful tool for investigating neural correlates of such emotions. Zentner *et al.* (2008) reported around 30 positive emotions that are evoked in a typical Western listener when listening to music. These emotions included feelings of wonder (e.g. happy, allured, moved), transcendence (e.g. inspired, feeling of spirituality, thrills), tenderness (e.g. in love, tender, affectionate), peacefulness (e.g. calm, relaxed, serene, soothed), power (e.g. energetic, strong), and joyful activation (e.g. joyful, animated, amused). Whereas the study by Zentner *et al.* (2008) relied on self-reports, the next sections will appeal to functional neuroimaging studies to explore two neural systems which seem to generate two different classes of emotion: (1) a diencephalon-centered affect system taken to generate reward-related feelings of pleasure, and (2) a hippocampus-centered affect system taken to generate attachment-related emotions such as joy, love, and happiness.

The diencephalon and emotion

The diencephalon is situated on top of the brainstem, and was phylogenetically differentiated in the course of the development of ovulation, thermoregulation, lactation, etc. The main components of the diencephalon are (dorsal and ventral) thalamus, hypothalamus, epithalamus, habenular complex, pineal gland, and subthalamic nucleus (Nieuwenhuys *et al.* 2008).

The hypothalamus controls and regulates endocrine functions, initiates and modulates vegetative reactions (via projections to pre-ganglionic autonomic neurons in the brainstem and the spinal cord), and generates basic behavioral patterns critical for immediate survival, such as defensive and attack behavior (e.g. Roeling *et al.* 1994; Canteras 2002; Nieuwenhuys *et al.* 2008). Importantly, the hypothalamus is involved in homeostatic activity, including the generation of "bodily need states" (Escalona 1963; Panksepp 1998) and the motivation to engage in activities that satisfy such bodily need states. For example, the hypothalamus plays a role in the regulation of water–electrolytic balance, blood pressure, thermoregulation (in mammals), as well the arousal of thirst and hunger. In addition to these functions that are critical for immediate survival, the hypothalamus is also involved in functions related to the survival of the species, such as maternal and sexual behavior. Panksepp (1998) denoted the system underlying the satisfaction of drives and urges related to the survival of the individual and the species the *SEEKING system* (the hypothalamus also plays a role in several other functions not elaborated here, such as food intake, circadian rhythm, wakefulness and sleep, and the stress response).

The satisfaction of bodily need states is a powerful source of pleasure, and it appears that the hypothalamus not only generates urges but also initiates neural activity that gives rise to feelings of pleasure when such urges are satisfied. The most effective sites in self-stimulation paradigms in rats are located in the *lateral hypothalamus* (Olds 1958) which partly projects via the *medial forebrain bundle* to the *ventral tegmental area* (VTA) in the midbrain, in which dopaminergic neurons innervate the *nucleus accumbens* (NAc; see also Kringelbach *et al.* 2007). Importantly, this so-called *reward pathway* (or *reward circuit*) can also be activated by other brain structures (including, for example, the amygdala and the orbitofrontal cortex), via projections to the lateral hypothalamus, for example. Thus, this pathway can be activated by virtually any rewarding stimulus, and activation of this pathway results in feelings of pleasure, reward, or fun (even if there is no immediate urge or homeostatic need). For example, monetary rewards, sexual activity, intake of drugs, sugar intake, drinking water when dehydrated, or the omission of an anticipated negative consequence are perceived as pleasurable, and correlate with activity of this reward pathway (Berridge *et al.* 2009; Nicola 2007). The studies reviewed in the next section indicate that music listening can also activate this pathway, and so presumably can other forms of art.

Music and reward-related experiences of pleasure

Using positron emission tomography (PET), Blood and Zatorre (2001) investigated the neural correlates of intensely pleasurable music-evoked experiences involving, for example, goosebumps and shivers down the neck, arms, or spine. Such experiences are also referred to as *musical frisson* (Levinson 2004), other researchers used terms such as *chills* (Panksepp 1995; Grewe *et al.* 2007b), *thrills* (Goldstein 1980; Sloboda 1991), or *skin orgasm* (Panksepp 1995).[xvii] Blood and Zatorre (2001) reported changes in regional cerebral blood flow (rCBF)[xviii] during musical frissons when participants were presented with a piece of their own favorite music (using normal CD recordings; as a control condition, participants listened to the favorite piece of another subject). Increasing intensity of frissons correlated with increases in rCBF in brain regions thought to be involved in reward and emotion, including the insula, orbitofrontal cortex, the ventral medial pre-frontal cortex, and the ventral striatum (presumably the NAc). Similarly, another PET study by Brown *et al.* (2004) reported activation of the ventral striatum (in addition to the subcallosal cingulate cortex, the anterior insula, and the posterior part of the hippocampus) during listening to two unfamiliar, pleasant pieces contrasted with a resting condition.

Activation of the ventral striatum in response to pleasant music (presumably involving the NAc) was also observed in several studies using functional MRI. One of these studies investigated the valence dimension (Koelsch *et al.* 2006) using joyful instrumental dance tunes. Unpleasant stimuli were permanently dissonant counterparts of the original musical excerpts. Pleasant music elicited increases of blood oxygen level-dependent (BOLD) signals in the ventral striatum (presumably including the NAc; activity changes in response to unpleasant music will be reported later).

Other functional MRI studies reported activity changes in the ventral striatum (1) during happy (in contrast to neutral) music (Mitterschiffthaler *et al.* 2007), (2) correlating with valence ratings (Trost *et al.* 2012), (3) due to the pleasantness emerging from the predictability of music (Menon and Levitin 2005), and (4) due to positive music-evoked memories (Janata 2009). The study by Menon and Levitin (2005) reported that activation of the ventral striatum (which hosts the NAc) was connected to activity in the VTA and the hypothalamus. This suggests that the hemodynamic changes observed in the ventral striatum reflected dopaminergic activity. As mentioned above, the NAc is innervated in part by dopaminergic brainstem neurons (located mainly in the VTA as well as in the substantia nigra), and is part of the so-called reward circuit. Further support for the assumption that the hemodynamic changes in the ventral striatum (reported in the above-mentioned studies) involved dopaminergic neural activity stems from a PET study by Salimpoor *et al.* (2011). That study showed that strong music-evoked pleasure (including "musical frissons") is associated with increased dopamine binding in the NAc (the experimental paradigm of that study was similar to the one used by Blood and Zatorre 2001).

Importantly, activity in the NAc (as well as activity in the ventral pallidum; Berridge *et al.* 2009) correlates with motivation- and reward-related experiences of pleasure, for instance during the process of obtaining a goal, when an unexpected reachable incentive is encountered, or when individuals are presented with a reward cue (reviewed in Berridge *et al.* 2009 and Nicola 2007). As mentioned above, in humans NAc activity has been reported, for example for monetary rewards, sexual activity, intake of drugs, sugar intake, drinking water when dehydrated, or the omission of an anticipated negative consequence (Berridge *et al.* 2009; Nicola 2007). Therefore, it has previously been suggested that NAc activity correlates with the subjective feeling of *fun* (Koelsch *et al.* 2010b), although more detailed information about the functional significance of the NAc is needed to determine the role that the NAc possibly plays for other emotions as well.

The NAc also appears to play a role in invigorating, and perhaps even selecting and directing, behavior in response to stimuli with incentive value, as well as in motivating and rewarding such behavior (Nicola 2007). The NAc is considered as a "limbic motor interface" (Nieuwenhuys *et al.* 2008), because (1) the NAc receives input from limbic structures such as amygdala and hippocampus, (2) injecting dopamine in the NAc causes an increase in locomotion, and (3) the NAc projects to other compartments of the basal ganglia, which play an important role in the learning, selection, and execution of actions. This motor-related function of the NAc puts it in a key position for the generation of a drive to move to, join in, and dance to pleasant music, although the neural basis for this drive needs to be specified.

It is important to note that in three of the mentioned studies (Brown *et al.* 2004; Menon and Levitin 2005; Koelsch *et al.* 2006) participants did not report "frissons" during music listening, suggesting that dopaminergic pathways including the NAc can be activated by music as soon as it is perceived as pleasant (i.e. even in the absence of extreme emotional experiences involving "frissons"). Results from the reviewed studies thus suggest that music can easily evoke experiences of pleasure, or fun, associated with the activity of a reward pathway involving the hypothalamus, the VTA, and the NAc. This potential of music opens interesting research perspectives that could provide more systematic knowledge for the use of music therapy in support of affective disorders related to dysfunctions involving the mesolimbic reward pathway, such as depression and Parkinson's disease (Koelsch 2010).

Music-evoked emotions and the hippocampus

The previous section described that music can evoke subjective experiences of fun involving the NAc, similar to other rewarding stimuli such as chocolate, drugs, and sexual activity. However, the review of functional neuroimaging studies on music and emotion reveals a particularly noticeable feature, namely (additional) activity changes in the (anterior) hippocampal formation in a large proportion of those studies. As will be argued further below, such hippocampal activations are presumably due to the generation of tender positive emotions such as joy, love, or happiness. Before the possible role of the hippocampus in emotion is elaborated further, functional neuroimaging studies on music-evoked emotions reporting activity changes within the hippocampal formation will be reviewed.

The first study reporting music-evoked activity changes in the hippocampal formation (as well as in the amygdala) was the PET study by Blood and Zatorre (2001), in which increasing intensity of music-evoked frissons correlated with decreases in rCBF in the amygdala and the hippocampus (see Figure 17.1). This PET finding of hippocampal activation during listening to music was corroborated with functional MRI. In the aforementioned functional MRI study by Koelsch *et al.* (2006), unpleasant music elicited increases of BOLD signals in the amygdala, the hippocampus, the parahippocampal cortex, and the temporal poles (a decrease of BOLD signal was observed in these structures in response to pleasant music). Activity changes in the (right) anterior hippocampal formation were also reported in a study by Mitterschiffthaler *et al.* (2007) in response to sad (in contrast to neutral) music.

In line with this finding by Mitterschiffthaler *et al.* (2007), Trost *et al.* (2012) reported that BOLD signal values correlated with felt sadness in the right Ammon's horn of the hippocampal formation; similar correlations were observed for felt tenderness, peacefulness, transcendence, and nostalgia.[xix] However, although these emotions have rather low arousal, and although sadness was rated to have lower valence than the other mentioned emotions, ratings of felt valence, of felt arousal correlated (positively) with BOLD signals in the anterior hippocampal formation.[xx] This indicates that BOLD signals in the hippocampal formation not only correlate with negative emotions, but also with positive emotions. The seemingly contradictory observation that activity changes in the hippocampal formation can be observed in response to both positive as well as negative emotions will be dealt with later in this chapter.

Similar to the study by Koelsch *et al.* (2006), a functional MRI study by Baumgartner *et al.* (2006) also reported activity changes in the hippocampus, the parahippocampal gyrus, and the temporal poles (that study used a combined presentation of fearful or sad pictures together with fearful or sad music). With regard to the use of music to elicit emotions, it is also interesting to note that brain activations were stronger during the combined presentation of pictures and music than during the presentation of pictures alone. For example, activation of the amygdala was only observed in the combined condition, but not in the condition where only pictures were presented. Based on the studies by Koelsch *et al.* (2006) and Baumgartner *et al.* (2006), as well as on a study by Fritz and

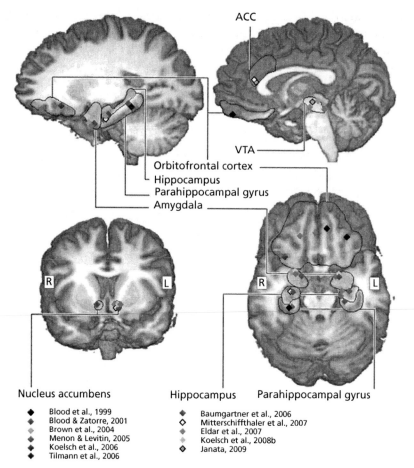

Figure 17.1. Illustration of limbic [amygdala, nucleus accumbens, anterior cingulate cortex (AAC), and hippocampus] and para-limbic structures (orbitofrontal cortex, parahippocampal gyrus). The diamonds represent music-evoked activity changes in these structures (see references in figure and text for details). Note the repeatedly reported activations of amygdala, nucleus accumbens, and hippocampus, reflecting that music is capable of modulating activity in core structures of emotion (see text for details). Top left: view of the right hemisphere; top right: medial view; bottom left: anterior view; bottom right: bottom view.

Koelsch (2005), it was suggested that the network comprising amygdala, hippocampus, parahippocampal gyrus, and temporal poles (which was observed in all of these studies) plays a particular role for emotions evoked by music (Koelsch 2010).

Similar to the study by Baumgartner *et al.* (2006), a functional MRI study by Eldar *et al.* (2007) reported that activity changes in response to music in both the amygdala and the hippocampus can be markedly increased when the music is presented simultaneously with film clips (the film clips were neutral scenes from commercials; positive music was also taken from commercials, and negative music mainly from soundtracks of horror movies). The combined conditions—positive music with neutral film, as well as negative music with neutral film—were not rated as more positive or negative than when music was presented alone (note that film clips played without music were rated as neutral). Nevertheless, activity changes in the amygdala were considerably larger for the combined (film and music) presentation than for the presentation of film clips alone, or music alone. Analogous response properties were observed in the areas of the ventro-lateral frontal cortex for both positive and negative music, and in the hippocampus for negative music combined with the film clips. Notably, emotional music on its own did not elicit a differential response in these regions (perhaps the combination of emotional music with neutral film clips stimulated fantasies about positive or negative things that might happen next, increasing the overall emotional activity). To discuss what the reported activity changes in the hippocampal formation in response to music might reflect, the next section will first provide information about the role of the hippocampus for emotion.

The hippocampus and emotion

The hippocampus consists of cortex (in contrast to the diencephalon, the VTA, and the NAc). The hippocampus is phylogenetically later differentiated than the diencephalon, and far more developed in mammals than in fish, amphibians, and reptiles (Salas *et al.* 2003). In contrast to the six-layered neocortex, the hippocampal cortex is transitional mesocortex consisting of three to five layers (Nieuwenhuys *et al.* 2008). The hippocampal formation is situated around the diencephalon and consists in primates of the well-developed retrocommissural hippocampus (which is the main portion of the hippocampal formation), a supracommissural part, and a pre-commissural part rostral to the septum verum.

In textbooks, the function of the hippocampal formation is usually considered with regard to learning and memory, spatial orientation, novelty, familiarity, and expectancies (for reviews of the involvement of the hippocampus in these functions see Nadel 2008). However, such textbooks, as well as the prevailing neurobiological theories on emotion, tend to ignore that the hippocampus also plays an important role in emotional processes. This notion was first proposed by James Papez, based on the observation that hippocampal lesions (caused by injection of the rabies virus into the hippocampi of cats) lead to marked changes in emotional behavior (Papez 1937). Papez mentioned that "since the Negri bodies, the essential lesions of rabies, or hydrophobia, have their site of predilection in the hippocampus and the cerebellum and since disease is characterized by intense emotional, convulsive, and paralytic symptoms, there seems to be offered an important clue to the probable location of the emotive mechanism. [. . .] The hippocampus participates in some important way in the central production of the emotive process" (Papez 1937, p. 733). Later in that article, he proposed that "the hypothalamus, the anterior thalamic nuclei, the gyrus cinguli, the hippocampus, and their interconnections constitute a harmonious mechanism which may elaborate the functions of central emotion, as well as participate in emotional expression" (Papez 1937, p. 734). Later on, MacLean supported this hypothesis in his *Theory of the Triune Brain* (MacLean 1990), based on the observation that typical aural symptoms of epileptic seizures triggered by epileptic foci located in the rostral hippocampal formation (as well as in other limbic structures) include a variety of strong emotions (see also Ploog 2003). Subsequently, however, the notion that the hippocampus plays an important role in emotion was hardly considered by neurobiological theories on emotion (except in a theory from W. A. Siebel, according to which the hippocampus is the neural correlate of "genuine emotions"; Siebel 1994). Nevertheless, several groups emphasized that emotional processes interact with the memory function of the hippocampus (McGaugh and Roozendaal 2002; Phelps 2004; Squire *et al.* 2007), that the hippocampus is implicated in familiarity (Squire *et al.* 2007), and that the hippocampus is involved in the establishment of preferences for places (Panksepp 1998).

The hippocampus has dense reciprocal connections with structures involved in the regulation of behaviors essential for survival (such as ingestive, reproductive, and defensive behaviors), and with structures involved in the regulation of activity of the autonomic, hormonal, and immune systems. Such structures include the amygdala, the hypothalamus, thalamic nuclei, the septal-diagonal band complex, the cingulate gyrus, the insula, and autonomic brainstem nuclei. Efferent connections project to the NAc, other parts of the striatum, as well as to numerous other limbic, paralimbic, and non-limbic structures (Nieuwenhuys *et al.* 2008). The functional significance of these connections places the hippocampus (along with other brain structures) in a pivotal position for emotional processing, and it has previously been noted that the key to understanding the function of the hippocampus lies in the fact that it has major projections not only to cortical association areas but also to subcortical limbic structures (Nieuwenhuys *et al.* 2008).

Attachment-related (tender positive) emotions

Little is known about the quality of emotions generated by the hippocampal formation. Here, the hypothesis is endorsed that the hippocampal formation generates attachment-related affects which are perceived by humans as *tender positive feelings* (Koelsch *et al.* 2007). The latter term is derived from Charles Darwin's *The Expression of Emotions in Man and Animals* (Darwin 1872), in which Darwin wrote that "tender feelings [...] seem to be compounded of affection, joy, and especially of sympathy" (Darwin 1872, p. 247).[xxi] These feelings are "of a pleasurable nature," and it is interesting to note that Darwin writes in this chapter also about the "wonderful power of music" (Darwin 1872, p. 250; an idea which is elaborated in more detail in *The Descent of Man*).

Attachment-related behavior includes kissing, caressing, hugging, softly touching, softly vocalizing, and in animals behaviors such as licking, grooming, nest-building, and pup retrieval. Attachment-related affects are also related to inclusion in close-knit social groups and communities. Extant research indicates that social contact and group inclusion are fundamental human needs (Baumeister and Leary 1995) whose fulfillment or disruption are major causes of affective activity (Turner 2000). Notably, at least in humans, attachment-related affects include love, an emotion that is not dealt with in most publications on neurological models of emotion (one of the few exceptions is Panksepp's *General Psychobiological Theory of Emotions*; Panksepp 1998).

Several lines of evidence point to the involvement of the hippocampus in attachment-related affects:

(1) Lesions of the hippocampus lead to impairment of maternal behavior in rats (Kimble *et al.* 1967).

(2) The hippocampus is damaged by chronic emotional stressors, particularly by helplessness and despair (Oitzl *et al.* 2010; Warner-Schmidt and Duman 2006). The hippocampus is unique in its vulnerability to emotional stressors, and is presumably the only brain structure in which severe emotional stress can lead to the death of neurons (in addition to neuronal death, the volume reduction of the hippocampus in response to severe chronic emotional stress is due to reduced neurogenesis in the dentate gyrus of the hippocampal formation).

(3) Dysfunction and structural damage of this structure has been observed in depressive individuals (Videbech and Ravnkilde 2004) and in individuals suffering from post-traumatic stress disorder such as Vietnam veterans who witnessed extreme violence or committed extremely violent acts against other individuals (Bremner 1999); similar findings have been reported for individuals who were sexually abused as children (Stein *et al.* 1997).

(4) Individuals with flattened affect and reduced tender positive emotionality show reduced hippocampal activity in response to emotion-evoking stimuli (Koelsch *et al.* 2007).

The fact that lesions of parts of the hippocampus sometimes do not lead to clear emotional impairment does not rule out that the hippocampus plays a role in the generation of emotion: first, emotionally relevant parts of the hippocampal formation might have been spared; second, emotional functions might have quickly reorganized; third, emotional flattening might have gone unnoticed. In this regard, it is interesting to note that no one would argue that the basal ganglia are critically involved in motor processes; yet, if damage to the internal capsule is avoided, even large bilateral lesions of the striatum or globus pallidus do not necessarily result in motor deficits (MacLean 1972). It should also be mentioned that Klüver and Bucy (1937) reported that bilateral (note, not unilateral!) removal of the temporal lobes of macaques, including the amygdala and the hippocampal formation, caused severe changes in cognition and emotional behavior. Interestingly, they described this changed condition as "*Seelenblindheit*" ("psychic blindness"). Notably, such behavior is not observed when only the amygdala is removed.

According to our experience from experiments using music as a stimulus to evoke emotions, hippocampal activity is often related to feelings described by the participants as touching, or being moved. This stays in contrast to the diencephalon-generated pleasure, which is rather associated with feelings such as fun (the diencephalon-centered pleasure experienced when satisfying a homeostatic need, e.g. drinking a glass of water when thirsty, will hardly be described as "touching"). Note that, although it is important to differentiate the feelings related to the activation of the "reward circuit" (including the lateral hypothalamus, as well as the mesolimbic dopamine pathway involving the VTA with projections to the NAc; see p.000) from the attachment-related (tender positive) emotions that involve activity of the hippocampus, both are naturally not mutually exclusive (usually, being joyful is fun). We (Koelsch *et al.* 2010b) have previously noted that feelings arising from activity of the former circuit (involving the NAc) might perhaps best be referred to as "fun," and that attachment-related (tender positive) emotions such as "joy," "love," and "happiness" require the involvement of hippocampal activity.

Another important differentiation between diencephalon-centered affects and hippocampus-centered affects is that the diencephalon-centered affects satiate: once an organism has satisfied bodily needs and achieved homeostasis, the organism is satiated, and stimuli that were incentives before can even become aversive (because too much of a chemical compound, for example, can be harmful for an organism). This stays in contrast to the hippocampus-centered tender positive affects, which do not get satiated. Note that a brain system for attachment-related affect that does not satiate is evolutionarily adaptive, because, for example, feeling attached to a child, loving a child, and feeling the joy of being together with the child are emotions that serve the continuous protection and nurturing of the offspring. Similarly, the need to belong to a social group and the feeling of social inclusion (both of which do not appear to satiate), serve the formation and maintenance of social bonds, thus strengthening social cohesion.

Whether this conception of the quality of hippocampus-centered affect is already sufficient, or needs to be expanded, it is important to recognize the relevance of the hippocampus for the generation of emotional processes. Note that, although it is suggested here that attachment-related tender positive emotion originates in the hippocampus, the hippocampus might also play a role in negative emotion: For example, in the face of danger, hippocampal activity appears to be inhibited (Koelsch 2010) in order to (1) focus resources on behavior relevant to deal with the threatening situation, for example on flight or fight behavior, and (2) prevent hippocampal damage due to (severe) emotional stressors (see p.240). That is, perhaps the increase in the BOLD signal in the hippocampal formation in response to unpleasant, fearful, or sad music reported in the studies by Koelsch *et al.* (2006), Baumgartner *et al.* (2006), Eldar *et al.* (2007), and Mitterschiffthaler *et al.* (2007) was due to a mechanism that protects the hippocampus by virtue of inhibitory neuronal activity. Such inhibition might contribute to the generation of fear and unpleasantness (Koelsch *et al.* 2010b; Koelsch 2010), and lead to emotional pain associated with social loss, sadness, and depression (Stahl 2002; Henningsen and Löwe 2006). In the study by Trost *et al.* (2012), the largest correlation between emotion ratings and BOLD signal values (in terms of the number of voxels) was observed for valence (followed by tender positive emotions such as peacefulness and tenderness). This indicates that BOLD signals in the hippocampal formation not only correlate with negative emotions but also with positive emotions. This supports the notion that changes in activity in the hippocampal formation can be due to the generation of emotion (reflected as a positive correlation between BOLD signal values and ratings of positive emotion), as well as due to the inhibition of such processes (reflected as a positive correlation between BOLD signal values and ratings of negative emotion).

As mentioned above, it is well established that the hippocampus plays an important role for learning and memory, spatial orientation, novelty, as well as expectedness, but it is also important to note that, at least in some of the reported functional neuroimaging studies that used music to investigate emotion, it is unlikely that the reported hippocampal activations were simply due to such processes. For example, in the study by Blood and Zatorre (2001), rCBF changes in the anterior hippocampal formation were observed even when analyzing responses only to stimuli that participants themselves brought into the experiment (supporting Figure 5 of Blood and Zatorre 2001), thus every subject was very familiar with the music included in that analysis. In the study by Trost *et al.* (2012), familiarity ratings correlated with activity changes in the right subiculum, whereas correlations with emotion ratings were observed in the Ammon's horn of the hippocampal formation. This argues for the notion that the processes related to the generation of emotions (reflected in activity changes located in the Ammon's horn) are not simply processes related to familiarity or memory (reflected in activity changes located in the subiculum).

The potential of music to evoke activity changes in the hippocampal formation related to emotions of joy has important implications for music therapy: As mentioned above, patients with depression or post-traumatic stress disorder show a volume reduction of the hippocampal formation (associated with a loss of hippocampal neurons and blockage of neurogenesis in the hippocampus; Warner-Schmidt and Duman 2006), and individuals with flattened affectivity (i.e. a reduced capability to produce tender positive emotions) show reduced activity changes in the anterior hippocampal formation in response to music (Koelsch *et al.* 2007). Therefore, it is tempting to speculate that music can be used therapeutically in order to: (1) re-establish neural activity (related to positive emotion) in the hippocampus, (2) prevent the death of hippocampal neurons, and (3) stimulate hippocampal neurogenesis.

The potential of music to evoke joy and happiness is probably related, at least in part, to the engagement of social functions by music making (and, although presumably to a lesser extent, also by music listening): The "Seven Cs" enumerated above are inherently related to social connection and inter-individual attachment. Participating in these functions fulfills human needs, and can evoke both strong positive attachment-related emotions as well as strong feelings of reward and pleasure. Music is special in that it can facilitate engagement in all of these social functions at the same time. In this regard, music serves the goal of fulfilling social needs, that is, needs that are related to survival functions and that are of vital importance for the individual. This is presumably one explanation for the emotional power of music.

Notes

i   For studies investigating peripheral-physiological effects of music-evoked emotions see, for example, Steinbeis *et al.* (2006), Sammler *et al.* (2007), Grewe *et al.* (2007b), Koelsch *et al.* (2008a, 2011), Orini *et al.* (2010).

ii   For the concept of basic emotions see, for example, Ekman (1999).

iii   For a review see Koelsch and Stegemann (2012). For example, a study by Koelsch *et al.* (2011) showed a decrease of cortisol levels due to reduced stress before and during surgery. Release of cortisol increases glucogenesis in the liver (leading to higher levels of blood sugar) and enhances lipolysis (leading to increased fat metabolism) and protein catabolism.

iv   Negative mood effects are described in the phenomenon of "appression" by Siebel and Winkler (1996, section 9.6.5).

v   For a study showing an increase of positive mood due to music making in a group see Koelsch *et al.* (2010a).

vi   For a study on EEG correlates of emotional mimicry during viewing facial expressions see, for example, Achaibou *et al.* (2008).

vii   Some (Hatfield *et al.* 2009) assume that mimicry, in turn, is a precursor of contagion.

viii The sensory–motor level represents reflex systems responding to stimuli that are innately preferred or avoided. The schematic level includes learned preferences/aversions, and the conceptual level includes recalled, anticipated, or derived positive–negative estimates.

ix   These checks include relevance detection (including a novelty check), implication assessment, coping potential determination, and normative significance evaluation. Note that some of these checks, such as normative significance evaluation, can only be performed by cortical structures.

x   For a functional MRI study on music-evoked autobiographical memories and emotional effects see Janata (2009).

xi   See, for example, LeDoux (2000) for neural correlates of evaluative conditioning, and Platel *et al.* (2003) for possible neural correlates of a semantic and an episodic musical memory. See Groussard *et al.* (2010) for a comparison between a semantic musical memory and a semantic language memory.

xii   For details see, for example, Huron (2006) and Meyer (1956); for neuroscientific studies investigating this issue see Steinbeis *et al.* (2006) and Koelsch *et al.* (2008a,b).

xiii The explanation of the mere exposure effects in terms of classical conditioning (Zajonc 2001) is weak, because this does not explain the decrease of preference following over-exposure.

xiv Perlovsky (2007) also argues that meaning emerges in part from such understanding.

xv   A study by Istók *et al.* (2009) reported that Finnish students associated the "aesthetic value of music" most strongly with the adjectives beautiful and touching.

xvi Studies on the empirical aspects of aesthetics are extremely sparse. For neuroscience studies approaching this issue by investigating neural correlates of judgments of beauty see Jacobsen *et al.* (2006) and Müller *et al.* (2010).

xvii Huron (2006) noted that listeners can find music "thrilling" without necessarily experiencing goosebumps, and that the term "chills" is best reserved for the phenomenological feeling of coldness, which often, but not necessarily, accompanies a frisson.

xviii The activity of nerve cells correlates with the regional flow of blood; therefore changes in rCBF are taken to reflect neural activity.

xix The reported Montreal Neurological Institute (MNI) coordinates of the peak values of correlations of BOLD signal values and emotion ratings are located with 80–90% probability in the Ammon's horn of the hippocampal formation according to the probability map provided by Amunts *et al.* (2005).

xx Eighty to ninety per cent probability according to the probability map provided by Amunts *et al.* (2005); the correlation with arousal was located in the right hippocampal formation, the correlation for valence in the Ammon's horn bilaterally. An additional correlation between BOLD signals and tension ratings was located in the right subiculum.

xi Darwin means sympathy in the sense with which nowadays the word empathy is often used, e.g. feeling either pity for the grief of someone else, or feeling the happiness or good fortune (Darwin 1872, p. 250). Note that, later on, he describes sympathy as a separate or distinct emotion (Darwin 1872, p. 249).

References

Achaibou, A., Pourtois, G., Schwartz, S., and Vuilleumier, P. (2008). Simultaneous recording of EEG and facial muscle reactions during spontaneous emotional mimicry. *Neuropsychologia*, **46**, 1104–13.

Allen, R., Hill, E., and Heaton, P. (2009). "hath charms to soothe…": an exploratory study of how high-functioning adults with ASD experience music. *Autism*, **13**, 21–41.

Amunts, K., Kedo, O., Kindler, M., Pieperhoff, P., Mohlberg, H., Shah, N.J., Habel, U., Schneider, F., and Zilles, K. (2005). Cytoarchitectonic mapping of the human amygdala, hippocampal region and entorhinal cortex: intersubject variability and probability maps. *Anatomy and Embryology*, **210**, 343–52.

Armstrong, T. and Detweiler-Bedell, B. (2008). Beauty as an emotion: the exhilarating prospect of mastering a challenging world. *Review of General Psychology*, **12**, 305–29.

Baumeister, R. and Leary, M. (1995). The need to belong: desire for interpersonal attachments as a fundamental human motivation. *Psychological Bulletin*, **117**, 497–529.

Baumgartner, T., Lutz, K., Schmidt, C., and Jäncke, L. (2006). The emotional power of music: how music enhances the feeling of affective pictures. *Brain Research*, **1075**, 151–64.

Berridge, K., Robinson, T., and Aldridge, J. (2009). Dissecting components of reward: liking, wanting, and learning. *Current Opinion in Pharmacology*, **9**, 65–73.

Blood, A. and Zatorre, R. (2001). Intensely pleasurable responses to music correlate with activity in brain regions implicated in reward and emotion. *Proceedings of the National Academy of Sciences of the United States of America*, **98**, 11818–23.

Blood, A., Zatorre, R., Bermudez, P. and Evans, A. (1999). Emotional responses to pleasant and unpleasant music correlate with activity in paralimbic brain regions. *Nature Neuroscience*, **2**, 382–7.

Brandão, M., Tomaz, C., Leão Borges, P., Coimbra, N., and Bagri, A. (1988). Defense reaction induced by microinjections of bicuculline into the inferior colliculus. *Physiology and Behavior*, **44**, 361–5.

Bremner, J. (1999). Does stress damage the brain? *Biological Psychiatry*, **45**, 797–805.

Brodal, A. (1947). The hippocampus and the sense of smell: a review. *Brain*, **70**, 179.

Brown, S. and Volgsten, U. (2006). *Music and Manipulation: on the Social Uses and Social Control of Music.* Oxford: Berghahn Books.

Brown, S., Martinez, M., and Parsons, L. (2004). Passive music listening spontaneously engages limbic and paralimbic systems. *NeuroReport*, **15**, 2033–7.

Cacioppo, J. and Hawkley, L. (2003). Social isolation and health, with an emphasis on underlying mechanisms. *Perspectives in Biology and Medicine*, **46**, S39–S52.

Callan, D., Tsytsarev, V., Hanakawa, T., Callan, A., Katsuhara, M., Fukuyama, H., and Turner, R. (2006). Song and speech: brain regions involved with perception and covert production. *NeuroImage*, **31**, 1327–42.

Canteras, N. (2002). The medial hypothalamic defensive system: hodological organization and functional implications. *Pharmacology Biochemistry and Behavior*, **71**, 481–91.

Craig, A. (2002). How do you feel? Interoception: the sense of the physiological condition of the body. *Nature Reviews Neuroscience*, **3**, 655–66.

Craig, A. (2003). A new view of pain as a homeostatic emotion. *Trends in Neurosciences*, **26**, 303–7.

Cross, I. and Morley, I. (2008). The evolution of music: theories, definitions and the nature of the evidence. In S. Malloch and C. Trevarthen (eds), *Communicative Musicality: Exploring the Basis of Human Companionship*, pp. 61–82. Oxford: Oxford University Press.

Dalgleish, T. (2004). The emotional brain. *Nature Reviews Neuroscience*, **5**, 583–9.

Daltrozzo, J. and Schön, D. (2009). Conceptual processing in music as revealed by N400 effects on words and musical targets. *Journal of Cognitive Neuroscience*, **21**, 1882–92.

Darwin, C. (1872). *The Expression of Emotion in Man and Animals*. London: John Murray.

Davies, S. (1994). *Musical Meaning and Expression*. Ithaca, NY: Cornell University Press.

Ekman, P. (1999). Basic emotions. In T. Dalgleish and M. Power (eds), *Handbook of Cognition and Emotion*, pp. 45–60. New York: Wiley.

Eldar, E., Ganor, O., Admon, R., Bleich, A., and Hendler, T. (2007). Feeling the real world: limbic response to music depends on related content. *Cerebral Cortex*, **17**, 2828–40.

Escalona, S. (1963). Patterns of infantile experience and the developmental process. *Psychoanalytic Study of the Child*, **18**, 197–243.

Fitch, W. (2005). The evolution of music in comparative perspective. *Annals of the New York Academy of Sciences*, **1060**, 29–49.

Fitch, W. (2006). The biology and evolution of music: a comparative perspective. *Cognition*, **100**, 173–215.

Fritz, T. and Koelsch, S. (2005). Initial response to pleasant and unpleasant music: an fMRI study. *NeuroImage*, **26**(Suppl. 1), 271.

Garcia-Cairasco, N. (2002). A critical review on the participation of inferior colliculus in acoustic-motor and acoustic-limbic networks involved in the expression of acute and kindled audiogenic seizures. *Hearing Research*, **168**, 208–22.

Goerlich, K., Witteman, J., Aleman, A., and Martens, S. (2011). Hearing feelings: affective categorization of music and speech in alexithymia, an ERP study. *PLoS One*, **6**, e19501.

Goldstein, A. (1980). Thrills in response to music and other stimuli. *Physiological Psychology*, **8**, 126–9.

Grewe, O., Nagel, F., Kopiez, R., and Altenmüller, E. (2007a). Emotions over time: synchronicity and development of subjective, physiological, and facial affective reactions of music. *Emotion*, **7**, 774–88.

Grewe, O., Nagel, F., Kopiez, R., and Altenmüller, E. (2007b). Listening to music as a re-creative process: physiological, psychological, and psychoacoustical correlates of chills and strong emotions. *Music Perception*, **24**, 297–314.

Grieser-Painter, J. and Koelsch, S. (2011). Can out-of-context musical sounds convey meaning? an ERP study on the processing of meaning in music. *Psychophysiology*, **48**, 645–55.

Groussard, M., Viader, F., Hubert, V., Landeau, B., Abbas, A., Desgranges, B., Eustache, F., and Platel, H. (2010). Musical and verbal semantic memory: two distinct neural networks? *NeuroImage*, **49**, 2764–73.

Harlow, H. (1958). The nature of love. *American Psychologist*, **13**, 673–85.

Hatfield, E., Cacioppo, J., and Rapson, R. (1993). Emotional contagion. *Current Directions in Psychological Science*, **2**, 96–100.

Hatfield, E., Rapson, R., and Le, Y. (2009). Emotional contagion and empathy. In J. Decety and W. Ickes (eds), *The Social Neuroscience of Empathy*, pp. 19–30. Cambridge, MA: MIT Press.

Henningsen, P. and Löwe, B. (2006). Depression, pain, and somatoform disorders. *Current Opinion in Psychiatry*, **19**, 19–24.

Herrick, C. (1933). The functions of the olfactory parts of the cerebral cortex. *Proceedings of the National Academy of Sciences of the United States of America*, **19**, 7–14.

Hillecke, T., Nickel, A., and Bolay, H. (2005). Scientific perspectives on music therapy. *Annals of the New York Academy of Sciences*, **1060**, 271–82.

House, J., Landis, K., and Umberson, D. (1988). Social relationships and health. *Science*, **241**, 540–5.

Huron, D. (2001). Is music an evolutionary adaptation? *Annals of the New York Academy of Sciences*, **930**, 43–61.

Huron, D. (2006). *Sweet Anticipation: Music and the Psychology of Expectation*. Cambridge, MA: MIT Press.

Istók, E., Brattico, E., Jacobsen, T., Krohn, K., Müller, M., and Tervaniemi, M. (2009). Aesthetic responses to music: a questionnaire study. *Musicae Scientiae*, **13**, 183–206.

Jacobsen, T., Schubotz, R. I., Höfel, L., and Cramon, D. Y. (2006). Brain correlates of aesthetic judgment of beauty. *NeuroImage*, **29**, 276–85.

Janata, P. (2009). The neural architecture of music-evoked autobiographical memories. *Cerebral Cortex*, **19**, 2579–94.

Jürgens, U. (2002). Neural pathways underlying vocal control. *Neuroscience and Biobehavioral Reviews*, **26**, 235–58.

Juslin, P. and Västfjäll, D. (2008). Emotional responses to music: the need to consider underlying mechanisms. *Behavioral and Brain Sciences*, **31**), 559–75.

Juslin, P., Liljeström, S., Laukka, P., Västfjäll, D., and Lundqvist, L. (2011). Emotional reactions to music in a nationally representative sample of Swedish adults. *Musicae Scientiae*, **15**, 174–207.

Kimble, D., Rogers, L., and Hendrickson, C. (1967). Hippocampal lesions disrupt maternal, not sexual, behavior in the albino rat. *Journal of Comparative and Physiological Psychology*, **63**, 401–7.

Kirschner, S. and Tomasello, M. (2009). Joint drumming: social context facilitates synchronization in preschool children. *Journal of Experimental Child Psychology*, **102**, 299–314.

Kivy, P. (1991). *Music Alone: Philosophical Reflections on the Purely Musical Experience*. Ithaca, NY: Cornell University Press.

Kivy, P. (1999). Feeling the musical emotions. *British Journal of Aesthetics*, **39**, 1–13.

Klüver, H. and Bucy, P. (1937). "Psychic blindness" and other symptoms following bilateral temporal lobectomy in rhesus monkeys. *American Journal of Physiology*, **119**, 352–3.

Koelsch, S. (2010). Towards a neural basis of music-evoked emotions. *Trends in Cognitive Sciences*, **14**, 131–7.

Koelsch, S. (2011). Towards a neural basis of music perception—a review and updated model. *Frontiers in Psychology*, **2**, 1–20.

Koelsch, S. and Stegemann, T. (2012). The brain and positive biological effects in healthy and clinical populations. In R. MacDonald, D. Kreutz, and L. Mitchell (eds), *Music, Health and Well-being*, pp. 436–56. Oxford: Oxford University Press.

Koelsch, S., Kasper, E., Sammler, D., Schulze, K., Gunter, T. C., and Friederici, A. D. (2004). Music, language, and meaning: brain signatures of semantic processing. *Nature Neuroscience*, **7**, 302–7.

Koelsch, S., Gunter, T. C., Wittfoth, M., and Sammler, D. (2005). Interaction between syntax processing in language and in music: an ERP study. *Journal of Cognitive Neuroscience*, **17**, 1565–77.

Koelsch, S., Fritz, T., Cramon, D. Y., Müller, K., and Friederici, A. D. (2006). Investigating emotion with music: an fMRI study. *Human Brain Mapping*, **27**, 239–50.

Koelsch, S., Remppis, A., Sammler, D., Jentschke, S., Mietchen, D., Fritz, T., Bonnemeier, H. and Siebel, W. A. (2007). A cardiac signature of emotionality. *European Journal of Neuroscience*, **26**, 3328–38.

Koelsch, S., Kilches, S., Steinbeis, N., and Schelinski, S. (2008a). Effects of unexpected chords and of performer's expression on brain responses and electrodermal activity. *PLoS One*, **3**, e2631.

Koelsch, S., Fritz, T., and Schlaug, G. (2008b). Amygdala activity can be modulated by unexpected chord functions during music listening. *NeuroReport*, **19**, 1815–19.

Koelsch, S., Offermanns, K., and Franzke, P. (2010a). Music in the treatment of affective disorders: an exploratory investigation of a new method for music-therapeutic research. *Music Perception*, **27**, 307–16.

Koelsch, S., Siebel, W. A., and Fritz, T. (2010b). Functional neuroimaging. In P. Juslin and J. A. Sloboda (eds), *Handbook of Music and Emotion: Theory, Research, Applications*, 2nd edn, pp. 313–46. Oxford: Oxford University Press.

Koelsch, S., Fuermetz, J., Sack, U., Bauer, K., Hohenadel, M., Wiegel, M., Kaisers, U. X., and Heinke, W. (2011). Effects of music listening on cortisol levels and propofol consumption during spinal anesthesia. *Frontiers in Psychology*, **2**, 1–9.

Konečni, V. (2003). Review of *Music and Emotion: Theory and Research*. *Music Perception*, **20**, 332–41.

Kringelbach, M., Jenkinson, N., Owen, S., and Aziz, T. (2007). Translational principles of deep brain stimulation. *Nature Reviews Neuroscience*, **8**, 623–35.

LeDoux, J. (2000). Emotion circuits in the brain. *Annual Review of Neuroscience*, **23**, 155–84.

Levinson, J. (1990). *Music and Negative Emotion*. Ithaca, NY: Cornell University Press.

Levinson, J. (2004). Musical chills and other delights of music. In J. Davidson (ed.), *The Music Practitioner: Research for the Music Performer, Teacher, and Listener*, pp. 335–52. Farnham: Ashgate Publishing Ltd.

Lundqvist, L.O., Carlsson, F., Hilmersson, P., and Juslin, P.N. (2009) Emotional responses to music: experience, expression, and physiology. *Psychology of Music*, **37**, 61–90.

MacLean, P. (1952). Some psychiatric implications of physiological studies on frontotemporal portion of limbic system (visceral brain). *Electroencephalography and Clinical Neurophysiology*, **4**, 407–18.

MacLean, P. (1972). Cerebral evolution and emotional processes: new findings on the striatal complex. *Annals of the New York Academy of Sciences*, **193**, 137–49.

MacLean, P. (1990). *The Triune Brain in Evolution: Role in Paleocerebral Functions*. New York: Plenum Press.

McGaugh, J. and Roozendaal, B. (2002). Role of adrenal stress hormones in forming lasting memories in the brain. *Current Opinion in Neurobiology*, **12**, 205–10.

Menon, V. and Levitin, D. (2005). The rewards of music listening: response and physiological connectivity of the mesolimbic system. *NeuroImage*, **28**, 175–84.

Messner, B., Jipson, A., Becker, P., and Byers, B. (2007). The hardest hate: a sociological analysis of country hate music. *Popular Music and Society*, **30**, 513–31.

Meyer, L. (1956). *Emotion and Meaning in Music*. Chicago: University of Chicago Press.

Mitterschiffthaler, M. T., Fu, C. H., Dalton, J. A., Andrew, C. M., and Williams, S. C. (2007). A functional MRI study of happy and sad affective states evoked by classical music. *Human Brain Mapping*, **28**, 1150–62.

Moors, A. and Kuppens, P. (2008). Distinguishing between two types of musical emotions and reconsidering the role of appraisal. *Behavioral and Brain Sciences*, **31**, 588–89.

Müller, M., Höfel, L., Brattico, E., and Jacobsen, T. (2010). Aesthetic judgments of music in experts and laypersons—an ERP study. *International Journal of Psychophysiology*, **76**, 40–51.

Nadel, L. (2008). Hippocampus and context revisited. In S. Mizumori (ed.), *Hippocampal Place Fields: Relevance to Learning and Memory*, pp. 3–15. New York: Oxford University Press.

Nicola, S. (2007). The nucleus accumbens as part of a basal ganglia action selection circuit. *Psychopharmacology*, **191**, 521–50.

Nieuwenhuys, R., Voogd, J., and Huijzen, C. V. (2008). *The Human Central Nervous System*. Berlin: Springer.

Noy, P. (1993). How music conveys emotion. In S. Feder, R. Karmel, and G. Pollock (eds), *Psychoanalytic Explorations in Music*, pp. 125–49. Madison, CT: International Universities Press.

Oitzl, M., Champagne, D., van der Veen, R., and de Kloet, E. (2010). Brain development under stress: hypotheses of glucocorticoid actions revisited. *Neuroscience and Biobehavioral Reviews*, **34**, 853–66.

Olds, J. (1958). Self-stimulation of the brain: its use to study local effects of hunger, sex, and drugs. *Science*, **127**, 315–24.

Orini, M., Bailón, R., Enk, R., Koelsch, S., Mainardi, L., and Laguna, P. (2010). A method for continuously assessing the autonomic response to music-induced emotions through HRV analysis. *Medical and Biological Engineering and Computing*, **48**, 423–33.

Overy, K. and Molnar-Szakacs, I. (2009). Being together in time: musical experience and the mirror neuron system. *Music Perception*, **26**, 489–504.

Panksepp, J. (1995). The emotional sources of "chills" induced by music. *Music Perception*, **13**, 171–207.

Panksepp, J. (1998). *Affective Neuroscience: the Foundations of Human and Animal Emotions*. New York: Oxford University Press.

Papez, J. (1937). A proposed mechanism of emotion. *Archives of Neurology and Psychiatry*, **38**, 725–43.

Patel, A. (2006). Musical rhythm, linguistic rhythm, and human evolution. *Music Perception*, **24**, 99–103.

Patel, A. (2008). *Music, Language, and the Brain*. Oxford: Oxford University Press.

Perlovsky, L. (2007). Neural dynamic logic of consciousness: the knowledge instinct. In L. Perlovsky and R. Kozma (eds), *Neurodynamics of Cognition and Consciousness*, pp. 73–108. Berlin: Springer.

Phelps, E. (2004). Human emotion and memory: interactions of the amygdala and hippocampal complex. *Current Opinion in Neurobiology*, **14**, 198–202.

Platel, H., Baron, J., Desgranges, B., Bernard, F., and Eustache, F. (2003). Semantic and episodic memory of music are subserved by distinct neural networks. *NeuroImage*, **20**, 244–56.

Ploog, D. (2003). The place of the Triune Brain in psychiatry. *Physiology and Behavior*, **79**, 487–93.

Rainville, P. (2002). Brain mechanisms of pain affect and pain modulation. *Current Opinion in Neurobiology*, **12**, 195–204.

Rilling, J., Gutman, D., Zeh, T., Pagnoni, G., Berns, G., and Kilts, C. (2002). A neural basis for social cooperation. *Neuron*, **35**, 395–405.

Roeling, T., Veening, J., Kruk, M., Peters, J., Vermelis, M., and Nieuwenhuys, R. (1994). Efferent connections of the hypothalamic "aggression area" in the rat. *Neuroscience*, **59**, 1001–24.

Salas, C., Broglio, C., and Rodrguez, F. (2003). Evolution of forebrain and spatial cognition in vertebrates: conservation across diversity. *Brain, Behavior and Evolution*, **62**, 72–82.

Salimpoor, V., Benovoy, M., Larcher, K., Dagher, A., and Zatorre, R. (2011). Anatomically distinct dopamine release during anticipation and experience of peak emotion to music. *Nature Neuroscience*, **14**, 257–62.

Sammler, D., Grigutsch, M., Fritz, T., and Koelsch, S. (2007). Music and emotion: electrophysiological correlates of the processing of pleasant and unpleasant music. *Psychophysiology*, **44**, 293–304.

Scherer, K. (2001). Appraisal considered as a process of multilevel sequential checking. In K. Scherer, A. Schorr, and T. Johnstone (eds), *Appraisal Processes in Emotion: Theory, Methods, Research*, pp. 120–44. New York: Oxford University Press.

Scherer, K. (2004). Which emotions can be evoked by music? What are the underlying mechanisms? And how can we measure them? *Journal of New Music Research*, **33**, 239–51.

Scherer, K. and Zentner, M. (2001). Emotional effects of music: production rules. In P. Juslin and J. A. Sloboda (eds), *Music and Emotion: Theory and Research*, pp. 361–92. Oxford: Oxford University Press.

Scherer, K. and Zentner, M. (2008). Music evoked emotions are different–more often aesthetic than utilitarian (comment). *Behavioral and Brain Sciences*, **31**, 595–96.

Schön, D., Ystad, S., Kronland-Martinet, R., and Besson, M. (2010). The evocative power of sounds: conceptual priming between words and nonverbal sounds. *Journal of Cognitive Neuroscience*, **22**, 1026–35.

Siebel, W. (1994). *Human Interaction*. Langwedel: Glaser.

Siebel, W. (2009). Thalamic contentedness. *Interdis—Journal for Interdisciplinary Research*, **2**, 37–9.

Siebel, W. and Winkler, T. (1996). *Noosomatik V: Noologie, Neurologie, Kardiologie*, 2nd edn. Wiesbaden: Glaser.

Siebel, W. A., Winkler, T., and Seitz-Bernhard, B. (1990). *Noosomatik I: Theoretische Grundlegung.* Langwedel: Glaser und Wohlschlegel.

Singer, T. and Lamm, C. (2009). The social neuroscience of empathy. *Annals of the New York Academy of Sciences*, **1156**, 81–96.

Slevc, L., Rosenberg, J., and Patel, A. (2009). Making psycholinguistics musical: self-paced reading time evidence for shared processing of linguistic and musical syntax. *Psychonomic Bulletin and Review*, **16**, 374–81.

Sloboda, J. A. (1991). Music structure and emotional response: some empirical findings. *Psychology of Music*, **19**, 110–20.

Squire, L., Wixted, J., and Clark, R. (2007). Recognition memory and the medial temporal lobe: a new perspective. *Nature Reviews Neuroscience*, **8**, 872–83.

Stahl, S. (2002). Does depression hurt? *Journal of Clinical Psychiatry*, **63**, 273–304.

Stein, M., Koverola, C., Hanna, C., Torchia, M., and McClarty, B. (1997). Hippocampal volume in women victimized by childhood sexual abuse. *Psychological Medicine*, **27**, 951–9.

Steinbeis, N. and Koelsch, S. (2008a). Comparing the processing of music and language meaning using EEG and FMRI provides evidence for similar and distinct neural representations. *PLoS One*, **3**, e2226.

Steinbeis, N. and Koelsch, S. (2008b). Shared neural resources between music and language indicate semantic processing of musical tension-resolution patterns. *Cerebral Cortex*, **18**, 1169–78.

Steinbeis, N. and Koelsch, S. (2008c). Understanding the intentions behind man-made products elicits neural activity in areas dedicated to mental state attribution. *Cerebral Cortex*, **19**, 619–23.

Steinbeis, N. and Koelsch, S. (2011). Affective priming effects of musical sounds on the processing of word meaning. *Journal of Cognitive Neuroscience*, **23**, 604–21.

Steinbeis, N., Koelsch, S., and Sloboda, J. (2006). The role of harmonic expectancy violations in musical emotions: evidence from subjective, physiological, and neural responses. *Journal of Cognitive Neuroscience*, **18**, 1380–93.

Tillmann, B., Koelsch, S., Escoffier, N., Bigand, E., Lalitte, P. Friederici, A. D., and Von Cramon, D. Y. (2006). Cognitive priming in sung and instrumental music: activation of inferior frontal cortex. *Neuroimage*, **31**, 1771–82.

Tomasello, M., Carpenter, M., Call, J., Behne, T., and Moll, H. (2005). Understanding and sharing intentions: the origins of cultural cognition. *Behavioral and Brain Sciences*, **28**, 675–91.

Tracey, I. (2005). Nociceptive processing in the human brain. *Current Opinion in Neurobiology*, **15**, 478–87.

Trehub, S. (2003). The developmental origins of musicality. *Nature Neuroscience*, **6**, 669–73.

Trost, W., Ethofer, T., Zentner, M., and Vuilleumier, P. (2012). Mapping aesthetic musical emotions in the brain. *Cerebral Cortex*, **22**, 2769–83.

Turner, J. (2000). *On the Origins of Human Emotions: a Sociological Inquiry into the Evolution of Human Affect.* Stanford, CA: Stanford University Press.

Videbech, P. and Ravnkilde, B. (2004). Hippocampal volume and depression: a meta-analysis of MRI studies. *American Journal of Psychiatry*, **161**, 1957–66.

Warner-Schmidt, J. and Duman, R. (2006). Hippocampal neurogenesis: opposing effects of stress and antidepressant treatment. *Hippocampus*, **16**, 239–49.

Wiech, K., Ploner, M., and Tracey, I. (2008). Neurocognitive aspects of pain perception. *Trends in Cognitive Sciences*, **12**, 306–13.

Wiltermuth, S. and Heath, C. (2009). Synchrony and cooperation. *Psychological Science*, **20**, 1–5.

Zajonc, R. (2001). Mere exposure: a gateway to the subliminal. *Current Directions in Psychological Science*, **10**, 224–8.

Zentner, M., Grandjean, D., and Scherer, K. (2008). Emotions evoked by the sound of music: characterization, classification, and measurement. *Emotion*, **8**, 494–521.

Section 3

The powers of music

Chapter 18

Section introduction

Bernardino Fantini

Music plays, and has apparently always played, a significant role in individual and collective human life, especially on occasions of emotionally intense events and socially relevant activities. No culture or historical period, past or present, is devoid of music in its diverse forms or traditions. The reason for this pervasiveness seems to be linked to the extraordinary power music has over the physiological mechanisms of the human body and over mental processes. Raising and controlling emotions, or, according to the vocabulary of the period, passions or affects, has been an essential object of study for music theory and a constant aim of music making throughout history.

The third section of this volume explores from an interdisciplinary perspective, but with a particular historical interest, the ways in which different cultures have sought to manage or manipulate the emotional power of music and how philosophy, medicine, and music theory have interpreted the causes of such a formidable power. Historical analyses provide a sense of how musical activities have been socially embedded, particularly as such activities reflect alternative conceptions of the nature and power of music, but also the interpretative models of the emotional power of music based on the concepts, beliefs, and metaphors present in a given culture.

In Chapter 19, Bernardino Fantini discusses the use of music as a metaphor for various non-musical phenomena, as well as the use of metaphors or analogies to provide some insights into the nature of music. In diverse historical periods, music, science, and medicine seem to have shared the same fundamental "epistemic styles" or "forms of thought," the same interpretive models of natural phenomena, the same metaphors and images. Concepts like "mechanism," "harmony," "cycle," or "arrow" play a metaphorical role in the elaboration of theories, which each era suggests as general models of natural or artificial systems. These metaphors are not, or are not only, rhetorical artifices, but have a heuristic role since they can specify and make more comprehensible the fundamental theoretical paradoxes of thought, suggesting some general interpretative models. For example, the metaphor of the "arrow of time" provides a possible definition of enigmatic concept of "time," as it suggests the one-way flow, "asymmetry," or irreversibility of time in physics and the idea of an evolutionary pathway for explaining the diversity of living beings.

In order to illustrate this, Fantini considers two "models of living" or definitions of life. The metaphor of "elementary fibers," developed in the 17th century identifies the "elementary fiber" as the ultimate element in the organization of the body and as the headquarters of all physiological function, including motility and sensibility. The second metaphor is the idea of the "organism" or "economy," which became central at the end of the 18th century with the origin of biology as a specific scientific domain. This model explains the essential properties of living organisms on the basis of a "complex, harmonious, and balanced organization," which constructs itself from a seed. In music, the model of "elementary fibers" always in movement in a sort of "perpetuum mobile" suggests a physical response of the body to the vibrations of sound, resulting in an alteration of emotional status. In the Baroque period what characterizes both music and living systems is movement, and the correspondence between the movements of music and the movements of bodies seemed a natural basis for the emotional power of music. Starting from the Classical period, form instead of movement became the fundamental property of a musical composition. A form is the result of the dynamic equilibrium within a complex structure, which derives from a theme (a "germ") and develops in a series of tension-building and relaxing moments. This produced a direct link between the representation of emotion in musical structure and the emotional effects of music.

Before the Scientific Revolution, which started in the 17th century and produced the two explanatory models discussed by Fantini, the philosophical and musicological panorama was dominated by the classical theory of the elements and humors and by the Platonic and Aristotelian philosophical systems. Philosophers, physicians, as well as theologians agreed on the idea that music itself possesses emotive properties, in its composition and structure. As wine or a drug can produce an exalted or lethargic state of the mind, music also can have a "psychotropic" power, which needs to be controlled in order to maintain the "social order." The theoretical and political aspects of the classical theories on the emotional power of music are discussed in the chapters contributed by Laurence Wuidar, Brenno Boccadoro, and Penelope Gouk.

In Chapter 20 Laurence Wuidar presents an overview of the historical debate on music and emotion, from the period of ancient Greece up to the Baroque theories of *Affektenlehre*. The author explains how certain conceptions of emotions and their relation to music were dominant during these periods, focusing particularly on the religious and medical discourse of the Renaissance concerning the power of music on the soul and body. Aristotle assumed Plato's ethical and educational considerations while also devoting part of his philosophical reflection on music to its hedonistic dimension, as music generates an intense pleasure. This explains why it was believed necessary in musical, medical, and political circles to control the production of music. The second part of Wuidar's chapter is then centered on specific cases with regard to the relationship between music, medicine, and theology, including the relationship between music and demonology found in the theological and medical literature. In particular, in order to control the hedonistic aspects of music, priority had to be given to the text. Music emotional effectiveness should serve and enrich the discourse, enabling holy words fully to penetrate the soul and body of the faithful.

The power of musical discourse was modeled on ancient rhetoric, not only with respect to the alliance between text and sound but equally with respect to the figures carried by pure sound. The so-called *Figurenlehre* could be defined as a system of associations between musical "nouns" and affections. A "grammar of the affects" also constitutes the core of the arguments used by Renaissance humanists to explain the emotional power of music, using at the same time musical and medical concepts, as discussed in Chapter 21 by Brenno Boccadoro. According to the neo-Platonic philosophy of Marsilio Ficino, harmony acts on the inferior faculties of the soul, which are independent of the will. In this context, Boccadoro discusses a few classical myths of the musical treatment of "excessus mentis," that is a deep alteration of the psychic equilibrium, as in fury or ecstasy. The fundamental idea is that harmony is a concordance of discordant (*crasis*) opposites, a conciliation of antagonistic qualities, which parallels the crasis of the humors in the body. This suggests an "elementary" conception of musical grammar, analogous to the physics of elements and the medicine of the humors. The same elementary conception characterizes the "elements of musical grammar" combined in the body of the melody. The theory of affects assumed by humanists, based on the heritage of the ancient theories, rests on the simple principle of imitation and correspondence: the transfer of forms across different domains. Renaissance theorists attribute the qualities of harmony to the soul and qualities of the soul to harmony. Thanks to this parallelism, the forms of expression of major passions, like anger or melancholy, encourage constant and easily traceable rhetorical expressions in the musical repertoire of Renaissance and early Baroque music. In such a way, the theory of affects in music becomes an ensemble of objective criteria, a method, and a series of shared rules.

The use of music as a tool for social control is the focus of Chapter 22 by Penelope Gouk. According to Gouk the power of music to affect people's "passions" was a commonplace of Renaissance thought, even though the physiological and psychological underpinnings of this power were not to become the focus of medical attention until the Enlightenment. This belief implicitly informed early modern efforts to regulate the potentially disruptive influence of music on individuals and collectivities. Like other authors in this section, Gouk highlights the relevance of the Aristotelian idea that "music is capable of creating a particular quality of character in the soul." Discussing a series of examples from late 16th-century France and mid-18th century Scotland the chapter explores the extent to which early modern Europeans considered music as a vehicle for achieving social transformation through control of the passions. In agreement with the medical theories of the time, music's power over the passions is explained in terms of its effects on the central nervous system, as music can alter the level of sensibility and excitation of the nerves by virtue of the impressions it makes on the ear. An excessive sensibility led to nervous disorders such as melancholia and other diseases associated with luxury, hence the need for proper regulation of music "under the direction of taste and philosophy."

The direct use of music in a medical context is the basis of the old tradition of music therapy, which underwent a radical resurgence of interest in the 18th century. This social and cultural phenomenon is discussed in Chapter 23 by Jackie Pigeaud, who isolates three different traditions of music therapy, attributed to the traditional figures of Asclepius, Herophilus, and to the biblical narrative of Saul and David. Asclepius cured "frenetics" (that is, the insane) with the aid of the *symphonia*, an instrumental musical composition. The physician Herophilus, the first to measure the pulse, found in the movement and regular beat of the body the target of the efficacy of the music. Finally, Saul's hypochondriac or hysterical condition found an effective relief in music, thanks to the "antagonism" between the pathological condition of the soul and the equilibrating harmony of music.

Analyses of the medical, literary, and philosophical writings of the 18th century allow us to perceive the importance accorded to "iatric" music in this period. In this context, attention was mainly directed towards two diseases, tarantism and nostalgia. The first appeared to be a physical malady and the second a moral malady, but both, in different fashions, showed the influence of music on human behavior.

A careful and original analysis of the introduction into the medical discourse of the concept of nostalgia and its influence across the 18th and 19th centuries is given in Chapter 24 by Jean Starobinski. The author underlines how, despite looking the same, an emotion, once named, is no longer exactly the same. A new word brings order to the unknown, which before had no form. A name brings with it a concept, with a precise definition, that calls forth additional definitions: it becomes a material for tests and experiments. There are few occasions where one finds terms destined to be added to the emotional lexicon, but this is the case for the word "nostalgia," which designated a pathological entity suffered by Swiss soldiers when they had "lost the sweetness of their homeland." Even though it can produce direct negative influences on the body, nostalgia was understood as a derangement of the imagination, as a pain of the memory. The fragment of a melody heard in the past suffices to exacerbate the suffering. A "little phrase," a simple popular melody, like the "Ranz des vaches," had the singular power of provoking the illusion of seeing a countryside from the past, doubled by the painful emotions of separation. However, in the heard melody there is no objective content, or specific figure, able to cause such a sentiment. Music is only a "*signe mémoratif*" (Rousseau), a call of memories of the past, and its emotional power results from a conventional association between the present condition and past experiences.

Finally, in Chapter 25, Ulrik Volgsten discusses the emotional power of music in a very modern context, the potential endangerment of individual and collective identities threatened by the various agreements for the protection of the intellectual property (copyright). Music is an important component in the construction and development of human identity, both on an individual and collective level, thanks to its affective and emotional qualities. Volgsten accordingly suggests that these identity functions can be severely restricted by today's copyright laws, because music becomes subject to the private rights of multinational corporations and media conglomerates and loses its independence as a dynamic cultural expression and individual "self-object." Volgsten argues that the emotional responses to music can be explained by viewing music listening as an embodied experience that engages sensory–motor processes. He states that since music simply wouldn't exist without the embodied engagement of the listeners, any claim to the rights of music that disregards the listener must be rejected as anticultural and contrary to the definition of music as an emotional experience.

The contributions by the authors in this section provide exciting new insights and hypotheses on the historical role of music in individual life and collective behavior. Future advances on this important issue depend on a much higher degree of collaboration and exchange between scholars coming from different disciplinary perspectives and interested in the reconstruction of the emotional role of music through history. Careful historical investigations can contribute widely to the present-day questionings about the nature of music and the causes and modalities of its strong emotional power. The answers provided in the different historical periods by the different philosophical, medical, and musical traditions to fundamental questions like "What are the mechanisms of action of the 'emotional power of music'? Are they physiological, psychological, or socio-cultural? What is the nature of the emotions embodied in or produced by music? How does music produce and/or communicate emotions at the level of the composer, the performer, and the listener?" can be of a great utility.

Of particular note is the historical tradition of providing specific rhetorical figures in the conveyance of emotions. Current approaches to musical expression tend to eschew this degree of specificity, appealing instead to generalized musical features such as tempo or instrumental attack. Perhaps agreement on rhetorical figures will emerge in the future. But certainly when it comes to appreciating the music of the past, we must acknowledge the extent to which participants in music engage with the musical conventions of their times and the ways these may overlap with more "natural" sources of affect. A similar concern must be recognized with regards to the relationship between global formal structures (the difference, say, between sonata or binary form) and emotional impact.

Also worth noting is the continuity of belief in the therapeutic powers of music. Further exploration and confirmation of these powers is an ongoing concern, and we should expect to see future research closely examining the kinds of disorders that music can effectively alleviate, as well as the general impact of musical engagement on the development of psychological capacities. Again, the role of music in social coordination, while embraced by cultures across the world, has yet to be fully tackled by scientific methodologies.

Overall, the questions highlighted here underline the importance of multidisciplinary research on the relationship between music and the emotions. Accurate historical analyses, based on the multiplication of well-documented case studies, can isolate the main discontinuities in the understanding of the emotional power of music and the emergence of the various interpretative models on the nature of music, its meaning, and its emotional power.

Chapter 19

Forms of thought between music and science

Bernardino Fantini (translation by Kristen Gray Jafflin)

Introduction

The relationship between music and science has been analyzed, studied, or parsed on several levels throughout the centuries. First mention should be given to the direct use of scientific knowledge in musical theory—in the numerical, Pythagorean formulations of harmony and consonance, in the application of geometrical propositions in Renaissance-era treatises, in musical references during the Scientific Revolution[i] and in the use of computers and of chaos theory in composition.

A second level of analysis is found in the scientific study of the influence of music and in attempts to explain the "reasons for musical emotions" based on physiological and psychophysiological models. This theme, which is found in Greco-Roman culture, fascinated people in the 16th and 17th centuries (Ettmüller 1714; Browne 1729; Albrecht 1734; Bachmann 1792), notably in discussions on the extraordinary effect of music on people suffering from tarantula bites—a subject that received great attention from many famous doctors (Senguerdius 1667; Platner 1669; Grube 1679; Albinus 1691; Baglivi 1696a, pp. 539–80; Vallerius 1702/1999; Mead 1774, pp. 133–51).[ii] Doctors and physicians sought to give a scientific response to the question that Shakespeare poetically expressed in *Much Ado About Nothing*: "Now divine air! Now is his soul ravished! It is not strange that sheep's guts should hale souls out of men's bodies?" The search for the reasons behind music and, more generally, the psychological and physiological effect of musical sounds on humans and their behavior found its apogee in Helmholtz's work (Helmholtz 1870, 1877, 1995); even in the 21st century this subject has excited the interest of psychiatrists, ethnologists, and anthropologists, and even more recent research on cerebral localizations.

A third level of contact between music, science, and medicine is clearly found in the application of music to therapy (i.e. music therapy), which seems to date back to the first forms of civilization and of therapeutic relations. Such applications have also excited great interest in the domain of studies of "alternative" therapies and medicine.

These different connections between music, science, and medicine have endlessly fascinated musicologists, historians, and theoreticians, notably because of the immutable loosening of disciplinary boundaries. Nevertheless, there exists another level of interaction between these topics which is less well known, and which, after a cursory examination, seems to be fundamental, at least during certain historical periods. This level, which we can define as epistemic, concerns the use by music and science of the same "styles of thoughts," of the same interpretive models, and of the same metaphors and images. It concerns a series of common elements that are often not defined with precision and are sometimes inconsistent, but that are shared in a given culture, producing a series of common elements, which form a sort of territory allowing communication and "objective" evaluation, with reciprocal and constant exchanges between the different domains of knowledge.

The philosophy of science has widely shown the fundamental role that "forms of thought," styles of explanation, images, and metaphors play in scientific creation and communication. The idea of style was widely diffused in musical and musicological treatises, considering that the term "style" included elements of communication, writing, and method (forms of notation, social practices, interactions with technology and with the physiology of performers, etc.).[iii] A style is needed to encompass constructive methods, forms of communication, and criteria for the evaluation of results, for music and for science; these are, by definition, necessarily public and collective activities (even at the level of social organization), lending an enormous, central space to individual creativity.

Notions like "mechanism," "harmony," "cycle," or "arrow" are metaphors in the elaboration of the theories which each era needs as general models of natural or artificial systems. Each era has its emblematic metaphors and, in modern science, Galilean mechanics and the chemical laboratory have the same function as Julien Offroy de la Mettrie's machine man, Albrecht von Haller's sensibility and irritability, Charles Darwin's fight for life, Ernst Haeckel's primordial plasma, or even the telephone exchange, the computer, or the computer program for biology in the 20th century. These metaphors are not, or are not only, rhetorical artifices, but have a heuristic role since they specify the fundamental theoretical paradoxes of thought, suggesting a general interpretive model that can be contradicted by theories or observations. And if the proposed models and interpretative solutions change radically, due to scientific revolutions, the perception of fundamental paradoxes can establish continuities with contemporary theorizing. According to this point of view, it is useful to break with the historical schema, which tends exclusively to stress discontinuity, discoveries, and revolutions, and, on the contrary, to seek the continuity that underlies these changes.[iv]

When we speak of continuity, we evidently are not referring to the persistence of proposed theoretical solutions, given that these solutions are progressively abandoned, but rather to the persistence of perceived problems and ideological schemas, which are all the result of observations and theoretical elaboration. Knowledge consists not only of facts and empirical evidence but also of problems, hypotheses, paradoxes, innovations, and surprises. Changes in "paradigms," in style, in revolutionary moments in the development of science, as in that of art, are also moments of re-evaluation, of representation of old aporiae.

In order to illustrate this, one could consider two "models of life," which were of great importance in the history of biology and medicine and which also played a fundamental role in the history of musical theory. The first model is that of "elementary fibers," which was found in the medical domain in antiquity but which was more thoroughly worked up after the development of "microscopic anatomy" in the 17th century. This idea, built on microscopic, anatomical observations, identifies the "elementary fiber" as the ultimate element in the organization of the body and as the headquarters of all physiological function, including motility and sensibility. The second example concerns the idea of the "organism" or "economy," also present in classical antiquity as an interpretative model, but which became central in the second half of the 18th century. This model explains the essential properties of living organisms on the basis of a "complex, harmonious, and balanced organization," which constructs itself from a seed.

The theory of fibers

In the 17th century, "solidist" theories, which were opposed to the traditional Galenic humoral theories, explained the normal and pathological functions of living beings according to differences in the form of solids or of elementary particles. This was after the development of microscopic observations, which had shown a complex weft beneath the apparent homogeneity of surface organs. Therefore, the fundamental idea of medical physiology became the reduction of an organ's vital functions to the movements of miniscule machines, connected together in a complicated but well-regulated edifice.

The anatomists, who came to discover the "fabric of the body," its parts, and their connections along with Versale, had a tendency to conceive of the organism as a perfectly built and balanced mechanical structure, ready to act by means of springs and levers put into action through sensibility and contractility, by hydraulic pressure or by mass. In his *Zootomia democritaea*, Marc-Aurèle Severino (1645) proposed replacing the "dissectio" with the "resolutio ad minutum," the decomposition of the body into its constitutive elements, while Marcello Malpighi (1675) finalized this methodology in proposing a "structural anatomy." His disciple, Giogio Baglivi, who is considered to be the founder of the solidist school, revived the former methodological school and tied all physiological and pathological phenomena to quantitative variations in the "tones" of the body's solids, and especially its fibers (Baglivi 1700). As a consequence, doctors sought to apply the laws of mechanics to physiology, in studying forces, the resistance of fluids and solids, and the oscillation of fibers, rather than chemical processes. Finally, Giovanni Alfonso Borelli, the paradigmatic figure of "medical mathematics," applied statistics and mathematics to the theory of muscular movement and proposed mechanical explanations for the body's functions (Borelli 1710).

According to this type of explanation, everything is matter and motion in the sublunary world. Every susceptible person vibrates, and the body's fibers vibrate in unison with exterior movements. If love kindles and the heart burns and consumes itself for Monteverdi during the Renaissance, in the 17th century we vibrate with all our cords and we quiver with fury. The dynamic between warmth and coldness, typical of humoral medicine and of Renaissance music, was replaced by the dynamic "tension–release," typical of mechanical interpretations of life and form. The relationship between tension and release, specific to solidist medical schools, from the Hellenic era's Alexandrian school, had already generated many metaphors, even musical ones, in the past, and had been used by Boethius and Oresme in their interpretation of the states of the soul.[v] In metaphorical language, one associated the vibrations of a tightrope with the trembling produced by strong emotions like love, fury, and fear.

In the 1620s and 1630s, the discovery of the laws of vibration and the regularity of the pendulum's vibrations in the domain of physics almost immediately found an application in the study of vibrating cords (the laws of Mersenne) and in musical theory. Along with the other arts, music participated in the Scientific Revolution in furnishing problems and interpretive models. Ideas about music, about the nature of sound, about the reasons for its extraordinary effects, were integral parts of the repertoire of the intellectual elite of the 17th and 18th centuries—of the construction of a new image of the world, founded on the dynamics, the movement, the forces, and the physical nature of natural phenomena.

Francis Glisson (1672) introduced the idea of irritability in the second half of the 17th century, but it was mainly in the 18th century that it found such extraordinary success in the medical sciences, particularly thanks to Albrecht von Haller, who made it the central explanatory concept of his physiology (Haller 1751, 1756–60). The idea of irritability indicates a property that permits the different parts of the living body to react independently from the conscious mind, the central nervous system, and the whole of the organism. Vital forces, notably the capacity to respond to stimulation, are, so to speak, "decentred," even to the point that they become the characteristic property of the structural element of the body, the elementary fiber. Living, flexible, tensile, elastic, and above all irritable fibers are the seat and the cause of all reactions to exterior stimuli that produce expressions, emotions, and different vital phenomena. According to Haller, "fiber for the physiologist is like the line for the geometrician,"[vi] the measure allowing the whole of sensible objects to be built.

As early as the 19th century, the historian, Charles Daremberg, remarked that the displacement of stimulation to the level of fibers constituted an important change because "we began to no longer consider the faculties as beings residing in the parts, but as properties of those parts" (Daremberg 1870, p. 653).

Thus, the fibers found throughout the whole body, and not only inside the nervous system, react to sensory stimulations, to light, to colors, and to sounds. Music acts at two moments and in two manners, namely as a truly physical impact on sensitive fibers and as a cognitive and cultural activity, which elicits immediate stimulation based on the "memory" of past experiences. An immediate action, at the level of "diffuse sensibility" ("a music which knots the stomach"), is followed by a "mediated" action, based on the intellectual and emotional elaboration of memories and images ("such music makes us think or dream"). The "physicality" of sound and of its perception establishes a strict correspondence between the interior and the exterior, founded on the correspondence of vibrations. This correspondence is associated with the profound aesthetic and cultural significance of musical work. Therefore, music has two levels of action: physical and cognitive.

Objects, especially exterior movement like the movement of air provoked by the vibration of strings, imprint vibrations on the elementary fibers that form the nerves and the whole of the body. The sensation is assumed to be felt through the vibratory movement of nerves, such that madness is caused by confused vibrations or an excess of nerves. The same sympathetic relationship exists between the vibrations of instruments and that of nerves, which induce sensations, as that which induces a string to move when it is approached by a vibrating string.[vii]

The natural magic of numbers and proportions is replaced as the foundation of music by the materiality, the "physicality" of sound and vibrations, capable of "stirring the sentiments" and touching the "sensitive strings" of those listening. Attention to the purely physical nature of sound and of song, which showed itself above all in the fascination with the Baroque voice, is central to the aesthetic and social interpretation of music in the 17th and 18th centuries.

The medical theory that draws the most on music's effect on the body thanks to the "consonance" between musical vibrations and the vibrations of the body's fibers is that proposed by Giorgio Baglivi, who dedicated an essay to the phenomenon of tarantism, in magic as in medicine (Baglivi 1696a). Baglivi was a great clinical reformer (Baglivi 1696b) but equally a great anatomist. He was a disciple of Malpighi, who maintained that mechanical models of the structure of the body were the only heuristically fruitful ones and, in consequence, thought that all phenomena, physiological as well as pathological and mental, must be attributed to the structure and the movements of the parts of the body, of which the fiber constituted the elementary unit. According to Baglivi, the different body parts only appear to be at rest, because all the parts and elementary fibers are constantly in motion and, repose is the consequence of antagonistic activities, which cancel each other, as with the balance between two physical forces. The organism is represented as a machine formed of elementary fibers in perpetual oscillation, a horologium oscillatorium.[viii] Sensations are transmitted to the brain, which responds to them in regulating the body's action, thanks to an "oscillatio," an undulating movement allowing transmission through the nerves. Fibers oscillate "naturally," thanks to a "vis innata," an innate force that resides in the fibers themselves, and a "vis elastica," which acts as a spring (elater). The stimulating force, such as the circulation of blood, maintains these fibers in perpetual agitation, ready to react to "vibrations" that come from outside. Acute illnesses are due to an excess of "tension" in the fibers, whereas chronic illnesses are provoked by their relaxation. In limiting the properties and vital functions of these elementary fibers to their oscillations, Baglivi proposes a physically dynamic interpretation of life. Therefore, the body's parts are in "perpetual motion,"[ix] and it is unnecessary to specify how important the model of "perpetual motion" is to musical practice and theory in the Baroque period, between 1650 and 1750.

This theoretical model corresponds to a style of life, described by Jean Starobinski (1989) as the style "of all activities without end, which the 18th century shows us: whether it concerns the pursuit of pleasure, the expansion of commerce or the exploration of nature, no possession can ever be held as definitive, because the possession inscribes itself in the moment, and the moment immediately passes." The Baroque theoretical and aesthetic model, in art as in music, is not accumulation but dynamism: flexible and always varied movement, sinuous and perpetual, which could continue forever. The unity and coherence of the whole finds itself in the unique and unifying impulse, which directs all activities towards a common goal. The constancy and sinuosity of rhythm, the magnitude and interior vibrations of melodies, the materiality of vocal and instrumental timbres, and the movement produced by the harmonic tension between the tonic and the dominant all characterize Baroque music and constitute its individuality. The formal unity is the result of the succession and reunion of parts in movement. The driving force of Baroque music is the harmonic sequence, which ensures the continuity and direction of movement and advances a fluid and continuous rhythm, regular as a heartbeat, natural because it does not need exterior forces to sustain itself but seems to generate itself, an almost automatic movement because each phrase's movement contains the source of the movement of the succeeding phrase.

Scientific images are used in language and in literary and musical metaphors, and they remain even after the end of the scientific theory that gave birth to them. According to William Cooper, "Souls have a sympathy with sounds […]. Some string in us is touched in unison with what we hear, and the heart responds" (*The Task*, 1875). Madame Bovary, in Flaubert's eponymous novel (1857), "allowed herself to rock with the melodies and felt herself vibrate with all her being, as if the bows of the violins were drawn across her nerves."

The idea of organization

Starting in the second half of the 18th century, a new style of thought emerged in the domain of science, notably concerning the whole group of scientific problems that Jean-Baptist de Lamarck (1802) and Treviranus (1802) grouped under the name "biology." The new "discourse on life," which gained precision at the end of the 18th and the beginning of the 19th centuries, evinced a fundamental discontinuity in the history of biological and medical thought. This happened when the fundamental and constant aporia between form and matter, between mechanical or chemical processes and the processes and functions that seemed to achieve a precise finality between "inorganic" systems and "organized" systems, provoked the passage from a science of order, in which natural history and nosology had dominated, to a science of organization and of the dynamic processes at its base.

The traditional division of nature into three parts, namely the animal kingdom, the vegetable kingdom, and the mineral kingdom, was abandoned because, according to Lamarck, "through this division, the beings included in each of these kingdoms are compared to each other, as if they were on the same line, while some have an origin very different from other. I have found it more suitable to employ another primary division, because it allows one to better identify all the beings that are subject to it. Thus, I distinguish all natural productions included in the three kingdoms mentioned above, and I divide them, I say, into two principal branches: 1) into organized, living bodies, and 2) into inanimate, lifeless bodies."[x]

In the same manuscript, Lamarck defines the content of the new scientific discipline with precision:

> It is to these singular and truly admirable bodies that we give the name of living bodies; and the life that they possess, as well as the faculties that they acquire from it, essentially distinguishes them from the

other bodies of nature. They offer in themselves and in the diverse phenomena that they present the material for a specific science that has not yet been founded, which does not even have a name, of which I have proposed some bases in my Philosophie zoologique, and which I will name biology.

Living beings and organized bodies, animal and vegetable, constitute the first of these two branches. Lamarck goes on: "As everyone knows, these beings have the ability to nourish themselves, to develop and to reproduce, and are necessarily subject to death." Among the products of nature, there is "a multitude of particular bodies that, whatever difference there be between them, all have one manner of being, which is at once common to them and particular." These bodies have in common an "interior phenomenon that we call life" and all possess "an organization allowing this physical phenomenon to occur." In passing from inorganic systems to living systems, nature made a passage that created an unbridgeable gap. According to Lamarck, between raw materials and living bodies there is: "an immense hiatus which does not allow us to place these two sorts of bodies on the same line, and which makes one think that the origin of the one is very different from that of the other."

The *Dictionaire des sciences médicales*, which was extraordinarily popular during the first decades of the 19th century defines life as follows:

> Consequently, life is the mode of activity and existence for organized bodies, and it is characterized by the fact that beings belonging to it begin by being born, grow, end in death, and, over their lifespan, which is limited, maintain their individual life by nutrition and their life as a species by reproduction. Only organized bodies have life; minerals exist, but only vegetables and animals live. [...] In effect, vegetables and animals are both called organized or living bodies, depending on whether we are concerned with their mode of material composition, which is an organization, or with their mode of activity, which is a life. (Chaussier and Adelon 1819)

Biology and medicine are not sciences with a specific object that can be described in chemical or physical terms, but rather are sciences of relationships between these objects in space and time, relationships which find their theoretical principle in the notion of "organization" and, as a consequence, in that of evolution.

In his *Considérations sur les corps organisés*, Charles Bonnet (1762/1985), a Geneva-born naturalist, made a categorical distinction between "crystallization" and "organization":

> The two great operations of nature are organization and crystallization: when nature ceases to organize, it crystallizes. [...] We know that they have different origins and obtain growth in a different manner. Organized beings grow by intussusception[xi] and convert the matter with which they nourish themselves into their own substance. Crystallized beings only grow through the mechanical apposition of parts of the same type. The first are preformed and only their seed develops itself, the second are formed daily.

The chemical dynamic of life is "directed" by an organization, the seed, which realizes itself, constructs itself thanks to the subordination of the physical and chemical laws to a design, to its coherence as a whole. The seed is the organism in potentia, an a priori which realizes itself in an individual form over the course of its development.[xii]

In the medical domain, François-Xavier Bichat (1801) proposed the famous semi-tautological definition of life in his *Recherches physiologiques sur la vie et sur la mort*: "Life is the whole of functions which resist death." In effect, according to Bichat, inorganic bodies and forces act ceaselessly on living systems, eventually destroying them in consequence.[xiii] This occurs because living beings possess a permanent principle of reaction: "This principle is that of life; unknown in its nature, it can only be appreciated through its phenomena: however, the most general of these phenomena is this habitual alternative action on the part of external bodies" (Bichat 1801).

Even if Bichat carefully avoided formulating hypotheses regarding the nature of the principle that animates living beings, affirming that knowledge of first causes is not accessible to human beings, he considers equally necessary to study phenomena determined by this principle and the specific properties that it allots to the living matter in which it is present: "We can, without knowing the principle of life, analyze the properties of the organs animated by it."

In this era, an essential dualism is established in "life science" between "the principle" and "the properties." Life becomes an abstract entity, independent of the living being inside of which it manifests and realizes itself. First organization and then evolution by natural selection and genetic program insert themselves into the structures they guide and control the function and relationships between organs.

According to the embryologist Karl-Ernst von Baer, architectural considerations about the organism as a whole prevail over analytic factors and organic development; development presupposes that the life form's organic project exercises control over analytic factors: "the essence of the generative animal form conditions the offspring's development" (von Baer 1828–1837, p. 148). An initial blastema, animated by a nisus formativus, has the essential capacity to form organic structures.

This same style of thought characterizes the work of Johannes Müller, the physiologist who founded the German school of biology. To explain the permanence and development of organic forms he suggested the existence of an "essential force" and the organization's continuity over time, because the production of a new organism necessarily depends on the "creative force" of a pre-existing organism. There is a "pre-established harmony between the organization and the faculties… The seed is the all in potential and when it develops, all the integral parts appear in reality. […] The seed is gifted with an essential force, capable of increasing the minimum of this specific force and of the matter which accompanies it through the assimilation of matter" (Müller 1838–1840, p. 23).

Cellular theory would complete this hypothesis by associating an organism's development and function with the presence of a pre-existing organism of the same type: "omnis cellula a cellula" (Virchow 1855). That which is transferred from one cell to the next during reproduction is not matter but the organization's form. The particular disposition of all internal parts constitutes the foundation of the organization and thus of life. There are no longer "elementary fibers," but elementary organisms, cells, the whole of which forms the body. Nonetheless, each cell is in itself a distinct organism, which can have an independent life. The organism as a whole is no more than a "cellular republic," according to Virchow, a state formed by the association of individual cells.

Therefore, the seed contains in itself the possibilities for the construction of the individual, the realization of its form and functions. The living being's organization is the result of the "development" of an "idea," a "vital design." Each individual's life is the "realization of its project," the manifestation of all its possibilities, contained in a project transmitted at the moment of reproduction. And the seed contains its own end as well, because living beings have a birth, a development, and an end, a limit set in time and space, and they cannot endure forever as dynamic, organized processes. Each individual necessarily has a limited and specific lifespan, which will be determined by the nature of the seed that gave birth to it. In the same way, each biological species has a typical lifespan determined by its specific life cycle.

This new style of scientific explanation finds a fascinating parallel in a new aesthetic system, in a new principle of construction which emerges in music during this same historical period, so-called classical music, the period tied to the names of Haydn, Mozart, and Beethoven and based on the construction of the "sonata form," the principal formula for the construction of musical structure.

This form isn't built through apposition, as in sinuous Baroque sequences, but "from inside," from a "seed," which is an "idea" of the final form of the individual composition in its totality.

In Baroque music, we find a "grammar of affects" (Boccadoro 2004); we can isolate known and formalized representation (*Affektenlehre*) of particular emotions or of the complex emotions that succeed them. The sequence of affective representations—and the sequence is the Baroque form par excellence—resulted in a structure inside of which the play of all the representative elements was determined by the composer, and often the interpreter's, choices, according to their taste and the necessary duration of the piece. Each element was interchangeable with the others, on the sole condition of respecting the constraints imposed by the rules of composition. On the contrary, in "classical" music, starting in the second half of the 18th century, it is the organization's coherent ensemble that reunites the structural elements, the phrase, the harmonic successions, and the rhythms in a unique pattern.

Musical objects acquire their own organization, an internal architectural structure, which articulates the acoustic space and the temporality inside of which acoustic phenomena are produced. The form determines relationships of a new type between the elements of the composition, which depend on the organization's plan and must coexist inside the whole structure and respect an internal hierarchy. As with biological organisms, the modification of a part entails the need to modify all the other parts of the piece in order to respect the formal organizational plan.[xiv]

In the "new" music at the end of the 18th century, the phrase and the motif can still represent and be seen as a sign, a symbol of affect, of emotion. Therefore, an emotional grammar continues to maintain a sense and an importance not due to the nature of the elements comprising the piece themselves (intervals, harmony, timbre, etc.) but solely due to their relationship with the whole organization and the function that the theme serves inside that organization. Each motif or grammatical element preserves the power to represent an emotion, but this role no longer constitutes its nature, which is now that of holding a place inside a form, of tying itself to other phrases and motifs. Thus, the relationship between the different parts of the whole form determines the nature of each constitutive element.

In the sonata form, if a theme has a significance when it appears in an exposition it is not by virtue of its own characteristics but because it obeys formal rules which govern all the elements of the composition in its very form, in the tones comprising it, in the changes it undergoes according to the function it holds inside the form, and, finally, in the modifications it is subject to throughout its development. The theme is only tied to a representation in so far as it is part of the formal organization that, through its relationship to the theme, is first and foremost.

The famous ta-ta-ta-ta theme of Beethoven's *Fifth Symphony* has an intrinsic representative value, which corresponds to a classical rhetorical figure,[xv] but its formal value depends on the fact that the theme is the nisus formativus of the symphony, specific to this sole composition. As Arnold Schönberg (1967, p. 103) noted, "a theme is not at all independent and auto-determined. On the contrary, it is closely bound to consequences which must be grasped, and without which it is insignificant." Nevertheless, the theme is not really "insignificant," but has an expressive value in itself, that gesture which enables the incipit of the exposition, on which it imposes a direction and characteristics.

The form's construction is determined by the characters contained in embryonic form in the idea from which the composition draws its inspiration and dynamic force, which is capable of constructing the "development." This is why each composition is individual, an "organic whole" like a biological individual, different from all others because its characteristics are determined by the "project" contained in the idea, the seed, and, as a result, it is necessarily unique.

The new notion of form, which articulates itself at the end of the 18th and the beginning of the 19th centuries, underscores the coherence and organization of the whole 'organism', the internal logic that animates a work of art, as it animates a biological individual. A composition's intrinsic logic connects each constitutive element to all the others, and the logic of the whole construction is privileged through its relationship with each event. Each element finds its value in its relationship with the whole, and each event is evaluated according to its integration into the whole. This is why even banal elements, like a little theme of four notes "which knocks at the door," a small military march, a cry in the street, a waltz in the salon, takes on a new, stronger signification at the heart of the general form of an individual composition.

Each composition becomes an individual; it is no longer possible to use one opera's aria or one instrumental composition's movement in another work or symphony, as was habitually done in the 18th century, because each part of a composition is directly derived from the seed and tied to the "whole" of the organization, outside of which it loses its characteristics and value. Because, in a musical composition, the development is determined by the very nature of the idea, the theme, the seed, which is its directing idea, the form has specific boundaries, it cannot be an endless sequence. Once all the potential for development inherent in the seed that determined the form and functions of the whole is exhausted, the structure and the dynamic cannot continue forever, which was, in principle, the case in Baroque music. Instead, once accomplished, its project must necessarily come to an end.

The definition of music as "organized sound,"[xvi] equally common in modern day treatises, has a significance which goes beyond a superficial reading, thanks to the complexity of the idea of "organization." At the foundation of the musical form, there are rules of organization and development for musical matter that determine the interior tempo of a form that grows according to its own needs and develops according to specific rules.

The coherence and autonomy of a composition are determined by the internal legality, by the formulae of organization that can be tied to a musical style, which is the case for the sonata form, or to each particular composition, as in the music of the 20th century. In effect, during the present era, the existence of a specific "formula of organization" still remains the sole organizing principle, a principle that seems to be permanent in a world where all constitutive and formal elements are put into question.

The theoretical and practical elements of "internal legality" present in a composition allow a subsequent and conclusive confrontation between musical thought and biomedical thought, yet again centered around the idea of organization. The famous physiologist and epistemologist Claude Bernard discusses the theoretical bases of biological organization in detail:

> Organization results from a mixing up of complex substances reacting on each other. For us, it is the arrangement that gives birth to the living matter's immanent properties. This arrangement is special and very complex but nevertheless does obey the general chemical laws of the grouping of matter. In reality, vital properties are only the physicochemical properties of organized matter. (Bernard 1878/1966, pp. 32–3)

In seizing on the paradox, Bernard seems to ask himself what ensures the maintenance of the form, the continuity of the organization, what determines the "vital properties?" What ensures the "internal legality?" He answers these questions by proposing a theoretical dualism that distinguishes "physico-chemical conditions" from "morphogenetic laws."

Vital phenomena have their rigorously determined physico-chemical conditions, but, at the same time, they are subordinated and follow each other in a chain, following a law fixed in advance: they repeat themselves eternally with order and regularity and harmonize themselves to achieve a result, which is the organization and the growth of the individual animal or vegetable (Bernard 1878/1966, p. 51).

Returning to and developing Xavier Bichat's famous metaphor, Bernard affirms that "life is a conflict" and its manifestations result from the two factors: "pre-established laws," due to atavism or heredity, which determine phenomena related to succession, to agreement, and to harmony, and fixed "physico-chemical conditions," necessary for the production of phenomena (Bernard 1878/1966, p. 66). Even if laboratory-based experimental physiology could totally control "physico-chemical conditions," it could not master morphogenetic laws, which result from the "prior state" of biological systems, transmitted through heredity. Claude Bernard concludes by saying that, because of this, certain philosophers and physiologists could write that life is only a memory: "the seed seems to preserve the memory of the organism that proceeds it" (Bernard 1878/1966, p. 66).

It is this seed, the carrier of heredity, that establishes the "internal legality," as Louis Pasteur would affirm with his "germ theory":

> Life is the seed with its future, and the seed is life. Life cannot be defined. What we can say most clearly is that it is the seed and its future. To ask where it comes from is to ask where the seed comes from (Pasteur 1922–1939, p. 29)

Life results from a unique and unifying impulse, which directs all activities towards a common end. The unity of the form, in biology as in music, results from the succession and the reunion of parts in movement in an organic whole.

However, this "organic whole" is not really a vital force, because it does not actively interfere in the chemical processes, which are instead subject to their own rigid determinism that can be studied in a rigorous fashion in the laboratory. The power to control is thus separate from the executive power responsible for the production of vital phenomena. The only vital force that Bernard acknowledges is "a legislative vital force, in no ways executive." "To summarize our idea, we could metaphorically say: the vital force directs the phenomena it does not produce; the physical agents produce these phenomena, which they do not direct" (Bernard 1878/1966, p. 52).

Nevertheless, we cannot separate the two aspects of the conflict, which characterize life. Morphology and phenomenology, form and function, morphogenetic laws and chemo-physical determinism are intrinsically linked and inseparable:

> In considering the question in an absolute manner, one must say that life is neither a principle nor a result. It is not a principle because this somewhat dormant or expectant principle would be incapable of acting by itself. No more is life a result because the physicochemical conditions that superintend its manifestation would not know to inscribe any direction to it, any determinate form [...] Neither of these two factor can explain life in isolation. Accordingly, for us, life is a conflict. Its manifestations result from a close, harmonious relationship between the conditions and the constitution of the organism. (Bernard 1878/1966, pp. 344–5)

Life is a conflict, a tension, an internal battle. The dynamic is the result of conflict between two opposed, or simply different, principles, which must integrate and create an "organic," "harmonious" whole. The dynamic is the result of an essential tension, contained in embryonic form in the seed, which produces the organization, the form. Life and the dynamic will exist as long as this essential tension is present. As Charles Rosen's (1976, 1988) studies demonstrate, the logic of the dramatic tension in the works of Haydn, Mozart, and Beethoven, the capacity to sustain the tension through harmonic and rhythmic mutations and through melodic movements in order to trigger and surpass the conflict, the technique of expanding the dynamic from a small detail, which must contain in itself a tension capable of generating the development, are the central characteristics of the classical style.

Beyond the use of already very productive metaphors, models, and images, music, science, and medicine appear profoundly to share styles of thought and explanation. The similarities and differences, perhaps more important that theoretical and historical analysis can discern, seem to present common modes of knowledge, of creation, and of appreciation of beauty.

Note

i For a paradigmatic example of the relationship between science and medicine during the scientific revolution see Mersenne (1627).

ii For a recent critical review on this subject see Di Mitri (2006).

iii The most fruitful analysis of the role of style in the history of music remains Rosen (1976, 1988)

iv On this point, it is useful to consult Canguilhem (1988).

v On this issue see Boccadoro (2002).

vi "Fibra enim physiologo id est, quo linae geometrae," in Haller (1755).

vii For the history of the concept of the fiber see Grmek (1970, 1989).

viii The use of this expression is probably directly tied to the success the concept "regulation by oscillation" had in the 17th century, after Christian Huygens' invention of the pendulum clock, which received theoretical treatment in his *Horologium oscillatorium* (1673), and quickly became a model for the universe.

ix "Quae vivunt, quae vegetant, & quae sensibiles mutationes vitae, & interitus subeunt, in perpetuo sunt moto" (Baglivi 1696a, caput XIII, p. 577).

x Lamarck MS 742–2, p. 17, "Discours de l'an 1809," in Vachon (1972).

xi This term, introduced by Louis Bourguet (1729) in his *Lettres philosophiques*, indicates the type of growth of living beings, which seems to increase through the generation of new parts from inside, contrary to the growth of crystals, which occurs through "apposition" on the exterior surface.

xii For Bonnet, this model also explained the formation of monsters in nature, which were the result of the "non-realization" of that which was inscribed in the seed, through accidental causes.

xiii This principle had been affirmed a just a few years earlier by Lamarck (1797): "There exists in all living being two powerful forces, which are very distinct and always in opposition to each other, of a sort that each of them perpetually destroys the effects that the other has just produced."

xiv In discussing comparative anatomy, Georges Cuvier (1810, p. 330) wrote: "All organs from the same animal form a unique system, in which all the parts stand, act, and react on each other; and there can be no modifications in one of these parts which does not lead to similar modification in all the others."

xv This is the *epizeuxis o subjunctio*, the immediate and therefore emphatic repetition of a word, a note or a motif (cf. Mattheson 1739/1954, p. 243).

xvi Starting at the end of the 18th century, life is also often defined as "organized matter."

References

Albinus, B. (1691). *Dissertatio de tarantismo*. Frankfurt an der Oder.

Albrecht, J. W. (1734). *Tractatus physicus de effectibus musicee in corpus animatum*. Leipzig: Martini.

Bachmann, C. L. (1792). *De effectibus musicae in hominem*. Erlangen: Kunstmann.

von Baer, K. E. (1828–1837). *Über Entwicklungsgeschichte der Thiere. Beobachtung und Reflexion*, Königsberg: Bornträger.

Baglivi, G. (1696a). De anatome, morsu. & effectibus tarantulae. In *Opera omnia medico-practica et anatomica*, pp. 539–80. Leiden: Anisson & Joannis Posuel.

Baglivi, G. (1696b). *De praxi medica ad priscam observandi rationem revocanda. Libri duo. Accedunt dissertationes novae*. Rome: Typis Domimici Antonio Herculis.

Baglivi, G. (1700). *De fibra motrice et morbosa*. Perugia: Costantino.

Bernard, C. (1878/1966) *Leçons sur les phénomènes de la vie communs aux animaux et aux végétaux*. Paris: Baillière et Fils. (Reprinted 1966 with a preface by G. Canguilhem. Paris: Vrin.)

Bichat, X. (1801). *Recherches physiologiques sur la vie et la mort*. Paris. (English translation by F. Gold, London: Longman, Hurst, Rees, Orme and Browne, 1815.)

Boccadoro, B. (2002). *Ethos e varietas: trasformazione qualitativa e metabole nella teoria armonica dell'antichità greca*. Firenze: Leo S. Olschki.

Boccadoro, B. (2004). Eléments de grammaire mélancolique. *Acta Musicologica*, **76**, 25–65.

Bonnet, C. (1762/1985) *Considérations sur les corps organisés: où l'on traite de leur origine, de leur développement, de leur reproduction, &c. & où l' on a rassemblé en abrégé tout ce que l'histoire naturelle offre de plus certain & de plus intéressant sur ce sujet*. Amsterdam: Marc-Michel Rey. (Reprinted 1985 with text reviewed by F. Markovits and S. Bienaymé. Paris: Fayard.)

Borelli, G. A. (1710) *De motu animalium*, editio novissima [additae sunt post finem partis secundae Johannis Bernoullii Meditationes mathematicae de motu musculorum]. Leiden: Petrum van der Aa.

Bourguet, L. (1729). *Lettres philosophiques sur la formation des sels, & des cristaux, et sur la génération, et le mechanisme organique des plantes, & des animaux etc.*. Amsterdam: François l'Honoré.

Browne, R. (1729). *Medicina Musica: or, A Mechanical Essay on the Effects of Singing, Musick, and Dancing, on Human Bodies. Revis'd and Corrected. To which is annex'd a New Essay on the Nature and Cure of the Spleen and Vapours*. London: Printed for J. Cooke.

Canguilhem, G. (1988). *Idéologie et rationalité dans l'histoire des sciences de la vie*, 2nd edn. Paris: Vrin.

Chaussier, F. and Adelon, N. P. (1819). Organisés (corps). In *Dictionaire des sciences médicales*, pp. 235–49. Paris: C. L. F. Panckoucke.

Cuvier, G. (ed.) (1810). *Rapport historique sur les progrès des sciences naturelles depuis 1789, et sur leur état actuel: Présenté à Sa Majesté l'Empereur et Roi, en son Conseil d'État, le 6 février 1808, par la classe des sciences physiques et mathématiques de l'institut…*. Paris: Impr. Impériale.

Daremberg, C. (1870). *Histoire des sciences médicales, comprenant l'anatomie, la physiologie, la médecine, la chirurgie et les doctrines de pathologie générale*, vol. II. Paris: J.-B. Baillière.

Ettmüller, M. E. (1714). *Dissertatio de effectibus musicae in hominem*. Leipzig: J. G. Bauch.

Glisson, F. (1672). *Tractatus de natura substantiae energeticae*. London: Brome.

Grmek, M. D. (1970). La notion de fibre vivante chez les médecins de l'école iatrophysique. *Clio Medica*, **5**, 297–318.

Grmek, M. D. (1989). La notion de fibre vivante. In *La première révolution biologique*, pp. 159–88. Paris: Payot.

Grube, H. (1679). *De ictu tarantulae et vi musicae in ejus curatione*. Frankfurt: Daniel Paul.

von Haller, A. (1751). *Primae lineae physiologiae*. Gottingen: Ab. Vandenhoeck.

von Haller, A. (1755) *Dissertation sur les parties irritables et sensibles des animaux* (translated from the Latin by S. Tissot). Lausanne: Marc-Michel Bousquet.

von Haller, A. (1756–1760). *Mémoires sur la nature sensible et irritable des parties du corps animal*. Lausanne: Marc-Michel Bousquet.

von Helmholtz, H. (1870). *Die Lehre von den Tonempfindungen als physiologische Grundlage für die Theorie der Musik*. Braunschweig: F. Vieweg. (1st edn 1863)

von Helmholtz, H. (1877). *Causes physiologique de l'harmonie musicale*. Paris: Germer Baillière.

von Helmholtz, H. (1995). On the physiological causes of harmony in music [A lecture delivered in Bonn during the winter of 1857]. In von Helmholtz H. L. F. (ed.), *Science and Culture. Popular and Philosophical Essays*, pp. 46–75. Chicago: Chicago University Press.

Lamarck, J.-B. (1797). *Mémoires de physique et d'histoire naturelle, établis sur des bâses de raisonnement indépendantes de toute théorie, avec l'exposition de nouvelles considérations sur la cause générale des dissolutions; sur la matière du feu; sur la couleur des corps; sur la formation des composés; sur l'origine des minéraux; et sur l'organisation des corps vivans*, p. 248. Paris: Muséum d'Histoire Naturelle.

Lamarck, J.-B. (1802). *Hydrogeologie, ou, recherches sur l'influence qu'ont les causes sur la surface du globe terrestre: sur les causes de l'existence du bassin des mers, de son déplacement et de son transport successif sur les différents points de la surface de ce globe: enfin sur la nature et l'état de cette surface.* Paris: Muséum d'Histoire Naturelle.

Malpighi, M. (1675). *De viscerum structura exercitatio anatomica: accedit dissertatio ejusdem de polypo cordis.* London: J. Martyn.

Mattheson, J. (1739/1954). *Der vollkommene Capellmeister.* Hamburg: C. Herold. (Facsimile edition 1954, Kassel: Bärenreiter.)

Mead, R. (1774). De la tarentule. In *Recueil des oeuvres physiques et médicinales*, pp. 133–51. Paris: Bouillon.

Mersenne, M. (1627). *Traité de l'harmonie universelle où est contenu la musique théorique et pratique des anciens et des modernes, avec les causes de ses effets, enrichi de raison prises de la philosophie, et des mathematiques.* Paris: Bandry.

Müller, J. (1838–1840). *Handbuch der Physiologie des Menschen für Vorlesungen*, 2 vols. Coblenz: Hölscher.

Pasteur, L. (1922–1939). *Oeuvres complètes*, vol. VII (ed. P. de Vallery-Radot). Paris: Masson et Cie.

Platner, F. (1669). *Dissertatio physico-medica de tarantismo.* Basel: Ex Typographia Deckeriana.

Rosen, C. (1976) *The Classical Style. Haydn, Mozart, Beethoven.* London: Faber and Faber (revised version).

Rosen, C. (1988). *Sonata Forms.* New York: W. W. Norton & Company. (French translation 1993, *Formes sonate.* Paris: Actes Sud.)

Schönberg, A. (1967). *Fundamentals of Musical Composition*, London: Faber and Faber.

Senguerdius, W. (1667). *Disputatio philosophica inauguralis de tarantula.* Leiden: Elsevir.

Severino, M. A. (1645). *Zootomia democritaea, idest anatome generalis totius animantium opificii: libris quinque distincta, quorum seriem sequens facies delineabit.* Nuremberg: Literis Endterianis.

Starobinski, J. (1989). *L'invention de la liberté.* Geneva: Skira.

Treviranus, G. R. (1802). *Biologie oder Philosophie der Lebenden Natur für Naturfoscher und Arzte*, 1st edn. Göttingen: Röwer.

Vachon, M. (ed.) (1972). Discours de l'an 1809. In *Inédits de Lamarck, d'après les manuscrits conservés à la bibliothèque centrale du Muséum d'histoire naturelle de Paris*, pp. 208, 284. Paris: Masson.

Vallerius, H. (1702/1999). *Exercitium philosophicum de tarantula.* Uppsala. (Italian translation 1999, Esercizio filosofico sulla tarantola. In *La tarantola iperborea*, pp. 25–72. Lecce: Besa Editrice.)

Virchow, R. (1855). Cellular-Pathologie. *Archkiv für Pathologische Anatomie und Physiologie*, **8**, 1–15.

Chapter 20

Control and the science of affect: music and power in the medieval and Renaissance periods

Laurence Wuidar (translation by Kristen Gray Jafflin)

Introduction

The subject of "music and emotion" poses, among others, the question of whether it is possible to objectify "emotions" or if it was ever possible to do so historically, notably within musical theory. This question lends itself equally well to a variety of approaches: psychological or anthropological, cognitivist or historical, aesthetic or sociological. How we think about emotions has varied throughout history, and the latter underscores modes of thought by collecting facts, as science collects data. Today, cognitivists investigate the subject, "emotion and music," which has a past, a history. Dialogue with historians of music could, if not enrich current research, which is based on its own methods, reveal the heart of the question. Integrating historians into the current debate in the cognitive sciences of affect returns to the question of whether going to visit a museum simply induces an aesthetic pleasure or if it also changes how we see the world. Does the historian's presence only apply a varnish of culture or can he or she make us see the subject in a new light?

The musical literature prefers to use the terms "affect" and "passion" rather than the term "emotion." The passions are the center of preoccupations found in ancient Greek theory, passions of the soul, which reverberate in the body. Humans as a whole are rational and passionate animals, impassioned and thus suffering. And those who speak of suffering also need to find remedies to cure, or at least regulate and temper, that suffering—which has been one of music's roles from antiquity to the present.

The different components of musical language receive an emotive characterization: musical scales, intervals, rhythms, and instrumentation. One of the codes of this language is the relationship between the characteristics of these components and the affect that they convey. Plato discussed this, as did the ancient, medieval, and Renaissance musical literature up to Baroque-era discussion of the ethos of tones, which corresponded to a change at the heart of musical language, namely the historical evolution from modes to tones during the 17th century. A particular mode suits a particular circumstance; a particular piece of music leads the listener to take up arms, while another, in contrast, calms him. The same principle holds for the rhythmic component: certain rhythms are noble, others vulgar. Thus, music has moral qualities (a theory denied by the Epicurean school), which is why it has its place in Plato's *Republic* and in Aristotle's *Politics*, which presents a hierarchy of different types of music according to their different ethical characters.

Music not only represents emotions but also provokes them. Isidore of Seville says no more than this: "Musica movet affectus, provocat in diversum habitum sensus" (*Etymologie*, book III, XVII). The theory of ethos is inseparable from the power of music: the power to affect, to move. Music is the art of movement that only exists in the passage of time, in contrast to the visual arts and the art of setting emotions in movement. The effects of music are exerted as much on the moral plane, directing the individual towards evil or towards good, which explains why music plays a primary role in education for the Greeks and why singing is encouraged in places of worship, music being a means of attaining a higher reality. The delight serves a precise goal, by moving the listener it leads the listener to contemplation. For Aristotle and the Peripatetics, music imitated the passions and was therefore recognized as much for its cathartic as for its educational value. From the Greek theory about the musical ethos of modes, recovered and updated during the Renaissance, to the Baroque era's rhetorical theory of affect (the *Affektenlehre* which has occupied generations of musicologists[i]), passions and affects have been the object of study for musical theorists, who have defined them and determined the interactions between a musical given and its effects on the human soul and body. Each musical mode not only has its particular color but also incites the listener to a particular mood, state of mind, or bodily action. These topics roam the history of musical theory in a tangle of medical, moral, and musical notions. A particular musical mode, namely the laying out of notes in relation to each other according to a determined scale, translates into a particular sentiment, affect, or passion and evokes it. The listener cannot be passive; music's power affects her whether she wants it to or not. Music acts on a level below volition and reason. The proof is that it also acts on animals, as "evidenced", for example, by the myth of Orpheus. From this fact, a particular given piece of music leads to a particular behavior, and another leads certain deranged behavior to a just temperance.

From ancient times, and into the Renaissance, authors considered that the effects of music on the passions or soul had a medical dimension. This viewpoint changed during the Baroque era, when the magico-medical perspective was abandoned for the theater of the passions: music represented affects; certainly it strongly moved the listener, its transforming power was not at all questioned, but music depicted theater of the passions that unfolded in the sacred and profane world in their smallest modulations. After the 1600s, the discourse on affects becomes confused with musical rhetoric: think of the first list of musico-rhetorical figures published by Burmeister (1599), a list extended in his *Musica poetica* (Burmeister 1606) and later by Germanic theorists.

The goal was always to touch the listener, but while Marsilio Ficino's generation thought very concretely in terms of physical effects on the body and psychological effects on the soul, Johannes Mattheson's generation progressively abandoned the idea of a musical pharmacopoeia. The composer stirred the listener, but questions of dilating or contracting the spirits through musical compositions no longer appeared. Composers arranged their discourse, from the exordium to the conclusion, with their invention serving adequately linked themes, eventually arriving at the refutation of certain themes to the profit of others to reach a conclusion that convinced the listener. Listeners continued to laugh and to cry: the composer, as a good orator, made emotions flow and provoked them. The object was still to move listeners and to create emotional empathy. At the heart of this musical rhetoric, figures played an essential role outside of the role of the plan and structure of the whole piece. They were not simple ornaments; the range of emotions they express has even been compared with the human face. These figures were intrinsically tied to emotions: it was emotions that, in primis, conveyed them. Joy, sadness, and doubt were all represented by specific musical figures, and it is in the representation of emotions that the union of rhetoric and music found its most perfect correspondence. The catalogue of affects aided the composer's creativity as much as it theorized relations between affects and sounds.

Like any good orator, the musician controlled and directed the listener's emotions, and musical theorists borrowed rhetorical terminology and traced the power of music along the same lines as words, until all parts of musical discourse were part of the art of affect. In vocal music, the goal of the music was to represent a text's affects by its own means; theorists determined these means, one of the principles being to depict the "verba affectuum" musically. It was thus that Johannes Nucius (1613) named the verbs expressing feelings, emotions, and affects, such as rejoice, enjoy, cry, fear, shout, wail, and laugh in his *Musicae poeticae sive de Compositione Cantus*. The "verba affectuum" served the composer's creativity by showing him what type of musical tone to use and what tempo to choose so that the music fitted the text. In each case, the criterion was respecting the movements of the soul and their adequacy for musical rhetoric's "loci topici." Throughout the 18th century, the duty of theorists was, on the one hand, to formalize poetic, rhetorical, and musical relations, notably by determining the translation of a the affects of a text into sound, and, on the other hand, to explain examples taken from past and present musical tradition with reference to musico-rhetorical categories. Seventeenth- and 18th-century theorists analyzed past and present music to confirm musico-emotional correspondences by tracing these analogies in the works of the masters, from Lassus to Johann Sebastian Bach. From the Greeks to the Baroque era, music maintained this privileged link with affects and passions through the very definition of the passions.

Moving and stirring

Certain pieces of music transport people into a state of limpness and weakness. This observation, made by Plato in *The Republic* (X, III), simultaneously implies the physical, psychological, affective, and institutional dimensions of music. It serves as a basis for reflection on the power of music and on the relationship between music and civil and religious power: Aristotle inherited this tradition, as did musical and Christian philosophical thought up to the Renaissance. It suffices to think of Monteverdi, who referred to Plato's *Republic* to justify the musical style known as *stile concitato*. In effect, music is capable of provoking physical and psychological attitudes, and when Monteverdi described three musical styles, *concitato*, *molle*, and *temperato*, in the famous preface of his *Madrigali guerrieri e amorosi* in 1638, he referred to the ancient idea and the Platonic correspondence between affects and musical styles. There is not only a correspondence between the two, but music also acts profoundly on the soul and on the character that it modulates. This is why Plato forbade Lydian melodies in the city: these melodies did not agree with women, and agreed even less with the city's watchmen because this type of music only induced weakness and limpness. In the same way, rhythms possess their own characters and impose this character on the people who hear them. In *The Republic* (XI), Plato distinguishes rhythms for baseness, for violence, for insanity and rhythms opposed to these negative states. Whether at the melodic or rhythmic level, music conveys a particular character or affect and is capable of transmitting it to the citizen's soul or body. That's why the legislator must rule on this matter. That is also why composers must know human characteristics before they are able to express themselves or to express them in music. The moral characters are to music what the letters are to literature: one must know them before one is able to compose. If music forms souls, it combines itself with gymnastics, which forms bodies. Elsewhere in *The Republic* (XVII), Plato explains how music and gymnastics are united in the search of comprehensive education for the whole person: we mustn't look after the soul without treating the body or treat the body while forgetting the soul. Music and gymnastics are complementary both because the first shapes the soul and the second the body and because both contribute to the temperance of human character. Those who only interest themselves in music have too slack a character, and those who only do gymnastics too hard. To avoid this excess of slackness or brutality, it is necessary to temper the character so that slackness becomes gentleness and brutality courage. Harmony and the just temperance of gentleness and courage are synonymous with a well-tempered man: thus the city's goal is to educate the man to become a perfect musician. Plato pursues this reasoning on musical education and legislation in Book VII of *The Laws*: proof that music was part of the legislator's discourse on behalf of the city and on behalf of sacred rites, music also having the power to attract the gods' favors.

Aristotle picked up on Plato's ethical and educational considerations while also devoting part of his philosophical reflection on music to its hedonistic dimension. Music generates pleasure (cf. *Politics*, VIII, 5, 9): it is educational but also a game and entertainment, releasing tensions arising from daily work and relieving the soul and the body of the day's fatigue. Thus, the function of music is to temper everyday rigors through a gentle pleasure. Music is medicine for the soul and for the tired body, and, following Platonic thought, it mimics the moral character of human beings. Rhythm and melody imitate anger, gentleness, courage, temperance, and their opposites, Aristotle continued (cf. *Politics*, VIII, 5, 18) and it insinuates them into the soul by means of the senses. If music is sad, the man cannot *not* be sad (cf. *Politics*, VIII, 5, 22–3): this clearly indicates its power to direct beings and their affects.

... et omnes affectus spiritus nostri

Christian thought inherited these Platonic and Aristotelian conceptions: Christian authors applied themselves to solving the same questions about the ethical value of music and about its potential hedonistic danger, particularly with regards to the specific problem of faith and spiritual elevation towards God. St Augustine, who had an important influence on medieval and Renaissance Christian musical thought, notes in his *Confessions* (§49, ch. 33, bk X) that music has a link with the entire range of human affects ("et omnes affectus spiritus nostri"). And this link is elusive: a person can realize the correspondence between music and the range of their sentiments, but can never completely explain why and how this link works. Thus a place is made in Christian musical philosophical thought for the recognition of the intrinsic ineffability of music and the mysterious relationship between musical and human components. Evidently, this did not keep authors from describing the characteristics of music suitable for the liturgy: a music that would seize the senses to speak to the soul and understanding faculties and conduct humans to God in the right way.

St Augustine reaffirmed the link between music and affects in another passage of *Confessions*, which demonstrates how central this link is to his philosophical and theological thought on musical fact. While he discourses on the difference between words sung by humans and God's creative word, St Augustine demonstrates in a synthetic manner and gets to the heart of music's effect on humans. We are thus at the heart of a major theological and philosophical problem, that of the eternity of the creative word, and St Augustine undertakes to determine the essence of musical effects by exposing the listener's or composer's attitude when faced with musical fact. "On the part of the listener or the singer, the wait for future notes and memory of past notes modifies affect and strains the senses" ("Neque enim sicut nota cantantis notumve canticum audientis exspectatione vocum futurarum et memoria praeteritarum variatur affectus sensusque distenditur"; *Confessions*, XI, 31, 41). St Augustine shows his skill as a commentator on the human psyche, with individuals and their experiences constituting the point of departure for his speculative constructions. The temporal components of music and the listener's or singer's attitude are described in the union of the faculties of the soul and the progress of the music. The past, the present, and the future, expressed by the music that makes humans more conscious of their passage, take into account affect and the senses because each is tied to a precise musical stage: memory, real sound, and waiting. Thus memory of past sound, reason, the listening body of present sound, and tension in awaiting future sound are all put into movement in a musical act, which has as a major property the stirring of affects and the senses.[ii] St Augustine is simultaneously interested in the interior and exterior mechanism, psychic and physiological, psychological and physical, the alchemy of the soul and the chemistry of the body, and he couldn't help thinking of all human and musical components as a coherent and inseparable ensemble. Affect and the senses, their modification, and their movement are also what signals the distinction between the sung word of humankind and God's creative word: the latter being affected by nothing, undergoing no modification, knowing no movement, being eternal and immobile.

This modification of affects, described by Greek philosophers and confirmed by the first Christian thinkers as a fundamental and intrinsic link between music and humankind is also found among medieval musical theorists. At the beginning of his treatise on music, Boethius returns to the heart of this manifestation of emotion: the accelerating heartbeat is a sign of strong emotion. The heartbeat, the lifeblood—the movement produced by the heart's beating and the movement produced by the arts of tempo (poetry and music)—shows the subject's interior states through its fluctuations. It communicates emotions without resorting to discursive language: it's this dimension that Boethius presents in the opening of his *De musica*.

Musica enim hominum movet affectus

In the medieval era, musical theorists concerned themselves with a synthesis of ancient ideas, transmitted by Boethius, and of patristic ideas. The reader finds immutable speculative chapters on the origin of music, on the Boethian tripartition of music into *musica mundana*, *humana*, and instrumental, on the amazing effects of music, supported through reference to Orpheus and David, and on the excellence of the musical art, which positions human beings on the side of the choir of angels that they imitate. Thus, in what is considered the oldest of medieval treatises, Aurelian of Reoma's *Musica disciplina* (*c.* 840–50), we find in chapter 10 the traditional cosmic conceptions of the music of spheres immediately followed by a discussion of the influence of music on humans: music moves the affects and provokes diverse sensations ("Musica enim hominum movet affectus, in diversum habitum provocat sensum"). It restores the soldier's energy, and the more valiant the trumpet's sound the more valiant and prompt the soldier is. This topic, found in the musical literature, is also found in other forms of literature. For example, in the writings of theologians musical science meets, on the one hand, the affects of the faithful led to contemplation by melodies that imitate the angels' songs and, on the other hand, Christian virtues. The ideas are always the same: music's power to stir is real, therefore it is necessary to use it well, and music reflects the different components of humankind: it is the mirror of the microcosm that it imitates in all its characteristics, and that it influences through its proper character.

Bernard of Clairvaux offers a perfect medieval example of Christian musical thought in his letter CCCXCVIII *A l'Abbé Guy et aux religieux de Montier-Ramey*. The community in question asked Bernard of Clairvaux to compose an office destined to be read or sung for the feast of St Victor, it was the occasion for him to theorize the musical rules of worship and of ecclesiastical song. The text is brief but condenses the key traditional element that defined the relationship between the passions and affects in good music for the Church for the modern reader. This is why it can be taken as a model for understanding how religious music engaged the passions: the goals and the description of music adapted to them persisted beyond aesthetic and stylistic exchanges. Church music owed it to itself to reflect Christian virtues in a mirror of sound in order to help the intelligence, the heart, the soul, and the body attain their just respective dispositions. Thus, music had to render the content of thoughts agreeable and profitable, it had to edify and elevate, to stir in order to move towards God. In order to do this, Church song had to be composed in the right temperament: "neither too lascivious nor too rustic," the song had to be grave and to follow the middle road ("Cantus ipse, si fuerit, plenus sit gravitate; nec lasciviam resonet, nec rusticitatem"; Bernard of Clairvaux, letter CCCXCVIII). That's how it could affect the emotions of the faithful. The song, through its temperance, tempered people's passions: it "lifts sadness and mitigates anger" Bernard of Clairvaux continued in the same letter to Abbé Guy ("Tristitiam levet, iram mitiget"). Finally, this testimony also summarized the proper use of the senses: "music charms the hearing to move the heart" to the affects that the pious text conveys; to do this musical characteristics must also be defined. The "gentle, and in no way lascivious" sonorities charm through their sweetness and touch the heart by caressing the ear ("Sic suavis, ut non sit levis; sic mulceat aures, ut moveat corda"). This letter, chosen for its value as an example, summarizes the issues of liturgical music in the framework of the discourse about affects, moving and stirring the listener. In this sense, Christian musical philosophy inherited Platonic thought: music touches, affects, and modifies people and it must be the model of temperance in order to temper.

We can find many testaments, by theologians and even by popes, of theological critiques of changing musical styles over the course of history. Church music had to sustain the sense of words; its goal was to stir in the "right" direction, to nourish piety, to elevate the soul to God by the movement of the senses, to bring the sense of words from the ear into the heart, and to help the mind understand the words. In other words, music had to *affect* the mind, the soul, and the heart through the body. All music contrary to piety, reverence, veneration, gravity, sobriety, and the grandeur of the praised object, and thus all music that betrayed just sentiments, just emotions, just affects, and the right religious direction had to be banished. Affection, the affects, and the passions are full categories in medieval treatises, whether they concern musical theory or theology.

Quod in Deo non sunt passiones affectuum

At this stage it is worth considering another example on the definition of affects in a larger domain than music. Specific to the sensitive being, the passions are clearly defined by different disciplines. For Thomas Aquinas, in his comments to Denys the Aeropagite, the passions are the movements of a sensitive appetite (cf. *In Dionysii de divinis nominibus*, 4, 25). The angelic doctor enumerates the consequences they could have in his chapter "Quod in Deo non sunt passiones affectuum": all passion implies a corporeal transformation; in all passionate states, the subject, whether animal or rational animal, is out of his habitual dispositions. Above all, passion is a movement, and all passionate movement is directed towards a determined object: sadness, joy, hope, desire, fear, and anger (cf. *Summa contra Gentiles*, I, 89). The soul is the seat of passion. However, as we have seen, in the Pythagorean and Platonic tradition, music acts on the soul. Through rhythms and specific melodies, human affects are cured and the soul led back to its original equilibrium, as Iamblichus says in the *On the Pythagorean Way of Life*. He continues: music turns pain, anger, jealousy, fear, excitation, depression and impetuosity's movements into their opposites. Music transforms destructive and disharmonious movements into harmony. Boethius, in the preface to *De institutione musica*, explains how this functions. The sense of hearing, the window to the soul as with the other corporeal senses, allows music to descend into the soul, into the mind. Once it arrives in the soul, music molds it according to the content it conveys.

Human passions express a suffering that calls forth release, the return to a harmonious state of being. In Christian culture, this is the key message of the Passion of the Christ—Christ's suffering on the cross for the benefit of humankind—and it isn't by chance that the Passion could be placed in analogy with music at different levels. The Passion is intimately tied to affects: Easter is synonymous with *passage*, thanks to the cross for eternal rest, to which each believer is invited until their passage into God through the ecstasy of contemplation—then, all affects are directed towards God.[iii] At the musical level, certainly, we find all the pieces of music composed for Eastertide, which translate the different steps of the Passion up to Christ's last seven words on the cross. But musical analogies are also found in the sacred literature: at the moment of the Passion, Christ is transformed into a stringed instrument, the tuning keys are the nails in the wood of the cross, and the instrument's seven strings are strung on Christ's body, each of the instrument's strings being one of Christ's last words on the cross.[iv] This theme, found in the sacred medieval literature, is again found in the imagery of 17th-century sacred literature: for example in the work of Benedictus van Haeften (1635, p. 228), the allegory of Christ playing on his cross becomes a musical instrument on which strings are strung. The theme echoes the human ideal of the accord between the soul's passions: what humans seek is to rejoin the passions' rest; thus they are like perfect musicians, and their souls are like well-tuned psalteries. This ancient image is a classical one found in diverse literary genres up to the musical theoretical literature written at the end of the 17th century (e.g. Berardi 1689, p. 25).

Not all music is affective, not all music conveys an affect: although the theme of the representation of the passions in music has been one of the dominant themes since the Greek affirmation of the cathartic value of sound, in parallel to this there is also discussion of mathematical abstraction, of combinatory music that both traces the cosmic order and reveals the universal structure of things. Music is not only a language that moves, it is also the secret glory of the universe's musician-organizer. These two cultural aspects are inseparable and constitute two lines of European musical thought in the Platonic and Pythagorean tradition that continue up to the 18th century. However, the one does not exclude the other. For example, the music of Johann Sebastian Bach magnifies the combinatory order at the heart of an effective discourse of affects, testifying to a single sacred mathematics, sometimes using cryptic devices not made to be audible, which directly and fully touches the listener, transporting him or her toward celestial contemplation through the hold of the senses and emotions (in sacred music, as we already said, the *delectare* is at the service of spiritual elevation).

The discourse on music and emotions reflects the physical and psychological aspect of music, leaving aside its mystical combinations and divine mathematics. That discourse focuses on one goal of music: to transport the listener, to move her physically and psychological, and to stir her through the emotions conveyed at the heart of its movement, which direct the movement of the listener's soul and body.

Musica movet affectus

We have already seen this *motto* of Isidore of Seville, used by medieval authors, and we should now consider this idea, that movement is intrinsically tied to the notion of affect, for a moment. For centuries, European musical culture constructed a science of affects, with the musical literature theorizing about how its musico-emotive shape was put into practice through partitions. For musical theorists, the minimal definition of affect was *movement*. Thus Berardi (1689, p. 9), describes the soul's passions: reason and the senses are its poles, thoughts its points, desires its circles, and affects its movements. A clever geometry of the passions emerges, in which the affects are a subcategory in which the soul is set in motion. Geometry maps reason and emotions. Reason and the senses are the poles of the soul's geography, thoughts are settled by being concentrated on an element contrary to the desires, the metaphor of the circle that determines them reflects the soul's continual confinement and fettering in the circle of desires, at once closed and infinite.

Rest is not opposed to movement, it is tranquil, serene, non-passionate movement, and music leads to this rest, in the appeasing of desires when the just temperament carries a temperate affect: balanced by the serenity of a well-tempered affect.

Since the writings of Plato and Aristotle, authors have emphasized that it is when a person is fatigued or sad that music shows its virtue in bringing them help. A Renaissance theorist (Bocchi 1580, p. 7) clearly expresses this theory in his *Discorso sopra la musica*: "the pains and difficulties that we experience each hour of our life are numerous, we could not support them if their bitterness were not diminished by something sweet [music],"[v] Music tempers and transmutes the bitter taste of afflictions into sweetness, but also acts on a strictly medical level.

Musical science and medical art

In all cases, the reasonings are founded on the power of music. Until the 17th century, the musician becomes the interface, the receptacle, and the mediator between the listener and higher realities. The catalogue of the amazing effects of music is a topic in the encyclopedic and musical literature that was developed from ancient and biblical authorities: music acts on stones, plants, animals, and human beings. Thus sings the Music in Claudio Monteverdi's *Orfeo* (1607), posing its powers over hearts and minds, birds and waves in the opening, until, through the sound of the lyre, the breeze stops. Music heals sciatica, viper and tarantula bites, melancholics, frenetics, the apoplectic, the insane and the deaf… It tempers drunkenness and anger, it reawakens the somnolent and quiets lust. It frees entire cities from the plague and leads to peace between people.

It is exactly because music is so powerful that religious and civil powers must legislate about it, as the Greeks had already testified.[vi] Such acts were also found in Renaissance European culture, whether by civil powers, in Calvinist countries for example, or by ecclesiastical powers, with Catholic countries offering a perfect example. The musical object thus was theorized in parallel by musical treatises and by the guardians of public and moral order.

Still during the Renaissance, music was already a science, based on mathematical rules, and medicine an art, based on experimental knowledge. As with all the sciences, music was divided into two lines: practical and speculative, the music played and sung, on the one hand, and contemplation of universal principles and of musical laws and structure, on the other. As with all sciences, practice could not be dissociated from theory, practical music from speculative music. With the birth of counterpoint, music began to represent in its whole the harmonious union of opposites, the deep voice was united with the high void, and different rhythmic values of notes' particular heights matched each other. Music testified to the concordant discord, opening the way to numerous political and interstate, conjugal and friendly, metaphors.

This definition of music, from the ancient Platonic idea, to Renaissance-era encyclopedism wherein music always constitutes the key to universal harmony, is singularly current in the context of interdisciplinary encounters. In a system that believes in the possibility of the universal and of unity, music is also that which improves all the sciences because it carries in itself the fundamental and foundational components of all that is rhythm, respiration, meter, proportion, tempo, and movement. Not that life without music would be a mistake; even more fundamentally, nothing can be without music, no being and no thing.[vii] Without music, we cannot truly understand the sciences, the discipline, and ourselves. Isidore of Seville expressed this thought in a synthetic manner: "Itaque sine Musica nulla disciplina potest esse perfecta" (*Etymologie*, bk III, XVII). In itself, music is a key to the meeting of knowledge: it allows the judge to apprehend the just and unjust through their harmonies and dissonances, the doctor to know the just temperance of medicines and the vital beat of the systole and the diastole through the *arsis* and the *thesis*.

Black bile and the *fantasia,* foolish attitude and the *gaillarde*

Let us limit ourselves to two examples, the doctor and the legislator, because when we speak of music's power over affects, the essential question is its medical and moral power. Music translates emotions into its own language, eventually adding audible or inaudible symbolic elements to its language. From the moment when this representation of emotions provokes them, it is necessary to theorize its effects and research their cause. We must frame, define, understand, and contain if we are to reproduce and use through a science of affect a model of the causes and effects that systematize the relations between modes and affects, and between intervals and their effects on the soul and the body, at the individual and collective level.

Pontus de Tyard (1555) gives us an example in his *Solitaire Second*; in it he describes how guests' mental and physical attitudes changed upon hearing Francesco da Milano improvise a fantasy on the lute during a banquet. While listening to the work, the guests could not help but slip down their seats or even rest their heads on their hands, a corporeal attitude classified since antiquity as the external mirror of melancholy. Black bile, dominated by negative influxes from the planet Saturn, invaded the audience when it heard the fantasy. The description highlights the guests' physical behavior. The listener's body, in addition to his fantasy and his imagination, is in play: music controls the body.

Music drives the body to a state of liquefaction and the spirit to dissolution in the black humor that characterizes speculative people, such as the alchemist and the musician. It also unchains the body, inducing it to dance. The moralizing secular literature seized on this subject; Simeon Zuccolo da Cologna (1549), offers a good example. Dance is a manifestation of madness, a villainous entertainment that turns human nature upside down in conferring bestial characteristics to it … It induces madness under the effects of wine and music. Music is thus the cause of dancing, an animal manifestation in men. The author recounts the following about a *gaillarde*, a lively type of dance music, as indicated by its name: "Upon hearing this bizarre music that issues from fantastic instrumentalists, such as those who have drunk too much, everyone begins to jump and to dance, to make gestures and signs of elation with their hands, feet and tongues […]. They spring and jump, small jumps, twists and rapid twirls, they act like horses, jump, trot, gallop and run from here to there."

Musical drunkenness leads to dancing and induces and encourages uncontrolled behavior. The rational animal loses his reason: music denies it to him. The unbridled body is the exterior index of a deeper power that touches human reason. The power of music provokes reactions, emotions, and uncontrolled behavior, putting morality in peril; thus music must be controlled.

Acoustic sin and legislation

This is the principal aim of ecclesiastical legislation about dancing. Four centuries of theologico-moral literature in Europe attempt to resolve the question of whether dancing is a mortal sin and establish criteria for tracing the boundary between healthy and obscene dancing.[viii] Doing so required determining the condition of the dance, when, who, how, according to the morality of intention and of just measure. During the Renaissance, more than ever, dance teetered between vice and virtue, between dance as an attribute of the devil—evil or even master of the dance—and the blessed ones' dance in Paradise. These categories run through the history of relations between dance and music: there is a lascivious music that leads to shameless dancing, the dance of Salome becomes the very example of dance's eroticism, but there is also a measured music that leads to well-regulated dancing. The Church took on the duty of defining who could dance, what they could dance, and when they could dance.

It was necessary to control the body, to monitor before punishing. If music led to dancing or to any other mental or physical attitudes through the simple fact of permeating the listener's senses, it was also necessary to define what music was acceptable to the Church. The ancients had already categorized which type of music was acceptable for honoring and pleasing the gods, which in any case represented its principal function.

The different councils charged themselves with announcing the precepts of church music. It was necessary to control what the assembly of the faithful, a determinate social body, could hear: the holy words in appropriate melodies. On this subject, St Augustine gives a decisive testimony that would mark musical history. In the above-mentioned book X of his *Confessions*, Augustine described the sins of the five senses and remedies to those temptations: chastity as a response to sexual pleasures, fasting to the earthly sweet foods. Gluttony is to taste what night visions are to sight. The sin of hearing is that which Augustine has the hardest time resisting. The description and commentary are eloquent and speak not only of simple speech but also of song. Just as food is necessary to survival, song is useful because it magnifies the holy words. Thus, it is necessary to know how to use it and in what measure. The vital can transform itself into pleasure: in eating, we can exceed what is necessary; pleasure's shadow is always present. Giving life to the holy words in song can even slide towards a pure pleasure of the auditory sense.

Not without hesitation, Augustine recognizes the benefits of church music: it moves people, bringing them to tears, and it exalts the holy words. The description of acoustic sin is interesting for several reasons: the author begins by distinguishing his relationship with music before and after his conversion. Before, he couldn't resist the power of sound and let himself be invaded by it; after, thanks to divine aid, he could keep the positive effects of music without suffering the negative effects. Thus, a supernatural, divine intervention is necessary for music to not act against someone's will or without their knowledge. In effect, Augustine tells how he enjoyed church music, without realizing it. It wasn't until later, after reflection, that he discovered that he had sinned through the pleasure felt while hearing the melodies and paying more attention to the melodies than to the sacred words. Aside from the relationship with will, denied when faced with the power of music, Augustine presents an element that would mark the history of European music until the 18th century.

The danger of music, its power of seduction, its ability to ravish the senses, in both senses of the term, is located at the very heart of "good" music. It isn't a simple dichotomy between church music that follows established criteria to lead to contemplation versus diabolic music, bad because it is the acoustic reflection of lascivious temptations. On the contrary, the danger lies at the very heart of church music. The question is resolved through a clear distinction of musical components: there are, on the one hand, the words and, on the other, melodies suitable for reinforcing the effects of the words on the listener. These latter represent the irrational aspect of music—but their suavity is the key to a deeper penetration of text in the heart of the listener; only they are responsible for acoustic sins, thus only they must be regulated, hence the importance of defining them. The melodies must not enter the listener's senses alone, i.e. without the words. Thomas Aquinas would pick up this idea, which was the basis for his rejection of the use of musical instruments in church music.[ix] This would set off European culture's distrust of instrumental music as well as the moral hierarchy between vocal music and pure music up to the Baroque era. This explains the precepts announced during the 22nd Session of the Council of Trent, which required that the text be clearly understandable: as it is necessary to banish all lascivious music, it is necessary that the words sung be intelligible, the aesthetic criteria of simplicity supports an ethical goal. It is the union of melody and holy words that acts on the assembly of faithful, which also recalls the Constitution of the Council of Vatican II (in Chapter VI, dedicated to holy music).

The underlying idea is the same: the criteria of beauty must be framed, a pleasing language, which fits with sensibilities, must be spoken. Does this mean that the councils defined what moves a determinate social body? The Council of Trent legislated about church music in terms of simplicity and the priority given to sung text: the sacred text must not be lost in the complexity of musical polyphony, which makes the words lose their sense for the listener. Similarly, Vatican II advocated simplicity with regard to the efficacy of a communal song. A given community's collective sentiments are thus directed by a determinate music in its aesthetic contours.

From Augustine to Vatican II, the ancient Greek theory of musical catharsis served faith: music leads to a saintly devotion, it moves to tears and incites piety. The power of music, its role at the heart of the liturgy, and the Church's control over it travels through time. It is what the social body of the faithful hears and what it sings as a community that is controlled to ensure that the power of music is as effective as possible in the pursuit of pastoral and contemplative ends.

In all cases, music serves and enriches the *logos*. Its effectiveness serves the text, its power is a means of enabling holy words fully to penetrate the soul and body of the faithful, who, when they take part in communal song, feel themselves to be part of a communion of faith.

"Una forma che muove a pieta"

This effect is not only an endowment of the sacred domain; profane music combines the power of the text and that of sound in the same manner, the one reinforcing the other. The repertoire of Renaissance and Baroque music is packed with poetico-musical figures that touch listeners and act on their emotions. An especially famous example is Arianna's *lamento* on the words "lasciatemi morire" by Claudio Monteverdi.[x] Yesterday, like today, listeners are captured by the effect of musical language: they cannot remain neutral, the state of their souls is transformed independently from their will in accordance with the affect conveyed by the text and the music. At the end of the 17th century, 70 years after the composition of the *lamento*, some musical theorists applied themselves to understanding how music acted and to define the affect by its musical causes. They isolated the components of musical language that provoke this determinate affect and those that give a rational definition to emotion. According to Berardi (1689, p. 39), Monteverdi "uses the diminished fifth in a form which moves the listener to piety" ("una forma che muove a pietà"). The words "lasciatemi morire" split the sound of the interval, with the words speaking of a depressed spirit while at the same time the sound invades the body.

The power of musical discourse at the moment when it was modeled more and more on ancient rhetoric is not only that of the alliance between the text and the sound but equally that of pure sound. Theorists of musical rhetoric in the 17th century and above all in the 18th century would establish the equivalent status of vocal and instrumental musical: instruments speak the same language—formalized in its micro-elements and in its structure—as the voice. The application of the codes of rhetorical discourse and divisions to music aimed to determine the figures and structures of musical language, and its linguistic codes and divisions apply as much to vocal music as to music without a text. But let us return to the Renaissance, when the debate between affect and music was still part of medical thought.

Musical treatment

In addition to pastoral and rhetorical debates about the power of music to represent emotions, another relation between music and its effects on affects was developed in the medical literature. The idea dates back to Pythagoras. The human body is composed of four elements—earth, water, air, and fire—in harmonious proportion, and the Platonic soul is composed of the same numbers as music. Illness, of the soul or the body, is a dissonance, and the doctor's goal is to re-establish harmony. If music produces effects on the soul, and thereby on the body, we possess a tool for treating the sick person, but we must know the rules of the musical pharmacopoeia.

"A harmonious medicine composed by consonances and dissonances"

During the Renaissance, authors drew on the knowledge of the ancients and developed diverse analogies about the microcosm, human beings as an image of the macrocosm, and musical instruments: it was necessary to know how to accord the passions and to temper the affects, and possibly to re-tune and re-temper them. Thus humans and the universe were sometimes compared to a lyre, sometimes to an organ. These metaphors are found in both the medical and the musical literatures.

A example summarizing both musical analogies and the basis of the epoch's musical theory is taken from a work of Fioravanti (1564, p. 54). It recalls that all forms of infirmity were thought to arise from four principal causes, which were none other than the four humors—wet, dry, hot, and cold. These qualities were properties of the four elements that comprised all bodies ever created, including the human body. The body, the author continued, is a stringed instrument, and a disharmony between one of the organs is sufficient to break the harmony between the whole.

A century later, this idea was still present in musical theory: in musical treatises, it was normal to find a chapter on the capacity of music to treat infirmities and to preserve health. Both curatively and preventively, music served all good doctors, teaching them the proportion of members and of humors so that they could hear the harmony between different parts of the body. Once this harmony was understood, the doctor could act and prescribe an appropriate medication, in tempering the hot, dry ingredients with cold, wet ones to create "*a harmonious medicine composed by consonances and dissonances*" (Berardi 1689, p. 46).

A human being is the reflection of the world; therefore they carry within themselves the proportions of universal harmony. They are the mirror of the universe, and the properties of the celestial spheres can be read in them. Reciprocally, the planets send their influence down to the sublunary world: the effect of the Moon on the tides was an incontestable testimony of this power over centuries of debate about the stars' power over people. These planetary influences could be directed and controlled by people; they never constrained, because if they did so they would deny free will; they not only inclined but could also be called upon, provided one knew how to do so. A natural philosopher who knew the rules for manipulating nature to serve his fellows was a scholar, an artist, a magician, and a musician using the laws of nature. Marsilio Ficino (1492) first theorized this figure of the doctor–artist, giving a first rational comprehensive framework in Chapter 21 of his *De vita*. Even if he was a confirmed Platonic, Ficino was the first modern author to set down a rational theory of magico-astral medicine in which music held a primordial place.

"Planets don't suffer and feel no pain" (but listen to music)

This theory argues that the power of music must be combined with the power of the stars in order to control the influences of the stars with the goal of re-establishing harmony in the sufferer's head.[xii] For a melancholic dominated by Saturn, a music possessing the characteristics of the black planet is suitable: for example, a heavy, serious song that imitates the qualities of the star responsible for melancholy. Music plays a double role in this process: it disposes the individual's spirit to receiving the planet's influence, and it attracts the planet's influence.

The power of sound acts on the rational animal on a sub-rational level: the proof is in its effects on non-rational animals, deer and elephants being common examples in ancient and Renaissance theory. In the docudrama *L'histoire du chameau qui pleure* [The Story of the Weeping Camel] (2004) we see a musician care for his camel and make it cry in the desert plains of Mongolia. That music also acts on the planets is the other aspect of the extent of its effects. It acts on planets through its capacity to imitate, through the similar character found in musical semantics and in planetary attributes. Imitation enables invocation. This no longer concerns the imitation of emotions to allow for an emotional affinity: the stars don't feel anything and thus are not felt. Tommaso Campanella (1620) recalls this poetically in his *De sensu rerum* (III, 4): planets don't suffer and feel no pain. This sensitive dimension radically differentiates the senses from the stars, which recognize things and beings from the sublunary world, which see through their radiance and hear through their movement, which sense but don't experience. Music is the interface between celestial and human bodies in these interactions between the powers of the stars and human ills arising from planetary influences.

In parallel to the magio-medical literature of natural philosophy, another type of literature referred to the power of music to act on affects. It was a genre that reunited theology and medicine, namely treatises on demonology written for (and generally by) exorcists, doctors of the soul charged with liberating the bodies of the possessed for the health of the soul. Unlike the musical theory of ethos, the traditional relationships between music and medicine and those between music and magic, the particular links between diabolic possession, a large preoccupation in Renaissance society, and medicine have not sparked the interest of either historians or musicologists. However, it is not illogical, given the place reserved for music in medieval and Renaissance knowledge, that music found a place in these works.

As late as the beginning of the 18th century, a musical theorist like Domenico Scorpione (1701, p. 78) concluded his list of the effects of music by mentioning its power against diabolical spirits. The story of Saul being liberated from evil spirits by David's harp (Kings 1: 16) served as a point of departure, of proof, and of justification for the use of music to drive out the devil. One of the principal questions that concerned treatises in demonology was that of the sign, a key element in Renaissance culture. There were different kinds of signs that one needed to know how to distinguish and decrypt: the sign that marked the pact with the devil defined a witch or wizard, and it was not the same as that which marked possession. Possession was the invasion of an individual by the devil without that person's consent. Once the sign was decoded, one needed to know if it was a real or imaginary possession.

Music as a sign

Signs of possession were categorized and catalogueed so that they would be recognizable. It was important to not make an erroneous diagnosis: the individual's health and their soul's salvation depended on it. A category related to language invariably appears among these signs. This was one of the topics of the theoretical literature on the practice of exorcism. A peasant or some other illiterate person who spoke in Latin or Greek could only be possessed by the devil: they would never have learned such a scholarly language, and the fact that they spoke it was a sign of diabolic intervention. Disproportion between an individual and their capacity or knowledge indicated an exceptional event, which was not natural and testified to the supernatural. Music as a sign of demonic possession found itself at the heart of the language problem: an illiterate person who sang musically or who played a musical instrument could not be a natural phenomenon. Once the sign of possession was recognized, it was possible to treat with an adapted remedy.

The devil could also appear in music, as, for example, in the story of a group of people going to San Michele in Bosco in the Bolognese hills, who heard a wonderful sound come out of a cloud, as reported by Girolamo Menghi (1595, pp. 63–4): the people lifted their eyes and saw a black servant, who had not received any musical training, playing the viola da gamba better than all the country's professional musicians. The devil had taken the form of a servant of color with the musical voice of a perfect viola da gamba player: he used this beautiful music to trick people, he unsettled the sense of hearing, played with the auditory imagination and also possibly provoked emotions—from fear to wonder—by means of musical trickery.

Music as an antidote

The invaded body and the troubled imagination had to be treated, whether in the case of possessions or of musical apparitions of the devil. Music served yet again as an antidote to malignant powers. The first treatise for exorcists, the famous *Malleus maleficarum,* which appeared in at least 34 editions in Europe between 1486 and 1669, took the story of David treating Saul with the sound of his harp as its point of departure for affirming that the medical power of music was equal to that of plants and herbs. Music, as with any other corporeal element, contained a natural virtue (*Malleus maleficarum* II, II, V) that one simply needed to know how to use in order for its efficacy to appear. After the appearance of this treatise, even the authors who were most skeptical about the effectiveness of plants and herbs in exorcising the devil agreed that musical harmony had this power. For its part, the musical literature conveyed the same idea. A little before the publication of the first edition of *Malleus maleficarum,* the theorist Johannes Tinctoris affirmed that music had the power to exorcise the devil when he listed the effects of music in his treatise *Complexus effectuum musices*: "Musica diabolum fugat." This is an assertion that is found in the entire Renaissance musical literature: "Musica est maximum Diaboli tormentum" (Cerreto 1601, p. 176). Music is the devil's supreme torment because it is harmony, and the devil flees from all that is harmonious.

Beyond the words, obviously historically connoted, the devil is all forms of evil, of dissonance, of dissension, of discord, and of disharmony that one would like to temper, to calm, and ideally to drive away. The catalogue of the medical effects of music concluded by affirming its maximum power, up to the 18th-century literature: the power of music even triumphs over infernal spirits ("la forza della musica fino de'Spiriti Infernali trionfa"; Scorpione 1701, p. 77) and, due to this power, the evil spirit gives way ("per la musica cede lo spirito maligno"; Goretti 1612, p. 17).

Conclusion

To provoke and to induce, to understand and to rationalize: the role of music in relation to affects passes through a theory of emotions on the part of musical theorists and, to a lesser extent, on the part of civil, and religious authorities seeking to control the effects of music. The questions asked during the Middle Ages and the Renaissance are, in part, identical those we are still asking today.

The Middle Ages and the Renaissance carried a double message: on the one hand, that of an encyclopedic knowledge, as opposed to our hyper-specialization and, on the other hand, a capacity to think about the unity of the individual and of the individual with the world. As for medieval and Renaissance musical thought, it talks about music as an encyclopedia, as the harmonious person's ideal and as the perfection of all the sciences. Seeing these cultural models across the window of history categorizes us. Does it not allow us to see things in terms of rupture, fractures, and radical epistemological and paradigmatic changes and to see these same things in terms of continuity and legacies? We no longer believe—since in the end in medicine as in the other sciences it is in part a question of belief—that we need the reunion of the spirits of herbs, the pharmacist, the doctor, and the patient for a medicine to be effective and to re-establish the harmony of the soul, of tormented spirits, of discordant bodies, and of badly tempered affects. And yet, the idea, for example, that the patient must believe in the prescribed remedy doesn't sound entirely false to our contemporary ears.Musical science may have had as its goal bringing attention to the being—a mixture of consonance and dissonance, a rhythmic harmony of systole and diastole, and an accurate meter of voices articulated in words—and recognition of its purpose, namely harmony. Speculative music had the ability to contain the arts and the sciences and to speak to different social actors, from legislators to doctors. The possibility of musical science to tell us about a being's essence and its finality petered out in the 18th century. In this era, music became exclusively an art, but neither a being's essence nor its finality can be dictated by sciences today. Neither the totalizing faculty of musical science nor its encyclopedism is possible today: instead, the spread of science has become its segmentation, hence the need for interdisciplinarity.

Notes

i   The theme of music and emotions, of sounds and affects, has been an integral part of musicological discourse for a century, and debates continue. I do not claim to present a historiographical summary. The reader will find the principal bibliographic references in the entries "Affect" and "Rhetoric" in the *New Grove Dictionary of Music and Musicians* (2001).

ii   We must retain the notion of will or the voluntary act, as the three dimensions of mind are memory, reason, and will.

iii   See St Bonaventure, *Itineriarium mentis in deum* [*The Journey of the Mind into God*], VII, pp. 2–4.

iv   See St Bonaventure, *Vitis mystica* [*The True Vine*], VII–XIII.

v   "Sono molti i dolori, e gli affanni, che nella vita ad ogni hora si devono provare né si potrebbero in modo alcuno agevolmente, se non fosse scemata con qualcosa di dolce la loro amarezza."

vi   In *De Musica* (37) Plutarch says that a penalty was given to those who played in the Myxolydian mode.

vii   Isidore de Séville, *Etymologie* (bk III, XVII), taken up again among others in the Renaissance by Aaron (1523).

viii   This question is analyzed in Arcangeli (2000).

ix   *Summa theologica*, II, question XCI.

x   Claudio Monteverdi, *Madrigali a 1, 2, 3, 4 e 6 voci, con altri generi di canti, settimo libro*, Venice, 1619.

xi   The literature has become abundent since Walker's (1958) pioneering study—see, for example, Tomlinson (1993), Boccadoro (2000, 2004, 2006), Gouk (2000), Voss (2002), and Gozza (2004).

xii   I present a bibliography on the theme of music and astrology in Wuidar (2008).

References

Aaron, P. (1523). *Thoscanello de la musica*, bk 1, ch. 1 (pages not numbered). Venice: Bernardino et Matheo de Vitali.

Arcangeli, A. (2000). *Davide o Salomè? Il dibattito Europeo sulla danza nella prima età moderna*. Treviso-Roma: Fondazione Benetton Studi Ricerche.

Berardi, A. (1689). *Miscellanea musicale*. Bologna: Giacomo Monti.

Boccadoro, B. (2000). Arsilio Ficino: the soul and the body of counterpoint. In P. Gozza (ed.), *Number to Sound. The Musical Way to the Scientific Revolution*, pp. 99–134. Boston: Kluwer Academic Publishers.

Boccadoro, B. (2004). Eléments de grammaire mélancolique. *Acta Musicologica*, **LXXVI**, 25–65.

Boccadoro, B. (2006). Musique, médecine et tempéraments. In J.-J. Nattiez (ed.), *Musiques, une encyclopédie pour le XXIème siècle*. Paris: Actes Sud.

Bocchi, F. (1580). *Discorso sopra la musica*. Firenze.

Burmeister, J. (1599) *Hypomnematum musicae poeticae*. Rostock: S. Myliander.

Burmeister, J. (1606). *Musica poetica*. Rostock: S. Myliander.

Campanella, T. (1620). *De sensu rerum*. Frankfurt: Apud Egenolphum Emmelium.

Cerreto, S. (1601). *Della prattica musica vocale, et strumentale*. Naples.

Ficino, M. (1489) *De vita libri tres*. Florence, Antonio di Bartolommeo Miscomini.

Fioravanti, L. (1564). *Capricci medicinali di M. Leonardo Fieravanti medico Bolognese* …. Venice: Lodovico Avanzo.

Goretti, A. (1612). *Dell'eccellenze e prerogative della musica*. Ferrara: V. Baldini.

Gouk, P. (2000). Music, melancholy, and medical spirits in early modern thought. In P. Horden (ed.). *Music as Medicine: the History of Music Therapy since Antiquity*, pp. 173–94. Aldershot: Ashgate.

Gozza, P. (2004). Platone e Aristotele nel Rinascimento: la psicologia della musica di Ficino e Giacomini. *Il Saggiatore Musicale*, **11**, 233–52.

van Haeften, B. (1635). *Regia via crucis*. Antwerp: Balthasaris Moreti.

Menghi, G. (1595). *Compendio dell'arte essorcistica*. Bologne: G. Rossi.

Nucius, J. (1613) *Musicae poeticae sive de compositione cantus*. Neisse: Scharffenbergus.

Scorpione, D. (1701). *Riflessioni armoniche divise*, 2 vols. Naples: De Bonis.

Tomlinson, G. (1993). *Music in Renaissance Magic*. London, Chicago University Press.

de Tyard, P. (1555). *Solitaire second, ou prose de la musique*. Lyons: de Tournes.

Voss, A. (2002). Orpheus *redivivus*: the musical magic of Marsilio Ficino. In M. J. B. Allen and V. Rees (eds), *Marsilio Ficino, his Theology, his Philosophy, his Legacy*, pp. 227–41. Leiden: Brill.

Walker, D. P. (1958). *Spiritual and Demonic Magic from Ficino to Campanella*. London, The Warburg Institute.

Wuidar, L. (2008). *Musique et astrologie après le Concile de Trente*. Turnhout: Brepols.

Zuccolo da Cologna, S. (1549). *La pazzia del ballo*. Padua: Fabriano.

Chapter 21

The psychotropic power of music during the Renaissance

Brenno Boccadoro (translation by Kristen Gray Jafflin)

You ask me, dear Canigiani, why I so frequently combine the study of medicine with that of music. What possible relationship can there be between remedies and the *kythara*? Astrologers may perhaps relate one or the other discipline to the convergence of Jupiter, Mercury, and Venus, on the grounds that medicine pertains to Jupiter and music to Mercury and Venus. On the other hand, our Platonists relate all this to the same God, Apollo, whom the ancient theologians believed to be both the inventor of medicine and supreme master in the art of playing the *kyithara*. In the Orphic *Hymns,* this is the God who, by his vital rays, bestows health and life and dispels all ills. Furthermore, by the sound of the strings of his lyre, that is their vibrations and power, he regulates all that exists, generating by the *hypate*, a grave note, winter; by the *neate* [namely *nete*], the highest note summer, spring and autumn by the Dorians that are the middle notes. To the extent that this God is both the patron of music and the inventor of medicine, it is not surprising that both arts are often practiced by the same men. Moreover, the soul and the body are in harmony by virtue of a certain natural consonance, just as the elements of the soul, as those of the body, are in mutual accord. It is this harmony that the harmonious circuits of the fevers, the humors and the rhythm of the pulse emulate.

Plato and Aristotle have taught and we ourselves have often experienced, that solemn music preserves and restores the harmony to the different parts of the soul, while medicine preserves the harmonious concert of the different parts of the body. Since the body and the soul respond and harmonize with each other, as we have stated, it is not difficult for the same person to simultaneously cultivate the harmony of the different parts of the soul and of the body. That is why Chiron practiced both disciplines; that is also why it is written that the prophet David healed the soul and body of the delirious Saul with this lyre. That the same result could be obtained in respect of other conditions affecting the soul as much as the body had been proven by Democritus and Theophrastus, and demonstrated in practice by Pythagoras, Empedocles, and the physician Asclepius. Nor is this surprising; for, like sound song emanates from imaginations in the mind, the impulse of the fantasy and the desire of the heart and, as it touches and tempers the air, it also affects the aerial spirit of the listener, the link between the body and the soul: it easily entrances the imaginary, affects the heart and penetrates to the innermost recesses of the mind, and even arrests or sets in motion the humors in the body, as well as the limbs. This was indeed demonstrated by Timotheus as he provoked Alexander the Great with his sounds to fury, to then appease him again. I need not dwell on the marvels wrought by Pythagoras and Empedocles who becalmed slackness, anger, or frenzy with grave and dignified music or, by using different modes, roused the sluggish souls from their torpor; nor shall I dwell on that which is related of Orpheus, Arion, and Amphion.

In truth, to return to our subject, the first form of music resides in reason, the second in the imagination, the third in discourse; then follows song, the song is followed by the movement of fingers in instrumental music, the instrumental music by the movement of the entire body in gymnastics and dance. Thus the music of the soul is extended into all limbs, music that the orators, poets, painters, sculptors, architects emulate in their creations. Given such communion between the music of the soul and the body, it is not surprising that one and the same man could thus temper both the soul and body. Finally, he who has learned from the Pythagoreans, the Platonists, Hermes Trismegistus, and Aristoxenus that the soul and body of the world, just as that of any living being, are composed of musical proportions, he who has been taught by the Holy Scriptures of the Jews, according to which God has ordered the universe "in accordance with the number, the weight and the measure," will not be surprised that harmony enthralls nearly all living beings. Neither will he find any reason to blame Pythagoras, Empedocles, or Socrates for having continued to sound the strings of the *kythara* in their old age. By contrast, he would qualify Themistocles who, at a banquet refused the lyre offered to him, as lacking in culture. In *Alcibiades,* our Plato has demonstrated that music belonged to the learned, those who cultivate the Muses, affirming that these governed music and that music derived its name from them. Plato wholly rejects the doleful or shallow melody, convinced that it debased the soul, rendered it lascivious or choleric. He only retains the higher and firm forms of music as constituting a most salutary remedy for the spirit, the soul, and the body.

As for myself, to tell you something of your dear Marsilio, after the study of theology and medicine, it is with this intention that I frequently immerse myself in serious music, through song and the playing of the lyre [viola da braccio]; ignoring completely all other delectations of the senses, expelling all pains of the soul and body, elevating my spirit as far as I can towards the sublime spheres and towards God, confident in the authority of Hermes Trismegistus and Plato, who declare that music was conferred on us by God in order to subdue the body, temper the soul, and praise God. I know that, above all, this is the precept of David and Pythagoras and, in my view, the objective they attained.

From Marsilius Ficinus to Antonio Canigiani, learned and sagacious man (Ficino 1990, pp. 161–3).

In this letter Marsilio Ficino (1433–99) answered his friend Canigiani's question about the motives that had led him to so diligently mix the study of medicine with that of music. A modern intermediary of this venerable chapter of ancient heritage, so exalted by the best authors, Ficino wasn't the only musicologist to investigate this subject. Discussion of the causal properties of musical harmony could emerge in contexts as diverse as natural philosophy, humoral medicine, architectural theory, white magic, and, *de iure*, in any technical treatise of musical theory. But everyone knew that it was in the works of Ficino, that one could find all the indications necessary, from the technical plan to its psychophysiological background.

Medicus mediceus, doctor to the Medicis in Florence, new adoptive father of ancient ideas on the melancholic spirit, author of the first Latin edition of the complete works of Plato, father of Florentine neo-Platonism, translator of Plotinus, Porphyry, Iamblichus, and the writings of Hermes Trismegistus, Ficino was famous as much for the universality of his knowledge as for the technicality of his competences. In a commentary on open musical digressions in Plato's works, he collected knowledge of the musical domain, unrivalled in his time, in a thorough study from the Greek of the principal ancient theoretical sources, Theon of Smyrna, Ptolemy, Nicomachus of Gerasa, and Aristides Quintilian. A musician in his spare time, he wielded the mathematical theory of harmony as successfully as his viola da braccio, with which he accompanied his Orphic songs—sparkling eyes lifted to the sky, like St Cecilia in ecstasy.

Enlivened by the breath of his enthusiasm, Ficino's memoir condenses the essential *ex auctoritate* arguments cited by scholars for centuries to prove the reality of the psychotropic power of music in less than a page. A red thread links all the examples cited: the causal value attributed to melody. For 17th-century rationalists, good sense teaches us to recognize the effect of *habitus* in these phenomena, or the consequence of a particular *synthesis* of the elements of the writing into a complex "unity," impossible to reduce to general rules. Descartes' example, "a dog whipped five or six times to the sounds of the violin will flee if it hears that instrument" (Adam and Tannery 1969) proves that the effective virtue that terrifies the animal's *vis imaginativa* is independent of the organization of sound in the melody: the sense of the music is a subjective psychological value, elaborated through the listener's individual experience, accidentally associated with a stimulus so the melody acts as a memory sign: seasoned with a good dose of whiplashes, a different melody would produce the same effect. Ficino was not yet there, or he didn't want to go so far. His explanation for the tarantism of Puglia shows that the power that treats the patient's tarantula bite has its source in a *virtus immutandi* radiating from the sun to the sublunary world through the intermediary of the mathematical organization of the melody. Ficino knew the argument about *habitus*, but he cited St Augustine to show that it was a "vulgar" conception of art, involving memory and the body: "Thus we discover that the vulgar art is nothing more than a memory of examined objects that pleased us, joined to our body and our activity's experience."[i]

Everyone knew Aristotle's proposition about the pleasure the elderly feel when they hear songs learned during their youth. But instead of invoking the associative action of memory, of the type that the 18th century would call "nostalgia" or "*Heimweh*," the authors limited themselves to a very physiological analysis invoking the pleasure felt in reminiscing about a period of life governed by a better proportioned temperament. Remarks about the fascination music exercised over animals—nightingales, bees, deer, dogs, bear, horses, camels, dolphins, and elephants—show that harmony acts on the inferior faculties of the soul, which humans share with them and which are independent of the will.

Melody treats because its action paralyses free will; there is no question of relying on critical thinking or an individual's personal inclination. The most instructive example is perhaps the inescapable story of Empedocles and Anchites, which Ficino doesn't fail to mention to his friend Canigiani:

> A young man rushed, sword in hand, at Anchites, Empedocles' guest, because he had condemned his father to death during a public trial; his passion and his anger were so great that he wanted to strike him with his sword, as if Anchites, instead of the judge, had killed his father. Empedocles, tuning his lyre on the sport, immediately played a peaceful, calm song and made this music heard, "this drug [*nepenthes*] calming the pain and anger and dissolving all the ills," as the poet said, thus sparing the life of his host and stopping the young man from murder. The story says that the young man later became one of Empedocles' most remarkable disciples.[ii]

Ficino knew very well that a common denominator tied all the elements in this scene together in the same intertextual relationship: the idea of harmony as a concordance of discordant (*krasis*) opposites. Homer's verse, put into Empedocles mouth by Pythagorean hagiography, invited the reader to another mythic banquet: the Homeric episode of an evening with a heavy atmosphere, made leaden by the recital of the Greeks' misfortunes, during which Helen tried to drown the guests' black humor in wine drunk from a vessel in which she had mixed carefully proportioned ingredients meant to give the drink the active virtue of a irresistibly powerful drug, "calming pain" (*nepenthes*) and keeping whoever "had lost father and mother" from shedding tears.[iii] The followers of Pythagoras knew that *nepenthes* was an attribute of Apollo, god of harmony, inventor of medicine and the lyre. Qualifying with this hallowed term the virtue of an air accompanied by this instrument meant placing the power of music above that of the most powerful narcotic ever imagined in history.

We don't know the composition of this beverage, but it is certain that it issued from a mixture (*krasis*, crasis) of opposed ingredients. The intertextual link tying the wine's sedative action and Empedocles' song passed precisely through the intermediary of this nodal point. The intrusion of harmonic models into oenology was inevitable in the literary genre of the banquet. Signs such as the rising temperature during the juice's fermentation, the spirit's effervescence, sweating, and the drinkers becoming red led ancient authors to point to the fire set free in the organism by the wine when accounting for drunkenness. Ancient ethics thus turned to the cooling power of water and of mathematical harmony to put a brake to the excesses caused by this heating power.[iv] Using the cup as a unit of measurement and on average three cups of wine for every two of water, Plutarch (*Quaestiones conviviales*, III, 9, 657b) made a wine "in the fifth" producing a "musical" intoxication, moderated by the numeric values of this interval (3:2).

The communication route between oenology and medicine was entirely found in the analogy between the "spirits" of wine and the spirits circulating in the organism and the bloody crasis. As to the idea of excess, it ruled all, from the relations between the humors to those between the two numeric terms of dissonance. Helen's wine, the overflowing anger of Empedocles' host, overheated by wine and yellow bile, and the crasis of the high and low notes of the lyre's chord all point to one sole principle: the idea of harmony as the discordant concordance of antagonistic forces (*krasis*, *harmonia*, crasis).

Harmony

The soul, wine, the crasis of the humors, and the crasis of melody, appeared as so many manifestations of the same principle tying different domains of knowledge together: the definition of harmony as the reconciliation of antagonistic forces, a definition that contained in embryo everything that authors imagined during twenty centuries of theorizing about harmony. This tradition's principal characteristic lies in what we would not be wrong to define as an "elementary" conception of musical grammar as a field parallel to the physics of elements. Everything began in the 5th century BC, when the Pythagoreans discovered that the consonance produced by the two extremes of a musical interval was the acoustic translation of a privileged numeric relationship tying an even and an odd number. This marriage of even and odd in musical intervals appeared to be a particular case of the mixture (*krasis*) of contrary elements in the physical world. Aristotle (*Metaphysics,* A v, 986a 15) pronounced himself explicitly on this point: the Pythagoreans regarded even and odd as "elements of the number" and the sky and the world as a living being derived from their harmonization: the elements of the number are even and odd, the former being limited and the later unlimited. Rather than explaining the world's diversity through the mixture of air, water, earth, and fire, they reduced the physical body to a musical mixture of even and odd. Despite what Aristotle said about the impossibility of extending the category of opposition to numbers, numeric values designating the high and low extremes of intervals are contrary to each other; one designates a high sound and the other a low sound; and a numeric relationship designates a specific relationship that can be seen as contrary to another, for example, when a relationship designates a consonant interval and another a dissonant interval. That is why, as Ficino noted, "Plato favors the number 12," because in addition to its roots, 7 and 5, it contains the form of the fifth (3:2) and the fourth (4:3), two odd and even elements (2 and 3) that, tempered according to just proportions, generate the octave, the most perfect of consonances (2:3 × 3:4 = 6:12) (Allen 1994, p. 183). The same elementary conception would characterize the "elements of musical grammar" combined in the body of the melody: sound intervals, modes, and *tonoi*.

The principle governing consonance is the capacity of even and odd numbers to blend into one—the same way that the human marital bond is born from the desire to fuse bodies in a primordial, androgynous unity. Ficino stated this in a well-known passage from his *Commentary on Plato's Symposium* harmony is love, and the odd number makes love to the even in the two extremes of the musical interval, because, by virtue of its central unity, the odd number is masculine, while the even is feminine due to the gaping opening, symbol of the womb, which opens at its center. Marital harmony varies in intensity depending on the quality of the relationship:

> We see the same thing in music, where artists research how much numbers love each other. Between one and two [namely the second 9:8], between one and seven [the seventh 7:4], they find almost no love. In contrast, between one, three, four, five, and six [the third 5:4; the fourth 4:3, the fifth 3:2 and the sixth 27:16], they find a very ardent love, and they find the most ardent love between one and eight. (Ficino 2002, p. 58)

Marriage is happy in a fifth (3:2), consonant thanks to the unity that measures both extremes without excess or defect, but it degrades into complex dissonances like 256:243, ending in a divorce in incommensurable relationships like √2:1, which theory qualifies as *alogoi*, or *absurdi*, terms derived from *ab* and *surdus*, devoid of logic and "deaf," inaudible.

There was hardly any area other than musical theory that could verify this thesis, wonderful and absurd at the same time:[v] the mixture of even and odd numbers in rectangular (*heteromekes*) ($n + 1:n$) relationships generates musical intervals allowing one to clearly hear that the different qualities of the "loving" relationship binding even and odd, masculine, in the physical body[vi] were simply a consequence of the ability of extremes to mix together into one, thanks to the mediating role of unity. The habit of isolating the qualities of numbers by averaging configurations of stones (Greek *psephoi*, Latin *calculi*, root of "calculation") distributed on a surface plane led the Pythagoreans to attribute this love to the kinship established by a common unifying module in the two extremes of the interval, such as in a fifth (3:2), where the consonance arises from the mediating action of the arithmetic unity (1) tying the two extremes 2 and 3, as shown in Figure 21.1.

The next step consisted of extending the whole to a planetary scale. Synonymous with "communication" and "transitive causality," the mediating action of the unity of extremes offered a reduced model for all phenomena of action at a distance crossing the machine of the world. All that could be interpreted in terms of this relationship was brought back to a problem of consonance and dissonance: from the sympathetic vibration of strings to magical enchantments, passing by way of homeopathy, allopathy, magnetism, astrology, the soul's and body's music, the crasis of the four humors, the voyages of the *spiritus phantasticus* into the regions of the *anima mundi*, prophetic

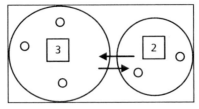

Figure 21.1 The mathematical ratio of the fifth represented as the harmony between the numbers 2 and 3. The small circles represent unities and the arrows their mediating action on each extreme.

irradiation, the soul's causality, the action and passion of like for like, the mimetic relationship between the text and its incarnation in the sonorous body of a musical composition, and the psychic power of modes.

Aristotelianism, neo-Platonism, science, and magic

During antiquity, the theory of the power of music received support from Plato and Aristotle, who arrived at their conclusions by different means. The Renaissance only prolonged this debate by drawing in an eclectic manner from these two traditions. The first model referred to in explaining this power was purely arithmetic and rationalist. The theory of art on which they drew came from Aristotle: it considered musical creation to be the incarnation of an idea conceived in the mind and imposed with "violence" on outer material. The theory of affects was a *techne*: it assumed objective criteria, a method, knowledge of rules, and imitation of canons cited as models of perfection by musical criticism. Aristotelianism sees the action of music in terms of a sympathetic relationship between the agent and the patient: in the mind of a well-meaning author, like Zarlino (1558, II, 8, p. 74), affect is the effect of a causal action exercised through the harmonic and arithmetic proportion that the essential chords of the modes share with the crasis of secondary qualities in the temperament. Counterpoint or melody is limited to representing affect to the listener's imagination without the intervention of other magical or supra-rational factors foreign to the form. On the ethical plane, passion is a positive good if it is measured.

Thus, the same Pythagoreanism could support the Aristotelian definition of ethos as simple imitation of forms as well as it could the sympathetic magic so dear to Ficino and to the tenants of occult, neo-Platonic, hermetic, and alchemist philosophy. Following Plotinus, Ficino imagined an animated world, with a soul, a body, and a nervous system of numeric correspondences spreading its net over all its members, thus tied together in an uninterrupted system of sympathetic resonances. The constitutive elements of this theory were not new. Ficino had expressly affirmed them when referring to "his" Platonics and to the "Arabs." But the synthesis was without precedent, as was the explanation of its operative causality, which, beneath its inoffensive appearance, defied all that orthodoxy banned. Musical theory played an important role in this synthesis. The mediating action exercised by the unity of the interval's extremes offered an efficient model leading back to the problem of consonance and dissonance in all transitive phenomena traversing the machine of the world: the analogy of the macro- and microcosm, the powers of astrology, the voyages of the *spiritus phantasticus* in the regions of the *anima mundi*; the *excessus mentis*, the prophetic irradiation of divine fury, the operations of magic, the virtues of stones and talismans and the contagious power of celestial and sonorous music manifested in its elements' force. According to the letter to his friend Canigiani, the therapeutic power of music had its source in the solar virtue of Apollo, who transmitted life and health to the whole universe through the harmony of his zither (12:9:8:6), producing "winter with the deepest chord" (the *hypate*, *mi*), summer with the highest (the *nète*, *mi'*), autumn with the *mèse* (*la*), and spring with the *paramèse* (*si*) (Ficino 1990, p. 651). The common denominator of the universe, number harmony, affected both "the parts of the soul among themselves" and those of "the body," namely the humors and the animal spirits. Due to the *consonantia* that tied the soul to the body, music treated the body by acting on the soul. And thanks to this same consonance, the harmony of the soul expressed itself in the body and in all that it did. Hence the intersections between music and medicine: the music of the beating heart, which scans the *thesis* and the *arsis* of ancient meters; the concert of the humors; the "harmonic rhythm" of fevers in feverish rigors when the excess heat appears in intervals of consonant time; articulated in tetrads of days, conjoint and disjointed, like the tetrachords of Greek music, during crises.

This doctrine, which Ficino was among the first to revisit, could have invoked Censorinus' specula-tion on the harmonic development of the fetus following days 6:8:9:12 of pregnancy. In its turn, this thesis naturally led to an anthropometric analysis of the body, well-known among architects and sculptors, and to analogies between metric and members that transformed the body into a poem: because temperament, in its manner, *speaks*; as it expresses itself in the body and in all that it does, it expresses itself in art and music.

Ficino pushed *Timaeus*'s anthropomorphism to its final consequences. Like Plotinus, he imag-ined a dancing world, having a soul, a body, and a frame of harmonic relations. He based the record of the intelligible and the sensible on a vitalist base, which engaged the efficient cause responsi-ble for the transformation of natural bodies into the same material. The model was found in its entirety in a summary of ancient Pythagoreanism given in Aristotle's metaphysics, which main-tained that the world was born from the encounter of even and odd in a living cell containing the driving principle of its growth. And an even more eloquent indication figured in a fragment of this same Pythagoreanism conserved in the Hippocratic regimen—which Ficino knew as well as medicine—on the development of the embryo following the dichotomy of an androgynous sperm cell, divided according to the proportion of the octave's fifth and fourth (Joly and Byl 1984, p. 132). Hence the astonishing image of ligaments tying the soul to the universe, like a baby in the womb:

> Thus, we are tied as if by three cables to the entire machine … as the embryo in the womb is attached by ligaments to the whole maternal body, and therefore senses through the intermediary of its soul, body and spirit the passions of the mother's soul, body and spirit. (Ficino 1964, XIII, ii, p. 209)

Through its intelligence (*mens*), the soul is tied to superior intelligences; through its imagination, it accords itself with the imagination of celestial souls; through its body, it communicates with the body of the world. The image of a cable refers to the mediating action of the *spiritus*. The "node" and mediating element of the soul and body. In the Pythagorean tradition, as seen in the works of Nicomachus, Iamblichus, and many others, the metaphor of the "node" designated the brake imposed on matter by a number: *tu numeris elementa ligas* recalled Boethius when referring to the demiurge's action in organizing chaos. Here the *spiritus* is qualified as such. *Spiritus* is to the soul and the body what unity is to the extremes, a transitive link assuring communication between opposites. It is the vehicle of harmony and even its link.

Ficino extended its transitive power to all domains of being, from the *spiritus phantasticus* tying imagination to the soul of the world to the *aer fractus ac temperatus* that breathed in the body of counterpoint. As in music, where love between the sounds isn't a function of their contiguity in the range or universe, similar parts thus sympathize through their resemblance despite being separated by different parts. The relationship of soul and body is not linear: in the world's soul, the idea of harmony is pure; incarnated in the artist's imagination in moments of creative ecstasy, it is covered with corporeal images, just as the sky is covered with clouds, and borrows the non-verbal language of the body. The universe is thus *liber* and *scriptura,* a cryptographic forest of hieroglyphic images communicating through a weft of harmonic resonances. Hence the principle of signatures, the very foundation of magical epistemology, wherein a simple analogy between two heterogeneous objects can serve as a conjunction between the most unthinkable things. The nut reflects the human brain, gold the Sun; body parts communicate with the sky. The metaphor of the incarnation applies to "bodies" and "soul" of the symbols, in a sort of Cratylism where the sign directly reflects the thing, as the soul expresses itself in bodies. Hence the poetics of *imprese*, of symbols, the *Wortmalerei* in Franco-Flemish music and in the madrigal, which clothes the text's soul in a sonorous garment to the measure of its character. The elements of musical grammar are no exception. In the last part of *De vita triplici*, pharmaceutical indications on the *ethos* of the elements of musical writing enter into a general discussion of the making of talismans, sonorous supports charged with astral energy whose physical activity had never been theorized before with such intensity.

Through its evolving form, counterpoint constitutes the most faithful imitation of the arithmetic figures seen in celestial revolutions, which it shares with the intelligence of planetary demons, which imagine the revolutions of the world's machine mathematically. At the same time, magic accorded a purely transitive role to the form. Streaming to Earth from the celestial vault in an uninterrupted circuit, *affectus* was no more than the effect of an energetic, autonomous fluid, superior to the pure quantity, which the mathematical organization of the mode can only divert towards the listener. The melody became a complex talisman crossed by a circuit of occult energies, independent of its mathematical frame. It lost its active role to become the instrument of heaven. The same can be said for the soul of the musician, which was more than just a simple intermediary or "medium" of exchange with unpredictable energies, housed in the interval between sky and earth. The spirit breaths where it wants to, *flat ubi vult*; the musician is a fowler destined to tend grace's traps. But he ceases to create beauty. Like the alchemist, he hastens or delays the conditions of natural activity; he "commands" the great machine of the world by obeying it; he operates, seizes the opportune moment and the short-lived occasion for capturing astral influences; he sets off the chain of natural causalities, even if it means not being able to stop it, like the sorcerer's apprentice. Hence the story about the *virtus immutandi* of *vis imaginativa*, able to bind or unbind matter to alter its own body and the body of others through the force of its affects and favorable constellations. The aesthetic of affects found therein all the phenomena that could not be explained by pure Aristotelianism: the contagious force of affect manifested by the form, the voyages of the imaginative spirit, inspiration, and melancholic genius. To the methodical artist who proceeds through calculations, academics opposed the image of the inspired one who creates *per ingegno proprio agitato e commosso da alcun vigore interno e nascoso il quale si chiama furore ed occupazione di mente* (Bruni 1436, cited in Chastel 1975). On the one hand, the "gift," on the other, the "study"; on the one hand art, on the other science. Affect responds to "gift," mathematical organization to form. The consequence of these divorces was subjectivism and abdication of the need to follow the rules, which, taken to its extreme, could have compromised the very possibility of a theory of affects.

Musica humana

A tight relationship ties the theory of affects to reflection on the soul and its powers. In the space of this chapter it is impossible for us to give a detailed report of internal variants of eclectic theory, which had dominated psychology in the Middle Ages and the Renaissance after Albert the Great, without resorting to a perfunctory summary. So, to avoid too long an account, we limit ourselves to Ficino's conceptions.

The composition of the body is broken into four humors, correlating to the four elements, the four seasons, and the four ages of life: black bile (earth) [cold dry]; phlegm (water) [cold humid]; blood (air) [hot humid]; yellow bile or choler (fire) [hot dry]. The tomb of the soul, the temperament is the place of the indeterminate movement of corporeal matter, opaque to reason and eternally torn by the tension of antagonistic forces. Taken individually, the humors are enemies; the purer they are, the more they oppose each other: the unlimited hegemony of the black humor produces death from a chill, just as the predominance of fire reduces one to dust. Duly tempered by their opposites, they produce a more or less stable equilibrium, the oscillations of which explain the somatic and psychic variations of all individuals; equality of antagonistic forces produces a universally colorless apathy while, for its part, the oscillation of the crasis creates an excess and a more or less pathogenic defect. For specialized medicine, this notion could have dispensed with a musico-mathematic interpretation, but among the partisans of physical reflections on *intentio* and *remissio formarum* inaugurated by the *calculatores* in Oxford and Paris—Bradwardine, Burdian, and Nicole Oresme—it led to an ideal geometry, the quality of the temperaments being the result of a critical point, *tonos*, or a happy medium, placed at the meeting of each pair of opposites on a continuous, infinitely divisible line. Others, like Ficino and Agrippa, didn't hesitate to tie the crasis to a harmonic progression of whole numbers.

The soul is commonly divided into its superior faculties and its inferior faculties:

Among the superior functions are found intellectual and rational activity, divided, according to the authors, into a "*ratio cogitativa*" and a "*ratio intellectualis*," faculties that approve or reject information delivered by the inferior faculties. Reason ascends from the quantity and quality of species up to the genres. It corrects the forms of the intervals, deformed by perception, and it separates causes from effects. It speaks and discusses: in vocal music it perceives the poetic text and determines the "fantastic" significance of sound. Reason oscillates between the intellect (*mens*) and the body: we call it "cogitative" when it is seduced by a sensitive soul and "intellectual" when it rises towards the universal. For authors who recognized free will, the soul is free thanks to reason.

Among the inferior faculties, the vegetative soul ensures safe nutrition, growth, and procreation. The sensitive soul governs life, movement, and sensation. We habitually divide it into a mechanical faculty (local movement and the power of appetite) and a cognitive faculty (interior senses):

The mechanical faculty contains concupiscible power and irascible power. The first has no goal beyond the blind satisfaction of its own desires; the second turns away from objects that it cannot attain with anger and indignation.

The soul's cognitive faculty contains the five external senses, the *spiritus* and the internal senses: *sensus communis, imaginatio-phantasia, memoria.*

The spiritus

Medical reflections on the spirit came to the Renaissance through Aristotelian, Galenist, and Arabic traditions. The spirit was seen as a bloody vapor produced by the combustion of food, which was diffused by the arteries and the nervous system. *Quasi spiritus* and *quasi corpus*, it contributed to thoughts and the breath's substance, and, thanks to its hybrid nature, it served as an intermediary between the soul and the body. This tradition usually distinguished three sorts of spirits, distributed in the organs according to their degree of heat and humidity: natural spirits, vital spirits, and animal spirits. The vital spirit distributed animal heat throughout the body. It produced the animal spirit in the ventricles of the brain, which were then diffused throughout the body, to the very peripheral organs of the senses and the muscles, by the nervous system. This latter constituted the seat of mechanical activity, of sensory perception, and, according to the authors, of some inferior psychological functions, like appetite, common sense, and imagination. Having a physical nature, it is subject to generation and corruption, to movement in category and quantity, to local movement and to qualitative transformation (*alteratio, alloiosis*). In effect, it contains the powers of the four elements (hot–cold, dry–humid…), grouped in pairs around a golden mean. The actions of physical bodies cause it to oscillate in opposing affections, delivering the impressions perceived by the senses to the superior faculties. It knows fire through fire, air through air, and earth through air. Sometimes active, sometimes passive, it ensures the psychosomatic exchange between the soul and body, especially in moments of passion: heated by bile, it multiples the speed of operation of the intellect; when it cools down, it paralyses thought, generating sleep, tears, and despair.

For Ficino and Agrippa, the aerial nature of the spiritus allowed it to be quickly absorbed by a sonorous melody. As the soul and the body form two extremes of the same "consonance" and the spirit is their "average," it is the place of harmony in the body. Jumps in its temperature constitute a "movement in category and quality," the measure of which "oscillates" between pairs of qualities on a continuous, infinitely divisible line, just as melody oscillates between high and low notes. And like melody, it holds the powers of the four elements, tempered by the octave's fourth and fifth proportions.[vii] In essence corporeal, it must be purified and regenerated through cathartic remedies, among which is found planetary music.

For a good number of authors, the border between the tradition of medical spirits and that of the spirit as the body mediating the spirit of the world was fluid. Many authorized sources supported this belief, including the passage of Plato's *Timaeus* on the chariot of the soul (41d–42d) and the Aristotelian thesis (*De generatione animalium* 736b–737a) of ethereal pneuma contained in the male's seed (*De generatione animalium* II, 3, 736b). But the idea of extending this physiology to the soul has its roots in Stoic and neo-Platonic pneumatology (Proclus). The fantastic spirit is a subtle garment surrounding the soul with a luminous substance. Like the imagination, it can project images and spectral apparitions. It constitutes the substratum of dreams and fantasies. But its luminous matter has the same nature as the cosmic fire (*ether*) that makes the stars shine, and its form is spherical, like celestial wheels and the propagation of sound in space. Just as the bloody spirit ties the soul to the body, it reunites body with the soul of the world. Unlike the bloody spirit, it can separate itself from the body, live an autonomous life, incarnate itself in another body, or serve as a mediator between the imagination and the stars. During sleep and ecstasy, it can wander into imaginary regions to participate in visions of which, in reality, it is the protagonist (Dodds 1933, pp. 310–21; Walker 1958; Klein 1970, p. 53). For Plotinus, who didn't hesitate to reduce "the enigmatic sense of the harmony of the spheres" to the destiny written in the soul by the planets during their descent to Earth by way of the spheres, when the *spiritus* could hear and remember the harmony of the spheres this opened the way to a musical interpretation (*Enneads*, IV, 3 11–12, p. 579). Hence art as anamnesis, inspiration, creative frenzy, and interplanetary voyages, of which the Dream of Scipio is an example.

Internal senses

Vague and confused, the sonorous image conveyed by the external ear ear passes through one door after another through the passage of the inner senses, which progressively distil universals by purifying the residues of matter. *Intentio* attains common sense, which distinguishes it from all the other sensory perceptions except reciprocal sensations. Fantasy or the imagination—two faculties that are often confused—extracts the qualities and quantities of sensitive objects. The body's representative in the concert of the internal senses, the imagination, can suffer the repercussions of the indeterminate movement of the humors. Its *vis imaginativa* can either shape the embryo during pregnancy or exercise a deforming power on the body, as was the case for King Cippus, who woke up to find himself with two horns after having dreamed of a battle between bulls. At times of ecstasy and inspiration, it runs from one form to another in a prurient and volatile manner. It juxtaposes incoherent images, coordinated by parataxis, without regard for genre or species.

Raised in ecstasy, the imagination can be see as the organ *par excellence* of knowledge; but it can also be the most myopic of the soul's faculties when it is cold. Certainly, it can imagine a song without hearing it or mentally compose counterpoint, but it defines crudely. In an eloquent passage of *Platonic Theology*, Ficino declares that, if men were reduced to imagination, they would speak through grunts and gestures like animals. As with the memory, it can only envision an indeterminate image from a semantic point of view; it speaks the body's non-verbal language of gestures and the voice's inflection. That's why it possesses codes for all the arts of spectacle, like dance and song, and it is very highly developed among artists.

Memoria

Just as wax retains the imprint of a seal, memory preserves present or absent sensations, separated by imagination from sensitive objects. Music has a sense and even an affective value thanks to this faculty because it extracts forms from time, allowing us to measure the present in terms of the past and the unknown in terms of the known. Ptolemy's theory of affects instructed the Renaissance on its role in a passage dedicated to how the melody shifts from one system to another during "modulation" (*metabole*). The conflict between the melodic configuration recorded by the memory and the form produced in modulation generates an alteration that makes the conductor forget the song's accustomed and expected thread, producing the excess necessary for *pathos* (Ptolemy 1982, II, 6, pp. 55, 20*ff.*; Porphyry 1980, pp. 169, 9*ff.*). The affective impact is thus directly proportional to the contrast and the complexity of the relationship tying the conflicting forms.

Furthermore, memory is a mnemonic and even a musical art. The last of the internal senses, it speaks through images, like fantasy, and images are the best vector for memorization. The spirit's librarian, the intellect, has the power to shape and engrave in the soft wax of memory shelves and compartments called "places," sorts of pictures or symbolic mental images (*notae, voces, signa*) distributed in the rooms of a well-proportioned museum that the orator, the artist, and the musician must be able to roam through in their imagination over the course of their performance. Memory nourishes itself with associations and recognizes itself when its objects are articulated following a pre-established order of succession: thus it isn't surprising that its adepts have borrowed connections used for arranging its places from musical harmony. In one of his letters, dated 1458, Ficino compares memory's operations to the activity of the digestion, which assimilates *intentiones* after having harmonized into a unitary form with "order," "proportion," and "connection," just as food is cooked by the blood (Ficino 2005, p. 656).[viii] It digests dishes more easily when a well-ordered prayer and a sweet song have made them more digestible. But the role of harmony is not limited to furnishing a purely functional structure to the edifices of memory: according to Notker's tropes and Guido d'Arezzo's solmization, in which *voces ut re mi fa sol la* serve as mnemonic sign (*notae*) for sounds found in the memory, the history of memory met that of music; musical history in the *loci topici* is subject to "cavati," solmization, which serves performers as an aid to imagination during freely improvised hexachordal fantasies. These compositions are described as *automata* because the places in the memory where they are composed activate thought without reflection, like so many involuntary automatisms. During the 16th century, the places were incarnated in polyphony and ended up being confused with the conventional typology of affects maintained by *habitu* and intertexuality.

Critical judgment

Imagination communicates with the power to satisfy one's desires, the organ of the souls' concupiscible and irascible virtues, and constitutes the theatre *par excellence* of affects. All conditions come from the pleasure and pain felt by these two functions. Certain sonorous images elicit good conditions, like joy, which dilates the heart. Their absence leads to hope, love, desire, and lust. The presence of an undesirable object, like grief, contracts the spirit, macerates the soul, and provokes melancholy and often death; when a terrifying object is situated in the future, it provokes fear. Pain and pleasure can produce mixed conditions, creating joy and hate at the same time, as when other's woes cause us to rejoice and their prosperity distresses us; hot-tempered passions, pleasure, and vengeance; hate, which is deep-rooted anger; passionate desire, which is offended by anything that harms the object of its love.

In addition to these faculties, the imagination is the primary target of the power of music: weak in dialectics, it approves of any kind of melody, whether good or bad, without reservation; it's an easily seduced courtesan. If human beings were reduced to imagination, music would make of them what it wanted, as the Sirens' song did to Odysseus. Hence the delicate problem of the listener's free will with regards to music, which manipulates the senses like a drug. Some authors divide the power to satisfy one's desires into natural, sensitive, and voluntary faculties, which, in theory, incite the soul to follow or avoid the path approved by the senses. But more often the body drives the will; thus, like beasts, humans become slaves to their senses. Psychological theories that are most sensitive to music, like neo-Platonism, tie this tension to a harmony of opposites—which explains the role played by harmonic theory in ethics. Psychic equilibrium is regarded as the result of a confrontation between form—reason and intellect—and potentially infinite, patient matter—the sensitive soul. While the sensitive soul chafes and feels joy or pain, the intelligent reasons (the *ratio cogitativa* for Ficino), notes the dispositions: sometimes it resists them, expelling the affects, and sometimes it consents to them, blindly surrendering itself to the body. The listener is thus a slave to the senses thanks to the power of the sensitive soul, but he is free thanks to his intelligence.

In song, the psychic double of the ego, sound responds to inferior faculties and the role of the moderating element sometimes echoes the musical number, sometimes the text (as for Calvin); because sound is indeterminate from a semantic point of view and speech determines it, as in the soul the understanding virtue measures affect. In perception, rational power responds to the text while imagination perceives the fantastical and indeterminate significance from the concept of the sound: hence the thesis regarding the supremacy of speech to "pure" music. As the rational soul is superior to the body, the text is more intelligent than its sonorous vehicle, and poetic music is more rational than music without words. Furthermore, it suffices to push the combination of soul and harmony to its final consequences to conclude, like Calvin, that pure music and dance embody the irrational, manipulative component of melody.

Ethos

The theory of affects that the humanists constructed on the ruins of the ancient theory rests on a very simple principle, resulting in a final analysis of imitation: the transfer of forms across the different domains of harmony. We find this principle in Ficino, who was among the first to assimilate artistic creation into the formative virtues of the *vis imaginativa* for the body. The soul expresses itself in the body and in all that it does: like a mother whose imagination fashions her child with the same face as the statue that she loves, the composer's imagination designs a form which takes shape in the work as if through metempsychosis, determining rhythms and harmony according to the author's temperament. Leonardo made similar comments about painters, who "*dipinge sé stesso.*" The text is the rational part of melody, counterpoint its body; and just as the temperament expresses itself in the body, melody weds itself to the text's affect. In its turn, the representation of affect to the listener's imagination through the *ekphrasis*, the *descriptio*, and the appropriate elemental powers awaken corresponding images which are found in the fantasy and the memory in a state of vacancy in their turn. Pythagoreanism reduces this network of mimetic duplication to a problem of consonance and dissonance. The relationship between harmony, which acts, and the soul, which suffers, is reciprocal, and it works in the two senses during the Renaissance, attributing the qualities of harmony to the soul and the qualities of the soul to harmony. Thus, the soul is a sort of harmony, and harmony is a sort of soul. A fragment of Aristotle's book critiquing the Pythagoreans, preserved by the author known as pseudo-Plutarch, qualified the 12:9:8:6 form of Dorian harmony in terms of "harmony's body," and a study of vocabulary showed that the word *melos* could send animals towards "anatomical members." Ficino explicitly affirmed this in an astonishing passage of *De vita*, where he regards the counterpoint as a *spiritual duplicate* of the singer's soul, a kind of daimon, endowed with an articulated body and with all the psychic faculties of living beings:

> In effect, the very matter of song is much purer and more analogous to the sky than the matter of a drug; here it concerns a hot or tepid air, which still breathes and, in a certain sense, is endowed with life, being alive in a certain fashion, composed of certain articulations and appropriate members, like an animated being, and it is not only the carrier of movement that conveys affect but also has a signification, like the spirit; so that it can be defined as an air-born and rational animal species […] (Ficino from *De vita*, III, 21, in Ficino 1576/1962, I, p.563).

This anthropomorphic metaphor—which we find everywhere from Leonardo, to Vincezo Galilei's treatise on counterpoint, and even in the Artusi–Monteverdi quarrel—had more success than one would imagine. It provides the composition of a "frame" [skeleton] (Kepler 1619/1969) of articulated members and a nervous system made up of more or less constant numeric relationships based on the affect. It furnishes the conceptual framework with which the Renaissance arranged its remarks on the *ethos* of the elements of writing, i.e. the harmonic system: the register, notes, intervals, modes, the *tonoi*, and their mixture in the body of the melody.

Renaissance authors knew, having learned it in a well-known paragraph from pseudo-Plutarch, that a melody's character raised a particular synthesis of syntactic elements, too complex to fall under the rules of a recipe. But they also knew that the case was different for the components of the synthesis considered in themselves, which were to the melody what the elements were to the body.

The theory of affects is the best proof of this. Thanks to this parallelism, knowledge of medical symptoms characteristic of major mental illnesses, like anger or melancholy, allows some summary conclusion about their rhetorical expression in the repertoire of the era. Let us confine ourselves, for reasons of space, to the black humor, which was incarnated in a typology of conventional rhetorical formulae and which represent the equivalent of a *typus melancholiae* well known in the iconographic tradition. Isolating music's black humor in the score signifies, first of all, taking stock of imagery concerning its symptoms, such as they were described in literature and poetry: poets referred to everything concerning cold when calling forth thoughts of melancholy in the listener's imagination: ice, the marble of tombs (cf. *Giunto alla tomba* by Tasso), the beloved's heart of stone, heat that set the imagination ablaze, and its alternation with cold that paralyzed the movement of the spirit, not to speak of forms dedicated to lamentations, like "alas," "addio," "lasso," and "misera."

As to the "physiognomic" analysis of the body of the melody, the method that Ficino recommends we use is an anatomy of the polyphonic animal in which it takes shape. We begin the dissection with the register, the song's matter. Ficino pushed the metaphor of incarnation to its final consequences, endowing counterpoint (*concentus*) with four humors:

> Just as experienced doctors mix together certain liquids following a true proportion in which several different matters reunite in only one new form […], very learned musicians temper deep notes [the bass] like cold materials, very high notes [the soprano] like hot materials, moderately deep notes [the tenor] like humid materials and moderately high notes [the alto] like dry materials, in proportions that create a sole form from many and that secures a celestial virtue in addition to its vocal virtue. (*Timaeus*, II, xxxi, p. 1455)

Thus we recognize a composition's black humor from its deep register, as the repertoire of compositions of this sort for four or more basses shows. In effect, a good number of authors regarded the oscillation of the melodic line from deep to high as the consequence of a movement "in the quality's category" (*alloiosis, alteratio*), according to the definition of qualitative transformation Aristotle gave in his treatise, *On Generation and Corruption* (319b 10). The register is thus to music what the color spectrum is to the visual arts: the simple transposition of one single melodic formula leads to a change of character.

The theory of affects is thus a pharmacopoeia with two components, the categories of high and low, of what climbs and of what falls (Kepler 1619/1969, p. 75), of joy and of pain, of *durum* and of *mollis*.

The register's quality, still indeterminate in the qualitative movement of the voice, assumes a first determination with the note, followed by the stop of the alteration (*alloiosis*) on a degree of fixed tension. Then it is broken into a kaleidoscope of individual species in the intervals, following their grandeur and the quality of the relationship tying the two extremes together. The grandeur of the melodic interval translates the "quantity" of the melody's movements (*intentio, remissio*) into a quality. The passage from a note at one given level of tension to another, involving an augmentation and a diminution of qualitative movement, led authors to attribute an exuberant, sanguine, and choleric *ethos* to large intervals, as with the fifth for Kepler, the octave, and others, and a plaintive character to softer intervals, like the semi-tones and the softened intervals enclosing a semi-tone—the minor third and sixth and increased and diminished intervals. This doctrine could draw on the authority of a known thesis in physiognomy, according to which:

> Those who walk with big steps are magnanimous and efficient; [those who proceed] by compact, little steps are inefficient, stingy, petty, fake pains, and are dark of spirit.[ix]

We find a musical application of this doctrine in a known testimonial by Mersenne (1636/1975, p. 173):

> Semi-tones and dieses represent tears and groans because of their small intervals, which indicate weakness; this is because small intervals made by ascending or descending notes are like children, dotards, and those who are recovering from a long illness, who cannot walk with large steps and who cover little ground over a large period of time.

As to the mathematical reasons governing *ethos* of intervals, the quality of harmonic relationship responds to a principle that humoral medicine had shared with harmonic theory since their common origins in fragments of Alcmaeon of Croton: the excess and defect in the crasis of even and odd.

In effect, we know that, rather than constructing a world with elements, Pythagoreanism combines even and odd, "elements of the number" for which the academic version of this maths substitutes, without truly differentiating, the one and the indeterminate dyad.[x] The principle is the same: the one unifies and tunes, while the dyad restlessly divides and duplicates quantities into multiples and submultiples. The matrix of the otherness of movement and illness, it contains the cause of the future and the deformation of the idea in the transitory reality of discernible phenomena. The odd is limited, while the even is unlimited (*apeiron*), in the image of the dichotomy of the infinite nature of a geometric magnitude. In a well-known passage of his *Physics* (III, iv, 203, a1), Aristotle explained the reason for this strange identity between even and odd: deformation of rectangular numbers (*heteromekeis*) in the even *gnomon*. Ficino repeated this explanation in a passage of his *De numero fatali*: "That is why," Ficino declared, "it being given that equilateral numbers give rise to odd number when put together and that oblongs give rise to even numbers with the binary in the lead, the first are good children, while the others are bad children."[xi]

The *gnomon* is a right-angled figure, square or rectangular, formed by the distribution of unities around a series of squares arranged around the unity and the duality (Figure 21.2).

Figure 21.2 An example of a *gnomon*.

Placing odd numbers around the unity proves that the addition of odd numbers produces "squared" numbers ($1 + 3 = 4 = 2 \times 2$; $1 + 3 + 5 = 9 = 3 \times 3$...), and placing even numbers around the duality produces a sequence of rectangles (2; $2 + 4 = 6 = 3 \times 2$; $2 + 4 + 6 = 12 = 3 \times 4$...). Contrary to its odd-numbered counterpart, the even *gnomon* calculates by ceaselessly alternating the relations of the sides, ceaselessly crossing the limits of the preceding form.

Thanks to Boethius, the Pythagoreans' pebbles would fill the pages of treatises on the mathematical causes of dissonance for ten centuries. Perfectly arbitrary, this operation proves that the sides of the uneven gnomon, converted into lengths of strings, produce a series of unisons, while the even gnomon produces the relationships of the *genus superparticolaris* ($n + 1/n$): the octave (2:1), the fifth (3:2), the fourth (4:3), the major third (5:4), the minor third (6:5), all the way up to the micro-intervals (81:80...). This confirms the even's deforming action: no relationship is equal to itself; furthermore, an interval's dissonance is directly proportional to the complexity of the "excess" (*hyperoche*[xii]) separating the numerator from the denominator: mathematicians of harmony can decree that the octave if more perfect that the fifth because its major extreme exceeds the minor extreme by a whole number ($2:1 = 1 + 1/1$); while the fifth is no more than a half, the fourth no more than a third ($4:3 = 1 + 1/3$), the minor third no more than a fourth ($5:4 = 1 + 1/4$), and the syntonic comma not more than an eighty-first ($81:80 = 1 + 1/80$). Finally, these manipulations explain the relationship of the even number to otherness: the dyad divides because it produces "specific" forms, enclosed on themselves, dissident and reluctant to integrate themselves into the society of sounds, beginning with the true third (5:4), too narrow to go into the octave three times.

The analogy between this phenomenon and the disequilibrium produced by the dissonance of humoral excess and defects is striking. It encouraged authors in the idea that pathos went hand in hand with dissonance, in accordance with an explicit declaration of the author of Aristotle's *Problems* (XIX, 6, 918a 10–15). As seen in Mersenne's work, the black ink of melancholy permeated semi-tones and dieses. For 16th- and 17th-century authors, including Kepler, the presence of a semi-tone qualified the ethos of minor intervals of a soft type (like the third and the minor sixth) as melancholic; its absence explained the joyous character of the major correlates. It was the same for false intervals, diminished or altered by the temperament: the oenological expression "fermentation of consonances" (consonantiarum fermentatio) refers to the melancholic intoxication induced by Phyrgian and Hypophyrigian modes due to the presence of an interval with too strong a comma (Kepler 1619/1969, III, p. 79).

The equivocation *mixis/krasis* could only encourage theorists to apply the mathematical notion of excess to the analysis of relationships between the humors. Otherness and identity govern the *spiritus* and convey the "ratione quadam harmonica temperatus" that encloses the "powers" of the fifth, the fourth, and the octave, and a doctor–musician like Ficino had no reason to not reduce the humors' crasis to a series of consonant intervals:

> To maintain the body well, if I may express myself thus, we need eight parts of blood, four parts phlegm, two of yellow bile, and one of black bile. So that, if through chance the blood is hot and humid to a degree, or maybe even a little hotter, the bile would have three degrees of heat and the phlegm three of

humidity; this way, in effect, the phlegm's humidity and the bile's heat could relate to the blood's proportion […]. (Ficino 1576/1962, II, lxxxxvii, p. 1481)

The equality of rights of the conflicting qualities is perfect because of the consonance of the geometric progression 8:4:2:1 generated by the *proportio dupla*, which is the most perfect form of consonance. In accordance with the *genus multiplex*, the series grows while preserving the identity of the initial sound, in the safety of the norm or the ideal straight line—a progression like 1:3:9:27 would have produced four different sounds. Furthermore, the octave "contains all consonances," as proven by the parallel categories of degrees of heat and of humidity lent to the humors.[xiii] Therefore Ficino could consider the generation of passions as a series of gaps or dissonances in the soul constituted from this basic series, 8:4:2:1, to be seen as the system's neutral point, a sort of "degree zero" for apathy:

> However, it [namely black bile] shouldn't completely mix with the phlegm, especially if it is too cold and too abundant, so as not to chill, but should rather be mixed with bile and blood until one sole body is born from the three parts, proportionally composed of two times more blood than the two others so that they are eight parts blood, two parts bile, and also two parts black bile. The other two should somewhat enflame the black bile and, once aflame, it should shine without burning, to avoid burning it or agitating it too violently as a harder material would normally do if it was too warm, and to avoid it becoming chilled when, in contrast, it is chilled to the maximum in the same fashion. (Ficino 1576/1962, I, v, p. 497)

A fundamental difference distinguishes this numerical formula from that of the ideal temperament, described above: the wish to reduce the concert of the humors to a three-voice counterpoint, following the elimination of the phlegm, which is curiously absent from the list of humors. In any case, even three humors are too many: Ficino contrives to reduce the series' terms to two through a coalition of yellow bile and black bile versus the blood. In effect, the proportion he mentions is not the quadruple 8:2 but the *double* 8:2 + 2 = 8:4—as proved by the expression *dupla sanguinis ad reliqua duo*. It is instructive to ask the reasons for this enigmatic magical formula. All of the attributes, all of the allegories, whether visual or sonorous, surrounding melancholy during its imposing trajectory in the history of Western thought returns to dualist models representing the exact antithesis of the ancient idea of harmony as the conciliation of antagonistic forces: Saturn's *ethos*, "unstable and dissonant star" (Ficino 1576/1962, III, 22, p. 565);[xiv] the figure of "concentration" like the oscillation of the spirit transported between Saturn's orbit and the "center" of the Earth; and the road to wisdom, like the passage between Scylla and Charybdis. Furthermore, the melancholic complexion *affectus producit varios*, and the purpose was to express the *varietas* of mental images through an indeterminate oscillation of the spirit on a continuous scale comprising mania and dejection, and this using a formula that could translate the paradoxical idea of a measure of deviation. A eurhythmic distribution of humors, in these conditions was shown to be irrelevant. Besides which, the *proportio dupla* imagined by the author didn't pretend to conciliate extremes at all, which proves an explicit declaration in *Commentaire au Timaeus* according to which the two extremes not tied together by *two* intermediary means *minime congruunt* (Ficino 1576/1962, II, xviii, p. 1445).[xv] But Ficino preferred emptying the body of the harmony at its heart. The solution was entirely founded on the mathematical theory of harmony. Interpreting the concept of *extremitas* to the letter, he reduced the proportion to two extremes, creating an interval without identity or measure in its center. The proportion concerned was not the octave form but the indeterminate dyad (*dyas aoristos*), matrix of otherness, indeterminate movement, *varietas*, and dissonance. Nothing was more logical than imagining the contrary power in conflict in the temperature as a confrontation of even and odd numerical elements (2:1) and conceiving of an oscillatory movement between contrary affective qualities as a geometric line, continuous and infinitely divisible, in the intermediary interval. The formal expression of the unstable dynamic of melancholic humor came to be confused with the archetype of dissonance and conflict. The history of music can prove this. If polyphony is a body, the body of melancholy is a deformed chimera of heterogeneous parts, or even better, in the words of Tasso, who was well placed to speak, a "hydra with a thousand heads," producing a new head each time the sufferer came to decide on an idea for reducing the mental tension:

> And I firmly hold that the venture to vanquish the Chimera wasn't any more taxing that the attempt to overcome melancholy, which can be equated more with the Hydra than the Chimera because, as soon as the melancholic has curtailed one thought, two more shoot up in its place, which pierce and lacerate him with their deadly bites. (Tasso 1958, pp. 48–9)[xvi]

Notes

i   St Augustine, *De vera religio*, 39, 53, cited in Ficino (1964, t. 2, XII, v, p. 175).

ii   As told by Iamblicus in *Vie Pythagorique* (Dumont *et al.* 1988, pp. 330–1).

iii   Homer, *Odyssey*, IV, 221 (Pigeaud 2008, p. 76).

iv   Hence the term *krasis*, "temperament," designating wine in modern Greek and in Apulian Greek (*krasí*).

v   Applying the predicate of its opposite to the number would signify that a number exists that is the opposite of the number. Making the quantity the elementary substratum of the quantity includes that the number is the number's element.

vi   In effect, Ficino supports Plato's preference for the number 12 due to its "elements" 2 and 3, whose "temperament" generates the fifth (3:2), the fourth (4:3), and the octave, the most perfect consonances ($2:3 \times 3.4 = 6:12$) (Allen 1994, p. 183).

vii   In *Timaeum*, II, xviii, p. 1454; Marsilii Ficini expositio in interpretatione Prisciani Lydi super Theophrastum, *Opera omnia*, 2, (Ficino 1580/2005, p. 1821); *Epistula de rationibus musicae* (Ficino 1937, p. 54).

viii   For a mnemotechnic use of solmization see the passage from Lodovico Dolce's (1575, p. 24) dialogue, *Dialogo nel quale si ragiona del modo di accrescere et conservar la memoria* cited by Castelli (1986, vol. II, p. 383).

ix   "Qui longis passibus incendunt magnanimi sunt et efficaces; parvi autem et restricti passus inefficaces, parci, parvae mentis sunt, dolorum artifices et obscurae mentis" (Foerster 1983, II, 75, p. 97).

x   And especially for Ficino, as the confusion between "pair/even" and "dyad" in the *Epistula de rationibus musicae* (Ficino 1937, p. 52), shows: "Omnino autem meminisse oportet auditum unitate quidem ubique mulceri, dualitate vero quasi divisione quadam semper offendi. Quamobrem quotiens voces duas maxime discernit ut duas, offenduntur maxime. Ubi vero discernit minus, minori ibi offensio provenit." "We should remember that hearing delights in unity, while it is still wounded by division. That's why, each time it discerns two notes as two separate entities, it experiences an extreme suffering." [our translation].

xi   *De numero fatali* XIII 14–16, p. 213: "Cum igitur ex imparibus unitate duce aequilateri fiant, ex paribus autem duce binario nascantur inaequilateri, nimirum illi quidem filii boni, hi vero mali censetur."

xii   Philolaus in Dumont *et al.* (1988, p. 463).

xiii   From a quantitative point of view, the progression is geometric 1:2:4:8. Qualitatively, by multiplying the respective quantities by their degrees of heat and humidity, it is harmonic 12:8:6. Either: 8 (parts of blood to eights degrees of heat): 12 (four parts phlegm by three degrees of heat):6 (two parts yellow bile per three degrees of heat). 12:8:6 = re la re' = fifth and octave.

xiv   "Contra influxum eius [saturni] hominibus communiter peregrinum et quodammodo dissonum nos armat Iupiter". (Against its influence [of Saturn], the wandering star, and somewhat dissonant for men, guards us from Jupiter.)

xv   "That we place an average in the middle of opposites;" as Empedocles sings, "when two opposites oppose each other without mediation, they only weakly harmonize [. . .] That's why Plato always inserts two means between opposites [. . .]."

xvi   "E per fermo non fu più faticosa operazione di vincere la chimera che '1 superare la malinconia, la qual più tosto a l'Idra ch' a la Chimera potrebbe somigliarsi, perch'a penail malinconico ha tronco un pensiero che due ne sono subito nati in quella vece, da' quali con mortiferi morsi è trafitto e lacerato".

References and bibliography

Aristotle [or pseudo-Aristotle]. *Problèmes* [**Problems**], translated and edited by P. Louis. Paris: Les Belles Lettres, 1993.

Baldry, H. C. (1932). Embryological analogies in early cosmogony. *Classical Quarterly*, **26**, 27–34.

Boccadoro, B. (2002). *Ethos e varietas. Trasformazione qualitativa e metabole nella teoria musicale dell'antichità Greca*. Florence: Leo Olschki.

Boccadoro, B. (2004). Eléments de grammaire mélancolique. *Acta Musicologica*, **76**, 25–65.

Castelli, P. (1986). Marsilio Ficino e i luoghi della memoria. In G. Garfagnini (ed.), *Marsilio Ficino e il ritorno di Platone*, vol. 2, p. 383. Florence: Casa Editrice Leo S. Olschki.

Chastel, A. (1975). *Marsile Ficin et l'art*. Geneva: Droz.

Descartes, R. (1969). *Oeuvres de Descartes. Correspondance: avril 1622–février 1638*, ed. C. Adam and P. Tannery. Paris: Vrin.

Dolce, L. (1575). *Dialogo nel quale si ragiona del modo di accrescere et conservar la memoria*. Venice: Gio. Battista et Marchio Sessa.

Ficino, M. (1576/1962). *Opera omnia*, 2 vols. Basel: Henrici Petri. Reprint 1962, Turin: La Bottega di Erasmo.

Ficino, M. (1580/2005). *Plotini opera omnia cum latina Marsilii Ficinii inerpretatione et commentatione*. Basle: Pietro Perna. (Reprinted 2005 with an Introduction by S. Toussaint, Villiers sur Marne: Phénix Éditions.)

Ficino, M. (1937). *Epistula de rationibus musicae*. In P. O. Kristeller *Supplementum Ficinianum*, pp. 52–54. Florence: Casa Editrice Leo S. Olschki.

Ficino, M. (1964). *Théologie Platonicienne de l'immortalité des âmes*, ed. R. Marcel. Paris: Société d'Édition les Belles Lettres.

Ficino, M. (1990). De Musica. In: Gentile, S. (ed.) (1990). Marsilio Ficino, lettere i, epistolarum familiarum, bk I, 92, pp. 161–3. Florence: Casa Editrice Leo S. Olschki. (French translation by B. Boccadoro.)

Ficino, M. (1994). De numero fatali. In J. B. Allen, *Nuptial Arithmetic: Marsilio Ficino's Commentary on the Fatal Number in Book VIII of Plato's Republic*. Berkeley: University of California Press.

Ficino, M. (2002). *Commentaire sur le banquet de Platon*, ed. P. Laurens. Paris: Société d'Édition les Belles Lettres.

Foerster, R. (ed.) (1983). *Scriptores physiognomonici Graeci et Latini*. Stuttgart: B. G. Teubner.

Garfagnini, G. (ed.) (1986). *Marsilio Ficino e il ritorno di Platone*. Florence.

Gozza, P. (2009). Renaissance mathematics: the music of Descartes. In P. Gozza (ed.), *Number to Sound*, pp. 155–72. Dordrecht: Springer.

Iamblicus (1988). Vie Pythagorique. In J.-P. Dumont, D. Delattre, and J.-L. Poirier (eds), *Les présocratiques*, pp. 330–1. Paris: Editions Gallimard.

Joly, R. and Byl, S. (eds) (1984). *Hippocratis de Diaeta*. Corpus Medicorum Graecorum. Supplementum. Berlin: Akademie-Verlag.

Kepler, J. (1619/1969) *Johannis Keppleri harmonices mundi libri V*. Linz: Sumptibus Godofredi Tampachii. (Reprinted 1969, Bologna: Forni.)

Klein, R. (1970). *La forme et l'intelligible*. Paris: Editions Gallimard.

Mersenne, M. (1636/1975). *Harmonie universelle*. Paris: Sebastien Cramoisy. (Reprinted 1975, Paris: Centre National de la Recherche Scientifique.)

Pigeaud, J. V. (2008). *Melancholia*. Paris: Manuels Payot.

Plutarch (1972). *Propos de table*, books I–III, ed. F. Fuhrmann. Paris: Les Belles Lettres.

Proclus (1933). *The Elements of Theology*, ed. E. R. Dodds. Oxford: Clarendon.

Porphyry (1980). *Ptolemaios und Porphyrios über die Musik*, ed. I. Düring. New York: Garland. (Reprint of 1934 edition, Göteborg: Elanders Boktryckeri Aktiebolag.)

Ptolemy (1982). *Die Harmonielehre des Klaudios Ptolemaios*, ed. I. Düring. Hildesheim: G. Olms. (Reprint of 1930 edition, Göteborg: Elanders Boktryckeri Aktiebolag.)

Ptolemy (1988). *Les préocratiques*, ed. J.-.P. Dumont, D. Delattre, and J.-L. Poirier. Paris: Editions Gallimard.

Siraisi, N. (1975). The music of pulse in the writings of Italian academic physicians (fourteenth and fifteenth centuries). *Speculum*, **50**, 689–710.

Tasso, T. (1958). Il Messaggiero. In *Dialoghi*, ed. E. Raimondi. Florence: Sansoni.

Walker, D. P. (1958). The astral body in Renaissance medicine. *Journal of the Warburg and Courtauld Institutes*, **21**, 119–33.

Walker, D. P. (1978). *Studies in Musical Science in the Late Renaissance*, pp. 63–80. London: The Warburg Institute.

Walker, D. P. (1987). Keplers Himmelsmusik. In F. Zaminer (ed.), *Hören, Messen und Rechnen in der Frühen Neuzeit*. Darmstadt: Wissenschaftliche Buchgesellshcaft.

Walker, D. P. (1988). *La magie spirituelle et angélique de Ficin à campanella*. Paris: Albin Michel.

Walker, D. P. (2009). The expressive value of intervals and the problem of the fourth. In P. Gozza (ed.), *Number to Sound*, pp. 201–15. Dordrecht: Springer.

Zarlino, G. (1558). *Istitutioni harmoniche*. Venice: Pietro Da Fino.

Chapter 22

Music as a means of social control: some examples of practice and theory in early modern Europe

Penelope Gouk

The power of music to affect people's emotions (or rather the "passions") and even behavior was a commonplace of Renaissance thought, even though the physiological and psychological underpinnings of this power were not to become the focus of medical attention until the Enlightenment (Gouk 2000). This belief implicitly informed early modern efforts to regulate music making and especially the movements of occupational musicians within society because of their potentially disruptive influence. For example, in 1572 the government of Elizabeth I instituted legislation requiring minstrels to be licensed, those not protected by a nobleman or other authority being classed as vagabonds and liable to prosecution (Marsh 2010, pp. 71–87). In fact this example is more about trying to limit the movements of musicians rather than prescribing the kinds of musical sounds people should be experiencing with a view to changing behavior. Nevertheless, as I will shortly describe, this latter goal was being pursued in France at around the same time that Queen Elizabeth passed her statute against vagabonds in England. It was a deliberate response to the unprecedented levels of religious and political disruption of the time, which seemed to threaten the very fabric of society.

Ancient models: Plato and Aristotle

Anyone thinking about music and social control in the early modern period would tend to look for precedents in antiquity, the most significant authors in this regard being Plato and Aristotle.[i] The two crucial texts by Plato are his *Republic* and the *Laws*, both of which are concerned with the nature of the best form of political organization and the proper kind of education for individuals that lead to a stable and harmonious community. Education of the republic's citizens includes early training in both gymnastics and *mousike*, which Andrew Barker (1984, p. 127) defines as "primarily an exposure to poetry and to the music that is its key vehicle." (For the rest of this chapter I will simply refer to "music" but will be using it in the broader sense of poetry set to a musical accompaniment.) The crucial point is that within Plato's ideal society the kinds of "music" that are performed must be firmly controlled by the law givers, the argument being that freedom of choice in music and novelty in its forms will inevitably lead to corruption and a breakdown of society. Plato's distrust of musical innovation is made concrete in his *Laws* where he describes what he thinks actually happened once in Greek society, namely that the masses had the effrontery to suppose they were capable of judging music themselves, the result being that "from a starting point in music, everyone came to believe in their own wisdom about everything, and to reject the law, and liberty followed immediately" (*Laws* 701a). (To Plato liberty is anathema since some people have much greater autonomy than others.) This close association between the laws of music and laws of the state exists because, according to Plato, music imitates character, and has a direct effect on the soul which itself is a *harmonia*. The consequence is that good music results in good character, and conversely inappropriate types of music may lead to a weak character. To achieve a good state some form of regulation must take place, the assumption being that if the right musical rules are correctly followed this will result in morally sound citizens.

It is fascinating to discover that Plato looks to Egypt with approval for its drastic control of music in society, claiming that its forms had remained unchanged for 10,000 years because of strict regulation that "dedicated all dancing and all melodies to religion" (*Laws* 799a). To prescribe melodies that possessed a "natural correctness," he thinks, "would be a task for a god, or a godlike man, just as in Egypt they say that the melodies that have been preserved for this great period of time were the compositions of Isis." (*Laws* 657a). (In fact as we shall see there were similar arguments made for the divine origins of sacred music in the Hebrew tradition.) Perhaps thinking himself to be a "godlike man," Plato lays down a series of strict rules governing musical composition and performance, a prescription that if correctly followed would ensure the virtue of citizens and the stability of the state, as well as the banishment of most professional musicians from society.

First, Plato wants to limit the kind of poetry that is set to music at all because songs have such a direct and powerful effect on people's morals. Thus any poems that portray wickedness, immorality, mourning, or weakness of any kind must be banned, leaving only music that encourages good and courageous behavior among citizens. The next thing to be curtailed is the range of musical styles allowed in the city, which Plato would confine to the Dorian and the Phrygian modes. Between them these two modes (which did not correspond to their modern equivalents, signifying much more than pitch organization) appropriately "imitate the sounds of the self-restrained and the brave man, each of them both in good fortune and bad." (Barker 1984, p. 131).[ii] Thirdly, as well as controlling the words to be sung and the manner in which they are performed, Plato would also regulate the kinds of instrument used for accompaniment, the two most important being the *lyra* and the *kithara*. Those that are forbidden include the *aulos* as well as a range of multistringed instruments capable of playing in a variety of different modes.[iii] Finally, Plato is emphatic in stating that the metrical foot and the melody must follow the words properly for the right effect to be achieved, rather than the other way around. Of course these rules are intrinsically interesting, since they tell us about what Plato thought was wrong with music of his own time. However, for my purposes they are also interesting because they seem to have had a discernible influence on would-be reformers of music and society in the early modern period (that is, between the 16th and 18th centuries) which I will come to shortly.

Turning now to Aristotle, we find his views on the educational and social aspects of music in a substantial passage at the end of the *Politics*. Although equally interested in the stability of the state, Aristotle is far less uncompromising than Plato in his view of music. He accepts that "music is capable of creating a particular quality of character in the soul" (*Politics* 1338a 9–37) but instead of excluding everything except morally improving music he suggests that a wider range of musical styles can be enjoyed in the regulated context of leisured entertainment, either by listening to professionals or engaging in performance oneself—at least to a limited extent. Learning music can form part of a liberal education, as long as students are not taught the spectacular technical practices of professionals that would enable them to participate in professional contests. Instead they should be taught the moral modes (especially the Dorian) while the other styles that are more invigorating and inspirational can be listened to in the pursuit of relaxation and harmless pleasure. In sum, Aristotle acknowledges the affective power of music but thinks if it is properly contained in the form of public or private entertainment it is not likely to be damaging either to the individual or to society as a whole. Again, just as I suggested that we can see the influence of Plato's views on music on some early modern thinkers, so we can find similar attention given to Aristotle's support of properly controlled musical practice.

However, before considering how these classical authorities were interpreted in early modern times, it should be noted that the Bible, specifically the Old Testament, also offered a window onto ancient musical and legislative practices. In particular we should note that early modern thinkers believed that King David, the charismatic leader of the Israelites, was inspired by the Holy Spirit not only to sing God's praises through voice and harp in the form of psalms but also to communicate divine laws to His (i.e. God's) chosen people. A similar unity between the law and song was also thought to be found among the Celts in ancient British and Gallic societies, a context in which the druids apparently played a leading role as guardians of customary law (Ahmed 1997). In short, early modern authors knew from their interpretations of ancient texts that some ancient communicative practices involving a fusion of music and poetry seemed to be much more emotionally powerful than anything in modern times. In certain cases this led directly to attempts to recreate these effects.

Music and social control in 16th-century France

The context in which my first historical example of music being recognized as a means of controlling society arises is France in the 1570s, a time which, according to Frances Yates, was "the darkest period of the struggle between Catholic and Huguenot," an episode in a bloody and protracted conflict known as the French Wars of Religion (1562–98) (Yates 1947, p. 69). In brief, between around 1540 and 1570 the Huguenots had effectively created a powerful new religious identity amongst communities of believers in Paris, Lyon, and other major cities across France (as well as Geneva of course, which remained the epicenter of Calvinist teaching long after Calvin's death in 1564). This success was in no small measure due to the practice of communally singing psalms in public, a sound that became unequivocally associated with a Protestant way of life. Psalms were a means through which Huguenots sustained themselves in the face of persecution, and attracted new converts to the Protestant cause (Diefendorf 1993). It was Calvin who was chiefly responsible for this development, since he regarded the psalms as the ideal instrument for restoring to Christianity the authentic and unadulterated worship of the ancient church. (This is one of the most important contexts in which the example of King David's rule of the Israelites and his creation of the psalms played a central role.) Calvin published his first psalter in 1539 and supported an initiative to produce a complete edition of the psalms set to simple melodies that was first published at Geneva in 1562, from whence some 27,400 copies were distributed across Europe. Thereafter thousands of copies continued to be issued at every major center of the Protestant book trade (Gouk 2005b).

It is against this background that we can see the sense of the French king Henri II in banning public singing of psalms in 1558 because they had achieved the status of insurrectionary hymns. By way of countering these practices Catholics became accustomed to sing the Te Deum to celebrate local victories of their own. The danger posed to the status quo by psalm singing can be shown with particular reference to Lyon, which was a nexus of tensions between a Catholic majority and Huguenot minority during this period. In Lyon in 1564 a royal ordinance of Charles IX made the singing of "dissolute songs" punishable by death, an action that was originally directed against Huguenot psalms, but soon came to have a wider application. In these early days of print culture the oral tradition of singing and crying the news elaborated in print was also a potentially disruptive force. As Kate van Orden puts it, "Through the expulsion or execution of vagrants, gamblers, and blasphemers, Charles IX hoped to cleanse the body politic in a process that emphasizes song as a transmitter of social disease and religious unrest" (van Orden 2000, p. 275).

Even as Charles IX attempted to control public order with anti-musical legislation, he was also receptive to the possibility of the creation of new music that would bring back into use "both the kind of poetry and the measure and rule of music anciently used by the Greeks and Romans."[iv] This lofty goal was presented to the king in 1570, in the form of a request made to the Privy Council by two men who had already spent several years experimenting with a form of poetry set to music that supposedly emulated ancient techniques of metrical composition, while using the modern French language. In 1570 Jean-Anton de Baïf and Joachim Thibault de Courville were successful in establishing the first publicly instituted academy in France, the *Académie de poésie et de musique* complete with its statutes and royal letters patent which outlined its broader aspirations as well as the details of day-to-day running and administration. As Charles IX or his officials observed in the Letters Patent of the academy, it was

> the opinion of many great personages, both ancient legislators and philosophers… that it is of great importance for the morals of the citizens of a town that the music current and used in the country should be retained under certain laws, for the minds of most men are formed and their behavior influenced by its character, so that where music is disordered, there morals are also depraved, and where it is well ordered, there men are well disciplined morally. (Quoted in Yates 1947, pp. 23, 319).

The formalization of Baïf's academy was not just intended to support poets and composers collaborating on new music, but was also planned to be part of a broader emulation of the ancient Greek academies where the study of philosophy and the arts was part of the education of the political elite, the ideal model, of course, being Plato's *Republic*. The academy had two classes of members, the "honest auditors" who were responsible for subsidizing composition and performance of the measured music, and the professional composers, singers, and players who were supported by this patronage. Baïf's larger aim was to create a new kind of song comparable to those used by Orpheus and the Gallic bards to establish law in their respective societies (Walker 1946). Once created, this music was to be imposed on citizens to regulate their behavior. It would banish disorder and restore health to the social body, and at the same time the minds of auditors would "be composed so as to become capable of the highest knowledge after being purged of the remnants of barbarism" (Yates 1947, pp. 23, 320).

Scottish Enlightenment theories of music and the body politic

These late 16th-century French examples of musical legislation leave us no doubt that "music" (i.e. especially verses set to music) was already assumed at this time to have a powerful effect on the passions. What is distinctively lacking in the 1570s, however, is a fully worked out doctrine of affections underpinned by a physiological model that could account for transformations in the human psyche. With hindsight we know that such discourses were developed during the 17th and early 18th centuries, a period when composers increasingly sought to develop a musical language of the passions that would strongly move their auditors. With these transformations in mind I now propose to turn to the writings of a mid-18th century Scottish physician and amateur musician, whose belief in the need for the right kind of music in polite society distinctly parallels Baïf's conviction in this matter.

Dr John Gregory expressed his views on music in a lecture given to the Aberdeen Philosophical Society in 1763, which he published in his *Comparative View of the State and Faculties of Man* (Edinburgh, 1765) nearly 200 years after Baïf's musical experiments in Paris.[v] This lecture shows us that Gregory, although neither a poet nor a composer himself, regarded music as a potentially powerful vehicle for self-improvement and social integration, a view that seems to chime with his own educational experience in Scotland and the Netherlands as a young medical student. In contrast to the turbulent times in which Baïf lived, Gregory's age was comparatively peaceable, with Lowland Scotland enjoying an unparalleled period of prosperity and expanding artistic culture.[vi] The thrust of Gregory's lecture is that music ought to play a more important role in social and personal development than it does at present, but in order for this to happen philosophers rather than professional musicians will have to be responsible for directing musical style, and indeed all the elegant arts.

Significantly, Gregory finds a model for this improvement in ancient Greece, in a period when music was taken seriously by its ruling classes. He notes that the laws and maxims of the early Greek states were written in verse, and "melody and poetry was the established vehicle of all the leading principles of religion, morals and polity" (Gregory 1788, p. 144). Indeed, Gregory stresses that bards like Orpheus were not only important figures in Greece but in other early periods of all civilized nations, notably among the Celts in Great Britain. Through the combination of powerful words and instrumental accompaniment, they moved the hearts and minds of their peoples towards right action. This power to regulate a society's passions represented a high point in civilization, the assumption being that societies lacking such music were more primitive and their people emotionally underdeveloped. However, Gregory notes that as Greek society became increasingly cultivated the use of music for mere entertainment made it an unsuitable skill for any man of high rank and character, and the power and dignity of music sank "into general corruption and contempt" (Gregory 1788, p. 151). Drawing a parallel with his own times, Gregory suggests that unchecked cultivation of music for its own sake undermines the moral health of a society, the solution being to strike a proper balance between the extremes of primitivism and decadence, a process that requires careful regulation.

Gregory's historical theories about the role of music in social development are closely intertwined with his theories of individual neurological and psychological development, which are found in the medical lectures he gave as professor of medicine at the University of Edinburgh between 1765 and his death in 1773. Gregory's lectures reflect the prevailing view of physicians at this time, namely that good health depends on the state of people's nerves, which need to possess a proper degree of excitation (i.e. sensibility) to develop and also to remain healthy (Lawrence 1979). This theory assumes that the central nervous system provides an anatomical basis for the integration of all bodily functions and for the communication of feeling between different bodily organs, known as "sympathy." The mind's interaction with the body relies on an extremely fine material substance or nervous energy which flows through the nerves, which most physicians including Gregory conceptualized as a network of hollow tubes continuous with the brain and spinal medulla.

Gregory thinks that music should be fundamental to children's education, since it is one of the means whereby the nerves acquire a proper degree of sensibility through the regular impressions music makes on the auditory nerve. Boys as well as girls should be musically educated since this can help produce "men of feeling" capable of influencing moral action in themselves and other people. Simple melodies are the most effective means of commanding the passions, but Gregory also points out that music can lead to a higher kind of pleasure arising from the cultivation of judgment and the intellect, rather than mere sensory gratification.

The danger, however (and this takes us back to medicine again), is that "when one practises music much, the simplicity of melody tires the ear" (Gregory 1788, p.181). This leads to the desire for variety and complexity, a condition that despite being essential for high standards of taste and performance eventually leads to weak nerves because there is too much stimulation from the kind of music which meets these exacting criteria, or indeed even simply too much music. Gregory believes that this condition of "weak nerves"—the basis of almost all diseases of civilization—typically affects women, who are more prone to emotion, and also the rich, because their lifestyle encourages intemperance of all kinds. Excessive sensibility leads not only to nervous disorders like melancholia, hysteria, and hypochondria, but also to diseases like smallpox and syphilis, which Gregory associates with luxury. This pathology reflects a widespread contemporary anxiety about the moral dangers that arise from the desires of a successful commercial society. Indeed, although there was a conflict of opinion about music's overall purpose and value among the intellectual elite, Gregory's assumption that there is a correspondence between musical, emotional, and social states, and the central role of the nerves in effecting this linkage, proves to be an integral part of Enlightenment medical orthodoxy. The step Gregory did not take, however, was to prescribe the kinds of music that children and also adults should be exposed to.

Conclusions

This brief summary has only begun to touch on the fascinating subject of music and the social control of emotions (or passions and affections). However, by discussing practice and theory in two very different times and places I hope to have drawn attention to some common themes that seem to recur in discourses on the power of music to affect both individual and collective action, at least in the early modern period.

One of these themes is a sense of corruption associated with certain kinds of modern music, and their potentially detrimental effects on society. Both Baïf and Gregory appear to think that something is lacking in present-day musical practice, or put another way they think that it can be positively damaging, a situation that arises from the wrong kind of people being responsible for musical production in society (Protestants in Baïf's case, professional musicians in Gregory's). This negative standpoint is coupled with a turning back towards ancient ideals of practice, an endeavor which in Baïf's case paradoxically leads to the creation of a new kind of music which aims to move listeners to right moral action. And although Gregory doesn't actually come up with any concrete proposals for new musical genres it is clear that he is distrustful of commercial music that has been created solely for the purpose of giving pleasure to the masses.

The second theme that connects my two protagonists is the linkage between music (i.e. with verses) and lawgiving, the assumption being that music has the potential to change society's behavior for the good if it is coupled with strong leadership. There is, however, a difference in attitude between the two men, which I think arises from the different times in which they lived. For Baïf and his contemporaries the ancients seem to be immediately relevant, setting an example that actually leads to a series of musical experiments promoted by the king himself (although the academy was in reality very short-lived and survived only a few years after Charles IX's death in 1574). Some 200 years later this immediacy seems to have abated, with Gregory adopting a much more historically nuanced position on the central role of music in ancient civilizations. That is to say, he admires figures such as David and Ossian (leader of the Celts) but does not argue for a return to ancient ways. Nevertheless he still accepts the possibility of changing individuals through music, believing that it has the power to alter development in the nervous system, a theory that at the time had no experimental foundation whatsoever.

Notes

i   For the following discussion I have relied chiefly on the interpretation of Barker (1984, pp. 124–182).

ii   The relevant passage in the *Republic* is 397–401b. In fact Plato was unique in describing the Phrygian mode as morally upright; most authorities associated it with frenzy.

iii The *lyra* was like a small U-shaped harp with strings fixed to a crossbar, while the *kithara* was a larger member of this family of instruments. The *aulos* was a single- or double-reed pipe.

iv Request for founding an Academy by Jean-Anton de Baïf and Joachim Thibault de Courville quoted by Yates (1947 p. 21).

v The following section is based on Gouk (2005a, pp. 191–207).

vi Not forgetting the failed Jacobite rising in 1745. See Johnson (1972).

References

Ahmed, E. (1997). *The Law and the Song: Hebraic, Christian and Pagan Revivals in Sixteenth-Century France*. Birmingham, AL: Summa Publications.

Barker, A. (1984). *Greek Musical Writings Volume I: the Musician and his Art*. Cambridge: Cambridge University Press.

Diefendorf, B. B. (1993). The Huguenot psalter and the faith of French Protestants in the sixteenth century. In B. B. Diefendorf and C. Hesse (eds), *Culture and Identity in Early Modern Europe (1500–1800): Essays in Honour of Natalie Zemon Davis*, pp. 41–63. Ann Arbor: University of Michigan Press.

Gouk, P. (2000). Music, melancholy and medical spirits in early modern thought. In P. Horden (ed.), *Music as Medicine: the History of Music Therapy since Antiquity*, pp. 173–94. Guilford: Ashgate.

Gouk, P. (2005a). Music's pathological and therapeutic effects on the body politic: Doctor John Gregory's views. In P. Gouk and H. Hills (eds), *Representing Emotions: New Connections in the Histories of Art, Music and Medicine*, pp. 191–207. Aldershot: Ashgate.

Gouk, P. (2005b). Harmony, health and healing: music's role in early modern Paracelsian thought. In M. Pelling and S. Mandelbrote (eds), *The Practice of Reform in Health, Medicine and Science, 1500–2000; Essays for Charles Webster*, pp. 23–42. Aldershot: Ashgate.

Gregory, J. (1788). *A Comparative View of the State and Faculties of Man with those of the Animal World*, 3rd edn. Edinburgh: W. Creech

Johnson, D. (1972). *Music and Society in Lowland Scotland in the Eighteenth Century*. Oxford: Oxford University Press.

Lawrence, C. (1979). The nervous system and society in the Scottish Enlightenment. In B. Barnes and S. Shapin (eds), *The Natural Order*, pp. 19–40. London: Sage Publications.

Marsh, C. (2010). *Music and Society in Early Modern England*, pp. 71–87. Cambridge: Cambridge University Press.

van Orden, K. (2000). Cheap print and street songs following the St Bartholomew's massacres of 1572. In K. van Orden (ed.), *Music and the Cultures of Print*, pp. 271–323. New York: Garland.

Walker, D. P. (1946). The aims of Baif's *Académie de Poésie et de Musique. Journal of Renaissance and Baroque Music*, **1**, 91–100.

Yates, F. A. (1947). *The French Academies of the Sixteenth Century*. London: Warburg Institute.

Chapter 23

The tradition of ancient music therapy in the 18th century

Jackie Pigeaud (translation by Kristen Gray Jafflin)

I would like to take a charming little book as the pretext for this chapter: *Traité des effets de la musique sur le corps humain* by Joseph-Louis Roger, doctor at the University of Montpellier. It was translated and enhanced with notes by Etienne Sainte-Marie in 1803 from the original 1758 Latin text *De vi soni et musices iatrica*.

Almost as soon as it was published, de Sauvages (1772) cited it.[i] The translator wasn't just anybody either. Etienne Sainte-Marie was a doctor in the faculty in Montpellier (Frimaire An XII), member of the health council of Lyon, of the Academy of Lyon, etc.; a very learned doctor; who was known for having given, in 1812, a speech on doctor-poets. And we will have a lot to say about poetry. In addition, it wasn't by chance that these two doctors came from the school of Montpellier, which was well known for its interest in culture and the arts. I am thinking, for example, of Barthez and his *Théorie du beau dans la nature et les arts* (Barthez 1895).[ii]

Roger's book is very interesting; but the preface and the abundant translator's notes make it doubly interesting. These allow us to perceive the importance accorded to "iatric" music, as it was called at the middle and the very end of the 18th century. Roger's book is divided into two parts: one part which is more properly physical and physiological; and a second more historical part, which then begins with a *histoire abrégée de la musique iatrique*. It is this second part, of course, which interests us the most today. But we must not forget that Roger was a good physiologist. As Sprengel wrote:

> I found for the first time in a little work that Joseph-Louis Roger published around this time,[iii] the idea that irritability only contains in itself a disposition to movements, and wasn't a sufficient reason for it, an idea which would later give birth to healthier and more useful ideas. Of the rest, the author thought he had made a very important discovery in telling us that all the muscular fibers of the body are in constant palpitation. (Sprengel 1815, t. 5, p. 549)

We should note in this passage the idea of *palpitation*. Sainte-Marie wrote, in making reference to this very book:

> Life exerts itself in us through a trembling analogous to that which sound establishes in a sounding body. This palpitation of the flesh and cellular tissue becomes sensible to touch in certain circumstances; for example, after lively affections of the soul, or a long march.... The sound that one hears in the ear, when one presses it strongly with palm of the hand, also arises from the same cause. *Thus we see an exact relationship between resonant trembling and vital trembling.* Sound's mechanical action on the fibers is a true exercise; *better put, it is the exercise that is the most relevant by its nature to these small movements which produces life itself in our organs.*

In this history of iatric medicine, I don't want to enumerate all the names. The doxography is somewhat reduced; as for antiquity thanks to Cassiodorus, we have the ensemble of the ancient tradition and its consistency; a tradition to which we continue to refer, with extremely precise relays. I think that, among them, I must immediately cite *De musica* by Aristides Quintilian in Meibomius's magnificent edition and translation from the 17th century. It was through this edition that Rousseau, for example, came to know Aristides Quintilian. For Rousseau, Meibomius is the link with antiquity.[iv] There are also some modern authors, who draw directly on the ancients. Among the modern authors cited by Roger are, essentially, Della Porta and Kircher. But it would be both fastidious and repetitive to enumerate all of this. Thus, we will proceed a bit differently.

There is no doubt that the attention drawn to two diseases, tarantula or tarantism and nostalgia, revived interest in *iatric music* in the 17th and 18th centuries. The first appeared to be a physical disease and the second a moral disease, but both, in different fashions, showed the influence of music on human behavior.

Tarantula

For the tarantula, we must begin by citing Baglivi's (1745) work:

> Music must be numbered among the most powerful means of lessening the suffering of the soul, following everyone's opinion, and we can repeat here Alessandro Alessandrini's reflection,[v] in chapter V of his treatise entitled *Dierum genitalium* Lib. VI. 'The sounds of instruments and the harmony of the voice were what Asclepius employed with the most success in cases of frenzy, of altered intelligence or of moral suffering.'[vi]

The effects of the tarantula's bite were impressive:

> A few hours after the bite, the patients experience first of all by an immense agony of the heart, a heavy sadness, but an even greater difficulty in breathing, they complain of a distressed voice, they begin with troubled eyes and when one asks them where it hurts, either they say nothing or they show that the area around the heart is affected by placing their hand on their breast, as though it were the heart that was affected before all other parts. (Baglivi, in Boucher 1851, p. 612.)
>
> Just as tarantulas are of various sizes, colors and virulence, those who are stricken are excited by and revel in diverse genres of sounds when they dance; and this affliction does not only concern sounds but also instruments: alii scilicet fistula pastorali, alii tympano parvo, cythara, lyra, cymbalo, fidibus, & tibicinibus varii generis. (Baglivi, in Boucher 1851, p. 624)

Baglivi tells the story of a patient bitten by a tarantula. They ordered musicians (*Cytharaedi*) to come; they asked her if she knew the color and the size of the tarantula; she wasn't even sure whether she had been bitten by a tarantula or by another beast, a scorpion, for example. So they tried two or three different genres of sounds; without result; "all the same, at the 4th different sound she heard, she immediately began to sigh, she jumped almost naked from the bed and danced for three days without interruption…" (Baglivi, in Boucher 1851, p. 628).

Baglivi makes much of Borelli's book, *De vi percussionis* (Borelli 1667). A golden book, according to him. He also cites Plutarch, *De sanitate tuenda praecepta* (Baglivi, in Boucher 1851, p. 637). Again, he said, a golden book:

> The effect the breath gives strength is proved by masseurs, who order athletes to resist frictions and to stop their breath every time when tending to the parts of the body that they knead and massage; as to the voice, which is a movement of the breath, if we fortify it, not superficially, but at its source in the level of the viscera, it adds to the heart, lightens the blood, cleans each vein, opens each artery, and prevents the condensation and solidification of superfluous humors from forming a sort of deposit in the vessels which receive and transform food …. (Plutarch 1985, p. 118)

Baglivi also cites Asclepius, who treated "with a hanging bed in order to (these are his own words) exhaust illnesses."[vii] For Baglivi, music was part of that type of exercise,

> which strike the air with vivacity, dispose it to lively undulations; these movements, or rapid undulations of the blood, communicated to the intellect by touch, excite diverse conditions, sometimes by violently exciting them to movement, sometimes by quietening them and leading them to rest. And, ideas are born in our spirits from the variety of sounds; some are incited to audacity; others to hilarity, others still to piety, and this arises because of the spirits and the humors, and not in another fashion.

Thus, music acts on the solids and liquids of our body. Animals feel it also. Strabon speaks of musicians who pacified irritated elephants (Baglivi, in Boucher 1851, p. 639). Baglivi also cites Theophrastus, who asserted that one could cure snakebites with music. Asclepius treated frenetics with the *symphonia*.

> And he was not astonished that music had so great a force to dissolve the spirits' or humors' empoisoned aggregate; since just as music affected hearing, an organ very close to the brain, essentially and immediately, and even more the brain itself, or the very small and very fine fibrils of the brain, which, while the spirits are at rest and almost disposed to necrosis, likely are deployed in the cerebral membranes under the effect of the continuous and violent contractions of music, and that they penetrate the fibril channels more easily and agilely, and thus recover their former intercourse with the humors and the solid parts. (Baglivi, in Boucher 1851, p. 640)

Another name that we must evoke is that of the great Athanase Kircher, the author of *Musurgia universalis, sive ars magna consoni et dissoni* (Kircher 1650), which Baglivi knew well[viii] and was cited by Roger (Schneider 1948). According to Kircher, musicians used to pass as much as possible from *la mineur* to *mi* in order to cure tarantula:[ix]

> But I believe that the fact that different people can be affected by different musical instruments must be attributed to the diversity of complexions and temperaments, either of tarantulas or of men, because those who are melancholic or who have been bitten by tarantulas with a particularly weak venom, are more sensitive to noisy dulcimers or to ringing instruments than to stringed instruments, because, when the humor is thick and slow, and when the spirits follow the disposition of the humor, a great force is needed to set it into motion and to disperse these spirits. Hence the story connected to Tarente: a young girl was struck by tarantism there who couldn't be moved to dance by any instruments other than the noise of tambourines, the explosion of bombards, the bursting sound of trumpets; and instruments of this type, which produce a violent sound, because the slow venom, in a body with a slow and cold complexion, refused to dissipate itself except through the large, violent effects. But, because of the mobility of the spirits, those of a choleric disposition and those of a sanguine disposition are easily cured by the harmony of the zither, of the lyre and of lutes and clavichords played together. (*Musurgia*, vol. II, pp. 218–19, cited in Schneider 1948, p. 100)

Sauvages (1772, ch VII, p. 268), whom Sainte-Marie also evokes, cites Baglivi at length, and adds this precision: "Musicians distinguish the false ill[x] from the truly ill because the truly ill have a delicate ear and perceive the smallest tonal error and the lightest dissonance, which the former do not do." But as we cite Sauvages, we must also say a few words about his *musomania*:

> This illness consists of a violent passion for music, such that those who cannot satisfy it fall into sadness, languor and a frenzied state, and don't recover their health until after their desire has been satisfied. When this passion affects patients' health, it is called *musomania*. All men are born with a penchant for music. Examples of healing through music: Bonet bears witness to it, but also Athena, Chrysippus, Desault… On this subject, one can see the learned dissertation of Louis Roger, Doctor from Montpellier, *De vi soni et musices iatrica*, published in 1748. (Sauvages 1772, ch VII, p. 271)

Referring to *Mémoires de l'académie des sciences pour l'année 1707* and *Mémoires de l'académie des sciences pour l'année 1708*, Sauvages reports two cases where delirium was cured through music.

Haller (1763, p. 305), first cites Claudius Roger, a 16th-century doctor: "Paulo aliter Georgius Cheyne [George Cheyne, 1671–1742] a musica docuit in fibris nerveis homotonas riri vibrationes, uti tremores sympathici chordarum se mutuo excitant. Per eas vero oscillationes possis credere, aliter & aliter systema nerveum adfici." Music treats delirium, rabies. For tarantula, Cl. Kaehlerus (1758) showed that the *bestiola* was innocent, and that this illness was of the same type as melancholy: Nunc quidem melancholicos laetis sonis hactenus adjuvari dedero, quod flexum ad mœstitiam animum ab ea obscura voluptate revocent, quam homines ejus temperamenti in tristibus ideis quaerunt.

"Today," wrote Sainte-Marie (1803, p. 327) in a note, "everyone knows that the tarantula is not the cause of the evils that we formerly blamed on it, and that its bite does not produce, as was said, this insatiable desire to dance to the sound of instruments… "[xi]

Return to the ancient tradition

Rather than lose myself in multiple allusions, which is the danger of this type of essay, I will concentrate on three fundamental paradigms in this return to the ancients. Those who made up Asclepius' tradition; those who followed Herophilus; and those of David and Saul.

Asclepius

Tradition has it that Asclepius cured frenetics with the aid of the *symphonia*. Here are some texts that make reference to this account:
Censorinus (*De die natali*, XII):

> The doctor, Asclepius, often restored the spirits of frenetics disturbed by the disease, to their natural state by means of the symphony. But Herophilus, professor of this same art, says that the vein's pulse is moved according to the pace of music and there is thus a harmony in the movements of the body and of the soul, music is undoubtedly not a stranger at birth. (Censorinus 1642, p. 76)

Martianus Capella (*De nuptiis philologiae et mercuri*, bk IX):

> Many Greek cities pronounced laws and public decrees to the sound of the lyre, I have rather often struck a healing melody for conditions of the soul and diseases of the body. In effect, I have cared for frenetics with the symphony, something that the doctor, Asclepius, imitated, when the poorly contained crowd of plebs was annoyed while the Fathers deliberated, a particularly full melody calmed the beginnings of sedition. Damon, one of my cultists, tamed some young people, who were drunk and even excited in an especially obscene manner, with solemn melodies; ordering the flute to play the spondee, he broke the madness of the drunken disturbance. What to say of the conditions of the body? Aren't they cured by assiduous care? The Ancients treated fever and injuries with a song. Asclepius, in the same manner, treated the deaf with a trumpet. Theophrastus used flutes for conditions of the soul. Does anybody not know that sciatica is cured by the sweetness of the aulos? Xenocrates alleviated the lymph nodes by melodious songs. It is certain that Thales, the Cretan, routed diseases and pestilence by the sweetness of the zither. Herophilus measured the veins of the ill through an analogy to tempos. (in Dick 1925, pp. 492–3)[xii]

However the question of what is meant by "symphony" in the preceding passage poses some big problems. Is it an instrument, or is it music, that is to say, to speak vulgarly, a piece of music, or a genre of music, *symphonic* music?[xiii] If we take Apuleius as an example, his *symphoniae* can only be musical instruments (*Metamorphoses*, 11, 9, 16): "Symphoniae dehinc suaues, fistulae tibiaeque modulis dulcissimis personabant." This question provoked a reaction from none other than

Claude Perrault, a skeptic who, for himself, relied on Cassiodorus. Perrault followed his physics of noise by an essay "*De la musique des anciens*" (Perrault 1727, pp. 295, 303). According to him, the ancients didn't know of symphonic music.

> Daniel chapter III, verses 5. 7. speaks of a musical instrument called *symphonia*, which it wants to make pass for something more perfect and more capable of composed harmony than the 3- or 4-string lyre and the psalterion, on which one could only play one part… Not long ago, this instrument, which Daniel called *symphonia*, was still used by our hurdy-gurdy players: one of the musicians touched it, while another played the top violin: this instrument was made in the form of an arc, on which three cords were strung: it only served as a drone: and those who struck it had nothing more to do than to follow the movement and cadence of the violin. This music represents that of the Ancients rather well, with regards to the harmony called "symphony", as it is defined by Cassiodorus: Symphonia est temperamentum sonitus gravis ad acutum, vel acuti ad gravem, modulamen efficiens, sive in voce, sive in percussione, sive in faltu.[xiv]

Perrault concludes: "This shows how little they (the Ancients) had advanced in knowledge in this area, even at the time of Cassiodorus, the writer of these words, who knew all that Antiquity had invented in music."

Herophilus' tradition: the *sphygmology*[xv]

The doctor, Herophilus, was without doubt the first to measure the pulse, if not to recognize its importance. In effect, the Hippocratic collection seems indifferent on the subject.[xvi] Herophilus, the effective inventor of anatomy, to whom we still owe numerous names for the parts of the body, was also the true discoverer of the pulse. Daremberg and Ruelle (1879) cite two contradictory texts from Galen on the Hippocratic origin of the pulse in Rufus of Ephesus' admirable manual; one where he says that Hippocrates first introduced the custom that prevailed after him of calling all movements of the arteries, whatever they were [σφυγμός, *De locis affectis*, II. III] and the other where he wrote that even though Hippocrates was not ignorant of the art of the examination, *he didn't give this name (the pulse) to all movements of the arteries* [*De diff. puls*, I, 2].

In fact, Galen, in our opinion, gives a decisive indication concerning Herophilus, in saying that he distinguished the *pulse* from *palpitation*: διαριζοντα σφυγμον παλμου (VIII K 716).[xvii] Galen continues, he named the movement of the arteries, which we perceive in us from birth to death, "pulse" (VII K 717). Therefore the heart's movement and palpitation of the brain or membranes aren't called "pulse." These two restricting definitions are crucial.[xviii] Henceforth it was acknowledged that a specific movement of the arteries called *pulse* (σφυγμός), existed.[xix] In truth, even if Hippocratic doctors perceived a pulse in the arteries, they would have felt it like a beat, more-or-less regular or more-or-less indistinct; their perceptions would have focused on the quality of the pulse. The analogy Aristotle gives us for the pulse, attributed to the heart, with the beating of the piercing abscess or with boiling, is interesting; it is an entirely empirical analogy, which concentrates on the quality, the picturesque nature of *sphygmos*. This means there is a movement, a beat in the body. Elsewhere, the text distinguishes the *pulse* from the palpitation of the heart and of respiration, considered as other movements (Aristotle, *Parva naturalia*, 479b) of the body, without raising the question of their regularity. What interests the author is the continuity, the permanence of the phenomenon. The Aristotelian author of *De spiritu* wonders if the pulsation was also produced in the arteries, and with the same rhythm and regularity as the beat of the heart and of breathing, and concludes that this does not appear to be the case (*De spiritu*, 482b, 483). To the proposition *there is a beat specific to the arteries*, Herophilus adds *there is a regularity, and even more there is a rhythm*. Herophilus, says Galen, considered the magnitude of the pulse, its rapidity, its power, and its rhythm (VIII K 625).[xx] We leave aside the other aspects to focus on rhythm. On this subject, Daremberg and Ruelle's publication of the Greek version of *Synopsis sur le pouls*, attributed to Rufus, is very important Daremberg and Ruelle (1879, pp. 219–32).[xxi] Here is what the abstract says about Herophilus:

> The pulse of new-borns is decidedly small; one distinguishes neither the diastole nor the systole. Herophilus says that this pulse is without defined proportion, neither that of a one to two, nor that of a one to one and a half, nor any other, but it is absolutely small; it doesn't seem any bigger than a needle point; it is thus rightly that Herophilus first called this pulse *without proportion*. When the child increases in age, and when the body begins to develop, the pulse grows with increasing age, that is to say, compared to the systole, the diastole is larger; of the rest, one can establish a proportion in using, as a means of demonstration, the metric measure; in fact, the first pulse that one can see in a new-born infant takes the meter of a foot at short syllables; it is brief in the diastole and in the systole, and one finds two tempos (*uu pyrrhique*) in it; among more aged individuals, the pulse is analogous to what grammarians call a *trochée* (-u): it has three beats: the diastole has two and the systole one.—In adults' pulse, the diastole is equal to the systole; one can compare it to a spondee (– –), which is the longest of feet with two syllables, and presents four beats. Herophilus calls this pulse *composed of equal beats*.—The pulse of men on the decline and of those who are approaching old age has three beats; the systole is twice the diastole and lasts longer (u- iamb). We see that the model is prosody. Each age has its own meter, even if it seems that there was a contradiction regarding the newborns pulse, qualified simultaneously as *alogos* and *pyrrhique*. Thereby was a norm instituted, according to each generation, which allowed the measurement of a pathological gap. A pulse with a regular rhythm is that which, in *each age*, preserves its natural motion; it was called *eurythmique*; on the contrary, *pararythmique* was the pulse that didn't maintain this motion. Daremberg and Ruelle (1879, p. 224–5)

Pseudo-Galen's *Medical Definitions* is even more precise (XIX K 409). In effect, this author distinguishes the *eurythmique* pulse from the *arythmique* pulse, that is to say without any rhythm, from the *cacorythmique* pulse (which had a rhythm contrary to the *eurythmique*), from the *pararythmique* pulse, that is to say, with a rhythm that doesn't correspond to the patient's age, from the *hétéroryth-mique* pulse, that is to say with the rhythm of another age; and from the *ecrythmique* pulse, that is to say with a rhythm that doesn't correspond to any age or circumstance (von Staden 1989, p. 279).[xxii]

Sainte-Marie (1803, p. 316) remembers the tradition:

> Rhythm exists in all of nature, and the human body is regulated by this universal principle. Each function of our economy has its own determined rhythm. The heart and the lungs strike a two-beat measure, marked in the first of these organs by the systole and the diastole, and in the second by the inhalation and the exhalation. *Therefore, the human body has been organized and animated after the laws of music,* because the principles of this art serve to explain the action of our organs. *Thus, one can consider the animal machine as a musical instrument, which has its tones and its harmony, its resonance and its particular timbre. This link did not escape the Ancients; and in their allegories we see that the god of music is also honored as the god of medicine.* Vaporous subjects and hypochondriacs have no rhythm in their physical faculties. All of their functions, all of their movements are unequal, irregular, brusque and imperfect. From this comes that malaise, that dejection, that weakness and that discordance of organs, which only sends the soul disagreeable and painful feelings, and produces inconstancy, bad harmony, and eccentricity. Don't we find here reason for the relief that music gives them in this regulated movement, which it imprints in their fibers, which, resonating in measure, finally fixes itself and gives rise to the habit of a more regular action.

Sainte-Marie relies on an observation:

> Music agitates all the humors, and especially the blood, as is shown by different observations. It acts on this fluid, first by rhythm; second by the mechanical action of sounds; third by the passions it produces in the soul. Rhythm's influences on circulation is attested to by the experiment that Grétry carried out

himself, and which I thought I recognized the accuracy of in repeating it myself. One places three fingers from the right-hand on the left-arm's artery, or on another of the body's arteries, and one sings an air to oneself, using the movement of the blood as a measure. After some time, one sings warmly an air with a different movement. One will feel the pulse quicken or slow down to put itself closer to the measure of the new song… Experiments have been done where a drum was beaten near a person with an open vein, and the blood came out of the vessel more quickly. (Sainte-Marie 1803, pp. 319–20)

Diseases of the soul; diseases of the body

I want to illustrate this with two stories.

The influence of music on the disease of the soul

I would like to speak a little about the Idyll 11, which Theocritus dedicated to the Cyclops: "There is no remedy for love, Nikias, nor ointment, in my opinion, nor powder, except Pierides' trade. That one is sweet and agreeable, but it is not an easy thing to find." [xxiii]

Three other poems concern Nikias. The Idyll 13, dedicated to Hylas; Epigram 8,[xxiv] and Idyll 28. We know practically nothing of Nikias. According to Theocritus, he was also a poet (cf. Idylls 11,6: 28, 7). Gow thinks that it wouldn't be absurd to suppose that he frequented the medical school at Cos. A scholium clarifies the following: "Theocritus approached the doctor, Nikias, of Milesian origin, who was the study companion of Erasistratus, who was also a doctor."[xxv]

The Cyclops complained. Polyphemus, "from the time when a nascent beard dressed his limps and his temples," was struck with love for Galatea. His love did not find expression in gifts of apples and roses… but in true fits of madness (ορθαις μανιας, verse 11). But he found a cure (Αλλα το φαρμακον ευρε). Seated on a high rock, with eyes turned to the sea, he began to sing. A song whose style may have seemed ridiculous: "What misfortune, that my mother didn't put me in the world with gills! I would dive to rejoin you…; at least I will learn to swim …." But an effective song (verse 67):

> Α ματηρ αδικειμε μονα, και μεμφομαι αυτα.
> ουδεν πηποχ ' ολως ποτι τιν φιλον ειπεν υπερ μευ
> και ταυτ ' αμαρ επ αμαρ ορευσα με λεπτον εοντα.
> Φασω ταν κεφαλαν και τως ποδας αμφοτερως μευ
> σφυζειν,[xxvi] ως ανιαθη, επει κηγων ανιωμαι.
>
> Ω Κυκλωψ Κυκλωψ, πα τας φρενας
> εκπεποτασαι;
> My mother made me wrong, alone, and I hate her for it.
> She never said a nice little word to you about me;
> and that even though she sees me wasting away day by day.
> I am going to tell her that I have a head and two feet that have palpitations,
> to vex her as I am vexed.
>
> O Cyclops, Cyclops, where has your good sense gone?
> - - - -/- - .. -.. -.

As Claude Meillier (1982, p. 177) wrote:

But there is likely an allusion to the doctor Herophilus' research on the role of nerves: the Cyclops, in trying to move his mother, whom he accuses of not intervening on his behalf with Galatea, asserts that he has *pulsations* in the head and legs (XI, 70–71), unless it means *palpitations*, a rather ambiguous term. Effectively, if there were a condition of this type, his state would not be reassuring, because, according to Galen, this is a harbinger of madness.

I agree regarding the ambiguous sense of σφυζειν, and the relation with Herophilus' thought. I am less in agreement with the conclusion. I think that we must delve further into Herophilus' thinking, and pay attention to the rhythm of the verses, to the importance of the spondees. What, the Cyclops reveals to us by the spondaic rhythm, without knowing it, is that he has recovered the rhythm of his age and of the health of his age; *that he is cured*. One feels it in the massive presence of the spondee.[xxvii]

Ω Κυκλωψ Κυκλῶψ, πα τας φρενας
εκπεποτασαι;

You will find another Galatea, perhaps even more beautiful…
‒ ‒ -/- ‒ .. -.. -.

The influences of music on diseases of the body

Roger, speaking of the influence of music on sciatica, evidently refers to Theophrastus, Aulus Gellius; and especially cites a passage from Caelius Aurelian (M.C., lib. V, cap. I, 23): "… loca dolentia decantasse quae cum saltum sumerent palpitando, discusso dolore mitescerent."

Sainte-Marie's translation of Roger, from Caelius' text, gives:

> Cælius Aurélien décrit très bien sa manière d'agir, en parlant d'un joueur de flûte qui avait enchanté, dit-il, les parties douloureuses, en leur imprimant une espèce de palpitation, ou de sautillement, au moyen duquel le principe de la douleur avait été chassé. (Sainte-Marie 1803, p. 204)

G. Bendz (1993), Caelius' last editor, gives the following text for treatment of sciatica: "Item alii[xxviii] cantilenas adhibendas probaverunt, ut etiam Philistionis frater idem memorat libro XXII De adjutoriis, scribens quendam fistulatorem loca dolentia decantasse,[xxix] quae cum saltum sumerent palpitando discusso dolore mitescerent."

The excellent editor and translator, Drabkin (1950), gives: "Other physicians prescribe music, as the brother of Philistion tells us in Book XXII of his work *On Remedies*. He writes that a certain piper would play his instrument over the affected parts and that these would begin to throb and palpitate, banishing the pain and bringing relief… "

Ingeborg Pape translates (Bendz 1993, p. 866, 32) as: "… dass irgendein Flötenspieler über den schmerzenen Stellen sein Instrument gespielt habe, die, als sie die Schwingung aufnahmen, dadurch Linderung erfuhren, dass der Schmerz durch das Pulsieren vertrieben worden war".

I return to the text, in which the sense of *saltum* and *palpitando* is difficult to discern: quae cum saltum sumerent palpitando discusso dolore mitescerent. For Caelius, the sense of *saltus* is, more or less, that of *pulsus*. It is beating (cf. MA, II, 11 = Bendz 1993, p. 136, 15):

> pulsus etiam inaequalis, hoc est aliquando saltus ordinatus aut inordinatus et pro aetate aut natura major aut tardior, aliquando etiam in inanitatem intercapedinatus.
>
> Wenn allerdings der Puls grösser wird und dabei weder langsam oder leer, sondern dem Alter des Kranken entsprechend ist, so fassen wir dies als eine typische Erscheinung des Abklingens einer Phrenitis auf…

Compare again 11 *in fine* (Bendz 1993, p. 136, 21): certius etiam quoties circa numerum aequales minoribus majores saltus efficiuntur ac velocibus et densis et vehemntibus, multo potius, si etiam multo majores atque celeres fuerint. Also MC, II, 88, which concerns a pulse that is beating violently and too strongly: cum pulsu magno ex vehementibus atque fortioribus saltibus confecto (Bendz 1993, p. 866, 21).[xxx]

I would propose, myself, to understand Caelius' text in this fashion—I gloss over more than I translate—"writing that a flute player had played above the painful parts, which, palpitating in absorbing the palpitation, that is to say, in re-absorbing the beating of the palpitation, [that is to say, in replacing σφύζειν with σφυγμος] became calm, the pain having left". In addition, *palpitando* is a ditrochaic sequence: (_-_-).[xxxi]

Don't we see Herophilus' influence here as well?

To return to Sainte-Marie, it is curious that we find in him Simmias' soul-harmony, Aristoxenus' theory: in the preface (Sainte-Marie 1803, p. VIII), he begins by writing: "Thus, all medical science is reduced to knowing how to tune and strum the lyre of the human body in such a manner that it makes true and agreeable sounds." And he cites Bacon: "Varia ista et subtilis *corporis humani compositio et fabrica* efficit ut sit *instar organi musici operosi et exquisiti*... Atque in eo constat plane medici officium, *ut sciat corporis humani lyram ita tendere et pulsare*, ut reddatur concentus minime discors et insuavis."[xxxii]

As I have said, the great initiator, by whom everyone in the 18th century was taught regarding these types of problems remains Aristides Quintilian and his great commentator, Meibomius (1652).[xxxiii]

David and Saul

Cassiodorus refers to the action of music on birds, serpents, and dolphins; recall Orpheus' lyre and the Sirens' song, and the following: "Quid de David dicimus, qui a Spiritibus immundis Saulem disciplina saluberrimae modulationis eripuit, novoque modo per auditum sanitatem contuli regi, quam medici non poterant herbarum potestatibus operari?" [What to say of David, who exorcised malignant spirits from Saul by playing a lilt with great curative powers, and who, when the doctors couldn't cure him using the virtues of herbs, returned the King to health by a new means, hearing?] (Cassiodorus 1650, p. 576.)

I cite Cassiodorus, but I must also cite Isidore of Seville (see Pigeaud 1984). In his *Etymologie* III, 17, 3, he writes:

> Music also pacifies excited spirits, as one reads concerning David, who rid Saul of an unclean spirit by means of the art of the melody (arte modulationis). For animals themselves, like snakes, birds and dolphins, music rouses them to listen to its own melody. But all that we say, and all the movements that we feel inside of ourselves, through the pulse and the veins, are associated, as has been shown, to the virtues of harmony by the intermediary of musical rhythms.

Evidently, we cannot understand this passage if we don't reflect on the analogy between prosodic rhythms and those of the pulse in the tradition of Herophilus. In Book IV, which is specifically medical, David is associated with Asclepius of Bithynia: "Sicut de David legitur... Asclepiades quoque medicus phreneticum quendam per symphoniam pristinae sanitati restituit."(*Etymologie* IV, 13, 3)

Roger assimilates the case of Saul to *hypochondria*. He writes:

> Perhaps it was a hypochondriacal or hysterical condition that Saul, who, according to the holy books, found such effective relief in music, experiences. [Kings, 16 v. 23] Richard Mead thinks that this illness was a furious mania, in which Saul had fallen through the just punishment of God; but I have as many reasons to believe that *it was a bout of hypochondriacal condition*, and the testimony of the Ancients conforms rather well to this idea; because these illnesses, according to Raulin [*Traité des affections vaporeuses du sexe*], were already frequent in the times of Democritus and of Hippocrates. (Roger 1758, pp. 248–9).

There remains a lot of work to be done on the tradition of iatric music. To return to the authors we began with, Roger and Sainte-Marie, perhaps we should evoke the *vitalism* of the Montpellier school. For example, Roger evokes Kau Boerhaave's hefty work *Impetum faciens d'Hippocrate* (Roger 1758, p. 117). However, to finish, I will turn to Roger (1758, pp. 220–1):

> The Ancients, in whose works we have preserved the most astonishing observation on the effects of music, employed simple melodies due to the imperfection of their instruments, *and had almost no notion of harmony*. It is to this great simplicity that their music owed all its advantages. Among others, they clung to I don't know what particular instinct to express all the movements, the agitations of the passions on their instruments; and by long practice, they acquired great skill in this effort. This art, which is entirely unknown to us, joined with the extreme simplicity of their music, which allowed everyone to easily follow the order of images, operated these miracles which have been transmitted to us ....

Notes

i   "On this subject, one can see the learned dissertation of Louis Roger, Doctor of Montpellier, *De vi soni et musices iatrica*, published in 1758."

ii   See, in particular, *Second discours*, p. 23 ss. Cf. and the note on *Mémoire sur l'utilité de la musique, tant dans l'état de santé que dans celui de maladie*, by M. Benoît Mojon, doctor of medicine and surgery, member of the Competitive Medical Society of Genova, translated from the second Italian edition, with notes, by C. D. Muggetti, doctor-surgeon from the School of Pavie, Paris 1803 in 8° of 48 pages and 10 for the foreword.

iii Sainte-Marie returned to Roger's work: *Specimen physiologicum de perpetua fibrarum muscularium palpitatione, novum phoenomenum in corpore humano experimentis detectum et confirmatum*, in 12., Gott. 1760.

iv   "Marc Meibomius gave us a beautiful edition of these seven Greek authors, with a Latin translation and notes." (*Dictionnaire de musique*; Rousseau 1995, p. 926). Cf. Aristidi Quintiliani, *De musica* Libri III. Marcus Meibomius restituit, ac notis explicavit, Amstelodami, apud Ludovicum Elzevirium, 1652 [referenced by S. Baud-Bovy in "Note sur la musique Grecque antique" (Rousseau 1995, p. 1658*ff.*)].

v   Alessandro Alessandrini was a jurist, born in Naples in 1461, died in Rome in 1523.

vi   We cite here from the translation by Boucher (1851, p. 297). See also p. 390 of Boucher's translation, where Baglivi puts *musica* with *rusticatio, navigatio, venatio, saltatio, equitatio, peregrinatio* and where he praises the *diæta Pythagoreorum*.

vii Lecto pensili, ut morbos (verba illius sunt) extenuaret (p. 638). In effect, this is the expression that Pliny attributes to Asclepius: jam suspendendo lectulos, quorium jactatu aut morbos extenuaret au somnos adlicerete . . . " H.N. XXVI, VIII, 14. Cf. also *extenuare* attributed to Asclepius, Caelius Aurélien, *MA*, I. 152, Bendz, p.g 106, 17. with relation to the pressure which "condenses and attenuates the nature of milk . . . "

viii In his *Dissertatio de tarentula*, Baglivi cites Kircher (see, for example., *Mund. magnet.* lib. 13. part. 8, in Boucher 1851, p. 625).

ix   Hinc quanto sonus majorem habuerit vocum notularumque dimanationem, atque acuti gavisque vocum, in Tono hemitoniis frequetibus referto, majorem permixtionem, tanto gratiorem futuram hoc morbo affectis musicam; ex celeritate enim motus vehementius musculus vellicat et consequenter ad saltandum vehementius sollicitat. Hin Cytharedi quantum fieri potest, variis vocum dimunutionibus et ut plurimum in tono phrygio, ob frequentia quibus constat hemitonia, modulationes adornare solent. *Musurgia*, vol. II, p.220 (Consect. II), cited in Schneider (1948 p.95). See also Cid (1787).

x   For example, religious nymphomaniacs.

xi   And he cites a long letter from the citizen, Philippe Guidi, "learned professor at the University of Naples."

xii We saw Asclepius cited by Baglivi (Sainte-Marie 1803, p. 215).

xiii On this question, I permit myself to refer to Pigeaud (1987, p.161).

xiv   In Cassiodorus (1650, p. 574). Apuleius is found among the authors cited by Cassiodorus, but also: Scripsit etiam Pater Augustinus de Musica sex libros in quibus humanam vocem, rythmicos sonos, & harmoniam modulabilem in longis syllabis atque brevibus naturaliter habere monstravit. Censorinus quoque . . . .

xv   Here we develop the argument of Pigeaud (1978). Since then, work on Hellenistic medicine has developed considerably. We now have an edition of fragments from Herophilus with commentary by Von Staden (1989) and on Erasistratus by Garofalo (1988). See also, for example, Grmek (1962)

xvi   Although we always cite, as Grmek (1962) remarks, the sentence: "it is better to feel the vessels than not to feel them." (Hippocrates, *Prorrh*, II, 10).

xvii   Herophilus attributed palpitation to a condition of the nerves, cf. Galen (VII K 59). (We designate sources following the use of Galen's works with the volume number and pagination found in Kühn's edition, K.)

xviii   Certainly, *Humeurs IV*, cited by Daremberg and Ruelle (1879, p. 615), advised the consideration of the σφυγμόι and the παλμοι. But Daremberg acknowledges that it is difficult to appreciate the positive value of this distinction. He thinks that σφυγμός designated a normal movement of the arteries, and παλμος the pathological movement.

xix   To distinguish between palpitation and spasm.

xx   We leave aside the problem of the cause of the pulse. On this subject, read Daremberg's note (Daremberg and Ruelle 1879, p. 615). Herophilus thought that the arteries had a diastolic and systolic movement, communicated by the heart. For him, the systole would be the active time (VIII K 747). The arteries contained air which they drew to all the parts of the body. Cf. Daremberg and Ruelle (1879, p. 627).

xxi   For connections to certain theories in the abstract with Soranus see Daremberg and Ruelle (1879, p. 66).

xxii   As von Staden says: "Whatever the provenance of Herophilus' theory of pulse rhythms might be, its impact was enormous, and his general analogy between metrical-musical rhythm and pulse rhythm became a topos of both medical and musical literature until the Renaissance."

xxiii   I will not insist on the bibliography. One story is told in *Bucoliques Grecs* (Theocritus 1925). See also the commentary of Gow (1950), Hutchinson (1988–1990, p. 179), and Erbse (1965).

xxiv   "Paieon's son also came to Milet to see a man who healed maladies, Nikias, who prayed to him each day and offered him sacrifices, and who sculpted this status out of fragrant cedar; Nikias had promised Aetion generously to award his practiced hand; Aetion dedicated all his skill to this work." (translated from the translation into French by Legrand).

xxv   προσδιαλεγεται δε ο θεοκριτοςιατρω Νικια, Μιλησιω τογενος, ος συμφοιτητης γεγονεν Ερασιστρου ιατρου οντος και αυτου (Gow 1950, p. 208).

xxvi   *Scholie:* σφυσδειν, αλγειν, M φλεγμαινειν L. ανιαθη, ινα λυπηθη βλεπονσα με πασχοντα οπερ λυπηρον μητρασιν. M. Grn.

xxvii   On this subject see Pigeaud (1978) and von Staden (1989, p. 281).

xxviii   Theophrastus. Frag. 87 (Wimmer) = Aulus Gellius IV. 13, 1_2; cf. *Chr.* I, 175–6; 178.

xxix   Cf. *decantatio tibiarum*, on the cure of madness (Bendz 1993, p. 534, 15).

xxx   *Palpitare* had already been used in reference to the heart by Cicero.

xxxi   This is the only occurrence, according to the index in Bendz (1993).

xxxii   *De dignitate et augmentis scientiarum*, IV, 2.

xxxiii   Aristidi Quintiliani, *De musica* Libri III (see note iv). Generally, says Aristides Quintilian, rhythm is perceived by three senses: sight, as in dance; hearing, as in song; and touch, as for the arteries' pulse (tactu, ut arteriarum pulsus . . . , p. 31; see also, p. 32: Ad rythmum enim in Musica componitur motus corporis, modulatio, dictio; p. 66: horum cuique convenientem medicinam musica adhibet, inscior paulatim ad rectam constitutionem subducens; p. 99: rursus qui in uno genere manet, singulis differentiis violenter animam retrahunt, coguntque ut varietatem subsequatur, illique adsimiletur. Qudocirca et in arteriaum motibus, qui eandem quidem speciem servant, at in temporibus parvam faciunt differentiam, licet rubati, nequauqam tamen sunt periculosi; verus qui aut valde temporibus variant, aut genera mutant, et terribilis sunt et exitiales . . . . For a modern edition, refer to Winnington-Ingram (1963). On Aristides Quintilian, it is profitable to read Croissant (1932, p. 117*ff*).

References

Baglivi, G. (1745). *Opera omnia*. Book I *De Praxi Medica*. Lyon.

Barthez, P. J. (1895). *Théorie du beau dans la nature et les arts*, 2nd edn (published posthumously). Paris: Vigot.

Baud-Bovy, S. (ed.) (1995) Note sur la musique Grecque antique. In S. Baud-Bovy (ed.), [J.-J. Rousseau] *Oeuvres complètes V. Écrits sur la musique, la langue et le théâtre*, p. 1658. Paris: Gallimard/Pléiade.

Bendz, G. (ed.) (1993). *Caelius Aurelianus, Akute Krankheiten* (Buch I–III), *Chronische Krankheiten* (Buch I–V), transl. I. Pape. Berlin: Akademie-Verlag.

Borelli, G. A. (1667). *De vi percussionis*. Bologna.

Boucher, J. (1851). *De l'accroissement de la médecine pratique*. Paris: Labé [translation into French of Baglivi 1745].

Cassiodorus (1650). *Opera omnia. De musica*. Geneva: P. Chouet.

Censorinus (1642). *De die natali*, XII. Edited with notes by H. Lindenbrog. Leiden.

Cid, F. X. (1787). *Tarantismo observado en España*. Madrid: M. Gonzalez.

Croissant, J. (1932). *Aristote et les mystères*. Liège, Paris .

Daremberg C. and Ruelle C.-E. (eds) (1879). *Œuvres de Rufus d'Ephèse*. Paris: Baillière.

Dick, A. (ed.) (1925). *Martianus Capella* [works]. Leipzig: Teubner. (Reprinted 1969 with corrections by J. Préaux.)

Drabkin, I. E. (ed. and transl.) (1950). Caelius Aurelianus, *On Acute Diseases and On Chronic Diseases*. Chicago: University of Chicago Press.

Erbse, H. (1965). Dichtkunst und Medizin in Theokrits 11. Idyll. *Museum Helveticum*, **22**(4), 232–6.

Garofalo, I. (1988). *Erasistrati fragmenta*. Pisa: Giardini.

Gow, A. S. F. (ed. and transl.) (1950). *Theocritus*, vol. II, commentary, appendix, indices, and plates. Cambridge: Cambridge University Press.

Grmek, M. D. (1962). Les reflets de la sphygmologie Chinoise dans la médecine occidentale. *Biologie Médicale*, February 1962 (number out of series), p. xxvi.

von Haller, A. (1763). *Elementa physiologiae corporis humani*, bk V, *De auditu*. Lausanne: Francois Grasset.

Hutchinson, G. O. (1988–1990). *Hellenistic Poetry*. Oxford: Clarendon Press.

Kaehlerus, Cl. (1758). *Swenska Acad. Handlung*, trim. I. p. 34 etc [as cited by von Haller (1763, p. 305)].

Kircher, A. (1650). *Musurgia universalis, sive ars magna consoni et dissoni*. Rome: Heirs of Francesco Corbelletti.

Legrand, E. (ed. and transl.) (1925) Theocritus *Bucoliques grecs. Théocrite*. Paris: Les Belles Lettres.

Meillier, C. (1982). La fonction thérapeutique de la musique et de la poésie dans le recueil des "Bucoliques" de Théocrite. *Bulletin de l'Association Guillaume Budé*, June, 177.

Perrault, C. (1727). *Oeuvre de physique et mécanique*. Amsterdam.

Pigeaud, J. (1978). Du rythme dans le corps, quelques notes sur l'interprétation du pouls par le médecin Hérophile. *Bulletin de l'Association Guillaume Budé*, **3**, 259–67.

Pigeaud, J. (1984). De la mélancholie et de quelques autres maladies dans les Etymologies d'Isidore de Séville. *Mémoires V, textes médicaux Latins.* University of Saint Etienne.

Pigeaud, J. (1987/2010). *Folie et cure de la folie chez les médecins de l'antiquité Gréco-Romaine: la manie.* Paris: Les Belles Lettres.

Plutarch (1985). *Œuvres morales.* Translated by J. Defradas, J. Hani, and R. Klaerr. Paris: Les Belles Lettres.

Roger, J. L. (1758). *De vi soni et musices iatrica.* (translated into French with added notes in 1803, as *Traité des effets de la musique sur le corps humain* by E. Sainte-Marie)

Rousseau, J.-J. (1995). *Dictionnaire de musique.* In S. Baud-Bovy (ed.), *Œuvres complètes V. Écrits sur la musique, la langue et le théâtre.* Paris: Gallimard/Pléiade.

Sainte-Marie, E. (ed.) (1803). *Traité des effets de la musique sur le corps humain* (translation into French, with added notes, of *De vi soni et musices iatrica,* J. L. Roger, 1758). Paris: Brunot.

de Sauvages, F. B. (1772). *Nosologie méthodique,* transl. M. Gouvion. Lyon: Jean-Marie Bruyset.

Schneider, M. (1948). *La danza de espadas y la tarantela.* Barcelona: Instituto Español de Musicologia

Sprengel, K. (1815). *Histoire de la médecine* (translated from the German following the 2nd edition by A. J. L. Jourdan). Paris.

von Staden, H. (ed.) (1989). *Herophilus, the Art of Medicine in Early Alexandria.* Cambridge: Cambridge University Press.

Winnington-Ingram, R. P. (1963). *Aristidis Quintiliani* De musica *libri tres.* Leipzig: Teubner.

Chapter 24

On nostalgia

Jean Starobinski (translation by Kristen Gray Jafflin)

Emotions come before the words that name them. Emotions only exist for our consciousness after they receive a name. These two propositions contradict one another and are equally true. We know that they are also true for the names of colors.

Despite looking the same, an emotion, once named, is no longer exactly the same. A new word brings together the unknown, which before had no form. Being named makes it a concept, it has a definition, and it calls forth an additional definition: it becomes a material for tests and experiments. The name of an affective state, if it is adopted and put into circulation, not only propagates itself in the vocabulary, it produces new emotions. We live passions whose words precede us and which we would not have felt without them. "There are people who would never have been in love, if they hadn't heard of love," writes de la Rochefoucauld (1678). This is primarily the effect of fashion or cliché, a thread of singular influences, a more-or-less conscious process of literary borrowing. Diffusion and generalization follow: each group, each society, sees, at a given moment, the call of several words reverberate almost without end, in a process which doesn't differ greatly from that of learning a language.

There are few occasions where one finds terms destined to be added to the emotional lexicon succeed and enter into the vocabulary of multiple languages. But this is the case for the word "nostalgia." A certain date and place can be assigned to its birth: Basel, 1688. An author: Dr Johannes Hofer, of Mulhouse. A work: *Dissertatio medica de nostalgia*. It was Johannes Hofer's doctoral thesis.[i]

The author wanted to devote medical reflection to the pain that the Swiss suffered when they had "lost the sweetness of their homeland." This pain, they had "long since named *Heim-weh* in their language," and "the French have designated as *la maladie du pays*." But, added Hofer, doctors had never properly studied this trouble. And as its study involved representing a new thing (*res nova*), it was necessary to have a name for it. This was what everyone had done before him when faced with a similar situation. "On reflection, no name is better, no name more suitable, for designating this object than that of *Nostalgia*, Greek in origin, and composed of two terms, of which the first, *Nostos*, means the return to the homeland, and the second, *Algos*, designates pain or sadness."[ii] Here, for once, a scholarly neologism which sounds well, which isn't too heavy, and which carries in it, from the beginning, the possibility of being adopted into the body of popular language, from which it wanted to distinguish itself! It would be accepted by the Académie française in 1835 (although Chateaubriand had used it much earlier).[iii] It competes with *Heimweh* in German and became established in English, Italian, Russian, etc.

The novelty, as shown, lay in the doctor's attention, in the decision that identified a state of suffering as a morbid entity and submitted it to the interpretations of the rational scholar. From the moment when, encouraged by the botanical system model, medicine entered the business of creating an inventory of illnesses, of classifying diseases, it had to search for all the varieties that could enrich the table of morbid genres and species (*genera morborum*). The medical tradition recognized diverse genres of melancholy. In 1621 Robert Burton carefully classified them in *Anatomy of Melancholy*. There was ample material on amorous melancholy, about which the doctor Jacques Ferrand dedicated a small scholarly treatise in 1616. The symptoms of lovesickness were well known:

> loss of appetite, fever, rapid pulse, etc. If the privation of a loved one caused a well-characterized sickness, shouldn't one list the suffering caused by the loss of a beloved place in the same manner? The elegiacs sang of grief at loss[iv] of love. And they also sang of *desiderium patriae*,—the grief at loss of the homeland: some magnificent verses from *The Odyssey*, and from Ovid's *Sorrows*, come to mind. Medicine, which writes of those who perished from love, ought not ignore those who perished from being far from their hometown. Did it not concern, in the two cases, the deadly effect of separation? (Hofer 1688)

For Johannes Hofer, nostalgia was a malady of the imagination. Therefore, he took up the notion of the *imaginatio laesa*, which had been frequently used during the Renaissance, and which had been invoked in all cases where the representation of the world and of the self seemed troubled. For many modern men, such as Thomas Willis, disorders of the imagination were the result of a material alteration in nervous fluids and in base instinct. Johannes Hofer (1688) proposed a sort of hydrodynamic vision, establishing the physiological response of an idée fixe materially:

> Nostalgia is born from a derangement of the imagination, when nervous fluids always flow in one sole direction in the brain, and, therefore, only awaken one sole idea, the desire to return to the homeland; this idea is linked to manifestations which are sometimes violent, sometime more moderate. […] Only a few external objects affect those suffering from nostalgia, and nothing makes a more lively impression on them than the idea of returning to their homeland. While in a normal state, the spirit can be moved by all objects, while in a nostalgic state, its attention is very diminished. It only feels attraction for very few objects and, for all intents and purposes, attaches itself to one sole idea. I would happily agree with those who invoke a share of melancholy here, because the vital spirits, expended on one unique idea, become fatigued and in part exhaust themselves, and therefore provoke erroneous representations.

Hofer cited two cases as examples. The first is that of a Bernese student living in Basel: this boy felt sadness, fever, and heart troubles. His state worsened day by day. He was on the brink of death. Someone recommended that he be carried back to his homeland on a stretcher. They did so. They had hardly left Basel before the symptoms retreated: the patient breathed better. He arrived at home cured. The second case was that of a woman who had been brought to the hospital following a serious accident. As soon as she regained consciousness, she had only one idea and one request: to return home. She became so weak that they returned her to her parents. A few days later, having received almost no treatment, she was completely better. For today's readers, the case of this young woman is analogous to the *hospitalism* observed among children.

The complete picture of the illness included constant sadness, agitated sleep (during which one revisited sites from the past), total insomnia, irritability when faced with injustices and bad treatment; in addition to which was added lassitude, insensibility to thirst and to hunger, feelings of fear, palpitations, frequent sighs, prostration, and, often, intermittent fever. Why, Johannes Hofer asked himself, were the young Swiss so often prone to nostalgia when they went abroad? Without a doubt because most of them had never before left their family home, and because they had never known a different milieu. It was difficult for them to forget the attention their mothers surrounded them with, the food they were offered each morning. Hofer mentions soups, milk, that is to say the food of infancy. For them, their birthplace was also the place of liberty. Instructed by the ample psychological literature of our century, we see in this picture "socio-emotional deprivation," the "need for mothering," and "regressive reveries."

As a good student of classical doctrines, Hofer took into consideration the change of air, which was part of the basic external causes of the illness: "The change in atmosphere isn't without effect on the blood and the nervous spirits; but the principal cause arises from strange mores and habits, from unaccustomed lifestyles." This implies that nostalgics didn't have the psychological resources necessary to accustom themselves to a different milieu. But didn't attributing nostalgia to a moral cause of this sort imply that the young Swiss were excessively weak? That is what the Zurich-born thinker, Johann-Jacob Scheuchzer, thought. He had another, entirely mechanical, explanation to propose. And it would find takers, because, after Hoffmann's systematic treatises, an entire scientific school, following Descartes and his disciples, sought to understand living organisms through the laws of motion and through the application of models from experimental physics. By resorting to a physical explanation, Scheuchzer shifted the debate. The "morale" of the patient was no longer in question. Now it was only necessary to invoke—that is to say, incriminate, a material necessity: atmospheric pressure. The Swiss live among the highest peaks of Europe. They breath, they take in, a light, subtle, rarefied air. In descending to the plain, they experience increased pressure, the effect of which is so much greater that their internal air ("which we carried with us") offered less resistance. A Dutchman, on the other hand, born in the plains, carries with him a heavy air that resists the pressure of weighty mists well. At sea level, the people of the Alps are literally oppressed by the atmosphere: the body undergoes a compression, circulation worsens, the heart receives less blood, sadness prevails, they lose sleep and appetite, soon a mortal fever arises. What is the remedy? If one cannot repatriate the patient, dismiss the soldier, or simply give him hope of return, the most logical treatment consists of lodging him on a hill or in a tower; one could also give him medicines containing "compressed air," which is effervescent air in water. New wine and beer, with their light bubbles, are also beneficial. At the same time, Scheuchzer's explanation rested on the stimulating effects of the Swiss climate. In them, one sees dawning the arguments that would make Switzerland a health resort for more than two centuries. Switzerland is a sanctuary for the ill (*asylum languentium*), Scheuchzer asserted in a paper from 1705. From all over Europe, individuals burdened by heavy air hasten to its mountains: they heal there: the body's channels expand, circulation improves, and all of the juices are gently set in motion. This reasoning makes us smile today. But can we blame an 18th-century doctor for his ignorance of the regulation of the gaseous equilibrium between the exterior and interior milieu? Having resolved to invoke physical causes, he could not speak a language other than that of the barometry and the hydrostatics of his epoch, concepts from which he speculatively applied to the human organism, without any experiment or recourse to measurable data. Dubos is included among those who accepted and propagated Scheuchzer's ideas: he mentioned *Heimweh* in his *Réflexions critiques sur la poésie et la peinture* (Dubos 1719), a work which figured in all the libraries of cultivated Europe for more than half a century. His explanation of it followed the medical ideas of the Zurich-born doctor, but also drew on Juvenal and Lucretius to illustrate and reinforce his theory:

> Our native air is a remedy for us. This disease, which is called *Hemvé* in some countries, and which gives the patient a violent desire to return home ("Cum notos tristis desiderat haedos"[v]: Juven. Sat. 11), is an instinct which warns us that the air in which we find ourselves is not as congenial to our constitution as that for which a secret instinct makes us yearn. *Hemvé* only becomes a mental suffering because it is really a corporal pain. The source of the indisposition and the illnesses is an air too different from that to which one is habituated.
>
> Non ne vides etiam coeli novitate et aquarum
Tentari procul a patria quicumque domoque
Adveniunt, ideo quia longe discrepat aër.
>
> Lucretius, lib. sexto

This air, although very healthy for natives of the country, is a slow poison for certain foreigners. Who hasn't heard of "Tabardillor," which is a fever accompanied by the most unfortunate symptoms and which strikes almost all Europeans a few weeks after their arrival in Spanish America? […] There is no cure for those who are stricken by this disease, which is very often mortal, other than bleeding them excessively and in bolstering them little by little with foods from their country. The same evil strikes the Spanish, born in America, on their arrival in Europe. Their father's native air becomes a poison for the sons. (Dubos 1719, 2nd pt, sect. 14, t. II, pp. 236–37)[vi]

But this doctrine found its opponents. François Boissier de Sauvages, the Montpellier-born author of *Nosologie méthodique*, which was an authoritative work,[vii] observed that separation and loss were sufficient to provoke nostalgic conditions, without adding exile to other skies or barometric variations. It was necessary to go beyond physical causes: "I have seen a beggar child, whose only country was the roads and crossroads, who died of this disease after having lost his father and mother. […] Little orphans, whose relatives can't remove them from our hospitals and take them home, almost all die of this illness, without receiving any relief from surgery or diet." Sauvages' conclusion, based on this evidence, was unambiguous: "It is necessary to seek the cure of this disease only in moral succor." Some of the means he suggested were identical to those which were habitually prescribed for melancholy: "Try to relieve the patient using games, amusements, spectacles, and offer them everything they desire." But in the most serious cases, the best remedy was returning patients to their families or country: "If the disease is serious and resists all remedies, the only thing capable of curing it is sending the patient into his country. However weak and battered they appear, they will have enough strength to raise themselves from their bed, when one allows them to believe that they will see their country again; their strength returns, and they are cured en route." (de Sauvages 1771, pt. II, pp. 684–6).

During the 18th century, we find nostalgia mentioned in almost all medical works that were meant to be exhaustive. (A singular chain of events: it's the word *nostalgia* and its medical fortune that make known, outside of Switzerland, the word *Heimweh*, which they proceed.) The case of nostalgia is all the more interesting because it became a privileged case in the debate concerning the influence of the physical on the moral, or, inversely, of the moral on the physical. The discussion would continue until the first decades of the 19th century. The cases highlighted in certain writings are striking: they resemble those that we consider psychosomatic today. This retrospective interpretation is legitimate, on the condition that we don't forget the more distant past. The debate concerned a very old problem, which traditional medicine had considered as falling under that part of medical knowledge defined under the name *hygiene*: what effect does a change in the quality of the air breathed have on one's health? Which disorders can the soul's passions produce? The air and the soul's passions were included in the list of "six unnatural things[viii] "that the doctor had to take into consideration when he sought to establish the predisposing causes of illnesses and when he made decisions concerning diet arising from this knowledge. A change of vocabulary has intervened in the medical language of today: *environment* has replaced *air*; *affective* reactions has replaced *passions*. We will return to our subject.

Nostalgia is a pain of the memory. A mere fragment of the past suffices to exacerbate the suffering. This fragment can be a melody that the sufferer had heard before. This melody calls forth an entire swarm of "accessory ideas," until a seemingly complete picture of the lost past forms.

In 1710, in a Latin dissertation on *Heimweh*, the Basel-based doctor Theodor Zwinger (1710) mentioned the outburst of intense grief that hearing "a certain rustic cantilena, which the Swiss peasants sing while herding their flocks in the Alps"[ix] engendered among expatriate soldiers. This song, sung during the hike up to the alpine meadows, was capable of suddenly kindling memories of the homeland. It was disastrous among those whose blood was already altered by a change of air, or among those subjects naturally inclined to sadness. This was why, affirmed Zwinger, when faced with the disastrous effects of this melody, the officers had no other recourse than banning it and severely punishing those who continued to play it, sing it, or whistle it. Hot fevers were one thing: the gravest threat was desertion. For captains serving abroad, who equipped the troops they commanded themselves at great cost, a desertion implied the loss of a part of their invested capital. They needed to silence these few notes that, once heard, led men to death or made them flee. They dreaded suicides. At the beginning of the 1700s, in an instantly famous treatise dedicated to professional diseases, Ramazzini (1700, ch. XL) mentioned a beautiful and terrible saying that prevailed in the armies: Qui patriam quaerit mortem invenit (He who seeks his country will only find death).[x]

A "little phrase," a simple popular melody, therefore, had the singular power of provoking an attack of hypermnesia: the illusion of seeing a countryside from the past, doubled by the painful emotions of separation. For 18th-century thinkers and philosophers, a physical explanation seemed necessary once again. Philosophers and doctors were once again tempted by the somatic model. A mechanical physiology of memory had to account not only for the reminiscence of a precise image but also for the reawakening of all "accessory ideas." Malebranche invoked the link between marked traces in the brain:

> The brain traces are so well tied to one another that none can be aroused without all those which were imprinted at the same time being aroused. (Malebranche 1997, II.I.5.ii)

Locke (1972, bk II, XXIII) and Hutcheson (1728, pt IV, p. 93) sought to prove that associations of ideas determined phobias and prejudices. An idea and an accidental circumstance could be linked so strongly that each repetition of the circumstance would necessarily invoke the idea. It was, in their opinion, the nefarious aspect of the association that prevented the healthy functioning of reason.

David Hartley (1755) made a proposal basing the psychology of association on the physics of vibration and resonance. One hears the harpsichord's resonance (as with Diderot) in the model proposed by Hartley. Here is how he formulated the theory of *idées complexes:*

> When multiple ideas are associated with one another, the visible idea, being clearer and more distinct than the rest, serves as a symbol for the others, it suggests them and ties them together: It somewhat resembles the first letter of a word, or the first words of a sentence, which one often uses to introduce the rest to the mind. […] Once words have acquired some considerable power to excite agreeable and pleasant vibrations in the nervous system, often by associating themselves with things, they can transfer a part of the pains and pleasure onto these indifferent things, being associated with them very often any other time. This is one of the principal sources of false pleasure and pain in human life. (Hartley 1755, vol. I, pp. 138–9 and vol. II, p. 34)

These associated reminiscences can acquire an intensity comparable to that of real feelings. Therefore, this is no longer a case of vibration "in miniature," which is produced in our "medullary substance": these are "living vibrations, equal to those excited by the objects imprinted on the sense" (Hartley 1755, vol. I, pp. 142–3). It became easy to understand phenomena of affective memory and of involuntary memory. John Gregory, in 1765, assigned a remarkable development to them:

> The passions are expressed naturally by different sounds; but this natural expression is capable of a very great range […] When a sequence of particular sounds or a certain melody strike an already tender-hearted soul, as with the musical expression of certain passions expressed in a piece of poetry, this regular association makes these sounds become, with time, a sort of natural and expressive language

for these passions. Melody, therefore, must be considered to a certain degree as a relative thing, founded on the association of ideas and the particular habits of different people and become through custom the language of sentiment and passions. We hear with pleasure the music to which we have been accustomed since our youth, perhaps because it recalls the days of our innocence and happiness to us. Sometimes we are singularly affected by certain airs, which appear neither to us not to others to be particularly expressive. This is because we heard these airs at a time when our soul was rather profoundly affected by some passion, which imprinted itself on everything present at that time; and although this passion has since entirely dissipated, together with the memory of its cause, nevertheless the memory of a sound which is associated with it often reawakens the sentiment, though the mind cannot recall the original cause. Similar associations are formed by the almost arbitrary way that different nations make use of particular instruments, such as bells, the drum, the trumpet, the organ, which, because of this use, excite among certain people ideas and passions that they don't excite among others. (Gregory 1769, pp. 153–5)[xi]

These lines clearly say that a melody can call forth a sentiment, while the circumstances which were previously associated with it, and which even determine the nature and intensity of the sentiment that actually seizes the hearer, remain unconscious. An element in the associative chain remains unknown, untraceable, and thus provokes the torment.

Rousseau, so preoccupied with the manner in which music could speak to feelings, couldn't remain unaware of these phenomena. During the evening of the harvest festival, in *Nouvelle Héloïse*, the "old romances" that the harvesters sing about provoke a surge of memory: "We can't keep ourselves, Claire from smiling, Julie from blushing, me from sighing, when we find in these songs rounds and expressions that we used in the past. Thus, in casting my eyes upon them, a thrill seizes me, all of a sudden an insupportable weight falls on my heart and leaves me a mournful impression that only disappears with pain."[xii] Writing to Maréchal de Luxembourg from Môtiers-Travers, Rousseau described Switzerland and made sure to tell his correspondent of a certain characteristic that was known to him. Note that he doesn't use the word (still technical and medical) *nostalgie*, but its synonym, *regret*, which had long been part of contemporary language:

It is extraordinary that so rude a country, which the inhabitants are so inclined to leave, nevertheless inspires in them so tender a love that grief at having left it leads almost all of them to return, and that this grief at the loss of it gives those who can't return a sickness, sometime mortal, which they call, I think, *Hemvé*. In Switzerland, there is a well-known song called the "ranz-des-vaches," which shepherds play on their horns and which they make reverberate in all the hills of the country. This air, which is a little thing in itself, but which recalls to the Swiss thousands of ideas about their native land, makes them shed torrents of tears when they hear it while abroad. It even makes so great a number of them die from grief that Roy issued an order forbidding the playing of the "ranz-des-vaches" among Swiss troops. But, Monsieur le Mareschal, perhaps you know all this better than me and the reflections that arise from it have not escaped you. I can't keep myself from noting that France is surely the best country in the world, where all the commodities and all the charms of life contribute to the well-being of the inhabitants. Nevertheless, as far as I know there has never been a *hemvé* or a "ranz-des-vaches" that made a Frenchman cry and die from grief at the loss of their country while in a foreign land, and this illness has lessened among the Swiss since they have begun to live more agreeably in their country.

As one sees here, Rousseau outlines an economic interpretation of nostalgia. It affects the poor: men exported by their country, according to him, along with cheese and horses. To these pages, which were well read, we add those found in the *Dictionnaire de musique* published in 1768, in the article "Musique." In accounting for the effects of the "ranz-des-vaches," Rousseau makes a very subtle allusion to the psychology of association and to the concept of the sign:

In this air, one would seek in vain energetic accents capable of producing such astonishing effects. These effects, which do not appear among strangers, only come from custom, from memories, from the thousands of circumstances, which, reawakened by this air in those who hear it and recall to them their former country, their former pleasures, their youth and their fashion of living, excite in them a bitter sadness to have lost all that. Therefore, the music doesn't act exactly as music but as a *memorial sign* ["signe mémoratif"]. (Rousseau 1995)

For Rousseau, as for John Gregory, music evokes a feeling or a landscape by an arbitrary link. Nevertheless, their conjectures are somewhat different. Rousseau doesn't go so far as to suppose that the associated cause remains unconscious. On the contrary, he admits that it is perceived in the most intense fashion. The recall is as complete as possible. The feeling awoken by music is accompanied by no shadow. Everything is perfectly clear. It is just that the world, reawakened in memory, is only an image, and thus is only the subjective residue of an irrecoverable reality. The "signe mémoratif" is turned towards a past place and time. It makes a familiar universe emerge from oblivion, but simultaneously adds to it the mark of impossibility. Touched by the "signe mémoratif", the consciousness is offered a reanimated and imminent past, which is immediately forbidden and out of reach. The pleasure of imagining a lost time and place is instantly surpassed by the pain of having lost them in reality. All of childhood reappears clearly in the background of a melody, marked by the sign of prohibition and leaving nostalgic prey to what Madame de Staël would name "the passion of memory": she saw in it "the most vexatious pain that can seize the soul" (de Staël 1807, bk. XIV, ch. 3, p. 390, author's translation).

In his *Anthropologie in pragmatischer Hinsicht*, Kant (1798) evoked nostalgia as an example of "tender-hearted invention." "The illusion provoked by the strength of human imagination often goes so far that one thinks one sees or experiences outside of oneself what is simply in one's head." If the nostalgic finds a cure in returning to his country, it isn't because he finally receives the objects whose absence made him suffer; it's because he finds that they no longer exist. He is made peaceful by deception. In truth, he didn't desire the place of his youth but his youth itself. We will always miss our past, but the past isn't given back to anyone:

> The Swiss, as with the Westphalians and the Pomeranians of certain regions […] are seized by home-sickness (*Heimweh*), above all when they move to other countries; it arises in recalling images of care-free times and of sociability between neighbors during their youth, the effect of an ardent desire (*Sehnsucht*) for places where they have known the simplest joys of existence. Visiting these places later, they find their expectations very disappointed, but also cured by it. They persuade themselves that everything at home has changed considerably. In fact, this is because they can't make their youth return. In connection to this, it is noteworthy that this homesickness affects the children from a province that is poor, but where the ties of fraternity and kinship are more solid than among people who concentrate on improving their own fortunes and take as their motto: *patria ubi bene*.

For authors from the second half of the 18th century, the sense of hearing was implicated in a great, associative magic. Thus, music was found to be gifted with a new power: it opened a retrospective space to desire. The noise of springs and the babble of brooks could act like music. Any noise could delude. In a text that he wrote for the Supplement of the *Encyclopédie méthodique*, the physiologist Albrecht von Haller evoked the role of certain inflections of the voice. The first signs of nostalgic disorders were recognizable in false recognition in the auditory domain, which today we call "acoustic paramnesia": "One of the first symptoms is finding the voice of a person whom one loves in the voice of those with whom one converses and seeing one's family in one's dreams."[xiii]

Auenbrugger (1761), the inventor of chest percussion, saw correlations of the same type as found for nostalgia in the lungs: "The body languishes, such that all ideas are concentrated on an useless aspiration, and the periphery of the lungs makes a dull sound in response to percussion. I have opened numerous cadavers of patients killed by this complaint, and I always found the lungs joined to the parietal pleura, the tissue of the lobes situated next to the dullness presenting a callous thickening and a more or less marked purulence." For us, it sounds like an infection, likely tuberculosis. In a more global (some, today, would say "holistic") and above all more imaginative vision, Auenbrugger established an affinity between the gloomy mood of the nostalgic and the mute sound of the chest. A same funereal veil obfuscated the thoughts and the lungs of a nostalgic: the dullness of the chest was the corporeal translation of sadness.

From the end of the 18th century, just up to the time when bacteriology became preponderant, nostalgia, considered to be a potentially fatal disease, was a universally recognized concept in scientific medicine. It was thought that all people and all social classes could be subject to it, from the Lapps of Greenland to Africans torn by force from their villages and thrown into slavery.

How was the diagnostic of nostalgia made? I will borrow Boisseau and Pinel's (1821) description, which has the advantage of being brief. It reviews numerous symptoms that had already been mentioned by Hofer:

> The principal symptoms […] consist of a sad, melancholy air, a dull look, sometimes haggard eyes and an inanimate countenance, a general disgust and an indifference to everything; the pulse is weak and slow; or, on the other hand, fast but barely perceptible: an almost constant drowsiness: during sleep, the patient may burst into tears; it is almost impossible to leave the bed; an obstinate silence, refusing drinks and food, emaciation, stagnation and death. The illness isn't brought to this last degree for all; but if it isn't directly fatal, it becomes fatal through indirect means. Some are strong enough to overcome it; for others, it lasts longer and, by consequence, prolongs their stay at the hospital; but this prolonged stay almost always becomes fatal for the patient, because sooner or later they catch one of the diseases which are spread in such a terrible manner in military hospitals, like dysentery, remittent fever, adynamic fever, ataxic fever, etc.

Thus, nostalgia could take either a simple or a complicated form. It could be fatal in itself or as the proximate cause of another infection. Initially, moral causes brought on the illness. It was generally accepted that an obsessive idea could cause mental irritation and even a lesion of the brain. The lungs and the digestive system suffered the consequences. Auenbrugger's ideas from almost half a century earlier were fully accepted. Around 1800, French doctors in particular would insist that the brain and the nerves played a role in the translation of sad thoughts into organic lesions. As the nervous system was a consolidated network, and as it ruled the body, all cerebral troubles translated themselves on the visceral level. "The brain and the epiglottis are simultaneously affected. The former concentrates all its force on one sole order of thoughts, on one sole thought; the later becomes the seat of uncomfortable impressions, of spasmodic constrictions" (Percy and Laurent 1819) Because, according to Bégin (1834), this "persistent, encephalitic excitement" would come to "react not only on the epiglottis, but also on all the principal viscera, which are affected sympathetically." Nostalgic thoughts were translated into visceral lesions as a mechanical after-effect. The concept of *reaction*, already very fashionable during the 18th century in similar usages,[xiv] allowed the reconciliation of unity and duality: the unity of energy and the duality of a body in motion, with the addition of the directional opposition of their movements. Cabanis systematically resorted to this idea in his *Rapport du physique et du moral* (1800), where nervous ganglions and the brain were considered as "centers of reaction."

During the Revolution and the Empire in France, nostalgia was principally an illness of soldiers. "Perhaps no era," wrote Percy and Laurent (1819), "had more plentiful examples of nostalgia than the French revolution […] The young Frenchman, suddenly carried away to the camps, often against his will, found the hard work, and sometimes the enormous disasters in which he was involved, worthy causes for transferring his thoughts to the past […] At the smallest sorrow, at the smallest setback, the adolescent recalled domestic happiness, and this memory, which at first consoled him, soon became the source of the most frightful ills. This evil didn't spare even the oldest and bravest servicemen." During this period of mass conscription, military life began with a very brutal separation. Draftees needed to leave their families, their villages, and their linguistic milieu. For many, this extraction was difficult to bear. Therefore, the illness, which had formerly affected Swiss soldiers obliged to leave their valleys because they couldn't win their livelihood there, reappeared *en masse*. An example reported by the historian Marcel Reinhard (1958) makes it clear how seriously nostalgia was taken, and how much it was feared: "18 November 1793, in alarming political and military circumstances, the deputy to the Minister of War, Jourdeuil, informed the commander in chief of the army of the North of decisions which would galvanize the troops and strengthen their numbers. Among the rigorous measures figured the suppression of convalescent leave, with one thought-provoking exception: leave would be exceptionally accorded to patients who were stricken with 'nostalgia or homesickness.' The illness must have been considered grave to justify such an exception, despite the situation." Military doctors—Boisseau, Larrey, Percy, and Laurent—made the most significant contributions to the literature on nostalgia. Thus, Boisseau gives us the reason for the exception mentioned above in the orders given by Jourdeuil: "Every soldier who is profoundly affected must be given sick leave before his organs are irremediably injured. In carrying out this just act, one saves for the State a citizen who can be made into a good defender" (Boisseau and Pinel 1821) Other doctors proved themselves less magnanimous, they thought they could manipulate emotions as they pleased: it was sufficient, they thought, to dangle the promise of a return home before the nostalgic; he would let himself be tricked by words, and it wouldn't be necessary to discharge him. Others thought they had achieved excellent results in increasing the number of musicians, entertainers, storytellers, and professional jokers in the army. Finally, some recommended acting in a severe manner and using threats: they knew that it was customary sometimes to try these means for mental maladies. In his study, Reinhard (1958) recalled that the military doctor, Jourdan Le Cointe, author of a work entitled *La santé de Mars* (1790), had proposed severe measures: nostalgia could be defeated by pain or terror. One would swear to the nostalgic soldier that a "hot iron applied to the stomach" would cure him at once. A Russian general had done this in 1733, when his army, which was advancing on Germany, was stricken by nostalgia: "He had it said that the first who were found ill would be buried alive; this punishment being executed the next day on two or three, there was no longer a single melancholic found in all the army."

Therefore, three methods: discharge, false promises, and threats. And to justify each of these methods, doctors once again habitually referred to the idea of reaction. The new idea, the new impression, communicated by those skilled in the art, reacted on the organism or on the morale of the individual.

An important question concerned how to distinguish the true nostalgic from the simulator. The problem had already been discussed in the work of Meyserey, and de Sauvages also discussed it in his *Nosologie*. Simulated melancholy had already become a morbid species, among others. It was a pseudo-sickness, but sufficiently typical to be listed. When a soldier didn't dare expose himself to the danger of battle, nor to risk the punishment reserved for deserters, what other choice did he have if not to intensely desire to show the signs of an illness, which was the only legal means of fleeing an intolerable situation? Among "true" nostalgics, the illness was already a search for refuge. Hence, how could the doctor distinguish simulated from true nostalgia? The problem would foreshadow one that doctors would pose at the end of the 19th century in attempting to recognize simulated paralysis, as opposed to hysterical paralysis, which was thought to be tied to either organic dispositions or to the effects of suggestion. Simulated paralysis was conscious, whereas the mechanisms producing hysterical paralysis escapes conscious thought. For the doctors of the Grande Armée, simulated nostalgia was voluntary, whereas the true nostalgic suffered involuntarily from painful memories of a lost country and the organic consequences of his moral suffering. They thought they had identified a certain number of signs, which allowed the detection of cheaters: they didn't manifest modifications of the pulse, feverish looks, fever, or emaciation, which authenticated the illness.

If the soldiers of the army of the Revolution furnished the principal contingent of victims of nostalgia, they were also found outside the borders of France, among those who had fled the Revolution: the émigrés. Madame de Staël makes reference to them in *De la littérature*. When he attempted to understand the motives of those who fomented the reaction against the principles of the Revolution, Benjamin Constant evoked grief at the loss of childhood and of the circumstances surrounding it. He was the first to give "political reaction," the concept of which was just making its appearance, an explanation analogous to that which Kant gave for nostalgia: the object of homesickness is less a determinate place than a moment in life. Those who participated in the reaction sought to "regress." And this was a regression both in the sense of a refusal of institutional progress and in the sense of a return to past life: "These reactions, which make useless revolutions anew from disastrous revolutions, arise from the human spirit's tendency, when grieving the loss of something, to encompass everything surrounding that object in its grief. Thus in our memories of childhood or of happy times that are no more, indifferent objects are mixed with those which are dearest to us, and the charm of the past attaches itself to all the details. The man who has seen the edifice of his individual happiness collapse in the general upheaval believes that he can only retrieve it by re-establishing everything which shared its fall; even the inconveniences and abuses become precious to him because, from afar, they appear to be intimately linked to the advantages, the loss of which he bemoans." Grief at the loss of a moment of personal life, of an era of "individual happiness" becomes grief at the loss of the entire world surrounding it through the unfurling of the associative network of memory. Hence the illusion of the "sweetness of life" tied to the image of the *ancien régime*.

In their general table of diseases, Percy and Laurent (1819) didn't forget the nostalgia found among émigrés. "This melancholy didn't spare those unfortunate souls who were obliged to seek asylum from the violence of one party in foreign lands." Nevertheless, these authors, judiciously, thought it necessary to mention that material resources could mitigate the disease's symptoms. For those émigrés who maintained "a remnant of ease," the "memories were more sweet than bitter, and they tempered the painfulness of grief at the loss of their country by the hope of return to it." Nostalgia sometimes led its victims to a form of suicide: "However, some can't resist the desire to re-enter France, and expose themselves to certain death in order to see that which is dearest to them in the world again."

Percy and Laurent rightly made a distinction between soldiers, who were forcibly recruited, and émigrés, who had some independent means. The former experienced military discipline and the perils of war in a situation of quasi-captivity, without the small freedom that more substantial resources would have assured them. The means available to the others allowed them a certain independence; they could form personal projects and dispose of their time as they pleased. Over the course of the 19th century, it became clearer and clearer that nostalgia arose from a double cause: separation from one's accustomed milieu and restriction of one's freedom. In the navy and the British merchant marines, nostalgia among the sailors—which was accompanied by fever and hallucinations, hence its name, *calenture*—was almost as serious a problem as the recruitment methods were brutal. We know that the method of impressment (taking men into the navy by force and with or without notice) was frequently practiced in the large ports. Sometimes it incited mutinies, and more frequently depression of the most serious kind (see Rosen 1975). The same despair led either to a revolt or to a decline.

As a less harsh military regime established itself, as sailors were treated better, as corporal punishment became less frequently applied, French and English military hospitals would see the number of diagnosed nostalgia cases decrease. The diminution of the exercise of constraint was accompanied by a proportional diminution in the frequency of nostalgic sicknesses.

Notes

i   The president of the jury being J.-J. Harder, to whom the *Dissertatio* has often been attributed in error. Another error, which is still current, concerns the publication date alleged without proof to be 1678.

ii   "Neque verò de nomine deliberanti convenientius occurrit, remque explicandam praecisius designans, quam *Nostalgias* vocabulum, origine graecum, et quidem duabus ex vocibus compositum, quorum alternum *Nóstos* reditum in patriam, alterum *Algos*, dolorem aut tristitiam significat. Ut adeò ex vi vocis Nostalgia designare possit tristem animum ex reditûs in patriam ardenti desiderio oriundum." We cite from the collection of texts outstandingly presented and commented on by Ernst (1949).

iii Other terms were proposed, by Hofer himself, of which the viability was doubtful: *nostomania, philopatridomania*. In 1710, the doctor Theodor Zwinger, in his dissertation (where he is the first to mention the effect the *Cantilena helvetica*, that is to do the *Kühe-Reyen* or the *Ran des vaches*), gave a Greek form to *Heimweh* with the designation *pathopatridalgia*, totally unsuitable for leaving medical jargon.

iv   Translator's note: Here and elsewhere, I translate the French word, "regret," as "grief at loss," which better captures the emphasis on loss than its English homonym.

v   Dubos erroneously mentions Satire 13. It concerns a little slave, son of a cowherd, who served drinks to Juvenal's guests. The complete citation is the following: "Suspirat longo no visam tempore matrem/Et casulam et notos tristis desiderat haedos" (verses 152–3). "He sighs after his mother, whom he had not seen for a long time; he is sad and misses his hut and his kid-goats to which he was familiar."

vi   It is from Dubos that Jaucourt borrows the essence of the article "Hemvé" of the *Encyclopédie méthodique* (Boisseau and Pinel 1821).

vii The eighth class of diseases (Folios) includes four orders. The second order (Oddities, Glooms, defined as "desires or depraved aversions") included ten conditions, among which is nostalgia. It is placed between antipathy and night-terror antipathy. The article is subdivided into (1) simple nostalgia, (2) complex nostalgia, (3) false nostalgia of Meyserey.

viii They are: (1) air, (2) food (both drinks and solid food), (3) sleeping and waking, (4) exercise and rest, (5) excretion and retention, (6) the passion of the soul.

ix   Extracts in Ernst (1949).

x   Chapter XL concerns diseases of soldiers. Ramazzini names "the illustrious Barnstorff" as his informant for these materials.

xi   This idea was in wide circulation. One reads in Boswell: "Much of the effect of music, I am satisfied, is owing to the association of ideas. That air, which instantly and irresistibly excites in the Swiss, when in a foreign land, the *maladie du pays*. has, I am told, no intrinsic power of sound. And I know from my experience that Scotch reels, though brisk, make me melancholy, because I used to hear them in my early years, at a time when Mr. Pitt called for soldiers 'from the mountains of the north', and numbers of brave Highlanders were going abroad, never to return" (*Life of Johnson*, Hill and Powell 1934–1964, vol. 3, p. 198).

xii *La nouvelle Héloïse*. In Rousseau (1961, vol. II, p. 609).

xiii In the article "Nostalgie" in the Supplement of the *Encyclopédie méthodique*. Haller's article is added to an article by Jaucourt, who contents himself with summarizing Dubos' pages on "Hemvé."

viv Notably for Diderot. See Starobinski (1989).

References

Bégin, L.-J. (1834). Nostalgie. In *Dictionnaire de médecine et de chirurgie pratiques*, vol. XII. Paris: Mequignon-Marivs, J. B. Bailliere.

Boisseau, F. G. and Pinel, P. (1821). Nostalgie. In *Encyclopédie méthodique*, vol. X. Paris: C. L. F. Panckoucke.

Dubos, J.-B. (1719). *Réflexions critiques sur la poésie et sur la peinture*, 2 vols. J Paris: Mariette.

Ernst, F. (1949). *Vom Heimweh*. Zurich: Fretz and Wasmuth.

Gregory, J. (1769). *Parallèle de la constitution et des facultés de l'homme avec la condition et les facultés des autres animaux*. Paris: Bouillon.

Hartley, D. (1755). *Explication des sens, des idées et des mouvement tant volontaire qu'involontaires*, 2 vols, translated into French by H. Jurain. Reims: Delaistre-Godet.

Hill, G. B and Powell, L. F. (eds) (1934–1964). *Boswell, The Life of Samuel Johnson, LL.D.*, 6 vols. Oxford: Clarendon Press.

Hofer, J. (1688). *Dissertatio medica de nostalgia, oder Heimwehe*. Basel: J. Bertsch.

Hutcheson, F. (1728). *An Essay on the Nature and Conduct of Passions and Affections*. J London: Smith and W. Bruce.

Kant, I. (1798). *Anthropologie in pragmatischer Hinsicht*. Königsberg: Friedrich Nicolovius.

Locke, J. (1972). *Essai philosophique concernant l'entendement humain* [An Essay Concerning Human Understanding], translated into French by P. Coste. Paris: Vrin.

Malebranche, N. (1997). *The Search after Truth*. Translated into English by T. M. Lennon and P. J. Olscamp. Cambridge: Cambridge University Press.

Percy, P. F. and Laurent, C. (1819). Nostalgie. In *Dictionnaire des sciences médicales*, vol. 36, pp. 265–81. Paris: C. L. F. Panckoucke.

Ramazzini, B. (1700). *De Morbis Artificum Diatriba* [*Diseases of Workers*]. Modena: Antonio Capponi.

Reinhard, M. (1958). Nostalgie et service militaire pendant la Révolution. *Annales Historiques de la Révolution Française*, no. 1, 1–15.

de la Rochefoucauld, F. (1678). *Réflexions ou sentences et maximes morales* [*Maximes*], 136. Paris: Barbin.

Rosen, G. (1975). Nostalgia: a "forgotten" psychological disorder. *Psychological Medicine*, **5**, 340–54.

Rousseau, J.-J. (1961). *La nouvelle Héloïse*, pt 5, VII. In *Oeuvres complètes*. Paris: Gallimard/Bibliothèque de la Pléiade.

Rousseau, J.-J. (1995). *Dictionnaire de musique*. In S. Baud-Bovy (ed.), *Oeuvres complètes V. Écrits sur la musique, la langue et le théâtre*. Paris: Gallimard/Pléiade.

de Sauvages, F. B. (1771). *Nosologie méthodique, dans laquelle les maladies sont rangées par classes, suivant le systême de Sydenham, et l'Ordre des Botanistes*, transled from the Latin by M. Nicolas, 3 vols. Paris: Hérissant le fils.

de Staël, G. (1807). *Corinne ou l'Italie*, vol. 2. London: M. Peltier.

Starobinski, J. (1989). Action et reaction chez Diderot. In C. Lafarge (ed.), *Les dilemmes du roman. Essays in honor of Georges May*, pp. 73–87. Saratoga: Anma Libri.

Zwinger, T. (1710). De pothopadridalgia. In *Fasciculus Dissertationum Medicarum Selectiorum*. Basel: J. Ludovici Koenig.

Chapter 25

Emotions, identity, and copyright control: the constitutive role of affect attunement and its implications for the ontology of music

Ulrik Volgsten

Music is the shorthand of emotion
Leo Tolstoy

Lesser artists borrow, great artists steal
Jaco Pastorius quoting Igor Stravinsky

It is the thought of just such a listener that excites the composer in me
Aaron Copland

Introduction

In this chapter I tie together three lines of argument. In line with existing research, I show that music is an important component in the construction and development of human identity, both on an individual and a collective level. Moreover I argue that music fulfills these identity functions through its affective and emotional qualities.

In my second line of argument I claim that these identity functions become severely restricted by today's copyright laws. As, for instance, national copyright laws are increasingly forced to harmonize with the World Trade Organization's (WTO) global TRIPS (trade related aspects of intellectual property rights) agreement, music becomes subject to the private rights of multinational corporations and media conglomerates, whereby music loses its independence as a dynamic cultural expression and individual self-object.

Against the totalizing threat of today's copyright regime I claim, as my third line of argument, that the same principles that underlie music's power to fulfill human identity functions show that music cannot be reduced to an expression subject to private rights. Music is more than a material set of sounds with a predictable physiological effect. Nor can music be reduced to an immaterial cognitive object. Music's ontological status derives to an irreducible extent from the affective investment of its listeners.

Music, emotions, and identity

Music has the power to express emotions and arouse feelings in and to its listeners and performers. These emotions are often tied to aspects of identity formation on both an individual and a collective level. National anthems, as played at international sports events, are perhaps the most obvious examples of music as expression of collective identity today. But any music can serve such a function. For instance, many Finns will "identify" with Sibelius' *Finlandia*, just as many Swedes will feel "as one" when they hear an ABBA song. A *cante jondo* will immediately tell the Andalusian Rom where his or her heart is, as will a *Blekete* rhythm to an Ewe in Ghana—"this is *our* music!" Moving to subcultural group belonging, the examples multiply almost infinitely: Rockers, Hippies, Mods, Punks, Emos, fans of Italian madrigals, each have their own music.

In all these cases music may function as a *sign* for a particular group identity. Music signals or symbolizes group identity in one way or another. But music isn't just like any flag to wave or badge to wear. Music may function as a sign by way of *expressing* different *emotions*. Several philosophers have discussed the way music may be expressive of the emotions (e.g. Goodman 1976; Davies 1980; Kivy 1989; Robinson 1994 and Chapter 12 in this volume). By metaphorically exemplifying certain emotional properties, music may be heard as aggressive, cool, romantic, sad, happy, *duende*, melancholic, etc. What makes this emotional expressivity of music particularly suitable for signifying identity is that emotions are often interpreted and valued differently in different cultures, thereby acquiring different meanings in different cultural contexts (e.g. aggression may be positively valued in one culture and negatively valued in another, cf. Harré 1986). In other words, music may function as a sign of identity on a collective as well as on an individual level and it may do this particularly well because it expresses certain culturally interpreted and valued emotions.

A second reason music is so well suited for its expressive task is that hearing music may in certain ways feel similar to experiencing an emotion. The feeling shapes that lie at the bottom of our aural experiences of music are similar to those forming the substrate of emotions and have been described in neurophysiological terms as "temporal pattern[s] of changes in density of neural firing" (Stern 1995, p. 84; Køppe *et al.* 2008). In other words it is not just a case of music's formal shape, its particular "ebbs and flows," being similar to the "morphology of feeling" (Langer 1948, p. 193); rather than being just a formal matter, a shape similar to the shape of some emotion or other for our minds to recognize, this similarity enables music to *sound* the way emotions are *felt*. I will refer to these feeling shapes as "affect," reserving "emotion" for feelings with a representational content—despite their importance, affects do not determine either the intentional content of the emotions, what the emotions are "about," or the aesthetic significance of sound, "that which" turns sound into music. The important point is that the function of music as a sign for identity thrives on emotional qualities that we experience as coming from and/or taking shape deep inside of us, in our bodies and souls. This point certainly needs further clarification, and I will provide some as we go along.

Several sociologists of music subscribe to a hypothesis about the relation between music, emotion, and identity along lines similar to the one just sketched. Reed Larson (1995, p. 535) highlights how "[p]opular music listening allows adolescents to internalize strong emotional images around which a temporary sense of self can cohere." Simon Frith (1996, p. 257) extends this emotional function of music beyond adolescence, claiming that similarities between emotional experiences of music and certain kinds of identifications makes it possible to "place ourselves in imaginative cultural narratives." In this way music allows us to test out new ways of being ourselves. Tia DeNora (1999) adds further strokes to the picture by pointing out how music not only enables the testing out of possible identities, but also how music can serve as an emotional memory, a resource for retrieving and reassuring our self-identities, how "the past 'comes alive' to its soundtrack," as it were.

By way of its emotional qualities, music enables individual development in serving as a resource for making sense of oneself, for transcending and thus developing oneself, and for feeling secure about who one is, for feeling secure about one's self-identity. However, individual development always takes place in relation to others, even when mediated through solitary listening to music. As Joel Krueger shows in his contribution to this volume (Chapter 14), music "is a kind of social scaffolding." Krueger highlights the notion of "communicative musicality" (Malloch and Trevarthen 2009), referring to a human capacity for *empathy* and *attunement* that already exists in the newborn child and which builds on many music-like features. This capacity enables an early social interaction between infant and caregiver, which further "nurtures the child's psychological and physiological development" (Krueger, in Chapter 14). Whereas Krueger's main purpose is to emphasize how this capacity is exploited through music as a basic human resource for the creation of interpersonally shared experiences—in a way, how music functions socially—I will point out in some more detail how *the human being's development of a sense of self* is fundamentally not only social but also musical, or perhaps better, how it is *protomusical*. As we shall see, it is the protomusicality of our earliest human interactions that explains music's extraordinary aptness as a sign of identity on both a personal and a cultural level.

According to the developmental psychologist Daniel Stern (1985), human subjectivity can be explained as developing along a route of an increasingly articulated *sense of self*. Stern speaks of "the sense of an emergent self," "the sense of a core self," "the sense of a subjective self," and "the sense of a verbal self." These different senses of self develop at different stages in the infant's life, from about 2 months of age to the second year of life when the child starts to acquire a spoken language. The verbal sense of self then becomes a narrated self at about 3 to 4 years of age, when the child starts to articulate a reflexive self-identity. Whereas each successive level of self-sense pre-supposes the foregoing, later stages do not exclude former stages but rather act in concert. And although we may feel rather secure in our adult self-identities, all the preceding levels remain parts of our composite selves, in need of a more or less constant reassuring input for a positive sense of self to be sustained.

The development of the various senses of self is accomplished through the necessary interaction with others. The infant interacts vocally, by gesture, and bodily with other people in its direct environment (seeking attention when hungry or in a playful mood), and these interactions are felt by the interlocutors as temporal feeling shapes, as affect (often experienced as an enveloping mood or "atmosphere"). We feel in and with our bodies the action and behavior both of our own conduct and that of our interlocutors, the latter of which we also observe with our senses. Of particular significance is that the affects are articulated by changes in intensity, shape, and rhythm—qualities we normally associate with music. In other words, basic human interaction is protomusical (see also Volgsten 1999, 2006, 2012).

Interaction is felt as affect by the interlocutors. Affectively felt interaction is experienced as more or less meaningful because it leads to, or fails to lead to, anticipated goals. Meaningful interaction can thus be described as being "enveloped" in affective experience, variously articulated according to differences in protomusical quality (intensity, shape, rhythm) (see Stern 1995, 2004). To the extent that these shared moments of affective experience (contributing to the child's developing sense of self) are recognized as they are repeated, they function as what Even Ruud calls "self-objects", reinforcers of one's respective sense of self (Ruud 2003, 2006). As mentioned, a positive sense of self needs recurring reinforcement, even at an adult age, and one particularly apt way of achieving such self-reinforcement is through the affective experience of music. Thus, music may not only serve as a sign of self-identity, it may also function as a self-object. These two sides of the contribution of music to matters of identity and emotion are likely to reinforce each other reciprocally: a piece of music may, in its capacity to function as a musical sign of self-identity or cultural identity, also function as a self-object; and by doing this (i.e. functioning as a self-object) it secures its function as a sign of identity.

These functions are, needless to say, very much the same as described in the sociological reports mentioned above, by Larson, Frith, and DeNora. In his 500-plus page book on "strong emotional experiences," music psychologist Alf Gabrielsson (2008) recounts more than a thousand reports by people from a diverse array of social backgrounds and different ages (13 to 91), all testifying to the importance of unique emotional experiences of music in their lives. Although Gabrielsson does not press the point, he mentions the possibility that music in many cases functions as an identity reinforcer. The experiences reported by Gabrielsson are single and unique in their strong and vivid character. Yet this does not rule out the significance of the findings of Larson, Frith, and DeNora, that music may also fulfill important identity functions on a repeated and everyday basis. In their functions as self-objects, pieces of music are likely to be taken for granted, noticed as such by the listener only when *not* available for repeated use. The potential of music in this regard, of course, depends on the technologies that make it so readily available. Yet while a shift of emphasis from the collective to the individual may have been influenced by the development of mass media technology, this does not rule out the possibility that music may have had similar identity functions on a collective level (as those referred to above) in societies before the entry of sound recording and radio broadcasting.

Two musical examples that are likely to have served as a reinforcer of collective identity in their capacities as self objects could be mentioned here. First, the "plot archetype" identified by Anthony Newcomb (1992) in some of the symphonies by Beethoven, Schumann, and Mahler, expressing what Newcomb describes as a "renewed harmony to heal the wounds inflicted by mankind's alienation from nature," a progress from "Arcadia forward to Elysium." It is quite likely that this plot archetype fulfilled a culture-specific function as a collective sign of identity for certain groups in the West, from the early 19th century on (those groups for whom the experience of alienation from nature was negative). To the extent that this plot archetype was heard in the music by the listeners, it functioned as reinforcer of collective identity by means of the music's affective impact.

The second example highlights a similar function of music in a non-Western society. As Steven Feld (1981) reports from his travels in Papua New Guinea in the 1970s, the Kaluli speak of their music as a characteristic "lifting up over sound," which is only possible for a song that has become "hard." This view is directly related to their everyday environment in the forest, where sounds constantly shift figure and ground—an environment where only people who have overcome the softness of childhood and become hardened can survive. Again, the music is likely to have an affective impact, functioning as a self-object for individual recipients (confirming their becoming hardened), which in its turn adds to the music's capacity to function as a sign of collective identity.

Controlling musical expression through copyright

Music is more than a flag to wave or badge to wear when it comes to its role in construction and development of human identity. This holds both on an individual level of self and on a collective level of culture. Music may function as a sign for various identities by being expressive of certain emotions. Music may do this particularly well because it can express certain culturally defined emotions and because it (the music) can sound the way these emotions feel. These feelings are not just any subjective feeling that one may or may not experience as one hears music; these feelings, these affective experiences, are similar in important respects to those feelings that shape the human being's most fundamental sense of self. Finally, functioning as a self-object, music may indeed support and reinforce such positive feelings, or senses of self, at any time in life. This is likely to be so, more or less, for listeners in both Western and non-Western societies (both before and after the entry of technologically mediated music).

Now, given this description of the functionality of music, it is hardly surprising that music has been put under various forms of control (see Korpe *et al.* 2006; Moreno 2006; Gouk, Chapter 22 this volume). For totalitarian regimes through all ages, the signs and the feelings of both collective and individual identities have been seen as sources of possible resistance, which must therefore be kept in constant check. Any change in the balance of power—including the strength of the senses of politically conflicting selves, as it were—may topple a dictatorship, which is why a total ban on music has been a common controlling device and tool of terror. In today's capitalist democracies the control is of a different kind and serves different purposes, but it is nonetheless a restrictive and inhibiting control of music's basic human identity functions. This control is administered under the regime of copyright.

Copyright law emerged as a means to regulate the economic interest of the printing trade (of which music print played a marginal role for a long time), replacing an older system of feudal privileges. The first copyright law was the British Statute of Queen Anne of 1709, intended according to its subtitle as "An Act for the Encouragement of Learning." A similar care for public education and utilitarian ends is stated in the American constitution, according to which one of copyright's main purposes is: "[t]o promote the Progress of Science and Useful Arts" (Mills 1996). Similarly, the revolutionary laws in France of 1791 and 1793 were formulated with the intent of distributing the texts of great French author's to the broad public (Hesse 1991). In its literal intent, these laws were formulated with the benefits of the collective, the people, as their main object. As a consequence, copyright law differed from ordinary property law in limiting the extension to a certain number of years after the author's death. The economic interest of the individual artist was thus of secondary importance (it appears in German legislative thinking during the 19th century, along with a growing need to "protect" music print), whereas the interests of printers and publishers are not mentioned at all. However, legal practice differs from juridical theory and cultural politics.

One aspect of copyright legislation that merits attention due to its consequences, which have turned out to be quite contradictory to the formative intents of the law, is the "alienability" of the right. In contrast to a human right, the composer of a piece of music may sign away his or her copyright. The consequence is that copyrights more often than not end up in the hands of the media industry. A composer's right to his or her work, be it a symphony or a pop song, lasts until 70 years after the death of the composer. This means that composers cannot expect full remuneration until 70 years after their own death. The argument for this absurd construction is of course that the 70 years extension of the right makes the composition (or perhaps better, the *composition-as-right*) a more attractive commodity on the market of rights, and that the composer can thereby get a better price for the composition (*-as-right*).[i] Whatever we think of this, it shows that the copyright system is constructed to (in practice) facilitate the alienation of the right to the music away from the composer and into the hands of the publishers. Given the economic conditions of most of today's freelancing individuals on the music scene, copyright law serves the corporate media industry far better than it serves creative composers.[ii]

A second problem with today's copyright law is its threat against the right to freedom of expression, of musical expression. An increasing number of legal cases show that charges of plagiarism are leveled against use of musical material that in the past would have counted as basic musical building blocks, as musical material. Whereas charges of plagiarism in the past usually involved entire pieces of music (Pohlmann 1962), composers today risk being accused of plagiarism when using short phrases that may have similarities with other short phrases in copyrighted compositions (Demers 2006). In a recent case of plagiarism in Sweden, the defendants were expected to prove their own innocence, and although a musicologist called to witness could ensure the court that the snippet of music at trial showed more similarity to a traditional and well-known folk song than to the plaintiff's claimed "original," they lost the case.[iii] The defendants had to pay for the estimated loss in sales that the 20-year-old "original" was claimed (by the plaintiff) to have suffered. The plaintiff was the internationally well-known record company EMI (controlling the rights of the "original" composer), whereas the name of the defendants' minor local label is by now a forgotten part of the past, since the fines forced the company into bankruptcy (Edlund 2006).

The ensuing problem facing today's composers is—strange as it may seem in the digital era—a diminishing availability of musical material, bound up with a growing anxiety to avoid using material that may be copyrighted already. If you aren't tied up to a company powerful enough to house its own team of lawyers, the mere risk of being accused of plagiarism, of being sued and having to pay the expenses just to show you are innocent, will be enough for many to refrain from using musical material with the slightest reminiscence of anything familiar (Klein 2000; McLeod 2005). While anxiety of influence hails originality, the copyright side of the coin burdens creativity with a counterproductive cautiousness. And this is not only an issue for popular music.[iv] As Robin Hartwell (1993) points out, there has been a

> shift from the eighteenth century, where the grammar of harmony was common to most composers and originality lay in its usage, through Wagner, where the musical grammar itself was valued for its originality, to the twentieth century, where the basic materials of music—chords, tone-colours, etc.— are perceived as the intellectual property of the composers. (For example, one has the sensation that Messiaen has patented certain modes, chord formations and orchestral colours. To work with these materials is to run the danger of committing an act of plagiarism.)

Now Messiaen's chords aren't patented or even copyrighted, but it would be an economically risky affair for any composer to try to use a Messiaen chord sequence, however short, without clearing the rights in advance (a task a publisher would hardly accept, unless you are already a commercially successful composer, cf. McLeod 2005). What the cases above show is that the companies that control copyright in effect also control much of the basic materials available to the aspiring composer—and very much the same companies also control the media channels necessary for communicating this content—which in consequence means that copyright is on the dangerous road of becoming nothing less than (what we may call) a musical *communication right*.[v]

The third problem with copyright that I want to point out is related to the main topic of this chapter. That copyright controls musical expression has consequences not only for composers and musicians, but also for the listener, for culture at large. It is almost a commonplace to say that our identities largely equal the narratives that we weave about ourselves. These narratives aren't just made up of words (Shaw 1994). As we have seen, they may also include such non-verbal signs or symbols as music. When these signs and symbols become "immaterial," communicated to an important extent through media, copyright becomes a threat against nothing less than the right of "free development of personalities," as stated by the United Nations' Universal Declaration of Human Rights (sect. 22). This becomes even more serious when we see how music functions, not only socially as a sign for identity but also psychologically as an identity-strengthening self-object. Copyright thus threatens to become not only a communication right, but also a right to our private and collective identities, a right to our memories, a right to culture in the widest sense of term.

So what can we do about this situation? Perhaps the most serious obstacle today in coming to terms with these problems is the WTO's multilateral TRIPS. The TRIPS agreement—with its world-wide compass—refers in the preamble to its members "*recognizing* that intellectual property rights are private rights," and the same members "*desiring* to reduce distortions and impediments to inter-national trade" (italics in original): each signatory of the TRIPS thus "recognizes" the seemingly undisputable fact that intellectual property rights are private, therefore "desiring" to overcome the distortions to international trade that might exist in the signatory's own national law (Anon. 1994). The problem is the very peculiar notion of "private right" that emerges in the TRIPS agreement.[vi]

The emphasis on private rights in the agreement is articulated against its implicit opposite, the public and collective, connoting such anti-individual and anti-personal institutions as the state and its "apparatuses." In addition, culture too is regarded as public, collective, which means that culture fares poorly by the TRIPS standard. On the other hand, corporations and conglomerates are private and have the same rights as persons, no matter how non-individual they are (we shall shortly see that the TRIPS actually favors corporations over persons). So whereas global trade cor-porations are private, local culture is non-private. Since copyright to music amounts to a private right, the owners of the rights have the right to legal protection. But whereas the music of local cultures per definition is non-private, these cultures cannot be expected to gain any protection of their music at all on the magnitude of TRIPS.

The corporate interests underlying the TRIPS agreement have even deeper consequences for the interpretation of what counts as private. It is important to be aware that the agreement explicitly denounces the personal, or what the law calls, "moral rights" of composers (Anon. 1994, art. 9, sect. 1); economical rights are the only rights that count as private rights.[vii] That the moral rights of the composers, their "personal" rights, are not accepted as private rights by the TRIPS agreement, points toward another potential contradiction of the term "private." Against the private (and its conglomerates) stand not only the collective, but also the individual person. This can be seen further on in the TRIPS preamble, where it says that it "recognizes the underlying public policy objectives of national systems for the protection of intellectual property."[viii] Though vaguely formulated in its seeming tolerance, one gathers from what follows in the text, that in the end copyright protection is so important, that if any member would want to, say (in the TRIPS' own words), "adopt measures necessary to protect public health and nutrition," it may do so only (and here I quote the TRIPS again) "*provided that such measures are consistent with the provisions of this Agreement*" (Anon. 1994, art. 8, italics added). Given that the TRIPS agreement explicitly considers public health and nutri-tion as subordinate to the private rights of international trade, one should not be surprised to find culture (where the individual and public are intermingled) even lower down the rank. Public health, like musical culture, is in the direct interests of people, not of private corporations. One can thus see that the TRIPS agreement in effect differentiates between private and personal interests. The former are protected, the latter are not (unless they are invested in private copyrights).

As we have seen, national laws are constructed so as to channel away the rights from composers and into the hands of the industry. This is bad enough. The TRIPS agreement is even more prob-lematic, since it does not permit any changes whatsoever in the construction of national legislation that would go against its paragraphs. As a compulsory agreement for the members of the WTO, TRIPS threatens any nation which does not comply with its rules with sanctions. If a country like Sweden should want to change its copyright law in a more liberal direction, the country would face the risk of being sanctioned by other members in export fields *other than music*, such as steel, paper, cars, or cellphones (Korten 1995, pp. 174*ff*.; May and Sell 2006, p. 4; Li 2009).[ix] In conse-quence, the TRIPS agreement backbinds democratic legislation on cultural matters at the national level (and of course also at an international level).

Thus, what seems to be fairly neutral formulations of TRIPS turns out not to be so at all. Not least should we keep in mind that the TRIPS agreement deals with "intellectual property rights" as "private rights." What then, one may ask, are intellectual property rights rights to? An answer that readily suggests itself is that a copyright is a right to a composer's work. The composer *owns* his or her work, just like he or she may own a pair of shoes, and copyright enshrines in statute the composer's right to this property.

However, if we turn to the TRIPS agreement, we will find that the question of what a work is, is neatly circumvented. The term "work" is specified as "musical," "literary," "photographic," etc. or even more generally as "artistic." From this formulation the text makes a conceptual leap to the statement that "[c]opyright protection shall extend to expressions and not to ideas… as such" (art. 9, sect. 2). Originally a metaphysical distinction set out within idealistic philosophy at the end of the 18th century, "expressions" are materializations of abstract but specific, immaterial "forms," single-handedly "created" by, and thus "owned" by, their authors. Ideas, on the other hand, are the non-specific, formless "contents" of the same expressions, and thus common property (Fichte 1793). Once this ontology of form and content is accepted and extended to music, focus can be directed towards the multifarious materializations of the forms (prints, performances, recordings), over which the copyright owner has exclusive power. The TRIPS agreement, like the law, is about "expressions," which in practice means locutionary *action*. It is about the private right to control what people *do* (print, perform, record). But in contrast to national law, TRIPS is not negotiable. In effect it is an international agreement about the private right to control culture.

This is important to keep in mind when considering today's media coverage of the topic. In their attempts to catch the interest of the public, mass media often describe the ongoing file-sharing debate in ordinary property terms, as instances of "theft," where downloading (by the ridiculously self-dubbed "pirates") amounts to "stealing" music that someone else "owns" (the individual "forms" that are "materialized" in recordings and performances). In a similar vein the secretary of the Nobel committee recently raged against the "attacks on artists' property rights" by public domain defenders. Even cultural theory scholars (who should know better) frequently speak about musical "ownership" as if it were a question of owning a thing (e.g. Chanan 2000; Frith 2001). What this ease of metaphorical use indicates is that copyright rests for much of its public legitimacy on a widespread but unarticulated view of what a piece of music, a song, or a composition *is*, namely an immaterial "thing" that the copyright holder "owns." However, we must be aware that *copyright is not a property right* in any national law today. Copyright does not amount to owning a thing, as an ordinary property right does (a point quite obvious to the law scholar). However, the term "intellectual property right" invites this kind of confusion, as does the very fact that the TRIPS agreement unhappily concerns commerce regulated by property rights *along with* commerce regulated by copyrights and patents.

By thus turning the copyright debate into a question of the right to control one's property (the music one "owns") and protecting it against "theft," the current media debate moves the focus away from the culture versus commerce issue discussed here, seeking public legitimacy for the strengthening of copyright laws—such as the recent extension of protection from 50 to 70 years after the death of the composer—on ontologically dubious grounds.

Affect attunement and the role of the listener

The TRIPS agreement entirely disregards the individual and cultural functions of music. It explicitly disregards the composer and implicitly the audience. To the extent that rights are the correct way to deal with cultural matters (see Volgsten and Åkerberg 2006 for a suggestion that it need not be), composers' rights cannot be dismissed as easily as in the TRIPS agreement. Any claim to the right to music that disregards the way or ways music comes into being should be questioned by composers, performers, and listeners to music. As participants of musical cultures of the world, we should not accept the claims to "private" rights to music as stated by the TRIPS agreement (to which our national laws are obliged to harmonize). I will now spell out an argument for this claim.

My thesis, in brief, is that sounds do not become music until a listener hears them *as such*. However, music cannot be reduced to an exclusively cognitive matter, nor can it be reduced to an emotional effect or reaction. That a musical experience cannot be reduced to a mere rationalistic calculation of sounds, ultimately owing to an abstract immaterial form, has to do with the affective impact of sounds in time on the listener. As argued above, to hear is to feel, and for this reason we cannot ignore the affective part of music. But this does not mean that music can be reduced to a simple sensational effect (of a "Mozartean" kind or whatever) or somatic reaction. Music is not some kind of affect-inducing drug that we use in the same way as tranquilizers, narcotics, or alcohol. What speaks against such an explanation is our tendency to respond to music in a (more or less) active way, whereas we react to drugs (more or less) passively. We identify and relate our musical experiences to the characteristics of the stimulus in a much more detailed and meaningful way than we do when we have an alcohol- or drug-induced mood or experience (John Lennon's "Lucy in the Sky with Diamonds" or Lou Reed's "Heroin" rather confirm the rule; drug experiences are rarely related to the chemical structure, shape, or color of the particular drug). This is an important reason why music cannot be regarded as a commodity in any simple fashion.

Since it is listeners and audiences that turn sounds into music—the music that the commercial music business ultimately lives on—any claim to the rights of music that disregards the listener must be rejected as unjust and anti-cultural (since it unjustly constrains our personal and cultural identity developments and unduly ignores the listener's constitutive role for music). Which leaves us with the question, what does it mean to turn sounds into music? My argument is that similar processes are involved in the transformation of sounds into music as in the transformation of bodily movement and behavior into human action. In order to interpret someone as performing an action, we must regard this someone as a subjective agent. Action involves intentions, beliefs, and desires on the part of the agent. We thus have to ascribe non-objective properties to each and everybody that we take as a performer of action (see, for example, Davidson 1980; Dennett 1989). Likewise, though with a different scope of variety, hearing sounds as music requires that we ascribe non-acoustic properties to the sounds we hear. We ascribe "cultural" properties to "natural" sounds. However, this is not merely an outcome of some culture-dependent habit, but a consequence of a way of relating to sound that very likely has its origin in our psychological development, in the development of our senses of self, as described above.

The source of our human ability to experience sounds as music most likely springs from the protomusical interaction of our earliest social development. Our ability to experience music is to a certain point identical to our ability to experience or sense *an other*. The ability of a human being to sense an other is a sense that develops in parallel with the sense of self (Stern 1985, p. 70, note 1). Stern names the sense of core self a "self versus other," which, as it increasingly comes to acknowledge this other, develops into a "self with other" (Stern 1985, pp. 69, 100). In other words, our developing sense of a "core self" necessarily involves a simultaneous development of a "core other," against and with which our selves are articulated. Likewise we develop our sense of being a "subjective self" in relation to our sense of there being a "subjective other." Moreover, the relationship that enables the articulation of a self and other is *dialogical* in a way that is crucial also for music (though there are important differences, as we shall see).

Of particular importance for the development of the different senses of self, Stern says, is the role played by affect. As pointed out earlier, meaningful interaction between self and other is enveloped in affective experience (experienced as mood or "atmosphere"), and is variously articulated according to the protomusical differences of intensity, shape, and rhythm. At the level of developing a sense of a core self, caregivers often engage in repetitive playing with their children, a playing which takes the form of a "theme" with variations, experienced by the child as variations in affective tone. The caregiver's playing behavior is varied to keep the child's attention, but still kept within a range of similarity to avoid confusion and overstimulation. The caregiver must regulate his or her playing to keep within pleasurable limits for the child, and the child senses that its own behavioral response has consequences for the outcome of the play (already at this point there is a dialogical quality to the interaction, with intricate rhythmic qualities; see, for example, Beebe and Lachmann 1988; Jaffe *et al.* 2001; Trevarthen 2002). However, the child will sense that it does not have the ultimate power over the play, but that there is another "against" which it is interacting (Stern 1985, pp. 72*ff.*). As the child comes to remember different types of games due to their similar affective shapes, it will also notice different styles of variation, styles belonging to different persons that enable the child to develop a sense of self "with" specific others (Stern 1985, pp. 104*ff.*).

At the level of developing a subjective self, the child is becoming aware of its own affective states, the feeling states that identify the types of interaction with the other. Given the theme-and-variation type of interaction that Stern emphasizes, the child has already come to distinguish an other (a "core other"), and as the child's own feeling states are affected by the other's stylistically unique behavior, the child becomes able to ascribe similar affective states on the part of this other: "selves and others now include inner or subjective states of experience in addition to overt behaviors and direct sensations that marked the core self and other" (Stern 1985, p. 125). Relating affective experience to the outcome of interaction can now develop into an initial sense of intentionality, desire, and belief. The self and the other become subjective.

This development of a sense of a subjective self and a subjective other is further enhanced by the caregiver's ability to affectively "attune" to the child's behavior, for instance by "commenting" on a child's banging on a toy with a vocal "kaaaaa-bam, kaaaaa-bam" (Stern 1985, p. 140). The caregiver's vocalization is not a strict imitation or a mirroring of the child's behavior; by responding with a different kind of behavior (vocalization rather than bodily movement), the child senses that the response is not directed towards the outer specifics, but towards the inner feeling, the affective experience of the "banging": the child senses that the response to its affective experience is a behavior expressive of a similar affective experience on the part of the caregiver. This enhances the child's ability to differentiate between the affective experience and the activity that brings it about. The child comes to sense something like "*I* have an affective experience that *You* respond to with a similarly affective-laden behaviour, because *You* have noticed the affective experience that *I* have." Stern calls this "affect attunement," and the properties attuned to are the previously mentioned protomusical properties of intensity, rhythm, and shape (Stern 1985, pp. 138*ff.*). As a result, the child becomes able to ascribe subjective properties such as affect and intentionality both to itself and to the caregiving other.

Stern's notion of affect attunement thus amounts to more than the dialogical interaction between two protagonists. Affect attunement is the process by which I sense my own subjective states through the simultaneous identification of your subjective experiences. In Stern's example it is the caregiver that actively attunes to the child's playing. However, the child also attunes to the caregiver's "comments" (Stern shows the child's attention to the caregiver's behavior by letting the caregiver overemphasize or misattune, whereupon the child usually reacts negatively and often starts to cry, and later research has shown that infants actively respond by imitating and that they also have "the capacity to provoke an imitative response, thus sustaining an interaction"; Nagy and Molnar 2004).

The protomusicality of affect attunement is also what the self- and identity-strengthening functions of music rely on. Music tends to affect us much like the caregiver's playing with the child, and by the very same means at that. Music functions as a self-object in that it strengthens the listener's sense of a core-self, in a dyadic process wherein the music becomes a core-other with which we engage (or against which we complain if we want quiet). But there is more to the equivalence between the psychological development of our selves and our musical experiences. The experience of music is rather like that of the child's sense of a subjective other, the development of which Stern links to the child's perception of the caregiver's attuning behavior (the vocal "kaaa-*bams*"). The sense of a subjective other, as we have seen, involves the distinction between the physical stimulus (the bodily behavior, the musical sounds) and the affective experiences of oneself and that of the other. In Stern's case it is a matter of coming to sense that both "I" and "You" have similar affective experiences, affective experiences that are not identical with our observable behavioral (physical) interaction.

In the musical case, it is similarly a matter of ascribing to something other—sound—qualities in response to my own affective experience. Both my affective experience and the qualities I project in response are something different from the material sounds as well as the physical interaction (singing, playing) that brings the sounds to my ears. Neither my experience nor that which my experience is "of" (and which it is somehow similar to) is reducible to either the observable singing or playing behavior in a "live" situation, or (if it is not a face-to-face situation) the technical transmission through a mass medium (i.e. the observable cause of the affective experience). Nevertheless, the material sounds brought about by physical interaction are necessary for there to be anything to affectively attune to. The acoustic stimulus is the necessary but insufficient substrate for music (music cannot be reduced to a mere cognitive construct, or to abstract form)—a substrate which we attune to and on which we project the aesthetic qualities that eventually transfigures sound into music. In other words, music does not exist (or even subsist) in sound before a listener hears it.

Just like the sense of being a self requires the simultaneous sense of there being at least one other, the opposite is equally true: for there to be an other, a subjective other, for there to be a "You," there has to be an "I." And the same, I claim, holds for music. For there to be music with aesthetic qualities, there has to be a listener for whom the ascription of these qualities are part of the sense-making of the affective states that the attunement has brought about. But is the opposite also true? Is there no listener until there is music? The answer hinges on how we understand the dialogicity of music, an answer that will throw light on the ultimate difference between the constitution of other subjects and of music.

According to Mari Riess Jones, when we listen to music our attention is directed "along paths of implied motion to certain expected frequencies and times" (Jones and Yee 1993). Attention is "cast from some reference event at one point in time towards a target event scheduled for a later time" (Jones 1981a). Whether conscious or unconscious, attention to music is a temporal affair. It is as much about *when* it is to sound as what is to sound. Thus a musical event "that occurs 'too early' or 'too late' violates one's expectancy just as much as does the timely occurrences of the 'wrong' event" (Jones 1981b). The temporal aspects of music are found both in its small- and large-scale rhythmical as well as metrical properties. The listener catches on to any of the temporal levels of music in order to generate any expectancies about its future course. As Jones puts it, the listener's "attending rhythms become phase-locked to corresponding time spans marked within the event" (Jones and Bolz 1989). This phase-locking between the listener's internal rhythms and the various rhythmical layers of a piece of music "involves a synchronous interplay between an attender and an event in which the former comes to partially share the event's rhythmic pattern." In other words,

> the biological basis for responses to event time takes the form of attunement rhythms that selectively entrain, that shift over nested levels, and eventually are shaped by the event itself.... In effect, the structure of a temporally coherent event can function as a natural time keeper for the attender. Instead of a clock-timed world, the attender responds to a dynamic event-timed world in which time judgments depend on an event's characteristic timing and on how its structure confirms or disconfirms some expected course (Jones and Bolz 1989).

Although Jones calls this attunement (Jones and Bolz 1989), it is clear that the attuning is one sided, non-dialogical. It is the listener that attunes to the sounds of music, and not the other way round. I mentioned the face-to-face situation as one in which the singer or player attunes to the listener, and perhaps the children's song sung together is the paradigm example of this phenomenon (wherein both the child and the adult are listeners as well as performers). At the other extreme is the mass-mediated music where there obviously can be no such attunement (it comes close to what media theorists call "mediated quasi interaction"; see Thompson 1995). In many, if not most, cases, the extent to which we can talk about the music attuning to the listener is a matter of music's capacity to sound the way emotions feel. Or rather, it is a matter of us listeners hearing sounds *as music* sounding the way we feel (often experienced as an all-enveloping mood or "atmosphere," even when the music discloses its own world of expressed emotions or formal qualities—that is, when the different levels of attunement act in concert).[x] We hear the music *as if* it attuned to us, when the music either corresponds to or contradicts our own (present or remembered) moods or feelings or when the music seems to articulate entirely new ways of feeling. The music seems to attune to our feelings, it seems to attune with us. But literally it does not. Music is only dialogical in an imagined sense, and likewise so in its attuning capacity.[xi] It is the listener that ultimately creates the music, whereby in the same moment the listener is confirmed as a listener to *music*.

But doesn't Jones' description of the listener's attunement to the temporal procession of sound show that everything is already there *before* the listener attends? The listener's biological "attunement rhythms... selectively entrain," they "shift over nested levels" and are eventually "shaped by the event itself," that is, *the music itself* isn't it? Isn't Jones' description a description of music as a physical stimulus with formal structure, completely devoid of affective qualities at that? My answer is negative. There is no autonomous form. Existing apart from the listener is the *complex of elements* of a possible formal sound structure. What is heard is a temporally ordered pattern of tensions and relaxations, of rhythms, intensities, and shapes. It is *a plurality of* affective shapes, a becoming structure (becoming music) in the imagination of the perceptive listener, and the aesthetically relevant relationships between the elements (which are never purely formal as they are heard) are always open to question and cultural and aesthetic dispute.

But this is also the point at which the two types of interaction part: whereas the relation between parent and infant is dialogic, the relation between the music and the listener is quasi-dialogic. In contrast to Stern's example of the child's developing sense of a subjective self in relation to a subjective other (or the child and the adult singing together), the musical listener will not sense any intentions or affects which he or she will be able to ascribe to the music in the "literal" sense that we ascribe intentions and emotions to each other. Music, as both Kant and Adorno would say, is non-intentional, non-functional, displaying instead a typically musical "purposefulness without purpose." Music, in its "as-if-ness," rather *urges* the listener to ascribe subjective feelings or other aesthetic qualities to it (cf. Levinson 1982; Maus 1989; Walton 1994). And the same holds for more "objective" metaphors, such as a melody "moving" in a tonal "space," etc. But this urge in music is a projection by the listener, as are any aesthetic—"musical" or "extra-musical"—qualities ascribed to it (like the "aura" of Benjamin's art work). This latter often requires that the listener has reached the developmental level Stern calls a "verbal self" (Volgsten 1999, 2006, 2012), which in its turn requires that the listener has already engaged with other listeners in a community (as we humans normally do). For just as Wittgenstein has shown there are no entirely private languages, there are no entirely private ways of experiencing music. And if there is no private music, why should we accept any "private rights" to it?

This relativism of aesthetic qualities (which does not imply that anything goes) also has consequences for the idealist concept of the musical work as a transcendent object, i.e. as a formal expression independent of any materializing encounter with performers and listeners, (which seems to nourish the legitimating idea that music is some kind of immaterial "thing" which the copyright holder "owns"). As pure structure there can be no music to the sounds. Significant form (to borrow Clive Bell's phrase) is an aesthetic quality that can only be ascribed to music by a listener involved in affect attunement. As a consequence, the "work" is perhaps best regarded as a fictional character in an aesthetics dressed up as ontology (cf. Kania 2008). But even when the law and its superordinate trade agreements dissimulate their ontological biases, restricting their scope to the seemingly straightforward "expressions" of musical works, we have reason to ask ourselves: where shall wide-reaching decisions about music's availability be made—behind the locked doors of the WTO, or in some more democratic congregation? The question should be taken seriously by anyone who takes music seriously.

Notes

i   As Simon Frith (2001, p. 30) points out, "[l]ong before it was a record business, the music industry was a rights business" (see also MacMillan 2003, 2005).

ii   Even when considering the "mechanical rights" to sound recordings, "it is the producer (or the record company) who holds all rights of reproduction" (Théberge 2001, p. 11).

iii   The plaintiff's lawyer argued for the non-contingent similarity between the two melodies by playing them simultaneously; since many of the notes were identical and none of them dissonant, it was (he claimed) a clear case of plagiarism (Edlund 2006, p. 116).

iv   In 1989, a popular act on a WEA (now Time-Warner) subsidiary label, sampled an equally brief snippet as in the Swedish case mentioned above, of a Hyperion recording of a Hildegard von Bingen composition; WEA claimed the sample was "too brief to constitute a copyright issue," and after a preliminary hearing Hyperion backed off, not because they deemed the odds of winning the case too small, but because the cost of lawyers to pursue the case would be too high (quoted in Chanan 2000, p. 164).

v   A part of the copyright problem that should also be pointed out is the increasing references in recent lawsuits to artists' "trademarks." In the Swedish case just mentioned, the Supreme Court likened the act of (claimed) plagiarism to trademark infringement (Edlund 2006). In the same vein, US courts have judged it criminal to imitate the vocal styles of Bette Midler and Tom Waits, since their respective vocal styles are regarded as their trademarks. Whereas copyright has its primary source in the composer's work, trademarks are an entirely commercial affair that pays no attention whatsoever to any composer. So if you are a vocalist naturally sounding like any well-known star you are not to be congratulated, but warned: don't infringe on existing trademarks, stay quiet!

vi   The TRIPS agreement has been criticized for its tendentious use of the term "intellectual property" (Lemley 2005), and for using a rhetoric akin to that of natural rights to private property (Oddi 1996; May and Sell 2006, p. 163ff.). However, my criticism is not directed against the agreement's notion of private property, but against its notion of private rights.

vii   According to the *Berne Convention for the Protection of Literary and Artistic Works* (established in 1886
      and revised several times thereafter), composers' rights are divided into an "economical right" to remu-
      neration (Anon 1886–1979, sect. 11) and the "moral rights" to be credited as composer of the music,
      and prohibit changes and revisions of one's music.

viii The formulation has been interpreted as an attempt to balance the private property claims in favor of
      "public policy objectives" (May and Sell 2006), though in any "dispute settlement" its vagueness remains
      to be interpreted by the trade experts of the WTO panel. As one commentator puts it, in a WTO dispute
      settlement "[t]here is no provision for the representation of alternative perspectives, such as amicus
      briefs from nongovernmental organizations, unless a given panel chooses to solicit them. Documents
      presented to the panel are secret [and the] burden of proof is on the defendant" (Korten 1995, p. 176).

ix   As put by TRIPS proponent Jerome Reichmann (1997, p. 5): "Right holders who cannot translate
      substantive victories into effective remedial action at the local level may eventually trigger the WTO's
      dispute-settlement machinery if their own states chose to question the good faith of the accused state's
      judicial and administrative organs. Taken together, the enforcement and dispute-settlement provisions
      of the TRIPS agreement put teeth into the pre-existing intellectual property conventions, which rel-
      egated the issue of effective implementation of agreed minimum standards to a purely theoretical pos-
      sibility of litigation before the International Court of Justice. In the long term, one may well hope that
      these provisions will further the goal of adapting the international intellectual property system to the
      challenges of an integrated world market."

x   On the relation between moods, music, and Martin Heidegger's notion of *Stimmung* see Wallrup
      (2012). A crucial difference between Heidegger's notion and the way I use "mood" and "attunement"
      here is that the former does not relate to self-development and subjectivity.

xi   Of course we attune to each other when sing or play together, but this does not change the validity of
      the argument against copyrights as "private rights."

References

Anon. (1886–1979). *Berne Convention for the Protection of Literary and Artistic Works.* <http://www.wipo.
int/treaties/en/ip/berne/trtdocs_wo001.html> (last accessed 3 January 2010).

Anon. (1994). *Agreement on Trade-Related Aspects of Intellectual Property Rights.* <http://www.wto.org/eng-
lish/tratop_E/trips_E/t_agm0_E.htm> (last accessed 3 January 2010).

Beebe, B. and Lachmann, F. M. (1988). The Contribution of Mother-Infant Mutual Influence to the Origins
of Self- and Object Representations. *Psychoanalytic Psychology* 5(4), 305–337.

Chanan, M. (2000). *Repeated Takes. A Short History of Recording and its Effects on Music.* London: Verso.

Davidson, D. (1980). Psychology as philosophy. In *Essays on Actions and Events*, pp. 229–239. Oxford :
Oxford University Press.

Davies, S. (1980). The expression of emotion in music. *Mind*, **89**, 67–86.

Demers, J. (2006). *Steal this Music: How Intellectual Property Law affects Musical Creativity.* Athens, GA:
University of Georgia Press.

Dennett, D. (1989). Three kinds of intentional psychology . In *The Intentional Stance*, pp. 43–68.
Cambridge, MA: MIT Press.

DeNora, T. (1999). Music as a technology of the self. *Poetics*, **27**, 31–56.

Edlund, B. (2006). *Riff inför rätta.* Lund: Juristförlaget.

Feld, S. (1981). "Flow like a waterfall": the metaphors of Kaluli musical theory. *Yearbook for Traditional
Music*, 22–47.

Fichte, J. G. (1793). Beweis der Unrechtmäßigkeit des Büchernachdrucks. Ein Räsonnement und eine
Parabel. *Primary Sources on Copyright (1450–1900)*, ed. L. Bently and Martin Kretschmer <www.copy-
righthistory.org> (last accessed 25 January 2012).

Frith, S. (1996). *Performing Rites. On the Value of Popular Music.* Cambridge, MA: Harvard University Press.

Frith, S. (2001). The popular music industry. In S. Frith, W. Straw, and J. Street (eds), *Cambridge Companion to Pop and Rock*, pp. 26–52. Cambridge: Cambridge University Press.

Gabrielsson, A. (2008). *Starka musikupplevelser. Musik är mer än bara musik*. Hedemora: Gidlunds.

Goodman, N. (1976). *Languages of Art. An Approach to a Theory of Symbols*. Indianapolis: Hacket.

Harré, R. (1986). *The Social Construction of Emotions*. Oxford: Basil Blackwell.

Hartwell, R. (1993). Postmodernism and art music. In S. Miller (ed.), *The Last Post. Music after Modernism*, pp. 27–51. Manchester: Manchester University Press.

Hesse, C. (1991). *Publishing and Cultural Politics in Revolutionary Paris 1789–1810*. Berkeley: University of California Press.

Jaffe, J., Beebe, B., Feldstein, S., Crown, C., and Jasnow, M. (2001). *Rhythms of Dialogue in Infancy*. Boston: Blackwell.

Jones, M. R. (1981a). Only time can tell: on the topology of mental space and time. *Critical Inquiry, 7*, 557–76.

Jones, M. R. (1981b). Music as a stimulus for psychological motion: Part 1. Some determinants of expectancies. *Psychomusicology, 1*, 34–51.

Jones, M. R. and Boltz, M. (1989) Dynamic attending and responses to time. *Psychological Review, 96*, 459–91.

Jones, M. R. and Yee, W. (1993). Attending to auditory events: the role of temporal organization. In S. McAdams and E. Bigand (eds), *Thinking in Sound. The Cognitive Psychology of Human Audition*, pp. 69–112. Oxford: Clarendon Press.

Kania, A. (2008). The methodology of musical ontology: descriptivism and its implications. *British Journal of Aesthetics, 48*, 426–44.

Kivy, P. (1989). *Sound Sentiment: an Essay on the Musical Emotions*. Philadelphia: Temple University Press.

Klein, N. (2000). *No Logo*. London: Harper Collins.

Køppe, S., Harder, S., and Væver, M. (2008). Vitality affects. *International Forum of Psychoanalysis, 17*, 169–79.

Korpe, M., Reitov, O., and Cloonan, M. (2006). Music censorship from Plato to the present. In S. Brown and U. Volgsten (eds), *Music and Manipulation. On the Social Uses and Social Control of Music*, pp. 239–63. New York: Berghahn.

Korten, D. (1995). *When Corporations Rule the World*. West Hartford: Kumarian Press.

Langer, S (1948). *Philosophy in a New Key. A Study in the Symbolism of Reason, Rite, and Art*. New York: New American Library.

Larson, R. (1995). Secrets in the bedroom: adolescents' private use of media. *Journal of Youth and Adolescence, 24*, 535–50.

Lemley, M. A. (2005). Property, intellectual property and free riding. *Texas Law Review, 83*, 1031.

Levinson, J. (1982). Music and negative emotions. *Pacific Philosophical Quarterly, 63*, 327–46.

Li, M. (2009). The Pirate Party and Pirate Bay: how the Pirate Bay influences Sweden and international copyright relations. *Pace Law Review, 29*, 281–307.

McLeod, K. (2005). *Freedom of Expression*®: *Overzealous Copyright Bozos and Other Enemies of Creativity*. New York: Doubleday.

MacMillan, F. (2003). *Copyrights Commodification and Creativity*. <http://www.oiprc.ox.ac.uk/EJWP0203.pdf> (last accessed 3 January 2010).

MacMillan, F. (2005). Commodification and cultural ownership. In J. Griffiths and U. Suthersanen (eds), *Copyright and Free Speech. Comparative and International Analyses*, pp. 35–65. Oxford: Oxford University Press.

Malloch, S. and Trevarthen, C. (eds) (2009). *Communicative Musicality. Exploring the Basis of Human Companionship*. Oxford: Oxford University Press.

Maus, F. E. (1989). Agency in instrumental music and song. *College Music Symposium, 29*, 31–43.

May, C. and Sell, S. (2006). *Intellectual Property Rights. A Critical History.* Boulder, CO:: Lynne Rienner Publishers.

Mills, S. (1996). Indigenous music and the law. *Yearbook for Traditional Music,* **28**, 57–86.

Moreno, J. (2006). Orpheus in hell: music in the Holocaust. In S. Brown and U. Volgsten (eds), *Music and Manipulation,* pp. 264–86. *On the Social Uses and Social Control of Music.* New York: Berghahn.

Nagy, E. and Molnar, P. (2004). Homo Imitans or Homo Provocans? Human imprinting model of neonatal imitation. *Infant Behavior and Development,* **27**, 54–63.

Newcomb, A. (1992). Narrative archetypes and Mahler's Ninth Symphony. In S. P. Scher (ed.), *Music and Text,* pp. 118–36. Cambridge: Cambridge University Press.

Oddi, S. (1996). TRIPS—natural rights and a "polite form of economic imperialism." *Vanderbilt Journal of Transnational Law,* **29**, 415–70.

Pohlmann, H. (1962). *Die Frühgeschichte des musikalischen Urheberrechts (ca 1400–1800).* Kassel: Bärenreiter-Verlag.

Reichmann, J. (1997). Enforcing the enforcement procedures of the TRIPS agreement. *Virginia Journal of International Law,* **37**, 335–56.

Robinson, J. (1994). The expression and arousal of emotion in music. *Journal of Aesthetics and Art Criticism,* **52**, 13–22.

Ruud, E. (2003). "Burning scripts." Self psychology, affect consciousness, script theory and the BMGIM. *Nordic Journal of Music Therapy,* **12**, 115–23.

Ruud, E. (2006). The role of music in the development of identity. In B. Stålhammar (ed.), *Music and Human Beings,* pp. 59–69. Örebro: Universitetsbiblioteket.

Shaw, T. A. (1994). The semiotic mediation of identity. *Ethos,* **22**, 83–119.

Stern, D. (1985). *The Interpersonal World of the Infant. A View from Psychoanalysis and Developmental Psychology.* New York: Basic Books.

Stern, D. (1995). *The Motherhood Constellation. A Unified View of Parent–Infant Psychotherapy.* New York: Basic Books.

Stern, D. (2004). *The Present Moment in Psychotherapy and Everyday Life.* New York: Norton.

Thompson, J. (1995). *Media and Modernity: a Social Theory of the Media.* Cambridge: Polity Press.

Théberge, P (2001). "Plugged in": technology and popular music. In S. Frith, W. Straw, and J. Street (eds), *The Cambridge Companion to Pop and Rock,* pp. 3–25. Cambridge: Cambridge University Press.

Trevarthen, C. (2002). Origins of musical identity: evidence from infancy for musical social awareness. In R. Macdonald, D. Hargreaves, and D. Miell (eds), *Musical Identities,* pp. 21–38. Oxford: Oxford University Press.

Volgsten, U. (1999). *Music, mind and the serious Zappa. The passions of a virtual listener.* Dissertation. University of Stockholm, Skrifter från Musikvetenskapliga Institutionen.

Volgsten, U. (2006). Between ideology and identity. Media: discourse and affect in the musical experience. In S. Brown and U. Volgsten (eds), *Music and Manipulation. On the Social Uses and Social Control of Music,* pp. 74–100. New York: Berghahn.

Volgsten, U. (2012). The roots of music—emotional expression, dialogue and affect attunement in the psychogenesis of music. *Musicae Scientiae,* **16**(2), 1–17.

Volgsten, U. and Åkerberg, Y. (2006). Copyright, music and morals: artistic expression and the public sphere. In S. Brown and U. Volgsten (eds), *Music and Manipulation. On the Social Uses and Social Control of Music,* pp. 336–64. New York: Berghahn.

Wallrup, E. (2012). *Musical attunement: the concept and phenomenon of Stimmung in music.* Stockholm: Department of Musicology and Performance Studies.

Walton, K. L. (1994). Listening with imagination: is music representational? *Journal of Aesthetics and Art Criticism,* **52**, 47–61.

Coda

A multi-authored volume such as this is not the place to impose any particular conception of the relationships between music and emotion as authoritative or incontestably true. Our authors have been encouraged to review the existing alternatives as well as to develop new theoretical models. Our main hope is to have presented the multiplicity of viewpoints as clearly as possible, enabling the reader to draw his or her own conclusions.

Nevertheless, it is possible to extract some common threads from the variety of discussions we find in this volume. First, we often find that authors locate many sources of affect in a single piece of music, and that theoretical models must find ways to accommodate this plurality. Emotions are complex phenomena made up of a number of components—and music may latch onto several of these components simultaneously (for example appraisals, actions, feelings, empathic recognitions). Different routes to arousal may also be appropriate to different species of emotion (for example Scherer and Coutinho's distinction between aesthetic and utilitarian emotions or Koelsch's distinction between "fun" and "attachment" based emotions). Alternatively, some authors try to find ways to show that different routes to emotion are really aspects of the same basic phenomenon (for instance, as Colling and Thompson synthesize expectation and resemblance based routes to expressivity around a central notion of action resemblance).

With the aid of more sophisticated analytic tools, researchers are delving ever deeper into the mechanisms underlying the powers of music. On the human side of the music–emotion relation, we can observe greater use of continuous measures of self-report, as well as a plethora of physiological and neural observations, and even the use of such measures in the live generation of music (Cochrane). On the musical side we observe sophisticated musicological examinations of musical works themselves (Zoppelli; Spitzer), and the subtle nuances that accompany different performances (Leech-Wilkinson). Only by getting down to the details of the continuously varying nature of the musical event will we properly appreciate the special power of music to express and elicit emotions. It is in the details that neat theoretical models may find themselves unstuck, or that rich new possibilities can open up.

One mechanism now widely recognized as playing a crucial role in our musical experience is empathy. This is a competence that different authors analyze at different levels within the overall human economy, from an automatic physiological entrainment with the pulse of the music (Trost and Vuilleumier), to contagious arousal by means of perceiving a resemblance to feelings (Davies), to more person-level empathy for the performer (Scherer and Coutinho; Colling and Thompson), to social uses of music for interpersonal entrainment (Krueger; Volgsten). Given the obviously social nature of most musical engagement, it is clearly a serious limitation that research up till now has been largely focused on the single listener. This is partly due to the limitations of experimental methodologies, which technological developments should to some extent ameliorate. But it is also due to the theoretical difficulty inherent in mapping the highly complex ecologies of human to human interaction. We have really only just begun to explore the role of music in social groups, and we should hope to see more active investigation into this at both a theoretical and experimental level in the future.

Another relatively untapped area of investigation concerns cultural variations in musical experience. This volume has for the most part been focused on the Western musical tradition, and indeed classical rather than popular music (though see Cochrane's interviews in Chapter 3 with Risset on electro-acoustic music and Burwell on film music). While some of our researchers have been able to demonstrate notable cross-cultural similarities (e.g. Koelsch; Colling and Thompson) we cannot be confident of having reached true human universals, or even to have mapped the full range of musical–emotional possibilities until cross-cultural comparisons become more systematic and robust.

The same might be said of historical excursions. The past, as they say, is a foreign country. And while some historically accepted claims may appear to modern readers as stretching credulity (for example tarantism) or merely quaint (the four humors), there are many notions found in these treatises that are not alien to us—the recognition for instance of a basic resonance between the nature of music and the nature of human feeling. Indeed the structural similarities between the four humors and modern-day appeals to emotion dimensions suggests that musicians and theoreticians of the past may be thinking along similar lines after all.

In our introductions to the different sections of this volume we have already outlined some potential future directions of research with regards to the emotionally expressive, eliciting, and social powers of music. This tripartite organization respects a fairly natural distinction within the field as it is traditionally practiced, but not all research fits neatly into one or other of these boxes. Certainly, we should hope to see efforts towards an integrated understanding of the expressive, eliciting, and social powers of music in the future. For while the identification of novel influences or applications of musical experience encourages the fragmentation of research, it must be emphasized that all of these aspects of music exhibit deep mutual dependences. Large multidisciplinary projects such as this volume should help connections to be more easily discerned, and we hope to have inspired the reader with a sense of the possibilities that the area of music and emotion research has to offer.

Appendix to "Gender ambivalence and the expression of passions" by Christine Jeanneret

Così cruda e così fiera

Del Signor Cavalier Loreto [Vittori]

Texts and Translations

Loreto Vittori

1. Cosi cruda e cosi fiera
mi si mostra una beltà,
ch'il mio core homai spera
di trovar fede o pietà.

L'adorai con fè costante,
idolatra e notte e di,
ma quel core d'aspro diamante
la mia fede ogn'hor scherni.

2. Sallo ch'il core in preda al duolo,
rio di pianto ogn'hor versò
se ne pur un guardo solo,
dalla cruda egli impetrò.

E sarà sempre costei
al mio duol cruda ogn'hor più,
ahi, no, no, gli affanni miei,
giusto Amor, vendica tu.

1. So cruel and so proud
a beauty shows herself to me,
so that now my heart does not hope
to find faith or mercy.

I adored her with constant faith,
idolized night and day,
but this heart of harsh diamond
every hour mocks my faith.

2. Be aware that a heart in prey to pain,
river of tears every hour sheds
if not even a single glance,
of the cruel one he implored.

And she will always be
more cruel to my pain every hour,
alas, no, no, my dreads,
fair Love, do you avenge.

Mario Savioni

1.
Bizzarre pupille,
che far vi credete?
A tante faville,
voi pur arderete.

Chi le fiamme accende e aduna,
prender suole i proprî ardori
con incender tanti cori.
Non tentate la fortuna.

Da tomba il foco,
a chi gli da la cuna.
Non tentate la fortuna.

2.
Di tanta fierezza,
non più v'armate.
Soave dolcezza,
accresce beltate.

Non si vince un alma forte
con minaccie e con rigori,
fulminando tanti cori.
Non tentate più la sorte.

Dai proprî strali,
anco ha un arcier la morte.
Non tentate più la sorte.

1.
Bizzarre eyes,
what do you believe to do?
To so many sparks,
you'll burn too.

He who lights up flames and collects,
should take his own ardors
to set fire to so many hearts.
Do not tempt fortune.

Fire puts in a grave,
he who cares for it.
Do not tempt fortune.

2.
Of so much pride,
do not arm yourself anymore.
A gentle sweetness,
increases beauty.

A strong soul is not won
with threats and rigors,
striking with lightning so many hearts.
Do not tempt fate.

From his own darts,
also an archer will die.
Do not tempt fate.

Del Signor Mario Savioni [or Carlo Caproli]

Bizzarre pupille che far vi credete

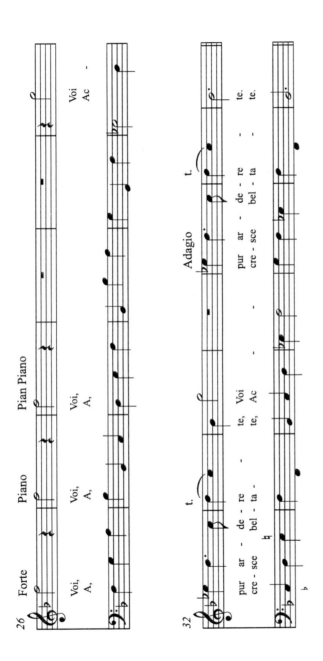

2a [strofa]

Index